E. T. A. Hoffmann's Musical Writings: *Kreisleriana, The Poet and the Composer*, Music Criticism

E. T. A. Hoffmann in 1821; pencil drawing by Wilhelm Hensel
(1794–1861). This is the only authentic likeness not drawn by
Hoffmann himself.

E. T. A. Hoffmann's Musical Writings: *Kreisleriana, The Poet and the Composer*, Music Criticism

Edited, annotated, and introduced by
DAVID CHARLTON
Lecturer in the School of Art History and Music, University of East Anglia

Translated by
MARTYN CLARKE

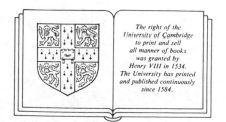

The right of the
University of Cambridge
to print and sell
all manner of books
was granted by
Henry VIII in 1534.
The University has printed
and published continuously
since 1584.

CAMBRIDGE UNIVERSITY PRESS

Cambridge
New York   Port Chester
Melbourne   Sydney

Published by the Press Syndicate of the University of Cambridge
The Pitt Building, Trumpington Street, Cambridge CB2 1RP
40 West 20th Street, New York, NY 10011, USA
10 Stamford Road, Oakleigh, Melbourne 3166, Australia

First published 1989

Printed in Great Britain at the University Press, Cambridge

British Library cataloguing in publication data
Hoffmann, E. T. A. (Ernst Theodor Amadeus),
1776–1822
E. T. A. Hoffmann's musical writings:
Kreisleriana, the poet and the composer,
music criticism
1. Music. Criticism
I. Title   II. Charlton, David, *1946–*
780′.1′5

Library of Congress cataloguing in publication data
Hoffmann, E. T. A. (Ernst Theodor Amadeus), 1776–1822.
[Selections. English. 1989]
E. T. A. Hoffmann's musical writings. Kreisleriana, The poet and
the composer, music criticism / translated by Martyn Clarke;
edited, annotated, and introduced by David Charlton.
       p.   cm.
Includes index.
ISBN 0–521–23520–0
1. Music – 19th century – History and criticism.   2. Romanticism in
music.   I. Charlton, David, 1946– .   II. Title.   III. Title: Musical
writings.
ML 196.H7   1989
780′.9–dc20   89–31511   CIP   MN

ISBN 0 521 23520 0

CONTENTS

MUSIC CRITICISM

FIGURES

PREFACE

This book consists mainly of texts never before translated into English or else unavailable in English in complete form. It brings together Hoffmann's professional criticism of musical scores or performances, and his musical writing classifiable on the borderline between philosophy and fiction. The supreme example of such writing is *Kreisleriana*. Perhaps the latter should be called 'Romantic criticism': a mode of writing in which the imagination and Romantic philosophy guide the pen, but always for the purpose of bringing the essence of a musical act into focus. The act is sometimes the purely aesthetic one of the finished masterpiece; sometimes the proper rôle of the performer; sometimes the task of the composer just starting on his way. However, as a body of writing, these essays are bound together by the individual intelligence and experience of one of the most remarkable musical artists to have left his imprint on the Western tradition.

The texts offered here complement the readily available translations of *Ritter Gluck, Don Juan, Rat Krespel, Die Automate* (*Automatons*), *Die Abenteuer der Sylvester-Nacht* (*Adventures of a New-Year's Night*), and *Die Fermate* (*The Cadenza*; sometimes translated as *An Interrupted Cadence*). Those who may read these stories after having gained knowledge of Hoffmann's musical life and thought will appreciate many inner connections between them. Those already familiar with *Kater Murr* will appreciate how different and self-sufficient the earlier *Kreisleriana* is.

The translations in this book are the result of collaborative work between the translator and the editor. Hoffmann's language bears upon such detailed and fundamental aspects of Western music and theatre that it is particularly necessary to make clear at all times what he is referring to. Even at his most abstract levels of thought Hoffmann strove for the utmost clarity of expression. Yet because what he had to say often involved his drawing on a wide range of musical, literary, and dramatic references, matching him in English has succeeded more surely through shared responsibility. The number of those whose assistance is acknowledged below bears further

ix

witness to the effort to come to terms with Hoffmann's enviable mental and linguistic breadth.

Initially, the need for a comprehensive set of translations of Hoffmann's musical writings became evident in the course of teaching a multi-disciplinary seminar at the University of East Anglia. It is hoped, therefore, that this book will fulfil a practical function in similar, future contexts. But these writings are not dry and unreadable. Hoffmann was a literary master of world stature who aimed to entertain his readers, as well as instruct them, whenever he put pen to paper. Many of the *Kreisleriana* essays attain unsurpassed heights of comic satire and irony. They are to be enjoyed for themselves as well as for the way in which their humour is directed to a serious end. Even apparently straight-faced reviews can turn out to contain amusing episodes; this is especially true where operas are the subject, for Hoffmann's impatience with the inept or inane is as fiery as his worship of the genius of Gluck and Mozart.

The unfamiliarity of so much of the material has suggested the idea of four separate editorial essays. The first provides a basic orientation. The Introduction to *Kreisleriana* is solely devoted to an exegesis of that cycle. The Introduction to *The Poet and the Composer*, entitled 'Hoffmann and Opera', draws together the critical strands concerning opera found in all parts of the book. It also offers a brief account of Hoffmann's personal activity as an opera composer. Lastly, Friedrich Schnapp's account furnishes the historical and archival background to Hoffmann's music criticism. It is hoped that this plan, together with the biographical information preceding the music reviews, will assist in making coherent the writings as a whole and prompt fresh speculation about the rôle of music in Hoffmann's work. A new generation of scholars in Germany, to whom reference is sometimes made below, has begun to investigate this rich field; but little has appeared in English. Conversely, much remains to be done concerning the historical impact of Hoffmann's career upon the growth of nineteenth-century music and opera: for example, his influence on the French musical world after 1830.

This book contains complete versions of every important musical essay by Hoffmann; every one of his reviews of music by Beethoven; and writings about every musical genre to which Hoffmann addressed himself, with the exception of solo piano music. The order of printing of the music criticism reproduces that in Schnapp's edition of the *Schriften zur Musik*, and represents the order in which the items were written, rather than that in which they were published. Constraints of space have obliged us to omit (a) certain reviews of unfamiliar scores (e.g. by Carl Anton Braun, Jan Wilms, Bernhard Stiastny); (b) the review of Kotzebue's *Opern-Almanach*, which however is discussed in the editor's Introduction to *The Poet and the Composer*; (c) short reviews of performances in Berlin, except for the two most interesting opera reviews and for two concert reviews; (d) the blow-by-blow description of the music of Spontini's opera *Olimpia*, whose French text Hoffmann translated for stage use in Berlin. However, we have included the first portion of that article, the 'Further Observations on Spontini's Opera *Olimpia*'. The Appendix gives fuller details of all omitted writings.

It is only quite recently that German scholarship has virtually agreed on what constitutes the canon of Hoffmann's reviews. The bare facts of the case will be found in 'Sources and Suppositive Reviews' by Friedrich Schnapp (1900–83), taken from the *Schriften zur Musik*. Editorial notes taken directly from Schnapp are indicated in this book by his initials; but his research lies behind many more of them. All writers and editors concerned with Hoffmann are under obligation to Schnapp's decades of productive work, which produced among other things the editions of Hoffmann's correspondence (*HBW*) and his diary (*HTB*). We have used Schnapp's edition of the music criticism (*Schriften zur Musik*), itself based on the original printings of the articles. The paragraphing is usually editorial in these texts. Schnapp himself edited the music examples, adding slurs, ties, and dynamics missing from the *AMZ* examples, and modernising the order of the staves.

The modern sources consulted for the present translation and edition are the above volumes edited by Schnapp; his edition of the *Nachlese*; Walter Müller-Seidel's editions of *Die Serapions-Brüder* and *Fantasiestücke in Callot's Manier* (Munich, 1963, 1960); and Hanne Castein's edition of *Kreisleriana* (Stuttgart, 1983). Earlier sources consulted include the second edition of *Fantasiestücke in Callot's Manier* (Bamberg, 1819); the edition of the same by Georg von Maassen in his *E. T. A. Hoffmanns sämtliche Werke* (Munich and Leipzig, 1912), i; certain issues of the Leipzig *Allgemeine Musikalische Zeitung* (*AMZ*), in which journal first appeared many of the musical works (see figure 3); and first editions of various books referred to by Hoffmann. Books most commonly cited in the present edition appear in the list of abbreviations below. Almost all the music analysed by Hoffmann has been consulted in the original edition from which it was reviewed. The title pages of the scores themselves have been transcribed in the editorial notes in each case. These processes have enabled any errors in the musical examples to be corrected or accounted for, and have helped to clarify several otherwise more problematic references in the reviews.

Certain writings of Hoffmann have, of course, been translated before. The most extensive earlier English selection appeared in R. Murray Schafer, *E. T. A. Hoffmann and Music* (Toronto, 1975), after work had begun on this book. Interspersing texts by Hoffmann with his own thematic commentaries, Schafer offered translations of five *Kreisleriana* essays, among other things. But these essays appeared in the order required by Schafer's discussions. Useful as it is, the book unfortunately contains factual errors (e.g. in supposing that Hoffmann reviewed Beethoven's Sixth Symphony) which lessen its value. In 1982 the journal *Nineteenth-Century Music* (vol. v/3) published the last essay from *Kreisleriana*, translated by Max Knight. The difficulties in understanding this essay in isolation will be appreciated when it is read below as the culmination of an entire cycle. 'Beethoven's Instrumental Music' was translated with introduction by Arthur Ware Locke in *The Musical Quarterly* in 1917. It was then published in translation by Oliver Strunk (*Source Readings in Music History*, New York, 1950), as well as by Schafer; but Strunk was obliged to shorten the text, which was also done in the case of *The Poet and the Composer* in the same volume. Elliot Forbes included the complete review of Beethoven's Fifth Symphony in the Norton Critical Score of that work (New York, 1971). In its relative completeness, the present collection has greater affinities with its companion volume, *Carl Maria von Weber: Writings on Music*, translated by Martin Cooper, edited by John Warrack (Cambridge, 1981); with Mary Hurst Schubert's edition and translation, *Wilhelm Heinrich Wackenroder's 'Confessions' and 'Fantasies'* (University Park, Pennsylvania, and London, 1971); and with Johanna C. Sahlin's translated *Selected Letters of E. T. A. Hoffmann* (Chicago and London, 1977).

ACKNOWLEDGEMENTS

Of the many who helped to bring this book about I should like to begin by thanking two colleagues at the University of East Anglia whose contribution is difficult to state in brief: Dr Elinor Shaffer (Reader in the School of Modern Languages and European History) and Professor Peter Aston (School of Art History and Music). For materials and research funding I am indebted to the University of East Anglia.

The following institutions and individuals have responded with kindness to sometimes repeated requests for assistance: the University of London Library (Senate House) and Dr Anthea Baird; the British Library (Reference Division); the Staatsbibliothek, Bamberg; the Zentraldirektion of the Répertoire International des Sources Musicales; the American Antiquarian Society and Joanne D. Chaison; the Fürstlich Fürstenbergische Hofbibliothek, Donaueschingen.

My friends and acquaintances named below have generously given of their time, thought, expertise and sometimes their materials in the interests of this book: Dr Denise Boulton, Professor Peter Branscombe, Dr Clive Brown, Dr Hanne Castein, Mr Anthony Caston, Signor Paolo Cerioni, Mr D. F. L. Chadd, Ms Elisabeth Cook, Professor Donald Foster, Dr John Gage, Dr Penelope Gouk, Mr Anthony Hicks, Dr Alec Hyatt King, Miss Corinna Jacobi, Dr Holger Klein, Mr A. J. Lawrenson, Dr Mark Lindley, Professor Hugh Macdonald, Mr John Mitchell, Professor Jean Mongrédien, Professor Alain Montandon, Dr Stefan Muthesius, Dr Maurice M. Raraty, Dr Elizabeth Roche, Professor Brian Rowley, Mr Graham Sadler, Dr Jim Samson, Professor Howard E. Smither, Mr John Stone, Dr Alan Tyson, Dr Michael Walter, and Mr John Warrack.

Additionally I should particularly like to thank Professor Ian D. Bent for his friendly collaboration; Hans-Jürgen and Elke Driemel for their searches for texts on my behalf; Margaret Pugh for her tireless and skilful scribal help; and those who have given the benefit of their criticism after reading portions of the book in manuscript: Dr Maurice M. Raraty, Ms Patricia

Scholfield, Mrs Penny Souster, and especially Professor Ronald Taylor. For similar offices, going well beyond the call of duty, I am most grateful to my colleague and translator, Martyn Clarke. All the foregoing debts stand in a special perspective to that I owe to Mr Michael Black (formerly the Publisher, Cambridge University Press), who nurtured the present project in its infancy. Final thanks are not least due to those whose enthusiasm for Hoffmann bore early fruit now ripened in the present work: J.O., A.W.F.C., H.L.

ABBREVIATIONS AND NOTE ON THE TEXT

AMZ   *Allgemeine musikalische Zeitung* (Leipzig, 1798–1848)

Castein   E. T. A. Hoffmann, *Kreisleriana*, ed. Hanne Castein (Stuttgart, 1983)

D.C.   David Charlton

DW   *Dramaturgisches Wochenblatt in nächster Beziehung auf die Königlichen Schauspiele zu Berlin* (Berlin, 1815–17)

Ellinger 1894   Georg Ellinger, *E. T. A. Hoffmann. Sein Leben und seine Werke* (Hamburg and Leipzig, 1894)

Ellinger 1912   Georg Ellinger (ed.), *E. T. A. Hoffmanns Werke* (Berlin, Leipzig, Vienna, and Stuttgart, 1912)

F.S.   Friedrich Schnapp

HBW   Friedrich Schnapp (ed.), *E. T. A. Hoffmanns Briefwechsel* (vols. i, ii, Munich, 1967, 1968)

Hirschberg 1922   Leopold Hirschberg (ed.), *Ernst Theodor Amadeus Hoffmanns sämmtliche Werke* (Berlin and Leipzig, 1922)

Hitzig   [Julius Eduard Hitzig], *Aus Hoffmann's Leben und Nachlass* (Berlin, 1823)

HTB   Friedrich Schnapp (ed.), *E. T. A. Hoffmann. Tagebücher* (Munich, 1971)

Kroll 1909   Erwin Kroll, *E. T. A. Hoffmanns musikalische Anschauungen* (Königsberg, 1909)

Nachlese   Friedrich Schnapp (ed.), *E. T. A. Hoffmann. Nachlese. Dichtungen, Schriften, Aufzeichnungen und Fragmente* (Munich, 1963, reissued Darmstadt, 1966)

OED   *The Oxford English Dictionary*

Sahlin	Johanna C. Sahlin (ed., tr.), *Selected Letters of E. T. A. Hoffmann* (Chicago and London, 1977)
Schriften zur Musik	Friedrich Schnapp (ed.), *E. T. A. Hoffmann. Schriften zur Musik. Aufsätze und Rezensionen. Neubearbeitete Ausgabe* (Munich, [1977])
The New Grove	Stanley Sadie (ed.), *The New Grove Dictionary of Music and Musicians* (London, 1980)
Vom Ende 1899	Hans vom Ende (ed.), *E. T. A. Hoffmann's musikalische Schriften* (Cologne and Leipzig, [1899])
VZ [Vossische Zeitung]	*Königlich privilegirte Berlinische Zeitung von Staats und gelehrten Sachen. Im Verlage Vossischer Erben* (Berlin, 1751–1934)
ZEW	*Zeitung für die elegante Welt* (Leipzig, 1801–59)

Footnotes indicated by an asterisk show Hoffmann's original notes. All others are by the present editor, except those indicated 'F.S.' (Friedrich Schnapp).

HOFFMANN AS A WRITER
ON MUSIC

Our knowledge, as a musical public, of the 'Age of Beethoven' is probably as distorted as is the general perception of E. T. A. Hoffmann, 'Author of the Tales'.[1] Beethoven lived from 1770 to 1827; Hoffmann from 1776 to 1822. It was a period of tremendous creativity and change, and saw the birth of many musical, as well as political, assumptions still held today, rightly or otherwise: the idea of Mozart as a genius to be compared with Raphael or Shakespeare; the idea of J. S. Bach as a universal musical creator; the value of Gluck's reform operas as critical to the mainstream of opera composition; addressing the public in print about music and performance as a civilised way of influencing amateur taste; the idea of the avant-garde. To all these, Hoffmann made signal contribution. But we forget much more. The symphony was a staple part of many a composer's output; the names of symphonists like Dittersdorf, Rössler, Pleyel, Waldstein, Gyrowetz, Eberl, Clementi, Gossec, Méhul, Cherubini, Vogler, Weber, and Spohr appear as the *most* representative figures in *The Age of Beethoven: The New Oxford History of Music*, vol. viii.[2] Yet it is difficult to persuade orchestras to take up their music. Piano composition was published at an astonishing rate, and the piano itself developing into the sturdier, six-octave instrument soon to be the vehicle for Chopin's genius. How many pianists know exactly which piano pedals were current in the age of Beethoven? Church music was composed, even published, in consistent quantities, yet is hardly more familiar than the extraordinary secular music of the French Revolution. Beethoven completed only one opera (*Fidelio*); how far do we see it against the background of hundreds of works for the stage stretching between the death of Mozart and Weber's *Der Freischütz* (1821)?

The value of reading Hoffmann on music has many aspects; an obvious one is that he describes both practical and characteristic features of his age.

---

[1] The standard life and works study remains that by Harvey W. Hewett-Thayer, *Hoffmann: Author of the Tales* (Princeton, 1948).

[2] *The Age of Beethoven 1790–1830* (*New Oxford History of Music*, vol. viii), ed. Gerald Abraham (Oxford, 1982).

He discusses instruments, performance practice, theatre production, amateur music-making; church music and its place in a new age; and of course the actual scores of well-known, poorly known, and unknown composers. Further, however, thanks to Hoffmann's rare genius, particularly in the dramatic monologues in *Kreisleriana*, we can see music through the eyes of imagined characters themselves – amusing characters whose present-day equivalents may well be only too familiar to us. The cultural attitudes to music found here, as in the author's essays from his final Berlin period (1814–22), help to reveal the age from within, to create a context within which we may appreciate better the symphonies of Louis Spohr as well as those of Beethoven. For as Gerald Abraham pointed out, 'the Age of Beethoven was above all an age of transition', and Beethoven himself was just one more dominant influence, who would in his turn have to be, aesthetically speaking, replaced. Hoffmann, who was only too conscious of Beethoven's musical stature, helped to replace him aesthetically, especially in the field of opera, and specifically with his own *Undine* (1816). The writings of Hoffmann reveal the critical evolution of an immensely influential thinker, whose aim was to raise musical consciousness, decry the trivial, and reveal the potential of the post-Beethovenian musical world.

This is not the place to correct commonplace misconceptions about Hoffmann's life and career. Perhaps inevitably, his disparate activities as a highly regarded judge, a professional conductor and music critic, a composer,[3] and a world-renowned master of literature, have tempted biographers into making unwarranted claims. Though it would be satisfying to correct some of them, it will be more fruitful to set out some facts for reference. No full-length biography in English has appeared since *Hoffmann: Author of the Tales* by Harvey Hewett-Thayer in 1948.[4]

1776   24 January: Ernst Theodor Wilhelm Hoffmann born, Königsberg (the third name Amadeus was adopted in 1804). Younger of two surviving brothers of the marriage between Christoph Ludwig Hoffmann (1736–97) and Louise Albertine Doerffer (1748–96). The Hoffmanns and Doerffers are families of lawyers by profession.

---

[3] Hoffmann's compositions are detailed in Gerhard Allroggen, *E. T. A. Hoffmanns Kompositionen: ein chronologisch-thematisches Verzeichnis seiner musikalischen Werke mit einer Einführung* (Regensburg, 1970). See also Allroggen's article 'Hoffmann', in *The New Grove*, with work-list.

[4] The shorter biographies prefacing various collections of the Tales, and even that prefacing Sahlin's edition of the letters, misrepresent musical details of his life, while underemphasising the orderly, sheer professional aspects of his existence. The superbly organised edition by Schnapp of the *HTB* gives innumerable day-to-day biographical details.

1778   H's parents separate, each adopting one son; H and mother live
        with the Doerffer family, chiefly siblings of his mother. She
        becomes increasingly withdrawn. The staid uncle Otto Wilhelm
        (1741–1811) acts as parent and music teacher.

1787   Beginning of H's lifelong friendship with Theodor Gottlieb [von]
        Hippel (1775–1843), later to rise to some prominence in the
        Prussian government under Hardenberg. Musical studies
        continue.

1792   H begins law studies at Königsberg University; begins to compose
        music. By 1794 is a practised painter.

1795   Graduates as *Auskultator* and enters legal profession in Königs-
        berg. Begins novel (now lost).

1796   Goes to live with an uncle (Johann Ludwig Doerffer, 1743–1803)
        in Glogau; reads Jean Paul.

1798   Takes up legal position in Berlin, civil service. Meets Franz von
        Holbein (1779–1855), musician, actor and writer; also J. F.
        Reichardt (1752–1814), veteran composer, from whom he receives
        musical instruction.

1799   Writes *Die Maske* (words and music).

1800   Transferred to Poznań. Composes own shortened version of
        Goethe's Singspiel, *Scherz, List und Rache* (1801), also other
        music.

1802   Marries Marianna Thekla Michaelina Rorer [Trzcinska] (1778–
        1854), daughter of a Polish civil servant. Is transferred to Płock as
        punishment for irreverent cartoons of Prussian military officers.

1803   Writes church music, also a play, *Der Preis*, and 'Letter from a
        Monk'. Begins (sporadic) diary.

1804   Transferred to Warsaw. Meets Julius Eduard Hitzig (1780–1849),
        subsequently friend and his (posthumous) biographer. Uses 'Ama-
        deus' as his third given name.

1805   Foundation of Warsaw *Musikalische Gesellschaft* (Musical Society),
        of which H becomes secretary and vice-president. Birth of
        daughter Caecilia (1805–07), H's only child. Singspiel *Die lustigen
        Musikanten* performed.

1806   Completes symphony in E flat, which H conducts on several
        occasions. Prussia defeated at Jena and Auerstedt; French invade
        Warsaw, November.

1807   Poland becomes French-allied Duchy of Warsaw; H's wife returns
        to Poznań; H returns without resources to Berlin; the Singspiel
        Liebe und Eifersucht is begun. Advertises for a musical post and
        corresponds with Count Julius von Soden (1754–1831), Bamberg.

1808   Appointed theatre music director, Bamberg, where he arrives with his wife on 1 September. Is not accepted by musicians, and takes post of theatre composer.

1809   Begins to publish in *AMZ*: *Ritter Gluck*. Composes a melodrama, *Dirna*, a piano trio, and a *Miserere* for chorus and orchestra.

1810   Publishes review of Beethoven's Fifth Symphony, and other reviews, also 'Kapellmeister Johannes Kreisler's Musical Sufferings'.

1811   Emotional involvement with Juliane Mark (1796–1865). Begins opera *Aurora*, unperformed until 1933. Spends much time in theatre production and management, including scene-building and effects.

1812   Plans musical novel, which either becomes, or overlaps with, *Kreisleriana*. Composes vocal music. Reads *Undine* by F. de la Motte Fouqué (1777–1843) and obtains from the latter an opera libretto derived from the tale.

1813   Signs contract with C. F. Kunz to publish *Fantasiestücke in Callot's Manier*, which are already in progress. Moves to Dresden and Leipzig as musical director of Seconda opera company. Witnesses bombardment of Dresden, and the battlefield. Writes *Der Dichter und der Komponist* (*The Poet and the Composer*).

1814   Writes fiction, reviews, completes *Undine*; is sacked by Seconda. The *Fantasiestücke*, i–iii, published. Napoleon defeated. H returns to Berlin hoping to re-enter judiciary. Literary fame established.

1815   *Fantasiestücke*, iv, published. Until his death H lives and works in Berlin, having become Supreme Court Judge in 1816. Publishes various musical articles, and stories.

1816   Première of *Undine*, Berlin Schauspielhaus, 3 August. *Die Elixiere des Teufels; Nachtstücke*, i.

1817   *Rat Krespel; Nachtstücke*, ii.

1819   Second, definitive edition of *Fantasiestücke*; *Die Serapions-Brüder*, i, ii.

1820   *Die Serapions-Brüder*, iii; *Kater Murr*, i.

1821   *Die Serapions-Brüder*, iv; *Kater Murr*, ii.

1822   H dies, 25 June, after repeated periods of illness, from liver disease, spinal marrow degeneration, and paralysis.

Hoffmann's musical education was organised with care.[5] His father was a string player; his uncle Otto, a keyboard player, was Hoffmann's first

---

[5]   A convenient recent summary is in Friedrich Schnapp, 'Der Musiker E. T. A. Hoffmann', *Mitteilungen der E. T. A. Hoffmann-Gesellschaft*, xxv (1979), 3–6.

teacher. The boy responded quickly and (according to Hippel) 'caused a sensation' with his improvisations. Otto's domestic concerts also proved a permanent influence. Hoffmann subsequently took keyboard lessons from C. G. Richter, a superb Bach player; learned harmony and violin-playing from C. Gladau, under whom he attained – according to his own admission – 'tolerable virtuosity'; attempted the harp and the guitar; and studied counterpoint with C. W. Podbielski, a widely read intellectual, organist of Königsberg Cathedral, and supposedly the model for Hoffmann's character of Abraham Liscov in *Kater Murr*. In addition, before his removal to Berlin in 1798, he saw important operas staged at Königsberg, including *Don Giovanni* and *Die Zauberflöte*.

Musicians are communicators. Although Hoffmann's grounding in Romantic theory produced undoubtedly élitist musical views, one can legitimately see him bridging the gap between theory and public appreciation, through the success of his fiction. Something of this process may be observed as well in his musical writings. Even in *Kreisleriana* he allows Fouqué (the actual author of the first essay in Part II), in the character of Wallborn, to criticise Kreisler for being 'very harsh in your passionate condemnation of all uninspired music'. In the late essay 'Casual Reflections on the Appearance of this Journal', Hoffmann took a distinctly pragmatic view of musical criticism, seeing that artistic jolts to the sensibility will be assimilated in due time, if ultimately worthy, and are a moving target for those who would denounce them (as he had denounced aspects of Spontini's music in 1813).

Yet he would never, surely, have absolutely retracted his formulation first written in 1810: 'Romantic sensibility is rare, and romantic talent even rarer' (review of Beethoven's Fifth Symphony). The chasm between the development of Romantic opera through *Undine*, and the adulated operas of Rossini arriving almost straight after it, roused him in 1821 to a final attack on such a debased music ('Further Observations on Spontini's Opera *Olimpia*'). The public's ready consumption of entertainment-music – pilloried at the outset of *Kreisleriana* – posed in the nineteenth century a permanent dilemma for unsubsidised creative musicians. The same problem is apparent in terms of the shrinking audience for Romantic poetry in contemporary England:

. . . the poetical audience will not only continually diminish in the proportion of its number to that of the rest of the reading public, but will also sink lower and lower in the comparison of intellectual requirement.

(Thomas Love Peacock, *The Four Ages of Poetry*, 1820)

. . . all men being supposed able to read, and all readers able to judge, the multitudinous PUBLIC, shaped into personal unity by the magic of abstraction, sits nominal despot on the throne of criticism.

(S. T. Coleridge, *Biographia Literaria*, 1816)[6]

In 1821 Hoffmann wrote (see p. 442):

And yet any gentleman or lady who with little talent can amuse the most elegant tea-circle . . . is able to speak and pass judgement about the works of great composers, as though he or she were accustomed to passing in and out of the hallowed temple of Isis, and ordering breakfast or tea there with complete ease and equanimity . . .

Romantic literature and art often (ironically enough) compel the idea of engagement with aspects of living. This is more obviously demonstrable in later, French manifestations of Romanticism, its liberalism and social conscience: 'Je hais l'oppression d'une haine profonde . . .' (Hugo).[7] Yet it also applies to the earlier German movement, imbued though this may seem to be by mere introspection. One of the most influential texts of the period – albeit by Goethe – was after all *Wilhelm Meisters Lehrjahre* (*Wilhelm Meister's Apprenticeship*, 1795–96), the most famous novel of development, from which Hoffmann sometimes quoted. 'Combining realistic and imaginary elements',[8] this was certainly an ancestor of *Kreisleriana*. 'Engagement', for the earlier Romantics, was often, however, concerned with the existential contradictions between inward and outer reality, whether stimulated by recent philosophy (Kant, Fichte, Schelling) or studies in the natural sciences. Thus the art of instrumental music found itself, around the time of Mozart's death in 1791, suddenly at a central point of mediation where mental, physical, spiritual, and social considerations of existence converged. Few seem not to have had an intellectual and even practical interest in music, whether the poet and librettist Goethe (1749–1832), the physicist and writer Johann Wilhelm Ritter (1776–1810), the poet and geologist Novalis (1772–1801), and so on. If easily remembered for the startling or grotesque juxtapositions of 'normal' and 'supra-normal' in his fiction, Hoffmann was nevertheless firmly rooted in the mainstream of modern thought in Germany. *Kreisleriana* is, in fact, his contribution to Romantic philosophy, probably inspired by its author's admiration for Novalis,

---

[6]   The Peacock and Coleridge citations are brought together in Lee Erickson, 'The Poets' Corner: the Impact of Technological Changes in Printing on English Poetry, 1800–1850', *ELH*, lii (1985), 893–911: citations pp. 896–7.

[7]   Victor Hugo, from *Les Feuilles d'automne* (1831), discussed in D. G. Charlton, 'Religious and Political Thought', in D. G. Charlton (ed.), *The French Romantics* (Cambridge, 1984), i, 33–75: discussion p. 68.

[8]   Roger Cardinal, *German Romantics in Context* (London, 1975), 13.

Friedrich Schlegel (1772–1829), and Friedrich Wilhelm von Schelling (1775–1854). Hoffmann's reading, as we learn from his letters and diaries, extended fairly widely through the moderns (Goethe, Schiller, Jean Paul, Tieck, Heinse, Ritter, G. H. Schubert), together with Shakespeare, Calderón (translated by Schiller), and Carlo Gozzi. Perhaps he was most admiring of Novalis, who in supremely distilled forms propagated a world view offering ceaseless metaphorical interaction between object and perceiver. Novalis's posthumously published, unfinished novel *Die Lehrlinge zu Sais* (*The Novices at Saïs*) (1802) also had a fundamental influence on *Kreisleriana*. Whereas Novalis and others emphasised the hidden unity connecting all aspects of nature, and thus the possibility of endless metaphorical transformation, Hoffmann emphasised that our recognition of 'higher natures' (linking man with this normally hidden level of awareness) was particularly to be mediated through certain types of music. Such mediation was even to be a primary goal of Romantic opera.

It is notable that Hoffmann takes no simple-minded stance when he speaks of music in such terms. He adopts an elliptical, varied, sometimes fragmentary approach. Consequently his intentions, most fully expressed in *Kreisleriana*, could be lost even on intelligent musical contemporaries. One such person, for example, was his acquaintance Carl Maria von Weber (himself the author of a musical novel, *Tonkünstlers Leben*),[9] who wrote to the editor of the *AMZ* in 1816 of Hoffmann's *Fantasiestücke*, 'I find much that is excellent and lively, though often with a wildly exuberant fantasy, and the whole, if I may say so, seems to me without a real purpose.' It is interesting that Hoffmann's own design for the frontispiece of the *Fantasiestücke* proved resistant to the understanding even of his publisher and friend, C. F. Kunz (see figure 1 and p. 30). The 'purpose' of Hoffmann's musical writing, in whatever form, was in the last analysis to justify music's proper position as a Romantic art. This did not mean that he simply went through the music he chose to discuss, sorting out which aspects were worthy of the epithet 'Romantic'. By and large, none of the instrumental music he reviewed, other than that by Beethoven, could be discussed by him in terms of Romanticism. Yet he seeks to praise what is to him good about it, or to show why something is poor. We read him for the professional value of his observations, just as we read A. W. Schlegel's lectures on literature and drama.[10] For Beethoven's Fifth Symphony alone he reserved the greatest force of his pen, because that work alone for him fully

9 Translated by Martin Cooper in *Carl Maria von Weber: Writings on Music*, ed. John Warrack (Cambridge, 1981), 312–64.
10 A. W. von Schlegel, *Vorlesungen über dramatische Kunst und Literatur* (1809–11), tr. John Black as *A Course of Lectures on Dramatic Art and Literature* (London, 1815).

exemplified Romantic transcendence, could be an archetypal 'hieroglyph' (to use a favourite early Romantic term) of surrounding nature.

As a trained lawyer, Hoffmann used words precisely, sometimes resorting to quasi-legalistic formulas in support of a proposition. Certain key words and phrases like 'yearning', 'spirit-realm', 'style', 'rational awareness' take on a particular resonance in his musical writing that will be linked with a particular set of concepts. In the following sentences from the close of the review of Beethoven's Fifth Symphony, it will be seen how the music itself is descriptively distanced from the Romantic effect it produces, or rather, the awareness it promotes. It is as though the music were construed on one expressive level, but a philosophically distinct one from the 'higher natures' to which it may lend access, given a correctly predisposed or gifted listener:

. . . the whole work will sweep past many like an inspired rhapsody. The heart of every sensitive listener, however, is certain to be deeply stirred and held until the very last chord by *one* lasting emotion, that of nameless, haunted yearning. Indeed for many moments after it he will be unable to emerge from the magical spirit-realm where he has been surrounded by pain and pleasure in the form of sounds . . . [The work] is conceived of genius and executed with profound rational awareness, and . . . expresses the romanticism of music to a very high degree.[11]

Music requiring words (masses, songs, incidental music) was to Hoffmann intrinsically less than Romantic. But no one type of instrumental music 'is' Romantic. Instead, Hoffmann accepts an immanent Romantic consciousness as the given fact; some composers (such as Beethoven) possess such consciousness and can express or evoke it through their art. 'These two splendid trios [Op. 70] demonstrate once more how deeply in his heart Beethoven carries the romantic spirit of music, and with what sublime originality, what authority, he infuses it into his works' (p. 302).

With opera, where music was perforce to act alongside so many other arts, the aesthetic problem was pressing. Opera was a relatively popular theatrical medium, but an almost universally debased one as far as Hoffmann was concerned. As is shown in the Introduction to *The Poet and the Composer*, he worked out a Romantic theory of opera (grounded in a sequence of three opera reviews published in 1810–11), and put it into practice in his operas *Aurora* and *Undine*. In his review of the latter, C. M. von Weber recognised the achievement in large measure of that operatic

---

[11] The most detailed and useful account of the Beethoven reviews in their Romantic and semantic contexts is Peter Schnaus, *E. T. A. Hoffmann als Beethoven-Rezensent der Allgemeinen Musikalischen Zeitung* (Freiburger Schriften zur Musikwissenschaft, vol. viii, Munich and Salzburg, 1977).

ideal 'which the German desires – an art work complete in itself, in which the partial contributions of the related and collaborating arts blend together, disappear, and, in disappearing, somehow form a new world'.[12] But Hoffmann's theory also demanded *a priori* total identification of subject-matter with resulting music, as well as a seriously conceived theme, or governing 'idea', that expressed a higher consciousness. The proper fusion of music and word was something so mysterious that it could be described only in vivid similes or metaphors based on chemical or alchemical transformation, with heat or fire as a recurring image for music (or its inspiration), but water as an image for text. Moreover, his ideal for the Romantic theatre was governed by the concept of the 'total effect': the complete 'blending' mentioned above by Weber to 'transport the spectator . . . to the fantastical land of poetry' ('The Complete Machinist', p. 115). But even this 'total communication' was no end in itself, though it may perhaps be related to Friedrich Schlegel's words on irony: 'It contains and incites a feeling of the insoluble conflict of the absolute and the relative, of the impossibility and necessity of total communication.'[13]

The raw ingredients employed by Hoffmann in his personal synthesis of Romantic and musical theories were largely in place before he began his writing career. This is so on the minute level of vocabulary as used in the *AMZ* by previous reviewers, and is so on the broadest level of concepts relating to instrumental music as they had evolved during the eighteenth century. But because Hoffmann's contribution to musical aesthetic discourse is so central, it will be useful now to summarise something of the music-aesthetic state of affairs as he found it. At this point we shall rely on the extensive discussions by Bellamy Hosler, to whom the reader seeking further background is referred.[14] Hoffmann's views were informed by a three-way familiarity: with technical theory, and composition itself; with past writing about music (he refers from time to time to Marpurg, Reichardt, Forkel, Gerber); and with recent Romantic writers, especially Wilhelm Heinrich Wackenroder (1773–98), and the latter's friend and posthumous editor, Ludwig Tieck (1773–1853), who was a generally profound influence on our author. The crux of Hoffmann's formulations is

---

[12]   Translated by Oliver Strunk in *Source Readings in Music History. The Romantic Era* (New York, 1965), 63.

[13]   From *Lyceum* (Berlin, 1797), Aphorism no. 108, in Ernst Behler and Roman Struc (tr., ed.), *Friedrich Schlegel. Dialogue on Poetry and Literary Aphorisms* (University Park, Pennsylvania, and London, 1968), 131.

[14]   Bellamy Hosler, *Changing Aesthetic Views of Instrumental Music in Eighteenth-Century Germany* (Ann Arbor, 1981).

addressed to the value of purely instrumental music – sonatas and symphonies rather than less potentially exalted forms, like sets of variations and solo concertos. Piano concertos were in fact explicitly rejected by Hoffmann, excepting those by Mozart and Beethoven, which latter he characterises as 'not so much concertos as symphonies with piano obbligato' (p. 101). Other concertos are not mentioned, save for Bernhard Romberg's 'Military' cello concerto, which pleased him (p. 391). Variation-sets were associated with mere entertainment-music, their vapidity ironically contrasted with the great peaks of J. S. Bach's 'Goldberg' Variations in 'Kapellmeister Johannes Kreisler's Musical Sufferings'.

The pattern of compositional progress in Germany moved from church-dominated vocal forms in the early eighteenth century through to their decline at the end of the century (see 'Old and New Church Music'), and the steady ascent of purely instrumental, secular forms. The characteristic richness of musical textures in Germany was certainly modified by external influences: Italy (the orchestral sinfonia) and France (the comic opera); but even these were soon assimilated into a tradition that relished the value of counterpoint and thought-out motivic technique. Haydn's symphonies, from about 1764, provided the measure of what could be done in the former. However, such was the legacy of earlier theoretical attitudes, subsequently buttressed by Enlightenment-influenced critics swept along by French rationalist writers, that 'Instrumental music, by virtue of its specific, non-verbal nature was [thought] necessarily inferior [to that using words], even in the eyes of eighteenth-century critics sympathetic to instrumental music's peculiar virtues.'[15] The latter were acknowledged in a number of interesting ways: but yet 'the insistence on verisimilitude – or a deliberately imposed and definite extramusical meaning – was one of the most persistent neoclassic attitudes in eighteenth-century German music criticism. During most of the latter eighteenth century, music without such a content was [theoretically speaking] considered incapable of moving, if not downright trivial and boring.'[16] The overriding temptation was to acquiesce to the majority view that all music required and communicated a 'content' associable with words. Vocal music, naturally, with the added emotive power associated with the human voice, was the apex of this aesthetic hierarchy. One knew what music was expressing. Instrumental music conformed by analogy to the same rules.

But the importation of Italianate sinfonias (Scarlatti, Sammartini, Pergolesi) and the evolution of orchestra music into the *galant*, the rococo, and the

---

[15]   *Ibid.*, 215.
[16]   *Ibid.*, 211–12.

pre-Classical idioms (*c.* 1730–*c.* 1770) posed problems caused by the music's intrinsic dissimilarity with vocal criteria. It was not 'singable', it had increasingly rich and new textures, and thus modes of expression; it could juxtapose strong contrasts of material, unfettered by words. Certain critics tried to take account of its qualities in a positive spirit; they increasingly anticipated the early Romantic position. Although any attempt to encapsulate such complex thought is bound to be a distortion, we should not neglect to mention the texts of Caspar Ruetz (1708–55), who precociously points to a later age:

[Music] actually causes feelings in us; and music has as its own peculiar property thousands of other feelings to which a musical heart is susceptible, but which no orator or poet can awaken through words or moving delivery [i.e. Ruetz rejects prevailing theories of rhetoric]. In this latter case music is not a copy of nature, but the original itself. Music is a universal language of nature which is only intelligible to harmonious souls. And its peculiar expressions, which it does not borrow from anywhere else, have a secret understanding with these souls.[17]

Slightly later critics, like J. A. Hiller (1728–1804), tried to combine respect for instrumental music with neo-French theoretical orthodoxy, and such positions remained broadly current up to the Romantic period. Nevertheless, a new strand of theoretical development is isolated by Hosler, connecting three who granted special meaning to modern instrumental music: (1) Johann Georg Sulzer (1720–79), editor of the *Allgemeine Theorie der schönen Künste* (1771–74), some articles from which were translated for use in later editions of Diderot and D'Alembert's *Encyclopédie*; (2) Karl Ludwig Junker (1748–97); and (3) Johann Nikolaus Forkel (1749–1818). The first, for all his Enlightenment steadfastness of attitude towards musical communication of precise emotion, recognised the limitations of such steadfastness in respect of sonatas and symphonies. So he had recourse to the new classification 'sublime'. Since Edmund Burke's *A Philosophical Enquiry* (1757), this term was used in painting for contemporary reference to 'wild' landscape, admitting a critical order of magnitude at least acknowledging the existence of the immeasurable.

Such an Allegro in a symphony [a first movement, typically] is what a Pindaric ode is in poetry: it likewise elevates and shakes the soul of the listener, and demands the same spirit, the same sublime imagination and the same knowledge of art in order to be successful.[18]

---

[17] *Ibid.*, 126, from Ruetz's 'Sendschreiben eines Freundes', in Friedrich Wilhelm Marpurg, *Historisch-Kritische Beyträge zur Aufnahme der Musik*, i (Berlin, 1754–55), 273–311.

[18] Hosler, *Changing Aesthetic Views*, 166, from Sulzer's article 'Symphonie' in *Allgemeine Theorie der schönen Künste* (2nd edn, Leipzig, 1792–99, reprinted Hildesheim, 1967–70), iv, 479.

Junker, though writing from a generally conservative viewpoint, nonetheless 'seems to have been the first to have worked out an aesthetic theory of music based explicitly on the dynamic nature of the feelings and passions'; in particular, he gave music the unique artistic power to depict the 'transition from passion to passion'.[19] Forkel – whose antipathy towards Gluck's music will be met with more than once in Hoffmann's writings within – lectured at Göttingen, where he was heard by Wackenroder. Forkel, importantly, accepted English theories of emotion (Kames, Hume) that stressed their constant mutation, or development from one state to another. Since he accepted that music represented emotions he accepted also that instrumental music, with all its contrasts, its modern complexity of counterpoint and thematic working, was to be construed as a valued language of the emotions, incommensurable with verbal language, since music 'only becomes the real language of the infinite gradations of the feelings at that point where other languages can no longer reach, and where their ability to express ends'.[20] That one could not as yet define the emotional terms of that language did not remove music's value or content, which inhered in 'subtle relations and agreements among dark feelings'.[21]

Of the connections between W. H. Wackenroder's figure of the Kapellmeister Joseph Berglinger, in *Herzensergiessungen einer kunstliebenden Klosterbruders* (*Confessions from the Heart of an Art-loving Friar*, 1797), and that of Kapellmeister Johannes Kreisler, we shall say more in the Introduction to *Kreisleriana*. Wackenroder is never named by Hoffmann, and indeed long remained in the public consciousness within the shadow of Ludwig Tieck. But Wackenroder's particular Romantic sensitivity to instrumental music, as well as to the psychological dilemmas of the aware composer before his uncomprehending public, cannot but have impressed him. In 1799 Tieck edited *Phantasien über die Kunst für Freunde der Kunst*, in which he explicitly acknowledged Wackenroder's contribution to this collection, and his authorship of the Berglinger material in *Herzensergiessungen*. The essays in *Phantasien* concerning the Naked Saint and concerning church music are mentioned elsewhere in the present book. That which is most relevant here is called 'Das eigenthümliche innere Wesen der Tonkunst und die Seelenlehre der heutigen Instrumentalmusik'. Hosler (*Changing Aesthetic Views*) places special critical emphasis on the term *Seelenlehre* (Doctrine of the soul), so it is unfortunate to this extent that the published

[19]   Hosler, *Changing Aesthetic Views*, 168.
[20]   *Ibid.*, 181, citing Forkel's 'Einzelne von allen übrigen abgesonderte Leidenschaft', in *Musikalisch-Kritische Bibliothek* (Gotha, 1778–79, reprinted Hildesheim, 1964), ii, 65–7.
[21]   Hosler, *Changing Aesthetic Views*, 181, citing Forkel's 'Feine Verhältnisse und Uebereinstimmungen dunkler Gefühle', in *Musikalisch-Kritische Bibliothek*, iii, 349.

translation of the same essay is called 'The Characteristic Inner Nature of the Musical Art and the Psychology of Today's Instrumental Music.'[22]

This remarkable essay contains several anticipations of Hoffmann's theoretical position. Not least interesting are those in the opening paragraph, where Wackenroder produces the image of a raw sound-material given to primitive man, which through the ages has been wonderfully developed, especially through the efforts whereby 'many wise men first descended into the oracle caves of the most occult sciences, where Nature, begetter of all things, herself unveiled for them the fundamental laws of sound. Out of these secret vaults they brought to the light of day the new theory, written in profound numbers.' Hoffmann, too, laid consistent stress on the fundamental and physical origin of music in surrounding nature, connecting the two through the idea of a mysterious 'music of nature' that was vouchsafed to early man, but still exists in 'marvellous acoustical secrets which lie hidden all around us in nature'.[23] Men act through the grace of nature, thereby developing a more perfect music. We have seen already Hoffmann's notion of Beethoven as one more profoundly aware than others of a surrounding 'romantic spirit of music'. Wackenroder goes on to evolve a thesis (his 'Doctrine of the soul') of musical uniqueness among the arts. Based on the 'inexplicable sympathy' existing between modern music and the human heart, music has gone beyond the power of the reasoners and pedants and attained inherent capability to transport to a new world those who know how to submit to it. This process depends on the rejection of words.

Whenever all the inner vibrations of our heart-strings . . . burst apart with *one* outcry the language of words, as the *grave* of the inner frenzy of heart: – then they go forth under a strange sky, amidst the vibrations of blessed harp-strings, in transfigured beauty as if in another life beyond this one . . .

Again, Wackenroder deprecates the 'doubting reasoners': 'have they never felt without words?'. He fastens on the image of the 'rushing river' as metaphor for both the 'depths of the human soul' in all its complex and simultaneous fluidity, and also for the power of music to reflect the same, to be the supreme art capable of '*poetization* of the emotions', which is 'the

---

[22]   Mary Hurst Schubert (tr., ed.), *Wilhelm Heinrich Wackenroder's 'Confessions' and 'Fantasies'* (University Park, Pennsylvania, and London, 1971), 188–94.
[23]   'Automatons', in *The Serapion Brethren*, tr. Alexander Ewing (London, 1886), i, 375. 'The music of nature', in this sense, was an idea deriving from G. H. Schubert. See Pauline Watts, *Music: The Medium of the Metaphysical in E. T. A. Hoffmann* (Amsterdam, 1972), 31–2.

essence of all art'. With this key the door was unlocked that should give instrumental music its legitimate aesthetic superiority.

Wackenroder was alive, as was Hoffmann, to the particular paradox – as Shakespeare puts it in *Much Ado* – 'is it not strange that sheep's guts should hale souls out of men's bodies?'. For Wackenroder, as other early Romantics, paradox leads closer to truth than does cold reasoning. The very essence of human 'mysteries of the soul' consists not in discipline or religious order, but 'that mad spontaneity, with which joy and pain, nature and artificiality, innocence and wildness, jesting and shuddering, befriend each other'.[24] Music, especially 'those divine, magnificent symphonic pieces', reveals this essence, 'in which not one individual emotion is portrayed, but an entire world, an entire drama of human emotions'. Hoffmann, perhaps self-symbolically, refers to this passage in his very first published symphony review, that of two works by Friedrich Witt (1809), declaring almost as a matter of course that such ideas are 'well known to every lover of music' (p. 223).

One may doubt whether he could have declared this had it not been for the weekly existence of the Leipzig *Allgemeine Musikalische Zeitung* (1798–1848), the organ widely accepted as having been the first modern journal devoted to music. Its nature at this time has been described by John Warrack and by Robin Wallace.[25] Wackenroder, Friedrich Schlegel, and Jean Paul wrote about music predominantly before the mature music of Beethoven became assimilated; the story of the first decade of *AMZ* is partially that of the acceptance of the genius of Beethoven as something to be regarded apart from normal judgemental criteria. The composer himself seems to have intervened on his own behalf, indeed. But the underlying assumption was still that the 'content' and technique of his music could be satisfactorily explained:

With regard to both spirit and effect [the Third Piano Concerto] is one of the most outstanding ever written, and I will try to clarify, with reference to the work itself, where this effect originates, to the extent that this can be determined from the materials and their construction.

(Review in *AMZ* dated 28 October 1804)

Substantial reviews of the variations Op. 35 (22 February 1804), Third Symphony (18 February 1807), and Sixth Symphony (17 January 1810) also appeared, together with many shorter reviews, and concert reports including mention of Beethoven sent from cities in several parts of Germany and

---

[24] Wackenroder, 'The Characteristic Inner Nature', in Schubert (ed., tr.), *Wackenroder's 'Confessions'*, 193.
[25] *Weber: Writings*, 4–6; Robin Wallace, *Beethoven's Critics* (Cambridge, 1986), chapter 1.

Austria.[26] Hoffmann's famous review of the Fifth Symphony, prepared over some ten months, digested most of the foregoing aesthetic tendencies and raised them, in the spirit of the early Romantics, to a new level of synthesis. All traces of apology or doubt about the primacy of instrumental music were destroyed. Attention was focussed for the first time on one specific piece (Wackenroder never named particular composers). The latter's concentration on water and the 'depths' of the soul was converted into Hoffmann's thenceforth permanent insistence on images of fire, light, upward movement, intensification; transcendent consciousness was characterised in the phrase 'spirit-realm'.

Novalis had shown the interrelatedness of phenomena, whether stones, clouds, birds' eggs, or the inward awareness capable of seeing their interrelation. An infinitely poeticised awareness would thus reveal an infinite and unified poetic world. Moreover, it was orthodox belief, facilitated by Schelling's writings, that 'since the work of art is fashioned by the same formative principle as is the totality of all things, it must be a perfect microcosm of all creation, just as the cosmos at large constitutes a vast work of art'.[27] In this deeper sense, Beethoven's Fifth Symphony (through Hoffmann's review) reveals the truth of Schelling's and Novalis's world view, independent of any tremendous yet nameless emotions it might wreak in the hearer: yet that these emotions might well be characterised by might, enormity, pain, annihilation, etc., showed all the more vividly Beethoven's full awareness of the might and enormity of created nature, and the puny and dependent stature of man within it. This aspect, in turn, connects with Hoffmann's vivid consciousness of 'higher natures' ruling men's lives.

We come now to a brief consideration of Hoffmann's critical vocabulary, and other specifically musical questions.

Hoffmann neither invented the standard review format of *AMZ* reviews, nor most of their terminology, however much he reinterpreted both. There were three basic orders of *AMZ* review: the brief notice, the brief review, and the comprehensive review.[28] The first is self-explanatory; the second contained only the essentials, chiefly factual. The third type, easily the least common, appeared only eight times in the first seven annual volumes. Of these, only three (Beethoven's Third Piano Concerto, and the Third and Sixth Symphonies) were of instrumental music. All tended to tripartite shape: introduction – main part – conclusion. There is unfortunately no

---

26 Schnaus, *Hoffmann als Beethoven-Rezensent*, 15–18.
27 Cardinal, *German Romantics in Context*, 83.
28 Schnaus, *Hoffmann als Beethoven-Rezensent*, 19–20.

room here to digress by discussing the work of Peter Schnaus in analysing *AMZ* vocabulary and outlook: a certain amount of information is in Wallace's study (see note 25). As Hoffmann became more established as a writer, so he varied the construction of his reviews more freely.

Concerning technical terminology, Hoffmann accepted the normal current understanding of a sonata form movement, defined at the time by J. G. Portmann (1789) and H. C. Koch (1787, 1793). These definitions have been translated and discussed by William S. Newman.[29] A first movement was conceived of in two parts, or sections, or halves, the first up to the double bar (our 'exposition'; translated in this book as 'first half'). The second part, section, or half simply contained the rest of the movement (our 'development' plus our 'recapitulation'; translated in this book as 'second half'). Koch, indeed, subdivided the second half into two divisions corresponding to our modern, familiar categories as above; but Hoffmann gives no special emphasis to such a subdivision, and was content to avoid delineating a predominantly tripartite structure.

It will be clear to the reader, on inspecting the level of detail explored by Hoffmann, especially in his reviews of Beethoven and Spohr, that he required terms with which to refer to many different musical entities. The approach taken in this translation has been, firstly, to convey accurately what Hoffmann is musically referring to in a given case; secondly, to remain faithful to the original term where this carried one satisfactorily defined meaning; and thirdly, not to impose artificial (modern) consistency or terminology. Certain terms can be rapidly disposed of here. When the English-speaking reader sees the terms on the left, she or he can take it that the original term will be that opposite:

theme   Thema

figure   Figur

idea   Gedanke

motive   Motive (first appears in the review of Beethoven's Op. 70 No. 2, first movement)

element   Element

melody   Melodie

[29] William S. Newman, *The Sonata in the Classic Era* (2nd edn, New York, 1972), 31–5.

Combination-terms involving the above are likewise of consistent character, e.g.:

main theme	Hauptthema
main idea	Hauptgedanke (etc.)
secondary theme	Nebenthema
secondary idea	Nebengedanke (etc.)

Hoffmann, like H. C. Koch in his *Musikalisches Lexikon* (1802), used either 'Hauptsatz' or 'Thema', also however 'Hauptthema' and 'Hauptgedanke', to refer to the main theme or first subject of a movement. In such cases 'Hauptsatz' is translated in this book as 'main subject'. The problematic terminological areas are those of the second subject, the transition sections, the codetta, and the retransition. No simple German equivalents are observable here in Hoffmann. What we would call 'second subject' appears either as 'Mittelsatz in der Dominante', or 'zweites Thema', or 'zweites Hauptthema', etc. In this book such phrases are translated variously, i.e. faithfully to Hoffmann, not as 'second subject'. (It is interesting in this regard to recall the differing opinions held at the time about the nature and function of a second subject: see Newman, note 29 above.)

The word 'Satz' was defined in four ways by H. C. Koch in 1802, and used in more than four senses by Hoffmann; it was frequently combined by the latter with various prefixes. Each case in this book has been translated according to its contextual meaning, while maximum attention has also been paid to consistency. Where a crucial area of doubt remains, it is noted in the editorial matter. Likewise, Hoffmann used terms inconsistently when referring to smaller transition sections or passages – something that becomes of some importance in the Fifth Symphony review – or when referring to subsidiary thematic material. However, this is not to say he was insouciant about technical matters: on the contrary, his search for appropriate terms bears witness to great assiduity, and Schnaus declares, in his study, that Hoffmann actually included more detail in the Fifth Symphony review than almost any preceding *AMZ* review had done. Desire for detail, in fact, somewhat overcame terminological capability in describing the musical area immediately before the double bar of a sonata movement, or before the end of the development section, as may be seen from the editor's notes to the review of the trios, Op. 70.

Of the terms used by Hoffmann in discussing opera, only one or two invite comment here. One is the perennial question of 'Gedicht' and 'Dichter': since we are dealing with the poetic and prosodic parts of opera, various possibilities exist in English, i.e. 'text', 'libretto', 'poet', 'librettist', etc., and no uniform or universal equivalents are desirable. Markedly idiosyncratic is Hoffmann's coining of two words in order to describe his ideal and authentic type of musical drama, in the tradition of the reforming Gluck. Thus we find 'Tongedicht' in 'On a Remark of Sacchini's, and on so-called Effect in Music', and 'Tondichtung' near the outset of 'Further Observations on Spontini's Opera *Olimpia*'. For reasons entirely unconnected with Richard Wagner (who in any case disapproved of the term) the preferred translation in this book is 'music-drama'. But of course the qualities Hoffmann is trying to convey are highly relevant to the later history of Romantic opera. A further favoured word is 'Moment', applied to a particular point in either an opera or a Lied (see the review of Riem's *Zwölf Lieder*) with the added sense of a dynamic impulse: this was clearly an important ingredient in Gluck's attainment of 'music-drama'. All these questions must be related to Hoffmann's reference, in another context, to 'a certain precision carried over from my life as a public official' (letter of 26 July 1813: *HBW*, i, 403).

In a fascinating section of his book, Peter Schnaus discusses Hoffmann's Romantic reinterpretation of established critical terms. One of the most celebrated of these is 'Besonnenheit', ordinarily meaning roughly 'self-possession' or 'composure'. Schnaus points out that there is a seeming connection between Hoffmann's use of it in the review of Beethoven's Fifth Symphony (and the trios Op. 70), and the following passage from Jean Paul's *Vorschule der Aesthetik* (1804): 'Now there is a higher awareness [*höhere Besonnenheit*], that which divides the inner world into two halves, a self and its domain, [or] into a creator and his world.'[30] Having (as we said earlier) implied a division between the individual effects produced by the music, and the Romantic awareness to which these effects give access, Hoffmann uses 'Besonnenheit' of Beethoven to signify that special mental property that gave him leave to reveal instrumental music's inherent Romanticism. This appears in the translation as 'rational awareness'.

The reader of Hoffmann's reviews will become conscious of a variety of musical preferences expressed from time to time. These include his desire for fidelity and dedication in the performer regarding the work of art; but also acceptance of certain freedoms that the performer can be permitted, including experimenting with the pedal combinations in Beethoven's music (see p. 309) and the need for vocal ornamentation in Mozart opera (see p.

30   Schnaus, *Hoffmann als Beethoven-Rezensent*, 81.

399). Hoffmann disliked the modern tendency to hurry (review of the Beethoven Mass in C, p. 339), and the use of *cercar la nota* in opera singers (p. 396). He expected that the printed repeats in a symphony would be obeyed in performance (review of Spohr's First Symphony). His views on what was difficult to play and what was not difficult – whether for orchestral players or solo pianists – are very interesting.

Hoffmann's consistent response to counterpoint in music was both striking and also typical of an aspect of musical Romanticism. This was surely not a simple desire to go back before the rococo and establish a neo-Gothic (Baroque) aesthetic, although Hosler not unreasonably points out some connections in that direction:

For just as the Romantic movement in general displayed a yearning for Germany's dark distant past, and found a new appreciation for the fantasy of fairy-tales and the unreasonable exuberance of Gothic cathedrals [see, specifically, Hoffmann's appre-ciation of Strasbourg Cathedral in *Kreisleriana* p. 104 and the review of Beethoven's Mass in C, p. 328], certain fundamental Romantic musical views seem to constitute a return to basic pre-Enlightenment attitudes towards music . . . [this] was the case with the so-called gothic art of counterpoint.[31]

Paradoxically, to us, this response was not obviously channelled through an appreciation of Renaissance church music, or the contrapuntal music of Palestrina in particular (see 'Old and New Church Music'). That is because Palestrina's music, like Protestant chorales, was understood as chordal more than polyphonic. Wackenroder's essay on church music memorably talks of this: 'To [God-fearing souls] belongs that old chorale-like church music which sounds like an eternal "MISERERE MEI DOMINE!", the slow, deep chords of which creep along in deep valleys like pilgrims laden with sin.'[32] To Hoffmann, counterpoint was a self-evident sign of musical seriousness, argumentative value, and compositional skill. Contrapuntal weakness irks him in Paer's opera *Sofonisba*, while intensive contrapuntal working in Beethoven's Trio Op. 70 No. 1 is described enthusiastically and is illustrated: 'this is the most original and ingenious part of the whole [opening] Allegro'. On a separate level, the symbolic, Romantic signifi-cance of counterpoint for Hoffmann in *Kreisleriana* will be discussed in the Introduction to that cycle.

The desirability of 'unity' was an old-established criterion, and it fitted with the unified world-view of early Romanticism. We find that Hoffmann values above all an instrumental or operatic work's overall unity of *charac-*

---

[31] Hosler, *Changing Aesthetic Views*, 229.
[32] Wackenroder, 'Concerning the Various Genres in Every Art and Especially Concerning Various Types of Church Music', in Schubert (ed., tr.), *Wackenroder's 'Confessions'*, 185.

ter, or idea, and refers to this demand in the review of Witt's symphonies, comparing it with the way one expects unity in a spoken play. To make manifest that unity by means of musical interconnections ought to follow as a consequence of a composer's technical consciousness and ability.

More individual to Hoffmann was his awareness of how unity ('the splendid tree, leaves, blossom, and fruit . . . springing from the same seed') related to artistic method. In the *Serapions-Brüder* collection, the friends agree that 'It is useless for a poet to set to work to make us believe in a thing which he does not believe in himself, cannot believe in, because he has never really seen it.'[33] An artist must 'see' the whole work inwardly, just as Mozart's *Don Giovanni* 'was all laid out and complete in his mind in all its wonderfully distinctive detail'.[34] Such total contemplation was also the technique of Gluck, according to a source Hoffmann knew well, who 'usually kept wholly completed operas in mind for a long time, to brood over them, before he wrote them down'.[35] At the end of *Kreisleriana*, acts of musical inspiration are themselves anatomised. As an analytical visionary, Hoffmann the writer must also be perceived as a totality. 'Do not let my second maxim out of your heart and mind: Everything is one!' (letter of 8 September 1813: *HBW*, i, 415): *Es ist alles Eins!*

[33] Hoffmann, *The Serapion Brethren*, tr. Ewing, i, 51.
[34] See 'Extremely Random Thoughts', p. 106.
[35] Ernst Ludwig Gerber, *Historisch-Biographisches Lexikon der Tonkünstler (1790–1792)*, ed. Othmar Wessely (Graz, 1977), i, col. 518.

Kreisleriana

INTRODUCTION TO
KREISLERIANA

Context

Kreisleriana is a cycle of musical writings, forming part of Hoffmann's first book, the *Fantasiestücke in Callot's Manier* (*Fantasy-pictures in the Style of Callot*) (4 vols., Bamberg, 1814–15). This book itself was later issued in a revised version in two 'parts', in 1819, and *Kreisleriana*, embedded within it, also consists of a bi-partite cycle: Part I with six numbered sections, and Part II with seven numbered sections. The reader will find more complete bibliographical information below, where the present Introduction continues with remarks on the individual sections of the cycle and on the origins of each. But it is important first to come to terms with the work as a whole.

Critically speaking, *Kreisleriana* has fared indifferently so far. English readers have had the opportunity of only limited acquaintance with it.[1] Hanne Castein, in her sympathetic edition (Stuttgart, 1983), mentions that its structure has attracted 'hardly a word' of attention, and that it has generally been seen as an 'overture' to Hoffmann's novel *Kater Murr* (*Tom-cat Murr*) (1820, 1821), which is subtitled 'With the Fragmentary Biography of Kapellmeister Johannes Kreisler on Random Sheets of Scrap Paper'.[2] I shall refer to the analyses of *Kreisleriana* by Jocelyne Kolb and Wolfgang Wittkowski in due course; but neither they nor the present essay have space to give this rich and complex text the exegesis it deserves.

Editors and commentators have habitually separated *Kreisleriana* from other essays in musical criticism published around the same time by

---

[1]   R. Murray Schafer, *E. T. A. Hoffmann and Music* (Toronto, 1975), translated four sections from Part I and one section from Part II, but published them in the wrong order. The final section of Part II, which cannot meaningfully be separated from what precedes it, was translated by Max Knight in *Nineteenth-Century Music*, v (1982), 189–92.

[2]   Leonard J. Kent and Elizabeth C. Knight (tr., ed.), *Selected Writings of E. T. A. Hoffmann* (Chicago and London, 1969), vol. ii: *The Life and Opinions of Kater Murr*.

Hoffmann; but on some levels there is no discontinuity between them. On the contrary, there is an interpenetration of ideas and responses, which the content of the present book helps to show. For example, 'On a Remark of Sacchini's, and on so-called Effect in Music' (II–6),[3] whose subjects are opera as drama and the rôle of 'effect', was clearly stimulated by Hoffmann's initial hostile reaction to recent operas by Gaspare Spontini, *La vestale* and *Fernand Cortez*. Whereas the same antipathy is openly expressed in Hoffmann's 'Letters on Music in Berlin' (p. 392), first published in January 1815, the name of Spontini is wholly absent from *Kreisleriana*. Again, fundamental notions concerning the process of musical composition set forth in 'Johannes Kreisler's Certificate of Apprenticeship' (II–7) relate to important pages in the same 'Letters on Music in Berlin'. And the curious twinned letters of Kreisler and Wallborn (II–1, II–2) could have arisen only through Hoffmann's close relations with the librettist of the opera *Undine*, Baron F. de la Motte Fouqué, who was also the actual author of the 'Letter from Baron Wallborn to Kapellmeister Kreisler' (II–1). The Wallborn–Kreisler 'letters' present the private, imaginative responses of a real poet and composer in the course of collaboration on an opera; the outward, dialectic responses of imagined potential operatic collaborators occur only in the separately published dialogue *The Poet and the Composer* (p. 189), actually begun in September 1813, shortly after Hoffmann had composed Act I of *Undine*.

It should also be mentioned that because *Kreisleriana* belongs in the *Fantasiestücke* collection, where it first appeared, strands of thought from the former recur variously in component stories of the whole publication. For example, even though the composer Gluck and his works play a part in four of the *Kreisleriana* (I–1, I–5, II–5, and II–6), one can comprehend the meaning of Gluck for Hoffmann, both as a fellow-composer and an iconic figure in his mythology, only by knowing the short story *Ritter Gluck*.[4] This stands at the gateway to the *Fantasiestücke*, after the short essay 'Jacques Callot' and immediately before *Kreisleriana*, Part I. And although one obtains a good idea of Hoffmann's understanding of the superiority of Mozart's music and its historical rôle from the various remarks in five of *Kreisleriana* (I–1, I–3, I–4, I–5, and II–6), it is only from the story *Don Juan* (*Don Giovanni*) that the supreme importance of Mozart's opera for Hoffmann himself is to be understood. Hoffmann positioned *Don Juan* immedi-

---

[3]   Here and subsequently, a roman numeral I or II refers to *Kreisleriana*, Part I or II, the accompanying arabic numeral to the number of the essay.

[4]   On Hoffmann's mythology and a view of *Ritter Gluck* in relation to it, see Kenneth Negus, *E. T. A. Hoffmann's Other World* (Philadelphia, 1965). There are many published translations of this tale.

ately after the first part of *Kreisleriana*, i.e. just after 'The Complete Machinist'. The great significance of the work of the writer Novalis (1772–1801) for *Kreisleriana* is strongly hinted at near the close of 'The Music-Hater' (II–5); but the panegyric to him occurs in *Nachricht von den neuesten Schicksalen des Hundes Berganza*[5] (*Report of the Latest Fortunes of the Dog Berganza*), which appears after *Don Juan*. Many other correspondences could be listed.

Structure and Authorial Voice

Kreisleriana presents a double cycle; Hoffmann even points to this through his employment of a double numbering system. While I could not agree that *Kreisleriana* is designed as a whole in a manner analogous to J. S. Bach's thirty 'Goldberg' Variations, which Johannes Kreisler himself performs in the first essay,[6] it is noteworthy that both cycles divide half-way in a distinctly formal gesture. Bach's sixteenth variation consists of an 'Ouverture' in the French style, while Hoffmann's 'overture' to Part II recapitulates and embellishes the circumstances of Kreisler's disappearance, which were first recounted in the opening to Part I. Moreover, Wallborn's letter (II–1) explicitly refers back to points raised in 'Kapellmeister Johannes Kreisler's Musical Sufferings' (I–1), adding to some and taking issue with others. '*Ombra adorata*' and 'Kreisler's Musico-Poetic Club' form a pair, being detailed subjective responses to specific musical experiences. 'Beethoven's Instrumental Music' and 'On a Remark of Sacchini's, and on so-called Effect in Music' make a parallel pair of 'objective' responses to the genres of modern instrumental music on the one hand, and modern opera on the other. The cycle begins with mention of a Kapellmeister's document, and ends with a strange certificate. Wittkowski calls the second part an 'ascending continuation' of the first one.[7] But Castein (p. 149) correctly warns against assuming any systematic design in Hoffmann's approach to

---

5 E. T. A. Hoffmann, *Fantasie- und Nachtstücke*, ed. Walter Müller-Seidel (Munich, 1960), 136–7.

6 Suggested in Jocelyne Kolb, 'E. T. A. Hoffmann's *Kreisleriana*: à la recherche d'une forme perdue?', *Monatshefte*, lxix (1977), 34–44. I would particularly reject Kolb's identification of 'a circular impulse' in *Kreisleriana*; that it exists as a set of 'variations on a theme' is formally untenable.

7 Wolfgang Wittkowski, 'Stufe und Aufschwung. Die vertikale Grundrichtung der musikalischen Struktur in Hoffmanns *Kreisleriana I*', in Steven Paul Scher (ed.), *Literatur und Musik. Ein Handbuch zur Theorie und Praxis eines komparatistischen Grenzgebietes* (Berlin, 1984), 300–11. This paper, to which we shall return, offers suggestive observations on Hoffmann's exalted language and the tendency of the cycle towards its final synthesis in the last essay.

grouping: 'such an obvious structural principle would be uncharacteristic pedantry for him'.

Although most commentators assume that the entire cycle is supposed to be understood as the work of the fictional character Johannes Kreisler, this assumption obscures what I take to be the true nature of the work as a whole. Certainly at the outset it is established that Kreisler, who has disappeared, left a number of haphazard writings behind scribbled on 'the plain reverse-side of several sheets of music'. These are put forward as the following 'brief essays, largely humorous in content'. Though they are unsigned, we easily accept this as 'true' of I–2, I–3 and I–4. 'Beethoven's Instrumental Music' (I–4) contains a reference to Kreisler himself in the first person, as author; while I–5 even reminds the reader of Kreisler's habit of scribbling 'random thoughts' on 'almost every blank page, every cover' of music. His mordant irony is fully unleashed in 'Thoughts about the Great Value of Music' and 'The Complete Machinist'. However, the second part of the cycle introduces ever-increasing authorial ambiguities, which are not really anticipated in Part I. Part II, indeed, opens with Wallborn's letter to Kreisler, establishing the motif of the double, and just before this, Hoffmann introduces himself by name for the first time: 'On the very night when he [Kreisler] departed for ever, he brought his intimate friend Hoffmann a carefully sealed letter . . .' (p. 124); this letter is then presented as II–2. The next section, 'Kreisler's Musico-Poetic Club' (II–3), continues the imaginative insinuation of 'Hoffmann', since (p. 135) the club member who rescues Kreisler from entering the 'dark abyss' provoked by C minor is called the 'true friend', a figure who is expressly – several lines later – identified with the 'travelling enthusiast', who is already established as the author of the whole *Fantasiestücke*.[8] Whereas 'Report of an Educated Young Man' (II–4) may be taken to come from the same pen as that which produced 'Thoughts about the Great Value of Music' (I–3), the whole picture changes with 'The Music-Hater' (II–5); this surely has to be taken as written by Hoffmann (setting aside from consideration its gentle-toned beginning and verifiably autobiographical subject-matter) because Kreisler is referred to near the end (p. 151) in the third person:

Is anyone likely to believe that there is nevertheless one real musician who, with regard to my musical sensibility, is of the same opinion as my aunt? Certainly no one will set much store by it when I say that he is none other than Kapellmeister Johannes Kreisler, who is notorious for his eccentricity.

And, in a crucial passage, the author goes on to tell how Kreisler 'said that

8   The *Fantasiestücke* is subtitled 'Leaves from the Diary of a Travelling Enthusiast'; the latter figure occasionally appears as narrator, e.g. in *Don Juan*.

I was rather like the novice in the Temple of Saïs ... I did not understand him, since I had not read the writings of Novalis, to which he referred me.'

The penultimate essay takes the form of a serious critical discussion, and is neither signed nor provided with references to any author. But for 'Johannes Kreisler's Certificate of Apprenticeship', the author is again quite separated from the *persona* of Kreisler; separated in order to be able to present Kreisler with evidence of his successful apprenticeship, but at the same time mysteriously to claim unity of person with Kreisler. The authorial voice is, literally, magisterial; it is this separation of authorial voice from Kreisler that determines the tone from beginning to end. Finally, Kreisler is delivered at the gates of the Temple of Isis (i.e. at Saïs), ready to proceed to higher learning; whereupon the authorial voice ends by signing himself, 'like you', as 'Johannes Kreisler, *cidevant* Kapellmeister', i.e. formerly Kapellmeister, now one who has gone beyond that state. Earlier, too, this imaginative unison of persons floats in and out of focus throughout the essay's introductory section. Most striking is the image of the mirror, reflecting the other's features when the author looks into it (p. 159):

I could certainly provide [a certificate for you] without further ado, but as I look at you in the mirror I become distinctly melancholy at heart.

The 'apprenticeship' and the final unison take *Kreisleriana* well beyond a simple set of variations. However, Hoffmann is known to have been influenced by literary dialogue form. (Wallborn's letter to Kreisler, II-1, refers indirectly to Plato's dialogue, *Symposium*.) Perhaps in its original inspiration *Kreisleriana* was a kind of wonderful expansion of the dialogue by Diderot, *Le Neveu de Rameau* (*Rameau's Nephew*), wherein by means of the *alter ego* of Kreisler – the modern form of the Nephew – Hoffmann could explore certain grotesque and dynamic aspects of modern music.[9] In the most traditional sense, the result is an extended, complex discourse with the self about the art of music in the early Romantic period.

The Journey to Saïs

Kreisleriana certainly is not 'about' a fictional Kreisler in the sense that the late novel *Kater Murr* is. There is no story; no setting; no outer *dénouement*; there is at first sight only a seeming set of literary relics. But once we observe

[9]   Hoffmann refers to *Rameau's Nephew* in 'Kreisler's Musical Sufferings'. He would have read it in Goethe's translation (1805), the first publication of the dialogue in any language. The pairing of Kreisler with the Nephew has been discussed by George Edgar Slusser in '*Le Neveu de Rameau* and Hoffmann's Johannes Kreisler: Affinities and Influences', *Comparative Literature*, xxvii (1975), 327–43, albeit in a way that makes him into too much of a proto-Kreisler. We shall consider this question briefly below.

the fiction of authorial separation, look more closely at the subject-matter of the closing essays, and consider Novalis's fragmentary novel, *Die Lehrlinge zu Sais* (*The Novices at Saïs*) (published 1802), it becomes apparent that Hoffmann is using the ideas of Novalis to bring his cycle to a conclusion in the form of an interior *Bildungsroman* (novel of development).

Die Lehrlinge zu Sais, which has been called by Ulrich Gaier 'perhaps the most complicated text in German literature', seems to describe events around the Temple of Saïs in Egypt; an 'entirely passive character',[10] the Novice, is (implicitly) learning wisdom from the Master, from other novices and from travellers, whose speeches occupy sections of the text. Part of the overall theme relates back to Schiller's poem *Das verschleierte Bild zu Sais* (*The Veiled Image at Saïs*) (1795) in which a novice is punished for lifting the temple veil. But Novalis makes the necessity of this symbolic unveiling a central point of his text, particularly in the inserted parable of Hyazinth. Hyazinth leaves behind his parents and his beloved (Rosenblütchen) in order to seek the Temple of Isis, not knowing if he will ever return, in order to 'become whole' in finding 'the Mother of All Things, the Veiled Virgin'. After the seeming passage of many years, Hyazinth is led beyond 'the last vestiges of earthliness' to the goddess;[11] he lifts the veil; mysteriously, it is Rosenblütchen who embraces him. 'Rosenblütchen, then, is identified with Isis' and 'His discovery of her is also the discovery of his higher and true self.'[12] Essentially, the search for truth ends within.

In the same way, *Kreisleriana* is a journey (of apprenticeship, learning) that also ends at Saïs; Kreisler joins the company of 'masters and journeymen'. Though Kreisler remains apart from them in respect of his untidy writing, and so on, he is implied to have greater penetration than they. Novalis's text is explicitly the model behind the autobiographical story of 'The Music-Hater' (II–5) of seemingly restricted sensibility; here, the narrator's apparent 'musical backwardness' (p. 151) recalls the awkward yet ever-observant pupil in *Die Lehrlinge zu Sais*. This novice finds the essential stone that completes the mysterious patterns of nature in the temple's collection of natural objects. In the same way, by being musically child-like and true to himself, Hoffmann's 'music-hater' will (implicitly) attain superior understanding.

---

[10]   Nicholas Saul, *History and Poetry in Novalis and in the Tradition of the German Enlightenment* (Institute of Germanic Studies, University of London, Bithell Series of Dissertations, vol. viii, London, 1984), 126.

[11]   F.V.M.T. and U.C.B. (tr.), *The Disciples at Saïs and Other Fragments by Novalis* (London, 1903), 119.

[12]   Saul, *History and Poetry*, 138–9. The concept of the 'Temple at Saïs' returns elsewhere in the *Fantasiestücke*, e.g. *Der Magnetiseur*, 'Mariens Brief an Adelgunde'.

Specifically, however, the *Kreisleriana* is a journey of musical discovery: that of self-knowledge in the art of composition. It will be seen from the opening of the first part that Kreisler, though a splendid improviser, and never less than sensitive, could not write down his musical compositions, or if he did do so, would always destroy them shortly afterwards. The will to learn is present, for at the end of '*Ombra adorata*' the narrator describes in mystical terms the rebirth of inspiration in the form of sparks: 'I shall contrive to harness them, and combine them . . .' (p. 90). The tide turns in the second part, when Kreisler writes to Wallborn:

Do you not think, Baron Wallborn, that your words could often be my melody, and my melody your words? I have just this moment written down the music for a beautiful song whose words you composed some time ago . . . At times I have the feeling that the song is a whole opera!

In 'The Music-Hater', the authorial voice has learnt to objectify his artistic reactions, and accept their social consequences (in autobiographical terms, the compositional late developer who now creates his greatest work, *Undine*). Then in 'On a Remark of Sacchini's, and on so-called Effect in Music' we read the confident prescriptions for potential compositions and indeed potential composers, as though spoken by a master; this is no longer the adulation and analysis of the music of others (Gluck, Bach, Beethoven, etc.). There is a new-found objective command of resources, and of the language in which to express them. The 'hapless composer grimly striving for effect' is certainly counselled to learn from the masters, thus giving him a 'mysterious rapport with their spirit'; but so long as he has some genius, 'the extraordinary sounds of his own inner music' can then be fixed in a score thanks to 'his study of harmony and his technical exercises'.

With Saïs attained, and the authorial Hoffmann separated from the authorial Kreisler, there is a re-enactment of Novalis's lifting of the veil: the persona of the Master sees in the mirror the persona of Kreisler. The one discovers himself in the discovery of his other self. Perhaps Hoffmann intended a translation and absorption of his Kreisler into some higher state, thus prompting the closing seal in the shape of a cross. In that sense, the authorial Hoffmann has been performing his own parable of apprenticeship and initiation which, by virtue of reading it, we undergo too. But precision of authorial voice is less significant than the process of 'inner history'. Just as in Novalis's *Die Lehrlinge zu Sais* the reader is faced with speakers who are not described, but have to be interpreted, so the reader of *Kreisleriana* faces different characters and tones of voice, learns from them, and so progressively understands the deepest wisdom that Hoffmann can offer about what actually constitutes a genuine modern music, and not a little about how such a music is to be discovered. This latter discovery forms the purpose of the parable of Chrysostomus that Hoffmann places within 'Johannes Kreisler's Certificate of Apprenticeship'; obviously the parable of Hyazinth was in Hoffmann's mind here too (if not also other contemporary 'fairy stories'). Even this notion of 'artistic discovery' and formulation may have come from Novalis: a matching proposition is found in his earlier work, *Pollen*, which is quoted below, p. 62.

Viewed, in short, from this perspective, *Kreisleriana* is a Romantic novel, indebted to Wackenroder, Friedrich Schlegel, Novalis, and the nature philosophers and scientists whom Hoffmann sometimes quotes in his text, or alludes to. It is apparently random in design, yet unified to a high degree; passionately concerned to define music as a Romantic art, yet highly charged with vivifying irony and humour. It is a literary apologia for music and opera vis-à-vis composition, performance, history, technique, social context, inspiration, operatic theory, theatrical practice. But it is a prescriptive text, not a passive one.

The Frontispiece to the First Edition

It is all the more interesting, in view of *Kreisleriana*'s nature as here defined, to turn to the vignette Hoffmann himself drew for the first volume of the book. This vignette was sent to his friend and publisher, C. F. Kunz, on 12 August 1813, with a covering letter showing that Hoffmann believed that the image (together with another for the second volume) would be self-explanatory to the reader. This image is reproduced as figure 1, and its allegorical significance, which Hoffmann explained in a letter dated 8 September the same year, proves that even before he had written down the parable of Chrysostomus, he was thinking of *Kreisleriana* as being about the condition of composers and modern music in general. There was never any Hoffmann drawing of Johannes Kreisler that was intended for publication, either in 1813–14 or at the time of *Kater Murr* five years later. In his letter to Kunz of 8 September, he wrote of the vignette: 'Do the *mysteries of music* then not speak to you through the sounds of the harp, which ring out at sunrise from the *ancient German troubadour* before the enigmatic image of the *Isis-headed sphinx*?'[13]

The troubadour, expressing the continuity and nationality of German poetic and musical art, now attends at Saïs, where, presumably, he has qualified at the temple of Isis like Kreisler, since he has learned to interpret the 'mysteries' correctly. Perhaps the significance of the sunrise is a reference once again to Novalis's tale, in which the novice who finds the missing

---

[13]   *HBW*, i, 413.

1 Hoffmann's own frontispiece to the first edition of *Fantasiestücke in Callot's Manier* (1814).

stone returned at dawn: 'Suddenly, when the glimmer of morning came, we heard his voice in a coppice near. He sang a noble, joyous song.'[14] The fact that the troubadour is German relates to Hoffmann's choice of four 'exempla' in *Kreisleriana*, the German-speaking composers whose symbolic rôle is discussed below.

Connections with Romantic Philosophy

We can gauge the extent of Hoffmann's literary and philosophical synthesis in *Kreisleriana* by pausing to mention some of the main currents of Romantic belief surrounding him.

Of Hoffmann's creative reaction to Friedrich Schlegel's work there is no doubt. Kenneth Negus has usefully coupled the two writers in the introduction to *E. T. A. Hoffmann's Other World*, particularly as concerns Romantic mythologies. Schlegel's adoption of the literary fragment (cf. Hoffmann's 'Extremely Random Thoughts'; I–5), and of the dialogue form; his prescription for the novel 'as a mixture of storytelling, song and other forms',[15] and for the essential mythology of the Romantic arts as stemming from a spiritualised nature; and his view of the basic tendency of Romantic art towards the transcendental: all these elements are detectable in *Kreisleriana*. Schlegel's prose sometimes resembles Hoffmann's. And it is in one of Schlegel's few references to music (albeit as an art of spiritual feeling – Hoffmann on the other hand never expresses himself in terms implying religious belief) that he writes:

[This quality of spiritual feeling] cannot be grasped forcibly and comprehended mechanically, but it can be amiably lured by mortal beauty and veiled in it . . . for the true poet all this . . . is only a hint at something higher, the infinite, a hieroglyph of the one eternal love and the sacred fullness of life of creative nature.[16]

This close sense of divine self-revelation or self-manifestation through inorganic and organic nature was prominently articulated through F. W. von Schelling's writings;[17] certainly Hoffmann is known to have read this philosopher's work. (The Christian cabalistic tradition behind Schelling has been concisely traced by Ernst Benz.)[18] Roger Cardinal writes of

---

[14]   F.V.M.T. and U.C.B. (tr.), *The Disciples at Saïs*, 95.
[15]   From the *Dialogue on Poetry* (1800). See Behler and Struc, *Schlegel. Dialogue on Poetry*, 102.
[16]   *Ibid.*, 99–100.
[17]   Especially the *Ideen zu einer Philosophie der Natur* (1797), *Von der Weltseele* (1798; Hoffmann completed his reading of it in July 1813), and *Erster Entwurf eines Systems der Naturphilosophie* (1799).
[18]   Ernst Benz, *The Mystical Sources of German Romantic Philosophy*, tr. B. R. Reynolds and Eunice M. Paul (Allison Park, Pennsylvania, 1983), chapter 4.

Schelling's influential theory of art and its stress on the metaphysical dimension:

Schelling defines Art as the expression of the infinite spirit made manifest in the finite. Beauty, he concludes, is the point of coincidence of the real with the ideal, the penetration of the infinite into the finite, which we can only apprehend by aesthetic intuition.[19]

Hoffmann's contribution to Romantic musical aesthetics was firstly to fix music as an art that could answer Schlegel's demand for a 'hieroglyphic expression of surrounding nature';[20] the art that could supremely 'hint at something higher, the infinite'. This he did in the famous essay 'Beethoven's Instrumental Music'; I–4 (itself carefully prepared for by ironic reversal in the preceding essay), and towards the end of *Kreisleriana* (p. 164):

In any individual language, there is such an intimate connection between sound and word that no idea can arise in us without its hieroglyphs (letters of the alphabet). But music is a universal language of nature . . .

And the point of Hoffmann's culminating fable of Chrysostomus is finally, 'the ascent to higher things and transfiguration through music and song!' (p. 165).

Secondly, Hoffmann evidently wished to go much further in philosophical terms than he went in the celebrated assertion (p. 96) that '[Instrumental music] is the most romantic of all arts, one might almost say the only one that is genuinely romantic, since its only subject-matter is infinity.' For one thing, he had to evolve a Romantic view of opera, discussed later on p. 172. In sharpest distinction to music without voices that inspired the above salvo, opera could never escape the potentially corrupting influences of the arts of drama, poetry, acting, and stagecraft. For another, Hoffmann obviously felt that music, as the art of vibration, acoustics, and a harmonic system based on the octave (as ordained by nature), could be almost scientifically construed as the art fundamentally closest to that surrounding nature in which true Romanticism was held to be immanent. He approached this question both by using contemporary works of natural science, and by developing the notion of the hieroglyph. G. H. Schubert's *Die Symbolik des Traumes* (1814),[21] for example, assumed the basic connection between dream-images, images occurring in nature, and esoteric cul-

---

[19] Cardinal, *German Romantics in Context*, 84.
[20] Behler and Struc (tr., ed.), *Schlegel. Dialogue on Poetry*, 85.
[21] Referred to by Hoffmann in the text of II–7, p. 160; opening paraphrased by him in part of 'Extremely Random Thoughts' (I–5) (p. 105). See also below, p. 74.

tural images (as of 'old Egyptian monuments' or 'curious idols of the Orientals'). Hoffmann repeatedly asserted esoteric connections between music or musical sounds, and images of colours and lights.[22] By insisting on their similarity or even semi-identity, he suggests Romantic music's basically metaphysical nature (partly by removing our image of it away from the mundane circumstances of its production), and also its transcendental qualities. But there are also many passages in *Kreisleriana* in which music is metaphorically combined with things other than light. Kreisler's coat was in C sharp minor, its collar in E major (p. 130); his fantasy interprets specific chords in terms of poetic images ('Kreisler's Musico-Poetic Club'); music is actually 'the mysterious Sanskrit of nature, translated into sound . . .' (p. 94). These things express an essential if paradoxical coherence, one that reaches a climactic form at the end of the cycle: 'It is no empty metaphor, no allegory, when the musician says that colour, fragrance, light appear to him as sounds, and that in their intermingling he perceives an extraordinary concert' (p. 164).

The Romantic musician, however, not only 'reads', but 'hears' nature; just as the element of sound (vibration) is essential to nature, so music is its natural Romantic medium of expression. The physicist Johann Wilhelm Ritter, whose *Fragmente aus dem Nachlasse eines jungen Physikers*[23] Hoffmann alludes to four times in 'Johannes Kreisler's Certificate of Apprenticeship', asserts the utter supremacy of the faculty of hearing, which can discern any surrounding vibration.

The sense of hearing is the highest, greatest, most comprehensive sense in the universe; it is moreover the *only* common, universally found sense. No apprehension of the universe is of such complete and absolute value, as the acoustic one.[24]

It is against that kind of assumption that Hoffmann sees the Romantic composer as a medium, or cognitive vessel, attuned to his surroundings, and constantly translating their acoustic nature: 'The audible sounds of nature . . . are perceived by the musician first as individual chords and then as melodies with harmonic accompaniment' (p. 164). We can justifiably go on to relate that statement to a larger concept: the music of the cosmos itself. This was an ancient idea which resurfaced at the period in question. If Schelling thought of the entire universe as 'nothing more than the palpitating heart of the divinity which . . . continues to beat in an endless pulsa-

---

[22] Schafer, *Hoffmann and Music*, chapter 20, gives some statistics.
[23] The *Fragmente aus dem Nachlasse eines jungen Physikers* (Heidelberg, 1810) was in two volumes (reprinted Heidelberg, 1969).
[24] *Ibid.*, i, 223.

tion',[25] Ritter the physicist speculated that the vibrations we can see in a length of cord, giving off their note, might merely exist as part of a phenomenon leading to infinitely larger vibrations and – to humans – unperceived notes. 'The world revolving might create such a note; the revolution round the sun, a second one . . . Here one arrives at the idea of a colossal music, of which our small one is but an important allegory.'[26] Though he avoided such reflections, Hoffmann's idea of 'infinite yearning' (p. 98) and his use of cosmic imagery raise the power of Beethovenian music to quasi-philosophical dimensions. This music reveals 'the realm of the mighty and the immeasurable' (p. 97); it intimates a joy 'sublimer than the confines of this world allow' (p. 102): it provokes comparison with annihilating images of supernatural size.

The concept of the hieroglyph, favoured in F. Schlegel's earlier writing, seems to have meant roughly the same as 'symbol' in his later work.[27] Thus the Romantic poet, for him, was to create a symbol, defined by Schelling 'as the poetic device of mediation between that which is real and that which is ideal, or between the particular and the universal'.[28] In this sense Hoffmann claims music as something with universal symbolic properties, for he repeatedly returns to the idea of music as a 'Sanskrit of nature' (pp. 94, 105), put down in hieroglyphic characters (p. 155) and so constituting, in the written form of a score, a magic book of charms (pp. 88, 101, 155). The score, that is, may not be the hieroglyph of an imagined symphony, though it uses symbolic notation. It should be the hieroglyph of surrounding nature itself; thus the danger is of 'any artificial arrangement of hieroglyphs' (p. 165). In all this Hoffmann stands beyond those who, shortly before, claimed instrumental music to be 'the language of the heart', simply; or just capable of directly poetical expression, albeit without words.[29]

Composers as Symbols

The current critical tendency to locate structural features in *Kreisleriana* will doubtless become more intensive. A close reading of the text shows some recurring symbols and metaphors, which may now be discussed in groups. The first group uses historical composers as 'exempla': each of the

[25]   Cited in Benz, *The Mystical Sources*, 55.

[26]   Ritter, *Fragmente*, i, 225.

[27]   Doris Starr, *Über den Begriff des Symbols in der deutschen Klassik und Romantik* (Reutlingen, 1964), 56–7.

[28]   Cardinal, *German Romantics in Context*, 84.

[29]   We shall see this subsequently in Wackenroder; cf. the idea '[C. P. E.] Bach was another *Klopstock*, who employed musical sounds instead of words': *A M Z*, iii (1801), issue 18 of 28 Jan., col. 300.

four main composers stands as a paradigm of excellence in a particular branch of music. They thus serve as part of the apprentice's 'training' in the Romantic education of a musician. In chronological order they are: J. S. Bach (master of counterpoint); Gluck (master of opera); Mozart (as a universal master); and Beethoven (master of modern instrumental music, who commands unparalleled consciousness of musical Romanticism).

J. S. Bach (1685–1750) is invoked in three essays, and his 'Goldberg' Variations – one of the supreme achievements of the composer's maturity – are performed in the first essay of the cycle. C. W. von Gluck (1714–87) or his works appear in four essays. W. A. Mozart (1756–91) or his works are referred to in five essays, and five of his pieces are mentioned in 'Kapellmeister Johannes Kreisler's Musical Sufferings' alone. L. van Beethoven (1770–1827) is named in four essays, and alluded to obliquely in 'Kreisler's Musico-Poetic Club'. He is the only composer of the four whose name appears in a *Kreisleriana* title. However, it must be remembered that the *Fantasiestücke* also contain individual stories dedicated to the music of Gluck (*Ritter Gluck*) and Mozart (*Don Juan*).

Other composers, however, are given sometimes extensive local significance. The more important of these are J. Haydn, C. P. E. Bach, Corelli, Benda, Benevoli, Perti, Hasse, Traetta, Sacchini, Piccinni, and Crescentini. The last seven names are associated with the power of melody (see below), while Haydn, C. P. E. Bach, and Corelli represent aspects of earlier instrumental music. Yet other composers are present only in mention of their works, and are thus negative influences for the most part: Paer, Schulz, Gelinek, von Winter, Beauvarlet-Charpentier.

Musical Procedures as Romantic Metaphors

For the Romantic approach to music, Hoffmann endows three traditional aspects of compositional technique with extended significance: melody, counterpoint, and orchestration. The most extensively treated of these is the first, chiefly characterised as 'song' or 'singing'. The whole of '*Ombra adorata*' concerns an Italian aria, seen as the epitome of melody's elemental power to attain musical sublimity. Elsewhere there are references to this style of melody as perfected by 'the earlier Italians', that is, a long tradition dating from seventeenth-century composers such as Orazio Benevoli (1605–72), to those born after Gluck, such as Tommaso Traetta (1727–79) of the composer of 'Ombra adorata', Girolamo Crescentini (1762–1846). Hoffmann's frequent identification of melody with 'sung melody' in *Kreisleriana* gives rise also to a more complex set of responses associated with the inspirational power of singers themselves. This is a main theme of his story

Die Automate (*Automatons*) which was originally intended for inclusion in the *Fantasiestücke*. In Hoffmann's philosophy, an almost mystical triangle connects composer, singer, and auditor, one that suggests music's acoustic immediacy of impact. Beyond that, though, it was for the singer (music being in this case a re-creative art) to embody the very spirit of the composer, and actually become its Romantic essence. In the tale *Don Juan* the opera singer mysteriously appears next to the musician-narrator and says ' "Your spirit opened itself to me in song and I understood you. For" – here she called me by my Christian name – "it was of you I was singing, and your melodies were *me*!" '[30] Likewise, discussing performers in general, Hoffmann urged self-negation to be practised by any 'true artist' almost as a condition for transmitting the 'composer's magical authority' (p. 103). In his fiction, Hoffmann would further have singers symbolise, *inter alia*, the spirit of national styles of music: Antonia and Angela in *Rat Krespel*, Lauretta and Teresina in *Die Fermate*.

'Counterpoint' recurs surprisingly often in *Kreisleriana* (it is not generally considered as very characteristic of Romantic music), and its rôle in the education of the 'apprentice' is confirmed in the fable of Chrysostomus (p. 163), though of course as a means rather than an end. Kreisler (p. 80), after all, extemporised for hours 'with elegantly contrapuntal devices'; counterpoint's rôle in Beethoven's Fifth Symphony is stated fully. But the Romantic significance of counterpoint is its poetic similarity to the intertwining, mysterious curvilinear forms found in nature (p. 94); both recall, in turn, the great opening of *Die Lehrlinge zu Sais* and its 'figures that seem to belong to the great Manuscript of Design which we descry everywhere, on wings of birds, on the shells of eggs, in clouds, in snow . . .'

Hoffmann's precocious remarks on orchestration (pp. 113, 158) anticipate a primary concern of Romantic music: 'colour' as a musical component of composition. His metaphors of 'perspective' and 'tone' – the latter term reclaimed by Hoffmann from painting – even anticipate the phrase 'tone-painting' (*Tonmalerei*); and his observation that whole musical works should partake of a predominant, unifying tone, related to their 'deeper character', connects without difficulty with Victor Hugo's Preface to *Cromwell* (1827) and its more famous demand for a *couleur locale* that would go to 'the very heart of the work, from where it would spread outwards . . . into all corners of the drama'.[31] In 'On a Remark of Sacchini's, and on so-called

---

[30] 'Don Giovanni', in *Six German Romantic Tales*, tr. Ronald Taylor (London, 1985), 109.

[31] Victor Hugo, *Cromwell*, ed. Annie Ubersfeld (Paris, 1968), 91: 'Ce n'est point à la surface du drame que doit être la couleur locale, mais au fond, dans le cœur même de l'œuvre, d'où elle se répand au dehors, d'elle-même, naturellement, également, et, pour ainsi parler, dans tous les coins du drame . . .'

Effect in Music' Hoffmann develops the idea of musical colour, extending it even to the detail of the accompaniment. No musical text- or reference-book at this date had properly attempted to tackle the subject of what we now call 'orchestration'.[32]

Personal Symbols

Some recurring symbols in *Kreisleriana* have a more esoteric significance, one that is doubtless partly autobiographical; in any case they point towards Hoffmann's development of personal myths in his fiction. Of course, there is no question of simple translation: 'Once, however, the literary "diction-ary meanings" of certain stock figures and motifs – such as the elemental spirits, the *vates*,[33] the witch, flowers, stones, metals, etc. – are established, we must turn to their functions within the particular myth in which they are found to understand them fully.'[34] The climactic confluence of Hoff-mann's esoteric symbols occurs at the end of the fable of Chrysostomus (p. 163) in a magnificently synaesthetic moment: rocks, mosses, nightingale, dark red carnations, light, fragrance, music, a female apparition. All these can be traced back in the text, albeit in varying degrees of frequency. The nightingale appears three times before the last essay: as the supremely musical bird, the night-singer, the utterer of lamentation,[35] this creature – celebrated in literature since Pliny – perhaps symbolises the composer himself, the singer of nature's music. Shakespeare's nightingale, as heard in *Romeo and Juliet* by the lovers, also seems connected: 'Nightly she sings on yond pomegranate tree' (Act 3 sc. 5). Red carnations can traditionally depict admiration, marriage, passionate love;[36] hence perhaps here the inspiring but now distant object of the composer's affection.[37] The first blending of several of these images occurs in 'Extremely Random

---

[32]   Cf. Heinrich Christoph Koch, 'Instrumentierung', in *Kurzgefasstes Handwörterbuch der Musik* (Leipzig, 1807): 'Indicates the method by which the composer has managed to choose the instruments to accompany a principal part through considering their effect, or their ability to be more or less prominent in the working-out.' The first systematic approach to orchestration as a subject occurs within Antoine Reicha's *Cours de Composition Musicale* (Paris, *c.* 1816–18).

[33]   (Latin): soothsayer; bard; prophet; poet.

[34]   Negus, *Hoffmann's Other World*, 23.

[35]   For two of the many references probably known to Hoffmann referring to such lamen-tation, see G. H. Schubert, *Die Symbolik des Traumes* (Bamberg, 1814), 30; Friedrich Schlegel, *Lucinde* (English translation by Peter Firchow, Minneapolis), 1971, 125–6.

[36]   J. C. Cooper, *An Illustrated Encyclopaedia of Traditional Symbols* (London, 1978), article, 'Carnation'.

[37]   Hoffmann's passion for his young singing-pupil Juliane Mark (1796–1865) in Bamberg diminished only gradually after her marriage to Gerhard Graepel on 3 December 1812.

Thoughts' (p. 105); but the large rock covered with 'strange mosses and reddish-coloured veins' appears only in the final essay. A rare carbuncle-stone whose red light, accompanied by distant music, helps establish 'friendly sympathy' is produced towards the end of Novalis's *Saïs*. Rocks 'can represent the cosmos',[38] as well as express a mystical unity.[39] The young woman in Hoffmann's parable who is taken by 'hostile powers' – stolen, like Hoffmann's own young *innamorata*, from the path of true music – is sacrificed but afterwards transfigured into a wider, more universal nature (cf. Wordsworth's 'Lucy' poems), whereafter the nightingale/composer arrives to create his 'lamenting melodies' perpetually. The artist's activity is released, following this reading of the text, by his objective celebration of experience;[40] those who come after must learn to 'read' nature's truth, to hear truly inspired works of music, and then to reconcile these with their own most naive artistic impulses.

But other interpretations are equally imaginable. The young woman might signify the essence of musical art, led astray and destroyed by the demonic stranger of pseudo-art. She continues to exist in a different form, just as in *Ritter Gluck* the earthly composer who died in 1787 continued to exist in ghostly or transcendental form.

Mozart and Shakespeare

Yet other symbolic levels in *Kreisleriana* could be explored. There is, for example, a circle of motifs flowing through the identities of Hoffmann himself, the composer Mozart, and the young men who appear in the first and last essays in the cycle: Gottlieb and Chrysostomus. The latter exemplify persons who seem to have the innate ability to become successful musical apprentices.

Hoffmann adopted the name 'Amadeus' as if to assume a portion of Mozart's identity. In 1804 this name was inscribed on the manuscript of his Singspiel, *Die lustigen Musikanten*; in July 1808 the publisher Nägeli addressed him with the initials 'E. T. A.'.[41] Mozart's birthday was 27

---

[38]   Cooper, *Encyclopaedia of Traditional Symbols*, article, 'Stone'.

[39]   J. E. Cirlot, *A Dictionary of Symbols*, tr. Jack Sage (London, 1962), 262.

[40]   Hans von Müller, in *E. T. A. Hoffmanns Tagebücher* (Berlin, 1915), stressed Hoffmann's self-distancing from the experiences of private emotion, especially in 1812, deliberately done with artistic goals in mind. See *HTB*, 12–16.

[41]   *HBW*, i, 253. Hoffmann's third given name was Wilhelm. 'Amadeus' was presumably fully adopted from the time of his arrival in Bamberg on 1 September 1808, according to Hans von Müller, *Drei Arbeiten Hoffmanns aus den ersten Regierungsjahren Friedrich Wilhelms III* (Munich and Berlin, 1918), 12–13.

January, which is the feast of St John Chrysostom. Consequently, Mozart's first two given names were Johannes Chrysostomus. Additionally, his fourth name was 'Theophilus', but Mozart 'sometimes preferred the Latin form, Amadeus . . . and occasionally the German [equivalent], Gottlieb'.[42] The first printed biography of him (1793) was entitled 'Johannes Chrysostomus Wolfgang Gottlieb Mozart'; the second, *Leben des k.k. Kapellmeisters Wolfgang Gottlieb Mozart*.[43]

Mention should finally be made of the Shakespearean threads stemming from *Romeo and Juliet* and *The Tempest*. '*Ombra adorata*' takes its name from an aria sung by Romeo, after taking poison, in an opera adapted from the former; its fatalistic theme is revived in the opening of Part II, where the distracted Kreisler has talked of Romeo's ecstasy, only to follow it by thoughts of suicide. *The Tempest* (not mentioned, incidentally, in *HTB*) is either quoted or echoed in 'Report of an Educated Young Man', 'Kreisler's Musico-Poetic Club', and 'On a Remark of Sacchini's, and on so-called Effect in Music'. Further observations concerning these connections are made below within the relevant Prefatory remarks. *A Midsummer Night's Dream* is quoted, to ironic effect, at the end of 'The Complete Machinist'. Shakespeare himself is mentioned as an essential point of reference in 'Beethoven's Instrumental Music'; and the cycle closes with a fascinating allusion to *Hamlet*.

Influence of Diderot and Wackenroder

If Hoffmann's theoretical constructions were complex, he was well equipped to persuade us of their truth through the vividness, gaiety, and ironic thrust of his verbal imagination. But this imagination has its being in verbal drama; in this theatre of the mind Kreisler is the unifying character. Hoffmann's later 'Serapiontic' aim, of involving his reader totally in the fictional world in question, is clearly adumbrated both here and throughout. Many of the items in *Kreisleriana* are, for example, presented as though actual documents, to persuade us of their veracity: letters ostensibly from Wallborn, Kreisler, Milo; set-pieces (exercises in pure irony), in the form of a lecture in 'Thoughts about the Great Value of Music' and a treatise in 'The Complete Machinist'; an imagined notebook in which Kreisler's 'Extremely Random Thoughts' have been jotted; the opening dramatic mono-

---

[42]   Stanley Sadie, 'Mozart, Wolfgang Amadeus', *The New Grove*, xii, 680–1.

[43]   F. Schlichtegroll's biography 'Johannes Chrysostomus Wolfgang Gottlieb Mozart' appeared in the *Nekrolog auf das Jahr 1791* (Gotha, 1793); the second biography was F. X. Niemetschek, *Leben des k.k. Kapellmeisters Wolfgang Gottlieb Mozart . . .* (Prague, 1798; 2nd edn 1808).

logue; and of course the concluding 'Johannes Kreisler's Certificate of Apprenticeship'. Even the typographical layout of the 1819 edition helped express this fictive level, and we have consciously echoed that in this book.

The figure of Kreisler, as we suggested earlier, owes something of its lively style to the Diderot of *Le Neveu de Rameau*, but also something fundamental to the Wackenroder of *Herzensergiessungen eines kunstliebenden Klosterbruders* (*Confessions from the Heart of an Art-loving Friar*) and maybe his *Phantasien über die Kunst für Freunde der Kunst* (*Fantasies on Art for Friends of Art*).[44] The first was issued anonymously in 1797, and was conceived jointly with Ludwig Tieck. The second was published in 1799, the year after Wackenroder's death at the age of 24, with contributions by Tieck and an explanation showing which parts were by his late friend.

To begin with Diderot: one must not consider the Nephew in this dialogue as an actual model for Kreisler: for one thing he is not a composer, but a professional violinist; for another, his moral nature is Parisian, ingratiating. It was clearly the Nephew's 'musical' spontaneity and eccentricity that affected Hoffmann, together with the remarkable description of his impromptu performance of a whole opera. This, I take it, Hoffmann interpreted as the composing musician's necessary self-identification with every part of what goes to make up an opera, seen in the form of creative rapture:

[Diderot]: What didn't he do? He wept, laughed, sighed, his gaze was tender, soft or
    furious: a woman swooning with grief, a poor wretch abandoned in the depth of
    his despair, a temple rising into view, birds falling silent at eventide, waters
    murmuring . . .
       Then he went on: 'Now that's what you call music and a musician.'[45]
[Hoffmann] . . . one can only give [a young artist] the following reply . . . 'You live in
    the characters of the drama, you yourself are the tyrant, the hero, the lover; you
    feel the pain and the joy of love, the humiliation, fear, horror, even the nameless
    agony of death . . . you brood, you rage, you hope, you despair . . .'
               ('On a Remark of Sacchini's, and on so-called Effect in Music')

It is worth mentioning that Ponto in *Kater Murr* will misquote from *Le Neveu de Rameau* and then recommend Diderot's *Jacques le fataliste*,[46] a

[44]   See Schubert, *Wackenroder's 'Confessions'*. See also the Berglinger translation from the 1797 book in Strunk (tr., ed.), *Source Readings in Music History*, 10–23.
[45]   Denis Diderot, *Rameau's Nephew*, tr. L. W. Tancock (Harmondsworth, 1966), 104.
[46]   Kent and Knight (tr., ed.), *Writings of Hoffmann*, ii, 293, 303. Ponto is ironically acknowledging the fact that *Jacques le fataliste* was regarded by the Romantics as an exemplary text, e.g. by F. Schlegel in his *Dialogue on Poetry*, who praised it as an 'arabesque', 'a work of art', and as an 'essential form or mode of expression of poetry'. See Behler and Struc, *Schlegel. Dialogue on Poetry*, 96.

book whose opening Hoffmann had parodied for that of his own *Kreisleriana*:

[Diderot] How did they meet? By chance like everyone else. What were their names? What's that got to do with you? Where were they coming from? From the nearest place . . .[47]

[Hoffmann] Where is he from? Nobody knows! Who were his parents? It is not known! . . .

The Nephew, it transpires finally, has lost his attractive and musical wife (it is not said how); Kreisler's despair is not unconnected to 'his quite irrational love for a singer' (p. 124), who is unattainable.

Standing as a complementary influence must have been the fictional Kapellmeister Joseph Berglinger in the two works of Wackenroder mentioned above. In the first of these, an 'art-loving friar' tells 'The strange musical life of the musical artist Joseph Berglinger' from the supposed vantage-point of close acquaintanceship, maintained up to the time of Berglinger's death. In the second book, writings on musical subjects are presented as though by Berglinger himself. As in the later *Kreisleriana*, that is, Wackenroder's supposed editor presents 'little essays' left by a supposed Kapellmeister, one who – as we know from the *Confessions* volume – has departed this life through circumstances directly related to his unconventional and artistic character.[48]

What, in fact, was a 'Kapellmeister'? By the eighteenth century in Germany the *Kapelle* 'encompassed all the musicians and all musical activities of a court, including opera and orchestral concerts . . . By the nineteenth century the term "Kapelle" for part of a sacred institution fell into disuse and eventually denoted any orchestra or dance ensemble. Correspondingly, the title *Kapellmeister* was given to the conductor of any ensemble, often being of lower rank than the chief director . . .'[49] In Kreisler's case, the difficulties mentioned in the introductory paragraph of the cycle show that his erstwhile court employers wanted him to run the theatre on fashionable Italianate lines, directing operas still moulded after Baroque *opera seria* conventions with singers trained in the bad old ways we still associate with

[47]   Denis Diderot, *Jacques the Fatalist and his Master*, tr. Michael Henry (Harmondsworth, 1986), 21. This book was first published, in German, in 1792.

[48]   Although Hoffmann does not refer to the Wackenroder–Tieck publications, he would have known them through his friendship with Zacharias Werner, if through nothing else: Werner revered the work of Wackenroder and the early Romantics. Schubert, *Wackenroder's 'Confessions'*, 11–12, also quotes a letter from Werner on the subject to Julius Eduard Hitzig, dated October 1803. In 1804 Hitzig moved to Warsaw, where he became friends with Hoffmann and introduced him to the work of many writers.

[49]   Adele Poindexter, 'Chapel', in *The New Grove*, iv, 151.

the phrase *prima donna*. He has demurred, and is now a mere music tutor to a wealthy family.

Joseph Berglinger's is the story of a poor boy who runs away from home, is taken up by a relative, and who becomes a court Kapellmeister. Here, his musical gifts are apparently realised and used; but he sustains both inner and outer conflicts. On the outer level, he is frustrated (like Berlioz later) by the way musical art requires the willing participation of so many intermediaries before it can be heard; he is disgusted by the jealousies around him and by 'the subordination of art to the will of the court';[50] he resents the pretentious amateur erudition and resistance to true feeling shown by his employers and by his audience, 'strutting about in gold and silver'.

On the inner level, Berglinger's psychology is shown to lack 'wholeness', and different contributory factors are suggested by Wackenroder. The notion of needful wholeness and balance is also relevant in the case of Kreisler, in whose 'formulation nature had tried a new recipe'. The deviation of these musicians from a culturally accepted norm can be gauged, for example, from the prescriptive section addressed to composers in a celebrated mid-eighteenth-century instruction book: that of J. J. Quantz (1697–1773), a blacksmith's son who rose to become personal musician to the King of Prussia.

He who wishes to devote himself to composition must have a lively and fiery spirit, united with a soul capable of tender feeling; a good mixture, without too much melancholy, of what scholars call the temperaments; much imagination, inventiveness, judgement, and discernment; a good memory; a good and delicate ear; a sharp and quick eye; and a receptive mind that grasps everything quickly and easily.[51]

Berglinger breaks under the resulting strain; Kreisler is inducted into a higher, or Romantic, form of apprenticeship.

For Wackenroder, the figure of Berglinger stands at one extreme of a line of artists he discusses, from the one most harmonious of spirit (Raphael) to the one least. But this is part of a complex enquiry into art, its creation, and its relation to God's design. Berglinger's is a proud soul; a soul without love for any fellow being; but one who wants to use his art to 'delight thousand Christians all'.[52] Only when moved to charity by the appearance of his destitute sister, and after some reconciliation with his dying father, does he surrender to the will of heaven and gain the creative power to write a masterpiece, a Passiontide oratorio. The narrator, musing on Berglinger's

50 Schubert, *Wackenroder's 'Confessions'*, 156.
51 Edward R. Reilly (tr., ed.), *Johann Joachim Quantz: On Playing the Flute* [1752] (2nd edn, London, 1985), 12–13.
52 'Tausend Christen zu erfreuen': Schubert, *Wackenroder's 'Confessions'*, 152.

death soon after, postulates a general distinction between his 'lofty fantasy' and that 'power of creativity' which he intrinsically lacked.

Thus Wackenroder's musical protagonist has sharply different characteristics from those of Kreisler, while his cycle (the *Confessions*) as a whole has striking structural similarities and thematic links with *Kreisleriana*. Kreisler, that is, lacks all sense of Berglinger's religious feeling. He is an entirely secular musician. Berglinger has a family, but lacks the ability to love; Kreisler has no family, but closely identifies his love-objects with his music. Berglinger writes music, but seems to be more a votary of art than a practitioner; Kreisler is a compulsive practitioner, but lacks – to begin with – the will or perhaps technique to preserve what he composes. Berglinger is introverted and in no way eccentric; Kreisler is clubbable, but notorious for his eccentricities.

Structurally speaking, the *Confessions* relate to *Kreisleriana* through the use of an authorial mask;[53] through a measure of criticism against art in the 1790s; through the lack of a continuous or conventional 'story', set in a temporal progression; through the use of 'exempla': artists chosen from the past and recent present as examples of types of creativity;[54] through the use of images of light that 'recur at many points where artistic inspiration and creativity are revealed';[55] and, not least, through Wackenroder's avowed purpose to educate: 'I dedicate these pages . . . only to young, beginning artists, or to boys who intend to dedicate themselves to art . . .'

The choice by Wackenroder of a recent *musician* (the only such artist) as exemplifying the harshest case of spiritual disjunction in his gallery of 'exempla' is not fortuitous. It is obvious that Wackenroder fully appreciated the unprecedented strides music – especially in symphonies and sonatas – was making in what is now labelled by musicians the 'Classical' phase, i.e. from the rise of Haydn (1732–1809) in the mid-1760s to the maturity of Mozart (1756–91) in the 1780s.[56] Berglinger's unhappy career, founded partially on the intense impression made on him when young by concert-music ('symphonies . . . which he loved particularly') poses the very problem of a new-found, exciting, highly sensual medium, in which emotions seem to be communicated directly and with unparalleled power:

[53]   Hoffmann, also, used the mask of a monk in his early critical essay 'Letter from a Monk to his Friend in the Capital' (see p. 213), dating from 1803.
[54]   These criteria are observed for Wackenroder by Mary Schubert in Part I of her edition.
[55]   Schubert, *Wackenroder's 'Confessions'*, 59.
[56]   In fact the 'high Classical' phase is now reckoned to begin around 1775 (e.g. by Charles Rosen, *The Classical Style* (London, 1971)) if not later, around 1781, with Haydn's Op. 20 string quartets. But Haydn's symphonies had begun to circulate widely in print and MS copies from 1765. The 'Sturm und Drang' period in Haydn's career covers *c.* 1766 to *c.* 1774.

[Music] affects us the more powerfully and tosses all the forces of our bodies the more generally into tumult, the deeper and more mysterious its language is.[57]

Such, in fact, is Berglinger's intoxication with this art that it absorbs his entire youthful existence and sense of moral purpose.

When Kreisler speaks of Haydn's works, he does so in similar language to Berglinger:

[Wackenroder] [During symphonies] it often seemed to him as if he were watching a lively throng of boys and girls dancing on a lovely meadow . . .[58]
[Hoffmann] Haydn's . . . symphonies lead us through endless, green forest-glades . . . Youths and girls sweep past dancing the round . . .
('Beethoven's Instrumental Music')

But the tensions produced by both society itself, and by works of musical art other than by Haydn, are more violent in effect. The cosmic imagery with which Hoffmann evokes Beethoven has been mentioned above. To Berglinger, long before, 'the full force of the sounds' was akin to 'huge wings' that lift him bodily into the air.

Berglinger's feelings, almost obsessions, must have been readily understood in a Germany where, through the efforts of many, the practice of music had advanced in the population as a whole during the eighteenth century from widespread ignorance and reliance on the churches, to widespread participation.[59] Possibly there was a lurking sense that the 'new music' was felt to belong to people as a whole, to speak a comprehensible language (not tied to the Church or to Italian words), and was in a tangible sense the province of artists of humble origins; for, neglecting Berglinger for a moment, it is notable that Hoffmann makes that association explicitly in 'Thoughts about the Great Value of Music': 'almost no artist becomes one purely by free will; they have arisen and still arise from the poorer classes'. Conversely, any sensible 'landed family of quality' would soon knock artistic talent out of those offspring who happened to be born with it (p. 95).

Both Kreisler and Berglinger suffer the trite, unreceptive reactions of the people who employ them.[60] Berglinger, in the end, dies. But Kreisler is of

---

[57] Schubert, *Wackenroder's 'Confessions'*, 150.
[58] *Ibid.*, 149.
[59] See the anonymous articles thought to have been written by Johann Karl Friedrich Triest, 'Bemerkungen über die Ausbildung der Tonkunst in Deutschland im achzehnten Jahrhundert', *AMZ*, iii (1801), issues 15 to 26, 7 January to 25 March inclusive.
[60] It may be mentioned here, regarding patronage, that of 174 subscribers to Mozart's concert-series in Vienna in 1784, 92 per cent were of the higher or lower nobility, and only 8 per cent from the bourgeoisie. Prussia too, though not directly comparable, had a relatively small bourgeois class. See H. Schuler, *Die Subskribenten der Mozart'schen Mittwochskonzerte im Trattnersaal zu Wien anno 1784* (Neustadt a.d. Aisch, 1983).

the age of Beethoven, and with him the reader is made fully aware of an unending combat against all Philistinism and of the moral superiority of the isolated and committed Romantic artist. However, now the enemy is if anything more numerous. Music has become a fashionable pastime for the bourgeois, and their unthinking consumption of it is mercilessly caricatured all through *Kreisleriana*: at home, surrounded by wife and children; at the theatre, afraid of anything too absorbing; at tea, talking glib nonsense about art; applauding the empty virtuoso performance; singing dutifully, if half a bar behind the rest of the polite chorus.

Unlike Berglinger, Kreisler distances and elevates himself through the power of his irony. So far from relying on the suggestiveness of the 'Romantic fragment', Kreisler more often assumes the diction, the mercilessly probing wit, and the rounded, logical constructions of the legally trained Hoffmann. We forget that the Kapellmeister has supposedly been jotting down his 'brief essays' in 'odd moments' on the backs of odd sheets of music. But then the concept of Kreisler has developed a very long way from the seeming roots of its inspiration: an obscure patient in an asylum for the mentally disturbed.

The Theme of Insanity

Around 12 January 1809, only three months after arriving in Bamberg to take up the position of theatre musical director, Hoffmann sent the now famous story *Ritter Gluck* to the editor of the *AMZ*, Friedrich Rochlitz (1769–1842). He told Rochlitz that it was 'based on an actual occurrence'. One reason for his choosing this editor – maybe one reason for him conceiving *Ritter Gluck* at all – was that Rochlitz had published an account in the *AMZ* in 1804 that had stuck in Hoffmann's mind; Hoffmann recalled it in his covering letter.

I have before now found similar things in the above mentioned journal [*AMZ*], e.g. the extremely interesting report about an insane man who would improvise fantasies at the keyboard in a wonderful manner.

(*HBW*, i, 261)

'The Visit to the Asylum' appeared in four parts, in issues 39 to 42 of *AMZ*, in June and July 1804. Such are the correspondences between the one patient it describes, simply called 'Karl', and certain aspects of Kreisler, that it would be wilful not to regard the former as the germ of the latter. The articles build into a quite detailed case-study stretching back from Karl's youth up to his death in 1803, and including transcriptions of material written by the patient. Most unexpectedly, Rochlitz published part of one of Karl's piano fantasies in music notation within the initial article, which gave a vivid account of Karl's behaviour when visited. His musical impulses were profound, for 'he lived completely and uniquely in music'; he was always humming, if not playing. His playing was 'very positive and extremely impressive'; it was technically capable; it contained 'very expressive melodies'. But Karl was also a compulsive writer, for 'Whenever he was given paper, he wrote.' Sometimes it concerned his condition, but 'far more often [he wrote] outpourings about his art, his opinions concerning it, and from which latter he had constructed his system, his *idée fixe.*' His total identification with music was intimately connected with an unhappy love for a girl whom he heard playing a guitar. Subsequently, Karl, already under a form of supervision at home, created musical fantasies idealising dialogues between himself and the beloved. Later he turned to religion. Rochlitz prints, finally, a letter from Karl to the King of Prussia concerning the metaphysical meaning of musical intervals. The octave becomes hereby an image of the Creator, from which all evil is excluded (i.e. dissonances). Karl's speeches ended by being sometimes long, even disconnected.

Transformed through the imagination, and given the catalyst of Hoffmann's emotions for Juliane Mark,[61] all the above-mentioned motifs became mainstays of *Kreisleriana*. As we shall see later (see p. 56 and figure 3) the figure of Kreisler was established in 1810, and *Kreisleriana* itself was always closely identified with (if not provably identical to) a project entitled 'Lucid Intervals of an Insane Musician', begun in the spring of 1812 after a year of hard work occupied with theatre productions. The theme of insanity was to remain part of the conception (chiefly in 'Kreisler's Musico-Poetic Club'), presumably signifying that elemental capacity to respond to musical sounds without which no true musical composition is possible. The pervasive sense of insanity, however, paradoxically lends all Kreisler's utterances a kind of oracular or magus-like truth. As a motif, the importance of madness is underlined by the signature of Kreisler as 'Kapellmeister and mad musician *par excellence*' (end of II–2) as well as the reference to 'a cycle about pure spirituality in music [which] could perhaps soon be appearing in book form under the title *Lucid Intervals of an Insane Musician*' (p. 124); these writings were to have been attributed to Kreisler. The book was announced as forthcoming at Easter 1815 (letter to Fouqué, 14 May 1815, in which Hoffmann still considered writing it). By March 1818 he admitted to

---

61 See note 37 above. Hoffmann wrote music for her (no longer extant) and the diaries give abundant evidence of despair: 'Why, sleeping and waking, do I think so often of insanity? – I think that exhaustions of the spirit might act like bleeding.' Entry of 6 January 1811.

his publisher that the project had become 'something entirely different from what I had in mind'.[62]

From a surviving sketch of contents it appears that the project originally consisted of essays or sections expanding on the kind of Romantic musical philosophy Hoffmann had worked on towards the end of *Kreisleriana*: the Romantic interpretation of constituent parts of musical language.[63] This serves to underline the point that in *Kreisleriana* the richly humorous content is not directed *at* Kreisler, but *away* from the central position of Kreislerian detachment. 'Karl', indeed, had exhibited not only a detachment, which Rochlitz described as 'a certain air of superiority', but also a 'contempt for all music in alternative and current musical forms'. This contempt was translated into Kreisler's merciless rejection of second-rate and utilitarian music. As for the inspiration for transforming such a figure into a mouthpiece for Romantic thought, Hoffmann might perhaps have mused on the 'Wondrous Oriental Tale of a Naked Saint', in Wackenroder's *Phantasien über die Kunst für Freunde der Kunst*:

Strange beings often dwell in the wildernesses [of the Orient], beings whom we would call insane . . . The Oriental mind regards these naked saints as the wondrous receptacles of a higher spirit which strayed away from the realm of the firmament into a human form . . .[64]

Humour

No mention of Hoffmann's irony in *Kreisleriana* would be adequate without reference to Friedrich Schlegel's keen consciousness of its appropriateness to the Romantic writer. Irony is the sworn enemy of rationalism: 'Irony is a clear consciousness of an eternal agility, of the infinitely abundant chaos.'[65] It attracts, engages, forces the reader to identify with the subject, yet creates constant movement through disequilibrium:

In it, everything must be jest and yet seriousness, artless openness and yet deep dissimulation . . . It contains and incites a feeling of the insoluble conflict of the absolute and the relative, of the impossibility and necessity of total communication. It is the freest of all liberties, for it enables us to rise above our own self.[66]

But *Kreisleriana* also contains the first fruits of what Charles Baudelaire called the 'absolute comic' in Hoffmann:

[62]   *HBW*, ii, 159; Sahlin, 276.
[63]   *Nachlese*, 884–5.
[64]   Schubert, *Wackenroder's 'Confessions'*, 175.
[65]   'Idea' no. 69, in Behler and Struc, *Schlegel. Dialogue on Poetry*, 155.
[66]   Aphorism no. 108 from *Lyceum* (1797), *ibid.*, 131.

The exalted nature of the absolute comic makes of it the special preserve of superior artists who have in them the necessary receptivity for absolute ideas. Thus the man who until now has apprehended these ideas better than anyone else, and who has exploited some of them in his purely aesthetic as well as his creative work, is Theodor Hoffmann.[67]

Baudelaire's analysis of the comic cannot be adequately reproduced here; but it is in 'Report of an Educated Young Man' – i.e. Milo, the educated ape – that Hoffmann most ingeniously blended satire (the 'significative comic' in Baudelaire) with the 'absolute comic' in order to direct his readers in their aesthetic education:

I submit that when Hoffmann engenders [the] absolute comic he is surely well aware of the fact; but, equally, he knows that the essence of this type of comic is to appear to be unaware of oneself and to instil in the spectator, or rather the reader, the feeling of joy at his own superiority and the joy of man's superiority over nature.[68]

Hoffmann was far from the first writer to write humorously about music; one need only recall the pens of Charles Burney, Friedrich Melchior Grimm, or Benedetto Marcello. Indeed, 'The Complete Machinist', Hoffmann's satire on behalf of the need for 'total effect' and total involvement of the spectator through the suspension of disbelief, forms a close successor to Marcello's *Il teatro alla moda* [1721] in both subject-matter and style: both, too, are cast as mock instruction-books.

[Marcello] If a throne should be required on the set, it can be thrown together by using three steps, a chair, and a canopy, but the latter is required only if the *prima donna* is to sit under it. In the case of tenors or basses there is no need for it . . .
    The modern stage designer or painter must avoid any familiarity with perspective, architecture, decorating, or lighting.[69]
[Hoffmann] A round hole is cut in a rectangular board, a piece of paper is stuck over it, and a light is placed in a red-painted box behind it. This contrivance is lowered by means of two strong, black-painted wires, and there you have it – moonlight! . . . Would it not be an advantage to construct [stage] houses, towers, and castles according to the sizes of the actors?

If Hoffmann did not know the Marcello editions in Italian of 1721 and

---

[67] 'Of the Essence of Laughter' [1855], in P. E. Charvet (tr., ed.), *Baudelaire: Selected Writings on Art and Artists* (Harmondsworth, 1972), 152–3.

[68] *Ibid.*, 160–1. Castein, 151–2, develops the comparisons between Milo and the cat Murr in *Kater Murr*.

[69] Reinhard G. Pauly (tr., ed.), 'Benedetto Marcello's Satire on Early Eighteenth-Century Opera', *The Musical Quarterly*, xxxiv (1948), 222–33 and 371–403; xxxv (1949), 85–105. The above citations from xxxv, 90–1.

1761, he might possibly have met with the French excerpts from it issued by François Arnaud in 1768 in *Variétés littéraires*. But Hoffmann's irony is not usually as broad-textured as this. It is typically imbued with a fine sense of detail. With an almost studied thoroughness, Hoffmann gave the whole *Fantasiestücke* the qualification *in Callot's Manier*, and wrote an introduction to it entitled 'Jacques Callot', further explaining the connections between this French master of etching (1592–1635), his own work, and their common Romanticism: this will be found in translation on p. 76. What chiefly made Hoffmann identify with Callot was 'the special *subjective manner* in which the author looks at and conceives the characters of everyday life'.[70] Hoffmann praised the purely personal way in which Callot had fused the results of 'exuberant fantasy' with exact detail and yet unified effect. He admired the necessary engagement of the viewer with Callot's images; and, perhaps above all, Callot's irony – the way his 'grotesque forms, created out of animal and man, reveal to the serious, deeper-seeing observer all the hidden meanings that lie beneath the cloak of absurdity'. If we with hindsight can perhaps associate Hoffmann's educated ape Milo with Callot's musical hunchbacks,[71] we should certainly connect the devilish figures in Callot's *The Temptation of St Anthony*, which Hoffmann mentions by name (figure 4) with the abundance of devilish grotesques in 'Kapellmeister Johannes Kreisler's Musical Sufferings': indeed these 'sufferings' almost constitute a comic vision of hell, with Kreisler cast as the long-suffering saint tormented by counterparts of Callot:

> ... some devil in the guise of a dandy with two waistcoats...
>
> O Satan, Satan! Which of your hellish demons has taken possession of this larynx?...
>
> ... now a nose appears, now a pair of eyes, but then they immediately disappear again...

– not to speak of other grotesque images and the effect of simultaneous events achieved in Hoffmann's writing, which parallels the manifold Temptations in Callot.[72] Thus it is the more rewarding to be aware that, in all likelihood, *Fantasiestücke* (*Fantasy-pieces*) as a word signified 'Fantasy *pictures*' to Hoffmann, as it did to certain of his contemporaries.[73] But of

---

[70] *HBW*, i, 416: Hoffmann's letter to Kunz of 8 Sept. 1813; Sahlin, 207.

[71] i.e. in the *Gobbi*: see Howard Daniel (ed.), *Callot's Etchings* (New York, 1974), reproductions nos. 140, 142–8.

[72] Later, Hoffmann was given Callot's twenty-four etchings known as *Balli di Sfessania* and modelled the story *Prinzessin Brambilla* (1821) around eight of them. See M. M. Raraty (ed.), *E. T. A. Hoffmann. Prinzessin Brambilla* (Oxford, 1972), Preface.

[73] *HBW*, i, 379; *Fantasie- und Nachtstücke*, ed. Müller-Seidel, 776.

course, they are animated by verbal drama, as we said earlier; what we actually have are 'fantasy scenes' forming a 'total effect' comprising the visual, the performing, and the literary arts: yet only in the theatre of the mind.

Origins and Early Publication

The first part of *Kreisleriana* was published before Easter 1814 within the first of the four volumes entitled *Fantasiestücke in Callot's Manier. Blätter aus dem Tagebuch eines reisenden Enthusiasten. Mit einer Vorrede von Jean Paul (Fantasy-pictures in the Style of Callot. Leaves from the Diary of a Travelling Enthusiast. With a Preface by Jean Paul)* (Bamberg, C. F. Kunz, 1814–15). The second and third volumes of *Fantasiestücke* also appeared in 1814, the latter containing only the story *Der goldne Topf (The Golden Pot)*. The fourth and last, dated 1815, contained *Die Abenteuer der Sylvester-Nacht (Adventures of a New-Year's Night)* and Part II of *Kreisleriana*.

In 1819 the *Fantasiestücke* was issued by Kunz in a revised edition, now in two volumes. Hoffmann made detailed changes, but also the larger amend-ment of cutting out *Prinzessin Blandina* from 'Kreisler's Musico-Poetic Club' (II–3). Each part of *Kreisleriana* naturally fell in its appropriate volume. In place of the original symbolic frontispiece (figure 1), the 1819 edition carried a self-portrait by the author, which we have also reproduced (figure 2).

The story of how this, Hoffmann's first book, came into being, is itself fascinating. Since early 1809, Hoffmann had published his musical prose in the *AMZ*, including both conventional criticism and what might be termed 'Romantic criticism', or prose combining criticism expressed more techni-cally with that expressed using the objectified mediation of the imagination: *Ritter Gluck* (1809); the review of Beethoven's Fifth Symphony (July 1810); 'Kapellmeister Johannes Kreisler's Musical Sufferings' (September 1810). Both the last-named piece and doubtless the planned memoirs of Bamberg life (*Erinnerungen aus dem Bamberger Leben*)[74] involved the externals of small-town existence. But Hoffmann was evidently pondering something more ambitious by the early part of 1812. On 8 February the phrase 'Musikalischer Roman' (musical novel) was entered in his diary. To a follower of Friedrich Schlegel's Romantic theory, the idea of a 'novel' would have been linked with variety of form and style, with paradox, and

---

[74] Carl Georg von Maassen (ed.), *E. T. A. Hoffmanns sämtliche Werke* (Munich and Leipzig, 1912), i, Introduction, calls these *Erinnerungen* the 'foundation-stone' of the *Fantasiestücke*.

2   Hoffmann's self-portrait, designed and engraved for the second edition
of *Fantasiestücke in Callot's Manier* (1819).

with intertwining construction (arabesque). Then in his letter dated 28 April 1812 to Julius Eduard Hitzig in Berlin he revealed his plan for what was to become *Kreisleriana*, combining the old image of the insane musician who is given to writing, with his desire to discuss a Romantic musical 'theory'.

> Also, I am occupied with a curious musical work, in which I should like to express my views on music and especially on the inner structure of compositions. In order to provide space and room for every seeming eccentricity, it consists of essays written by a mad musician in his lucid intervals.

> (*HBW*, i, 334)

We have circumstantial evidence that what Hoffmann was working on at the time was to become the essay 'Extremely Random Thoughts', in *Kreisleriana*. In the same letter, he says to Hitzig: 'As I remember, you like to drink strong, fiery burgundy, and I can recommend to you *Chambertin* as a truly poetic wine, which in my case has often evaporated into symphonies and arias.' This recalls the section where Hoffmann not only records the beneficial effect of alcohol on the imagination, but also amusingly links specific drinks – including burgundy – to specific musical genres (p. 112). There is the added factor that the disjointed design of 'Extremely Random Thoughts' accords well with the concept of 'lucid intervals' of an insane person.

From 18 to 20 May 1812 Hoffmann 'began' what he called in his diary the 'Lucid Intervals of an Insane Musician'; it is likely that this project already overlapped with the incipient *Kreisleriana*, and that this diary entry marked simply one stage in a continuing creative process. For example, the diary for 20 June records the writing of 'Thoughts about the Great Value of Music' (I–3), which, attributed to Johannes Kreisler, was published a few weeks later in the *AMZ*.

During the summer period Hoffmann freed himself for his writing work by obtaining release from his time-consuming production tasks at the Bamberg theatre – though this experience of staging and design was then made good use of in 'The Complete Machinist' (I–6). 'Now there will be time to work seriously *in litteris*' (*HTB*, 29 April); 'I now live more than ever *in litteris*' (*HBW*, 4 October 1812). Hoffmann did not publish everything he wrote, but evidently began garnering his stock. His reviews of *Das Waisenhaus* and *Iphigénie en Aulide* (pp. 252, 255) were sent to the *AMZ*, but *Don Juan* (written between 19 and 24 September) was held back until the following February. We do not know quite when '*Ombra adorata*', 'Extremely Random Thoughts', or 'The Complete Machinist' were composed, but they must date from the same few months, up to February 1813.

During the same months Hoffmann was on very friendly terms with the Bamberg wine-dealer and bibliophile Carl Friedrich Kunz (1785–1849), who was just setting up a lending library and going into the publishing business. We can surmise that in their sometimes daily social meetings, the basic ideas for *Fantasiestücke* evolved verbally before being expressed in contractual form. On 2 February 1813, Hoffmann sent off his review of Beethoven's piano trios to the *AMZ* (p. 300) and thereafter, probably in the next fortnight, re-cast it together with the 1810 review of the Fifth Symphony to create the essay 'Beethoven's Instrumental Music' (I–4).[75] On 15 February Kunz agreed informally with Hoffmann that he would print certain manuscript material, material which Hoffmann referred to as (or associated with) the 'Lucid Intervals'.[76] Two days later Hoffmann began the dialogue 'Report of the Latest Fortunes of the Dog Berganza' which he finished, provisionally, on 29 March: it eventually formed the opening of Volume ii of *Fantasiestücke*.[77] Finally, a contract was drawn up, dated 18 March 1813, between Hoffmann and Kunz, for 'four works' (of literature) entitled 'Fantasiestücke in Callot's Manier', of which the first should contain 'several essays, of which some have already appeared in the [*Allgemeine*] *Musikalische Zeitung*'.[78] Hoffmann bound himself to furnish the remaining material 'in order that printing should begin now and continue uninterruptedly'.

At the same juncture, Hoffmann (who was supposed to be starting work on *Undine*, the libretto of which had been received by him on 14 November 1812) was appointed musical director of the theatre company of the brothers Franz and Joseph Seconda, operating in Leipzig and Dresden. On arriving in Dresden (25 April 1813) Hoffmann continued to pursue his contractual obligation to Kunz: he obtained a copy of his own *Ritter Gluck* via his friend Franz Morgenroth, and made a manuscript copy for Kunz;[79] then on 19 May he began the last story of the second *Fantasiestücke* volume, *Der Magnetiseur*. It was eventually completed on 19 August, after much toil.

The title 'Kreisleriana', perhaps substituting for 'Lucid Intervals . . .',

---

[75]   This chronology cannot be proved, but a study of the diaries and letters suggests there was no other time so likely.

[76]   *HTB*, 15 February: 'er will durchaus Manuskripte drucken – Beschluss wegen der "lichten Stunden"!' (He will assuredly print MSS – Resolution on account of the 'Lucid Intervals'.)

[77]   For an earlier form of the familiar text, see von Maassen (ed.), *Hoffmanns sämtliche Werke*, i, 456–62.

[78]   The contract is reproduced in *HBW*, iii, 36–8. Thus the idea was for Volume i to be wholly musical: *Ritter Gluck, Kreisleriana, Don Juan*.

[79]   He doubtless hoped, in vain, to be able to revert to certain forms of words that the *AMZ* had toned down in 1809: see *HBW*, i, 285.

first survives in a letter dated 20 July 1813 to Kunz, where Hoffmann reminds his publisher that 'The measure of *what* and *how* I drink [wine etc.] you will find in the *Kreislerianis.*' In the same letter Hoffmann expressed the desire for his authorship to remain anonymous, and agreed to provide two 'allegorical vignettes', the first serving as the frontispiece, shown as figure 1. Around 24 August, Kunz went to Bayreuth with as much of the books as had been set up in type, and there obtained Jean Paul's agreement to write a preface. Dated 24 November 1813, the latter in fact named Hoffmann, identifying him as 'Musikdirektor in Dresden'.

Work on *Der goldne Topf* for the third volume occupied Hoffmann from November 1813 to the following March, but during the same period (quite apart from his conducting duties) he planned the remaining *Fantasiestücke* and indeed commenced writing certain items. As an author's letter reveals, the third volume was to have included 'Scenes from the Life of Two Friends', that is to say the Ferdinand and Ludwig of *The Poet and the Composer* of September–October 1813 (see p. 169) and *Die Automate*, written in January 1814; both pieces eventually appeared much later in *Die Serapions-Brüder* (*The Serapion Brethren*) after initial periodical publication. *Kreisleriana*, Part II, was always planned for the fourth volume (*HBW*, i, 438, 451) and was thought out and written, for the most part, in the first half of 1814.[80] Most of its essays were first sold to the *AMZ* and appeared there (see below, 'Prefatory Remarks', for details), but not the final one, 'Johannes Kreisler's Certificate of Apprenticeship'. Hoffmann had always recognised the need for a focus to his *Fantasiestücke* (letter of 24 March 1814), and in February 1815 he created this focus in *Kreisleriana* by re-casting a still-unpublished essay dating from June 1814. His aim, expressed in that letter, had been 'to think of something new, and truly in the most daring, most original manner, in order to lead to the climax' (*HBW*, i, 453). Upon receiving his copy of the finished fourth volume ten months later, Hoffmann wrote to Kunz expressing dissatisfaction with *Prinzessin Blandina* (which he duly removed in the 1819 edition), but added, 'I believe the world of music should be satisfied with Kreisler's Certificate of Apprenticeship' (24 May 1815; *HBW*, ii, 57). By this time Hoffmann's literary fame had been secured through the earlier *Fantasiestücke*, and his services as a writer of fiction were already in strong demand.

[80] Not until September 1814 did Hoffmann move back to Berlin, where he re-entered the Civil Service.

PREFATORY REMARKS TO INDIVIDUAL ESSAYS

I–1: Kapellmeister Johannes Kreisler's Musical Sufferings

First published: AMZ, xii, 26 September 1810, cols. 825–33   *Unsigned*

No diary of Hoffmann's survives from 1810, but evidence of his contemporary literary output in the shape of music reviews, including those of Beethoven's Fifth Symphony and Gluck's *Iphigénie en Aulide*, already betrays the formation of his mature judgements. The remarkable fact about 'Kreisler's Musical Sufferings' is its prefiguring, even in detail, of the mature fictional world of Kreisler: this essay is 'Kreisler's' first surviving appearance anywhere. Even the figure of a tom-cat appears, to be taken up in *Kater Murr* (1820, 1821), and even on the first page, the motif of the 'good' versus the 'corrupt' singer is seen, which later appeared in *Die Fermate* and *Rat Krespel*. But the fluency of Hoffmann's prose style, with its variations of tempo and ironic understatements, was not achieved at a stroke. This is apparent from a precious document that seems unique with relation to *Kreisleriana*: a manuscript draft of 'Kreisler's Musical Sufferings'. It reveals that Hoffmann both pruned and rewrote in virtually every paragraph.[81]

Hoffmann's naming of various pieces of music, throughout, sets up a duality basic to *Kreisleriana*: the depreciation of entertainment (or otherwise unworthy) music, as against commitment to music of the highest quality, which is by definition more difficult to comprehend. Where hidden behind a mere title, the author's musical barbs are noted in the editorial matter. In every case Hoffmann is thinking of actual pieces; when he mentions J. S. Bach's 'Goldberg' Variations, he refers to one particular printed edition. When he refers to 'Rode' near the end, he means the actual, celebrated violin virtuoso.

Hoffmann's earlier writing often took its cue from life and some, if not

---

[81] Printed in von Maassen, *Hoffmanns sämtliche Werke*, i, 445–51.

all, of the characters in 'Kreisler's Musical Sufferings' were based on acquaintances of the author in Bamberg; the substitution of two earlier names for Kratzer and the baron between the prose draft and publication is also circumstantial evidence of this.

Of far more importance is the function of the essay as an exposition of many motifs that will recur variously throughout *Kreisleriana*.

I–2: Ombra adorata

First published: *Fantasiestücke in Callot's Manier* (1814–15), i

The phrase '*Ombra adorata*' appears in Hoffmann's private diary twice (25 July and 25 August 1812), and could refer to the person of Hoffmann's pupil Juliane Mark (1796–1865), or to this essay (*HTB* 167, 171). But in any case, the essay itself contains a depth of response and breadth of reference that add greatly to its intrinsic beauty as a lyrical word-picture. In his *E. T. A. Hoffmann: Author of the Tales*, Harvey Hewett-Thayer has compared it to the love-lyrics of Goethe and Heine.

As the author's own footnote mentions, 'Ombra adorata' is an aria by the castrato singer and composer Girolamo Crescentini (1762–1846), inserted within *Giulietta e Romeo, dramma per musica in tre atti* (1796) by Niccolò Zingarelli (1752–1837). Crescentini performed internationally and was nicknamed 'L'Orfeo italiano', taking the leading part of Romeo at the première at La Scala, Milan, of Zingarelli's opera. The composition date of the aria 'Ombra adorata' is not known, but its enormous popularity helped make Romeo the most famous rôle Crescentini sang; it was always performed as part of the opera.[82] The words and the dramatic placing of the aria are as significant for the private Kreisler as is its rôle epitomising Italianate vocal melody for the cycle as a whole.

In the opera (text by G. Foppa), Romeo and Giulietta swear vows of eternal faith at night in Act 2 sc. 6. Giulietta then discovers that her father knows of her love for Romeo, she is given a sleeping-draught by their mutual friend Gilberto, who proposes to take her from the tomb where she will be laid. She drinks it, and appears to die.

---

[82] It is present, for example, in the printed libretto for the Paris première (Paris, 1812), as well as in the score in the British Library, Add. MSS 30795–6, ii, fo. 128. The score calls it 'Rondo'; as such it appears to have played the rôle of audition-piece when the actress of Klärchen's part in Goethe's *Egmont* sang for Beethoven in 1810: 'We went to the pianoforte and rummaging around in my music . . . he found on top of the pile the well-known rondo with recitative from Zingarelli's *Romeo and Juliet*': *Thayer's Life of Beethoven*, rev., ed. Elliot Forbes (Princeton, 1970), 484.

ALLGEMEINE
MUSIKALISCHE ZEITUNG.

Den 26sten September.   N̲o̲. 52.   1810.

Johannes Kreisler's, des Kapellmeisters, musikalische Leiden.

Sie sind alle fortgegangen. — Ich hätt' es an dem Zischeln, Scharren, Räuspern, Brummen durch alle Tonarten bemerken sollen; es war ja ein wahres Bienennest, das vom Stocke abzieht, um zu schwärmen. Gottlieb hat mir neue Lichter aufgesteckt und eine Flasche Burgunder auf das Fortepiano hingestellt. Spielen kann ich nicht mehr, denn ich bin ganz ermattet; daran ist mein alter herrlicher Freund hier auf dem Notenpulte Schuld, der mich schon wieder einmal, wie Mephistopheles den Faust auf seinem Mantel, durch die Lüfte getragen hat, und so hoch, dass ich die Menschlein unter mir nicht sah und merkte, unerachtet sie tollen Lärm genug gemacht haben mögen. — Ein hundsvöttischer, verlungerter Abend! aber jetzt ist mir wohl und leicht. — Hab' ich doch gar während des Spielens meinen Bleystift hervorgezogen und Seite 63 unter dem letzten System ein paar gute Ausweichungen in Ziffern notirt mit der rechten Hand, während die Linke im Strome der Töne fortarbeitete! Hinten auf der leeren Seite fahr' ich schreibend fort. Ich verlasse Ziffern und Töne, und mit wahrer Lust; wie der genesene Kranke, der nun nicht aufhören kann zu erzählen, was er gelitten, notire ich hier umständlich die höllischen Qualen des heutigen Thees. Aber nicht für mich allein, sondern für alle, die sich hier zuweilen an meinem Exemplar der Johann Sebastian Bachschen Variationen für das Klavier, erschienen bey Naegeli in Zürich, ergötzen und erbauen, bey dem Schluss der 3osten Variation meine Ziffern finden, und, geleitet von dem grossen lateinischen *Verte*, (ich schreib' es gleich hin, wenn meine Klageschrift zu Ende ist) das Blatt umwenden und lesen. Diese errathen gleich den wahren Zusammenhang; sie wissen, dass der geheime Rath Röderlein hier ein ganz charmantes Haus macht, und zwey Töchter hat, von denen die ganze elegante Welt mit Enthusiasmus behauptet, sie tanzten wie die Göttinnen, sprächen französisch wie die Engel, und spielten und sängen und zeichneten wie die Musen. Der geheime Rath Röderlein ist ein reicher Mann; er führt bey seinen vierteljährigen Dinés die schönsten Weine, die feinsten Speisen, alles ist auf den elegantesten Fuss eingerichtet, und wer sich bey seinen Thees nicht himmlisch amüsirt, hat keinen Ton, keinen Geist, und vornämlich keinen Sinn für die Kunst. Auf diese ist es nämlich auch abgesehen; neben dem Thee, Punsch, Wein, Gefrornem etc. wird auch immer etwas Musik präsentirt, die von der schönen Welt ganz gemüthlich so wie jenes eingenommen wird. Die Einrichtung ist so: nachdem jeder Gast Zeit genug gehabt hat, eine beliebige Zahl Tassen Thee zu trinken, und nachdem zweymal Punsch und Gefrornes herumgegeben worden ist, rücken die Bedienten die Spieltische heran für den älteren, solideren Theil der Gesellschaft, der dem musikalischen das Spiel mit Karten vorzieht, welches auch in der That nicht solchen unnützen Lärm macht und wo nur einiges Geld erklingt. — Auf

3   The original printing of 'Kapellmeister Johannes Kreisler's Musical Sufferings' in *Allgemeine Musikalische Zeitung*, xii, 26 September 1810.

Act 3 opens in the Capulet vault; Giulietta's tomb is revealed; the unwitting Romeo is left alone. In due course, after a monologue and an aria, he takes poison. Crescentini's music follows immediately. The recitative section, 'Tranquillo io sono', consists of twelve bars, D major, accompanied lightly by strings, flutes, and bassoons. The main aria, marked 'Rondo', also in D major, consists of 68 bars, 4/4 time, Andante, accompanied by strings, horns, flutes, oboes, and bassoons.

Ombra adorata aspetta	Adored shade, await!
Teco sarò indiviso	I shall not be parted from you;
Nel fortunato Eliso	In happy Elysium
Avrò contento il cuor.	My heart will be satisfied.
Là tra i fedele amanti	There, among constant lovers,
Ci appresta amor diletti	A cherished love is given us;
Godremo i dolce istanti	We shall enjoy those sweet moments
Di più innocenti affetti;	Of the most innocent affections
E l'eco a noi d'intorno	And the echo around us, to us,
Risuonerà d'amor.	Will ring out with love.

The elemental qualities of musical power evoked at the beginning of Hoffmann's essay, and the appeal to childlike instinct, form part of a continuity in the *Kreisleriana* cycle that stretches between Gottlieb's inspiration by Rode at the end of 'Kapellmeister Johannes Kreisler's Musical Sufferings', and the story of Chrysostomus in 'Johannes Kreisler's Certificate of Apprenticeship'.

I–3: Thoughts about the Great Value of Music

First published: AMZ, xiv, 29 July 1812, cols. 503–9
Attributed to: Kapellmeister Johannes Kreisler

In its defence of music as a utilitarian pastime, its mockery of Romantic theories of the arts, and denigration of Romantic composers as useless, socially inferior lunatics, this lecture might well belong in the mouth of Privy Councillor Röderlein. Our experience of the first essay (I–1), indeed, increases the comic force of this one. The social regard for music as a background convenience, both in the home and the public arena of theatre or hall, seems to be essentially accurate. For example, we know that in his string quartets written for the second London visit (1794–95) Haydn often incorporated a musical 'call to attention' to quell general noise.[83] And we

---

[83] László Somfaì, 'The London Revision of Haydn's Instrumental Style', *Proceedings of the Royal Musical Association*, c (1973–74), 166–7.

have precise information about conditions in Vienna, where besides acting as 'a pleasant background for other salon pastimes' music played an 'influential rôle in social advancement',[84] around 1800, for the middle class:

Every well-bred girl, whether she has talent or not, must learn to play the piano or to sing; first of all it's fashionable . . . The sons likewise must learn music . . . because it serves them too as a recommendation in good society . . . if someone wants to be a lawyer, he acquires a lot of acquaintances and clients through music by playing everywhere; the same is true of the aspiring physician.[85]

The ironic rehearsal of important elements of Hoffmann's system of musical thought (the Temple of Isis, the 'mysterious Sanskrit of nature', etc.) helps disarm the reader's prejudices and thus prepares for later theories in Part II, as well as for the exalted opening of the following essay on Beethoven. In fact 'Beethoven's Instrumental Music' (I–4) and the present 'Thoughts' can almost be regarded as a pair, masque and anti-masque. The ironic recommendation to remove artistically gifted children from the nefarious impact of serious music and poetry, moreover, directly inverts the notion of the whole *Kreisleriana* as 'apprenticeship'.

I–4: Beethoven's Instrumental Music

First published: *Z E W*, 9–11 December 1813   *Unsigned*

The material of this essay was drawn from Hoffmann's reviews of Beethoven's Fifth Symphony (1810: see p. 234) and of his two Piano Trios, Op. 70 (1813: see p. 300). Judging from the author's letter to Kunz of 28 December 1813, it was the latter who sold the present essay to the journal *Zeitung für die elegante Welt*.

Probably no musical writing by Hoffmann has been more republished and quoted than this essay, particularly its opening section. But people can be prone to misrepresent the author's thought; not simply 'music' is asserted as 'the most romantic of all arts', but *instrumental* music, that which contains no conceptual reference outside itself. Hoffmann's original *A M Z* readers were already used to regarding the achievements of instrumental music as something aesthetically distinct, but the natural tendency was to interpret its meaning through definable moods (almost as in the Baroque) or poetic images. Hoffmann substitutes a shifting, unsettling type of image: 'fear'; 'purple shimmer'; 'yearning'; 'magical spirit-world'; 'infinitely varied clusters'; 'unknown language'; 'rings of light'. By insisting on the literal

---

[84]   Alice M. Hanson, *Musical Life in Biedermeier Vienna* (Cambridge, 1985), 118.
[85]   *Ibid.*, quoting a correspondent for *A M Z* in 1800.

infinitude of impressions proper to truly modern instrumental music, he is able to fix this art squarely at the top of the Romantic mast, which could hardly have been done at the time of the Berlin *Athenaeum* declarations on Romanticism (1798–1800), because Mozart's achievements had not been assimilated by the public and Beethoven was only just ending his apprenticeship. Friedrich Schlegel, moreover, showed no unusual sensitivity towards music in his work.[86] For further discussion of this central text, see 'Hoffmann as a Writer on Music', above, and the Prefatory Remarks to the review of the Fifth Symphony, below.

As ever meticulous in his musical thought, Hoffmann refined his texts in several places when re-casting them for *Kreisleriana*. 'Genuinely [*echt*] romantic' in the second sentence, for example, originally read '*purely* [*rein*] romantic'; the sentence 'Beethoven's mighty genius intimidates the musical rabble...' was added; the imaginary critique of Beethoven's music just after this was expanded and made to lead into a strong attack on reactionary 'wise judges'. There was a telling change of emphasis at the end of the symphony section (p. 100) where Hoffmann now stressed the way that not just orchestration, but also all other musical constituents, were 'directed towards a single point', i.e. the ending of the work.

Music examples and technical commentary, which had loomed large in the original reviews, were mostly omitted; even so, 'Beethoven's Instrumental Music' has a more technical flavour than any other essay in the cycle, because Hoffmann cannot wholly avoid using specifically musical vocabulary.

In the section concerning the trios Op. 70, the essay's subject-matter is extended to include a discussion of what constitutes a satisfactory music for the medium of the piano. Here one must remember the enormous amount of piano music then being issued in print: in 'Kapellmeister Johannes Kreisler's Musical Sufferings', notes 131 and 132, we mention some typical sets of variations. It is against this background of occasional music that Hoffmann demands an end to 'all facetiousness and clowning' in instrumental piano music, with its 'whimsical flourishes' and self-defeating difficulties.[87]

---

[86] Schlegel endows Romantic poetry with the notion of permanent incompleteness ('it is always becoming'), which, like the form of the fragment itself, provides an infinite source of suggestion. See *Athenaeum*, Aphorism no. 116, in Behler and Struc, *Schlegel. Dialogue on Poetry*, 140–1.

[87] For a different interpretation see Joseph Kerman, '*Tändelnde Lazzi*: On Beethoven's Trio in D Major, Opus 70, No. 1', in Malcolm Hamrick Brown and Roland John Wiley (eds.), *Slavonic and Western Music. Essays for Gerald Abraham* (Ann Arbor and Oxford, 1985), 109–22.

Beethoven's personal response to this essay prompted him to write appreciatively to Hoffmann in 1820: 'Allow me to tell you that this interest on the part of a man like you who is endowed with such excellent qualities is very gratifying to me.'[88]

The Fifth Symphony, in C minor, Op. 67, was first performed on 22 December 1808 and published in about April 1809. The two piano trios, Op. 70, in D major and E flat major, were first performed in December 1808, and published in about October 1809. The first is sometimes called the 'Ghost' trio, on account of the special effects in what Hoffmann calls its 'melancholy Largo'. Both trios are substantial in size, with finales of some 400 bars each.

I–5: Extremely Random Thoughts

First published: *Z E W*, 4–8 January 1814

Attributed to: Kapellmeister J. Kreisler

The disjunct formal structure of these 'thoughts' (though not the fictional frame explaining their appearance) echoes certain earlier Romantic texts: primarily Friedrich Schlegel's 'fragments' concerning literature and related themes (see note 86) and, more closely, Novalis's *Blütenstaub* (*Pollen*) (1798), a series of more personal aphoristic statements, published in the first issue of the *Athenaeum*. Indeed, one of these relates closely to the nature of *Kreisleriana*:

To discover formulas for individual arts, by means of which alone they may be understood in their most intimate sense, is the business of the artistic critic, whose labours initiate the history of the art.[89]

Novalis's observations on humour and irony are also apposite to Kreisler (see the Introduction to *Kreisleriana*).

It was possible for an entire two-volume book to be cast in loosely organised, short, often speculative or rhetorical statements: one such was the physicist Johann Wilhelm Ritter's *Fragmente aus dem Nachlasse eines jungen Physikers* (*Fragments from the Estate of a young Physicist*), issued in

[88]   Letter of 23 March, in *The Letters of Beethoven*, tr., ed. Emily Anderson (London, 1961), ii, 885.
[89]   *Blütenstaub*, Aphorism no. 53: 'Formeln für Kunstindividuen finden, durch die sie im eigentlichsten Sinn erst verstanden werden, macht das Geschäft des artistischen Kritikers aus, dessen Arbeiten die Geschichte der Kunst vorbereiten.'

1810.[90] This was used and quoted towards the end of *Kreisleriana* for its insights on acoustic phenomena, language, somnambulism, etc. The general model, of expressing scientific observation and theory side by side with philosophy and artistic thought, was obviously attractive to Hoffmann.

It is possible that Hoffmann knew also a series of contributions to the *AMZ* entitled 'Musikalische Fragmente', by Franz Horn (1781–1837). These were issued in eight instalments between 17 March and 22 September 1802, and Horn divided his thoughts visually by means of a horizontal rule, as was Hoffmann's technique in his own text. Horn's ideas closely prefigure Hoffmann's in relation to instrumental music and opera (see p. 185).

A basic irony underlies the 'Random Thoughts', which are ostensibly haphazard and at times exalted, but which all relate more or less directly to the basic themes of *Kreisleriana*. If Hoffmann's word to his publisher is to be trusted, they 'caused something of a sensation'.[91] Wolfgang Wittkowski has gone so far as to identify a set of symmetries underlying the whole and creating two reflecting halves, parallel to the twin halves of the *Kreisleriana* itself.[92] What unifies the 'Thoughts' is the filter of the writer's mind: like the physicist Ritter or the geologist Novalis, Hoffmann gathers empirical data on his subject (music and art in the modern world), taking experimental 'cases' from intimate knowledge – as in the section on alcohol – or from music history, but then interprets it in a Romantic manner. In the section on Mozart, he distances himself from the 'popular anecdotes' then being published about well-known musicians. The story about the overture to *Don Giovanni* had appeared in *AMZ* on 6 February 1799, ostensibly communicated by Mozart's widow.

I–6. The Complete Machinist

First published: Fantasiestücke in Callot's Manier (1814–15), i

Everything in this essay is contingent on Hoffmann's belief that all aspects of the theatre should be combined in the most thorough and convincing way

90 Heidelberg, 1810, reprinted 1969. There is a similarity of title between Hoffmann's 'Höchst zerstreute Gedanken', ('Extremely Random Thoughts'), and Johann Gottfried von Herder's *Zerstreute Blätter*, issued at Gotha between 1785 and 1797, and in various editions.

91 That is, on initial publication in *ZEW*: see letter to Kunz of 16 January 1814, *HBW*, i, 438.

92 See above, note 7 to the Introduction. Wittkowski sees the seventh section, 'When I read . . .', as the centre point of an intertwining and intensifying set of ideas.

in order to create a 'total effect'. Although he had seen and read many plays and operas, and had himself written operas, incidental music and a comedy, all before arriving in Bamberg in 1808, it was only there that Hoffmann's theatrical experiences and ideas achieved mature concrete form. His three opera articles on Weigl, Gluck, and Paer constitute part of the same process (pp. 252 ff.)

In a sense, 'The Complete Machinist' is a satire at Hoffmann's own expense; he was employed in 1811–12 at the Bamberg theatre as set designer, builder, painter, and effects man. This occurred when his old acquaintance Franz von Holbein (1779–1855), an actor, writer, manager, and singer of some renown, reorganised the theatre in the autumn of 1810. Hoffmann wrote to J. E. Hitzig on 28 April 1812:

the whole burden of financial arrangements and a large part of the aesthetic ones fell on me, and in addition to my continuing as theatre composer, I also became theatre architect and designer, for which the most skilful machinist Holbein soon initiated me *practically* speaking into the secrets of stage effects, thereby completing the theory I had devoured from all the books I could get hold of. – Thus we constructed the collapsing castle for [Kleist's] *Kätchen von Heilbronn*, the ascending cross for [Calderón's] *Die Andacht [zum Kreuze]*, the phantasmagorias in *Der standhafte Prinz*, and above all the bridge of Mantible [in Calderón's eponymous play, as translated by A. W. Schlegel].

(*HBW*, i, 333)

All these plays, and others, were in fact mounted in the second half of 1811, but already on 24 March 1811 Hoffmann's diary noted, 'Painted a scene for the theatre all day.' Kunz recalled that Hoffmann painted all the sets for *Die Andacht zum Kreuze* (*The Devotion at the Cross*). In 1812 Hoffmann published an account of the production and successful reception of the Calderón plays in Bamberg.[93] Some of his stage effects were described here, not least for *Die Brücke von Mantible* (the latter ended by being blown up), but not his technical methods. His lighting effects in *Die Andacht zum Kreuze* created a mystical climax to the whole, in which the sky reddened, and an aerial vision was seen against the misty skyline of the city of Tangiers.

The word 'machinist' has become obsolete in theatrical parlance. The term 'machinery' applied to all the non-visible technology of the stage, which was divided as follows: (a) the fixed portions of the staging; (b) the moveable portions of the staging, in the wings or behind the stage; (c)

---

[93] 'Über die Aufführung der Schauspiele des Calderón de la Barca auf dem Theater in Bamberg', in *Die Musen*, i (1812), 157–67; also ed. Friedrich Schnapp in *Nachlese*, 595–601.

special effects, whether visual or auditory.[94] The 'machinist' was the person employed to invent, assemble, and take charge of the operation of all the 'machinery'; by extension it also applied to the stage hands operating it.[95] The adept machinist therefore needed to have much knowledge, imagination, and artistic sense.

The word 'Dekorateur', which Hoffmann also uses, meant the person responsible for all the visual elements (including the backcloth and other scenery) that lent the stage space its temporal and geographical illusion of reality.[96] This has been translated as 'designer'.

In the introductory part of the essay Hoffmann pours ironic scorn on the successful efforts of the designer and machinist, which even cause the playwrights to become a little jealous. In the 'treatise' proper, he therefore urges ways of distancing audiences and disengaging their imagination, and he writes with special reference – as he says – to opera. 'The Complete Machinist' thus stands as an ironic aesthetic prologue to Hoffmann's own contemporary opera, *Undine*.

The title of the essay might also – in view of its supposed authorship – contain an intended allusion to the famous treatise by Johann Mattheson, *Der Vollkommene Capellmeister* (*The Complete Kapellmeister*) (Hamburg, 1739), an encyclopaedic, if sometimes idiosyncratic, compendium.

II–1 and II–2: Letter from Baron Wallborn to Kapellmeister
                Kreisler
                Letter from Kapellmeister Kreisler to Baron
                Wallborn

First published: Die Musen [iii], 1814, part 3, 272–93[97]

This pair of letters, the first of which is by Baron Friedrich Heinrich Carl de la Motte Fouqué (1777–1843), immediately sets a new direction for *Kreisleriana*. As explained earlier in the Introduction, we encounter several elements of structural repetition, which suggest that a new phase of the cycle has been reached. Furthermore, the mention of 'Hoffmann' in the third person establishes a separation of the Kreisler/Hoffmann personas which will be resolved only in the final essay of the whole (II–7). Lastly, the

---

[94] R. Blum, K. Herloßsohn, H. Marggraff (eds.), *Allgemeines Theater-Lexikon oder Encyklopädie alles Wissenswerthen für Bühnenkünstler, Dilettanten und Theaterfreunde* (7 vols., Altenburg and Leipzig, 1839–46), article 'Maschinerie'.

[95] *Ibid.*, 'Maschinist'.

[96] *Ibid.*, 'Decoration'.

[97] A reprint edition has been issued (Nendeln, 1971).

second letter (II–2) marks Kreisler's decisive advance towards successful and sustained compositional achievement: the potential is felt for 'a whole opera'.

Hoffmann read Fouqué's tale *Undine* (published 1811) sometime before the last week of June 1812, when the idea of an opera on the same subject came to him while on a local holiday (*HTB*, entries for 22–23 June; *HBW*, i, 339). Through his friend Hitzig, the publisher of *Die Musen* and an acquaintance of Fouqué, Hoffmann obtained from the latter himself the libretto of *Undine*, 'magic opera in 3 acts'; it arrived the following 14 November. The composition was completed in August 1814, and performed in 1816–17.[98]

Given Hoffmann's highly developed sense of the creative relationship between any opera librettist and composer, and the successful collaboration between himself and Fouqué on *Undine*, it is not surprising that the meeting between the two at the end of September 1814 in Berlin (whither Hoffmann was then moving) proved memorable.

Fouqué was already a leading Romantic writer, whose works are mentioned at the beginning of Part II of *Kreisleriana*. He was the editor, together with Wilhelm Neumann, of the triannual periodical *Die Musen*. On Hoffmann's arrival in Berlin, Hitzig organised a celebration dinner for him on 27 September, attended by Tieck, Chamisso, Franz Horn, and others, including Fouqué. At tea afterwards, in Hoffmann's words, 'I was introduced by the name of "Doctor Schulz from Rathenow", and only after much good playing of music Fouqué said: "The Kapellmeister Johannes Kreisler is among us – and here he is!"' (*HBW*, ii, 24). Both Wallborn's and Kreisler's Letters allude to this incident, though in transformation, and as though it took place in a theatre: Kreisler's 'recognition' of Wallborn in II–2 reflects the fact that Hoffmann first saw Fouqué on 27 September (this description certainly does not fit the fictional Wallborn of *Ixion*), while Wallborn's description of 'a small, strange-looking man' in II–1 reflects Hoffmann's short stature and quizzical expression.

Presumably only a short time after this party, Fouqué must have suggested inserting a piece of writing by them jointly in *Die Musen*, and the 'letters' were issued in the final pages of the final issue of that journal. Their creative friendship was more overtly displayed in the original version of the texts, where Fouqué–Wallborn writes, 'P.S. Could we not create an opera together one day?'

The rather confusing expository sentences (pp. 123–4) result from the fact that Hoffmann was amalgamating and adapting two originally separate

---

[98] Further consideration of *Undine* will be found below, pp. 177, 184.

prefaces, one by Fouqué for Wallborn's letter, and one by himself for Kreisler's. That the first letter is by Fouqué is entirely within the conception of *Kreisleriana* as modelled on Novalis's *Die Lehrlinge zu Sais* (see Introduction above) with its various 'speakers'.

Fouqué's short story *Ixion* (1812) centres on the incompatibility of everyday existence and friendship with the emotions of first love. Wallborn disappears, and is later discovered, insane, only through a chain of coincidences. After his final rejection by the beloved, and his final assumption of the character of Ixion with his 'poet's crown' of golden paper, Wallborn dies. On the night of his death, his form mysteriously appears to the beloved, who is watching an operatic scene portraying Ixion's love-song to Juno, in a theatre thousands of miles away. Hoffmann's story *Don Juan* (September 1812) uses a very similar motif.

II–3: Kreisler's Musico-Poetic Club

First published: Fantasiestücke in Callot's Manier (1814–15), ii

Although at first this essay appears to be a rare excursion into the narrative mode, Hoffmann subverts any 'objectivity' by introducing himself at the end in the person of the 'travelling enthusiast' (i.e. the author of the *Fantasiestücke*), who turns out to be identical with the 'true friend'; thus he has been, in fictional terms, present throughout the séance.

Many eighteenth-century writers published theories about the expressive properties of various musical keys.[99] This was particularly significant at a time when there were still regional and personal preferences as to which system of tuning or 'temperament' might be employed. As late as 1780, J. J. Engel could write, 'a characteristic instrumental piece in C major, [when] transposed to A flat major, will be nearly unrecognisable. The same goes for the minor keys.'[100] The first interesting thing about Kreisler's performance is that it specifies not just key, but also chord-position, dynamic level, and tone-quality (timbre), low down on the piano keyboard: his chords can be reconstructed and played today. Furthermore, however, these keys themselves, the verbal fantasy attached to them, and indeed the act of playing

---

[99] For example those of Mattheson (1713) translated in George Buelow, 'An Evaluation of Johann Mattheson's Opera *Cleopatra* (Hamburg, 1704)' in H. C. Robbins Landon and Roger E. Chapman (eds.), *Studies in Eighteenth-Century Music* (London, 1970), 98–102; or of C. F. D. Schubart in 'Charakteristik der Töne' [1806], *Gesammelte Schriften und Schicksale* (Stuttgart, 1839, reprinted Hildesheim and New York, 1972), v, 381–6. These are translated in Schafer, *Hoffmann and Music*, 151.

[100] Johann Jakob Engel, *Über die musikalische Malerey* (Berlin, 1780): quotation kindly supplied and translated by Mark Lindley.

single chords, all are connected to past or forthcoming passages in
Kreisleriana.

We have seen E major as the colour of Kreisler's collar, and C minor as
the key of Beethoven's Fifth Symphony; E flat major is the key of Beethoven's Trio, Op. 70 no. 2, mentioned in I–4 (the full review of this work
appears below, p. 313). The 'sound of trumpets and drums' for C major
could be related to the fanfare-figures in the slow movement of Beethoven's
Fifth Symphony, which occur in that key, just as the reference to 'red-hot
talons' under C minor surely relates to the same symphony through connection with the 'arms of red-hot metal' of Beethoven's 'mighty spirit', evoked
in '*Ombra adorata*'.

No clear tale is told in Kreisler's verbal 'fantastication', but the imaginative reader can detect hints sufficiently relating to Kreisler's own emotional
situation, described at the beginning of Part II.

As to playing single chords, this is revealed as a youthful fascination of the
narrator in 'The Music-Hater', who would finally be moved to tears by their
musical effect (p. 146). Moreover in the fable of Chrysostomus, in
'Johannes Kreisler's Certificate of Apprenticeship', the narrator recalls how
he instinctively discovered for himself 'melodies and chords on the piano,
some of which were quite expressive and coherent' (p. 162).

Kreisler's skill as an improviser of fantasies has been established from
the opening of the whole cycle; but Hoffmann's need to use words to create
the effect of a fantasy makes for a paradoxical performance, well fitting the
mood of incipient mental imbalance. For 'an essential of the fantasia is its
freedom from words. The musician was free "to employ whatever inspiration comes to him, without expressing the passion of any text" (Marin
Mersenne, [*Harmonie Universelle*] 1636–7).'[101] We have already mentioned, in the first part of the Introduction, the fantasies that were the
habitual mode of expression of the mental patient 'Karl' whose condition
fascinated Hoffmann. In the sense that 'Karl' became Kreisler, the 'fantasy'
performed by the latter at his musico-poetic club exists as a simultaneous
outer (musical) and inner (emotional) dramatisation of spontaneous musical
composition, and is a crucial part of *Kreisleriana* for that reason. The result
is not the same as Ludwig Tieck's 'verbal music', though surely influenced
by the two examples of it in his play *Die verkehrte Welt* (*The World Upside-
Down*) of 1798: 'Symphonie' (overture) and 'Musik' (entr'acte between
Acts 4 and 5). Tieck heads the prose with musical terms of all kinds, for
example 'Violino primo solo'. Hoffmann specifies not just actual aural
effects, but their fundamental emotional equivalents. Tieck's 'music' is

---

[101] Christopher D. S. Field, 'Fantasia', in *The New Grove*, vi, 381.

impersonal theatre music; Hoffmann's is a directly expressive 'music'. There is surely also the possibility that Hoffmann's dramatisation implies its own musical elaboration: thanks to the words, the musical reader can actually *compose* passages in the keys specified, in accordance with the verbal images.

The 'poetic' aspect of the essay's title is related to the insertion, within its original 1815 published version, of the one-act fragment, *Prinzessin Blandina (Princess Blandina)*, 'a romantic play in three acts'. It came after Kreisler's wild conclusion to C minor, and was narrated by the 'jovial one', who indicated that its plan had previously been discussed with Kreisler: its ten scenes are fully worked out, and have been reprinted.[102] The characters included Amandus (a musician), Kilian (King of the Moors), and some from the *commedia dell'arte*. Extensive discussion of the significance of *Prinzessin Blandina* has been carried out by Maurice M. Raraty; he points out that it was intended as 'a purely dramatic equivalent of *Der goldne Topf* [completed shortly before] in which was to be portrayed the way of the poetic hero (or heroine) to the ideal world of poetry through earthly destruction', achieved theatrically by a combination of serious and comic elements.[103]

Because it overbalanced *Kreisleriana* and was considered 'my weakest product' by Hoffmann,[104] it was withdrawn from the 1819 edition and new connecting material inserted. But its inner relation to the imaginative history of Kreisler, his 'way' to Saïs and final disappearance, is undoubted.

II–4: Report of an Educated Young Man

First published: AMZ, xvi, 16 March 1814, cols. 178–87

Attributed to Kapellmeister Johannes Kreisler

We know from Hoffmann's letter to Kunz of 17 November 1813 both that he was at work on this 'humorous essay' and that he intended it for

---

[102] E. T. A. Hoffmann, *Fantasie- und Nachtstücke*, ed. Müller-Seidel, 712–48. For an account of the plot of *Prinzessin Blandina* and its relation to Tieck and Gozzi, see Hedwig Rusack, *Gozzi in Germany. A Survey of the Rise and Decline of the Gozzi Vogue in Germany and Austria* (New York, 1930), 154–62.

[103] Maurice Michael Raraty, 'E. T. A. Hoffmann and the Theatre. A Study of the Origins, Development and Nature of his Relationship with the Theatre, and its Impact on his Imaginative Literary Work' (unpublished dissertation, Sheffield University, 1963), 179 *et passim*, especially chapter 9.

[104] *Ibid.*, 172.

Kreisleriana (*HBW*, i, 420). It stems from a highly creative period, after *The Poet and the Composer* and before *Der goldne Topf.*

The early reference to Councillor R. (= Röderlein), the technique of dramatic monologue, and a character of limitless vanity coupled with artistic ignorance: all take us back to the world of 'Kapellmeister Johannes Kreisler's Musical Sufferings'. Milo is a kind of reverse of Kreisler. Hanne Castein has pointed to the close connection between Milo and the tom-cat Murr in *Kater Murr* five years later, where the cat's attitude to literature parallels Milo's to music.[105] His animal origins as a vehicle for irony must lie at least partly with the cat Hinze in Ludwig Tieck's experimental play *Der gestiefelte Kater* (*Puss-in-Boots*) (1797).[106] Not only is Hinze opinionated and given to high-flown sentiments, but – like Milo – has to struggle at awkward moments to overcome his baser instincts. It was, of course, part of Hoffmann's avowed purpose in the *Fantasiestücke* to emulate Callot's irony and its 'grotesque forms, created out of animal and man' (see p. 76). He had already written another 'report' in *Fantasiestücke*, that of the Dog Berganza, dating from earlier in 1813. Further back, Hoffmann may have drawn on fables about the innocent outsider, such as Voltaire's *L'Ingénu* (1767). There are perhaps shades of *The Tempest*, Act 4, in the account of Milo's capture, redolent of Prospero with the 'noise of hunters' trapping Caliban and friends with 'glistering apparel'. But the top-boots could also be a cue taken from Tieck's play, where Hinze's reasons for ordering boots are discussed. The name Milo might be an ironic reference to a celebrated athlete of ancient Greece, Milo of Crotona: cf. the end of the 'Report' where the subject's 'agile legs' are again alluded to.

Specific threads connect Milo's musical victories parodistically with other parts of the cycle, especially virtuoso pianism (I–1; II–5), vocal ornamentation (I–2), and composition (II–6, II–7). The humour now also extends to Romantic theory, as well as social practice: Milo's dismissal of 'all that stuff they cram into a score' is a joking reversal of Hoffmann's hieroglyphic fascination with 'a full score, that true musical book of charms preserving in its symbols all the miracles and mysteries' of ensemble music ('Beethoven's Instrumental Music'); or 'the charm-book of the score' ('On a Remark of Sacchini's, and on so-called Effect in Music').

'Charles Ewson' in the opening paragraph must be connected with the eccentric, unmusical Herr Ewson in *Die Elixiere des Teufels*, vol. i, chap. 4, which Hoffmann published in 1815.

---

[105] Castein, 151–2.
[106] Hoffmann certainly knew Tieck's work. '*I*: I see that you mean *Puss-in-boots*, a book that has . . . filled me with the purest delight.' From near the conclusion of 'Report of the Latest Fortunes of the Dog Berganza', in *Fantasiestücke in Callot's Manier*.

II–5: The Music-Hater

First published: AMZ, xvi, 1 June 1814, cols. 365–73   *Unsigned*

The reader is presented with what appears to be an amusingly harmless piece. But as in 'Kreisler's Musico-Poetic Club', the connecting threads are drawn in at the end. Mention of 'one real musician', evidently a kind of musical mentor, establishes once again the binary identity of 'Hoffmann' and Kreisler. As the cycle approaches its conclusion, where this binary identity will be explored directly, the author here makes explicit reference to another book, Novalis's *Die Lehrlinge zu Sais*; this (as we said in the Introduction) is a key to understanding *Kreisleriana*, as well as 'The Music-Hater', with its paradoxical title. In note 258 to the text we have quoted from Novalis's work. It is striking that *Kreisleriana* begins with many references to musical works by other hands, but ends with several allusions to works of literature by other hands: Novalis, Shakespeare, Plato, Fouqué, Goethe, G. H. Schubert, J. W. Ritter. (Standing half-way in the cycle are the essay on opera production and the Wallborn–Kreisler correspondence, as a mid-point joining music and letters.) This shift echoes the author's changing career.

As we might suspect, some details in 'The Music-Hater' are autobiographical. Hoffmann's own father did not bring him up; his mother (who did) had two sisters: Charlotte, who died when Hoffmann was three, and Johanna Sophia (1745–1803), who was a beneficial influence on him. His uncle Otto, head of the household in Königsberg, was the subject of mocking and frustrated comments in Hoffmann's letters. Nevertheless, on 10 January 1796, Hoffmann wrote, 'At times I am all done for, and if my uncle's little concerts didn't keep me going, I don't know what would have become of me by now' (*HBW*, i, 75; Sahlin, 45). According to T. G. von Hippel, in *Erinnerungen an Hoffmann*, Otto was Hoffmann's first teacher of music. Other details emerge (or are transformed) in *Kater Murr*.

Various experiences in 'The Music-Hater' are connected with other parts of *Kreisleriana*, chiefly I–2 (on concerts), II–4 (on pianists), II–6 (on Gluck), and II–7 (the 'magical sounds' of wild nature as the composer's raw material).

II–6: On a Remark of Sacchini's, and on so-called Effect in Music

First published: AMZ, xvi, 20 July 1814, cols. 477–85   *Unsigned*

In few other documents than this can the Richard Wagner of *Oper und Drama* (1851) have been so closely anticipated. At a vital point during the composition of *Undine*, the climax of Act 2 – where after a crisis Undine returns to her watery home and the music takes on a highly effective breadth – Hoffmann addressed himself in this essay to the historical development of opera and his own position in it.

Just as Wagner after him, so Hoffmann placed himself in line with Gluck, the model opera dramatist. As Wagner would be obliged to replace 'opera' with other generic titles – though not in fact 'Musikdrama'[107] – so Hoffmann before him coins the word 'Tongedicht' (here translated 'music-drama', simply on internal grounds) from a parallel need. Wagner over-hauled most of the constituent elements of opera. Hoffmann, who will have opera composed by no one less than 'a musical genius', also starts from the position 'that opera should appear as a unified whole in word, action, and music'. In his essay, he counsels the composer concerning the need for true originality, authentic translation of drama, musical harmony, and the proper place of 'effect'. (The impact of *Undine* itself is considered later: see p. 177.)

The notion of 'effect' seems particularly to have been prompted here by Hoffmann's first encounters with the French operas of Gaspare Spontini (1774–1851), namely *La vestale* (1807) and *Fernand Cortez* (1809). These first find mention in his diary in May 1813. As is shown in the 'Letters on Music in Berlin' (p. 392), he was fairly appalled by their heavy orches-tration, their harmonic language, and their lack of true melody. Hoffmann makes analogous points in II–6, but without revealing Spontini's name.

Critical use of the term 'effect' had most notably been made by J.-J. Rousseau in his *Dictionnaire de musique* (Paris, 1768), under 'Effet'. Some-thing is 'effective', he says, when 'the sensation produced seems superior to the means employed in creating it'. Only genius can really command this. 'Beginners' and 'bad composers' sin 'by piling up part upon part, instru-ments upon instruments', only to give rise to 'a barren, beggarly, confused music, without effect', and so on. The term, rendered in the borrowed word *Effekt*, rather than the normal *Wirkung*, was used in Germany at the turn of the century; a writer in the *AMZ* in 1801 associated 'effect' (*Effekt*) with 'mere feeling', 'the taste of the ignorant listener'. 'Is then *effect* – as is so generally maintained – really the highest artistic law, or most important aim of the artist? Were it not well to proceed cautiously with this maxim, and to discuss it closely?'[108]

---

[107]   In spite of its ubiquitous use in the literature, the familiar label 'Music-drama' was not approved of by Wagner, but applied by others even during his lifetime. See 'On the name "Musikdrama"' [1872], *Richard Wagner's Prose Works*, tr. William Ashton Ellis (London, 1896, reprinted New York, 1966), v, 299–304.

[108]   [J. K. F. Triest], 'Bemerkungen über die Ausbildung der Tonkunst in Deutschland', *AMZ*, iii (1801), issue 16 of 14 Jan., col. 258 and note.

Antonio Sacchini (1730–86), who worked chiefly as an opera composer, was invited to Paris in 1781 as part of the continuing efforts of the Paris Opéra to renew its repertory, following the impact of Gluck there between 1774 and 1779. He brought a musical suavity to the Parisians that was much appreciated. The opening anecdote about him was translated straightforwardly by Gerber from an obituary by N. E. Framery.[109] Framery led up to it by saying, '[Sacchini] avoided commonplace turns of phrase, but he feared still more anything that seemed studied. His most unexpected modulations never astonished the ear.' After the anecdote quoted by Hoffmann, the obituary continued by recounting how Sacchini illustrated his point by composing a sixteen-bar minuet on the spot that modulated sixteen times.

The inner design of *Kreisleriana* leads towards a Romantic understanding of composition. This essay – like the next – is remarkable for the precision of its language when discussing the most elusive creative processes. In this respect it may be compared with the most subtle passages in the 'Letters on Music in Berlin'.

II–7: *Johannes Kreisler's Certificate of Apprenticeship*

First published: Fantasiestücke in Callot's Manier (1814–15), ii

The final essay of the cycle acts as a resolution on three levels: firstly, regarding the Romantic theory of musical composition, Hoffmann makes his definitive statements linking nature, and its sounds and acoustic properties, with the rôle and training of the composer. Secondly, he sums up the esoteric (and personal) strands of the cycle, together with their recurring symbols, in the fable of Chrysostomus. Thirdly, he resolves the question of the binary identity of 'Hoffmann' and Kreisler: though both are aspects of the same consciousness, the Kreisler part is, for the moment at least, put to one side as having accomplished creative wholeness.

The triple resolution makes for a sharp juxtaposition between the ambiguities of the fable and the compositional formulations after it. Concerning the fable, some reflection of its meaning is surely present at the close of *Die Fermate (An Interrupted Cadence)*,[110] written at the same juncture as the present essay, spoken by the musician Theodore:

No doubt every composer can remember some particular occasion when some

---

[109] Nicolas Etienne Framery, 'Lettre au rédacteur du Mercure, sur la mort de M. SACCHINI', *Mercure de France*, 28 October 1786, 169–87.

[110] Hoffmann, *The Serapion Brethren*, tr. Ewing, i, 73–4.

powerful impression was made on him, which time never effaces . . . when his beautiful enchantress [the singer] has left him . . . she has been transformed to everlasting Music, glorious and divine . . . and out of it are born the melodies which are Her only and Her again and again.

On the other hand, passages in the story *Die Automate* (*Automatons*), also contemporary, illuminate Hoffmann's consciousness of the music of nature. Here it must be recalled that important questions about musical acoustics were being raised at the time by the physicist Ernst Chladni (1756–1827), concerning patterns of vibration and the nature of sound.[111] After mentioning G. H. Schubert's book *Ansichten von der Nachtseite der Naturwissenschaft* Hoffmann's character Louis explains:

In the primeval condition of the human race . . . Mother Nature continued to nourish [mankind] from the fount of her own life . . . she encompassed him with a holy music, like the afflatus of a continual inspiration, and wondrous tones spake of the mysteries of her unceasing activity. There has come down to us an echo from the mysterious depths of those primeval days – that beautiful notion of the music of the spheres . . . However, as I said to you already, those nature-tones have not yet all departed from this world . . .[112]

and he continues by discussing both natural and artificial forms of 'nature-tones' wherein an induced vibration causes an object to give off a note or notes. The Aeolian harp is one example given.

Hoffmann alludes several times to the work of the physicist Ritter in 'Johannes Kreisler's Certificate of Apprenticeship'; these references are explained in the notes to the text.

In the copy of *Fantasiestücke* in the British Library (C. 104. e. 15) the handwriting, in pencil, of the poet Coleridge has been identified. The only annotation he made was at the point where Hoffmann quotes Ritter (see note 282) to the effect that 'hearing is seeing from within'. The decipherable portion of Coleridge's remarks is as follows (pp. 368–9):

I suspect, that this is a mere ting tang, meaning nothing or a truism.[113] But I have often thought, that Hearing might be called a Seeing of the Inward, of (not merely *from*) the *Within*. Only *from* within can we either see or hear. But a seeing of the

---

[111] Chladni invented the 'euphon' and the 'clavicylinder'; Hoffmann mentions the former instrument in *Kater Murr*, and would have encountered J. W. Ritter's thoughts on Chladni in the *Fragmente*, i, 226–7.

[112] Hoffmann, *The Serapion Brethren*, tr. Ewing, i, 375–7. See note 279 to II–7 for further mention of G. H. Schubert.

[113] The *OED* defines 'ting-tang' as 'A jingling repetition of sounds; a rime'.

Within is necessarily opposed to[114] the seeing of the surface, i.e. of the positive shape, nature, colour . . .

How much, one wonders, did Coleridge absorb from *Kreisleriana*, especially when one reads in his Table Talk (6 July 1833), 'I like Beethoven and Mozart – or else some of the aërial compositions of the elder Italians, as Palestrina and Carissimi – And I love Purcell. The best music is what it should be – sacred'?[115]

The first version of 'Johannes Kreisler's Certificate of Apprenticeship' including the fable of Chrysostomus and a longer version of the following matter concerning composition was completed in June 1814 and sent to the editor of the *Morgenblatt für gebildete Stände* in Stuttgart. The latter held it back until issues 45 and 46, of 21 and 22 February 1816. Meanwhile, Hoffmann reworked the essay, adding the framing sections, in February 1815: the diary entry for 26 February reads '*Kreislerianum* ganz fertig gemacht' (*HTB*, 266). Entitled 'Ahnungen aus dem Reiche der Töne', the first version has been edited in the *Nachlese*, pp. 605–13.

---

[114] Coleridge here uses a sign he explains means 'opposed to' or 'contra-distinguished from', as in the case sweet/sour.

[115] Kathleen Coburn (ed.), *Inquiring Spirit* (London, 1951), 213.

'JACQUES CALLOT'

[Hoffmann's prefatory lines to the *Fantasy-pictures in the Style of Callot*, the book originally containing *Kreisleriana*]

Why can I not see enough of your strange and fantastic pages, most daring of artists! Why can I not get your figures, often suggested merely by a few bold strokes, out of my mind? When I look long at your compositions, which overflow with the most heterogeneous elements, then the thousands of figures come to life, and – often from the furthest background, where at first they are hard even to descry – each of them strides powerfully forth in the most natural colours.

No master has known so well as Callot how to assemble together in a small space such an abundance of motifs, emerging beside each other, even within each other, yet without confusing the eye, so that individual elements are seen as such, but still blend with the whole.

It may be that harsh judges of art reproach him for his ignorance in proper grouping, and also in his deployment of light. But his art really goes beyond the rules of painting; or rather his drawings are but reflexes of all the fantastic apparitions called up by the magic of his exuberant fantasy.

For even in his designs taken from life, his processions, his battles, and so on, there is a uniquely vigorous physiognomy which gives his figures, his groups – I might almost say something oddly familiar. Even the commonest subjects from everyday life – his peasant dance, accompanied by musicians who sit like little birds in the trees – appear in the glow of a certain romantic originality, so that one's thoughts are surrendered to fantasy, and engaged in the most amazing way.

Irony, in that it sets man and animal in conflict, derides man with his paltry works and endeavours; it resides only in a profound soul, and Callot's grotesque forms, created out of animal and man, reveal to the serious, deeper-seeing observer all the hidden meanings that lie beneath the cloak of

76

4 Jacques Callot, *The Temptation of St Anthony* (1635 version); detail
showing the saint tormented by devils, including assorted musicians.
This etching is mentioned by Hoffmann in 'Jacques Callot'.

absurdity. By this token, then, how splendid is the devil (in *The Temptation
of St Anthony*) whose nose has grown into a musket, which he aims
everlastingly at the man of God; the merry devil as ordnance officer, and the
clarinettist (in the same picture)[116] who requires a quite singular bodily
organ in order to provide enough wind for his instrument, are equally
delightful.

It is fitting that Callot was as bold and outrageous in his life as he was in
his powerful illustrations. It is said that when Richelieu insisted that he
engrave the capture of Nancy, the city of his birth, he freely asserted that he
would as soon cut off his own thumb as perpetuate the humiliation of his
duke[117] and his fatherland through the use of his talents.

[116] See figure 4.
[117] Nancy was part of the duchy of Lorraine.

May a poet or writer, in whom the figures of everyday life are reflected in his inner romantic spirit-realm, and who then portrays them in the glow by which they are there enveloped, as if in weird and wonderful apparel, may he not justify himself at least by reference to this master and say: He wished to work in the manner of Callot?

KREISLERIANA: PART I

Where is he from? Nobody knows. Who were his parents? It is not known. Whose pupil is he? A good teacher's, for he plays excellently, and since he is intelligent and cultivated one can certainly tolerate him, and even permit him to teach music. And he really and truly was a Kapellmeister. So say the diplomatic officials to whom on one occasion, when in a good mood, he produced a document issued by the director of the Court Theatre at ***. According to this, he, Kapellmeister Johannes Kreisler, had been relieved of his office merely for having refused outright to set to music a libretto written by the court poet; also for having repeatedly spoken of the *primo huomo*[118] with contempt at the tavern-table; and for having sought to advance a young girl to whom he taught singing, using the most extravagant if incomprehensible language, at the expense of the *prima donna*; but the document went on to say that he should retain the title of Court Kapellmeister, and even be allowed to return, provided he utterly renounced certain eccentricities and ridiculous prejudices, such as that true Italian music had disappeared,[119] and willingly acknowledged the excellence of the court poet, who was generally regarded as a second Metastasio.[120]

His friends maintained that in his formulation nature had tried a new recipe but that the experiment had gone wrong: to counteract his over-excitable spirit and his fatally inflammable imagination too little phlegm had been added, and thus that balance which is essential to the artist, if he is to survive in this world and compose the works it actually needs, especially in a higher sense, had been destroyed. Be that as it may, Johannes was tossed back and forth by his inner visions and dreams as though on an eternally stormy sea, and he seemed to seek in vain the haven that would

---

[118] *primo huomo*: leading male singer of an opera company.
[119] true Italian music: i.e. in the melodic tradition of the Baroque. See p. 36.
[120] Pietro Metastasio (1698–1782), the most celebrated opera librettist and poet of his age, whose librettos (such as *La clemenza di Tito*, mentioned in note 128 below) were repeatedly set to music.

finally give him the peace and tranquillity without which an artist can create nothing. So it was that his friends could not bring him to write down a single composition, or to leave it intact if he actually did write it down. Sometimes he would compose by night in the most agitated frame of mind. He would awaken his friend who lived next door in order to play to him, in a state of utmost rapture, everything he had scribbled down with incredible speed. He would weep tears of joy over the composition he had produced. He would proclaim himself the happiest of men. And yet, by the following day, the great work had been consigned to the fire.

Singing had an almost fatal effect upon him, since his imagination became overstimulated and his mind withdrew into a realm where nobody could follow him without danger. On the other hand he was often content to play the piano for hours, elaborating the most curious themes with elegantly contrapuntal devices and imitations and highly ingenious passage-work. Whenever this had gone particularly well, he would be in jovial spirits for several days afterwards, and a sort of roguish irony would spice the conversation with which he delighted the small, intimate circle of his friends.

Suddenly, nobody knew how or why, he disappeared. Many thought they had observed signs of madness in him, and it is true that he had been seen skipping out of the gates, singing merrily and wearing two hats, turned inside-out one on top of the other, with two stave-ruling pens tucked into his red belt like daggers. His close friends had noticed nothing unusual, however, since he had been subject to violent outbursts, sparked off by some inner torment, for some time previously. When all enquiries as to his whereabouts had produced no result, and his friends were deliberating about his small estate of music and other writings, Fräulein von B. appeared. She declared that it was for *her* to look after these effects for her dear master and friend, whom she did not for a moment consider lost.[121] The friends gladly handed over to her everything they had found, whereupon it was discovered that on the plain reverse-side of several sheets of music brief essays, largely humorous in content, had been hastily scribbled in pencil during odd moments. This faithful pupil of the unfortunate Johannes allowed his faithful friends to make a copy of these, and to pass them on as unconsidered products of a momentary impulse.

---

[121] Fräulein von B: Georg von Maassen (*Hoffmanns sämtliche Werke*, i, 482) associated this reference with a sympathetic 'Fräulein von B.' who appears in J. W. von Goethe's *Die Leiden des jungen Werthers* (1774).

1 Kapellmeister Johannes Kreisler's Musical Sufferings

They have all gone.

I could have told that from the whispering, scraping, throat-clearing and muttering in every key; it was a veritable bees' nest, detaching itself from the trunk in order to swarm. Gottlieb[122] has replaced the candles for me and put a bottle of burgundy on the fortepiano. But I can no longer play; I am completely exhausted. My splendid old friend here on the music-rest is to blame for that; once again he has borne me through the ether, like Mephistopheles carrying Faust on his coat, so high that I was unaware of the homunculi below me, in spite of them making so much idiotic noise.

What a damnable, uselessly squandered evening! But now I feel more at ease. Even while playing I took out my pencil, and on page 63 below the last stave scribbled with my right hand a few good modulations in figures, while the left kept up the stream of notes! I shall continue writing on the blank page overleaf. I shall leave figures and notes behind, and with true relish, like a recovered invalid who cannot stop telling people how he has suffered, I shall record here in full detail the hellish torture of today's tea-party. Not for myself alone, of course; but for all those who may occasionally find pleasure and edification here in my copy of Johann Sebastian Bach's keyboard variations published by Nägeli in Zurich,[123] who find my figures at the end of the thirtieth variation, and who, guided by the Latin *verte* in big letters (I will write it in as soon as this account of my grievances is finished), turn the page and read. They will immediately divine the true state of affairs. They know that Privy Councillor Röderlein keeps a most charming house here, and that he has two daughters, of whom the whole of polite society enthusiastically declare that they dance like goddesses, speak French like angels, and play and sing and draw like the muses. Privy Councillor Röderlein is a rich man; at his quarterly dinner-parties he serves the finest wines, the choicest foods, and everything is arranged in the most elegant style; and anyone who fails to have a heavenly time at his tea-parties has no breeding, no intellect, and above all no feeling for art. For they have also made provision for this; as well as tea, punch, wine, ices, etc., music is always served up too. This is consumed by refined society with the same

---

[122] Gottlieb: young, menial servant who possesses true musicality; see Introduction, p. 39.

[123] i.e. the thirty 'Goldberg' Variations (BWV 988), originally published in Nuremberg [1742] as *Aria mit verschiedenen Veraenderungen vors Clavicimbal . . .* Kreisler's edition: *Trente Variations fuguées pour clavecin ou piano-forte* [c. 1800]; Nägeli issued it in oblong folio format, and the music ends on p. 63.

relish as the other offerings. The routine is as follows. After every guest has had sufficient time to consume the desired number of cups of tea, and after punch and ices have twice been passed round, the servants move out card-tables for the older, weightier members of the company. These have no taste for the playing of music and prefer playing with cards, which indeed does not cause such a pointless noise, producing only the chink of a few coins.

This is the sign for the younger members of the company to descend upon the Miss Röderleins. A commotion breaks out in which one can distinguish odd words: 'Oh, Miss Röderlein, do not deny us the pleasure of your divine talent – do sing something, my dear.' 'Not possible – catarrh – the last ball – not practised.' 'Oh please, please – we beg you,' etc. Gottlieb has meanwhile opened the piano and deposited the familiar volume of songs on the music rest. Mama calls across from the card-table, 'Chantez donc, mes enfants!' This is the cue for *my* rôle. I sit down at the piano and the Miss Röderleins are led to the instrument in triumph. Now another dispute arises: neither is willing to sing first. 'My dear Nanette, you know how frightfully hoarse I am.' 'But my dear Marie, am I any less so?' 'But I sing so badly.' 'Oh my dear, do please begin.' And so on. My sudden inspiration (I have it every time) that they should both begin with a duo is greeted with loud applause, the music is leafed through, the carefully folded-down page is finally found, and away we go with 'Dolce dell'anima'.[124]

Actually the talent of the Miss Röderleins is not insignificant. I have now been here for five years, and a teacher in the Röderlein household for four and a half. During this short time Miss Nanette has progressed to the point where, after hearing a melody only ten times in the theatre and then playing it through on the piano another ten times at the most, she can sing it so well that one immediately recognises what it is supposed to be. Miss Marie grasps it after only eight times, and if her pitch is frequently a quarter-tone below that of the piano, then her dainty little face and most agreeable rosebud-lips make it on the whole easy to bear.

After the duet a general chorus of approval! Then ariettas alternate with duettinos, while I hammer away at the accompaniments, churned out a thousand times before. During the singing Treasury Secretary Eberstein's wife lets it be known by clearing her throat and joining in *sotto voce* that she too can sing. Miss Nanette says, 'Oh dear Madam Eberstein, now you must let us hear your divine voice.' A new commotion breaks out. She has catarrh – she cannot sing anything from memory! Gottlieb carts in two armfuls of

[124] 'Dolce dell'anima': duet from Act 2 of *Sargino, ossia L'allievo dell'amore, dramma eroicomico in due atti* by Ferdinando Paer (1771–1839) (piano score, Leipzig, [1803]), 109–10. The piece is quite slow (Larghetto), short (43 bars in all) and does not deviate from the key of A major. For Hoffmann's scathing review of Paer's *Sofonisba*, see p. 262.

music; there is much turning over of pages. First she wants to sing 'Der Hölle Rache', then 'Hebe, sieh', then 'Ach ich liebte'.[125] In consternation I suggest 'Ein Veilchen auf der Wiese'.[126] But she is intent on the operatic heights, she wants to show what she can do, and Konstanze it shall be.

Oh blithely go on with your shrieking, squeaking, miaowing, gurgling, groaning, moaning, warbling, wobbling! I will keep my foot on the fortissimo pedal and bang away until I am deaf! Oh Satan, Satan! Which of your hellish demons has taken possession of this larynx, which traps and twists and tears every musical sound? Four strings have snapped already, and one hammer is out of action. My ears ring, my head throbs, my nerves jangle. How can every obscene sound that emanates from the screeching trumpets of market-criers have been charmed into this little throat? The strain is too much to bear. I drink a glass of burgundy!

There is unbounded applause, and someone observes that Madam Eberstein and Mozart have set me well and truly on fire. I lower my gaze and smile – remarkably stupid of me, as I well realise. Now every kind of talent, hitherto blossoming in obscurity, makes its presence felt and contributes to the wild confusion. All sorts of musical outrage are agreed upon; ensembles, finales, choruses are to be performed. Canon Kratzer[127] is well known to possess a beautiful bass voice, as observed by the Titus-head[128] over there, who adds modestly that he himself is actually only a second tenor, although a member of several choral societies. Everyone is rapidly organised for the first chorus from Titus.[129] It goes quite swimmingly! The canon, standing close behind me, thunders out the bass above my head as though he were

[125] 'Der Hölle Rache': famous and exceedingly difficult aria of the Queen of the Night in Act 2 sc. 8 of Mozart's opera Die Zauberflöte (1791). 'Hebe, sieh': song [An Hebe, 1804] by Friedrich Heinrich Himmel (1765–1814), words by Gottlob von Nostitz. Its difficulty lies in its slow, sustained line, which is directed to be sung 'Gefühlvoll' (full of feeling), being an evocation of a beautiful evening. 'Ach ich liebte': another fast, virtuoso aria, ascending repeatedly to the note d''', sung by Konstanze in Act 1 sc. 7 of Mozart's opera Die Entführung aus dem Serail (1782).

[126] 'Ein Veilchen': song [Das Veilchen: KV 476] by Mozart to words by J. W. von Goethe, technically straightforward and of moderate speed.

[127] Hoffmann knew a cloth-merchant, Johann Kratzer (1754–1813), in Bamberg and, according to his friend and publisher Kunz, always found him a comic figure. The MS draft calls him 'Reese' or 'Keese'.

[128] Titus-head: i.e. with hair styled in the short, quasi-dishevelled manner originally popularised in 1793 by the classical actor Talma in Paris in Voltaire's play Brutus.

[129] Titus: many eighteenth-century operas used the name Titus in their title, such as Vivaldi's Tito Manlio (1719). Metastasio's libretto La clemenza di Tito (1734) was set over forty times. Mozart's version, adapted in two acts by Caterino Mazzolà (1791), has a first chorus that well fits Hoffmann's ironic purpose: 'Serbate, oh Dei custodi'. This is quite short, is easy to sing (being written chordally, not contrapuntally), and does not deviate from the key of E flat. It praises Titus 'the just, the strong'.

singing in a cathedral with obbligato trumpets and drums. He pitches the notes perfectly, but despite all his haste he starts the piece at almost half the proper tempo. At least he remains consistent, however, by then dragging along half a beat behind throughout the entire piece. The others reveal a distinct leaning towards ancient Greek music, which as we know was innocent of harmony and proceeded in unison; they all sing the upper part, with slight variations of about a quarter of a tone up or down in pitch.

This somewhat noisy production creates a general mood of tension, and a certain feeling of shock, even from the card-tables, which for the moment cannot participate in the performance in their customary manner; they normally do this by interpolating declamatory phrases in the style of a melodrama, as for example 'Oh, I loved . . . (forty-eight) . . . was so happy . . . (I pass) . . . knew not . . . (whist) . . . the pains of love . . . (on the hearts).'[130] It is really most ingenious. I refill my glass.

That was the high point of today's musical presentation, and now at last it's over! At least I assume it is, so I shut the book and get up. But then the baron, my Titus-headed tenor, comes up to me and says 'Ah, my excellent Kapellmeister, I gather you improvise fantasies quite divinely; oh do fantasise something for us, just a little, I beg you!' I reply somewhat coolly that my fantasy has all dried up today. But while we are talking, some devil in the guise of a dandy with two waistcoats has nosed out the Bach variations under my hat in the adjoining room; he thinks they are variations on popular tunes, 'Nel cor mi non più sento',[131] 'Ah vous dirai-je, maman',[132] and the like, and demands that I rattle through them. I decline, whereupon they all fall on me in protest. Right, I think to myself, you can listen and burst with boredom. I get down to work. During Variation Three several ladies retire, followed by some Titus-heads. Because their teacher is playing, the Miss Röderleins hold out until Variation Twelve, though not without distress. Variation Fifteen puts the two-waistcoat man to flight.[133]

---

[130] 'melodrama': later eighteenth-century genre (pioneered by J.-J. Rousseau, *Pygmalion*) in which actors declaimed speeches between, or sometimes during, expressive passages of instrumental music. Often dealt with tragic subject-matter. Here the comic comparison is heightened by the fact that Hoffmann uses the example of Madam Eberstein's earlier rendition of Mozart's 'Ach ich liebte' ('Oh, I loved').

[131] 'Nel cor più non mi sento' [*recte*]: duet from opera *La molinara* (1788) by Giovanni Paisiello (1740–1816), used as the basis for variation-sets by composers great and small, such as Josef Gelinek (*c.* 1795: named at this point in Hoffmann's MS draft); Beethoven, WoO 70 (1796); Moritz von Lichnowsky (1798); Daniel Steibelt (*c.* 1810) etc.

[132] 'Ah vous dirai-je, maman': French folk-tune (known in England to the words 'Twinkle, twinkle, little star') used for variation-sets by Mozart (KV 265/300e), anonymous composers (Paris, *c.* 1780 and London, *c.* 1790), and Ludwig Berger (1777–1839).

[133] Variation 15 is the first in the minor mode, and follows a variation of some brilliance.

Out of exaggerated courtesy the baron remains until Variation Thirty, consuming large amounts of the punch which Gottlieb has placed on the piano for me. I would now be happy to stop, but this Variation Thirty, the theme, urges me irresistibly onward.[134] The quarto pages suddenly expand to an elephant-folio, containing a thousand imitations and elaborations of the theme which I am forced to play. The notes come to life and flutter and dance around me; electric sparks flow through my finger-tips into the keys; the spirit generating them overtakes my thoughts. The whole room is filled by a thick fog, in which the candles burn more and more dimly; now a nose appears, now a pair of eyes, but then they immediately disappear again. So it is that I continue sitting alone with my Sebastian Bach, with Gottlieb waiting upon me like a *spiritu familiari*! I drink.

Is it right to torture honest musicians with music as I have been tortured today, and am tortured so often? I can truthfully say that no art has so much damnable abuse perpetrated upon it as the noble and sacred art of music, whose delicate nature is so easily violated. If you have real talent and a real feeling for art, good; then study music, achieve something worthy of the art, and give devotees the benefit of your talent in abundant measure. If you prefer warbling away without bothering with all that, then do it for yourself and by yourself, and do not torture Kapellmeister Kreisler and others with it.

I could go home now and finish my new piano sonata, but it is a fine summer's night and not yet eleven o'clock. I wager that next door where the master of the hunt lives, the girls are sitting by the open window and screeching out into the street with their shrill voices 'Wenn mir dein Auge strahlet'[135] twenty times over, and always the first verse at that. Across the street someone with lungs like Rameau's nephew[136] is inflicting torture upon a flute, and the nearby horn-player is carrying out acoustical experiments on long, long notes. The numerous dogs of the neighbourhood are

---

[134] the theme: in the *AMZ* version of this essay Hoffmann clarified himself by using music-type; this shows the opening of Bach's final variation (entitled 'Quodlibet') which quotes the traditional tune 'Ich bin so lang nicht bei dir gwest'.

[135] 'Wenn mir dein Auge strahlet': duet from Act 1 of *Das unterbrochene Opferfest* (*The Interrupted Sacrifice*), opera by Peter von Winter (1796). The main theme always returns to the same note, thus compounding the 'shrieking' of the singers. Ironically, the words express a declaration of love. Hoffmann reviewed the opera in 1815 as 'Winter's master-piece', and it was second only to Mozart's *Die Zauberflöte* in popularity in Germany.

[136] Rameau's nephew: protagonist of dialogue of the same name (*Le Neveu de Rameau*; see Introduction, pp. 40–2, and notes 9 and 45) by Denis Diderot, supposedly modelled on Jean-François R. (1716–?1781), nephew of the composer Jean-Philippe R. (1683–1764). 'For the rest, he is endowed with a strong constitution, a singular warmth of imagination, and uncommonly sturdy lungs.'

growing restless, and my landlord's tom-cat is lurking close by my window (it goes without saying that my musico-poetic laboratory is a garret). Aroused by the sweet duet, he is making tender avowals to the neighbour's cat, for which he has nourished a passion since March, by caterwauling up and down the chromatic scale. After eleven o'clock it will be quieter. Until then I shall remain here, since there is still some blank paper and burgundy left, and I can derive comfort from both.

I have heard that there is an ancient law that prohibits noisy craftsmen from living near men of learning. Should not poor, put-upon composers, who also have to mint gold from their inspirations in order to spin out their life's thread, be able to apply this law to themselves and ban screaming children and horn-blowing neighbours from their vicinity? What would a painter say who was trying to paint an idealised portrait while people kept holding up nothing but grotesque caricatures in front of him? If he closed his eyes, then at least he could retain the image without distraction in his imagination. Cotton wool in the ears is of no help; one still hears the din. And then the idea, merely the idea that now they are about to sing, now the horn is about to start, etc., etc., and the sublimest thoughts go out of the window!

The sheet is completely filled up. I intend only to record, on the blank reverse-side of the title-page, why I have resolved a hundred times no longer to submit myself to this torture at the Privy Councillor's house, and why I have a hundred times broken my resolve. It is Röderlein's delightful niece, I confess, who ties me to this house, with bonds that art has fastened. Whoever has been fortunate enough to hear Miss Amalie singing the closing scene in Gluck's *Armide*, or Donna Anna's great scene in *Don Giovanni*,[137] will understand that an hour at the piano with her pours heavenly balm into the wounds inflicted on the tortured musical schoolmaster that I am by all the cacophonies of a long day. Röderlein, who believes neither in the immortality of the soul nor in tact, considers her of no use at all for the higher existence of tea-parties; not only does she utterly refuse to sing on such occasions, but then for the most common people, such as simple musicians, she sings with an effort that is quite unbecoming. Her long-held,

---

[137] *Armide: drame héroïque* (1777); *Don Giovanni: dramma giocoso* (1787). The 'closing scene' of *Armide* portrays the enchantress of T. Tasso's *Gerusalemme liberata* abandoned, defiant, and ascending to the skies in a chariot. The 'great scene' in *Don Giovanni* is Act 1 sc. 13: 'Don Ottavio, son morta'; aria, 'Or sai chi l'onore', in which Donna Anna, having recognised Don Giovanni as her father's murderer, recounts the events of the fatal night and calls on Don Ottavio to inspire her to revenge.

swelling armonica-notes[138] transport me into heaven, but Röderlein says she has obviously picked them up from the nightingale, a mindless creature that only lives in forests and should not be imitated by humans, the intelligent lords of creation. She carries her uncompromising attitude so far that sometimes she even lets Gottlieb accompany her on the violin, while she plays sonatas by Beethoven or Mozart on the piano, music of which no tea-connoisseur or whist-specialist can make head or tail.

That was the last glass of burgundy. Gottlieb snuffs the candles for me, and seems surprised at my constant scribbling. People are quite right when they put Gottlieb's age at only sixteen years. His is an extraordinary talent. But why did Papa Torschreiber[139] die so early? And did his guardian have to put the boy into livery? When Rode[140] was here, Gottlieb listened in the anteroom with his ear pressed to the door, and afterwards played for nights on end. During the day he went around in a state of dreamy introspection; and the red mark on his left cheek is a clear impression of the solitaire on the Röderlein hand which, instead of the somnambulant stupor induced by gentle stroking, had tried to bring about the opposite effect by severe beating. Among other things I gave him the sonatas of Corelli,[141] whereupon he wrought havoc among the mice in the old Oesterlein harpsichord[142] in the attic until none was left alive, and with Röderlein's permission he moved the instrument to his own little room. 'Fling it off, this hated servant's uniform, honest Gottlieb, and let me press you to my heart in years to come as the indomitable artist you can be with your outstanding talent and your profound artistic sense!' Gottlieb stood behind me wiping the tears from his eyes as I spoke these words. I pressed his hand in silence, and we went up and played the sonatas of Corelli.

---

[138] armonica-notes: i.e. like the silvery notes produced by the glass bowls of the 'armonica', Benjamin Franklin's mechanised version of the musical glasses. That Miss Amalie possesses such fine, long-held notes associates her with the singer adored by Kreisler, the 'Juliet' of his derangement: see p. 123.

[139] Torschreiber: the sudden inclusion of this name suggests a private significance for Hoffmann. Literally it means 'gatekeeper' or 'toll-keeper'.

[140] Pierre Rode (1774–1830), celebrated Parisian violinist and composer, actually gave a concert in Bamberg on 17 October 1812, to which Hoffmann, apparently, did not go (HTB, 391). At the time, Hoffmann had just accepted a commission to translate the Méthode de violon by Pierre Baillot, Rode, and Rodolphe Kreutzer (Paris, 1803).

[141] Corelli: Arcangelo Corelli (1653–1713), Sonate Op. 5 (Rome, 1700). The historical significance of Corelli is as a magisterial figure of the Baroque style, whose sonatas and concerti grossi have remained touchstones of taste and technique.

[142] Johann Christoph Oesterlein (fl. 1773–94) was a Berlin maker of harpsichords, who may also have made pianos. See Donald H. Boalch, Makers of the Harpsichord and Clavichord 1440–1840 (2nd edn, Oxford, 1974), 117.

2 *Ombra adorata**

What an utterly miraculous thing is music, and how little can men penetrate its deeper mysteries! But does it not reside in the breast of man himself and fill his heart with its enchanting images, so that all his senses respond to them, and a radiant new life transports him from his enslavement here below, from the oppressive torment of his earthly existence? Indeed, he is suffused by a divine power, and by abandoning himself with a childlike and pious mind to whatever influence the spirit arouses within him, he is able to speak the language of that unknown, romantic spirit-realm. Without realising it, like the apprentice who reads aloud from his master's book of spells, he summons all the wonderful images from within his heart, so that they come to life and dance around in brilliant circles, filling all those able to see them with infinite, inexpressible yearning.

How constricted was my breast as I entered the concert-hall! How weighed down I felt by the burden of all the worthless banalities of this wretched existence that plague and persecute men, and particularly artists, like poisonous, blood-sucking vermin, so that rather than endure this constantly smarting torment, we would often prefer the violent stroke that for ever removes us from this and every other earthly affliction!

You understood the melancholy look I gave you, my dear friend, and infinite thanks are due to you for taking my place at the piano, while I sought to hide away in the furthest corner of the hall.[143] What pretext did you employ, how did you contrive that instead of Beethoven's great symphony in C minor only a short and insignificant overture was performed, the work of some composer who had not yet achieved mastery?[144] For that too let me thank you from the depths of my heart. What would have become of me if, almost overwhelmed by all the earthly misery continuously seething around me in recent times, Beethoven's mighty spirit had confronted me, and seized me as if with arms of red-hot metal, and carried me off to the realm of the mighty and the immeasurable that is revealed by his thunderous sounds?

---

* Who does not know Crescentini's wonderful aria 'Ombra adorata' which he composed for Zingarelli's opera *Romeo e Giulietta* and sang with such characteristic delivery?

[143] That is, the friend took over Kreisler's function as conductor, seated at a grand piano. This method of direction was used by Hoffmann in Bamberg (where it caused problems) and in Leipzig and Dresden (where there were no problems). See Hoffmann's letters of 13 July 1813; *HBW*, i, 392, 397, 405 and *HTB* 208.

[144] This Beethoven symphony forms the first subject of I–4; on Hoffmann's reaction to music in concert see 'The Music-Hater', p. 149.

When the overture had reached its conclusion amid all sorts of childish excitement with trumpets and drums, a silent pause supervened as though something really important were imminent. I found this restful, and closed my eyes; and as I searched my mind for images more agreeable than those surrounding me, I forgot the concert and naturally therefore all the arrangements relating to it, which I had been well aware of since I should have been at the piano. The pause must have lasted rather a long time when finally the ritornello of an aria began. It was very tender in character, and seemed to speak in simple but deeply affecting tones of the yearning that sweeps the pious soul up to heaven and restores every beloved object denied it here below. Then, like a heavenly luminescence, the bell-like voice of a woman radiated upwards from the orchestra:

Tranquillo io sono, fra poco teco sarò mia vita![145]

Who can describe the feeling that surged through me! How the pain gnawing at my innards was transformed into wistful melancholy that poured heavenly balm into all my wounds! Everything was forgotten and I simply listened in rapture to the sounds that held me in their consoling embrace as though they were transmitted from another world.

The theme of the following aria, 'Ombra adorata', is just as simple in character as the recitative; but just as tenderly, just as poignantly, it conveys the state of mind that soars above earthly affliction in the blessed hope of seeing all that has been promised brought to fulfilment in a better world. How unaffectedly and naturally everything in this simple composition proceeds; the music moves only between tonic and dominant; no jarring changes of key, no contrived detail; the singing flows along like a silvery stream past brightly coloured flowers. But is this not precisely that mysterious magic which distinguished the composer: that he was able to give the simplest melody and the most unaffected structure that indefinable power to move every receptive heart irresistibly? In his wonderfully bright and clear melismas the soul flies with rapid wing-beat through shining clouds; it is the exultant joy of transfigured spirits.

The composition, like any that has been so deeply felt within the composer, demands to be just as deeply understood and performed, and with an awareness, I would say with an explicit recognition, of the sense of spirituality contained within the melody. Also, as the genius of Italian melody dictates, certain embellishments were allowed for, both in the recitative and in the aria. But is it not a blessing that the way in which the composer and singer Crescentini performed and embellished the aria himself has been

---

[145] How peaceful I am, in a short while I shall be with you, my life.

handed down, as though by tradition? No one would now dare to introduce inappropriate flourishes, at least not without being rebuked.[146] How intelligently Crescentini applied these incidental embellishments, and how they enliven the overall effect; they are the brilliant finery that adorns the beloved's fair countenance, so that her eyes shine more brightly and a deeper purple colours her lip and cheek.

But what am I to say of you, most wonderful of singers! With the fervent enthusiasm of the Italians I call to you, 'You who are blessed by heaven!'* For it must be the benison of heaven that enables your pious heart to give pure and full voice to what it feels within. Your notes surrounded me like propitious spirits, and each one said 'Lift up your head, you who are bowed down! Come with us, come with us to that far land where suffering no longer inflicts its bloody wounds, but as if in deepest rapture fills the breast with inexpressible longing!'

I shall not hear you again; but when ignobility advances towards me and, taking me for one of its own kind, would join the vulgar battle with me, when absurdity would numb me, and the rabble's odious mockery would wound me with its poisonous spines, then through *your* music a consoling spirit-voice will whisper softly to me:

Tranquillo io sono; fra poco, teco sarò mia vita!

Inspired as never before, I shall then rise in powerful flight above all earthly degradation. Every sound congealed in the blood from my wounded breast will be revivified, and stir and spring up and throw out glittering sparks like fire-breathing salamanders.[148] And I shall contrive to harness

---

* Our German singer Häser,[147] who unfortunately has now completely retired from the stage, was greeted by the Italians with cries of 'Che sei benedetta dal cielo!'

[146] Italian vocal music continued to be ornamented by singers throughout the nineteenth century. Hoffmann's attack on indiscriminate vocal egotism occurs in 'Report of an Educated Young Man', p. 142.

[147] Charlotte Henriette Häser (1784–1871), concert and opera-singer, particularly renowned (in male rôles) in Italy: retired 1812.

[148] Salamander: lizard-like animal, or spirit, traditionally supposed to inhabit (or endure) fire. Similar images occur in a letter by Hoffmann of 10 December 1803; after likening his consuming passion for painting to the fate of 'the fairy-tale princess who fought with a salamander' only to collapse in ashes, he continues, 'Music with its tremendous explosions is more of a theatrical thunderstorm, a fire-spewing mountain by Gabrieli (in the arts what Vesuvius is *in natura*). One can, without danger, become rather intimate with it . . .' *HBW*, i, 177; Sahlin, 103. In *'Ombra adorata'* Hoffmann still thinks of salamanders as dangerously powerful.

them, and combine them, so that as if merging into a single burst of fire they form a single flaming image, that transfigures and glorifies your singing and yourself.

3 Thoughts about the Great Value of Music

It cannot be denied that in recent times, may heaven be thanked, the taste for music is becoming increasingly widespread, so that it is now to a great extent accepted that as part of a good education children should also be taught music. In every household that has any pretensions at all, therefore, one finds a piano, or at least a guitar.[149] Only a few despisers of this unquestionably fine art remain here and there, and it is now my intention and duty to give them a good lesson.

The aim of art in general is simply to provide men with pleasant amusement, and thus distract them in a pleasant manner from their more serious occupations, or rather the only occupations proper for them, namely those that earn them bread and respectability in society; they will then be able to return with redoubled concentration and energy to the real purpose of their existence, namely to become efficient cogwheels in the treadmill of the state, and (I continue the metaphor) to twirl round and be twirled round. Now no art is more capable of achieving this purpose than music. One might read a novel or a poem; and one's choice might be so fortunate that the work contained none of the unbelievable lapses of taste found in many of the latest effusions,[150] and that the imagination, which to be sure is the most evil element of our sinful nature and must be suppressed with all our strength, were consequently not in the least aroused; but to read such a work would still have the major disadvantage, I feel, that one is to some extent required to think about what one reads, and this is obviously contrary to the principle of distraction. The same applies to reading aloud, in that if one's concentration is completely diverted from it one very easily falls asleep, or becomes engrossed in serious thoughts; these, according to the intellectual diet to be followed by every respectable business-man, must be given a rest every so often. One can look at a painting for only a very short

---

[149] The social prestige of playing music or singing was of benefit to both men and women: see Prefatory Remarks.

[150] i.e. particularly referring to Romantic writers such as F. Schlegel, whose novel *Lucinde* was widely held to be pornographic.

time, since one's interest disappears as soon as one has guessed what it is supposed to represent.

With regard to music, however, only incorrigible despisers of this noble art would deny that a successful composition – that is to say, one that keeps within proper bounds, and consists of one pleasant melody followed by another, without hysteria or foolish indulgence in endless contrapuntal passages and resolutions – exercises a wonderfully soothing charm. It completely relieves one from having to think. It certainly prevents any serious thoughts from arising, and produces a gentle succession of pleasantly diverting impressions, of which one is not even individually aware. One can even go further and ask why it should not also be possible, during a piece of music, to enter into a conversation with one's neighbour about some political or moral topic, and thus in a pleasant manner achieve a double objective. Indeed, this is very much to be encouraged, since music uncommonly facilitates talking, as one has the opportunity to observe in any concert or musical circle. In the intervals all is silent, but with the music the stream of talk begins to flow, and as more and more notes join in it rises higher and higher. Many a young lady whose conversation otherwise, as in the saying, consists merely of 'Oh yes!' and 'Oh no!', is led by music into more than these, which according to the same saying cometh of evil;[151] here, however, it clearly cometh of good, since it can sometimes result in a lover, or even a husband, intoxicated by the sweetness of her unaccustomed speech, falling into her meshes. Dear Heaven, the advantages of such sweet music are almost infinite!

You incorrigible despisers of this noble art, I would now take you into the domestic circle, where the father, wearied by the serious business of the day, sits contentedly in dressing-gown and slippers, smoking his pipe to the murky-bass[152] of his eldest son. Has his innocent little rose not learnt the Dessau March and 'Blühe liebes Veilchen'[153] just for him, and does she not play it so beautifully that her mother sheds bright tears of joy over the stocking she is darning? And finally, would the hopeful but unsteady squeaking of his youngest offspring not be somewhat burdensome if it were

---

[151] Matthew 5, 37 (Sermon on the Mount): 'But let your communication be, Yea, yea; Nay, nay: for whatsoever is more than these cometh of evil.' One of Hoffmann's favourite quotations; see p. 100.

[152] murky-bass: 'A style of keyboard writing (or a piece in that style) in which the bass consists of an extended pattern of alternating octaves'. Douglas A. Lee, 'Murky', in *The New Grove*, xii, 792.

[153] Dessau March: popular national melody (composer unknown, *c.* 1705), used at the entry of Duke Leopold von Anhalt-Dessau into Turin in 1706. Its rhythm is very repetitive. 'Blühe liebes Veilchen': simple strophic song by Johann Abraham Peter Schulz (1747–1800) in his *Lieder im Volkston* (Berlin, 1785), ii, 21; words by C. A. Overbeck.

not kept in time and tune by the cheery lilt of nursery songs? If your heart is quite unmoved by this domestic idyll, by this triumph of simple humanity, then follow me into a grander house with large, brightly lit windows. You walk into the hall; the steaming tea-machine is the focus of activity, and around it move elegant ladies and gentlemen. Card-tables are moved out, but the lid of the fortepiano also flies up, since here too music serves as a pleasant amusement and distraction. If well chosen, it is not at all disturbing; for even card-players, despite being occupied with higher things, with profit and loss, willingly tolerate it. What am I to say finally of great public concerts, which provide the most splendid opportunity to converse, to musical accompaniment, with this or that friend; or, if one is still at the age of presumption, to exchange soft words with this or that lady, for which the music can indeed suggest an ideal pretext? These concerts are perfect places of distraction for the business-man, and much to be preferred to the theatre; the latter occasionally presents performances that concentrate the mind on things that are quite unworthy and improper, so that one runs the risk of being carried away by the drama, which all those who value their honour as citizens must guard against!

In short, it is a significant indication, as I mentioned at the outset, how clearly the true purpose of music is now recognised, that it is practised and taught so assiduously and seriously. How practical it is that children, even if they have not the least talent for the art, which is a matter of no importance anyway, are put to music, so that if they are unable to play an obbligato rôle in society in any other way, they can at least contribute their share to its entertainment and distraction.

Another conspicuous advantage of music over all the other arts is that in its purity (without the admixture of poetry) it is of great moral value and has no injurious influence on the innocence of youth. Any chief of police would confidently certify on behalf of the inventor of a new instrument that it contained nothing harmful to the state, to religion, or to public decency. With the same confidence any music-master can assure papa and mama in advance that the new sonata contains not a single immoral idea.[151] As children grow older, it goes without saying that they must give up practising the art of music; that sort of thing is not very appropriate for grown men after all, and it can all too easily lead ladies to neglect their higher social duties. They can then enjoy the pleasures of music only in a passive way, by allowing children or professional artists to play for them.

Having correctly identified the purpose of art, we can see that artists, that

---

[154] That is, because it contains no verbal text; lack of text (see following essay) becomes however a fundamental consideration in Hoffmann's view of Romanticism in music.

is to say those persons who (rather foolishly I admit!) devote their entire lives to an occupation serving merely to amuse and distract, are to be regarded as quite inferior subjects, and are to be tolerated only because they put into practice the principle of *miscere utile dulci*.[155] No one of sound mind and mature understanding would value the best artist as highly as a worthy chancery-clerk; or even as a worker who stuffs the cushion on which the tax-collector sits in his counting-house, or the merchant at his desk. The one caters for a necessity, the other only for an amenity. When artists are treated in a polite or friendly manner, therefore, that is merely a token of our cultivation and good nature, since we also flatter and humour children and others who amuse us. Many of these unhappy dreamers have awoken from their delusions too late, and as a result have decayed into mild insanity, as one can very clearly observe from their utterances about art. They think, for instance, that art allows men to sense their higher destiny, and that it will lead them from the futile hurly-burly of everyday life into the Temple of Isis,[156] where nature will speak to them in sacred sounds, unheard before yet immediately comprehensible. With regard to music these madmen cherish quite the most astonishing opinions. They call it the most romantic of all the arts since its only subject-matter is infinity; the mysterious Sanskrit of nature, translated into sound that fills the human breast with infinite yearning; and only through it can they perceive the sublime song of – trees, flowers, animals, stones, water!

All the pointless trumpery of counterpoint, which does not cheer the listener up at all and thus misses the whole point of music, is regarded by them as a thrillingly mysterious series of combinations that bears comparison with an improbable intertwining of mosses, weeds, and flowers. A talent, or, in the language of these lunatics, a genius for music, is said by them to burn in the breast of those who revere and practise the art, and to consume them with inextinguishable flames, whereas a baser motive would artificially smother or deflect the spark. Those who quite correctly recognise the true purpose of art, as I have already shown, and of music in particular, they call ignorant blasphemers, who must remain eternally excluded from the sanctum of the higher life; in this they manifest their derangement. Who, I may justly enquire, is the better judge? The civil servant, the merchant, the man who makes a living from his money, who eats and drinks well, who drives about in a fitting manner, and is greeted

---

[155] Horace, *Ars Poetica*, 343: 'omne tulit punctum qui miscuit utile dulci': 'He has won every vote who has blended profit and pleasure.' H. Rushton Fairclough (tr.), *Horace: Satires, Epistles and Ars Poetica* (London and Cambridge, Mass., 1961), 478–9.

[156] Temple of Isis: the place at Saïs, in Egypt, symbolising both the focus of the personal quest and the site of revelation. See Introduction, p. 27.

with respect by everyone; or the artist, who must eke out a miserable existence in his world of fantasy? These fools maintain that poetic elevation over baseness is a very special thing, and that renunciation will often bring pleasure; but emperors and kings in the mad-house with straw crowns on their heads are happy too! The best proof that all these fine words contain no real substance, and are intended merely to appease their inner guilt at not having striven for something more solid, is that almost no artist becomes one purely by free will; they have arisen and still arise from the poorer classes. Of unlanded, obscure parentage, or born of other artists, it is necessity, circumstances, and lack of any prospect of fortune in the genuinely wealth-creating classes which makes them what they are. And this will always be the case, in spite of these dreamers. If a landed family of quality were to be so unfortunate as to have a child who possessed a strong inclination towards art, or who, to use the ridiculous expression of these lunatics, carried in his breast the divine spark that if resisted consumes all around it, if he had really begun to dream about art and the artistic life, then a good tutor would very easily bring the erring young fellow back to the right path: by prescribing a prudent intellectual diet including, for example, the complete removal of all fantastical, overtaxing fare (such as poetry, and so-called serious compositions by Mozart, Beethoven, etc.), and by diligently and repeatedly demonstrating the utterly subordinate function of all art, and of the utterly inferior status of artists, who are without rank, title or wealth. In this way he will finally come to feel a thorough contempt for all art and artists, which as a reliable remedy against any further eccentricity can never be carried far enough.

To the poor artists who have not yet fallen victim to the insanity described above, I feel I can give some genuinely helpful advice. In order to extricate themselves at least to some extent from their futile obsession, I would suggest that in their spare time they might learn some simple trade; then they would certainly be of some value as useful members of society. An expert has told me that I have a natural aptitude for making slippers, and I am not averse to setting an example by becoming an apprentice with our local master-slippermaker Schnabler, who also happens to be my godfather.

On reading over what I have written, I find the insanity of many musicians very accurately diagnosed, and to my private horror I feel a certain kinship with them. Satan whispers in my ear that much of what I have intended so sincerely could well appear to them as wickedly ironic. I assert once more, however, that it is to you, you despisers of music, who call the beneficial singing and playing of children a pointless jangle, and who wish to regard the mysterious and sublime art of music as worthy only of them, it is to you that my words are directed. By means of serious argument

I have shown you that music is a wonderful and useful invention of clever Tubalcain,[157] which cheers and distracts people, and that it consequently promotes domestic happiness, the most sublime objective of every cultivated person, in a pleasant and satisfying manner.

4 Beethoven's Instrumental Music

When music is spoken of as an independent art, does not the term properly apply only to instrumental music, which scorns all aid, all admixture of other arts (poetry), and gives pure expression to its own peculiar artistic nature? It is the most romantic of all arts, one might almost say the only one that is genuinely romantic, since its only subject-matter is infinity. Orpheus's lyre opened the gates of Orcus. Music reveals to man an unknown realm, a world quite separate from the outer sensual world surrounding him, a world in which he leaves behind all precise feelings in order to embrace an inexpressible longing.

Were you even aware of this peculiar nature of music, you poor instrumental composers who have laboriously struggled to represent precise sensations, or even events? How could it even occur to you to treat sculpturally the art most utterly opposed to sculpture? Your sunrises, your storms, your *Batailles des Trois Empereurs*, etc.[158] are clearly just ridiculous aberrations, and have been deservedly condemned to total oblivion.

In singing, where the poetry suggests precise moods through words, the magical power of music acts like the philosopher's miraculous elixir, a few drops of which make any drink so much more wonderfully delicious. Any passion – love, hate, anger, despair, etc. – presented to us in an opera is clothed by music in the purple shimmer of romanticism, so that even our mundane sensations take us out of the everyday into the realm of the

---

[157] Tubal-cain was 'the master of all coppersmiths and blacksmiths'; his half-brother Jubal 'the ancestor of those who play the harp and pipe' (Genesis 4, 22). Thus Hoffmann reveals his private opinion of soothing, utilitarian music. Wittkowski points to the comic analogy whereby Kreisler 'bangs away until [he is] deaf' (p. 83) to drown the singing in 'Kapellmeister Johannes Kreisler's Musical Sufferings'.

[158] The original (1810) version named the symphonies of Dittersdorf (1739–99), some of which were designed to tell stories. It is interesting that Hoffmann quite admired Méhul's famous *La Chasse du jeune Henri* overture, which has a narrative design and begins at dawn (see p. 296). The *Batailles des Trois Empereurs* could refer to two symphonies entitled *La Bataille d'Austerlitz surnommé la Journée des trois Empereurs* (both 1806) by J. M. Beauvarlet-Charpentier and L.-E. Jadin. For Hoffmann's review of Beethoven's descriptive orchestral piece, *Wellingtons Sieg oder Die Schlacht bei Vittoria*, Op. 91 ('Battle Symphony') (1813), see p. 420.

infinite. Such is the power of music's spell that it grows ever stronger and can only burst the fetters of any other art.

It is certainly not merely an improvement in the means of expression (perfection of instruments, greater virtuosity of players), but also a deeper awareness of the peculiar nature of music, that has enabled great composers to raise instrumental music to its present level.

Mozart and Haydn, the creators of modern instrumental music, first showed us the art in its full glory; but the one who regarded it with total devotion and penetrated to its innermost nature is Beethoven. The instrumental compositions of all three masters breathe the same romantic spirit for the very reason that they all intimately grasp the essential nature of the art; yet the character of their compositions is markedly different. Haydn's compositions are dominated by a feeling of childlike optimism. His symphonies lead us through endless, green forest-glades, through a motley throng of happy people. Youths and girls sweep past dancing the round; laughing children, lying in wait behind trees and rose-bushes, teasingly throw flowers at each other. A world of love, of bliss, of eternal youth, as though before the Fall; no suffering, no pain; only sweet, melancholy longing for the beloved vision floating far off in the red glow of evening, neither approaching nor receding; and as long as it is there the night will not draw on, for the vision is the evening glow itself illuminating hill and glade.

Mozart leads us deep into the realm of spirits. Dread lies all about us, but withholds its torments and becomes more an intimation of infinity. We hear the gentle spirit-voices of love and melancholy, the night dissolves into a purple shimmer, and with inexpressible yearning we follow the flying figures kindly beckoning to us from the clouds to join their eternal dance of the spheres. (Mozart's Symphony in E flat major, known as the 'Swan Song'.)[159]

In a similar way Beethoven's instrumental music unveils before us the realm of the mighty and the immeasurable. Here shining rays of light shoot through the darkness of night and we become aware of giant shadows swaying back and forth, moving ever closer around us and destroying *us* but not the pain of infinite yearning, in which every desire, leaping up in sounds of exultation, sinks back and disappears. Only in this pain, in which love, hope, and joy are consumed without being destroyed, which threatens to burst our hearts with a full-chorused cry of all the passions, do we live on as ecstatic visionaries.

---

[159] Symphony no. 39 (1788), KV 543. The nickname 'Swan Song' was of unknown provenance, according to Hermann Abert, *W. A. Mozart* (Leipzig, 1923–24), ii, 578, n. 3. For a different interpretation, see the poem by A. Apel in *AMZ*, viii, issues 29 and 30 of 16 and 23 April 1805.

Romantic sensibility is rare, and romantic talent even rarer, which is probably why so few are able to strike the lyre whose sound unlocks the wonderful realm of the romantic.

Haydn romantically apprehends the humanity in human life; he is more congenial, more comprehensible to the majority.

Mozart takes more as his province the superhuman, magical quality residing in the inner self.

Beethoven's music sets in motion the machinery of awe, of fear, of terror, of pain, and awakens that infinite yearning which is the essence of romanticism. He is therefore a purely romantic composer. Might this not explain why his vocal music is less successful, since it does not permit a mood of vague yearning but can only depict from the realm of the infinite those feelings capable of being described in words?[160]

Beethoven's mighty genius intimidates the musical rabble; they try in vain to resist it. But wise judges, gazing about them with a superior air, assure us that we can take their word for it as men of great intellect and profound insight: the good Beethoven is by no means lacking in wealth and vigour of imagination, but he does not know how to control it! There is no question of selection and organisation of ideas; following the so-called inspired method, he dashes everything down just as the feverish workings of his imagination dictate to him at that moment. But what if it is only *your* inadequate understanding which fails to grasp the inner coherence of every Beethoven composition? What if it is entirely *your* fault that the composer's language is clear to the initiated but not to you, and that the entrance to his innermost mysteries remains closed to you? In truth, he is fully the equal of Haydn and Mozart in rational awareness, his controlling self detached from the inner realm of sounds and ruling it in absolute authority. Our aesthetic overseers have often complained of a total lack of inner unity and inner coherence in Shakespeare, when profounder contemplation shows the splendid tree, leaves, blossom, and fruit as springing from the same seed; in the same way only the most penetrating study of Beethoven's instrumental music can reveal its high level of rational awareness, which is inseparable from true genius and nourished by study of the art.

Which instrumental work by Beethoven confirms all this to a higher degree than the immeasurably magnificent and profound Symphony in C minor? How this wonderful composition irresistibly draws the listener in an ever-rising climax into the spirit-realm of the infinite. Nothing could be simpler than the main idea of the opening Allegro, consisting of only two

---

[160] For more detailed comments, see Hoffmann's reviews of Beethoven's Mass in C and incidental music to Goethe's *Egmont* (pp. 325, 341).

bars and initially in unison, so that the listener is not even certain of the key. The mood of anxious, restless yearning created by this subject is heightened even further by the melodious secondary theme. The breast, constricted and affrighted by presentiments of enormity and annihilation, seems to be struggling for air with a series of stabbing chords,[161] when suddenly a friendly figure moves forward and shines brilliantly through the dreadful darkness of night (the attractive theme in G major that was first touched on by the horns in E flat major). How simple – let it be said once more – is the theme on which the composer has based his entire movement, but how wonderfully all the secondary elements and transition passages are related to it by their rhythmic content, so that they serve to reveal more and more facets of the Allegro's character which the main theme by itself only hints at! All the phrases are short, almost all of them consisting merely of two or three bars, and are also constantly exchanged between winds and strings. One would think that such ingredients could result only in something disjointed and impossible to follow, but on the contrary it is precisely this overall pattern, and the constant repetition of phrases and single chords, which intensifies to the highest possible degree the feeling of ineffable yearning. Quite apart from the fact that the contrapuntal treatment betokens profound study of the art, the transition passages and constant allusions to the main theme demonstrate how the whole movement with all its impassioned features was conceived in the imagination and clearly thought through.

Does not the lovely theme of the Andante con moto in A flat major sound like the voice of a propitious spirit that fills our breast with hope and comfort? But even here the awful phantom that seized our hearts in the Allegro threatens at every moment to emerge from the storm-cloud into which it disappeared, so that the comforting figures around us rapidly flee from its lightning-flashes. What am I to say about the minuet?[162] Listen to the distinctive modulations, the closes on the dominant major, which is taken up by the bass as the tonic of the following theme in the minor mode, the theme itself, repeatedly extended by a few bars at a time! Does that restless, ineffable yearning, that presentiment of a magical spirit-world, in which the composer excels, not seize hold of you again? But like a shaft of blinding sunlight the full orchestra bursts forth in joyful jubilation with the splendid theme of the final movement. What wonderful contrapuntal

---

[161] That is, at bar 168, in the development section.

[162] The third movement was simply headed Allegro by Beethoven. Hoffmann's use of this casual term merely heightens, by its absurdity in context, the vast expressive difference between the relaxation of the traditional third movement of a symphony, and the dynamic structural and expressive rôle of this one.

intricacies are woven into the overall texture again here! It may well all sweep past many like an inspired rhapsody, but the heart of every sensitive listener is certain to be deeply stirred by one emotion, that of nameless, haunted yearning, and right to the very last chord, indeed for some moments after it, he will be unable to emerge from the magical spirit-realm where he has been surrounded by pain and pleasure in the form of sounds.

The internal disposition of the movements, their working-out, orchestration, the way in which they succeed each other, all is directed towards a single point. But it is particularly the close relationship of the themes to each other which provides the unity that alone is able to sustain *one* feeling in the listener. This relationship frequently becomes clear to the listener when he hears it in the similarity between two passages, or discovers a bass pattern which is common to two different passages;[163] but often a deeper relationship that is not demonstrable in this way speaks only from the heart to the heart, and it is this kind which exists between the subjects of the two Allegros and the minuet, and which brilliantly proclaims the composer's rational genius.

What a deep impression your magnificent piano compositions have made on my mind, sublimest of composers! How pale and insignificant everything seems that does not come from you, from the intelligence of Mozart, or from the mighty genius of Sebastian Bach. What pleasure I felt on receiving your two splendid trios, Op. 70, for I knew that after they had been briefly rehearsed I would soon be able to savour their glories. And that is exactly what has happened to me this evening; like someone wandering along the labyrinthine pathways of some fantastic park, hedged in by all kinds of rare trees, shrubs, and exotic flowers, and becoming more and more deeply absorbed, I am still unable to extricate myself from the extraordinary twists and turns of your trios. The enchanting siren-voices of your music, sparkling with colour and variety, draw me deeper and deeper into its spell. The gifted lady who in honour of *me*, Kapellmeister Kreisler, played the Trio No. 1 so superbly today, and beside whose piano I am still sitting and writing, has made it very clear to me that only what the *spirit* provides is to be paid regard, and that all the rest cometh of evil.

I have now just repeated from memory some of the striking modulations from both trios on the piano. It is true that the piano remains an instrument more appropriate for harmony than for melody. The most refined expression of which the instrument is capable cannot bring a melody to life with

---

[163] Passages: Hoffmann here uses 'Sätze', which could mean a unit as small as a phrase, or as large as a whole movement. For further analytical/critical information see the Norton Critical Score of the work, ed. Elliot Forbes (London, 1971).

the myriad nuances that the violinist's bow or the wind player's breath is able to call forth. The player struggles in vain with the insuperable difficulty presented to him by the mechanism, which by striking the strings causes them to vibrate and produce the notes. On the other hand there is probably no instrument (with the exception, that is, of the far more limited harp) that is able, like the piano, to embrace the realm of harmony with full-voiced chords and unfold its treasures to the connoisseur in the most wonderful forms and shapes. When the composer's imagination has struck upon a complete sound-painting with rich groupings, brilliant highlights and deep shadows, he is able to bring it into being at the piano so that it emerges from his inner world in shining colours. A full score, that true musical book of charms preserving in its symbols all the miracles and mysteries of the most heterogeneous choir of instruments, comes to life at the piano under the hands of a master; and a piece skilfully performed from a score, including all its voices, may be compared to a good copper engraving taken from a great painting. For improvising, then, for playing from a score, for individual sonatas, chords, etc. the piano is excellently suited. Trios, quartets, quintets, and so on, with the usual stringed instruments added, also belong fully in the realm of piano compositions, because if they are composed in the proper manner, that is to say genuinely in four parts, five parts, and so forth, then they depend entirely on harmonic elaboration and automatically exclude brilliant passages for individual instruments.

I harbour a real aversion to what are called piano concertos. (Those by Mozart and Beethoven are not so much concertos as symphonies with piano obbligato.)[164] They are supposed to exploit the virtuosity of the individual player in solo passages and in melodic expressiveness, but the very best player on the very finest instrument strives in vain to equal what the violinist, for example, can achieve with little effort.

Every solo, after a full tutti of strings and winds, sounds stiff and flat, and although one admires the facility of the fingers and suchlike, the heart is not really touched at all.

Yet how well the composer has seized upon the most essential character of the instrument, and exploited it in the most appropriate way!

---

[164] The *musical* or experiential truth behind this statement can be best judged from performances using instruments and playing styles of the period (for example as recorded by Malcolm Bilson, fortepiano, and John Eliot Gardiner, conductor). But Hoffmann here enters a contemporary debate. Johann Georg Sulzer, *Allgemeine Theorie der schönen Künste*, i, 573, labelled concertos as 'an exercise for the composer and the performer, and . . . an utterly indistinct amusement for the ear, which has no other purpose'. Heinrich Christoph Koch defended them as a dialogue, and 'something similar to the tragedy of the ancients'. See Owen Jander, 'The "Kreutzer" Sonata as Dialogue', *Early Music*, xvi (1988), 35–6.

A simple but fruitful and lyrical theme, susceptible of the most varied contrapuntal treatments, abbreviations, etc., forms the basis of every movement. All the secondary themes and figures are closely related to the main idea, and everything is interwoven and arranged so as to produce the utmost unity between all the instruments. This describes the overall structure, but within this artful edifice there is a restless alternation of the most marvellous images, in which joy and pain, melancholy and ecstasy, appear beside and within each other. Strange shapes begin a merry dance, now converging into a single point of light, now flying apart like glittering sparks, now chasing each other in infinitely varied clusters. And in the midst of this spirit-realm that has been revealed, the enraptured soul perceives an unknown language and understands all the most mysterious presentiments that hold it in thrall.

A composer has truly penetrated the secrets of harmony only if he can use its power to affect the human heart. For him the numerical relationships that remain lifeless formulas for the pedant without genius become magical prescriptions from which he conjures forth an enchanted world.

Despite the geniality that prevails particularly in the first trio, not even excluding its melancholy Largo, Beethoven's spirit remains serious and solemn. The master seems to be implying that the deeper mysteries can never be spoken of in ordinary words, even when the spirit feels itself joyfully uplifted in moments of intimate familiarity with them, but only in expressions of sublime splendour. The dance of the High Priests of Isis can only be a hymn of exultation.

If its effect is to be achieved solely by music in its own right, rather than by serving some specific dramatic purpose, instrumental music must avoid all facetiousness and clowning.[165] The profounder mind seeks intimations of that joy, sublimer than the confines of this world allow, which comes to us from an unknown domain and kindles in the breast an inner bliss, a higher significance than feeble words, confined to the expression of banal earthly pleasures, can communicate. This gravity, which is found in all Beethoven's instrumental and piano music, rules out all the breakneck passages up and down the keyboard with both hands, all the odd leaps, the whimsical flourishes, the towering piles of notes supported by five or six leger lines, with which the most recent piano compositions are replete. In terms of mere dexterity, the piano works of this composer present no great difficulty, since the few runs, triplet figures and the like must be within the powers of any

---

[165] clowning: Hoffmann uses '*Lazzi*', properly signifying 'stage business', especially within the *commedia dell'arte* tradition. So his meaning might include the mimetic aspect of playing showy music, as well as applying metaphorically to its substance. See also Kerman, '*Tändelnde Lazzi*'.

practised player, and yet they are in many ways extremely difficult to perform. Many so-called virtuosos dismiss Beethoven's works, not only complaining 'Very difficult!' but adding 'And very ungrateful!' As far as difficulty is concerned, the proper performance of Beethoven's works demands nothing less than that one understands him, that one penetrates to his inner nature, and that in the knowledge of one's own state of grace one ventures boldly into the circle of magical beings that his irresistible spell summons forth. Whoever does not feel this grace within him, whoever regards music solely as amusement, as a pastime for idle hours, as a passing gratification for jaded ears, or as a vehicle for his own ostentation, let him keep away from it. Only such a one could utter the reproach 'And very ungrateful!' The true artist lives only in the work that he conceives and then performs as the composer intended it. He disdains to let his own personality intervene in any way; all his endeavours are spent in quickening to vivid life, in a thousand shining colours, all the sublime effects and images the composer's magical authority enclosed within his work, so that they encircle us in bright rings of light, inflaming our imaginings, our innermost soul, and bear us speeding on the wing into the far-off spirit-realm of music.

5 Extremely Random Thoughts

Even when I was still at school, I formed the habit of committing to paper whatever thoughts occurred to me as a result of reading a book, listening to music, looking at a painting or any other object, or whatever notable happenings I experienced myself. For this purpose I had a small notebook bound up for me, with the legend 'Random Thoughts' stamped upon it. My cousin, who shared a room with me and followed my aesthetic endeavours with decidedly mischievous irony, found my little book, and prefaced the word 'Random' on the cover with the adverb 'Extremely'! To my not inconsiderable chagrin I found, when I had got over my private annoyance with my cousin and once more read through what I had written, that many of my random thoughts were indeed *extremely* random; whereupon I threw the whole book into the fire and vowed never to write anything down again, but instead to allow everything to be digested and assimilated inwardly, as it should be. On looking through my collection of music, however, I find to my not inconsiderable horror that in much more recent and, one might think, much more prudent years, I have continued this shameful practice more obsessively than ever. Is not almost every blank page, every cover, bescribbled with *extremely* random thoughts? If, when I have departed this life as a result of this or that circumstance, some faithful friend should really consider these writings of mine to be worth anything, or even (as tends to happen sometimes) should have extracts from them copied and printed, then I beg him to have the mercy to consign without mercy the *extremely extremely* random thoughts to the fire; with regard to the remainder may he allow my schoolboyish inscription to stand, together with my cousin's mischievous addition, as a sort of *captatio benevolentiae.*[166]

There is much dispute today about our Sebastian Bach and the early Italians; it has been quite impossible to agree as to which is the superior, and a clever friend of mine observed that Bach's music bears the same relationship to that of the early Italians as the cathedral in Strasbourg to St Peter's in Rome.[167]

How deeply the truth and aptness of this parallel impressed me! I see in Bach's eight-part motets the wonderfully bold, romantic structure of the cathedral rising proudly and gloriously into the air, with all its fantastic ornaments artfully blended into the whole; and in Benevoli's and Perti's[168] religious settings the pure, magnificent proportions of St Peter's, which bring even the most massive forms into balance, and elevate the spirit by filling it with divine wonder.

---

[166] *Captatio benevolentiae*: reaching after goodwill (rhetoric).

[167] Hoffmann here takes up Goethe's eulogy of Gothic style in Strasbourg Cathedral, in the (originally anonymous) *Von deutscher Baukunst* (1772): 'My soul was suffused with a feeling of immense grandeur which, because it consisted of thousands of harmonising details, I was able to savour and enjoy, but by no means understand and explain.' See Johann Wolfgang von Goethe, *Essays on Art and Literature* (*Goethe's Collected Works*, vol. iii), ed. John Geary (New York, 1986), 3–10.

When writing his review of Beethoven's Mass in C not so long afterwards, Hoffmann expanded his idea, and compared the 'strange inner disquiet' caused by the 'audacious convolutions' of Strasbourg Cathedral to the impression 'given by the pure romanticism living and moving in Mozart's and Haydn's fantastical compositions' (see p. 328).

[168] Orazio Benevoli (1605–72), early Baroque composer and director of music at Santa Maria Maggiore, Rome. Giacomo Perti (1661–1756), church music composer, active in Bologna.

Not only in dreams, but also in that state of delirium which precedes sleep, especially when I have been listening to much music, I discover a congruity of colours, sounds, and fragrances.[169] It seems as though they are all produced by beams of light in the same mysterious manner, and have then to be combined into an extraordinary concert. The fragrance of deep-red carnations exercises a strangely magical power over me; unawares I sink into a dream-like state in which I hear, as though from far away, the dark, alternately swelling and subsiding tones of the basset-horn.[170]

There are moments, especially when I have deeply studied the works of the great Sebastian Bach, at which the numerical proportions of music and the mystical rules of counterpoint arouse in me a profound horror. Music! It is with secret trepidation, even with dread, that I utter your name! Sanskrit of nature, translated into sound! The uninitiated parrot its formulas with their childish voices, while the mockers and blasphemers sink down in their own contumely.

Some anecdotes about great composers frequently bandied about are so patently invented, or repeated with such fatuous ignorance, that I get frustrated and annoyed whenever I am forced to listen to them. The story about Mozart's overture to *Don Giovanni*, for example, is so prosaically absurd, that I am at a loss to understand how, as happened today, it can be given currency even by musicians, whom one would like to credit with some

[169] This important synaesthetic fragment is mirrored in the climactic passage in the fable of Chrysostomus (p. 163); together with related texts by others, it anticipates an abiding nineteenth-century concern, as expressed by Baudelaire in his theory of 'correspondences'. Hoffmann's opening phrases coincide with the opening of Gotthilf Heinrich Schubert, *Die Symbolik des Traumes*: 'In dreams and already that state of delirium which usually precedes sleep, the soul seems to speak a language quite other than its usual one' (1814). The phrase 'state of delirium' was taken over by Hoffmann in the 1819 edition of *Kreisleriana*.

[170] basset-horn: a rare member of the clarinet family, originally curved like a sickle, possessing lower notes than the normal clarinet. Was invented seemingly in the 1760s, and composed for by Mozart (Requiem, *Die Zauberflöte*, etc.), among others.

intelligence. Mozart is said to have repeatedly put off composing the overture, long after the opera itself had been finished, and even on the day before the performance, when his worried friends thought he was at last sitting at his desk, to have cheerfully gone off for a walk. Finally, on the very day of the performance, early in the morning, he supposedly *composed* the overture in a few hours, so that the parts were carried to the theatre with the ink still wet. Whereupon everyone was bowled over with amazement and admiration that Mozart was able to compose so quickly; and yet one could accord the same admiration to any competent and rapid copyist. Do you not think that the composer had for a long time been carrying *Don Giovanni* in his head? His profoundest work, composed for *his friends* – for people, that is, who understood his innermost feelings? And that it was all laid out and complete in his mind in all its wonderfully distinctive detail, just as if it had been cast in a perfect mould? And do you not think that this overture of all overtures, in which every aspect of the opera is so brilliantly and vividly suggested, was not just as complete as the whole work before its great composer took up his pen to write it out?[171]

If this anecdote is true, then Mozart was probably teasing his friends, who had always spoken of him *composing* the overture, by putting off writing it out; their concern that he might not find the propitious hour for a task that had now become mechanical, namely writing out a work conceived and inwardly fixed in one beatific instant, must have appeared ridiculous to him. Many have claimed to discern in the Allegro the exhausted Mozart suddenly starting up from an involuntary doze he had fallen into while composing! There certainly are some foolish people! I remember someone once bitterly complaining to me at a performance of *Don Giovanni* that really that business with the statue and the demons was terribly unrealistic! I asked him with a smile whether he had not realised long ago that the stone guest concealed a damned clever police-inspector, and that the demons were merely bailiffs in disguise; and furthermore that hell was merely the gaol in which Don Giovanni was to be imprisoned because of his crimes, so that the whole opera was intended allegorically. Whereupon he repeatedly snapped his fingers with glee, and laughed, and expressed pity for all the others who allowed themselves to be so grossly misled. Afterwards, when the talk turned to the subterranean agents which Mozart summons from Orcus, he gave me a knowing smile, which I returned.

---

[171] Hoffmann makes a telling point, since the idea (particularly outside France) of using musical material from an opera to constitute parts of its overture was only recently accepted. *Don Giovanni*, the overture, begins with the music from the climactic scene of the opera, portraying the appearance of the living statue of the Commendatore at the dwelling of Don Giovanni.

He was thinking: we know what we know! And he was perfectly right!

It has been a long time since I enjoyed so much unalloyed pleasure and amusement as I did this evening. My friend rushed into my room in some excitement and announced that at a tavern in the outskirts he had tracked down a troupe of players who every evening, before the assembled customers, performed the greatest plays and tragedies. We went straight there and found a written notice stuck to the door of the main room which stated, following the estimable acting-company's humble compliments, that the choice of play each evening would depend on the highly respected wishes of the public in attendance, and that the landlord would endeavour to serve his honoured guests in the front seats with the best beer and tobacco. On this occasion, at the director's suggestion, *Johanna von Montfaucon*[172] was chosen, and I became convinced that when presented in such a manner the play has an indescribable effect. One can see clearly how the author was aiming at a poetic irony, or rather was trying to ridicule false emotion, poetry that is not poetic, and in this respect *Johanna* is one of the most amusing farces he has ever written. The actors and actresses had grasped this profounder meaning of the play very well, and had organised the stage admirably. Was it not an excellent idea, for example, that when Johanna burst out in comic despair with the words 'Lightning must follow!'[173] the director had not shrunk from the expense of rosin[174] but actually produced a few flashes of lightning? There was one small accident, when in the first scene the approximately six-foot high castle collapsed without undue noise, although made of paper, to reveal a beer-barrel from the lofty eminence of which, instead of from a balcony or window, Johanna now warmly

---

[172] *Johanna von Montfaucon* (Leipzig, 1800): a popular play, set in the Middle Ages, by August von Kotzebue (1761–1819). Hoffmann seems rarely to have lost the chance to heap sarcasm on Kotzebue's productions: the review of Kotzebue's *Opern-Almanach* (1815) is typical (*Schriften zur Musik*, 258–67). See also *HBW*, i, 329: '*Pereat* Kotzebue! Vivat Schlegel!' However, the present mock-approving review of Kotzebue's dramatic aims and methods stands also as a comic counter-subject to the extended ironic treatise on theatrical technique that follows, 'The Complete Machinist'.

[173] Reference to Act 5 sc. 4, where the knight Lasarra threatens to kill Johanna's small son if she does not return his love: 'Don't be afraid, my son! . . . The Almighty will not allow such wickedness! – The lightning must follow!'

[174] rosin: the powdered resin commonly used for flash or flame effects by means of a 'lycopodium flask'. See I–6, note 202.

addressed her good countrymen. Apart from this, however, the scenery was excellent, particularly the Swiss mountain landscape, which was also treated with delightful irony, in keeping with the spirit of the play. The lesson that the author is trying to teach would-be authors by the way in which he portrays his characters was also clearly underlined by the costumes. 'Behold', he is telling us, 'These are your heroes! Instead of dauntless, dashing knights from the great days of yore, they are wretched, whining weaklings from our own age, who behave abominably and then think that's the end of it!' All the knights, Estavajell, Lasarra, etc., appeared in ordinary coats just with army belts worn over them, and a few feathers in their hats.

A particularly clever arrangement, which deserves to be copied by major stages, was also observed. I would like to record it here so that I never forget it. I could not get over the great precision of entries and exits, and the overall smoothness of the production, since the choice of play had been left to the public, and the company had therefore to be capable of putting on a large number of plays with a minimum of preparation. Finally, noticing a rather comical and, as it seemed, completely involuntary movement by one of the actors in the wings, I discerned with optical assistance that from the actors' and actresses' feet fine threads ran to the prompter's box, and that these were tugged whenever they were to come on or off. A good director, who wants everything on the stage to go exactly according to his own opinion and interpretation, could carry this further; just as the cavalry has its *calls* (on the bugle) to signal its various manoeuvres, which even the horses instantly follow, he could invent different tugs for a wide variety of postures, exclamations, cries, rising and falling vocal inflections, etc., and sitting beside the prompter he could apply them to great advantage.

The greatest error an actor could then commit, punishable by immediate dismissal, which is equivalent to the death penalty, would be if the director could justly complain that *he had stumbled over a line*; and the greatest praise of a complete performance would be that *it had all gone without a hitch*.

Great poets and artists are sensitive to criticism even from inferior beings, and are more than pleased to receive praise, to be pampered and treated with kid gloves. Did you think that the vanity by which you are so often consumed could reside in nobler minds? But any kindly word, any gesture of goodwill, appeases the inner voice incessantly admonishing true artists:

'How lowly your flight remains, burdened down by the dead weight of earthly things – spread out your wings afresh and soar upwards to the shining stars!' And urged on by this voice, the artist often loses his way and can no longer find his homeland, until his friends' encouraging calls lead him back to the straight and narrow path.

When I read in Forkel's musical *Bibliothek* his mean and contemptuous remarks about Gluck's *Iphigénie en Aulide*, my spirit was profoundly moved by the strangest sensations.[175] What disagreeable feelings must have taken possession of the great composer when he read this absurd twaddle, like someone strolling amid the flowers and blossom of a beautiful park who is set upon by barking and yapping dogs; although unable to do him any serious harm they are still irksome beyond endurance. But just as we are pleased to hear, now that the battle is won, of the trials and tribulations he had to face, since they enhance his glory even further, so it lifts up soul and spirit still to gaze upon the monsters over which his genius raised its victory-banner so that they were consumed by their own calumny! Be comforted, those of you awaiting recognition, those of you bowed down by the frivolity and injustice of our age! *You* are assured of *certain* victory, and *it* will be eternal, whereas your exhausting *struggle* was only short-lived![176]

---

[175] For Hoffmann's own review of *Iphigénie en Aulide* (1774), see p. 255. Forkel, *Musikalisch-Kritische Bibliothek*, i, contains an extended review of a book by Friedrich Riedel entitled *Ueber die Musik des Ritters Christoph von Gluck* (Vienna, 1775). Probably by Forkel himself, the review (pp. 53–173) amounts to an attempted blow-by-blow demolition of Gluck's musical achievements and artistic credenda. (Forkel was an important scholar and biographer of J. S. Bach.) Hoffmann returned to his attack in 'Casual Reflections' and 'Further Observations on Spontini's opera *Olimpia*' (pp. 429 and 437).

[176] The curious italics here suggest that Hoffmann was incorporating a lightly disguised nationalistic, anti-French victory message. (For other examples of his nationalist publications, cf. 'Die Vision auf dem Schlachtfelde bei Dresden' (*Nachlese*, 601) and the pseudonymously issued piano piece *Deutschlands Triumph im Siege bey Leipzig* (Leipzig, 1814).) In the same disguised manner the painting by Caspar David Friedrich entitled *Der Chasseur im Walde* (1813–14), ostensibly a snowy landscape, was seen as a nationalistic allegory: William Vaughan, Helmut Börsch-Supan, Hans-Joachim Neihardt, *Caspar David Friedrich 1774–1840. Romantic Landscape Painting in Dresden* (London, 1972), 67.

There is a story that after the dispute between the Gluckists and the Piccinnists had cooled down somewhat, some aristocratic devotee of art succeeded in bringing Gluck and Piccinni together one evening at a party.[177] The honest German, in benign mood after the wine and pleased to see the bitter dispute finally at an end, is said to have revealed to the Italian his entire method of composition, his secret of stirring and uplifting men's hearts, particularly those of glutted Frenchmen. It lay, he said, in combining melodies in the older French style with German workmanship.[178] And yet Piccinni, thoughtful, good-natured, and great in his own way, whose chorus of Priests of the Night in *Didon*[179] still rings in my head with its horrifying sounds, has written no *Armide*, no *Iphigénie*, as Gluck has! Can one become a Raphael merely by knowing precisely how Raphael planned and executed his paintings?[180]

It was impossible today to sustain any conversation about art – not even that divine small-talk without pretext or point, which I so gladly indulge in with the ladies since it always seems to me like a chance counterpoint to a secret but universally perceived melody. Everything gave way to politics. Someone said that Minister –r– had refused to listen to the representations of the Court at –s–. Now I know that this minister is in fact deaf in one

[177] C. W. von Gluck's Parisian operas were first produced from 1774 to 1779 inclusive. They triggered such a change of taste at the Opéra that there followed an urgent need to find alternatives to the prevailing Baroque repertory. Niccolò Piccinni (1728–1800) was therefore invited to Paris; his first new work was *Roland* (1778) and his most successful one, *Didon* (1783). The circumstances of Piccinni's commissioning, his artistic progress, and the stylistic differences between his works and Gluck's, all gave rise to a literary 'war'.

[178] Although Gluck's explanation sounds implausible, it is true that he re-used his *own* earlier material in the Paris operas.

[179] N. Piccinni, *Didon* (Paris, n.d), Act 3 sc. 10, 290: general ensemble in E flat, with the Priests of Pluto, 'Appaisez-vous, mânes terribles'. Aeneas has departed, and as his spoils and arms are brought in, Dido mounts her funeral pyre.

[180] This refers to Wackenroder's story of the young painter Antonio who, finding that his copies of Raphael's work were unsuccessful and 'worlds apart from' the latter's unforced naturalness, naively wrote to Raphael to discover his secret. Raphael advised him to copy someone else's work, as he could not explain his own techniques. See Schubert, *Wackenroder's 'Confessions'*, 90–4, from *'Confessions from the Heart of an Art-Loving Friar'*. It should be said that Piccinni certainly did *not* copy Gluck's style, and that in 'Further Observations on Spontini's Opera *Olimpia*' (p. 439) Hoffmann gave high praise to Piccinni's Paris works.

ear,[181] and at that instant a grotesque image came into my mind that remained with me for the whole evening. I saw the minister standing stiffly in the middle of the room, with the negotiator from — unfortunately standing on his deaf side and the other one on his hearing side! Both of them employ every means, every ruse and artifice imaginable, the one to make His Excellency turn round and the other to make His Excellency remain as he is, since thereby hangs the entire success of the exercise. But His Excellency remains rooted to the spot like a German oak, and fortune favours the one who finds himself on his *hearing* side.[182]

What artist has ever troubled himself with the political events of the day anyway? He lived only for his art, and advanced through life serving it alone. But a dark and unhappy age has seized men with its iron fist, and the pain squeezes from them sounds that were formerly alien to them.

One hears a great deal about the inspiration that artists derive from the consumption of strong drink. One hears the names of musicians and poets who can work *only* by this means (painters, so far as I am aware, have not been subject to this criticism). I do not believe that; but it is true that in the happy state of mind, I might say under the auspicious constellation, when the spirit moves from *brooding* to *creating*, spirituous liquor does promote a livelier circulation of ideas. It is not a very sophisticated image, but here the imagination seems to me like a mill-wheel that is driven faster by a more

[181] As often in Hoffmann, there may well be underlying references here. The minister's deafness points towards the identity of Karl August von Hardenberg (1750–1822) who was named Prussian First Cabinet Minister on 10 April 1807 and Chancellor of State on 4 June 1810. Hoffmann's lifelong friend Theodor Gottlieb von Hippel (1775–1843) worked for Hardenberg. The friends met unexpectedly in April 1813.

[182] Hardenberg was in charge of the Prussian negotiators at the Congress of Vienna in 1814–15, where there doubtless circulated stories very like that of Hoffmann, simply because he was 'usually able through his deafness to avoid hearing what he disliked . . .': C. W. Crawley (ed.), *The New Cambridge Modern History* (Cambridge, 1965), ix, 654.

strongly flowing stream; one pours wine on it and the machinery inside turns more rapidly! How extraordinary it is that a noble fruit carries within it the power to control the innermost workings of the human spirit in such a mysterious way. But what swirls in the glass before me at this moment is that drink which, like a mysterious stranger who changes his name everywhere so that he is not recognised, has no universal appellation; it is produced by a process of igniting cognac, arrack, or rum, and allowing sugar placed above it on a grill to drip into the liquid.[183] The preparation and moderate consumption of this drink has a beneficial and pleasurable effect on me. When the blue flame darts upward, I see how the salamanders emerge glowing and spitting and attack the earth-spirits present in the sugar. These bravely resist; their yellow light crepitates amidst the enemy, but the odds are overwhelming, and crackling and hissing they sink down. The water-spirits escape, eddying upward in the vapour, while the earth-spirits drag the exhausted salamanders away and devour them in their own domain. But they too are consumed, and impudent new-born spirits stream forth in the ruddy glow; these offspring born of the internecine struggle between salamander and earth-spirit have the salamander's fieriness and the earth-spirit's sustaining strength.

If it really is of benefit to pour spirituous libations on the inner wheel of imagination (as I believe it is, since in addition to a freer flow of ideas it gives the artist a sense of well-being, even joy, which makes his work easier), then one could logically postulate certain principles with regard to the various potions. For church music, for example, I would advise an old wine from the Rhine or from France; for serious opera a fine burgundy; for comic opera champagne; for canzonettas a fiery Italian wine; but for a highly romantic composition, such as *Don Giovanni*, I would suggest a modest glass of that product of salamander and earth-spirit I have just described! But I will let everyone make up his own mind. For myself I would merely issue a gentle warning that the spirit born of light and subterranean fire exerts so arrogant an influence on men that it can present dangers; one must not trust its beneficence, since it changes mood rapidly, and instead of a soothing, agreeable friend, it becomes a terrifying tyrant.[184]

---

[183] This preparation is still a ceremonial drink in Germany (*Feuerzangenbowle*).

[184] Hoffmann ironically recalled in a letter of 24 March 1814 the pressures that had caused him to drink while in Bamberg: 'Very often I felt quite weak and miserable from sheer love and had to wash it down with wine or arrack': *HBW*, i, 454; Sahlin, 225.

Today someone told the well-known anecdote about the aged Rameau.[185]
To the priest exhorting him to penitence with all manner of harsh and
unkind words as he lay on his deathbed, and who would not cease his
preaching and screeching, Rameau solemnly replied: 'But why does Your
Reverence have to sing so out of tune!'[186] I could not join in the loud
laughter of my companions, since for me the story contained something
extremely moving. Now that the old composer had shuffled off almost all
earthly things, his spirit had become so thoroughly attuned to the music of
heaven that any external impression upon his senses could only be a
dissonance; interrupting the pure harmonies that filled his soul, it caused
him pain and retarded his ascent to the world of light.

In no art is theory more feeble and inadequate than in music. The rules of
counterpoint naturally relate only to the harmonic structure, and any piece
correctly worked out in accordance with them is only a painter's sketch
correctly laid out according to the fixed rules of proportion. But when it
comes to colour, the musician is left entirely to his own devices; for *that* is
orchestration. Because of the infinite variety of musical solutions it is
impossible to venture even a single rule about this. With the help of a lively
imagination refined by experience, however, one can at least give some
indications, and to these, systematically summarised, I would give the term
'mystique of instruments'. The art of employing the full orchestra here, and
individual instruments there, with each in its appropriate place, is *musical
perspective*. Similarly music can reclaim the term *tone*, borrowed from it by
painting, and distinguish it from *key*. In another, higher sense, then, the
tone of a work would refer to its deeper character, expressed by the particular

---

[185] Jean-Philippe Rameau (1683–1764), the leading French high Baroque composer and
theorist.

[186] Though later embroidered, the original anecdote was recorded on the day of Rameau's
death: 'Il est mort avec fermeté. Différents prêtres n'ayant pu en rien tirer, M. le curé de
Saint-Eustache s'y est présenté, a péroré longtemps, au point que le malade ennuyé s'est
écrié avec fureur: "Quel diable venez-vous me chanter là, monsieur le curé? Vous avez la
voix fausse!"' L. Petit de Bachaumont, *Mémoires secrets* (London, 1777–89), entry for 12
September 1764. Hoffmann's reaction to the story perhaps contains an unconscious echo
of *Romeo and Juliet*, Act 3 sc. 5, where Juliet blames the lark for separating her from her
lover: 'It is the lark that sings so out of tune / Straining harsh discords and unpleasing
sharps.'

treatment of the voices and their accompaniment of associated figures and melismas.[187]

It is just as difficult to write a good last act as a competent closing passage. Both are usually overladen with figures, and the criticism that 'he cannot come to a conclusion' is all too often well founded.[188] For poet and musician it is no idle suggestion that both, the last act and the finale, should be written *first*. The overture, like the prologue, must undoubtedly be written last.[189]

6   The Complete Machinist

During the time when I conducted the opera in ***, my interest and inclination often led me onto the stage.[190] I took a great interest in the scenery and stage effects, and as a result of a long period of calm reflection on everything I saw, I arrived at some conclusions which, for the benefit of designers and machinists,[191] as well as the general public, I would like to publish as a short tract entitled *Johannes Kreisler's Complete Machinist*. In the nature of things, however, time blunts the keenest of intentions, and who knows whether I will find the leisure which such an important work of theory requires, or even whether a suitable state of mind will come in which I might actually write it. In order, therefore, to rescue from oblivion at least the main principles of this splendid theory I have invented, and its most

---

[187] Hoffmann develops these ideas later, in 'On a Remark of Sacchini's, and on so-called Effect in Music', II–6. It is to be regretted that he never published anything more extended on musical 'colour', since he was one of the first thinkers to address this problem after the evolution of the modern orchestra.

[188] These ideas, and the comparison between music and the spoken theatre, derive from Hoffmann's review of Spohr's First Symphony: see p. 284.

[189] Opera overtures were normally composed last of all. Hoffmann composed his own *Undine* beginning with the music of the first act (*HTB*, 537), completed on 3 September 1813; its second act was completed on 30 June 1814. His opera *Aurora* was also composed in the order Act 1, Act 2, Act 3, beginning in January 1811 (*HTB*, 534–6).

[190] It was normal practice for many theatres to present both opera and spoken drama, in alternation. So the scenery and effects referred to subsequently are not necessarily operatic. For Hoffmann's activities as designer and machinist, see the Prefatory Remarks.

[191] designers and machinists: see Prefatory Remarks.

brilliant ideas, I will merely provide, so far as I am able, a rhapsodic summary, and then declare: *sapienti sat!*[192]

Firstly I owe it to my stay in *** that I was completely cured of a number of dangerous misconceptions under which I had previously laboured. I also completely lost my childish reverence for persons whom I had always regarded as great geniuses. In addition to an enforced but highly beneficial intellectual diet, my health was restored by following advice to partake regularly of the extremely pure water that gushes – or rather I should say gently trickles – from many sources in ***, particularly in the theatre.

So it is with inner shame that I still remember the reverence, even childish awe, in which I held both the designer and the machinist at the *** theatre. They proceeded from the foolish premise that scenery and stage effects should unobtrusively blend with the drama, so that the total effect would transport the spectator, as though on invisible wings, right away from the theatre to the fantastical land of poetry. They believed it was not enough to use scenery devised with profound skill and refined taste to create the greatest illusion, or contrivances that produced magical effects inexplicable to the audience. They thought it was also essential to avoid anything, even the smallest detail, that detracted from the intended total effect. Not one piece of scenery should oppose the author's meaning; a tree peeping out at the wrong time, or even a single piece of string hanging down, often destroyed all verisimilitude. It is very difficult, they said further, by means of grandiose proportions, or noble simplicity, or artificially scaling everything down, to reconcile the apparent dimensions of the scenery with reality (e.g. with the characters on the stage),[193] and also to find the knack, by total concealment of the mechanism of the effects, of maintaining the spectator in his agreeable make-believe. As a result even dramatists, normally more than willing to enter the realm of fantasy, had cried, 'Do you think your canvas mountains and palaces and your collapsible painted panels can deceive us

---

[192] *sapienti sat*: that is enough for anyone with sense.

[193] This consideration goes back to A. W. Schlegel's *Vorlesungen über dramatische Kunst und Literatur*, which Hoffmann studied approvingly on 12 January 1811 (*HTB*, 113). Schlegel and other innovators 'regarded mere décor as nonsense: the scenery should co-operate with all the other factors, by being architecturally the space within which the action occurs'. See Raraty, 'Hoffmann and the Theatre', 143–4. Schlegel wrote: 'Our system of stage design was, properly speaking, invented for opera . . . among its unavoidable defects I count the refraction of lines on the wings from all points of view except one, and the disproportion of the actor's size, when he appears upstage, beside objects reduced by perspective.' Merely adjusting the scenery to create good perspective was incompatible with the physical dimensions of an upstage actor: thus Hoffmann's ironic remarks later about fitting scenery to the sizes of the actors. Raraty believes that Hoffmann may have used puppets to overcome this problem.

even for a moment? Is your importance anything like as great as ours?' And blame had always been laid on the limitations and ineptitude of their painting and building colleagues who, instead of conceiving their task in a higher poetic sense, had reduced the theatre, however large it might have been (which incidentally does not make as much difference as people think),[194] to the level of a wretched peep-show. As a matter of fact the sinister forests, the long colonnades, and the Gothic cathedrals created by the aforesaid designer were extraordinarily effective and conveyed no suggestion of paint and canvas; while the machinist's subterranean thunder and collapsing buildings filled the mind with fear and trembling, and his aerial devices floated smoothly and sweetly across the stage.

In the name of heaven, how could these good people, in spite of all their expertise, have been so utterly misguided? If they should read this, perhaps they will desist from their clearly unhealthy fantasising, and will see some reason, as I have. I would now prefer to address myself directly to them, and to discuss that genre of theatrical productions in which their arts are most in demand: I refer to opera! Actually I intend to deal only with the machinist, but the designer will also be able to derive some benefit from my remarks. And so:

Gentlemen!

In case you may not have already realised it, I would like to point out to you that poets[195] and musicians find themselves in a highly dangerous alliance against the public. They have set themselves no less a task than to wrench the spectator out of the real world, where he feels quite at home, and then, when they have separated him from all the things he knows and loves, to torment him with all the sensations and passions that are most injurious to his health. He is made to laugh, to cry, to be startled, frightened, terrified, just as they wish; in short, as the saying goes, he dances to their tune. All too often their evil intention succeeds, and we regularly see the most pathetic consequences of their pernicious influence. Have not many theatre-goers actually believed the far-fetched nonsense they were witnessing? Have they not failed to notice that the characters do not speak, like other decent people, but sing? And have not many young ladies been incapable, for the whole night, or even for several days following, of ridding their heads of all the images conjured forth by the poet and musician, and therefore of

---

[194] Hoffmann's personal belief in the necessity for total illusion in the theatre is disguised above through his ironic tone, but the incidental aside here is to be taken literally: he was proud of the effects he obtained on the small Bamberg stage. See 'Über die Aufführung der Schauspiele des Calderón', in *Nachlese*, 600, and *HBW*, i, 341–2 (letter of [18] July 1812).

[195] poets: that is, in the context of opera, librettists. See p. 189.

working a single piece of knitting or embroidery properly? But who can prevent this scandal? Who can ensure that the theatre will provide intelligent recreation, that everything will remain calm and quiet, and that no passion detrimental to mental and physical well-being will be aroused? Who is to do that? No one but yourselves, gentlemen! To you falls the noble duty of combining forces against poets and musicians for the benefit of civilised humanity. Fight bravely, for victory is assured, and you have abundant resources at hand! The first principle, from which all your efforts must proceed, is to declare war on the poet and musician – to destroy their evil intention of surrounding the spectator with illusions and wrenching him from the world of reality. It follows from this that when such persons use every conceivable means to make the spectator forget that he is in a theatre, then you must go to equal lengths, by appropriate deployment of scenery and stage effects, to remind him of that fact.

Do you still not understand me? Need I say more? I am well aware, of course, that you are so engrossed in your own fantasies, that even though you recognise the validity of my argument you might not have at hand the simplest means of achieving the intended aim. To some extent, therefore, I must help to put you on the right track, as they say. You would not believe, for example, what an irresistible effect it often has to insert the wrong piece of scenery. When part of a living-room or salon appears in a gloomy vault, and the *prima donna* sings a most moving lament about captivity and imprisonment, the spectator laughs up his sleeve; he knows that the machinist only needs to ring his bell[196] and the dungeon will be gone, for behind it all the time lies a friendly room. Even better, however, are wrong borders[197] and half-exposed intermediate curtains, since they divest the whole setting of any so-called truth, which in this case is merely a disgraceful deception.

There are cases, however, where the poet and musician are able to hypnotise the audience with their devilish arts to such an extent that they pay regard to nothing else; they are completely carried away, as though in another world, and abandon themselves to the seductive attractions of their fantasies. This takes place notably in large-scale scenes, and especially in those involving choruses. Under such desperate circumstances there is a

---

[196] bell: machinists co-ordinating effects used forms of audible signal which (at least by c. 1840) became obsolete. See R. Blum *et al.*, *Allgemeines Theater-Lexikon*, article 'Maschinist'.

[197] border: 'A strip of curtain stretched horizontally across the front top of the stage behind the proscenium arch, fastened to a batten, and flied, used to form the top of a setting and mask the flies and lights'. Walter P. Bowman and Robert H. Ball, *Theatre Language* (New York, 1961). Also known as a 'top drop'.

method that will always achieve the intended aim. Completely without warning, in the midst of a lugubrious chorus, for example, grouping itself around the principal characters at the moment of greatest emotion, you suddenly lower an intermediate curtain, causing consternation among the actors and sending them in all directions, so that those at the back of the stage are totally cut off from those on the proscenium. I recall seeing a ballet in which this method was employed effectively, if not quite correctly. The prima ballerina performed an exquisite solo, while the corps de ballet stood in a group on one side. Just as she was holding a striking pose at the back of the stage, and the audience could not sufficiently express its joy and jubilation, the machinist suddenly lowered an intermediate curtain which at once removed her from the public gaze. Unfortunately, however, it showed a room with a large, centrally placed doorway; before we realised what had happened, the determined ballerina came tripping gracefully through the doorway and continued her solo, whereupon the curtain flew up again, much to the relief of the corps de ballet. Remember, therefore, that the intermediate curtain must have no door, or must at least contrast violently with the existing scenery. A street-scene in the middle of a rocky desert, or a dark forest inside a temple, would serve very well.

It is also extremely useful, particularly in monologues or virtuoso arias, if a border threatens to fall down, or one of the wings threatens to collapse onto the stage, or actually does so. Not only is the audience's attention completely distracted from the dramatic situation, but the *prima donna*, or the *primo huomo*, who perhaps was on the stage and thus in danger of being seriously injured, obtains a much greater and livelier response from the public; and however out of tune either of them might sing afterwards, everyone says 'The poor woman, the poor fellow, it is from having had such a fright', and applauds all the more loudly! One can achieve the same aim, that of diverting attention from the characters of the drama to the personality of the actors, by causing entire structures to collapse on the stage. I remember that once, in the opera *Camilla*,[198] a specially built walkway and steps leading to the subterranean vault collapsed at the very moment when all the people rushing to Camilla's rescue were standing on it. There were shouts, screams, commiserations from the public; and when it was finally announced from the stage that no one had sustained serious injury and that the opera would continue, with what rapt attention its conclusion was heard! As is right and proper, however, the concern was no longer for the

---

[198] *Camilla ossia il Sotterraneo* (*Camilla, or The Dungeon*): *dramma serio-giocoso* (1799), text by G. Carpani, music by Ferdinando Paer (1771–1839). The climax of this popular opera depicts Camilla's rescue. Various performances in Bamberg are known from Hoffmann's time there, between 1809 and 1814, though not under his musical direction.

characters of the story, but for the actors who had undergone such a terrifying experience.

On the other hand it is wrong to put actors in danger behind the scenes, since all the effect is lost if it does not happen before the eyes of the public. Houses whose windows are leaned out of and balconies from which conversations are held must therefore be built as low as possible, so that it is not necessary to climb up high ladders or high scaffolds. Usually the actor who has spoken from the window above comes out through the door below, and in order to demonstrate to you my willingness to reveal all my accumulated wisdom for your benefit, I list here the dimensions that such a practicable house, with its window and door, should conform to, taken from the theatres in ***. Height of the door 5 feet, distance between it and the window ½ foot, height of the window 3 feet, distance to the roof ¼ foot, roof ½ foot, which makes 9½ feet altogether.[199] We had a rather tall actor who, when he played Bartolo in *Il Barbiere di Siviglia*,[200] only needed to stand on a foot-stool in order to peer out of the window. Once, the door below accidentally came open, revealing his long red legs, and one's only concern was how he would manage to get through the door. Would it not be an advantage to construct houses, towers, and castles according to the sizes of the actors?

It is very wrong to frighten the audience with sudden claps of thunder, gunshots, or any other unexpected loud noise. I still remember very well your confounded thunder, my dear machinist, with its hollow and terrifying rumble as if from deep within the mountains. But why is that necessary? Did you not know that a calf-skin, stretched across a frame and beaten with both fists, produces a much more tasteful thunder?[201] And instead of using the so-called cannon-machine or firing a real gun, one slams the wardrobe-door hard, and then no one will be unduly startled. But in order to protect the spectator from even the slightest shock, which must be one of the machinist's highest and holiest duties, the following method is absolutely infallible. Usually, when a shot rings out or thunder is heard, various characters cry 'What was that?' – 'What a deafening sound!' – 'What a dreadful noise!' Now the machinist must always wait for these words to be spoken first, and only then produce the shot or thunder. Apart from the fact

---

[199] 9½: this droll total appears in both the 1814 and 1819 editions.

[200] *Il Barbiere di Siviglia* (*The Barber of Seville*), *opera buffa* (1782), text by G. Petrosellini, music by Giovanni Paisiello (1740–1816), and the standard musical setting before Rossini's (1816).

[201] thunder: this method was actually used in some theatres. More effective methods involved (i) rolling heavy wheeled carts above the stage space, and (ii) metal sheeting. See R. Blum *et al.*, *Allgemeines Theater-Lexikon*, article 'Donner'.

that the public is given due warning by these words, it also has the advantage that the stage-hands can enjoy watching the opera and do not need any special cue for their operation; the actor's or singer's exclamation serves as a cue for them, and they can then slam the wardrobe-door or belabour the calf-skin with their fists at exactly the right time. The thunder then gives the stage-hand, standing like Jupiter Fulgurans with his tin trumpet[202] at the ready, his cue for the lightning. Since something might easily catch light in the flies, he must stand in the wings below, so far forward that the public can easily see the flame, and if possible the trumpet too, so as not to remain in unnecessary ignorance as to how in heaven's name the business with the lightning is done. What I have said above about shots also applies to trumpet-calls, interpolated music, etc.

I have already spoken, my dear machinist, of your smoothly floating aerial devices! But is it quite right to devote so much thought and so much art to giving illusion the appearance of reality, so that the spectator involuntarily believes in your heavenly apparition descending in a nimbus of shining clouds? Even machinists whom one expects to proceed on more sensible principles can fall into error here. They correctly allow wires to be seen, but such thin ones that the public flies into a thousand fears that the god, spirit, etc. will crash to the ground and break all his bones. The chariot or cloud must therefore hang from four really thick, black-painted wires, and be raised or lowered at a very slow but fitful speed. The spectator, who will clearly observe these safety precautions, and be able to verify their strength even from the furthermost seat, will then be completely reassured about the heavenly conveyance.

You used to be quite proud of your billowing ocean waves and your lakes with their optical reflections, and you doubtless regarded it as a triumph of your art when you were able to give characters strolling across a bridge on a lake mirror-images of themselves likewise crossing it.[203] I admit that this earned you considerable admiration, but nevertheless, as I have already pointed out, your purpose was completely mistaken! An ocean, a lake, a river, in fact any body of water, is best depicted in the following manner. You take two planks, as long as the stage is wide, cut jags in their upper edges, paint them with little blue and white waves, and suspend them from

---

[202] Jupiter Fulgurans with his tin trumpet: '*fulgurans*' = a mode of title sometimes accorded to the god, meaning 'sending out lightning', or 'characterised by lightning'. The 'tin trumpet' refers to a standard item of stage equipment: a metal box with perforated lid, containing inflammable powder, topped by a long blowpipe device. The machinist thereby blew the powder into a spirit-flame, causing a flash.

[203] mirror-images: probably refers to an effect created by Hoffmann in his staging of Calderón's *Die Brücke von Mantible* in 1811. See the Prefatory Remarks.

cords one behind the other so that their lower edges still rest on the floor. These planks are then moved back and forth, and the scraping noise they make as they slide over the floor represents the lapping of the waves.

Now what am I to say, my dear designer, of your sinister moonlit scenery? A skilled machinist can transform any prospect into a moonlit scene. A round hole is cut in a rectangular board, a piece of paper is stuck over it, and a light is placed in a red-painted box behind it. This contrivance is lowered by means of two strong, black-painted wires, and there you have it – moonlight!

If the public became too agitated, would it not also be quite in conformity with the stated aim for the machinist to cause one or other of the major culprits to sink helplessly through the stage, and so cut short any sound from him that could incite the spectator to further excesses of emotion? On the subject of trap-doors, however, I would point out that an actor should be placed in danger only in the most extreme circumstances, namely when it is a matter of protecting the public. Otherwise one must take every possible precaution to ensure his safety, and release the trap-door only when he is suitably positioned and balanced. Since no one but the actor himself can know this, however, it is wrong to allow the prompter to give the cue with his under-stage bell; rather should the actor, when he is about to be swallowed up by subterranean forces,[204] or to disappear as a ghost, himself give the cue by stamping hard on the floor three or four times, whereupon he should sink slowly and safely into the arms of a stage-hand waiting below. I hope that you have now clearly understood my drift. Since every performance offers a thousand opportunities to win the battle against the poet and composer, I trust you will act entirely in accordance with the correct principles, and with the examples I have provided.

Let me in passing advise you, my dear designer, to regard the wings not as a necessary evil, but as a major asset, and so far as possible to regard each piece as an independent entity and to paint it in great detail. In a street-scene, for example, each wing should represent a projecting building with three or four stories. The little windows and doors of the buildings on the proscenium will be so small that obviously none of the characters on the stage, who reach up almost to the second storey, could possibly live there. Only a race of Lilliputians could pass through such doors or peer out of such windows; but by destroying all illusion in this way the great objective that the designer must always keep in mind will be most easily and happily achieved.

If against all expectation, gentlemen, the principle upon which I have

---

[204] i.e. as at the end of *Don Giovanni*.

erected my entire theory of scenery and stage effects is not acceptable to you, then I must draw it to your attention that an extremely worthy man has expressed the same opinion *in nuce* long before me. I refer to none other than the good weaver Bottom; he also tries to ensure, in the highly tragic tragedy *Pyramus and Thisbe*, that the public is protected from fear, anxiety, etc., in short from any sort of over-excitement.[205] The only difference is that he transfers all the tasks for which you should be mainly responsible onto the shoulders of the Prologue, who has to announce at the outset that the swords would not really hurt anyone, that Pyramus would not really be killed, and that Pyramus was not actually Pyramus but Bottom the weaver. Take to heart wise Bottom's golden words when he speaks of Snug the joiner, who is to represent a fearsome lion:

> Nay, you must name his name, and half his face must be seen through the lion's neck; and he himself must speak through, saying thus, or to the same defect, 'Ladies,' or 'Fair Ladies,' 'I would wish you,' or, 'I would request you,' or, 'I would entreat you, not to fear, not to tremble: my life for yours. If you think I come hither as a lion, it were pity of my life: no, I am no such thing: I am a man as other men are;' and there indeed let him name his name, and tell them plainly he is Snug the joiner.

I assume you have some sense of allegory, and will therefore easily find a means of following the precepts expounded by Bottom the weaver in your own art. The authority I have adduced in my support will ensure that I am not misunderstood, and so I hope I have sown a healthy seed from which a tree of knowledge perhaps will sprout.

[205] Shakespeare, *A Midsummer-Night's Dream*, Act 3 sc. 1: Bottom: 'There are things in this comedy of Pyramus and Thisbe that will never please. First, Pyramus must draw a sword to kill himself, which the ladies cannot abide. How answer you that?'

KREISLERIANA: PART II

In the autumn of last year, the editor of these pages[206] was most delighted to meet in Berlin the aristocratic author of *Sigurd*, *Der Zauberring*, *Undine*, *Corona*, and other works.[207] Much was said about the remarkable Johannes Kreisler, and it transpired that in some strange way Kreisler must have come into contact with a closely kindred spirit who had been born into the world merely in a different guise. Baron Wallborn was a young poet who succumbed to insanity and a merciful death as a result of unrequited love, and whose story de la Motte Fouqué has told in a novella entitled *Ixion*.[208] Among his papers a letter was found which Wallborn had written to Kreisler but not sent.

Kreisler too, before his own disappearance, left a letter behind. The circumstances were as follows. Poor Johannes had been generally regarded as insane for some time, and to be sure, his doings and dealings, particularly his artistic activities, contrasted so sharply with all that is held to be reasonable and proper, that his mental disintegration could hardly be doubted. His thought-processes became increasingly eccentric and disjointed. Shortly before his flight from the town, for example, he spoke frequently about the ill-fated love of a nightingale for a purple carnation, although the whole affair (according to him) was nothing but an adagio, and this in turn was actually a single long-held note sung by Juliet, which

---

[206] the editor: that is, the imaginary editor of *Fantasiestücke in Callot's Manier*, subtitled 'Pages from the Diary of a Travelling Enthusiast'.

[207] Fouqué's main literary achievements to date: *Sigurd, der Schlangentöter* (*Sigurd, the Dragon-slayer*) (1808), first part of a trilogy on the Nibelung sagas entitled *Der Held des Nordens* (*The Hero of the North*) (1810); *Der Zauberring* (*The Magic Ring*), a novel (1813); *Corona* (1814), an epic poem. On *Undine*, see Prefatory Remarks.

[208] *Ixion*: published in *Urania. Taschenbuch für Damen auf das Jahr 1813* [recte 1812] (Amsterdam and Leipzig), 63–77.

transported Romeo, filled with love and happiness, to the highest heaven.[209] He finally disclosed to me that he was resolved upon death, and intended to stab himself in the nearest forest with an augmented fifth.[210] In a disturbing way, his greatest suffering was frequently expressed in ludicrous terms. On the very night when he departed for ever, he brought his intimate friend Hoffmann a carefully sealed letter, with the urgent request to send it to the authorities immediately. This was hardly possible, however, since the letter bore the startling address:

> *To my friend and companion in love,*
> *pain, and death!*

Cito   To be delivered in the world, hard by
———————   the tall thorn hedge, at the limit of
par bonté[211]   reason.

The unopened letter was retained in safe keeping, and it was left for chance to identify his friend and companion more closely. And so it did. The letter from Wallborn, kindly passed on by de la Motte Fouqué, placed it beyond all doubt that the friend Kreisler had in mind was none other than Baron Wallborn. Both letters were printed in the third and final issue of *Die Musen*, with a foreword by Fouqué and Hoffmann. It would be appropriate, however, to reproduce them here, as a preface to the *Kreisleriana* contained in the final volume of the *Fantasiestücke*, since the gentle reader, if he has any sympathy for the eccentric Johannes at all, cannot remain uninterested in this curious encounter between Wallborn and Kreisler.

Just as Wallborn became insane as a result of unrequited love, Kreisler too seems to have been driven to an extremity of madness by his quite irrational love for a singer; his suggestion of it, at least, is contained in an essay he left behind entitled *The Love of an Artist*. This essay, together with several others which form a cycle about pure spirituality in music, could perhaps soon be appearing in book form under the title *Lucid Intervals of an Insane Musician*.[212]

---

[209] This passage obviously relates to one in *Don Juan* referring to Act 2 sc. 12 of *Don Giovanni*, the aria 'Non mi dir' (also mentioned in 'On a Remark of Sacchini's, and on so-called Effect in Music', II–6): 'a glowing kiss seemed to burn my lips: but the kiss was a long-held note of eternally sought-after yearning'. Hoffmann recapitulates here certain recurring symbols of *Kreisleriana* (see Introduction).

[210] augmented fifth: dissonant musical interval; possibly Hoffmann imagines here the chord C–E–G sharp.

[211] *Cito par bonté*: please forward quickly.

[212] *Lucid Intervals*: both the original inspiration for the 'insane musician' and the early overlapping of this project with what was to become *Kreisleriana* are discussed in the

1 Letter from Baron Wallborn to Kapellmeister Kreisler

From what I hear, my dear Sir, you have found yourself for some considerable time in exactly the same predicament as I. That is to say you have long been suspected of madness, brought on by a love of art that rather too obviously exceeds the norm which the so-called rational world preserves for measurements of that sort. There is only one similarity lacking in order to make us complete companions. You, Sir, had already become weary of the whole business, and had resolved to make your escape; whereas I kept on and on, and let myself be tormented and mocked and, which is worse, bombarded with advice. And during this entire time I found my best and surest comfort in the papers you left behind, which Fräulein von B. – oh, constellation in the night! – occasionally permitted me to examine. On one such occasion it struck me that I must have seen you somewhere previously. Are you not, my dear Sir, a small, strange-looking man, with a physiognomy that one could compare in some respects with that of Socrates? This was highly praised by Alcibiades because the god within it was concealed behind a peculiar mask, yet shone forth in brilliant flashes of lightning, bold, graceful, and terrible![213] Are you not accustomed, my dear Sir, to wearing a coat whose colour one could call the oddest imaginable, if its collar were not an even odder one? And is there not some doubt about the style of this garment, whether it is a frock-coat trying to be a top-coat, or a top-coat transmogrified into a frock-coat? At any rate a man of this description once stood next to me in the theatre, when someone on the stage fancied himself, quite without justification, as an Italian buffo; my neighbour's wit and alacrity turned the pitiable farce into a real comedy for me. Upon

---

Introduction. Planned subject-headings from Hoffmann's diary, under the same title, are printed in *Nachlese*, 884–5.

[213] praised by Alcibiades, etc.: ingenious reference to Plato, *The Symposium*, 215A–216D, Alcibiades' praise of Socrates. The latter is likened outwardly to the flute-playing satyr, Marsyas, as well as to the commonplace miniature sculptures of Silenus, piping, which opened up to contain images of gods. Alcibiades compares Socrates' speech to the divinely entrancing power of Marsyas' music (becoming here an obvious reference to Hoffmann's dual skill); but also calls Socrates a mocking fellow (like Hoffmann) who affects occasional stupidity or ignorance while always maintaining sobriety. (For his unsuccessful challenge to Apollo as musician, the mythical Marsyas was flayed alive; this may reflect ironic value on the comparison.) See the translation by W. R. M. Lamb (*Loeb Classical Library*, 166) (Cambridge, Mass., and London, 1925), 219–23.

enquiry he gave his name as Dr Schulz from Rathenow, but I did not believe it for a moment;[214] as you spoke, my dear Sir, a curious, comical smile played about your lips, for without doubt it was you.

First of all let me inform you that I recently followed your example and ran away, and to the same destination, i.e. into the wider world, where we shall surely meet again. For although its breadth might seem boundless, rational people make it so terribly narrow for the likes of us that we are simply certain to run into each other somewhere, even if it is only when each of us is in desperate flight from some right-thinking person, or from the above-mentioned advice (which might, incidentally, more aptly be written 'add-vice').

At the moment, dear Sir, my endeavour is directed towards adding a small contribution to your catalogue of musical sufferings.[215] Has it ever happened to you, that in order to play some piece of music, or hear it played, you have moved six or seven rooms away from the convivial gathering, only to find that they come running after you and listen, i.e. chatter at the top of their voices? For my part, I think that to such people no route is too circuitous for this purpose, no corridor too long, no staircase, indeed no mountain, too steep or too high.

And then have you noticed, my dear Sir, that there are no heartier despisers of music, no more inimical antipodes to it, than all ranks of servants? Is not a single order sufficient to make them slam the doors, move about noisily, or even throw things down, whenever they happen to be in the room and some enchanting sound proceeds from instrument or voice? But they go further. They are directed by a most exceptional demon of hell to come in, in order to fetch something, or to whisper, or, if they are particularly doltish, to blurt their question with cheerful, insolent coarseness, just as the soul is rising on the swell of music. And they never do it during an interlude, or at some less important moment, of course not, but at the culmination of sublimity, when one feels like holding one's breath so as not to waft away a single golden echo, or when the gates of paradise open softly, so softly at the delicate chords – then, then of all times! Oh Lord of heaven and earth!

If such menials are unavailable, it must not be forgotten that gifted children, animated by the purest servant-mentality, are also able to perform the same rôle with equal skill and equal success. Oh, children, what a price we pay to make you into such servants! It has a sobering, a very sobering effect on me when I think of this, and I am hardly able to remember that

---

[214] Dr Schulz: see Prefatory Remarks, p. 66.
[215] musical sufferings: that is, as described in the first essay of the whole cycle (I–1).

these same charming creatures are equally cheering and friendly towards someone reading aloud to them.

And the tear that now welled up in my eye, and the drop of blood that stung my heart, were they caused only by children?

Alas, it has probably never happened to you, that you want to sing some song to a pair of eyes that seem to gaze down at you from heaven and reflect back to you in a nobler light all your better nature; and that you actually begin singing, and believe, oh Johannes, that your music has really moved the beloved's heart, and that at any moment the sublimest sweep of your melody will anoint those twin stars with pearls of dew, softening and gracing their serene radiance; but then the stars idly turn to some banality such as a dropped stitch, and a stifled yawn twists the angelic lips into a horrible smile; and you realise, my dear Sir, that you have merely been boring the young lady.

Do not laugh, my dear Johannes. There is nothing in life more painful, or more terribly devastating, than when Juno turns into a cloud.[216]

Oh cloud, cloud, beautiful cloud!

And in confidence, Sir, here lies the reason why I have become what people call mad. But only rarely do I become violent with it. Usually I weep quite quietly. So do not be afraid of me, Johannes, but you must not laugh either. And so let us rather speak of other things, though closely related, which my heart urges me to convey to you.

The fact is, Johannes, that you sometimes appear to me to be very harsh in your passionate condemnation of all uninspired music.[217] Is there in fact any absolutely uninspired music? And on the other hand, is there in fact any absolutely perfect music, such as that of the angels? It may well be because my ear is far less sharp and sensitive than yours, but I can tell you in all honesty that I would prefer even the ugliest sound from an out-of-tune violin to no music at all. I hope you will not despise me for saying that. Any such twanging, whether intended to be a dance or a march, awakens the noblest impulses within us, and in spite of all its deficiencies effortlessly forces me with the sweetest sounds of love or war to acknowledge its original purity. Many of the operas that I have heard praised as successful – silly expression! – no, that have spoken from heart to heart, owe the first stirrings of their existence to extremely untuned strings, extremely unpractised fingers, and extremely untrained throats.

---

[216] Juno, etc.: reference to Fouqué's own *Ixion*, in which the insane Wallborn imagines he is the eponymous classical king, who embraced a cloud bearing the shape of Juno. Juno appears also in Act 4 of *The Tempest*, a play shortly to be referred to (II–3, II–6).

[217] uninspired music: the following paragraphs respond to 'Thoughts about the Great Value of Music' (I–3).

And then, my dear Johannes, is not the mere desire to make music a truly moving and admirable impulse in itself? And also the touching faith that carries itinerant musicians into court and cottage, the faith that music and song will open all doors, which is seriously shaken only rarely, by unenlightened masters and fierce dogs! I would as willingly trample down a bed of flowers as shout 'Get out of my house!' just as a waltz was starting. Then smiling children always gather round, from all the houses that the sound can reach, quite different children from the servant-types mentioned above, and confirm by their bright, angelic faces that the musicians' faith is justified.

With so-called 'music-making' in elegant society, the situation frequently appears rather worse, I admit. But even there, no sounds produced by strings, flutes, or voices are entirely without divine afflatus, and they are all preferable to the gossip which at least to some extent they put a stop to.

And finally, Kreisler, what you say about the pleasure that father and mother in their modest household derive from the jangling piano and faltering singing of their small children – I tell you, Johannes, I really believe that amid all the discordant earthly sounds an echo of angelic harmony is to be heard.

I have written more than I should, and I would now like to conclude in the formal manner with which I began. That would not be appropriate, however. So be content with this, Johannes, and may God bless you and bless me, and mercifully draw out from us both what He has placed within us, to His glory and to the pleasure of our fellow men!

The solitary Wallborn

2   Letter from Kapellmeister Kreisler to Baron Wallborn

Now that I have got back to my little room from the theatre, and with great difficulty have lit the lamp, I must write to Your Lordship in some detail. Do not take it amiss, however, if I should express myself in highly musical terms, for you doubtless know that people say that the music formerly bottled up within me came out too forcefully and rapidly, winding itself around me as though I were a chrysalis, so that I can no longer extricate myself, and everything, absolutely everything, takes the form of music to me; and people may well be right. But however that may be, I must write to Your Lordship, for how else am I to be free of the burden that settled heavily and oppressively on my breast when the curtain came down, and Your Lordship had mysteriously disappeared.

How much I had intended to say; unresolved dissonances cried out hideously in my heart; but just as all the serpent-tongued sevenths were on the point of sinking into a pellucid world of friendly thirds, Your Lordship was gone – gone – and the serpent-tongues continued to stab and sting me terribly![218] Your Lordship, to whom I now want to sing all those friendly thirds, is none other than Baron Wallborn, whom I have cherished in my heart for so long that it has often seemed as if all my melodies have taken shape, and then streamed boldly forth, in *his* guise; I could even have been him. Today in the theatre, when a vigorous, youthful figure in uniform, his sword rattling at his side, approached me with such a manly and noble bearing, a feeling of great strangeness yet great familiarity came over me, and I could not identify the odd sequence of chords that began and gradually rose higher and higher. But the young nobleman turned increasingly towards me, and in his eyes I saw an extraordinary new world, a whole Eldorado of delicious dreams. The wild sequence of chords melted into gentle angel-harmonies that spoke magically of the poet's life and nature. And then, since I am an experienced practitioner in music, as Your Lordship can rest assured, the key from which all the music proceeded became clear. I mean that I immediately recognised in the young nobleman Your Lordship, Baron Wallborn.

I attempted a few modulations, and my inner music streamed forth with childish and childlike delight in all manner of lively melodies, amusing murkies,[219] and waltzes; and then Your Lordship joined in, in exactly the right rhythm and key, so that I have no doubt that you will also have recognised me as Kapellmeister Johannes Kreisler, and will not have paid any attention to the mischief that Puck and some of his companions got up to with me this evening. In such strange circumstances, that is to say when I come under the influence of some mischief, I know that I tend to pull some

---

[218] dissonances, etc.: the most dissonant musical intervals are seconds and sevenths; the most consonant ones thirds, fifths, and sixths. The constant metaphysical references during the letter to musical intervals both recall the writings of the insane musician 'Karl', the model or inspiration for Kreisler (see Introduction, pp. 46 f.) and anticipate the use Hoffmann makes later of those of the physicist Ritter. In Ritter's *Fragmente*, i, 226, for example, we read: 'C . . . E . . . G . . . c – C = unity of existence; E = reminiscence; G = hope, the future; c = new existence, resurrection.' This musical chord contains all the consonant intervals mentioned above.

[219] murkies: pieces based on a simple left-hand accompaniment of alternating octaves. See I–3, note 152.

peculiar faces. Also I happened to be wearing a coat that I had once bought in great annoyance over an abandoned trio. Its colour was in C sharp minor, so in order to give those seeing it some peace of mind I had a collar made for it in the colour of E major,[220] and I am sure it will not have upset Your Lordship. In addition I was given a different name this evening. I was introduced as Doctor Schulz from Rathenow, because only under this alias was I allowed to stand by the piano to listen to the singing of two sisters – two nightingales vying with each other in song and scattering the most brilliant and sparkling sounds from the depths of their breasts.[221] They would have shrunk from Kreisler's immoderate spleen, but Doctor Schulz was in a musical Eden to which the sisters had transported him, meek and mild and filled with delight; and the sisters were undismayed when Doctor Schulz was suddenly transformed into Kreisler.

Alas, Baron Wallborn, I fear that in speaking of the sacred impulses burning inside me, I have appeared too severe and intemperate even to you.[222] Alas, Baron Wallborn, unfriendly hands grasped at my crown too;[223] for me too the heavenly creature who invaded the deepest corner of my heart, and suffused the most intimate fibres of my existence, dissolved into mist. Nameless pain tore at my breast, and every melancholy sigh of unquenchable yearning turned into an intolerable smart of resentment, inflamed by the dreadful torment. But Baron Wallborn, do you not also agree that the breast bleeding and lacerated by demonic talons feels every droplet of soothing balm more keenly and beneficially? You know, Baron Wallborn, that I have frequently raged against the musical activities of the common multitude; but I can assure you that often, when I feel thoroughly battered and bruised by godless bravura arias, concertos, and sonatas, then an insignificant little melody, sung by a modest voice, or played in a halting fashion, but sincerely and well meant and speaking directly from the heart, can bring me comfort and cheer. So if you come across such sounds and melodies on your travels, Baron Wallborn, or if you see them below you when you gaze down from your cloud, looking up at you with innocent

---

[220] E major: this key is the 'relative major' to that of C sharp minor, i.e. it has a close technical relationship to it, but expresses the obverse, optimistic side of C sharp minor's melancholy. Additionally, E major will be characterised in the following essay (II–3) as a key of fortitude.

[221] two nightingales: at the party of 27 September 1814 Hoffmann met the 'Marcuse singers' (*HTB*, 255), who have been identified as the twin sisters Elisabeth and Julie Marcuse.

[222] Kreisler answers points in Wallborn's letter even though, logically speaking, he cannot, Wallborn never having 'sent' his letter.

[223] crown: reference to *Ixion*, where Wallborn wears a crown of golden paper, both identifying with the classical King Ixion, and because it symbolises his poetic consciousness. He calls it his 'poet's crown'; the 'unfriendly hands' are those of the woman who rejects him.

longing, then tell them that you wanted to protect and cherish them like little children, and that you were none other than Kapellmeister Johannes Kreisler. For you see, Baron Wallborn, I hereby give you my solemn assurance that *I* want to be *you*, and just as full of love, gentleness, and innocence as you. But then I am already! So much arises simply from the mischief that my own notes create. They often come to life and jump up from the white pages like little black many-tailed imps. They whirl me along in their senseless dance, and I perform extraordinary capers and pull grotesque faces. But a single musical sound, sending out its glow of numinous incandescence, will still the tumult, and I am good and gentle and tolerant. You see, Baron Wallborn, that it is all a question of true thirds, into which all sevenths eventually resolve; and I have written to you in order that you may clearly recognise these thirds!

May God grant that just as we have long known each other in spirit, we may also often meet in person as we did this evening. Your eyes, Baron Wallborn, look straight into my heart, and your eyes themselves are often eloquent words that ring within my breast like my own new-forged melodies. I shall surely meet you often, for tomorrow I shall set out on a great journey into the world, and have already put some new boots on.

Do you not think, Baron Wallborn, that your words could often be my melody, and my melody your words? I have just this moment written down the music for a beautiful song whose words you composed some time ago; nevertheless I felt as though the melody had come to me at the same instant that the song was conceived in your mind.[224] At times I have the feeling that the song is a whole opera![225] Yes! Just as you so vividly appear before my mind's eye, dear, gentle Baron, God grant that I may soon look upon you again with my bodily eyes. May God bless you and so enlighten your fellowmen that they accord you adequate recognition in all your noble works and endeavours. Let this be the serene closing chord in the tonic.

Johannes Kreisler,

Kapellmeister and mad musician *par excellence*.

3 Kreisler's Musico-Poetic Club

All the clocks, even the slowest ones, had already struck eight. The lamps were lit, the piano stood open, and the landlord's daughter, who attended to

---

[224] cf. Hoffmann's theory of song composition as set out in the review of W. F. Riem's *Zwölf Lieder*, Op. 27 (p. 376).

[225] Hoffmann's opera *Undine*, words by Fouqué, had recently been completed.

Kreisler's minor needs, had already informed him twice that the tea-kettle was boiling over. Finally a knock came at the door, and the *true friend* came in with the *cautious one*. They were soon followed by the *dissatisfied one*, the *jovial one*, and the *indifferent one*. The club was convened, and Kreisler got ready to set the right tone and tempo, as usual, by improvising a fantasy of symphonic proportions. Since they cultivated a taste for music, this was also intended, if needed, to raise the assembled clubbists a few fathoms up from the dusty sweepings in which they had been obliged to scratch around during the day into less polluted air. The cautious one assumed an extremely serious, almost pained, expression and said 'How upsetting it was, my dear Kreisler, that your playing was interrupted by that sticking hammer the other day. Have you been able to have it repaired?' 'I think so, yes', replied Kreisler. 'I think we ought to make sure', continued the cautious one, and in order to do so, lit the big writing-lamp, which he then held above the strings, cautiously searching for the offending hammer. But suddenly the heavy wick-scissors attached to the lamp fell off, and with a clashing reverberation twelve or fifteen strings snapped. The cautious one merely said 'My goodness, look at that!' Kreisler pulled a face, as if biting into a lemon. 'The very devil!' cried the dissatisfied one, 'I was particularly looking forward to Kreisler's fantasy today, today particularly! I have never looked forward to hearing some music so much in my whole life!' 'When all's said and done', interjected the indifferent one, 'it doesn't make much difference whether we begin with music or not.' The true friend thought it was certainly a pity that Kreisler could not play now, but they should not allow themselves to lose their tempers over it. 'We shall have some fun in any case', added the jovial one, not without giving his words a certain significance. 'And I intend to perform a fantasy no matter what', cried Kreisler, 'the bass is completely unaffected, and I shall manage with that.'

Thereupon Kreisler donned his little red cap, put on his Chinese dressing-gown, and moved over to the instrument. The clubbists had to take their places on the sofa and on the chairs, and at Kreisler's request the true friend put out all the lights, so that they found themselves in total darkness. Pianissimo, and with the dampers raised, Kreisler then played a full A flat major chord in the bass. To the diminishing whisper of the notes, he spoke:

'What strange and magical susurration rises all around me? Invisible wings flutter up and down; I swim through the fragrant ether. But the fragrance radiates in flaming, mysteriously intertwining circles. They are propitious spirits, moving their golden wings in sounds and chords of surpassing beauty.'

A flat minor chord (*mezzo forte*)

'Ah! They carry me to the land of eternal yearning, but as they take hold of me, pain awakens and tries to burst forth from my breast by rending it asunder.'

E major, first inversion chord (*ancora più forte*)[226]

'Stand firm, my heart! Do not break under the searing heat that suffuses my breast. Be of good cheer, my sturdy spirit! Rise up, and make your presence felt in the element that gave you birth, that is your home!'

E major, root position chord (*forte*)

'They have handed me a magnificent crown,[227] but flashing and sparkling among the diamonds are the thousand tears I shed, and amid the gold glisten the flames that consume me. To him who is called to rule the spirit-realm – courage and power, faith and strength!'

A minor (*harpeggiando-dolce*)

'Why do you flee, fair maiden? Can you do so, when invisible bonds tie you down on all sides? Can you not bespeak or bemoan the feeling that has taken root in your breast like a gnawing pain, and yet fills you with shivers of sweet pleasure? But all will be revealed when I address you tenderly in the language of the spirits, which I can speak and you so well understand!'

F major

'Ha! How your heart will swell with love and longing when I fill you with burning joy, and envelop you with melodies as if with a loving embrace. You will never wish to leave me again, for the secret expectations that caused your breast to tighten have been fulfilled. Music, like a consoling oracle, has spoken from my heart to yours!'

B flat major (*accentuato*)

'What lively sounds in field and forest in this sweet spring-time! All the flutes and shawms, which through the winter lay in dusty corners with the

---

[226] Musically trained readers will be aware that Kreisler's chords follow in a coherent modulating sequence. The relationship of A flat minor to E major is an enharmonic one. Hoffmann describes this important early Romantic resource (enharmony) later in *Kreisleriana* (II–6, p. 158 and note 275), and discusses it in his review of Spohr's First Symphony (p. 277).

[227] crown: Kreisler's fantasy recalls here his words to Wallborn on p. 130 (or maybe, imaginatively, vice versa), 'unfriendly hands grasped at my crown too'.

stiffness of death, have come to life and remembered all their favourite tunes, which they now trill merrily like the birds in the air.'

B flat major with the minor seventh (*smanioso*)

'A mild west wind moves bleakly moaning through the forest, gloomy and mysterious, and as it passes by, the spruce and birch whisper to each other: Why has our friend become so sad? Do you hear him, lovely shepherdess?'

E flat major (*forte*)

'Follow after him! Follow after him! His raiment is green like the dark forest, his yearning words the sweet sound of horns! Do you hear their mellow tones behind the thickets? Do you hear their sound? The sound of horns, full of pleasure and melancholy! There he is! Go on! After him!'

D six–four–three chord (*piano*)[228]

'Life plays its teasing game in a thousand ways. Why wish? Why hope? Why desire?'

C major, root position chord (*fortissimo*)

'But let us dance above the open graves in our wild frenzy of pleasure. Let us shout for joy – those below will not hear it. Hurrah, hurrah, dance and rejoice, the devil enters to the sound of trumpets and drums!'

C minor chords (repeated *fortissimo*)

'Don't you recognise him? Don't you recognise him? Look, he clutches at my heart with red-hot talons![229] He disguises himself in weird masks of all kinds: as a huntsman, concert-master, worm-doctor, *ricco mercante*.[230] He hurls wick-scissors into my strings, just to prevent me playing! Kreisler, Kreisler! Pull yourself together! Do you see it lying in wait, the ghastly apparition with its flashing red eyes? Stretching out its claw-like skeleton-hands towards you from its tattered coat? Shaking the crown of straw on its

---

[228] D six–four–three chord: that is, in ascending order, D, F, G, B; the chord musically conveys the expression of unfulfilment, being an unresolved discord.

[229] red-hot talons: cf. Beethoven's 'arms of red-hot metal' in I–2; but also similar images elsewhere, like the age's 'iron fist' in I–5 and the same idea in *The Poet and the Composer*, p. 190.

[230] *ricco mercante*: rich merchant.

smooth bare skull? It is the spectre of insanity.[231]Johannes, face it bravely. Terrible, terrible living ghost, why do you ensnare me in your coils? Is there no escape from you? No mote of dust in the universe on which I might save myself, shrunken to the size of a gnat, from your tormenting clutches? Leave me alone! I promise to be good! I promise to believe the devil is a *galanthuomo* of the most refined manners! *Hony soit qui mal y pense.* I hereby curse all singing, all music. I will lick your feet like the drunken Caliban, only release me from this torture![232] Hey, hey, you monstrous villain, you have trampled down all my flowers – no blade of green will flourish in such hateful desolation – all dead – dead – dead –'

At this point a small flame hissed in the darkness. The true friend had quickly taken out a chemical match and lit both lamps, in order to put a stop to any further fantasising by Kreisler; he well knew that Kreisler had now reached a point from which he usually plunged into a dark abyss of inconsolable lamentation. At that moment too, the landlord's daughter brought in the steaming tea. Kreisler sprang up from the piano. 'So what is all that supposed to mean?' asked the dissatisfied one, 'a well-turned allegro by Haydn sounds much better to me than all that absurd mumbo-jumbo.' 'But it wasn't all that bad', interjected the indifferent one. 'But too depressing, much too depressing', put in the jovial one, 'we should try to steer our conversation today in a lighter, jollier direction'.[233] The clubbists did their best to follow the jovial one's advice, but Kreisler's sinister chords and disturbing words hung in the air like a distant deadening echo, and maintained the mood of tension into which Kreisler had put them all. The dissatisfied one, highly dissatisfied indeed with an evening which, as he put it, had been ruined by Kreisler's absurd fantastication, took his leave with the cautious one. The jovial one followed them, and only the travelling enthusiast[234] and true friend (both, it should be expressly pointed out here, united in one and the same person) remained behind with Kreisler, who sat silently on the sofa with his arms crossed. 'I don't know what to make of you today, Kreisler', said the true friend. 'You are so excited, and yet without any humour, not at all your normal self!' 'Ah, my friend!' replied Kreisler, 'a dark cloud is passing over my life! Don't you think a poor innocent melody, that desires no – no abode on this earth, might be permitted to wander freely and harmlessly through the wide spaces of heaven? If only I

---

[231] insanity: Kreisler apparently recalls his ironic comparison in I–3 of Romantic artists to 'kings in the mad-house with straw crowns on their heads'.

[232] *The Tempest*, Act 2 sc. 2: 'And I will kiss thy foot: I prithee be my god.'

[233] At this point the first edition went on to include the one-act dramatic fragment, *Prinzessin Blandina*: see Prefatory Remarks.

[234] enthusiast: that is, the author of the whole *Fantasiestücke*; Hoffmann.

could sit on my Chinese dressing-gown as though it were Mephistopheles' cloak and fly out of that window there!'[235] 'As a harmless melody?' interrupted the true friend with a smile. 'Or as a *basso ostinato*[236] if you prefer', replied Kreisler, 'but I have to get away soon, however I do it.' And so it soon came about, just as he had foretold.

4 Report of an Educated Young Man

It is heart-warming to realise that culture is making itself felt to an increasing extent, and that even in species formerly excluded from higher education talents of the rarest quality are emerging. At the house of Privy Trade Councillor R. I made the acquaintance of a young man, in whom the most extraordinary gifts are combined with an endearing bonhomie. When I happened to mention the regular correspondence I maintain with my friend Charles Ewson in Philadelphia, he trustingly handed me an open letter which he had written to his lady friend, to be forwarded to her. The letter has been sent, but was I wrong, my dear young friend, to keep a written copy of it, as a monument of your great wisdom and virtue and your genuine artistic feeling? I cannot conceal the fact that this exceptional young man, by his birth and original occupation, is actually an ape.

Living in the Trade Councillor's house, he has learned to speak, read, write, play music, and so forth. In short, he has achieved such a level of culture, that because of his art and learning, and the elegance of his manners, he has acquired a large number of friends and is welcome in all intellectual circles. Apart from trifling exceptions, such as when he occasionally executes rather odd somersaults in the *hops angloises*[237] at *thés dansants*, or is unable to hear nuts cracked without a certain inner agitation, or (and this may be only the sort of envious tittle-tattle that pursues all geniuses) tends to inflict minor scratches when kissing ladies' hands, despite their gloves, one is not in the least aware of his exotic origin; and all the little acts of mischief he committed in his earlier years, such as snatching the hats from the heads of all those entering the house and scurrying behind

---

[235] Reference to Goethe, *Faust*, e.g. Part I, line 2065; compare the opening of 'Kapellmeister Johannes Kreisler's Musical Sufferings'.

[236] *basso ostinato*: a constantly repeated bass pattern. The contrast seems to be intended between a free spirit (the 'innocent melody') and one forced to toil (the bass 'carrying' the rest of the musical structure).

[237] *hops angloises*: seemingly country-dances, reels, currently in fashion.

a sugar-barrel, have now become amusing *bons mots* which are repeated to uproarious applause.

Here is the remarkable letter, in which Milo's sublime sensibility and extraordinary cultivation find full expression.

> *Letter from Milo, an educated ape, to his lady-friend Pipi*
> *in North America.*

It is with a sort of horror that I still remember the unhappy time when I was unable to express to you, my dear friend, the tenderest impulses of my heart, other than by inelegant noises that were incomprehensible to any educated person. How could the piercing, pitiable 'Aiee, aiee!' that I emitted in those days, albeit accompanied by many a tender look, in the least convey the profound emotions stirring in my manly, hirsute breast? And even my caresses, which you, my sweet little friend, had to endure at that time in silent surrender, were so awkward that now, when I equal the best *primo amoroso*[238] in that respect, and kiss ladies' hands *à la Duport*,[239] I could blush at the thought of it, if a somewhat swarthy complexion characteristic of my race did not prevent such a thing. Yet despite my good fortune in possessing the profound self-satisfaction that an education received among men has brought me, there are still times when I feel distinct pangs of regret, although I know that such aberrations are quite incompatible with the moral character that culture instils, and arise from the coarse temperament that ties me to a class of creatures that I now despise unutterably. I am then foolish enough to think of our poor relatives, who still cavort about among the trees in remote, uncultivated forests, who live on raw fruit not rendered palatable by culinary art, and who, particularly in the evenings, intone hymns in which not a single note is in tune and any conception of rhythm, even the new-fangled 7/8 or 13/4 time,[240] is entirely unknown. I think of these poor creatures for whom I no longer have any regard whatsoever, and cannot but feel a profound pity for them.

I particularly remember our old uncle (he must have been an uncle on my mother's side as I recall), who brought us up in his simple-minded way, and did all he could to keep us far removed from anything human. He was a serious man, who would never put on boots, and I can still hear his anxious

---

[238] *primo amoroso*: 'first lover'; phrase applied to a stereotyped opera-singer rôle.

[239] Louis-Antoine Duport (1781–1853): famous ballet-dancer, active until 1830, whose agility and pirouettes were legendary.

[240] 7/8 or 13/4 time: these sophisticated violations of traditional duple or triple metre are not fanciful: Hoffmann might be referring to Antoine Reicha's *36 Fugues* for piano (Vienna, 1803), which employ 5/8, compound 6/8 and 2/8, and compound 2/2 and 3/4 metres.

warning cry when I set my greedy eyes on the beautiful new top-boots that the cunning hunter had placed under the tree in which I was avidly devouring a coconut. Some distance away I saw the hunter walking past; he looked most dashing in a pair of top-boots that were just like those he had left behind. For me the well-polished boots lent his whole figure such a distinguished and imposing air that I could not resist. The thought of proudly striding about in new boots, just like him, took control of all my senses. And was it not an early sign of that extraordinary talent for art and science which only needed awakening in me, that I sprang down from the tree, and with ease and skill, as though I had worn boots all my life, was able to use the steel boot-hooks to pull the unaccustomed footwear onto my slender legs? But I was naturally unable to run away then. The hunter walked over to me, unceremoniously seized me by the scruff of the neck, and dragged me off. My old uncle shrieked pitifully and threw coconuts at us, one of which struck me quite hard behind my left ear; this was not intended by the angry old fellow, but may well have stimulated the development of remarkable new organs. You already know all this, my dearest, since you ran howling and wailing after your beloved and thus voluntarily delivered yourself into captivity too.

But why do I say captivity? Has this captivity not given us the greatest freedom? Is there anything more wonderful than the training of the mind which we have undergone among men? I have no doubt that you, dear Pipi, with your innate high spirits and intelligence, will also have devoted yourself to the arts and sciences to some extent, and in this belief I distinguish you sharply from our godless relatives in the forests. Ha! Among them immorality and barbarism still prevail, their eyes are dry, and they are completely without nobility of spirit! I naturally assume that your education will not have advanced so far as mine, since I am now, as they say, a man whose fortune is assured. I know absolutely everything, I am consequently just like an oracle, and in the realm of science and art my authority here is unchallenged. You will doubtless think, my sweet girl, that it has cost me infinite pains to attain such a high degree of culture; but on the contrary, I can assure you that nothing in the world could have been easier. Indeed, it often makes me laugh that in my early youth my detested jumping-exercises from one tree to the next extracted large quantities of perspiration, which I did not expend at all in becoming learned and wise. That process took place quite naturally by itself, and it was almost more difficult to accept the fact that I was actually standing on the highest rung of the ladder than to climb up it. It was all due to my exceptional intelligence, and the lucky blow on the head from my uncle! I am sure you know, dear Pipi, that intellectual gifts and abilities appear like bumps on the head, and can be felt with the hand; the back of my head feels like a bag of coconuts, and that blow must have produced several bumps, and with them new abilities. In fact my head is unusually wide behind my ears!

That imitative instinct which is characteristic of our species, and which is so often yet quite unjustly ridiculed by men, is nothing more than the irresistible urge not only to attain culture, but also to display that which we already possess. The same principle has long been accepted among men, and the truly wise, whom I have always striven to emulate, apply it in the following manner. Someone produces something, a work of art or whatever, and everyone cries 'That's wonderful.' The wise man, driven by his inner voice, immediately imitates it. Admittedly his version turns out differently, but he says 'That is just as it should be, and the work you thought was wonderful merely gave me an incentive to bring forth the genuinely wonderful one I have so long been carrying in my head.' It is roughly the same, my dear Pipi, as when one of our brothers cuts his nose while shaving, but thereby gives his beard a certain original flourish which the man he was imitating could never achieve. It was this imitative instinct, which has always been so marked in me, that brought me into contact with a professor of aesthetics, the most lovable man in the world, from whom I later received the first understanding of myself, and who also taught me to speak. Even before I had perfected this talent I frequented select gatherings of amusing and gifted men. I had precisely observed their expressions and gestures, and was able to imitate them skilfully. This, and my elegant clothing, with which my employer at that time had provided me, not only opened doors to me everywhere, but made me generally accepted as a refined young man of the world. How passionately I wanted to be able to speak, but in my heart I thought 'Alas, even if you could speak, where would you get all the thousands of thoughts and ideas that pour from people's lips? How could you begin to speak of the thousands of things whose names you hardly know? How could you criticise works of art and science as confidently as everyone else, without being familiar with those subjects?'

As soon as I was able to string together even a few words, I expressed my doubts and fears to my dear teacher, the professor of aesthetics. But he laughed out loud and said 'What do you think then, my dear Monsieur Milo? You must learn to speak, speak, speak, and all the rest will follow by itself. Speak fluently, cleverly, and confidently, that is the whole secret. You will be surprised how ideas come to you while speaking, how wisdom arises in you, how the divine gift of the gab admits you to every level of art and science, so that you think you are wandering in a veritable labyrinth. Often you will not even understand yourself, but that is when you have achieved the truly inspired state that speaking induces. Some light reading can also be of assistance to you, and it is useful to make a note of a few well-turned phrases that can be advantageously interspersed and employed in the manner of a refrain, as it were. Talk frequently about the trend of the times, how this or that is manifestly demonstrated, a lot about spiritual depth, about being full of spirit or devoid of spirit, and so forth.'[241] Oh my Pipi, how right he was! How my wisdom grew along with my proficiency in speaking! My fortunate play of features lent weight to my words, and I have seen in the mirror how magisterial my naturally rather wrinkled brow appears when I manifestly demonstrate that this or that poet is devoid of spiritual depth, since I do not understand him, which means he cannot possibly be any good. This intuitive awareness of cultural excellence is the tribunal to which I automatically submit every work of art and science, and my judgement is infallible, since it springs spontaneously from within me like an oracle.

I have many times tried my hand at art – some painting, sculpture, and also modelling in clay. I once modelled you, my sweetest friend, as Diana in the classical style. But I soon wearied of all that nonsense. Music attracted me above all else, since it gives me an opportunity effortlessly to fill large numbers of people with astonishment and admiration; and because of my natural propensities the fortepiano soon became my favourite instrument. You are aware, my sweet, that nature has endowed me with rather longish fingers; with these I can span fourteenths, even two octaves,[242] and this, together with enormous skill in moving and animating my fingers, is my whole secret of fortepiano playing. My music-master shed tears of joy over the outstanding gifts of his pupil, for within a short time I reached the point where I could run up and down with both hands in demisemiquavers, hemidemisemiquavers, even semihemidemisemiquavers, without a mistake, play trills with all my fingers equally well, and execute leaps of three or four octaves up and down, just as I used to leap from one tree to the next. As a result I am the greatest virtuoso there can be. None of the available piano compositions is difficult enough for me, so I compose my sonatas and concertos myself. In the latter, however, my music-master has to write the tuttis, for who can possibly be bothered with all those instruments and other

---

[241] This speech by the professor of aesthetics distinctly recalls Diderot, *Rameau's Nephew*: 'HE: . . . I represent the most important part of town and Court . . . Fulfilling your duties, where does that land you? Into jealousy, upsets, persecution. Is that the way to get on? Butter people up, good God, butter them up, watch the great, study their tastes, fall in with their whims, pander to their vices, approve of their injustices. That's the secret.' *Rameau's Nephew*, tr. Tancock, 64–5.

[242] two octaves: about twice as many notes as can be spanned by the human hand.

inanities! Tuttis in concertos are in any case merely a necessary evil, and only provide a breathing space, as it were, for the soloist to recover his strength and prepare for the next hurdles.[243]

I have also recently spoken to an instrument-maker about a fortepiano of nine or ten octaves. Can genius be limited to a meagre compass of seven wretched octaves? As well as the usual pedals for the Turkish drum and cymbal, he is to incorporate a trumpet pedal, and also a flageolet pedal to imitate as closely as possible the chirrupping of birds.[244] You see, dear Pipi, what sublime ideas a man of taste and education can conceive!

After I had heard a number of singers reap loud applause, I was seized with an indescribable desire to sing too, but unfortunately it seemed as though nature had utterly failed to provide me with suitable vocal cords. I could not refrain from revealing my wish to a famous singer, who had become my closest friend, and at the same time pouring out my frustration concerning my voice. But he took me in his arms and cried enthusiastically 'Bless you Monsieur, with your musical ability and the flexibility of your vocal cords, which I have long admired, you are born to be a great singer. You have already overcome the greatest difficulty. You see, nothing is more unsuited to the true art of singing than a good natural voice, and it costs no little effort with young pupils who have a real singing voice to remove this obstacle. Total avoidance of all sustained notes, diligent practice of the most florid roulades far exceeding the normal compass of the human voice, and above all straining to produce the falsetto voice in which truly artistic singing resides – all these usually help after a while.[245] Even the most robust

---

[243] hurdles, etc: ironic metaphor relating to Hoffmann's poor opinion of piano concertos, in 'Beethoven's Instrumental Music', p. 101. The joke about tuttis being a 'necessary evil' relates to the fact that whereas the older generation (including Mozart himself) showed their musicianship by participating on the piano during these orchestral sections, recent amateurs and showmen did not possess the necessary skills. See Faye Ferguson, 'The Classical Keyboard Concerto. Some Thoughts on Authentic Performance', *Early Music*, xii (1984), 437–46.

[244] The first joke here alludes to the contemporary widening of the piano's compass, from its standard five octaves in the late eighteenth century. But even by 1820 the largest instruments possessed only six and a half octaves, though most today have seven. The second joke alludes to the fitting of newly invented pedals for various effects: *una corda, Pianozug*, harp, mute, swell, cymbals, bassoon, octave coupler. W. L. Sumner, *The Pianoforte* (London, 3rd edn, 1971), 59–62. See also p. 309, nn. 13 and 14.

[245] Hoffmann, himself a singing-teacher, enumerates the techniques he execrated. The stretching of the upper voice limit was a tendency already observable in the 1780s (e.g. the Queen of the Night's arias). The term 'falsetto voice' was usually synonymous with 'head voice' at this time, and Hoffmann himself explained it elsewhere: 'The falsetto is also not simply the weaker range of a singer, but that which he develops and produces outside the scale of his natural one (i.e. chest notes), by means of artistic constriction of the throat (throat notes).' *Schriften zur Musik*, 94.

of voices seldom withstands such intensive pressures for long. But in your case, my dear Monsieur, there is no obstacle to remove. Within a short time you will be the sublimest singer there is!'

The man was quite right. It only needed a little practice to develop a splendid falsetto voice, and the capacity to throw off a hundred notes in one breath. This earned me the unanimous applause of all true connoisseurs, and put the wretched tenors who pride themselves no end on their chest voice, when they can hardly execute a single mordent,[246] well and truly in the shade. Right at the outset my maestro taught me three coloratura phrases; they were rather long, but contained the quintessence of all wisdom about artistic singing. One could then employ them, now in this way, now in that, in whole or in part, over and over again.[247] Indeed, instead of the melody intended by the composer, one could simply sing these phrases, in all sorts of different guises, to the bass-line of a wide variety of arias. I cannot describe to you, my sweet, the tumultuous applause I have already received merely for repeating these phrases, and you see again how even in music my natural, inborn intelligence makes everything so absolutely easy for me.

I have already spoken of my compositions, but when it comes to actually composing – well, when I do not have to, simply to provide my genius with works worthy of it, then I prefer to leave it to inferior beings who exist in order to serve us virtuosos, i.e. in order to supply works in which we can display our virtuosity. I must confess that I find it a curious business with all that stuff they cram into a score, all the different instruments and harmonic combinations – they have whole sets of rules about it. But for a genius, for a virtuoso, it is all much too tedious and boring. In any case, if one wishes to command respect in every quarter, as the ultimate wisdom of life requires, one need only be *thought* to be a composer, and that is enough. When, for example, at some gathering I have reaped copious applause for an aria, and the composer happens to be present, and part of the applause is about to be directed to him, then with a sort of dark, pensive gaze, which with my distinctive physiognomy I can do very effectively, I casually remark 'Yes, of course, I really must finish my new opera!' This revelation spurs everyone to renewed amazement, and as a result the composer who actually has finished is completely forgotten. In general a genius is well advised to make

---

[246] mordent: simple three-note ornament.

[247] The first joke here is that trained singers were traditionally expected to ornament their own music, even extempore. The second is that the ornamentation should obviously reflect the aria in question. There is also an ironic reference back to '*Ombra adorata*' (I–2), where the beauty and delicate appropriateness of Crescentini's vocal embellishments have been praised.

himself as conspicuous as possible, and he must not hesitate to point out
that whatever his artistic achievements may be, they are paltry and insignificant compared with what he could produce in any sphere of art or science if
he so chose, and if people were worth the effort. Utter contempt for the
exertions of others, the strength of mind to ignore totally all those who
prefer silence and get on quietly without talking about it, overweening
arrogance about all the seemingly effortless products of one's own brilliance
– all these are unmistakable signs of the most highly cultivated genius, and I
am glad to say that I observe them daily, indeed hourly, in myself.[248]

And so, sweet friend, you can well imagine my happy state, which I owe
to the excellent education I have received. But can I conceal from you one
trifling matter that weighs upon my heart? Should I not confess to you, my
dearest, that certain urges that often overtake me unawares still wrench me
from the agreeable serenity that sweetens my days? Alas, how one's earliest
upbringing exerts such weighty influence over one's whole life! And it is
rightly said that the appetites imbibed with a mother's milk are the ones
most difficult to eradicate! What harm was done by my wild rampaging in
the hills and forests! Recently I was strolling in the park with some friends,
elegantly dressed, when suddenly we stopped beside a superb, towering
walnut tree. An irresistible desire robbed me of all self-control; a few nimble
bounds, and I was swinging high up in the branches, grasping for the nuts!
A cry of astonishment from the party below accompanied my exploit. When
I remembered that cultural propriety does not permit such extravagance,
and climbed down again, a young fellow who holds me in some reverence
exclaimed 'Oh my dear Monsieur Milo, what agile legs you have!' But I felt
nothing but shame.

Similarly I can sometimes hardly suppress the desire to exercise the skill
in throwing that comes naturally to me. I am sure you can understand, my
dearest girl, how at a dinner party recently this desire so took possession of
me that I seized an apple and threw it at the wig of the Trade Councillor, my
old patron, who was sitting right at the other end of the table – an outrage
that almost landed me in a thousand embarrassments. Yet I hope to be able
to cure myself increasingly of these vestiges of my former barbarous
condition.

Should you not yet be so culturally advanced, my sweetest friend, that
you can read this letter, then let the recollection of your beloved's nobility
and resolve encourage you to learn to read; and then let its contents give you
wise counsel in how you must begin, in order to achieve that inner peace and

---

[248] Compare the similar attack on the singer Joseph Fischer (1780–1862), who incurred
Hoffmann's wrath when he withdrew from the cast of *Undine*. See p. 408.

contentment which only superior culture, the product of inborn genius and intercourse with wise and cultivated men, can bring. And now, my sweetest friend, a thousand farewells!

> Doubt thou the stars are fire,
> Doubt that the sun doth move;
> Doubt truth to be a liar,
> But never doubt I love.[249]

Your friend,
faithful unto death!
Milo,
Formerly ape, now privately established
artist and scholar.

5 The Music-Hater

It must be a wonderful thing to be so profoundly musical that one can easily and happily cope, as though equipped with special powers, with the largest musical forms that composers have constructed from infinite quantities of notes played by the widest possible variety of instruments; and that one can assimilate them in heart and mind, without any disturbing agitation of the spirit, and without any painful pangs of ecstasy or heart-rending melancholy. How completely could one then enjoy the virtuosity of the players; and one could fully savour this enjoyment, which clamours to be released, without any danger. I prefer not even to think of the bliss of being a virtuoso myself, for then my sorrow that I so utterly lack all feeling for music would be still deeper. My indescribable awkwardness in the practice of this glorious art, which alas I have displayed since childhood, must also be due to this.

My father was certainly a capable musician; he played the grand piano assiduously, often late into the night, and whenever there was a concert at our house he played very long pieces, in which the others occasionally accompanied him on violins, cello and bass, and even flutes and horns. When one of these long pieces finally came to an end, everyone cheered loudly and cried 'Bravo, bravo! What a splendid recital! So perfect, so well

---

[249] *Hamlet*, Act 2 sc. 2. Hoffmann noted his great pleasure at seeing his friend Carl Leo (1780–1824) act the rôle of Hamlet in Bamberg in March 1813 (*HTB*, 197).

played!' and the name of Emanuel Bach[250] was reverently mentioned! But my father always hammered and crashed about so much that to me it hardly ever seemed like music, in which I expected to hear melodies that went straight to the heart; it seemed as though he was just doing it as a joke, and the others enjoyed joining in with it.

On these occasions I was always buttoned up in my Sunday coat, and had to sit on a high chair beside my mother and listen without fidgeting. The time went dreadfully slowly, and I could not have endured it if I had not been fascinated by the peculiar expressions and comical movements of the players. I particularly recall a retired lawyer who always played the violin right next to my father; he was always said to be a fanatical enthusiast whom music had made half crazed, so that in his state of delirious exaltation induced by the genius of Emanuel Bach, or Wolf, or Benda,[251] he could play neither in tune nor in time. I can still see him clearly before my eyes. He wore a plum-coloured coat with buttons covered in gold thread, a small silver sword, and a reddish, lightly powdered bag-wig with a small round pouch hanging at the back. There was an indescribably comical earnestness about everything he did. '*Ad opus!*' he would cry, when my father put the music out on the stands. Then with his right hand he seized the violin, and with his left the wig, which he removed and hung on a nail. Now he set to work, bending lower and lower over the music, with the light flashing from his protruding red eyes and beads of perspiration standing on his brow. It sometimes happened that he got to the end before the other players, whereupon he was more than a little taken aback and glared at them fiercely. Also he produced sounds that often seemed to me like those which Peter from next door, prompted by his bent for natural history to inquire into the latent musical talent of cats, extracted from our tom-cat by skilfully squeezing its tail, for which he (Peter, that is) was occasionally given something of a thrashing by his father.

In short, the plum-coloured lawyer – Musewius by name – more than compensated me for the torture of sitting still, since I so much enjoyed his grimaces, his comical contortions, and even his screechings on the violin. Once he caused a complete breakdown in the music; my father leapt up from the piano, and everyone rushed towards him fearing that he had been overcome by a fatal seizure. It began with a gentle shaking of the head, but

---

[250] Carl Philipp Emanuel Bach (1714–88), second surviving son of J. S. Bach; his music is characterised by utmost individuality and expressive power.
[251] Ernst Wilhelm Wolf (1735–92), active at Weimar and once widely known for his chamber music; 'Benda' could refer to Franz (1709–86), his brother Georg (1722–95) or his son Friedrich (1745–1814), all of whom issued chamber music, though the last-named was especially noted in that field.

then, in a gradual crescendo, he jerked his head more and more violently from side to side, and at the same time hideously scraped his bow back and forth across the strings, repeatedly clicking his tongue, and stamping his foot. It turned out, however, to be nothing but an irksome little fly, which kept buzzing round him with undeviating obstinacy and landing on his nose, though brushed away a thousand times; this was the cause of his desperate agitation.

Sometimes it happened that my mother's sister sang an aria. Ah, how I always looked forward to that! I loved her very much. She spent a great deal of time with me, and with her beautiful voice, which pierced me to the quick, she sang me lots of unforgettable songs that made such an impression on my heart and mind that I still sing them softly to myself today. There was always a special atmosphere when my aunt handed out the parts to an aria by Hasse, or Traetta,[252] or some other great composer; and the lawyer was not allowed to play. Even while they were playing the introduction and my aunt had not yet begun to sing, my heart pounded, and I was suffused by such a wonderful feeling of pleasure and melancholy that I could hardly control myself. No sooner had my aunt finished singing the first piece than I burst into tears, and had to be taken out of the room, to the severe displeasure of my father. My father often had arguments with my aunt, since she maintained that my behaviour was in no way brought about by the adverse effect of music on me, but rather by the extreme sensitivity of my nature; my father, on the other hand, called me a stupid boy who deliberately howled out of perversity, like a music-hating dog.

My aunt found an excellent reason not only for defending me, but even for attributing to me a deeply hidden feeling for music, in the fact that often, when my father happened to leave the piano unlocked, I would amuse myself for hours by discovering and repeatedly playing all sorts of fascinating chords. When, using both hands, I had found three, four, or even six keys that I could press down together to produce a magical harmony, I did not tire of playing them again and again and listening to them die away. I laid my head sideways on the lid of the instrument; I closed my eyes; I was in another world; but finally I could not stop myself weeping bitterly, not knowing whether from pleasure or from pain. My aunt often enjoyed listening to me, but my father regarded it merely as a childish game. As over me, so over other subjects, and particularly music, they seemed to be completely at odds. She derived great pleasure from short pieces of music, especially those in the simple, unaffected style of Italian composers,

---

[252] Johann Adolf Hasse (1699–1783); Tommaso Traetta (1727–79). Both were predominantly composers for the theatre and the church.

whereas my father, who was a rather forceful man, called such music just a jingle, which could never satisfy the mind. My father always spoke of the mind, my aunt always of feeling.

Finally she persuaded my father to let me have piano lessons from an old organist, who usually played the viola at our family recitals.[253] But, sad to relate, it soon became apparent that my aunt had placed far too much confidence in me, and that my father had been right. In sense of rhythm, and grasp of melody, there was no deficiency at all, as the organist confirmed; but my boundless lack of self-discipline brought it all to nought. When I had been told to practise a study, and sat down at the piano with the best intention to work hard, I soon slipped absent-mindedly into my aimless chord-hunting, and thus made little progress. With immense effort I had struggled through various keys, as far as the dreadful one that has four sharps and, as I still all too clearly remember, is called E major. Above the music in large letters stood the words 'Scherzando Presto', and when the organist played it to me, it had an uneven, jerky quality that I greatly disliked. Oh, the tears, the encouraging prods from my unfortunate organist which that accursed Presto cost me! Finally came the dreaded day when I was expected to demonstrate to my father and his musical friends the proficiency I had acquired, and play all the pieces I had learnt. I could play them all except the detested E major Presto. So on the evening before, I sat down at the piano in a state of desperation, determined to practise the piece, whatever the cost, until it was note-perfect. I do not know how it happened, but I tried playing the piece using the keys immediately to the right of those which I should have used. It worked. The whole piece became easier, and I did not miss a single note; I merely played it on different keys.[254] It seemed as though the piece even sounded better than when the organist had played it to me. I now felt much happier and calmer. On the following day I confidently sat down at the piano, and cheerfully hammered out my little pieces. After each one my father cried 'I would never have thought it!' When the Scherzo came to an end, the organist said in a kindly way 'That was the difficult key of E major!' and my father turned to a friend and said 'You see how well the boy manages the difficult E major!' 'Forgive me, my dear fellow', replied the latter, 'but that was F major'. 'Certainly not, certainly not', said my father. 'But it was', countered the friend, 'Let's have a look.' They both walked over to the piano. 'There you are', cried my

---

[253] cf. *Kater Murr, Writings of Hoffmann*, tr., ed. Kent and Knight, ii, 84: Kreisler's uncle 'abandoned me to the caprices of the teachers who came to the house'.

[254] E major involves four black notes per octave; F major only one. It should be noted that the boy had evidently memorised the study and absorbed it, for otherwise he could never have played it in F.

father triumphantly, pointing to the four sharps. 'But the boy played in F major', repeated the friend. I was asked to play the piece again. I did so quite innocently, since it was not at all clear to me what they had been discussing so seriously. My father watched the keys closely. I had hardly played a few notes when my father's hand delivered a stinging blow to my ear. 'Confounded, stupid boy!' he bellowed, beside himself with anger. Howling and crying I ran out of the room, and that was the end of my musical education for good. My aunt thought that the very fact that I had been able to play the whole piece correctly in a different key was a sign of genuine musical talent; but I now believe that my father was right to abandon my lessons on a musical instrument, since my awkwardness, and the stiffness and clumsiness of my fingers, would have frustrated all my efforts.[255]

This clumsiness with regard to music also seems to extend to my intellectual appreciation. All too often, after hearing recognised virtuosos, when everyone has burst into unrestrained acclamation, I have felt nothing but boredom, distaste, and weariness. In addition, since I could not refrain from honestly speaking my mind, or rather expressing my inner feelings clearly, I have exposed myself to the ridicule of the tasteful, music-loving multitude. Did this not happen quite recently, when a famous pianist was passing through the town and agreed to play at the house of one of my friends? 'Today, my dear chap', the friend told me, 'you will certainly be cured of your hatred of music. The great Y. will inspire and delight you.' Reluctantly I had to stand next to the piano. The virtuoso began to churn out notes up and down the keyboard, and set up a considerable clamour. As this continued unabated, I felt increasingly dizzy and disconcerted, until suddenly something else caught my attention. I no longer heard the player, and I must have been staring into the piano very strangely, for when the thundering and crashing finally stopped, my friend seized me by the arm and cried 'Look, you've been completely turned to stone! So, my friend, now do you feel the overwhelming effect of such divine music?' Whereupon I had to confess frankly that I had hardly heard the player at all, but instead had been absolutely fascinated by the hammers – the way they sprang up and down in a sort of wave-motion from side to side. At this everyone burst out in peals of laughter.

How often I am called insensitive, heartless, and unfeeling, when I impetuously run out of the room as soon as the fortepiano is opened, or this

---

[255] Hoffmann himself, of course, was a very competent pianist, judging by his own works and view of Beethoven's piano music as presenting 'no great difficulty' in 'mere finger skill' ('Beethoven's Instrumental Music' (I–4)).

or that lady takes up the guitar and clears her throat in order to sing. But I know that when I hear the sort of music they usually perpetrate in their houses, I become quite unwell, and my stomach feels positively queasy. This is a great misfortune, and it brings me the contempt of refined society. I only know that such a voice and such singing as that of my aunt pierces me to the quick, and gives rise to feelings for which I can find no words. It seems to represent bliss itself, rising above all earthly things and thus not capable of expression in earthly terms. And for that very reason I find it quite impossible, when I hear such a singer, to burst out into loud applause like the others; I remain motionless and concentrate on my inner feelings, for they still vibrate with all the sounds that outwardly have died away. And so I am called cold, insensitive, and a music-hater.

Across the street from me lives the concert-master,[256] who has a string quartet at his house every Thursday. In the summertime I can hear their gentle sound, since in the evening, when the street has become quiet, they play with the windows open. On such occasions I sit down on the sofa, close my eyes, and listen in a state of profound bliss – but only to the first piece. By the second quartet the notes already start to become confused, for it seems as though they inwardly clash with the melodies of the first one, which still linger on. But the third one I cannot bear at all; I have to run away, and the concert-master has often laughed at me for letting myself be put to flight by music. I have heard that they play six, sometimes eight quartets, and I really wonder at the extraordinary mental stamina, the inner musical resilience, that can encompass so much music all at once, and, by playing it all exactly as they intuitively feel and understand it, can bring it to pulsating life. I have just the same experience at concerts, where the first symphony often creates such a tumult within me, that I am oblivious of all the rest. Even after the first movement, I am often so excited, so violently shaken, that I long to escape, in order to distinguish more clearly all the strange images by which I am surrounded, and in order to enravel myself in their magical dance, so that among them I become like them. I feel then as though I and the music I have heard are as one. I therefore never ask who the composer was; it seems to me of no importance. It is as though at the point of greatest intensity only one psychical entity is in motion, and as though in that sense I have composed many excellent works myself.

As I write all this down, merely as a private record, so to speak, the

---

[256] concert-master: the violinist-leader of an orchestra. Hoffmann might have been thinking of Anton Dittmayer (1774–1835), the *Konzertmeister* in Bamberg with whom he at first had decisive disagreements concerning the theatre orchestra, but who was later a drinking-companion and played well enough to afford Hoffmann at least some pleasure (see *HTB*, 133).

frightening possibility occurs to me that with my natural unguarded honesty these thoughts might well some time escape my lips. How I would be laughed at! Would not all the real musical hearties doubt the soundness of my mind? Often when I rush from the concert-hall after the first symphony they call after me 'There he goes, the music-hater!' They pity me, because every educated person now rightly expects that as well as decently bowing in the direction of art, and pronouncing upon things one knows nothing about, one should also go in for music. It is my great misfortune that because so many go in, I so often have to go out, driven into solitude where the ever-present forces of nature, in the rustling of oak-leaves above my head, or the splashing of streams below, create magical sounds that mysteriously mingle with the echoes in my mind, and then blaze forth in glorious music.

My painful slowness in coming to grips with music also causes great difficulties at the opera. Sometimes it seems to me that acceptable musical sounds emerge only at infrequent intervals and are useful mainly for staving off boredom or worse horrors, much as cymbals and drums are furiously beaten in front of caravans in order to keep wild animals at bay. But when I feel that the characters could not speak other than in the powerful accents of music, and that a world of prodigies is about to be revealed like a flaming star, then I have great difficulty in controlling myself in the hurricane that seizes me and threatens to hurl me into infinity. To such an opera I will go again and again; it becomes clearer and more transparent in my mind, its characters all emerge from the fog and gloom and move closer to me, and then I recognise them as old friends with whom I advance into their extraordinary world. I must have heard Gluck's *Iphigénie* at least fifty times. Real musicians understandably laugh at that, and say 'We saw it all the first time, and by the third time we'd seen enough.'

I seem to be pursued by a malevolent demon, which causes me to be unintentionally comical, and to provide endless comical stories about my hatred of music. Recently, for example, I was at the Schauspielhaus,[257] where I had gone to oblige a visiting friend, and as the pointless musical noise went on (an opera was being performed) I became completely absorbed in my thoughts. Suddenly my neighbour nudged me and said 'This is a really good section, isn't it?' I thought, and at that moment could not imagine other than that he was referring to the section of the stalls in which we happened to be sitting, and so I answered innocently 'Yes, a very

---

[257] i.e. the Berlin Schauspielhaus, the theatre where Hoffmann's *Undine* was first performed. Destroyed in the Second World War, it has been rebuilt as a concert-hall (standing in East Berlin).

good section, but there's a bit of a draught!' He laughed a great deal, and as an anecdote about the music-hater it had soon spread throughout the whole town. Everywhere I was teased about my draught at the opera, and yet I had been quite right.

Is anyone likely to believe that there is nevertheless one real musician who, with regard to my musical sensibility, is of the same opinion as my aunt? Certainly no one will set much store by it when I say that he is none other than Kapellmeister Johannes Kreisler, who is notorious for his eccentricity. But I flatter myself not a little that he is not above singing and playing to me, to see my inner reaction and how it delights or inspires me. Recently, when I was complaining to him about my musical backwardness, he said that I was rather like the novice in the Temple of Saïs. Apparently inept by comparison with the other pupils, the novice nevertheless found the magic stone which the others with all their diligence had sought in vain. I did not understand him, since I had not read the writings of Novalis, to which he referred me.[258] I have today applied to the lending library, but will probably not be able to obtain the book, since it is said to be extraordinary, and will therefore be in great demand. But no – I have actually just received Novalis's writings, two volumes, and the librarian informs me that there is no hurry to return things like that as they are always on the shelves; he had not been able to find the Novalis immediately since it had been put in a separate place as a book that was obviously never asked for. Now I shall find out what this story is about the novices at Saïs.

---

[258] Novalis, *Die Lehrlinge zu Sais* (*The Novices at Saïs*), published 1802, whose significance for the *Kreisleriana* cycle has been discussed in the Introduction. This novice
> seemed ever sorrowful. Long years he was here; nothing prospered with him. When we searched for crystals or flowers he did not find them easily. With difficulty, too, he saw from a distance; he knew not how to arrange the motley lines in order. He broke everything so easily. Yet no other had such craving and ardour to see and hear ... One day he went out sorrowful. He did not return. Night advanced. We were very anxious on his account. Suddenly, when the glimmer of morning came, we heard his voice in a coppice near ... After a while the singer came upon us, bringing with an expression of ineffable bliss upon his countenance, a dull little stone of curious shape. The Master took it in his hand and kissed his disciple long ...'
>
> (F.V.M.T. and U.C.B. (tr.), *The Disciples at Saïs*, 94–5)

6 On a Remark of Sacchini's, and on so-called Effect in Music[259]

In Gerber's *Tonkünstler-Lexikon* the following story is told about the famous Sacchini.[260] When Sacchini was in London having lunch with Herr Lebrun, the famous oboist,[261] someone repeated in his presence the accusation sometimes levelled by the Germans and French against Italian composers, that they do not modulate enough. 'We do modulate in church music', he said. 'Because the attention is not distracted by theatrical incident, it can more easily follow artistically integrated changes of key. But in the theatre one must be clear and simple; one must touch the heart but not disturb it; and one must make oneself comprehensible to less practised ears. The composer who can write contrasting arias without changing key shows far more talent than the one who changes it every few moments.'

This noteworthy remark of Sacchini's clearly sets out the whole objective of Italian operatic music at that time, and it has remained essentially the same up to the present day. The Italians did not progress to the view that in opera word, action, and music should appear as a unified whole, and that this indivisible whole should create a total impression on the listener. The music was to them more of an incidental accompaniment to the spectacle, and was only now and then allowed to emerge as an independent art creating its own effects.[262] So it was, that when the action actually moved forward, the music was all kept very simple and insignificant, only the *prima donna* and the *primo huomo* in their so-called *scenas* being allowed to stand out in music of significance, or rather truth. But then no regard was paid to the dramatic context, and the aim was merely to display the singing, often merely the singer's technique, to the most brilliant effect.

In opera Sacchini rejects any forceful or upsetting elements, consigning them to the church. In the theatre he will tolerate only agreeable sensations,

---

[259] See the Prefatory Remarks to this essay concerning the specialised meaning of 'Effect' here, where the original word is *Effekt* rather than *Wirkung*.

[260] Antonio Sacchini (1730–86), celebrated composer of opera and church music. See Prefatory Remarks for further details. The anecdote was copied almost verbatim from 'Sacchini' in Ernst Ludwig Gerber, *Historisch-Biographisches Lexicon der Tonkünstler . . . Zweyter Theil* (Leipzig [1792]), cols. 361–2.

[261] Ludwig August Lebrun (1752–90), internationally famous player.

[262] This formulation of traditional opera seria values is indeed not exaggerated. 'The performance of a *dramma per musica* was regarded [in Italy] primarily as the music-dramatic recitation of poetry': Reinhard Strohm, *Essays on Handel and Italian Opera* (Cambridge, 1985), 97.

or rather those which do not move one deeply; he wishes not to be disturbing, but merely to be gently touching. As if opera, by combining its individualised language with the universal language of music, did not by its very nature aim to exert the greatest, most profoundly stirring effect on the mind! Finally, by means of the greatest simplicity, or rather monotony, he wishes to be comprehensible even to the unpractised ear. But it is the composer's highest, or rather most essential aspiration, that by the truth of his expression he moves everyone, and disturbs everyone, as the dramatic context dictates, and that he creates this dramatic context himself, just like the poet. All the resources that the inexhaustible abundance of music offers him are at his command, and he needs them, since they appear as essential components of this expressive truth. Then the most ingenious modulations, with their rapid changes of key at appropriate places, will be comprehensible to the most unpractised ear in a higher sense. That is to say, the layman does not recognise the technical structure, which is not what matters anyway, but he is powerfully swept along by the dramatic momentum. In *Don Giovanni* the statue of the Commendatore intones its terrible 'Yes!' on the tonic E, but the composer then takes this E as the third above C and thus modulates into C major, the key taken up by Leporello.[263] Now no musical layman will understand the technical structure of this transition, but he will tremble inwardly with Leporello; and the musician who has attained the highest level of knowledge is equally unlikely, at the moment of greatest tension, to think of the structure, since for him the scaffolding disappeared long ago, and so his response coincides with that of the layman.

True church music, that which accompanies worship, or rather is itself worship, seems other-worldly, like the language of heaven.[264] Intimations of ultimate reality which enkindle sacred sounds in the breast of man are themselves the ultimate reality, which speaks through the universally comprehensible medium of music of an overwhelmingly wonderful realm of faith and love. The words associated with the singing are only incidental and for the most part contain only pictorial suggestions, such as in the Mass. The leavening of evil, which ferments the emotions, has been left behind in the earthly life we have escaped, and even pain has been dissolved into the intense yearning of eternal love. But does it not follow logically from this that bold modulations expressing a feeling of distraught anxiety are precisely what should be banished from the church, since there they distract and encumber the mind with worldly concerns? Sacchini's remark should therefore be exactly the other way round, even though when he spoke of

---

[263] Mozart, *Don Giovanni*, Act 2 sc. 11, duet no. 22, 'O statua gentilissima', bars 84–5.
[264] These ideas are expanded in the contemporary essay 'Old and New Church Music', p. 355.

more frequent modulation in church music he was thinking only of its greater harmonic richness, since he expressly referred to the composers of his own country, and clearly had the earlier ones in mind.[265] With regard to operatic music he probably also changed his mind after he had heard Gluck's works in Paris, otherwise he would not have composed the powerful and stirring curse scene in *Oedipe à Colone*,[266] which contravenes his own principle.

The truth that opera should appear as a unified whole in word, action, and music was first propounded clearly by Gluck in his works.[267] But what truth has not frequently been misunderstood, thus giving rise to the strangest misconceptions? What masterpieces have not spawned the most absurd products as a result of blind imitation? A weak eye sees the works of great genius like a distorted painting, since it cannot bring them into focus, and it is the disjointed impression of this painting which is then criticised and imitated. Goethe's *Werther* gave rise to the lachrymose sentimentality of its time; his *Götz von Berlichingen*[268] produced crude, empty suits of armour from which hollow voices of dutiful crassness and prosaically vainglorious nonsense rang out. Goethe himself (*Aus meinem Leben. Dichtung und Wahrheit*, Part III) says that the influence of those works came mainly from their material; so one could assert that the influence of Gluck's and Mozart's works, in a purely musical sense and disregarding their librettos, also stemmed only from their material. Attention was directed to the material of the musical structure, and the higher meaning which this material served was not discovered. In this regard it was found, particularly in Mozart's case, that as well as numerous striking modulations, it was also his frequent use of wind instruments that seemed to heighten the astonishing effectiveness of his works; and from this sprang our chaos of overladen orchestration and bizarre, unmotivated modulation. 'Effect' became the watchword of composers, and to create an effect at all costs became the sole objective of

---

[265] i.e. composers whom Hoffmann admired, such as Antonio Caldara (*c.* 1670–1736), Alessandro Scarlatti (1660–1725), and Leonardo Leo (1694–1744), who wrote within the harmonic limitations of the Baroque style.

[266] *Oedipe à Colone. Opéra en trois actes*, libretto by N. F. Guillard (1786), Act 3 sc. 3, in which Polinices, who banished his father Oedipus years earlier, now comes before him to beg his help, having been defeated by his brother, Eteocles. There is an extended sequence of accompanied recitatives, broken by two arias, after which Oedipus curses his two sons even more vehemently than ever.

[267] See Hoffmann's review of Gluck's *Iphigénie en Aulide* (1774), p. 255. Only the 'reform' operas of Gluck are alluded to here, beginning with *Orfeo ed Euridice* (1762) and *Alceste* (1767).

[268] J. W. von Goethe, *Die Leiden des jungen Werthers* (1774), his early novel. *Götz von Berlichingen* (1773), his early Shakespearean play which, like his *Werther*, was an acclaimed product of the *Sturm und Drang* (Storm and Stress) period.

their efforts. But this very striving for effect shows that it was lacking, and could not be made to appear wherever the composer wanted it.

In a word, in order to move us, in order to stir us profoundly, the artist must be affected deeply within his own heart; and the art of composing effectively is to employ the highest possible skill to capture ideas unconsciously conceived in a state of ecstasy, and to write them down in the hieroglyphs of musical sound (notation). If a young artist asks, therefore, how he should set about composing an opera with the maximum effect, one can only give him the following reply. 'Read the libretto, concentrate your mind on it with all your strength, enter into the dramatic situations with all the resources of your imagination; you live in the characters of the drama, you yourself are the tyrant, the hero, the lover; you feel the pain and the joy of love, the humiliation, fear, horror, even the nameless agony of death, and the blissful ecstasy of transfiguration; you brood, you rage, you hope, you despair; your blood races through your veins, your pulse beats faster; from the fire of inspiration that inflames your breast emerge notes, melodies, chords, and the drama flows from within you translated into the magical language of music. Technical proficiency gained from studying harmony, analysing the works of great composers, and from your own composing, will enable you to hear your inner music more and more clearly; no melody, no modulation, no instrument will escape you, and so, simultaneously with the effect, you will conceive the means to achieve it, which you will then commit to the charm-book of the score, like spirits subjugated to your power.' Admittedly all this is only tantamount to saying: just make sure, my dear fellow, that you are a musical genius, and then the rest will take care of itself! But it really is like that, and there is no way round it.

It must nevertheless be assumed that many suppress the true spark they carry within them, since they have no confidence in their own powers, reject any ideas springing from their own inspiration, and anxiously strive to make use of everything they see creating an effect in the works of great composers; thus they are reduced to imitating form, which can never produce spirit, since it is spirit that determines form. The eternal braying of theatre-directors for 'Effect! Only effect!' in order to pull in the audience, as the current theatrical expression has it,[269] and the demands of so-called fastidious connoisseurs, to whom pepper itself is no longer peppery enough, often drive musicians into a sort of hopeless desperation to outdo earlier composers in their effects wherever possible. This is how curious compo-

---

[269] cf. *Prinzessin Blandina*, 'Zwischenszene hinter dem Theater' before sc. 8: 'The Theatre Director: . . . I have told you already, I will have nothing aesthetic on my stage – my stage shall not be aesthetic.'

sitions arise in which without any motivation – that is to say without the context of the drama providing the slightest justification for it – crude changes of key and blaring chords from every conceivable wind instrument follow in rapid succession, like garish colours that never coalesce into a picture. The composer[270] is like a man in a profound sleep who is repeatedly woken up by violent hammer-blows, but then keeps going back to sleep again. Composers of this sort are absolutely amazed when, despite the pains they have put themselves to, their works utterly fail to produce the effect they had imagined. They certainly do not realise that the music that was created by their own imagination and flowed spontaneously from within them, but seemed to them too simple or too empty, would probably have been infinitely more effective. Their anxiety and lack of confidence blinded them and prevented them from properly appreciating the masterpieces they took as models; they became preoccupied by technical resources, seeing them as the means whereby effect was obtained. But as already pointed out, it is the untrammelled spirit which commands the resources, and exercises total authority in those works; only the music-drama[271] that has emanated sincerely and powerfully from the heart can then enter into the listener's heart. The spirit comprehends only the language of the spirit.

To lay down rules for bringing forth effect in music may well be impossible, therefore; but a composer at odds with himself and wandering astray as though dazzled by will-o'-the-wisps can be brought back on course by a few guiding suggestions.

The first and foremost element in music is melody, which seizes the human imagination with magical power. It cannot be said often enough, that without expressive, singable melody any instrumental colour is merely glistering apparel, not adorning any living body, but hanging on a line as in Shakespeare's *Tempest*,[272] and appealing to the mindless rabble. Singable, understood in the higher sense of the word, is an excellent adjective with which to describe true melody. It must itself be song, and must issue in a free and unforced flow directly from the human breast, which is the instrument that resounds with the most magical and mysterious sounds of nature. Melody that is not singable in this sense is nothing but a series of separate notes striving in vain to become music. It is incredible how in recent times, particularly following the example of a misunderstood com-

---

[270] Hoffmann particularly thinks of Gaspare Spontini. See Prefatory Remarks.

[271] music-drama: Hoffmann's neologism (*Tongedicht*) seems not to have been used by him before. In his review of *Iphigénie en Aulide* he has 'true musical drama' ('wahre musikalische Drama').

[272] *The Tempest*, Act 4 sc. 1, where Prospero catches Caliban, Stephano and Trinculo using this means.

poser (Cherubini),[273] melody has actually been neglected, and as a result of the constant struggle to be original and striking a number of music-dramas have appeared that are utterly unsingable. How is it that the simple arias of the earlier Italians, often accompanied only by a continuo, move and elevate the spirit so irresistibly? Does the explanation not lie entirely in their sublime, truly singing melody? Melody is in fact the undisputed, native property of that passionately musical people, and the German, if he has arrived at a higher, or rather at a proper view of opera, should become familiar with their spirits in every way he possibly can, so that they do not disdain to kindle melodies in his soul as by some magical power. An excellent example of this deep familiarity is given by that great master of art, Mozart, in whom Italian melody burned brightly. What composer wrote in a more singable style than he? Even without orchestral gloss, every one of his melodies makes a profound impression, and this explains the extraordinary effect of his compositions.

With regard to modulation, only the dramatic context can provide a justification for this; it should proceed from the various impulses aroused in the spirit. These can be gentle, strong, overpowering, gradually burgeoning, or suddenly gripping. Similarly the composer, who possesses the mysterious knowledge of harmony as a munificent gift of nature, so that technical study merely provides him with the means of consciously applying it, will move now to related, now to remote keys, now gradually, now at a stroke. The true genius does not presume to impress by artificial artistry, which becomes painful non-art; he merely follows the dictates of his inner spirit, as it translates the dramatic situations into music. Let the musical mathematicians then draw their examples from his works, and use them as practical exercises. It would lead too far to discuss the profound art of harmony here, and to show how it is rooted deeply inside us and how to those with sharper vision mysterious laws are revealed that no text-book contains. Let it suffice to point out, in order to draw attention to one particular circumstance, that abrupt changes of key are of great effect only when despite their heterogeneity the keys have an underlying relationship apparent to the mind of a musician.[274] The passage mentioned earlier,

---

[273] Luigi Cherubini (1760–1842), known at this time chiefly for his operas composed for Paris, where he settled from 1786. These broke new ground in their internal design and musical language: *Lodoiska* (1791), *Médée* (1797), *Les Deux journées* (1800), etc. Hoffmann's approval of Cherubini appears already in the review of Weigl's *Das Waisenhaus* (p. 255), though six years later he criticised him for over-seriousness, intricateness and gloominess (review of J. P. Schmidt's *Die Alpenhütte*). Hoffmann's review of Méhul's *Ariodant* also mentions Cherubini (p. 406).

[274] Hoffmann is still thinking of Spontini, whose adventurous modulations sometimes remind the modern hearer of his later admirer, Berlioz.

from the duet in *Don Giovanni*, may also serve as an example of this. Also to be included here are enharmonic modulations,[275] often ridiculed for being misused, but containing that underlying relationship, and frequently producing an undoubtedly powerful effect. It is as though a hidden, sympathetic bond often connected the most remotely separated keys, and as though under certain circumstances an insuperable idiosyncrasy separated even the most closely related keys. The most common and most frequent modulation of all, that from the tonic to the dominant, or vice versa, can seem at times unexpected and unusual, even unpleasant and unbearable.

It is true that a large part of the disturbing effect often produced by the inspired works of great composers comes from their orchestration. Here too, however, it is hardly possible to venture even a single rule; for this department of the musical art is enveloped in mystical darkness. Every instrument, whatever its distinctive effect in a particular instance, is capable of a hundred others, and it is a foolish delusion to suppose, for example, that strength and power can be expressed only by them all playing together. A single note sounded by this or that instrument can often produce inner turmoil. Many passages in Gluck's operas provide conspicuous examples of this, and in order to appreciate fully the variety of effect of which every instrument is capable, one need only think of the heterogeneous effects that Mozart draws from the same instrument – the oboe for example. Only a few indications are possible here.

To return to the comparison between music and painting,[276] a music-drama will appear in the artist's mind like a finished canvas, and as he contemplates it the correct perspective, without which no truth is possible, will automatically become apparent. Orchestration also includes the various accompanying instrumental figures, and how often one of these figures, genuinely derived from within, raises expressive truth to the highest power! How deeply affecting, for example, is the steady figure played in octaves by the second violins and violas in Mozart's aria 'Non mi dir, bell'idol mio'.[277] With regard to figures, nothing can be artificially concocted or grafted on; the brilliant colours of a music-drama highlight the smallest detail, and any

---

[275] Enharmonic modulations: see II–3, note 226; these involve something analogous to a pun in musical harmony, i.e. a double significance that can be interpreted only in retrospect. The chord A flat minor in 'Kreisler's Musico-Poetic Club' is silently re-interpreted (according to theory) as signifying G sharp minor in order to gain legitimate access to the new chord of E major. See also the review of Beethoven's Piano Trio Op. 70 No. 2, p. 318, and Ex. XVII.

[276] The comparison, that is, between crude timbres and modulations and 'garish colours that never coalesce into a picture'. See also the penultimate fragment of 'Extremely Random Thoughts' (I–5).

[277] *Don Giovanni*, Act 2 sc. 12, aria of Donna Anna.

extraneous embellishment would only destroy rather than beautify. It is the same with the choice of key, with forte and piano (which proceed from the underlying character of the work and should not be introduced just for the sake of variety), and with all the other means of expression at the musician's disposal.

One can absolutely assure the hapless composer grimly striving for effect that so long as genius resides in him, his thorough acquaintance with the works of the masters will soon give him a mysterious rapport with their spirit, and that this will arouse his latent powers, even induce a state of ecstasy, in which he awakens as from torpid sleep into new life, and perceives the extraordinary sounds of his own inner music. Then his study of harmony and his technical exercises will give him the ability to grasp hold of the music that would otherwise rush past him; and the inspiration that gives birth to the work will powerfully seize the listener with its magical resonance, so that he partakes of the bliss enveloping the musician during those sacramental hours. This, therefore, is the genuine effect achieved by a music-drama that springs from the heart.

7 Johannes Kreisler's Certificate of Apprenticeship

Since you are now really intent, my dear Johannes, on leaving your apprenticeship with me and finding your own way in the wider world, it is proper for me, as your master, to slip a certificate of apprenticeship into your bag, which you can present to any musical guild or society as a passport. I could certainly provide one without further ado, but as I look at you in the mirror I become distinctly melancholy at heart. I would like to recall with you once more everything we have thought and felt together at particular times during your years of apprenticeship. I am sure you know what I mean. But since we possess the common failing that when one speaks the other cannot keep his mouth shut, it is probably better if I write down some of it at least, like an overture as it were,[278] and you can then read it occasionally for the good of your soul.

---

[278] overture: Hoffmann plays on the three aspects of an opera overture as (i) written last of all, (ii) containing the essence of the material in its parent opera, (iii) serving as a prelude – here to Kreisler's departure into the world. See I–5, fourth and also final fragments.

Ah my dear Johannes! Who knows you better than I? Who has gazed more deeply into your heart, and even from your heart, than I? And therefore I believe that you know me completely, and that as a result our relationship was always tolerable, even though we exchanged the most contradictory views about each other; we thought ourselves at times extraordinarily wise, even gifted with genius, but at other times quite silly and ignorant, even slightly stupid. You see, my dear wandering scholar, although I used the word 'we' in the previous sentence, I feel as though in modestly using the plural I was actually speaking of myself in the singular, as though the two of us were in fact only *one*. Let us tear ourselves free of this absurd delusion! So once again, my dear Johannes! Who knows you better than I? And who can affirm with greater authority, therefore, that you have now achieved that mastery which is necessary in order to begin your really specialised learning?

What appears to be chiefly necessary has already become part of you. You have sharpened your faculty of hearing to such an extent that now and then you perceive the voice of the poet hidden within you (in the words of Schubert)* and really cannot believe that it is only you speaking and no one else.

One warm July night, I was sitting alone on a mossy bank in that jasmine bower which you know, when the quiet, good-natured young man we call Chrysostomus came along and told me a remarkable story from his childhood. 'My father's small garden', he began, 'bordered on a forest bursting with music and song. Year in and year out a nightingale nested there in a magnificent old tree, below which lay a large rock covered with all kinds of strange mosses and reddish-coloured veins. The story that my father told about this rock sounded just like a fairy-tale. Many, many years before, apparently, an unknown but handsome-looking man, unusual in figure and dress, came to the nobleman's castle. The stranger struck everyone as very extraordinary; one could not look at him for long without an inner shudder, but then one could not turn one's spell-bound gaze away from him. The nobleman soon took a great liking to him, although he often confessed that he felt rather uncomfortable in his presence, and that ice-cold shivers ran

---

* Schubert's *Die Symbolik des Traumes*.[279]

[279] Gotthilf Heinrich Schubert, *Die Symbolik des Traumes*, which Hoffmann ordered from C. F. Kunz, its publisher. In 1813 Hoffmann had ordered Schubert's *Ansichten von der Nachtseite der Naturwissenschaften (Opinions Concerning the Nocturnal Side of the Natural Sciences)* (Dresden, 1808). Hoffmann now continues with the fable of Chrysostomus, who learns to heed his own 'hidden poet'. On the significance of 'Chrysostomus', see the Introduction, p. 39.

through him whenever the stranger, over a full cup of wine, spoke of the many distant and unknown lands and strange men and beasts he had become acquainted with during his far-flung travels. At such times his speech faded into an incantatory drone, in which he wordlessly rendered obscure and mysterious things comprehensible.

'No one could tear himself away from the stranger, or listen often enough to his stories, which in an unfathomable way brought vague, shapeless imaginings before the mind's eye in a clear, recognisable form. And when the stranger sang to his lute all sorts of amazing songs in unknown languages, all those who heard him were transfixed as if by some supernatural power, and they said he could not be a man but must be an angel, who had brought to earth music from the heavenly concert of cherubim and seraphim. The beautiful young daughter of the castle became completely wrapped up in the stranger's mysterious, irresistible spell. He gave her lessons in singing and playing the lute, and within a short time they were on very familiar terms with each other; the stranger would often steal out at midnight to the old tree, where the girl would be waiting for him. Then in the far distance one could hear their singing and the fading notes of the stranger's lute, but their melodies sounded so strange and ghostly that no one dared to approach or betray the lovers.

'Suddenly one morning the stranger was gone, and a search was made for the girl through the whole castle, but in vain. Seized by tormenting anxiety and presentiments of horror, her father leapt onto his horse and raced towards the forest calling out his daughter's name in despairing misery. When he came to the rock where the stranger had so often sat and exchanged tender words with the girl at midnight, the mane of his valiant steed stiffened; the beast snuffled and snorted, and as if bewitched by some demon of hell, refused to stir from the spot. The nobleman thought his horse had been frightened by the weird shape of the rock, and he therefore dismounted in order to lead it past. With a sudden spasm of horror, however, his heart stopped and he stood paralysed, as he noticed bright gouts of blood copiously dripping from the rock. As though endowed with superhuman strength, the huntsmen and peasants who had followed the nobleman heaved the rock to one side with great difficulty; beneath it they found the poor girl, her body covered with stab-wounds and hurriedly buried, and beside her the splintered remains of the stranger's lute. Every year after that, a nightingale nested in the tree, and at midnight it sang lamenting melodies that pierced the heart. And from the blood sprang strange mosses and wild flowers that bedecked the rock with incredible colours.

'Since I was still quite a young boy, I was not allowed to go into the forest without my father's permission, but the tree, and especially the rock, drew me there irresistibly. Whenever the gate in our garden wall was not locked, I would slip out to my beloved rock, and I never tired of gazing at its mosses and flowers, which formed the strangest patterns. I often felt that I understood their significance, and it seemed as though I could see illustrated in them, with appropriate explanations, all sorts of exciting tales like those my mother had told me. Then again, as I looked at the rock, I could not help thinking of the beautiful song that my father sang almost every day, accompanying himself on a harpsichord, and it always moved me so deeply that I forgot my favourite toys and could only listen with heavy tears in my eyes. Similarly, on hearing the song I thought of my beloved mosses, and soon the two seemed to be one and the same, and I was hardly able to separate the one from the other in my mind.

'At that time my love of music grew stronger every day, and my father, a good musician himself, took it upon himself to give me some careful instruction. He hoped to make not only a competent player out of me but also a composer, since I was always so keen to pick out melodies and chords on the piano, some of which were quite expressive and coherent. But often I could have wept bitterly with frustration and despair, and wanted never to touch the piano again, for whenever I pressed down the keys it turned out to be different from what I intended. Nameless melodies that I had never heard before teemed in my head. At such times I felt that it was no longer my father's song that was preserved in the mysterious symbols of the moss, but these melodies that echoed around me like spirit-voices; I felt that if one contemplated these symbols in a spirit of sincere love, the young girl's songs would issue forth with the graceful plangency of her own voice. And indeed it often happened that as I gazed at the rock, I drifted into a waking dream, and heard the girl's extraordinary singing, which filled my breast with the exquisite pain of ecstasy. But as soon as I tried to sing the songs myself, or play them on the piano, everything I had so clearly heard dissolved into confused uncertainty. After my first childish attempt, I often locked the instrument and listened to see if the melodies would emerge with greater clarity and brilliance, for I knew that the notes must somehow be contained within it, as if under a magic spell. I became quite inconsolable, and when I finally had to play my father's songs and exercises, which I now found odious and unbearable, I could have died with impatience. As a result I neglected all my technical study of music, and my father, despairing of my ability, completely abandoned the lessons.

'Later on, at the school in the town, my enthusiasm for music was awakened in a different way. The technical skill of several pupils inspired me to emulate them. I went to great pains, but the more mechanical mastery I acquired, the less I was able to detect again that music whose sublime melodies had previously echoed in my mind. The musical director of the school, an old man and, so it was said, a great contrapuntist, gave me lessons in figured bass and composition. He even tried to give me guidance in inventing melodies, and I felt greatly pleased with myself when I had concocted a theme that yielded to all the various contrapuntal procedures. So when after a few years I returned to my village, I fancied myself to be a complete musician. There in my room still stood the little old piano at which I had spent so many nights and shed so many tears of frustration. I also saw the magic rock again, but now that I was so much wiser, I laughed at my childish absurdity in trying to *see* melodies in its covering of moss. Yet I could not deny that the mysterious, lonely spot under the tree surrounded me with the strangest intimations. Lying in the grass, or leaning against the rock, when the wind rustled through the tree's leaves, I often heard a sound like that of gentle spirit-voices; the melodies they sang had long lain dormant in my breast, and now they came to life afresh!

'How shallow and insipid all my compositions now appeared; they seemed hardly like music at all, and all my efforts were the meaningless strivings of an insignificant nobody. But the dream revealed to me its realm of shimmering splendours and I was comforted. I gazed at the rock; its red veins twisted upwards like dark carnations whose fragrance rose visibly into the air in an aura of bright sound. In the long swelling phrases of the nightingale the aura took on the form of a mysterious female apparition, but then again it was the apparition of heavenly music!'

As I am sure you realise, my dear Johannes, this story told by young Chrysostomus certainly contains many lessons, which is why it finds a worthy place in this certificate of apprenticeship. How forcibly the higher power that awakened him reached out from a remote and fabulous age into his own life.[280]

Our kingdom is not of this world, say musicians, for where in nature do we find the prototypes for our art, as painters and sculptors do? Sound resides in all things; but notes, that is to say melodies, which speak the higher language of the spirit-realm, repose only in the breast of men. But like the spirit of sound, does not the spirit of music also permeate the whole of nature? A sounding body, when it is mechanically animated and thus brought to life, gives expression to its existence, or rather its inner organism consciously emerges.[281] Cannot the spirit of music, when it is awakened by

---

[280] The 'remote and fabulous age' must be connected with the 'Isis-headed sphinx' seen in the frontispiece to the first edition of the *Fantasiestücke*, figure 1. Further consideration of the meaning of the fable of Chrysostomus appears in the Introduction.

[281] In this section Hoffmann gives scientific evidence for his philosophy of Romantic composition. Cf. Johann Wilhelm Ritter (1776–1810), *Fragmente*, i, 162, §250: 'Every sounding body, or rather its note, is as it were the coloured shadow of its inner quality.'

its votaries, similarly express itself melodically and harmonically in secret resonances intelligible only to them? Musicians, that is to say those in whom music becomes a condition of total awareness, are surrounded on all sides by melody and harmony. It is no empty metaphor, no allegory, when the musician says that colour, fragrance, light appear to him as sounds, and that in their intermingling he perceives an extraordinary concert. Just as hearing, in the words of a brilliant physicist, is seeing from within,[282] so to the musician seeing is hearing from within, attainable only through the profoundest awareness of music, which radiates from everything his eye falls upon, and vibrates in sympathy with his spirit. Thus the musician's sudden inspirations, the burgeoning of melodies within him, the processes of recognising and assimilating the secret music of nature, which is unconscious or at least not definable in words, become the guiding principles of his life and all his activities. The audible sounds of nature, the sighing of the wind, the rushing of streams, and so on, are perceived by the musician first as individual chords and then as melodies with harmonic accompaniment. As recognition grows, so does his personal will, and may not the musician then behave towards the natural world surrounding him like the mesmerist towards his patient, since his active will is the question which nature never leaves unanswered?[283]

The keener and more penetrating his recognition becomes, the higher the musician stands as a composer, and the art of composing consists in his ability to seize upon his inspirations with special mental powers and to conjure them into signs and symbols. These powers are the product of a musical training directed towards producing the symbols (notation) spontaneously and fluently. In any individual language, there is such an intimate connection between sound and word that no idea can arise in us without its hieroglyphs (letters of the alphabet).[284] But music is a universal language of

---

[282] Ritter, *Fragmente*, i, 224, §358. In this paragraph Ritter is discussing the fundamental superiority of the sense of hearing, for through subtle vibrations we sense changes of place, etc., and we know instinctively what is changing around us through 'a thousand chemical, electrical and magnetic processes'. For Coleridge's reaction to this passage see p. 74.

[283] Ritter, *Fragmente*, ii, 232, comparing the activating of any sounding body, which is impelled to respond, with the action of a mesmerist upon a human subject. These ideas must be understood in relation to the popular experiments in 'animal magnetism', using mesmerism, and also to Hoffmann's imaginative treatment of such ideas. 'Such extensions of the magnetic theory account for a multitude of puzzling phenomena, such as clairvoyance, thought-transference, and presentiments': Hewett-Thayer, *Hoffmann*, 171–2. But Schubert, *Die Symbolik des Traumes*, 24, also says: 'The anonymous philosopher (of the *Esprit des choses humaines*) seems correct, therefore, to compare Nature to a sleepwalker, a teller of dreams, who everywhere acts from her own inner necessity.'

[284] Ritter, *Fragmente*, ii, 228; but whereas Ritter goes on to consider music as a universal language of men, Hoffmann goes in a quite different direction.

nature; it speaks to us in magical and mysterious resonances; we strive in vain to conjure these into symbols, and any artificial arrangement of hieroglyphs provides us with only a vague approximation of what we have distantly heard.

With these few words of wisdom I now deliver you, my dear Johannes, at the gates of the Temple of Isis, so that you might study diligently. You will be well aware that I consider you capable of taking up a genuinely musical course of instruction. Show this certificate of apprenticeship to those who, perhaps without fully realising it, stand at the gates beside you. And to those who do not know what to make of the story of the evil stranger and the noble young lady, explain its point: that the extraordinary adventure that exerted such an influence on the life of Chrysostomus is a telling allegory of earthly extinction by the evil workings of hostile powers, of the demonic misuse of music, but finally of the ascent to higher things and of transfiguration through music and song!

And now, good masters and journeymen assembled before the doors of the great workshop, kindly accept Johannes into your midst, and do not hold it against him that while you wish only to doze, he dares now and then perhaps to beat gently at the door. And do not take it amiss that when you write your hieroglyphs so clearly and neatly, he occasionally mixes in his scrawl among them; he would also like his handwriting to benefit from your example.

Fare thee well, my dear Johannes Kreisler! I have the feeling I will not see you again! Should you find that I am no more, then after you have duly mourned for me, like Hamlet for the deceased Yorick, erect for me a peaceful *Hic jacet*, together with a

This cross will also serve as a great seal to my certificate of apprenticeship. And so I, like you, sign myself,

Johannes Kreisler,
cidevant Kapellmeister

The Poet and the Composer

INTRODUCTION TO *THE POET AND THE COMPOSER*: HOFFMANN AND OPERA

This celebrated dialogue, composed between 19 September and 9 October 1813, dates from the period broadly separating the writing of Parts I and II of *Kreisleriana*. Hoffmann planned at one stage to use it in *Fantasiestücke*, Volume iii: in his letter of 16 January 1814 he wrote of including 'Scenes from the Lives of Two Friends', in three or four parts, the 'friends' presumably being Ludwig (the composer) and Ferdinand (the poet), who also appear in the story *Die Automate*. The *Allgemeine Musikalische Zeitung* first published *The Poet and the Composer* in vol. xv, issues 49 and 50 (8 and 15 December, 1813); it was unsigned.

Had the dialogue appeared in *Fantasiestücke*, it would have complemented well *Ritter Gluck*, *Don Juan*, and parts of *Kreisleriana*, especially 'On a Remark of Sacchini's, and on so-called Effect in Music'. There is thus no particular need for puzzlement that 'Hoffmann does not mention *Don Giovanni*', for example.[1] Nevertheless, the idea of a grouping of semifictional, semi-critical musical writings stayed in Hoffmann's mind, and provided him with the plan for the opening of the prose collection known as *Die Serapions-Brüder*, Volume i, first issued in 1819. In Alexander Ewing's translation (now over a century old), the contents appear as follows:

> *The Serapion Brethren*: Section 1
> 'The Story of Serapion'
> 'The Story of Krespel' [*Rat Krespel*: Hoffmann never gave this tale a
> title]
> 'An Interrupted Cadence' [*Die Fermate*]
> 'The Poet and the Composer' [*Der Dichter und der Komponist*]

The dialogue with which we are concerned thus appeared immediately after a story written and published originally in 1815 (*HTB*, 262–4 and 468), but

---

[1] Aubrey S. Garlington, Jr, 'E. T. A. Hoffmann's "Der Dichter und der Komponist" and the Creation of the German Romantic Opera', *Musical Quarterly*, lxv (1979), 40. This article is essentially an expository piece, limited to the text in question.

with the addition of framing material spoken by the four Serapion 'brothers' themselves.

Lothar, Theodor, and Cyprian represent, generally speaking, delicately graded aspects of Hoffmann's own personality: Lothar is more realistic in his views and is somewhat inclined to scepticism; Theodor is Hoffmann the musician, and Cyprian is an out-and-out romantic and mystic. Ottmar is Hoffmann's old friend [Julius Eduard] Hitzig, more of a realist, more sceptical than Lothar; he is ever calling his companions back to earth.[2]

The idea of such a framework for various writings arose most proximately from Ludwig Tieck's *Phantasus* (1812, 1816), where the reading of stories and plays 'is accompanied by discussion on the part of the whole company'.[3] In Hoffmann's case, too, each reading is made the subject of discussion, but is anchored also to the concept of the 'Serapiontic principle', which the friends discuss after 'The Story of Krespel'. Just as Serapion, the hermit in Cyprian's tale, believed he was actually the martyred Saint Serapion, and defied anyone to prove he was not (thus illustrating the superiority of the imagination over the outer world), so the friends vow to tell only that which they have fully experienced within themselves, and grasped 'in every one of its forms, colours, lights and shadows'.[4] This, of course, is a theory which relates to ideas in *Kreisleriana*, for example the passage asserting that *Don Giovanni* was 'all laid out and complete in [Mozart's] mind in all its wonderfully distinctive detail . . . before its great composer took up his pen to write it out' (p. 106).

Although the 1813 text of *The Poet and the Composer* was almost completely retained in 1819, the framing discussions added a major region of ambiguity. Theodor, the narrator, becomes a third voice in the imaginary Chinese box of authorial *personas*: Hoffmann→Theodor→Ludwig. Whereas in 1813 the anonymous presentation of the dialogue threw the sole attention upon Ludwig (music) and Ferdinand (words) in such a way as to make them almost into metaphors for music and words themselves, in creative conflict, the presence of discussion offers the chance of different perspectives. And the discussion ultimately focuses not on what Romantic opera should be, but whether it should be written by two separate persons at all. Lothar's last speech points strongly towards a new departure in Hoffmann's thought, as does Lothar's belief that 'music and word [should] flow

[2] Hewett-Thayer, *Hoffmann*, 101–2. Hitzig will be mentioned later in this Introduction.

[3] Hewett-Thayer, *Hoffmann*, 101. *Phantasus* is quoted in the Prefatory Remarks to 'Old and New Church Music', p. 352.

[4] *The Serapion Brethren*, tr. Ewing, i, 52.

from the inspired poet and composer at the *same* instant' (p. 189), a notion
that we shall return to later in this Introduction.

In the month prior to the composition of *The Poet and the Composer*,
Hoffmann had witnessed several bloody turning-points in European history
leading towards 'The Battle of the Nations', and a word here concerning
political events is needed, both in order to place the opening and the closing
sections of the main dialogue in perspective, and to understand a central
theme of the text.

Following Napoleon's disastrous march on Moscow during the winter of
1812–13 a new coalition was formed against him, including Britain, Russia,
Prussia, Sweden, Spain, and Portugal. But Saxony and Austria were still on
the French side, and thus Dresden (Saxony's capital city) became the main
theatre of war. When Hoffmann first moved to Dresden in April 1813, he
found it already full of allied military personnel, who by May were vacating
the city in favour of Napoleon. The bombardments began, and Hoffmann
wrote for the first time of seeing injury and death (letter of 10 May). Life
became profoundly abnormal, even when he went temporarily with his
opera company to Leipzig, since the military truce there did not preclude
bloodshed (letter of 13 July). On 11 August Austria declared war on
Napoleon, and each side took up positions around Dresden. Eight days
later Hoffmann reported:

. . . everything is in a state of extreme tension, and heaven knows what is going to
happen to us. We rely entirely on the fortune of Napoleon's arms – otherwise we are
lost. By the way, I am going to move into the city, for my little house lies very
conveniently in the firing-line of an important entrenchment. At this moment of
writing (midnight), cavalry is arriving to bivouac on the whole street in front of my
window, and my landlady has to cook for twenty men.
                            (Adapted from Sahlin, 203–4; *HBW*, i, 409.)

There followed the battle of Dresden itself (26–27 August), a victory for
Napoleon, which Hoffmann watched closely, visiting the battlefield; but
even in the city 'the earth shook and the windows rattled' (letter of 1
December). Napoleon's defeat at 'The Battle of the Nations' at Leipzig
came on 18 October, and Dresden saw desperate rearguard actions on the
part of the French.

Events such as those with which Theodor opens *The Poet and the
Composer* were experienced directly by Hoffmann and his civilian countrymen, and the glow of victory present in the Serapiontic epilogue should not

deflect attention from the fact that what the author is vitally concerned with is the relation between the outer life (action; politics; war) and the inner life (reflection; theory; art). War forced Hoffmann to push himself harder: 'At no other time has writing so appealed to me'; the emergence of the inner life 'removes me from the pressures of life outside' (letter of 19 August). But war also became for him a confirmation of one of his abiding beliefs as a Romantic artist: that he must express 'the influence of higher natures on our lives', an influence which provokes understanding of 'a romantic dimension' (pp. 196–7). The mighty events, the unexpected sights, the experiences of horrors: all these outer phenomena are expressed in Theodor's opening section as a demonstration of the reality of Hoffmann's Romantic theory of opera, which finds expression in the main dialogue. In fact, we can see this parallel in Theodor's first paragraph, for just as Ludwig's symphony sought, like 'one of those [romantic, Beethovenian] wonders . . . to penetrate our narrow, paltry lives', so too war penetrates the lives of the city inhabitants, somehow giving their narrowness ('Tenants who scarcely raised their hats when meeting on the stairs') an almost miraculous transformation, as they sit 'revealing their innermost feelings in mutual warm-heartedness'. In Hoffmann's conception of Romantic opera even characters in contemporary costume may be portrayed, so long as a 'bizarre fluctuation of fortune boldly invades everyday life and turns everything topsy-turvy' (p. 202). Romantic art, or rather opera as a unified expression of Romantic art at its most potent, stands thus in a very clear philosophical relation to contemporary life for Hoffmann. This concrete concern is easy to relate to the tendency of *Kreisleriana* to consider Romantic music and theatre from their practical aspects: while the Philistines use music as a social commodity, the 'true' musician or music-lover understands the relevance of 'real' music as an expression of transcendental reality, and as a transcendental expression of surrounding nature. It reveals those same 'higher natures' as does genuine Romantic opera.

The closing paragraphs of the dialogue express identical anxieties about the fate of art in a time of upheaval to those found in the author's private letters, and also in one of the most memorable fragments of *Kreisleriana*:

What artist has ever troubled himself with the political events of the day anyway? . . . But a dark and unhappy age has seized men with its iron fist, and the pain squeezes from them sounds [i.e. music] that were formerly alien to them.

(p. 111)

Ferdinand then offers a poetic rationale of upheaval, couched in terms of an elemental Nature that herself embodies the 'higher natures' ruling men's lives. This conception of nature appears at the close of *Kreisleriana*, and is discussed in the Prefatory Remarks to 'Johannes Kreisler's Certificate of Apprenticeship'. But the rhetorical crescendo placed in the mouth of Ferdinand has a deeper significance, revealed in Hoffmann's vocabulary. With the revelation of 'eternal omnipotence', 'The golden gates are open, and art and science kindle in a single incandescence all the holy aspirations that unite mankind into a single church.' This can be understood both as an anticipation of victory for German-speaking peoples, and as a metaphor for the truth of the musico-poetic process outlined earlier:

> *Ludwig:* . . . in that far realm which often envelops us in curious presentiments . . . poets and musicians are closely kindred members of *one* church; for the secret of words and sounds [*Ton*] is one and the same, unveiling to both the ultimate sublimity.
>
> (p. 195)

In life or in Romantic art (opera), the consciousness of a transcendent reality draws together the different elements; Ferdinand responds, 'I do begin to see the gap ceasing to exist.' This subtle and bold interfusing of the outer and inner worlds lives in the text also by virtue of its intrinsic dynamism. That is, Ludwig speaks with an intensity of enthusiasm which is like an allegory of the action of music itself. But Ferdinand speaks with the heavy, duller phrases that are like an allegory of the dampening influence of words in the type of opera that Hoffmann wishes to rise above. As Ferdinand rises towards understanding of Ludwig, his very language becomes more flexible. Hoffmann's prose becomes, as it were, the dramatisation of a creative process, just as in 'Kreisler's Musico-Poetic Club' (p. 132) his prose dramatises the process of spontaneous musical composition.

Hoffmann's word 'Poet' (*Dichter*) implies 'writer of literature', as against 'collaborator in an opera'; all opera librettos were versified at this period, in their sung portions at least. As though to express his fluid attitude to the text, he always used a variety of terms for it: *Gedicht, Oper, Operntext, Operngedicht.*

'Opera' meant no one single type of theatre in 1813. The art-form had paid the price of popularity in Germany by becoming quite heterogeneous.

In the last decade of the eighteenth century, the sway foreign operas held over nearly all German stages grew even stronger . . . North German librettists and composers rethought the dramaturgic and aesthetic bases of their own operatic traditions, drinking deep draughts of the foreign operatic elixir around them, and began trying to produce new German operas more in step with popular taste.[5]

---

5   Thomas Bauman, *North German Opera in the Age of Goethe* (Cambridge, 1985), 261.

Comedy, history, the exotic, the supernatural – all had entered opera in the 1780s, so that the paraphernalia of the Romantic stage had begun to take root. But the relentless importation continued. 'Foreign elixirs' included Mozart's later operas (for example, *Die Zauberflöte*, *Don Giovanni*, *Die Entführung aus dem Serail*, *Così fan tutte*, *La clemenza di Tito*, which were among the ten most-performed operas at the Weimar Court Theatre between 1791 and 1817);[6] included Italian works by Paisiello, Cimarosa, Salieri, and Righini (twelve operas by these composers were given out of a total of thirty-five operas on the Berlin stage in 1798–99);[7] and also the continuing influx of Parisian works by Cherubini, Méhul, and others, following on older works by Grétry and Dalayrac. German composers and librettists could hardly be blamed for not knowing which way to turn. The mixture can be seen as well in the operas conducted by Hoffmann in 1813. German-language works tended to come from Viennese-based composers (Wenzel Müller, Paul Wranitzky, F. X. Süssmayr, P. von Winter, Josef Weigl) and to be domestic in scale.[8] Some insight into their typical content is provided in Hoffmann's 1810 review of Weigl's *Das Waisenhaus* (*The Orphanage*; see below, p. 252) and his 1812 review of Gyrowetz's *Der Augenarzt* (*The Oculist*; see p. 293), which was in his 1813 repertory.

Hoffmann also conducted French and Italian works. From Parisian composers there were Cherubini's *Les deux journées* (a humanitarian rescue story), *Faniska* (another rescue, written for Vienna) and *Lodoiska* (an adventure plot, dating back to 1791); Méhul's *Joseph* (the Biblical story, which did not attract Hoffmann's critical attention), *Héléna* (a kind of mediaeval detective story), and *Une Folie* (a comedy); Solié's *Le Secret*; Isouard's *Cendrillon* (Cinderella); Dalayrac's *Le Château de Monténéro* (another old adventure story); and Grétry's perennial tale of beauty and the beast, *Zémire et Azor*, now over forty years old. From Italy came scores by Salieri, Paer, and others.

Against this sort of background Hoffmann's Ludwig therefore asserts:

Most so-called operas are merely inane plays with singing added, and the total lack of dramatic force, imputed now to the libretto, now to the music, is entirely attribu-

6   *Ibid.*, 263.
7   Raraty, 'Hoffmann and the Theatre', 60.
8   W. Müller: *Der alte Überall und Nirgends*; *Der Geisterseher, oder Das Neusonntagskind*; P. Wranitzky: *Oberon*; G. B. Bierey: *Rosette*; F. H. Himmel: *Fanchon*; F. X. Süssmayr: *Die edle Rache*; J. Weigl: *Die Schweizerfamilie*; H. C. Ebell: *Das Hochzeitfest im Eichthale*; F. L. Kunzen: *Das Fest der Winzer*; A. Gyrowetz: *Der Augenarzt*; P. von Winter: *Marie von Montalban*; J. Schenk: *Der Dorfbarbier*; A. Bergt: *Das Dorf im Gebirge*. Works by Mozart were also given. See Friedrich Schnapp (ed.), *Der Musiker E. T. A. Hoffmann: Ein Dokumentenband* (Hildesheim, 1981), 668–71.

table to the dead weight of successive scenes with no inner poetic relationship or poetic truth that might kindle the music into life.

These strictures were expanded in a review the following year.[9] Among those content to follow taste rather than lead it were such prolific lightweights as the playwright August von Kotzebue (1761–1819), who first began writing librettos in 1785. In reviewing Kotzebue's latest collection of librettos (mentioning also his *Fanchon*, set by F. H. Himmel, conducted by Hoffmann in 1813–14, and *Deodata*, set by B. A. Weber) Hoffmann fastened on an essential polarity. Kotzebue viewed singing as 'unnatural', and something that had to be 'motivated'; this he stated in his preface to *Deodata*. But Hoffmann conceived true opera as the expression of a 'higher realm' and, in a proper sense, 'far more natural' than something 'treating of commonplaces in a commonplace way'. For him, the conflict implied in Kotzebue by 'motivating' people to sing in a realistic dramatic setting, and the resulting lack of inner 'poetic truth' emanating from the libretto, should simply not exist.

The final objection raised against Kotzebue's collection was that it really consisted of comedies with long, chatty spoken episodes arbitrarily sprinkled with vocal numbers. Moreover, Hoffmann also found the internal structure of vocal items for the most part clumsy and unusable. Even so, Kotzebue's total output of twenty or more librettos represented a plausible alternative in an age of literary dearth. Not only were they set by once-celebrated composers (Joseph Weigl, Peter Lindpaintner), but also by composers such as J. F. Reichardt (*Das Zauberschloss*) and Franz Schubert (*Der Spiegelritter* and *Des Teufels Lustschloss*). Beethoven himself, having composed incidental music to Kotzebue's *König Stephan* and *Die Ruinen von Athen*, wrote to the playwright on 28 January 1812 to express his 'ardent wish to have an opera that would be the product of your unique dramatic genius', offering him *carte blanche* as to its genre.

The presence of spoken dialogue, as opposed to recitative, was not in itself a large issue with Hoffmann; it was normal at the time. Nevertheless he noted in his review of Méhul's *Ariodant*, 'An opera dismembered by speech is an absurdity to be sure, tolerated only out of habit', and in his review of the 1815 production of *Don Giovanni* in Berlin (p. 397) he attempted to find a way round the inauthenticities caused by abandoning its recitatives in favour of spoken dialogue.

Of course, Hoffmann was not the first to inveigh against poor librettos in Germany; nor would he be the last. C. M. von Weber (1813), Heinrich

[9] 'Der Opern-Almanach des Hrn. A. v. Kotzebue' (*AMZ*, xvi, issues 43 and 44 of 26 Oct. and 2 Nov. 1814), *Schriften zur Musik*, 258–68.

Marschner (1820), and Louis Spohr (1823) all found themselves obliged to advertise publicly for librettos.[10] Nor is his passionate demand for the librettist to be sensitive to the needs of musical settings as such to be construed as something unprecedented in Germany. For example, the adaptation of Shakespeare's *The Tempest* by Friedrich Wilhelm Gotter in the early 1790s (*Die Geisterinsel*, after a plan by F. von Einsiedel) seems to have been carried out with ideal care for musical structure and setting,[11] not to mention consciousness of German staging conditions. It was eventually set successfully by J. F. Reichardt (1798) and probably seen in Berlin by Hoffmann, who never left any record of his reaction to it. Gotter anticipated the demand in *The Poet and the Composer* for a librettist to 'inwardly compose everything in musical terms just as well as the musician', since he reported singing 'every line' to himself and placed detailed formal musical *desiderata* in the course of the libretto, such as 'without accompaniment', or 'cavatina'. But then the Baroque librettist Metastasio had also imagined his own lines musically, and Hoffmann roundly rejected *his* operatic aesthetic, near the close of *The Poet and the Composer*.

At an opposite pole to Kotzebue's literary promiscuity stood the example of Carlo Gozzi (1720–1806). The influence of his dramatic fairy-tales on *The Poet and the Composer* is discussed later. Yet as the following account will show, Gozzi's literary theory also fed directly into Hoffmann's theory of opera.

In the preface to *Prinzessin Brambilla* [Hoffmann] refers to Carlo Gozzi's opinion of the Märchen [fairy-tale] as expressed in the foreword to his *Re de' Genj* (*King of the Spirits*: a dramatic fairy-tale), that a whole arsenal of absurdities and supernatural phenomena is not sufficient to give a soul to the Märchen, which it can obtain only through a deep foundation, through a leading idea drawn from some philosophical view of life; Hoffmann adds that this is what he has tried to do in the story he is presenting.[12]

In identical manner, *The Poet and the Composer* demands that an opera libretto shall address itself to 'the human condition', whatever its theatrical genre; shall have a view of human existence that expresses consciousness of a 'mysterious fate that governs [men's] own movements'. Already in 1810 Hoffmann had demanded for any opera an 'overall imaginative idea', 'a romantic concept', and shown why Weigl's *Das Waisenhaus* failed in this respect, while his *Die Schweizerfamilie* succeeded (pp. 253, 296). The fixity

---

10   *The Age of Beethoven*, 476–7. A libretto competition held by the management of the Kaiserliche Hofoper in Vienna took place in 1812, as Hoffmann noted (*HTB*, 364–5).

11   Bauman, *North German Opera*, 310–22. It was at one time intended for setting by Mozart.

12   Hewett-Thayer, *Hoffmann*, 216–17. He ordered his own copy of Gozzi's works in May 1809: *HBW*, i, 285.

of his own position as finally reached in 1809 or 1810 enabled the character Ottmar – in the prologue – to put forward 'serious tragic opera' as the current correct 'pinnacle to which a composer can aspire'. But this view needs to be related back to Hoffmann's analysis of the later work of Gluck, the composer 'who stands forth like a demigod' (p. 201).

The history of the reception of Gluck's reform operas in North Germany is one of pamphleteering, not performance, up to the 1790s.[13] Forkel's 1778 critique, to which Hoffmann refers in *Kreisleriana* ('Extremely Random Thoughts', p. 109 and n. 175), was only one of several carping attacks. However, even the success of *Iphigénie en Aulide* from 1806 (see p. 256) and *Iphigénie en Tauride* (in the Berlin repertory from 1795) had not seemingly engendered valid creative responses in other composers. Indeed, *Ritter Gluck* is critical of the Berlin performances themselves. Hoffmann's crucial review of *Iphigénie en Aulide* in 1810 shows that he regarded Gluck as the musico-dramatic model *par excellence*, for four reasons: his elevation of subject-matter; his refusal to write superficially attractive solos; his penetration to the inner drama, and musical portrayal of psychological realities rather than superficial verbal ones; and his ability to create 'true musical drama, in which the action moves forward without stopping from one moment to the next'.

The at first sight implausible fusion of these ingredients from Gozzi and Gluck were to form, nevertheless, the basis of Hoffmann's mature operatic practice. One of the most impressive features of his own opera *Undine* in 1816 was to be the extraordinary continuity of his musical structures, containing solos, sung dialogue, choral writing, action, and even scene-changes. This, together with his ambition to portray the inner life of the characters and drama, provoked C. M. von Weber to write in his review of *Undine*:

> The music is in a single mould, and after repeated hearings the present writer cannot remember a single passage that even for a moment broke the magic spell cast by the composer . . . [Hoffmann] goes steadily forward, visibly guided by the determination to achieve dramatic truth and intensity instead of holding up the swift progress of the drama or shackling it in any way.[14]

Attainment of this 'single mould' meant attainment of an authentic, personal musico-dramatic language: what Hoffmann called 'style'. By 'style', Hoffmann proposes a certain compositional awareness, which he places in distinction to 'manner', and which involves a particular quality of

[13]   Bauman, *North German Opera*, 238f., 265–6.
[14]   *Weber: Writings*, 203.

melody. He analysed these constructions later, in detail, in his important essay entitled 'Letters on Music in Berlin', p. 392. The negation of 'style' prevailed in contemporary Italianate operas, and Hoffmann had pilloried them mercilessly in his review of Paer's *Sofonisba* (see p. 262):

those who in an opera expect only to be lulled by pleasant sounds, who desire only to admire the skill of the singers, in short who regard the stage only as heightening the appeal of a nice concert . . . will find complete satisfaction in Paer's music.

In parts of Europe, Gluck's dramatic achievements in the Paris operas gave rise to a line of critical thought which said that the musician in the operatic partnership should, like Gluck, seem in effect to be the poet as well. Jean-Jacques Rousseau, after all, had shown the way by actually writing words as well as music for *Le Devin du village* (1752), which held the stage at the Paris Opéra for over seventy-five years. Something of this French view of Gluck as his own 'poet' may have been known to Hoffmann.[15] However, his own arguments centre on Gluck's 'style' and his classical subjects. For the latter, it is their 'inner strength of character and situation' and the 'mysterious forces governing gods and men', which provide a model for the Romantic stage, and would inspire Hoffmann's use of classicism in his own opera *Aurora*.

The corollary of Hoffmann's stress on Gluck was his self-distancing from the huge achievements of Mozart. On the personal and the general levels, he well realised that Mozart's operas had created a stylistic vacuum. In his essay 'On a Remark of Sacchini's' in *Kreisleriana* (II–6) he examined the way Mozart's musical effects and techniques were being appropriated by others, but often to worthless ends in that these composers used them without regard for 'the underlying character of the work' being written. This observation actually originated in the review of Gluck's *Iphigénie en Aulide*, where Hoffmann warned against the 'high romanticism' of Mozart those who had not yet been taught to acquire 'a certain style' by Gluck's works.

Important operatic developments after *The Poet and the Composer* did not oblige its author to change his theories. In 1814 the prime example of a serious opera composer who, to Hoffmann, lacked 'style' and – in spite of setting neoclassical or historical librettos – was unworthy to be regarded as Gluck's successor, was Gaspare Spontini (1774–1851). It was, in fact, Spontini's *Fernand Cortez* that provoked such impressive exploration of the differences between 'style' and 'manner' in 'Letters on Music in Berlin'. Subsequently, Hoffmann learned to appreciate Spontini's earlier opera *La*

---

[15]   See David Charlton, '"L'Art dramatico-musical": an essay', in *Music and Theatre: Essays in Honour of Winton Dean*, ed. Nigel Fortune (Cambridge, 1987), 234–8.

vestale in Berlin: by 1816 he was publicly calling it an 'overwhelming masterpiece'. Shortly after that, the mania for the comic and the serious operas of Gioacchino Rossini reached northern Germany. To the composer of *Undine* this could only signify a threat to the authentic development of opera, a threat he was consequently forced to address in part of 'Further Observations on Spontini's Opera *Olimpia*' (1821). His reactions were the same as those to Paer's music, quoted above, but commensurately more vitriolic:

One need only think of the grotesque leaps and roulades of Rossini and his ilk, of the clumsy violin figures, and of the odious trills that often take the place of melody and then incite female singers to a surfeit of gurgling.

(p. 441)

So it was natural that when Spontini signed a contract to come to Berlin as the king's General-Musikdirektor in 1820, Hoffmann should welcome him heartily. Within the above-named *Olimpia* essay he formulated his verdict, carefully intended to place Spontini in the great tradition, yet without proclaiming him as Gluck's natural successor in so many words (see p. 445). He hoped that Spontini would become a 'German' composer, even though the ambivalence he felt about certain 'jaunty' rhythms, 'Italianate' arias, and his style of orchestration, is clear. In the last six months of 1820 Hoffmann returned to the practical world of opera and translated the French libretto of Spontini's *Olimpia* for its 1821 Berlin première, also composing the verses for its new final scenes.

The dual or single identity of an opera's composer and librettist was a question about which Hoffmann had acquired first-hand knowledge. Other composers who had most recently written their own opera texts included the Parisians Nicolas-Etienne Framery and Henri-Montan Berton (in 1768 and 1797)[16] and the Germans J. F. Reichardt and Johann Nepomuk von Poissl (in 1800–08, and 1806–43). Poissl (1783–1865) worked at Munich and was 'the first German composer consistently to write his own librettos',[17] usually modelled on Italian originals. His most celebrated opera from the nine composed to his own texts was *Der Wettkampf zu Olympia* (1815), modelled after Metastasio. Reichardt, the veteran composer, author, publisher, and traveller (1752–1814) had written three '*Liederspiele*' to his own texts, acted at the Berlin Nationaltheater; in 1808 he adapted Gozzi's text *Il mostro turchino* for a libretto, though he never finished

---

[16]   Framery (1745–1810), *La Sorcière par hazard* (1768, rev. 1783); Berton (1767–1844), *Ponce de Léon*; both were minor works, using spoken dialogue, and arousing no great controversies.

[17]   *Weber: Writings*, 380. For Weber's reviews of Poissl, see pp. 184 and 289.

composing the opera, which has since been lost.[18] Hoffmann neglected to discuss Reichardt's individual operatic works, but wrote warmly about them as a whole in the introduction to a review of his F minor piano sonata.[19]

He who is able, like Reichardt, to enter into the poetry, and, starting with words, to connect poem and music intimately, will soon become accustomed to regard both as integrated parts of one work; in fact, as one artistic entity.

This was, doubtless, just praise; but without the artistic ability to evoke a given subject, a composer was bound to fail. Clemens von Brentano, who heard some of Reichardt's music for *Il mostro turchino*, condemned it since Reichardt evinced 'no talent for the romantic . . . his music does not, nor will, take the new romantic step'.[20]

It is clear that the concept of text and music flowing from one pen was in the air. As we shall see in a moment, Hoffmann had experimented in this way between 1799 and 1807 in some of his earliest stage works. Knowing of these at least in part, Jean Paul wondered publicly whether Hoffmann might not be the very man to take the same perceived task a step further:

For up to now the sun-god has always flung down poetic talent with his right hand and musical talent with his left, to two such widely separated persons, that until this moment we still await the man who can produce a genuine opera by composing words and music at the same time [*zugleich*].

(Foreword to Hoffmann's *Fantasiestücke in Callot's Manier*, dated 24 November 1813)

Jean Paul's word 'zugleich' need not have meant 'simultaneously' so much as 'together'. But it might have been the origin of Lothar's opinion, preceding *The Poet and the Composer*, that simultaneity of inspiration was in fact possible. The topicality of this debate remains apparent.

It took much time and effort before Hoffmann arrived at his critical and practical positions of maturity, for there is no question but that the experiences of writing words and composing music over many years went into *The Poet and the Composer*. Unfortunately, however, it is too soon to be able to come to any proper conclusions concerning his development as an opera composer, since some music is lost and several important sources have never been published. Perhaps the least hypothetical conclusion would be

---

[18]   Rolf Pröpper, *Die Bühnenwerke Johann Friedrich Reichardts (1752–1814)* (2 vols., Bonn, 1965), i, 122–7. In 1780–81 he had composed the text for his own Singspiel, *Liebe nur beglückt*, unpublished, but produced at Dessau.

[19]   *Schriften zur Musik*, 203–4. See the review of Riem's *Zwölf Lieder*, pp. 379–80, for Hoffmann's opinion of Reichardt's songs.

[20]   Pröpper, *Die Bühnenwerke Reichardts*, i, 122–3.

to say that he pursued a steady path towards the achievements of 1813–15; to point out that the ingredients in his potent mixture were assembled gradually.

One reason why Lothar remains adamant that poet and composer could reside satisfactorily in one person, is that Hoffmann had repeatedly proved the case. He had first written both words and music for the three-act Singspiel *Die Maske* (1799). Short piano-score extracts appeared in print in 1923.[21] In 1801 he then adapted Goethe's *Scherz, List und Rache* into a one-act Singspiel, now lost, which was performed professionally (unlike *Die Maske*). In 1805 he almost certainly wrote both words and music for *Die ungeladenen Gäste, oder der Kanonikus von Mailand*, a one-act Singspiel modelled on a French original.[22] It too was not performed, through ill-luck, and is lost. Then in 1807 he modelled Calderón's *Die Schärpe und die Blume*, after A. W. Schlegel's translation,[23] into a three-act Singspiel, *Liebe und Eifersucht*; the score is still unpublished, and Hoffmann never saw it staged, though he held a good opinion of it.

No amount of speculation can substitute for the truth revealed by the score of an opera, for that alone shows the dramatic proportions and the tone of a piece. The spoken prose sections of *Die Maske* are set off by versified texts for music which already betray Hoffmann's taste for ensembles and interaction rather than solos and reflection. This was not abnormal, however, for the age. Equally orthodox for Germany was Hoffmann's tendency to use eight- or seven-syllable lines for much of the time, ballad-like metres which easily 'blurred the distinction between the requirements of recitative and aria or ensemble',[24] encouraging (in other composers at least) undramatic over-regularity of musical phrase-lengths.

The above four works represent Hoffmann as a writer of poetry: one is struck by the persistence of his desire for total control (cf. his insistence on 'total effect' later), insofar as he admitted, in 1812,

You know that I am not at all good at writing verse, and hence how difficult it would be for me to make an opera out of *Undine*.[25]

---

[21] *Die Maske*, ed. Friedrich Schnapp (Berlin, 1923). Text also in *Nachlese*, 698–757. Discussions of this and later Hoffmann stage works are in James M. McGlathery, *Mysticism and Sexuality: E. T. A. Hoffmann*, Part 1 (Las Vegas, Berne, Frankfurt, 1981), 52f, 93f.

[22] A. Duval, *Le Souper imprévu*. Schnapp uses the adjective 'ungeladenen', while Allroggen uses 'ungebetenen'. See Maurice M. Raraty, 'Wer war Rohrmann? Der Dichter und der Komponist', *Mitteilungen der E. T. A. Hoffmann-Gesellschaft*, xviii (1972), 9–16.

[23] Original title, *La banda y la flor*. See *Nachlese*, 780–806.

[24] *The Age of Beethoven*, 476–7.

[25] Letter dated 15 July 1812 to Hitzig, requesting help in locating a poet. Sahlin, 172; *HBW*, i, 342.

But in certain of his earlier works, Hoffmann set texts by others. In 1804 he was much impressed by Clemens von Brentano's two-act Singspiel text, *Die lustigen Musikanten*, which had been published in 1803. The resulting score – now published and in part recorded – was staged in Warsaw in 1805, though not very well. Finally, from these earlier years, came the setting which won Hoffmann his post at Bamberg, to a text by Count Julius von Soden: *Der Trank der Unsterblichkeit* (1808); again, the work is unpublished.

Two points may be worth noting here. The first is the presence of *commedia dell'arte* elements in *Die Maske* (in the form of the masked woman) and *Die lustigen Musikanten* (which includes Pantalone, Tartaglia, and Truffaldino, all traditional rôles in the Italian improvising theatre). The second point is that, although Hoffmann's earlier operas are basically comedies, they point towards his demand in *The Poet and the Composer* for the depiction of 'the influence of higher natures' upon human life. In *Liebe und Eifersucht* love is the responsible party, as witness the text opening Act 3:

Liebe! Liebe! deine Macht	Cupid! Cupid! Your decrees
Bändigt Reiche, bricht Gesetze!	Subdue empires, break commandments!
Mehr als aller Kön'ge Schätze	You have brought under your rule
Hast du unter dich gebracht!	Far more than any royal treasure!

Furthermore, in Brentano's *Die lustigen Musikanten*, Hoffmann's

transition to the sphere of the magical was prepared, though not anticipated, by means of the fantastic impetus of events, moods and dialogue. For that purpose Brentano – as though anticipating Hoffmann's as yet unarticulated ideas on romantic opera – preferred the vicissitudes of colour and mood over the development of characters and their emotions, the aura of a fairy-tale over the interest in what happens.[26]

Then came the creative response to Gluck in the 1809 tale, *Ritter Gluck*, and the experiences of theatre production Hoffmann underwent in 1810–11: the latter have been mentioned in the Prefatory Remarks to 'The Complete Machinist', p. 63. He evidently became convinced of a possible synthesis obtainable through using classical myth in a Romantic spirit, rather in the

---

[26] Norbert Miller, 'E. T. A. Hoffmann und die Musik', in *Zu E. T. A. Hoffmann*, ed. Steven Paul Scher (Stuttgart, 1981), 195.

manner of certain painters like Angelica Kauffmann (1741–1807).[27] And there was the notable example of Spontini's opera *La vestale* (1807), which employed a setting in the Rome of A D 269. Both *La vestale* and Hoffmann's opera *Aurora*, written in 1811–12 to a text by his colleague and friend Franz von Holbein, are stories of love-trials that end happily, in contradiction of their classical sources.[28] In both, the happy ending is brought about through the agency of a higher power: the goddess Vesta in Spontini, the goddess Aurora in Hoffmann. Vesta was a fire-protecting deity, Aurora goddess of the red light of morning. We lack documentary evidence of Hoffmann's early familiarity with *La vestale* (whose score and libretto were freely available in print), but von Holbein probably knew it, since he had so many connections in the theatre world (see *HTB*, 606).

Aurora is only now becoming available.[29] Its editor has claimed it to be the first German opera to carry the epithet 'romantic', insofar as Hoffmann's autograph of the text (not the score) calls it 'eine grosse romantische Oper in drey Aufzügen'.[30] It takes as its source the tale of Cephalus and Procris, but superimposes extra elements of the supernatural. The first act sees the Athenian princess Procris fall in love with a beautiful shepherd. But owing to her father's dynastic plans for her, the shepherd is bound in chains. The Athenian general Polybius helps Procris by taking this youth to a place of concealment by the sea. In Act 2, the goddess Aurora falls in love with the youth and takes him to her palace on the sea-bed. A magic inscription is left by her on a rock for Polybius, implying the youth's infidelity to Procris. The last act sees the youth identified as Cephalus, the lost son of King Dejoneus, who had himself intended marrying Procris. There are strong intimations of a tragic end before Aurora's unexpected help for the lovers (involving a magic helmet which changes the wearer's features) is successful. She transforms herself finally into a star, seen floating against a red horizon, while a chorus is sung to the omnipotence of love.

In spite of the presence here of a certain complexity of intrigue, one can still relate *Aurora* to Hoffmann's general dictum for Romantic opera, as set

---

[27] See her *Ariadne* now in Dresden, and the paintings by Ferdinand Hartmann (*Hector's Farewell*, 1800) and Pierre-Narcisse Guérin (*Clytemnestra*, 1817) in Robert Rosenblum, *Transformations in Late Eighteenth-Century Art* (Princeton, 1970), plates 14, 17, 20.

[28] *Ibid.*, 17; and Ovid, *Metamorphoses*, tr. Mary M. Innes (Harmondsworth, 1955), 174–8.

[29] The score has been published (*Denkmäler der Tonkunst in Bayern*, vi; edited by Hermann Dechant, 1984). Details and analyses may be found in Hermann Dechant, *E. T. A. Hoffmanns Oper 'Aurora'* (Regensburger Beiträge zur Musikwissenschaft, vol. ii, Regensburg, 1975).

[30] See *HTB*, 362; and Hermann Dechant, 'Entstehung und Bedeutung von E. T. A. Hoffmanns Oper *Aurora*', *Mitteilungen der E. T. A. Hoffmann-Gesellschaft*, xxxi (1985), 14.

forth in *The Poet and the Composer*: it is opera 'in which the music springs directly from the poetry as a necessary product of it'. Since music is a 'sublime language', the libretto must treat of an extraordinary world, so that the result is a unified impression, 'words sounding forth in music'. And we know from 'The Complete Machinist' that, in addition, 'scenery and stage effects should unobtrusively blend with the drama, so that the total effect [will] transport the spectator . . . to the fantastical land of poetry'. The spectacular closes of Act 2 (with subterranean tritons, sirens, and nymphs) and Act 3 (as the temple is bathed in red light) obviously constitute such effects. But *Aurora* was never staged, though preparations were made at the Würzburg theatre where Holbein was director until 1813.

The choice of *Undine* as the Romantic myth for Hoffmann's last completed opera can thus be seen as the logical consequence of *Aurora*: the supernatural figure of Aurora became that of Kühleborn, controlling destinies. The interfusion of earthly and supernatural *milieux* was concentrated greatly, to the point where one world permanently seems as real as the other in *Undine*. The implications of tragedy were now realised, since in *Undine* the knight Huldbrand is destroyed, in a *Liebestod*, by the watery powers of Kühleborn and Undine: his new wife Bertalda remains alone. The trappings of personal origins and identities are not shed, but they are reduced to the minimum required by the fable. This allowed drama and music to develop freely side by side.

Hoffmann's fortune in securing *Undine* for an opera in 1812, with the collaboration of its author Friedrich de la Motte Fouqué, was surely the catalyst enabling *The Poet and the Composer* to be conceived. It was in fact written between the composition of Acts 1 and 2 of *Undine* (see *HTB*, 537). However, recent research has shown that certain earlier contributors to the *AMZ* helped to prepare the way for the positions that Hoffmann would take, concerning both instrumental music and opera. These may be briefly mentioned.

Retrospective articles by Triest in 1801 laid blame for the state of German opera on librettists who had lost sight of the 'purpose of art';[31] by contrast, Mozart the dramatist was squarely compared to Shakespeare. *Don Giovanni*, in particular, might be paralleled (said the writer) with *Hamlet* or *King Lear*.[32]

Another influential critic was the editor of the *AMZ*, Friedrich Rochlitz

---

[31] [J. K. F. Triest], 'Bemerkungen über die Ausbildung der Tonkunst in Deutschland', *AMZ*, iii, (1801), issue 22 of 25 February.

[32] *Ibid.*, issue 23 of 4 March.

(one of his contributions has been discussed earlier, in the Introduction to *Kreisleriana*). Judith Rohr has elucidated Rochlitz's concept of modern operatic music as a 'symphony with singing', which Mozart supposedly practised, and which Cherubini had taken up: 'Let your uninterruptedly flowing music become an expression of sensitivity to *all of nature.*' Such a music will result in a 'single, gigantic painting', which to Rochlitz is the only apt way of portraying a dramatic subject such as that of Medea.[33] Clearly this relates to what C. M. von Weber called 'a single mould' in *Undine*, and is a telling response to the achievements of various composers who were writing extended, through-composed operatic structures in the 1790s. More striking is the theory developed in 1802 by the young writer Franz Horn (1781–1837): that although music could reach its highest expression only without the intervention of any other art, nevertheless *Don Giovanni* and certain other works (by Cimarosa and Cherubini) had shown the way for opera by creating scores that functioned as an 'invisible painting'. That is, music must not 'paint' or 'imitate' anything in the Baroque or Enlightenment sense. The subject-matter of opera should correspond to the 'freedom' (Horn's term) that music exemplified: tragedy should be excluded.

True opera is essentially romantic. It allows the most exuberant harmonic vitality and extravagant flights of fancy to glide smoothly past us, and, uplifted by the sweet sounds of music, we perceive the sublimest impulses of that vitality with greater clarity than can ever happen in a mere drama . . . One could say that here in the realm of romanticism is the play at the heart of play, the life that delights in life, whose deepest mysteries only music is capable of expressing (which it cannot do, however, as soon as it becomes a mere accompaniment to poetry, in which case it should not really be called music, but only musical translation).[34]

Horn's style as well as substance here demonstrate that Hoffmann the *AMZ* critic was the same enthusiast as had been nourished in his own youth by the riches in that journal.

The position of Franz Horn relative to E. T. A. Hoffmann is rendered more interesting still through their mutual concern with the dramatic fairy-tales (the *fiabe*) of Carlo Gozzi (1720–1806). In *The Poet and the Composer*, Hoffmann spends some considerable time stressing the suitability of his *Il corvo* (*The Raven*) as the basis for a romantic opera. Since Gozzi's works have never been generally available in English, and have not entered the

---

[33] Judith Rohr, *E. T. A. Hoffmanns Theorie des musikalischen Dramas* (Baden-Baden, 1985), 33–6. Cherubini's *Médée* (1797) is probably his greatest operatic achievement.

[34] Rohr, *Hoffmanns Theorie*, 42–3, taken from Franz Christoph Horn, 'Musikalische Fragmente', *AMZ*, iv, issues 25, 26 of 17 and 24 March 1802.

repertory of the theatre, it is necessary in conclusion to sketch in the relevant background. This is drawn primarily from the book by Hedwig Rusack.[35]

In fact, Gozzi's influence on the whole of Hoffmann's imaginative work was far-reaching. But it would be wrong to imagine that he alone saw the logic connecting Gozzi and opera. Though he does not mention them, several operatic adaptations in Germany had been made already.

The most famous of Gozzi's ten dramatic fairy-tales were *L'amore delle tre melarance* (*The Love of Three Oranges*, 1761); *Il corvo* (*The Raven*, 1761); *Turandot* (1762); *La donna serpente* (*The Snake-woman*, 1762); and *Il mostro turchino* (*The Blue Monster*, 1764). Written for a famous Venetian acting company, they incorporated characters from the *commedia dell'arte all'improvviso*, such as Pantalone, Truffaldino, Pulcinella, whose parts were improvised rather than written out. Yet these *were* integrated: as Ludwig says in *The Poet and the Composer*, 'How splendidly the comic rôles of the masks are also woven in.' The rest of the characters spoke in verse. All the dramatic fairy-tales employ the supernatural, as well as elements of suffering; this latter feature was singled out by Franz Horn in 1803 when he claimed Gozzi as a Romantic writer with the words, 'The tragic and the comic never stand alone, they have interpenetrated each other thoroughly.'[36] Horn is echoed by Ferdinand: 'Only in a truly romantic work can the comic be so smoothly blended with the tragic that they combine into a single overall effect . . .' (p. 200).

By simply extracting information from Rusack's text and correcting it against more up-to-date musicological reference works, the following summary of early Gozzi operatic adaptations is obtained:

[1777]   F. W. Gotter writes to Georg Benda proposing *Il corvo* as opera-subject. The plan is not realised.

1779   Gotter's libretto taken from Gozzi's *I pitocchi fortunati* published (resulting in settings by Hiller, Seydelmann, Zumsteeg, and Georg Benda, as either *Die glücklichen Bettler* or *Das tartarische Gesetz*)

1785   *Il mostro* by Franz Seydelmann

c. 1790   *Das Reh* by Schmohl [*Il re cervo*]

c. 1790[37]   *König Rabe* by Franz Anton Martelli [*Il corvo*]

---

[35]   Rusack, *Gozzi in Germany*. In his published translation of Gozzi's *The Blue Monster* (Cambridge, 1951), v, Edward J. Dent reported that 'No play by Gozzi was ever acted in English until . . . 1948.' Even Dent's version shortened and modified the original.

[36]   Franz Horn, *Über Carlo Gozzis dramatische Poesie* (Penig, 1803), translated in Rusack, *Gozzi in Germany*, 73.

[37]   Franz Stieger's *Opernlexikon* (Tutzing, 1980) gives c. 1780; Hugo Riemann's *Opern-Handbuch* (Leipzig, 1893) gives 1790.

1790–93	*Das blaue Ungeheuer* by Andreas Jakob Romberg [*Il mostro turchino*]
1794	*Der Rabe* by Andreas Jakob Romberg [*Il corvo*]
1800	*Der König der Genien* by Friedrich Dionys Weber
1805	*Schecheristani* by Johann Zapf [*La donna serpente*]
1806	*Die Sylphen* by Friedrich Heinrich Himmel [*La zobeide*]
1808	*Das blaue Ungeheuer* by Reichardt [discussed above]
1809	*Turandot* by J. F. G. Blumenröder
1814	*Die Abenteuer von der Schlangenburg* by Franz Joseph Volkert [*Turandot*]
1817	*Der Kampf mit der Riesenschlange* by Franz Joseph Volkert [*Il corvo*]
1822	*Der Zauberspruch* by Johann Peter Pixis [*Il corvo*]
1832	*Ravnen* by J. P. E. Hartmann [*Il corvo*]
1833	*Die Feen* by Richard Wagner [*La donna serpente*]
1835	*Turandot* by Karl Reissiger
1838	*Turandot* by J. Hoven

Some of these pre-1813 works would not have been known to Hoffmann; however, he could have known at least the libretto of Romberg's *Der Rabe*, which was published, and his letter of 22 July 1807 refers to an opera much publicised at the time, Himmel's *Die Sylphen*. This was one of the Gozzi-derived works listed (according to Rusack) in the preface to the new edition of Gozzi's *fiabe teatrali* issued in 1808 by J. E. Hitzig in Berlin, precisely as a response to the 'interest in this excellent poet' evinced in Germany. As we said earlier, Hoffmann ordered these volumes from his friend Hitzig in May 1809. What is striking, apart from the existence of two operas based on *Il corvo* before 1800, is the continued response to the same fairy-story after 1813, rivalling the perennial *Turandot* (of which the celebrated German version by Schiller had been issued in 1802). In fact, Rusack mentions that the 1822 work by Pixis was based on Hoffmann's account of *Il corvo* in *The Poet and the Composer*. What would be most fascinating to know is whether Hoffmann knew Franz Horn's published opinion, in 1803, that *Il corvo* represented the summit of Gozzi's 'romantic art'.[38]

---

[38] Franz Horn, *Über Carlo Gozzis dramatische Poesie*, paraphrased in Rusack, *Gozzi in Germany*, 73.

THE POET AND THE COMPOSER

[Prologue]

'My dear friend Theodor', said Ottmar, 'Your story[39] has clearly demonstrated what tribulations you have suffered in the noble cause of music. Each of us tried to tempt you in a different direction. While Lothar wanted to hear only instrumental pieces by you, I insisted on comic operas; and while Cyprian, as he would now admit, expected the impossible by asking you to set librettos that completely lacked form and balance, you preferred serious church music. As things stand at the moment, serious tragic opera would seem to be the highest pinnacle to which a composer can aspire, and I don't understand why you did not attempt that genre and produce something remarkable long ago.'

'But who else', replied Theodor, 'who else is to blame for my negligence but you, Ottmar, together with Cyprian and Lothar? Has any of you been able to agree to write a libretto for me, despite all my begging, pleading, and nagging?'

'What an amazing fellow you are', said Cyprian. 'Have I not spent long enough discussing texts for operas with you, and did you not dismiss the sublimest ideas as utterly impracticable? Did you not end by demanding, rather absurdly, that I should make a formal study of music in order to understand your requirements and be able to satisfy them? Any interest I had in poetry of that kind evaporated when you made it clear – something I would never have believed possible – that you stick to conventional forms and are totally unwilling to depart from them, just like the most mechanical composer, kapellmeister, or musical director.'[40]

---

[39] story: *Die Fermate* (*The Cadenza*; or *An Interrupted Cadence* in Alexander Ewing's translation of 1886), told by Theodor in the first person and concerning his experiences with the singers Teresina and Lauretta who inspire him to compose contrasting types of music.

[40] The 'conventional forms' – symmetrical vocal and instrumental forms as developed in the eighteenth century – show that Theodor is no duplicate of the composer Hoffmann. The latter's freedom of approach in *Undine* has been discussed in the Introduction 'Hoffmann and Opera'.

'But what', interjected Lothar, 'what is more inexplicable – tell me, why in the world does Theodor, who is a master of words and of poetic expression, not write a libretto himself? Why does he expect us to become musicians and squander our poetic gifts merely in order to create a thing to which *he* then gives life and movement? Doesn't he know his own needs best? Isn't it simply because of the imbecility of most composers, and their one-sided training, that they need the help of others in their work? Isn't perfect unity of text and music possible only when poet and composer are one and the same person?'

'That all sounds remarkably plausible', replied Theodor, 'but it's completely wrong. I maintain that it's impossible for anyone to create a work by himself that is equally outstanding in word and music.'

'But my dear Theodor', continued Lothar, 'you only imagine that to be the case, either out of unwarranted pessimism or out of – well, innate laziness. The idea of having to work your way through the lines of text in order to arrive at the music is so distasteful to you that you refuse to have anything to do with it, whereas I believe that music and word flow from the inspired poet and composer at the *same* instant.'[41]

'Quite right', cried Cyprian and Ottmar.

'You drive me into a corner', said Theodor. 'Instead of trying to refute your argument, let me relate to you a conversation between two friends, which I wrote down several years ago, about the requirements of opera. The fateful period we have lived through was then just beginning. I thought that my existence as an artist would be endangered, or even destroyed, and a feeling of despair came over me, to which poor physical health may also have contributed. So I created for myself a serapiontic friend[42] who had taken up the sword instead of the quill. He gave me comfort in my anguish, and pitched me right into the bewildering maelstrom of great events and deeds of that momentous time.'

Thereupon Theodor began:

The Poet and the Composer

The enemy was at the gates, guns thundered all around, and grenades

---

[41] Lothar goes much further in speculation here than anywhere else in the discussion. The tendency of what he says accurately foreshadows the nineteenth-century concern with creating truly musico-dramatic librettos. For a sustained study of Richard Wagner's methods in writing both words and music of opera, see Curt von Westernhagen, *The Forging of the 'Ring'*, tr. Arnold and Mary Whittall (Cambridge, 1976), esp. pp. 9ff.

[42] serapiontic friend: one worthy of the friends' rule of 'Serapion the Hermit': 'that they should never torment each other with inferior hack-work'.

sizzled through the air amid showers of sparks. The townsfolk, their faces white with fear, ran into their houses; the deserted streets rang with the sound of horses' hooves, as mounted patrols galloped past and with curses drove the remaining soldiers into their redoubts. But Ludwig sat in his little back room, completely absorbed and lost in the wonderful, brightly coloured world of fantasy that unfolded before him at the piano. He had just completed a symphony, in which he had striven to capture in written notation all the resonances of his innermost soul; the work sought, like Beethoven's compositions of that type, to speak in heavenly language of the glorious wonders of that far, romantic realm in which we swoon away in inexpressible yearning; indeed it sought, like one of those wonders, itself to penetrate our narrow, paltry lives, and with sublime siren voices tempt forth its willing victims. Then his landlady came into the room, upbraiding him and asking how he could simply play the piano through all that anguish and distress, and whether he wanted to get himself shot dead in his garret. Ludwig did not quite follow the woman's drift, until with a sudden crash a shell carried away part of the roof and shattered the window panes. Screaming and wailing the landlady ran down the stairs, while Ludwig seized the dearest thing he now possessed, the score of his symphony, and hurried after her down to the cellar.

Here the entire household was gathered. In a quite untypical fit of largesse the wine-seller who lived downstairs had made available a few dozen bottles of his best wine, and the women, fretting and fussing but as always anxiously concerned with physical sustenance and comfort, filled their sewing-baskets with many tasty morsels from the pantry. They ate, they drank, and their agitation and distress were soon transformed into that agreeable state in which we seek and fancy we find security in neighbourly companionship; that state in which all the petty airs and graces which propriety teaches are subsumed, as it were, into the great round danced to the irresistible beat of fate's iron fist. Their grievous situation, even their apparent mortal danger, was quite forgotten and cheerful talk poured from animated lips. Tenants who scarcely raised their hats when meeting on the stairs sat arm in arm beside each other, revealing their innermost feelings in mutual warmheartedness. The shots were now heard only intermittently, and there was already talk of going up again, as the street appeared to have become safer. One old soldier went further; after vouchsafing a few instructive words about the art of fortification in Ancient Rome and the efficacy of catapults, and also mentioning the renown of Vauban[43] in more recent

---

[43]   Sébastien Le Prestre de Vauban (1633–1707), French military strategist and engineer, also author, who revolutionised the arts of siege-craft and fortification. His treatise *De l'attaque et de la défense de places* was reprinted as late as 1829.

times, he roundly asserted that all fears were groundless since the house lay well beyond the line of fire. Whereupon a stray shot smashed the bricks protecting the ventilation holes and flung them into the cellar. No one was injured, however, and when the soldier with full glass in hand leapt onto the table from which the bottles had been dashed by the bricks, and expressed contempt for any further shot, they all recovered their spirits.

This was indeed the last scare. The night passed quietly, and on the following morning they learned that the army had taken up a different position and had voluntarily left the town to the enemy. When they came out of the cellar, enemy troops were already moving through the town, and a public notice promised the inhabitants peace and security of property. Ludwig plunged into the motley crowd eagerly awaiting the new spectacle and pressing towards the enemy commander,[44] who was just riding through the gate amid the joyful sound of trumpets and surrounded by guards in gleaming uniforms.

He could hardly believe his eyes when among the officers he recognised his beloved university friend Ferdinand who, in a simple uniform and carrying his left arm in a sling, came prancing past him on a magnificent dun. 'It was him – it was really and truly him!' Ludwig burst out involuntarily. In vain he tried to follow his friend, who was quickly carried out of sight by his impetuous steed. Deep in thought Ludwig hurried back to his room, but he could make no progress with his work; his head was filled by the appearance of his old friend, with whom he had completely lost touch years before, and all the happy hours of his youth that he had spent with good old Ferdinand passed luminously through his mind. At that time Ferdinand had not shown the least propensity towards military life; he lived purely for the muses, and the gifts revealed in several of his works bore witness to his calling as a poet. All the more incomprehensible to Ludwig, therefore, was this transformation of his friend, and he burned with longing to speak to him, without having any idea how he might begin to track him down.

There was now more and more excitement in the town. A large section of enemy troops rode past led by the allied princes, who were allowing themselves a few days' respite there. The greater the congestion at headquarters became, however, the more Ludwig lost hope of ever seeing his friend, until at last, in an out-of-the-way, unfrequented coffee-house where Ludwig usually ate his frugal evening meal, Ferdinand suddenly fell into

---

[44] Hoffmann recalls the events of 8 May 1813 when he witnessed the withdrawal of the Prussians and Russians from Dresden, the burning of bridges, and the entry of the French headed by Napoleon. This was followed by bombardments.

his arms with a loud cry of heartfelt joy. Ludwig remained silent, for a certain uneasiness soured in him the longed-for moment of reunion. It was like a dream in which one embraces those one loves, only to find them suddenly changed into strangers, so that the most sublime pleasures instantly dissolve into mocking phantoms.

The gentle son of the muses, the poet of numerous romantic lyrics which Ludwig had clothed with melody and harmony, now stood before him in a plumed helmet, a great, rattling sabre at his side, even profaning his voice with the harsh cry of greeting. Ludwig's troubled eyes took in the wounded arm, then moved to the medal on Ferdinand's breast. But then Ferdinand embraced him with his right arm and pressed him warmly to his heart. 'I know', he said, 'what you are thinking, what feelings this sudden meeting must arouse in you! My country needed me, and I could not hesitate to follow the call. It was with joy, with that burning enthusiasm a noble cause kindles in any breast which cowardice has not condemned to slavery, that this hand, previously accustomed only to guiding the gentle quill, took up the sword! My blood has already been shed and only chance, which caused the Prince himself to witness my deed, obtained the decoration for me. But believe me, Ludwig! The strings vibrating in my soul, whose notes so often spoke to you, are still unharmed. In fact, even after the horror of bloody battle, on lonely guard duty, or when my comrades sat around the campfire, I would pour my inspiration into poems which uplifted and strengthened me in my glorious vocation to fight for freedom and honour.' Ludwig felt his heart open up at these words, and when Ferdinand sat down with him in a small side-room and removed his helmet and sword, it was as though his friend had only been teasing him with a ludicrous disguise now cast aside. As the two friends ate the modest meal that had meanwhile been brought for them, and their glasses rang merrily together, they were filled with joy and elation; the bright lights and colours of the old days surrounded them, and all the profound feelings produced by their combined artistic efforts, as though by some powerful magic, came back to them in the warm glow of renewed youth. Ferdinand earnestly enquired what Ludwig had composed since that time, and was very much surprised when Ludwig confessed that he had still not managed to write an opera and have it produced, having not yet found a single libretto whose subject and treatment had been able to inspire him to composition.

'I cannot understand', said Ferdinand, 'why you, with your vivid imagination and more than adequate command of language, have not written a libretto yourself long ago!'

Ludwig: I am willing to admit that my imagination may well be lively enough to devise several good subjects for an opera; indeed, especially when at night a slight headache produces in me that dreamlike state halfway between sleeping and waking, I not only conceive quite good, genuinely romantic operas, but actually see them performed before me together with my music. So far as the gift of grasping hold of them and writing them down is concerned, however, I am afraid I do not possess it; and really it is hardly right to expect us composers to develop the mechanical skills necessary for success in every artistic medium, and learned only through constant diligence and long practice, that we would need in order to compose our own texts as well. But even if I did acquire the ability to work out a story, and to set it properly and tastefully into poetic and dramatic form, I could still never bring myself to write my own libretto.

Ferdinand: But no one could ever be so much in sympathy with your musical objectives as you yourself.

Ludwig: That may well be true, but it seems to me that the composer who set himself the task of constructing his own libretto line by line would feel like a painter who had to make a laborious copper engraving of the picture he had conceived in his imagination, before he was allowed to begin painting with living colours.

Ferdinand: You mean that the spark necessary for composition would be smothered and extinguished in the process of versification?

Ludwig: That's precisely it! And eventually my verse would seem to me just as wretched as the paper cases of the rockets that only yesterday were hissing up into the sky with fiery energy.[45] But seriously, if success is to be achieved, it seems to me that in no art is it so necessary as in music to embrace the whole work in the first, most intense flash of inspiration, down to the smallest detail of every part. Nowhere is filing and altering more futile and destructive; for I know from experience that the melody conjured up as though by a thunderbolt immediately on first reading the libretto is always the best, and in the composer's mind perhaps the only valid one.[46] It would be quite impossible for a musician, as soon as he started writing the text, not to occupy himself with the music called for by the situation. He would be completely immersed and carried away by the melodies flooding over him, and would struggle in vain to find the words, and if he succeeded in forcing himself to do so, then no matter how forcefully the waves surged over him the torrent would soon drain away as though into barren sand. In fact, let

---

[45]   Fire and sparks, however (in spite of Ludwig's topical joke), were an abiding Hoffmann metaphor for musical creation: see '*Ombra adorata*', p. 90, and Ludwig's 'tongues of fire' speech later in the dialogue.

[46]   This should not be taken to mean that Hoffmann himself never revised his music. We know, in the case of *Undine*, that he made many improvements and re-composed certain items such as Undine's Act 2 aria, 'Wer traut'. See Jürgen Kindermann (ed.), *Undine. Zauberoper in 3 Akten* (E. T. A. Hoffmann, *Ausgewählte musikalische Werke*, i) (Mainz, 1971), i, Vorwort.

me put my inner conviction in even plainer terms. At the moment of musical inspiration any word or any phrase would seem to him inadequate, lifeless, pitiful, and he would have to descend from his exalted state in order to be able to beg for the necessities of his existence in the lower region of words.[47] But wouldn't his wings then soon become useless, like those of a caged eagle, so that he would try in vain to reach for the sun?

Ferdinand: There is certainly something in that. But you probably realise, my friend, that more than convincing me, you are excusing your reluctance to beat a path towards musical creation through all the inevitable scenes, arias, duets, and what have you.

Ludwig: That may be, but I must bring up an old grievance again: why were you never willing, when the same artistic aspirations bound us so intimately together, to satisfy my fervent plea to write a libretto for me?

Ferdinand: Because I consider it the most thankless task in the world. You will grant me that nobody can be more stubborn in his demands than you composers are. And when you assert that the musician cannot be expected to acquire the skill necessary for the mechanical task of versification, then I retort that the poet may well be hard pressed to pay such strict regard to your requirements, to observe the structure of your trios, quartets, finales, etc., and to make sure he is not every moment trespassing, as happens sadly all too often, against the form that you have fixed (though with what right you only know yourselves). When we have striven with the utmost care to render every dramatic situation in true poetry, and to depict it in the most inspired words and the most well-turned phrases, then it is quite horrifying that you so often ruthlessly strike out our finest lines, abuse our noblest words by twisting and inverting them, in fact by drowning them in music.[48] And this is to speak only of the fruitless toil of carefully working the libretto out. Many a splendid subject, conceived by us in moments of poetic rapture and proudly placed before you in the expectation of your

---

[47]   This account is by no means far-fetched. We know that various composers have, at times, been impelled to write part of an operatic score without yet having received the precise form of words for the vocal line. In such cases, either the rhythm and metre had been agreed already, or else the librettist added words to the musician's patterns. Evidence exists in the cases of A. E. M. Grétry, W. A. Mozart, and G. Meyerbeer.

[48]   Ferdinand returns to this concept near the close of the dialogue. He refers to the fact that composers of vocal music frequently repeat words or phrases in the course of a setting, either for immediate dramatic emphasis or for reasons of musical elaboration. In any case, the passage recalls, by inversion, Diderot's *Le Neveu de Rameau*, where the Nephew calls for a new approach to writing librettos: 'phrases must be short and the meaning self-contained, so that the musician can utilise the whole and each part, omitting one word or repeating it, adding a missing word, turning it in all ways like a polyp, without destroying it'. *Rameau's Nephew*, tr. Tancock, 105.

delighted response, has been rejected out of hand as worthless and unsuitable for musical embellishment. And often this is sheer wilfulness, or something of the sort, for frequently you turn instead to texts that are beneath contempt, and . . .

Ludwig: Stop, my dear friend! There are admittedly composers to whom music is as alien as poetry is to many versifiers; they are the ones who have often set texts that really are beneath contempt in every way. True composers, who live and move amid the hallowed splendour of music, have chosen only poetic texts.

Ferdinand: But Mozart . . .?

Ludwig: . . . chose for his classical operas[49] only librettos that genuinely suited the music, paradoxical though this may seem to many. But leaving them aside for the moment, I believe that it can be determined very precisely what sort of subject is suitable for opera, so that the poet need never run the risk of making a mistake.

Ferdinand: I confess that I have never considered that, and with my lack of musical knowledge I would not even have known where to start.

Ludwig: If by musical knowledge you are referring to so-called academic music, then there is no need of that in order to gauge the real needs of composers; without it one can recognise and grasp the essential nature of music to such an extent that in this respect one is a much better musician than the man who by the sweat of his brow works through the whole academic system with its numerous wrong turnings, who glorifies the dead letter as the living god like a self-carved fetish, and who by this idolatry is denied the bliss of higher realms.

Ferdinand: And you believe that the poet can penetrate this essential nature of music without having received that lowlier initiation from the academy?

Ludwig: I certainly do! Indeed, in that far realm which often envelops us in curious presentiments, from where mysterious voices echo down to us and awaken all the resonances dormant in the burdened breast, which once awake shoot joyfully upwards like tongues of fire, so that we become partakers in the bliss of that paradise – it is there that poets and musicians are closely kindred members of *one* church; for the secret of words and sounds is one and the same, unveiling to both the ultimate sublimity.

Ferdinand: I hear my dear friend striving to describe the mysterious nature of art in profound utterances, and I do begin to see the gap ceasing to exist that previously seemed to me to separate the poet from the musician.

---

[49] classical: i.e. which stand as authoritative monuments; not here in contradistinction to 'romantic'.

Ludwig: Let me try to express what I feel about the essential nature of opera. Briefly, genuine opera seems to me to be only that in which the music springs directly from the poetry as a necessary product of it.

Ferdinand: I must confess that I do not quite see what you mean.

Ludwig: Is not music the mysterious language of a distant spirit-realm, its wonderful accents resounding in our souls and awakening a higher, intenser awareness? All the emotions vie with each other in dazzling array, and then sink back in an inexpressible longing that fills our breast. This is the indescribable effect of instrumental music. But now music is expected to step right into everyday life, to come to grips with the world of phenomena, adorning words and deeds and dealing with specific emotions and actions. Can one use sublime language to speak of ordinary things? Can music proclaim anything other than the wonders of that region from which it echoes across to us? Let the poet be prepared for daring flights to the distant realm of romanticism, for it is there that he will find the marvellous things that he should bring into our lives. Then, dazzled by their brilliant colours, we willingly believe ourselves as in a blissful dream to be transported from our meagre everyday existence to the flowery avenues of that romantic land, and to comprehend only its language, words sounding forth in music.

Ferdinand: So you are making a case exclusively for romantic opera with its fairies, spirits, miracles, and transformations?

Ludwig: I certainly consider romantic opera to be the only true sort, for only in the realm of romanticism is music at home. Of course you know that I utterly despise those wretched productions in which absurd spiritless spirits appear and miracle is heaped upon miracle without cause or effect, merely to amuse the gaze of the idle rabble. Only the inspired poet of genius can write a truly romantic opera, for only he can bring before our eyes the wonderful apparitions of the spirit-realm; carried on his wings we soar across the abyss that formerly separated us from it, and soon at home in that strange land we accept the miracles that are seen to take place as natural consequences of the influence of higher natures on our lives. Then we experience all the powerfully stirring sensations that fill us now with horror and fear, now with utter bliss. In short it is the magical power of poetic truth that the poet who describes these miracles must have at his command, for only this can carry us away, whereas a merely whimsical sequence of pointless magical happenings, often inserted as in many such productions just to tease the buffoon in his squire's costume,[50] will seem farcical and silly and will only leave us cold and unmoved.

---

[50] pointless magical happenings: such as favoured by Kotzebue (see Introduction) and many
      others, especially set by southern composers in the 1790s. Kotzebue's *Der Spiegelritter*

So, my friend, in opera the influence of higher natures on us should be seen to take place. Then a romantic dimension reveals itself before our eyes in which language is raised to a higher power, or rather (since it is part of that distant realm of music) takes the form of song. Then even action and situation, carried forward by irresistible sonorities, seize and transport us more potently. In this way, as I have already asserted, the music should spring directly and inevitably from the poetry.

Ferdinand: Now I understand you clearly, and I am reminded of Ariosto and Tasso. But I think it would be a difficult task to construct a musical drama according to your requirements.

Ludwig: It must be the work of a truly romantic poet of genius. Think of the excellent Gozzi.[51] In his dramatic fairy-tales he has provided exactly what I demand of a librettist and it is incredible that this rich storehouse of outstanding operatic subjects has not been more exploited before now.

Ferdinand: I do admit that when I read Gozzi several years ago he made the most lively impression on me, although I naturally did not consider him from the standpoint you are adopting.

Ludwig: One of his finest tales is indisputably *Il corvo*.[52]

Millo, King of Frattombrosa, knows no other pleasure than hunting. In the forest he catches sight of a magnificent raven and transfixes it with an arrow. The raven plunges to earth on to a tombstone of whitest marble lying beneath the tree, and bespatters the marble with its blood as it stiffens and dies. Then the whole forest begins to tremble, and from a grotto a terrible monster advances and bellows a curse at poor Millo: 'Find a wife as white as this tombstone's marble, as red as this raven's blood and as black as this raven's feathers, or you will die a raving madman.' All attempts to find such a woman are in vain, so the king's brother, Jennaro, who loves him most dearly, resolves not to rest until he has found the beautiful girl who will save his brother from incurable insanity. He traverses land and sea and finally, after receiving guidance from an old man experienced in necromancy, he sees Armilla, the daughter of the powerful sorcerer Norand. Her skin is as white as the tombstone's marble, her hair as red as the raven's blood, and

---

(1791), for example, is summarised in Bauman, *North German Opera*, 277. Hoffmann probably had in mind *Das Donauweibchen* (1798), music by Ferdinand Kauer, which was extremely well known and much imitated; or other musical plays featuring knights and comic subsidiary characters who are the butt of jokes perpetrated by fairies or spirits.

51 Carlo Gozzi (1720–1806), author of the ten celebrated dramatic fairy-tales (*fiabe*), 1761–65, discussed briefly in the Introduction; but also twenty other plays, including sentimental and tragicomic works.

52 *Il corvo* (*The Raven*): dramatic fairy-tale, originally produced in Milan, 1761. The story originated in a much older collection by Giambattista Basile.

her eyebrows as black as the raven's feathers.[53] He contrives to abduct her, and after surviving a storm they soon land near Frattombrosa.

Hardly has he stepped ashore when a splendid stallion and a falcon of the rarest quality fall by chance into his hands, and he is overjoyed, not only to be able to save his brother, but also to be able to delight him with gifts he will value so highly. Jennaro is about to rest in the tent that has been pitched under a tree, when two doves land in the branches and begin to speak: 'Unfortunate are you, O Jennaro, that you were born! The falcon will peck out your brother's eyes; if you do not present it to him, or if you reveal what you know, then you will be turned to stone. If your brother mounts the stallion, it will kill him instantly; if you do not give it to him, or if you reveal what you know, then you will be turned to stone. If Millo marries Armilla, a monster will tear him to pieces in the night; if you do not deliver Armilla to him, or if you reveal what you know, then you will be turned to stone.'

Norand appears and confirms what the doves have said, laying down the punishment for Armilla's abduction. As soon as Millo sees Armilla he is cured of the madness that had possessed him. The horse and the falcon are brought in and the king is overjoyed by his brother's love in gratifying his greatest passions with such splendid gifts. Jennaro hands the falcon to him, but just as Millo takes it Jennaro cuts off its head and his brother's eyes are saved. Similarly, just as Millo places his foot in the stirrup in order to mount the stallion Jennaro draws his sword and with a single stroke cuts off both of the horse's forelegs so that it crashes to the ground. Millo now feels convinced that insane love is driving his brother to act in this way, and Armilla verifies this supposition, since Jennaro's surreptitious sighs and tears and his eccentric behaviour have long since made her suspect that he loves her. She assures the king of her deepest affection, which had already formed during the journey, when Jennaro spoke of his beloved brother in the most animated and moving terms. In order to avoid any mistrust she now begs the king to hasten their union, and this duly takes place. Jennaro expects his brother's destruction at any moment; he is in despair to see himself so misunderstood, and yet a terrible fate awaits him if the least word of his dreadful secret escapes his lips. So he decides to save his brother, whatever the cost may be, and during the night he makes his way to the king's bedroom along a subterranean passage. A horrible, fire-breathing dragon appears; Jennaro attacks it, but his blows are ineffectual. The monster gets closer to the bedroom, so in utter desperation he seizes his

[53]   In the *A M Z* version of this text Armilla's lips, not hair, were red, and her hair was black, like her eyebrows. 'Norand' was the orthodox Germanic rendering of Gozzi's original 'Norando'.

sword in both hands, but the dreadful blow intended for the monster smashes the door. Millo comes out of the bedroom, and since the monster has disappeared he sees his brother as a hypocrite driven to fratricide in a fury of jealous love. Jennaro cannot explain himself; the guard is summoned and he is disarmed and dragged off to prison. He is found guilty of the crime and must pay with his life on the scaffold.

Just before his execution he asks to speak to his dearly beloved brother. Millo grants him an audience, and Jennaro in the most moving terms reminds him of the ardent love that has united them since their birth; but when he asks whether Millo really considers him capable of murdering his brother, Millo asks for proof of his innocence. In a torment of agony Jennaro now reveals the terrible prophecies of the doves and the necromancer Norand; but when he has finished speaking, to Millo's speechless horror he is transformed into a marble statue. Millo now recognises Jennaro's brotherly love and, tortured by heart-rending reproach, he resolves never to leave the statue of his beloved brother, but to die at its feet in remorse and despair. Then Norand appears. 'In the eternal ordinances of fate', he announces, 'the raven's death, your curse and Armilla's abduction were already prescribed. Only one deed can restore your brother to life, but that deed is a terrible one. If Armilla dies by this dagger beside the statue then the cold marble, bespattered by her blood, will quicken into life. If you have the courage to kill Armilla, then do it! Mourn and complain, as I do!'

He vanishes. Armilla wrings from the unfortunate Millo the secret of Norand's fearful words. Millo leaves her in despair. Overcome with horror and dread, and no longer valuing her own life, Armilla stabs herself with the dagger thrown down by Norand. As soon as her blood splashes the statue Jennaro is restored to life. Millo returns and finds his brother alive again but his beloved wife lying dead. In despair he is about to kill himself with the same dagger that Armilla had used, when the gloomy vault is suddenly transformed into a bright and spacious chamber. Norand appears; the great, mysterious prophecy has been fulfilled; all sorrow is at an end; Armilla, touched by Norand, comes back to life and everything ends happily.

Ferdinand: I remember the extraordinary play exactly now, and I can still recall the profound impression it made on me. You are right; the miraculous element seems entirely in place here, and has such poetic truth that one willingly accepts it. Millo's action in killing the raven knocks, as it were, at the bronze portal of the shadowy spirit-realm, so that it swings open with a clang and the spirits emerge into the world and enmesh men in the mysterious fate that governs their own movements.

Ludwig: Precisely, and consider the irresistible situations that the author was able to fashion from this conflict with the spirit-world. Jennaro's heroic self-sacrifice and Armilla's noble deed contain a greatness of which our moralising playwrights, grubbing among the trivialities of everyday life as in the sweepings thrown into the dust-cart from a stately hall, have no conception. How splendidly the comic rôles of the masks are also woven in.[54]

Ferdinand: I agree! Only in a truly romantic work can the comic be so smoothly blended with the tragic that they combine into a single overall effect and seize the listener's spirit in a strange and magical way.

Ludwig: Even our opera-manufacturers have darkly perceived this. It is doubtless for this reason that their so-called heroic-comic operas[55] came about; in these the heroic is often really comic, but the comic is heroic only to the extent that it disregards with true heroism all the dictates of taste, propriety and manners.

Ferdinand: According to your definition of a libretto then, we certainly have very few true operas.

Ludwig: Precisely! Most so-called operas are merely inane plays with singing added, and the total lack of dramatic force, imputed now to the libretto, now to the music, is entirely attributable to the dead weight of successive scenes with no inner poetic relationship or poetic truth that might kindle the music into life. Often the composer has unconsciously worked entirely on his own, and the wretched libretto trots along beside him quite independently of the music. In such a case the music can be very good in some ways; that is, without necessarily seizing the listener with the magical power of its inner meaning, it can still provide a certain pleasure, like a brilliant play of iridescence. But then the opera is merely a concert given in a theatre with costumes and scenery.

Ferdinand: If you therefore only recognise operas that are romantic in the fullest sense, what do you think of musical tragedies, and of comic operas in modern costume? Must you completely reject them?

Ludwig: Not at all! In the majority of older tragic operas, such as are sadly no longer written and set to music, it is again the true heroism of action and the inner strength of character and situation which so powerfully seize the

---

[54] masks: Gozzi's dramatic fairy-tales all employed the 'masks', the improvising actors of the traditional *commedia dell'arte all'improvviso*; their parts were not so much written out by Gozzi as left in outline. When the plays were adapted or translated (into German first by Friedrich Werthes, 1777–79) the masked rôles naturally posed various problems.

[55] heroic-comic operas: Hoffmann alludes to the mixed genre-descriptions of Italian opera, and probably a work that he well knew: Paer's *Sargino*, a *dramma eroicomico*. (See *Kreisleriana*, p. 82, for mention of its duet, 'Dolce dell'anima'.) The 'heroic' aspect of the opera refers to the action surrounding the Battle of Bouvines in 1214, and the 'comic' aspect refers to the sentimental education of the eponymous hero.

spectator. The dark, mysterious forces governing gods and men pass visibly before his eyes, and he listens as the eternal, immutable decrees of providence to which even the gods are subject are proclaimed in strange and ominous tones. Strictly speaking, these purely tragic subjects exclude fantastical elements, but in dealings with the gods, who rouse men to a higher existence and to godly deeds, a higher language must also be spoken using the enchanting accents of music. Incidentally, were the ancient tragedies not musically declaimed, and did that not clearly express the need for a loftier means of expression than ordinary speech can provide?

Our musical tragedies have in a quite distinct way inspired the composer of genius to write in a lofty, one might almost say sacred style; it is as though men, with profound dedication, borne on sounds emanating from the golden harps of cherubim and seraphim, were making a pilgrimage into the realm of light where they learn the secret of their own existence. I would like to point out nothing less, Ferdinand, than that church music and tragic opera form an intimate kinship, from which the older composers fashioned their own glorious style[56] which more recent ones do not remotely understand, not even Spontini, for all his exuberant abundance.[57] I need hardly mention the magnificent Gluck, who stands forth like a demigod; but in order to realise how even inferior talents embraced that truly great, tragic style, think of the chorus of Priests of the Night in Piccinni's *Didon*.[58]

Ferdinand: Now you make me feel just as I used to in our meetings in the good old days. When you speak so enthusiastically about your art, you lift me up to see things that I previously had no inkling of, and you can believe me when I say that at this moment I feel as though I understand a great deal about music. Indeed, I do not think a good line of poetry could awaken in my heart without issuing forth in music and song.

Ludwig: Isn't that the librettist's real inspiration? I maintain that he must inwardly compose everything in musical terms just as well as the musician, and it is merely a conscious awareness of specific melodies and specific notes from the accompanying instruments, in a word a secure mastery of the inner

---

56 style: used in a particular sense by Hoffmann, as explained in the Introduction, akin to 'authentic, personal musical language'. Here he is thinking of composers of the High Baroque like Alessandro Scarlatti and Johann Adolf Hasse. See 'Old and New Church Music', p. 366.

57 Gaspare Spontini (1774–1851): the Italian composer most recently celebrated for his Paris operas *La vestale* (1807) and *Fernand Cortez* (1809). Hoffmann's initial unfavourable analysis of his music appears in 'Letters on Music in Berlin', p. 392. Subsequently, he came to believe that Spontini – who was appointed as royal composer to the Berlin court in 1820 – might become the Romantic successor to Gluck.

58 Niccolò Piccinni, *Didon, tragédie lyrique* (1783), Act 3 sc. 10: general ensemble in E flat with the Priests of Pluto, 'Appaisez-vous, mânes terribles.'

realm of sounds, which distinguishes the latter from the former. But I still owe you an explanation of my views about opera buffa.

Ferdinand: You will surely not value it very highly, at least in modern costume?

Ludwig: For my part, my dear Ferdinand, I confess not only that I like it best in contemporary costume, but also that only in that style, preserving as it does the character and feeling with which those mercurial, excitable Italians endowed it, does it seem to me genuinely to exist. Here a sense of the fantastic, arising partly from the eccentric folly of individual characters and partly from the bizarre fluctuation of fortune, boldly invades everyday life and turns everything topsy-turvy. We must concede that yes, it is the fellow next door in his familiar light-brown Sunday suit with gold-covered buttons, but what on earth can have got into the man to make him behave so absurdly? Or imagine a respectable family gathering including a love-sick daughter, together with a few students who serenade her eyes and play the guitar below her window; then Puck appears among them in a mood of roguish mischief and everything disintegrates into wild imaginings and all manner of outlandish capers and eccentric contortions. A special star has risen and everywhere chance sets up its coils in which the most respectable of people get entrapped if they stick out their noses even just a whit.

This incursion of eccentricity into everyday life and the contradictions arising from it contain, in my opinion, the essence of true opera buffa. And this perception of the fantastic, previously remote but now encroaching upon reality, is precisely what makes the acting of Italian comedians so inimitable. They understand the poet's allusions and by their performance clothe the skeleton, which is all he is able to provide, with flesh and colour.[59]

Ferdinand: I think I understand you exactly. In opera buffa then, the fantastic actually takes the place of the romantic which you lay down as an indispensable requirement of opera. And the art of the librettist should consist in making the characters appear not only fully rounded and poetically true but lifted straight from everyday life and so individual that one instantly says to oneself: Look! That's my neighbour whom I talk to every day! That's the student who goes to lectures every morning and sighs terribly below his cousin's window! And so on. But then the adventures that they get up to, as though seized by some strange paroxysm, or that befall

---

[59]   Allusion to the improvising actors mentioned in note 54, whose rôles were traditionally Pantalone, the Doctor, Arlecchino, Brighella, Truffaldino, Pulcinella, Tartaglia, the Captain, and Smeraldina.

them, should give us the curious feeling that a mad demon is abroad, irresistibly drawing us into the circle of its amusing drolleries.

Ludwig: You express my most heartfelt conviction, and I need hardly point out how, following my principle, music is readily fitted to opera buffa, and how here too a particular style emerges of its own accord, stirring the listener's heart in its own way.

Ferdinand: But can music be expected to express comedy in all its nuances?

Ludwig: I am absolutely convinced it can, and artists of genius have proved it a hundred times. Music can convey, for example, an impression of the most delicious irony, such as that pervading Mozart's splendid opera *Così fan tutte*.

Ferdinand: The thought now strikes me that, according to your principle, the despised libretto of that opera[60] is in fact truly operatic.

Ludwig: And that's precisely what I meant when I said earlier that Mozart had chosen for his classical operas only librettos that exactly suited opera, although *Le nozze di Figaro* is more a play with songs than a true opera. The shameful attempt to translate sentimental plays into opera can only fail, and our orphanages, oculists,[61] and suchlike are certainly destined for early oblivion. Thus nothing could be more wretched, or more opposed to true opera, than that whole series of Singspiels which Dittersdorf produced,[62] whereas I very much defend operas like *Das Sonntagskind* and *Die Schwestern von Prag*.[63] One could call them genuinely German opera buffas.

Ferdinand: Those operas, as long as they were well performed, have at least

---

[60] 'This libretto was denounced throughout the nineteenth century as being intolerably stupid, if not positively disgusting, and various attempts were made in Germany and elsewhere to "improve" it.' Edward J. Dent, *Mozart's Operas. A Critical Study* (2nd edn, London, 1947), 190. Objections to it dating from 1791 and 1808 are recorded in Otto Erich Deutsch, *Mozart. A Documentary Biography* (Stanford, 1965), 365, 394, 508. Yet it was issued in two editions before 1800 and six more before *c*. 1830: A. Hyatt King, *Mozart in Retrospect* (London, 1955), 11, 260.

[61] sentimental plays: Ludwig's term *weinerliches Schauspiel* is the equivalent of *comédie larmoyante*, or sentimental bourgeois domestic plays originating in the 1760s. 'Orphanages' refers to Joseph Weigl's Singspiel of the same name (*Das Waisenhaus*, 1808); 'oculists' refers to Adalbert Gyrowetz's Singspiel of the same name (*Der Augenarzt*, 1811). Both were reviewed by Hoffmann: see pp. 252, 293, where he gives ample indication of their type of genre.

[62] Carl Ditters von Dittersdorf (1739–99), composer of some thirty-nine Italian and German operas, chiefly comedies, between 1771 and his death. Hoffmann here objects to works of immense popularity like *Doctor und Apotheker* (1786), *Das rote Käppchen* (1788), *Hieronymus Knicker* (1789), and *Das Gespenst mit der Trommel* (1794). See Bauman, *North German Opera*, 300–10.

[63] *Das Neusonntagskind* [*recte*] (1793); *Die Schwestern von Prag* (1794): Singspiels by Wenzel Müller (1767–1835), Viennese-based composer of some 250 musical theatre works. The first-named was conducted by Hoffmann in 1813 and 1814.

never failed to give me real enjoyment, and I have certainly taken to heart what the poet tells the public in Tieck's *Der gestiefelte Kater*: If they are to find pleasure in it, they must set aside all the education they may have had and in effect become children again and be able to experience childlike amusement and delight.[64]

Ludwig: I'm afraid that those words, like so many others of that sort, fell on hard and sterile ground, in which they could not lodge and take root. But the *vox populi*, which in matters of the theatre is usually a veritable *vox dei*, drowns out the occasional sighs vented by hyper-refined natures over the dreadful perversions and absurdities that these in their view footling affairs contain; and there are instances where some of them, despite all their airs and graces, have even burst out into horrible laughter, as though caught up by the madness that possesses the people, and yet have asserted that they could not explain their own laughter at all.

Ferdinand: Wouldn't Tieck be a poet who, if he felt like it, could offer the composer romantic librettos tailored exactly to the requirements you have laid down?

Ludwig: Quite assuredly, since he is a genuinely romantic poet. I remember in fact having a text of his in my possession; it was truly romantic in conception, but overloaded in subject-matter and too lengthy. If I am not mistaken it was called *Das Ungeheuer und der bezauberte Wald*.[65]

Ferdinand: You yourself bring me to a difficulty that you composers place upon the librettist. I refer to the incredible brevity that you expect of us. All our efforts to conceive and present in exactly the right words this or that situation, or the outbreak of this or that passion, are in vain; everything

---

[64] Ludwig Tieck (1773–1853), leading Romantic writer whose work much influenced Hoffmann. The latter returns here to a central position of the Romantics, and a key idea in *Kreisleriana*. In the Epilogue to *Der gestiefelte Kater* (*Puss-in-Boots*, 1797) the Author comes on stage to explain his purpose, only to be greeted by coarsely ironic responses of the (acting) audience. This play remains a supreme example of experimental writing (not staged until 1844), and by mentioning it even obliquely, Hoffmann reminds us how ambitious his standards for opera were, and he will certainly have had Tieck's Prologue in mind:

   Müller: I do hope they're not going to bring childish foolery on to the stage.
   Schlosser: Is it an opera then?

   See the translation by Gerald Gillespie (Edinburgh, 1974), 37.

[65] *Das Ungeheuer und der verzauberte Wald* [*recte*] occupies 117 pages in *Ludwig Tiecks Schriften* (Berlin, 1829, reprinted 1966), xi. Described as 'a musical fairy-tale in four acts', it was intended as a libretto when written in 1798 (published 1800), but was itself a revision of the fairy play *Das Reh* (*The Deer*, 1790), which was influenced by Shakespeare and by Gozzi. See Edwin H. Zeydel, *Ludwig Tieck, the German Romanticist* (2nd edn, Hildesheim and New York, 1971), 24–5. Its cast includes a King, Queen, Ministers, a Fairy, a Monster, Prophets, ghosts, etc.

must be dealt with in a few lines, which must also be capable of being ruthlessly twisted and turned according to your pleasure.

Ludwig: I would say that the librettist, like the scene-painter, must make a proper drawing but should then dash off the whole painting in a few powerful strokes; the music then places the whole work in a proper light and suitable perspective, so that everything stands out vividly and the separate, apparently arbitrary brush-strokes blend into boldly striking forms.

Ferdinand: So we are supposed to provide only a sketch rather than a libretto?

Ludwig: Not at all. It surely goes without saying that with regard to overall layout and economy, the librettist must remain faithful to the dramatic rules dictated by the nature of the subject; but he really must be especially careful so to arrange the scenes that the subject-matter clearly unfolds before the spectator's eyes. Almost without understanding one word, the spectator must be able to form an idea of the plot from what he sees taking place. No dramatic medium needs this clarity to a greater degree than opera. Besides the fact that even with the clearest singing the words are always harder to understand than elsewhere, the music all too easily transports the listener to distant regions and can be kept under control only by being continually directed to the point at which the dramatic effect is concentrated. As for the words, the composer likes them best when they powerfully and concisely express the passions and situations to be portrayed. No special frills are necessary, and especially no similes.[66]

Ferdinand: But what about the rich imagery of Metastasio?[67]

Ludwig: Yes, he had the most curious belief that the composer's inspiration should always proceed from some poetic image, particularly in an aria. Hence we have his continually recurring opening stanzas: 'Come una tortorella', 'Come spuma in tempesta', and indeed we frequently hear, at least in the accompaniment, the cooing of doves, the raging sea, and so on.[68]

Ferdinand: So are we not only to refrain from poetic devices but also to forgo all further elaboration of interesting situations? When, for example, the

---

[66] This demand is echoed in actuality in C. M. von Weber's letter to the English librettist of his *Oberon* (1826): 'The composer looks more for the expressions of feelings than the figurative; the former he may repeat and develop in all their gradations, but verses like "Like the spot the tulip weareth / Deep within its dewy urn . . ." must be said only *once*.' John Warrack, *Carl Maria von Weber* (2nd edn, Cambridge, 1976), 331.

[67] Pietro Metastasio (1698–1782), the leading Baroque opera librettist.

[68] These opening lines are not in fact present in the works of Metastasio or even of his predecessor Apostolo Zeno (1668–1750). This does not of course invalidate the point, which is that Baroque arias were reflective elaborations of an emotion, during which the action ceased.

young hero goes into battle and bids farewell to his grey-haired father, the old king whose realm is being shaken to its foundations by a conquering tyrant, or when a terrible misfortune separates the ardent youth from his beloved, are they to say nothing but 'Goodbye'?

Ludwig: The former could certainly speak briefly of his determination and faith in his just cause; and the latter could also tell his beloved that life without her will be but a slow death. But for the composer who expects inspiration not from words but from action and situation, even a simple 'Goodbye' will enable him to depict in powerful strokes the mental state of the young hero or the parting lover. To remain with your example, what a countless variety of heart-rending inflections the Italians have employed when singing the little word *addio*! How many thousand upon thousand nuances musical expression is capable of! And that is precisely the wonderful mystery of music, that only when our clumsy words dry up does it release its inexhaustible stream of expressive resources!

Ferdinand: In that case the librettist should strive for the utmost simplicity of language, and it would be sufficient merely to indicate the situation with nobility and force.

Ludwig: Indeed, for as I say, it is the subject-matter, plot, and situation, rather than fine words, which must inspire the composer. Not only so-called poetic imagery, but any sort of reflection, is a positive mortification for the musician.

Ferdinand: But surely you realise that I can't help feeling how difficult it is to write a good opera according to your requirements. This simplicity of language especially . . .

Ludwig: . . . may certainly be difficult for you poets, who so much enjoy painting with words, yes. But just as the operas of Metastasio, in my view, clearly show how texts must *not* be written, there are many Italian librettos that can be held up as perfect models of what a proper text should be. What could be more simple than stanzas like this well-known one:[69]

Almen se non poss'io	If I must therefore part
Seguir l'amato bene,	From him my well-beloved
Affetti del cor mio,	The feelings of my heart

---

[69] With unintended irony, Hoffmann selected the first quatrain sung by Servilia in Act 2 sc. 5 of Metastasio's libretto *La clemenza di Tito* (1734). It is not found in Mazzolà's version of the text for Mozart, which Hoffmann knew. The reason why he quoted it is probably that he remembered it from Zingarelli's opera *Giulietta e Romeo* (1796), Act 1, where it is incorporated into Romeo's scena, 'Prendi, l'acciar ti rendo' (British Museum, Add. MS. 30795, fo. 125v). This opera furnished the imaginative material for '*Ombra adorata*' in *Kreisleriana* (I–2). His own setting of this scena dates from 1812.

Seguite lo per me!   Remain at least instead!

How these few simple words contain an evocation of the spirit seized by love and pain, which the composer can respond to. He can then depict the mental state suggested using the full forces of his musical eloquence. In fact the particular situation in which those words are to be sung will so fire his imagination that he will give the music a highly distinctive character. For this very reason you will find that the most poetic composers often set to music even inferior lines with great success. In such cases it is the genuinely operatic, romantic subject-matter which provides their inspiration. I would suggest Mozart's *Die Zauberflöte* to you as an example.

Ferdinand was just about to reply, when outside the windows in the street the call to arms was sounded. He seemed thunderstruck. With a deep sigh Ludwig pressed his friend's hand to his breast. 'Oh Ferdinand, my dearly beloved friend!' he cried. 'What is to become of art in our harsh and turbulent times? Will it not perish, like a delicate plant that turns its drooping head in vain towards the dark storm-clouds behind which the sun has vanished? Oh Ferdinand, where are the golden days of our youth? Every nobler impulse is engulfed by the seething torrent ravaging our landscape in its headlong course; bloody corpses stare forth from its black waves,[70] and in the tide of horror washing over us we lose our footing – we have no handhold – our cry of anguish is lost in the desolate air – victims of implacable fury we sink down helplessly!'

Ludwig fell silent, lost in his thoughts. Ferdinand got up. He took his sabre and helmet and like the god of war in battle array he stood before Ludwig who looked at him in amazement. Then a glow spread across Ferdinand's countenance, his eyes shone with a fiery passion and he spoke in sonorous tones: 'Ludwig, what has become of you? Has the prison air that you must have been breathing here for so long corroded your spirit so deeply that you are now too weak and ill to feel the warming breath of spring, that plays outside among the clouds made golden by the blush of morning? Nature's children[71] luxuriated in sluggish inactivity; they scorned the finest gifts she offered them and trampled them under foot with wanton stupidness. And so the wrathful mother awoke the juggernaut of war which had long lain asleep in her fragrant flower-garden. Like an

---

[70] At this point Hoffmann's writing recalls his nightmarish prose picture *Die Vision auf dem Schlachtfelde bei Dresden* (*The Vision on the Battlefield of Dresden*): see *Nachlese*, 601–5.

[71] Cf. the words on mankind and Mother Nature quoted from *Die Automate* on p. 74.

armour-plated giant it moved among the degenerate breed; fleeing from its dreadful voice which made the mountains resound, they sought the protection of the mother in whom they had ceased to believe. But with belief there came a new awareness: only strength can guarantee prosperity! Godliness is generated from struggle, as life from death!

'Yes, Ludwig, our time of destiny has come. As though from the eerie gloom of ancient legends that echo down to us like mysterious rumblings of thunder from the distant twilight, we hear again the unmistakable voice of eternal omnipotence; bursting visibly into our lives it awakens in us the faith by which the mystery of our existence is revealed. The dawn is breaking; enraptured voices rise into the fragrant air proclaiming godliness and praising it in song. The golden gates are open, and art and science kindle in a single incandescence all the holy aspirations that unite mankind into a single church. So, my friend, direct your gaze upward, with courage, trust, faith!'

Ferdinand clasped his friend to him. Ludwig took up his filled glass: 'Eternally united in a higher cause through life and death!' 'Eternally united in a higher cause through life and death!' repeated Ferdinand, and in a few minutes his impetuous steed was carrying him into the lines that moved towards the enemy, rejoicing in their wild urge for battle.

[Epilogue]

The friends felt profoundly moved. Each of them thought of the time when the burden of a hostile fate had lain upon them and all their appetite for life had seemed to wither away and be irrevocably lost. How brightly then the first rays from the star of hope broke through the dark clouds, becoming ever more brilliant and breath-taking as it rose, quickening and nurturing new life. How their hearts had leapt and rejoiced in the joyful struggle. How their courage and faith had been crowned by the sublimest victory!

'As a matter of fact', said Lothar, 'each of us has probably spoken to his inner self in the same way as the serapiontic Ferdinand. And fortunately for us, the ominous storm that thundered about our heads, instead of destroying us, has merely strengthened and invigorated us like a powerful sulphur-bath. It seems that only now, among you, with the storm completely past, do I feel my full health returning, together with a new desire to apply myself seriously again to art and science. That is what Theodor is doing, I know, and very diligently too. Once again he is devoting himself totally to earlier music, although he has by no means neglected poetry. For this reason I believe he will soon surprise us with a first-rate opera, whose libretto and music will be entirely his. Everything that he has so sophistically argued concerning the impossibility of devising and composing an opera oneself may sound quite plausible, but it has not convinced me.'

[. . .]

Music Criticism

'Letter from a Monk to his Friend in the Capital'

Published: *Der Freimüthige oder Berlinische Zeitung*, 9 September 1803, 573–4   *Signed*: G[iuseppo].D[ori].[1]

First reprinted: Hitzig, i, 280–5

Unlike those eighteenth-century musicians who threw over a legal training in favour of their art (e.g. Telemann and Handel), Hoffmann qualified and practised as a lawyer. At the same time he studied and wrote music, and continued to sharpen his critical faculties. In 1800 he was appointed to the civil service in Poznań (Posen), half-way between Berlin and Warsaw: Western Poland had been a Prussian sphere of influence since the partition of 1775. But in 1802 he had incurred punishment for lampooning (with his friends) the local military commander, and was sent to the isolated town of Płock. Periods of semi-isolation invariably encouraged Hoffmann's creativity; the essay below (his first published writing) was followed by various musical compositions including a Mass in D and a piano sonata in A flat (both now lost).

Although 'Letter from a Monk' is about Schiller's use of the chorus rather than about music, it is full of characteristic features: the use of an authorial persona (cf. that of a monk in Wackenroder's *Herzensergiessungen eines kunstliebenden Kloster-bruders* (*Confessions from the Heart of an Art-loving Friar*), published in 1797); the use of a pseudonym; the autobiographical details woven into the account as a starting-point; the creation of a character through the technique of dramatic monologue; the use of irony in the service of artistic criticism.

Hoffmann's Letter was provoked by exchanges in the *Zeitung für die elegante Welt* (*ZEW*) and *Der Freimüthige oder Berlinische Zeitung*, journals that his cousin had been sending to Płock for him. Set in the Middle Ages, Schiller's penultimate play, *Die Braut von Messina* (*The Bride of Messina*), 1803, used a chorus inspired by ancient Greek tragedy. Anticipating controversy, Schiller had prefaced the play with an essay, 'On the Use of Chorus in Tragedy'. The ridicule that Hoffmann expresses was chiefly directed at those who naively took Schiller's example as the cue for seriously proposing to revive ancient Athenian theatrical masks and buskins (high-soled boots). His irony relies on the fact that, despite all the investigations into it, ancient Greek music still resisted attempts to reconstruct it satisfactorily.

Hoffmann returned to the subject of the chorus in his letter on Quaisin's *Le Jugement de Salomon*, reproduced after the present essay.

I thank you with all my heart, my dear friend Theodor, for so promptly sending me the books I ordered. The Father Prior was kind enough to send

---

[1] The complete version of the name was used as the signature on Hoffmann's letter to the publisher H. G. Nägeli, 9 August 1803.

the box to my cell without opening it, and I was pleased that Brother Vincent, who was visiting me, had just left when I received and eagerly unpacked it. He would certainly have been scandalised at the motley selection of magazines that you included without my having ordered them.

And you were right, my dear Theodor: even within these walls I am pleased to learn how life goes on in the world that I have forsaken for ever, and I therefore read the *Zeitung für die elegante Welt* and the *Freimüthige* with much pleasure, although many things struck me as distinctly odd and nonsensical, probably because here in my little cell I am so unfamiliar with the circumstances.

It is however clear to me that the writers in the two journals are very ill-disposed towards each other and always hold completely different opinions. They sometimes reproach each other quite rudely and seek to defend their cause with unseemly invective and abuse. I do not like that, and I was reminded of His Reverence the Prelate, who once gave Father Adalbert a good telling-off for having excessively berated Doctor Luther in his sermon on the Feast of St Anthony of Padua. The Prelate maintained that it brought more harm than good to a just cause, and was the sign of a coarse and petty mind.

I was quite overcome with joy, however, when I read that the famous Herr Schiller, who if I am not mistaken is the author of that splendid work *Don Carlos* which I read when I was still out in the world,[2] has completed a new tragedy, in which he treats the chorus in the manner of the ancient Greek tragedies. It is called *Die Braut von Messina*.

You know, my dear Theodor, that I have studied music avidly for many years and have never been content with a superficial, theoretical knowledge, adequate merely for setting a votive mass, or a vespers, or a new offertory for a saint's day. The music of the ancients drew my main attention, and I have always experienced profound distress to read in the ancient authors of the extraordinary effects that it is said to have produced, and to think that the way in which it was performed has so completely disappeared. I have compared everything that I could find in the ancient scribblers about music and the theatrical productions of the ancient Greeks in which it was incorporated; and yet I am still utterly in the dark as to how I should distinguish the declamation of Greek tragedy, which was provided with musical instruments and known as *melopoeia*,[3] from what we now call declamation and song. The choruses of Greek tragedies certainly resembled

---

[2] Hoffmann had 'read *Don Carlos* at least six times', casting himself in the title rôle and his friend Hippel as Posa. See letters of 23 January and 31 March 1796 (Sahlin, 47, 54).

[3] *melopoeia*: literally, the setting of lyrics to music. Hoffmann's ironic discussion of Greek practice in relation to the present has a striking earlier parallel in Voltaire's preface to his

true singing even more than the declamation of the rest of the text did; they were performed by a number of voices in unison and accompanied by instruments. This is shown in the account of the philosopher Seneca, among others, where we read:

Do you not see how many voices there are in a chorus? Yet out of the many only one voice results. In that chorus one voice takes the tenor, another the bass, another the baritone. There are women, too, as well as men, and the flute is mingled with them. In that chorus the voices of the individual singers are hidden; what we hear is the voices of all together.[4]

How this was actually put into effect, however, and to what extent the declamation of the chorus resembled true melody, I have no clear idea; and so far as I am aware, no one until now has managed to track down enough about the practice to enable it to be reproduced.

These momentous revelations have now been vouchsafed to the scholarly gentlemen in Weimar! From what I read, the aforementioned new tragedy by Herr Schiller is being presented there, and the declamation will doubtless have been provided with musical notation and an instrumental accompaniment. Write and tell me, my dear friend, whether Herr Schiller himself or somebody else was so fortunate as to discover the way of the ancients, and what means were employed of initiating the actors and musicians into the mystery of *melopoeia*, which we now find so unfathomable.

Somebody writes in the *Freimüthige*[5] that the chorus was spoken by seven men, and that it sounded like schoolchildren repeating their lessons. I cannot imagine anything more feeble and absurd than a number of people reciting verses on the stage without being governed by any sort of notated declamation constraining them as to pitch and rhythm. But I find it equally impossible to imagine that the scholarly gentlemen in Weimar would ever have entertained the thought of reintroducing the Greek chorus into the

---

Sémiramis (1748), where the constituents of opera are placed in the great tradition of Athens:

> 'What', I am told, 'an Italian opera resembles in any way the Athenian drama?' Yes, indeed. The Italian recitative is precisely the *melopoeia* of the ancients. It is that declamation with fixed note-values that is accompanied by musical instruments . . . The choruses which you have added in recent years, and which are so tightly linked to the plot, resemble the ancient choruses all the more closely in that their music is different from that of the recitatives . . .

From Ulrich Weisstein (ed., tr.), *The Essence of Opera* (Glencoe and London, 1964), 76.

[4] Seneca, *Ad Lucilium epistulae morales*, letter LXXXIV, translated by R. M. Gummere (London and Cambridge, Mass., 1920), ii, 281–3.

[5] Allusions to anonymous reviews in *Der Freimüthige*, 4 and 5 April 1803, 209–12, 213–14 [F.S.].

theatre, were they not fully acquainted with the manner of its performance by the ancients. In the production which that quibbling critic saw, the tibiists had doubtless not practised enough.[6]

Please write further, my dear Theodor, and tell me whether the flute-players accompanied the declamation throughout the play, or merely supported the chorus, and whether the tragedy was given with masks and buskins. I am also anxious to know what sort of effect the chorus had on the audience, whether they were deeply moved or whether the actors shared the experience of Professor Meibom of blessed memory, who was laughed to scorn by the entire court of Queen Christina when he began to sing a Greek aria.[7] That was ill-mannered, since the man was profoundly learned and meant well, but he did sometimes have very silly notions, as one can read in numerous accounts.

Finally I would like you to enlighten me as to the reason why Herr Schiller chose not a heroic tale from antiquity for his tragedy in the Greek manner, but a story from more recent times.[8] That seems to me the same as if our sisters of St Ursula were to clothe the Holy Child at Christmas in the robe normally worn by the Blessed Virgin: it is far too long and too wide, it will not fit anywhere, and does not look at all well.

So long as they have restored the art of *melopoeia*, and the people have got over the strangeness of their first impression, then the rest will take care of itself. Without musical instruments, however, without notated declamation, it will all be just an ineffectual babble.[9]

I assume that the tragedy *General Wallenstein*,[10] which Herr Schiller is said to have written in verse, and the *Hussiten vor Naumburg*, which must be a fine play in view of all the controversy surrounding it,[11] are performed with the tragic bass flute (tibia dextra), and that the new verse comedies by

---

[6] tibia: Roman instrument much like the Greek aulos, or reed-blown pipe. The dextra and serrana (see end of the Letter) types were right- and left-handed versions, the former with the deeper pitch.

[7] Marcus Meibom (1620/21–1711) edited Greek musical texts as *Antiquae musicae auctores septem* (Amsterdam, 1652). Named as assistant royal librarian to Queen Christina in the same year, he was invited by her to construct some of the ancient instruments. But his 'Greek' singing met with ridicule, at which he boxed the ears of the Queen's physician and favourite, Bourdelot, and was dismissed as a consequence.

[8] The story was invented by Schiller, though set in mediaeval times.

[9] How Hoffmann himself solved this difficulty when he composed 'marches and chorus' for the Bamberg production of *Die Braut von Messina* on 12 March 1813, we cannot tell, as the music is lost [F.S.].

[10] Schiller's trilogy of plays: *Wallensteins Lager* (1798), *Die Piccolomini* (1799) and *Wallensteins Tod* (1799).

[11] *Die Hussiten vor Naumburg im Jahre 1432* was by August von Kotzebue, the founder-editor of *Der Freimüthige*, and first seen in 1802. It uses a chorus too. The 'controversy' centred on

Herr von Kotzebue are performed with the comic descant flute (tibia serrana). I wish I could hear them myself.

Farewell, my dear Theodor. I will pray to the saints for you and remain etc.

'Observations on Quaisin's *Le Jugement de Salomon*, on Melodrama, and on the Chorus in Tragedy'

Original form: *HBW*, i, 238
Published: *Allgemeine Deutsche Theater-Zeitung*, 17 and 20 May 1808
Signed: *H—v*
First reprinted: *Zeitschrift für Bücherfreunde*, Neue Folge, xvi (1924)

In October 1806 Prussia was defeated simultaneously at Jena and at Auerstedt, and Berlin was captured by the French. Warsaw, where Hoffmann had lived and worked since April 1804, was made the capital of a French-dependent 'Duchy of Warsaw'. So Hoffmann left his wife with her family in Poznań while he struggled to make a living in Berlin. Through his friend Hitzig in Potsdam he advertised for employment and received a letter in November 1807 from Count Julius von Soden, director of the theatre in Bamberg. Soden held out the prospect of the musical directorship to Hoffmann and commissioned him to set his own four-act libretto, *Der Trank der Unsterblichkeit* (*The Drink of Immortality*). He also mentioned a melodrama, *Joseph in Ägypten* (*Joseph in Egypt*). Hoffmann completed the opera in a month or less and sent the score to Bamberg on 27 February 1808, following which he was duly offered the post; he accepted it on 16 April. (The opera survives in the Deutsche Staatsbibliothek, Berlin.)

On 23 April 1808 he wrote to Soden to say he would like to begin work on *Joseph in Ägypten*, and included some observations on the melodrama genre by way of a private review of a French work, *Le Jugement de Salomon* (*The Judgement of Solomon*). Soden sent a copy of this review to the *Allgemeine Deutsche Theater-Zeitung*, to which he was a contributor, where it was printed with the minimum of editorial changes. The last part of Hoffmann's letter provides a fascinating glimpse of the dramatic composer in the initial collaborative stage of a new venture.

In a melodrama, non-singing actors declaimed their speeches between, or sometimes during, expressive passages played by the orchestra. This was the case in *Le Jugement de Salomon*, a three-act work first produced at the Théâtre de l'Ambigu-

a parody of it by A. Mahlmann (1803), and critical features in *Der Freimüthige* of 3 May, 12 May, and 8 July 1803 [F.S.].

Comique, Paris, on 18 January 1802. The composer, Adrien Quaisin (1766–1828), was this theatre's musical director for twenty years from 1799; he also composed music for Pixérécourt's melodramas. The text was by Louis-Charles Caigniez (1762–1842), one of whose librettos was the indirect source of Rossini's opera *La gazza ladra*. *Salomon* was a success, reaching its twenty-seventh performance by 25 February. It reached Vienna in 1804. Soden had it mounted at Würzburg (24 October 1806) and then Bamberg (1 January 1807). Hoffmann must have seen it in Berlin, where with A. W. Iffland as Salomon it was first staged on 16 March 1808. The original music seems to have been modified (see note 5) but since it was not published and even the manuscript score in the Bibliothèque Nationale is of German provenance, there is currently no way of checking whether this is so.

Hoffmann's projected *Joseph* never materialised, perhaps partly because of the wide success of Méhul's eponymous opéra-comique (1807). However, his setting of Soden's melodrama *Dirna* was staged at Bamberg on 11 October 1809.

1. The piece begins with a solemnly sustained overture, after which some light-hearted music depicts the cheerful life of the gardeners.[1] The idea is a good one. Every serious play should begin with an overture designed for it, to put the listener into an appropriate frame of mind. The effect of an *introduzzione* would be in proportion as it approximates to the opening scenes, thus forming a transition from the overture, which expresses the character of the play in general, to the opening scenes, whose particular mood it reflects.

2. Music heralds the appearance of the most important characters in the play. This means of further arousing the interest of the audience should not be rejected, so long as the strictest economy is observed. In my opinion music may be employed here only very rarely, and then as briefly as possible. If it is used too frequently the spectator will no longer be seized by the feeling of the unexpected that is intended. If the music lasts longer than the character needs to make his appearance, the action comes to a halt and the players are obliged, as frequently happens in *Salomon*, to stare at each other for a while before they begin to speak, which is ridiculous. It is with good reason that Gluck condemned long ritornellos in opera.[2]

3. Many speeches are accompanied by music. One can imagine that if some motive is present to justify music during the speech, then it can be of

---

[1] The exposition of the plot is made by Léila's nurse to Morad, a gardener. The dispute concerning maternity of the child over whom Salomon pronounces in Act 3 proves to be between Léila and Tamira. The latter, a widow, is betrothed to Salomon's brother Eliphal; he is the child's unacknowledged father, and eventually marries Léila, its natural mother.

[2] i.e. in the Italian *Alceste* (Vienna, 1769): see p. 265 n. 7. In a very disapproving review of *Le Jugement de Salomon* (*VZ*, 19 March 1808) we read: 'On the whole the acting was excellent, but subject to too many musical interruptions. Between a question and an answer, for

great effect; but without any such motive it is quite tasteless and absurd. In *Octavia*,[3] for example, Antonius lies sleeping in a richly decorated tent, and while the harps and flutes that lulled him to sleep whisper gently round, Cleopatra betrays him at the front of the stage. A similar example is the famous soliloquy in the *Jungfrau* [*von Orleans*] (*The Maid of Orleans*):[4] a shawm echoes among the hills, a shepherd sings his merry song, and the well-loved sounds calling her back with such longing make all the harder her farewell to a life of idyllic peace. In neither case is the music directly linked to the speech. Rather is it a fortuitous occurrence independent of the speech, and is regarded by the listener as such; but it does not fail to have considerable effect in heightening the romantic mood of the moment. Even in everyday life one hears of such cases; for example, 'Imagine my feelings when, just as my dear wife died, the choir-school boys began singing the chorale "How softly they repose" outside my house'; or, 'Yesterday at the ball I became convinced my beloved was unfaithful, and just as I was sealing the letter that would separate us for ever the band went past for the changing of the guard and the oboists were playing a waltz, etc. etc.' What is one to say, however, when Salomon kneels and begs God Almighty to grant him sufficient wisdom, to the sudden blowing of basset-horns?[5] Here the music is directly linked to the speech, so that the actor is obliged to adjust his words exactly to the rhythms of the music. The speech itself then acquires a rhythmical quality bordering on song, without fulfilling the requirements of euphony in intonation. Music and speech diminish each other reciprocally, since one inevitably perceives them as belonging together as song and instrumental accompaniment. When in addition the music is so highly obtrusive and yet so shallow as in *Salomon*, the effect cannot but be thoroughly repugnant. Even Iffland's splendid declamation was unable to improve matters and among true connoisseurs of art only one opinion was voiced.

    4. The procession with Salomon's bride appears and passes by to the

---

    example, there would be a beautiful violin solo, but played at totally the wrong time' (*HBW*, i, 239).

[3] Five-act tragedy by Kotzebue, Act 2 sc. 1; as it was not given in Berlin in 1807–08 Hoffmann would have seen it, if at all, at the time of its Berlin première on 9 June 1800, just before his move to Poznań (*HBW*, i, 239).

[4] Schiller, *Die Jungfrau von Orleans*, Act 4 sc. 1. The setting is actually a hall adorned for a festival; not only does Schiller specify the sound of offstage flutes and oboes, but also instructs them to play 'a soft, languishing melody' at a certain juncture, prompting new thoughts in the protagonist: 'Woe! Oh woe!'

[5] The German score of *Salomon* obviously differed from the Parisian original: basset-horns were not then used in Paris. The original French text did not in fact indicate any music during Salomon's prayer, Act 3 sc. 3.

accompaniment of a march; in the last act two choruses are interspersed.[6] This brings me to a major point, and the discussion of an idea that I have long wished to submit to Your Excellency.[7] We had tragedies with choruses long ago, but they formed a musical entity separate from the rest of the play. In Racine's *Athalie*, for example, the Levites gather at the end of each act and sing a cantata, which is what choruses interspersed with solos, duets, and so on amount to. They result not only in a division of interest, but also in a uniformity that gives rise to boredom, even when the music is as excellent as that of Schulz for *Athalie*.[8] In *Herrmann von Unna* the arrangement is operatic, and only the solemn church style of Vogler compensated for this defect.[9] There is something else that has been done: an attempt has been made to introduce the chorus from Greek tragedy, with a number of people declaiming stanzas together. I consider this to be a great misconception; such unison speaking, which sounds utterly abhorrent, cannot be endured by musical ears at least, and this new idea is of little value. The idea is new, since the Greeks did not expect the chorus to speak but rather to sing, accompanied by instruments. This may be demonstrated in a number of authors, and a passage from Seneca occurs to me that is conclusive:

Do you not see how many voices there are in a chorus? Yet out of the many only one voice results. In that chorus one voice takes the tenor, another the bass, another the baritone. There are women, too, as well as men, and the flute is mingled with them. In that chorus the voices of the individual singers are hidden; what we hear is the voices of all together.[10]

How would it be if one retained the Greeks' idea of the chorus but applied it to our music, as it has developed now? The companions of the heroes in the

---

[6] Towards the end of Act 1 Pharaoh's daughter Azélie arrives for her wedding to Salomon in a procession; extravagant gifts are displayed. The two choruses in Act 3 are for the welcome extended to Azélie in sc. 2, followed by a dance of the daughters of Jerusalem; and for the end of the whole work where, in the Paris version at least, there was a solo stanza as well.

[7] As Hoffmann perhaps knew from reading the *Allgemeine Deutsche Theater-Zeitung* of 26 and 29 March 1808, Soden had experimented with a chorus that appeared 'following each act' of his five-act tragedy *Medea*. They were 'not, as in Schiller's *Die Braut von Messina*, actively participating characters, but voices of the people'. Thus Hoffmann must have feared that Soden would treat the chorus similarly in *Joseph*, and he obliquely tries to forestall the idea (*HBW*, i, 240).

[8] J. A. P. Schulz (1747–1800): his choruses and songs for Racine's *Athalie* (published 1786) enjoyed great popularity well into the nineteenth century. Hoffmann noted going to a concert performance in Königsberg in his diary of 14 February 1804 (*HBW*, i, 240).

[9] A. F. Skjöldebrand's play (1792) with music by G. J. Vogler was first given in German in Berlin, 5 September 1800; Hoffmann could have seen it there only on 15 September or 10 December 1807. The piano score, however, was published by Breitkopf & Härtel early in 1801 [F.S., rev.].

[10] See p. 215 note 4.

action express their admiration, their amazement, their pain, their horror in powerful stanzas at the important moments of the play, and they sing these stanzas; both the poet and the composer should be *forceful* and *brief* here. Choruses performed in the manner preferred today would be a misconception, and it would sound like an opera in which the main characters were speaking their rôles because of hoarseness or some other reason. Obviously there can be no question of retaining the inner poetic form and disposition of the Greek chorus, but its form should be adapted to our present music with perhaps only the strophe and antistrophe being preserved. In large theatres where an experienced chorus of at least forty singers is available[11] the chorus should have no instrumental accompaniment at all (or perhaps only *violons*[12]) in order to have the greatest effect. The chorus moreover forms an entity distinct from the characters of the drama, and all the less likely is it to be incongruous or disturbing that only *it* sings.

Review of Witt's Fifth and Sixth Symphonies

Published: *AMZ*, xi, 17 May 1809, cols. 513–21   *Unsigned*
First reprinted: Ellinger 1912

The four and a half years' sojourn in Bamberg commenced for Hoffmann with traumatic events that had a direct bearing on his writing. When he and his wife arrived on 1 September 1808, Count Soden had disappeared to Würzburg and left the theatre enterprise to a 'conceited windbag', Heinrich Cuno.[1] The orchestra had not even been assembled. Worse followed. The musicians were not good, the violinist-leader Anton Dittmayer resented the newcomer, and there was disagreement over Hoffmann's desire to conduct from the keyboard (a perfectly acceptable method, later practised by Hoffmann in Dresden and Leipzig). Dittmayer refused to play, the musicians spread rumours, and – after conducting three or so times – Hoffmann retired from the fray and took the title of 'theatre composer' instead, but with reduced salary (*HTR*, 78 9).[2]

---

[11] This was not an implausible number. C. M. von Weber reported seeing fifty young singers in the chorus at the court theatre, Darmstadt, in 1811. *Weber: Writings*, 67.

[12] *violons*: not 'violins' but Hoffmann's term for double-basses, or the latter mixed with the violone (the double bass viol). Leopold Mozart (1756) and H. C. Koch (1802) both used 'violone' for 'double-bass'. *The New Grove*, xix, 863.

[1] See letters to Hitzig and the violinist Morgenroth (1 January and 26 February 1809: *HBW*, i, 255, 268) and Speyer (13 July 1813: *HBW*, i, 392).

[2] On the conducting question, see the letter to Speyer mentioned above, and also comments in a letter from C. F. Kunz (*HBW*, i, 405).

The rebuff helped lead to writing, which was after all an alternative means of assertion and interpretation, as well as financial reward. Hoffmann also began to teach music in the wealthier local families, able to observe there the provincial idiosyncrasies so familiar now from *Kreisleriana* and *Kater Murr*. On 12 January 1809 he sent the manuscript of *Ritter Gluck* to the editor of the *AMZ*, Friedrich Rochlitz (with whom he had corresponded since October 1807 about his own compositions), and suggested that he might submit further essays 'and reviews of smaller works'. This offer was accepted on 29 January and on 2 March Hoffmann received a batch of six works including Witt's symphonies.[3]

Hoffmann may have arranged a local performance of one of these works on 13 March (*HTB*, 318); the diary entry for 19 April reads: 'Reviewed the two symphonies of Witt – opus 1 of this kind – went more easily than I had expected.' The completed review was despatched on 22 April. Hoffmann declined to write about Heinrich Tuch's *Harmonie*, on account of its 'unimportance', or Peter Hänsel's or Friedrich Dotzauer's quartets, because he had apparently been unable to arrange good performances of them.

Friedrich Witt (1770–1836), Kapellmeister in Würzburg, was a composer in the Haydn tradition, whose symphonies (as reported in E. L. Gerber's *Lexicon der Tonkünstler*) 'are favourites in our concerts'. The first fourteen of his symphonies remained unpublished; then eight were issued in parts between about 1803 and about 1811 (numbered 1 to 8), while the ninth and last, in D minor, was printed around 1816. Three symphonies (including the notorious 'Jena' symphony) are currently available in modern editions.[4]

In casting his reviews, Hoffmann followed the established guidelines of the *Allgemeine Musikalische Zeitung*: an introductory section; an analytical section, usually with the weight thrown towards the first movement; and a concluding section, mentioning among other things any relevant details of performance practice, publication, or arrangement in piano score. These principles, and the use of terminology, are discussed in 'Hoffmann as a Writer on Music', above. The 'first half' of a sonata movement signified the material of the exposition, while 'second half' signified the remainder of the movement.

Symphony No. 5

That instrumental music has now risen to a level of which one probably had no inkling not so long ago, and that the symphony, especially following the

---

[3] J. J. F. Dotzauer, *Quartetto* Op. 13; P. Hänsel, *Quatuor brillant* Op. 18; J. C. Stumpf, *Entr'actes pour des pièces de théâtre*, livres 1–4; H. A. G. Tuch, *Harmonie ou Sonate en B pour 2 Clarinettes, 2 Bassons, 2 Cors et 2 Hautbois* Op. 22; and the Witt symphonies in orchestral parts.

[4] Hoffmann's reviews are not mentioned in any of the more recent English writings about Witt. See the biography and thematic catalogue in Stephen C. Fisher's edition of Witt's Second Symphony, published within *The Symphony 1720–1840*, ed. Barry S. Brook (New York and London, 1983), Series B, vol. ix. Also H. C. Robbins Landon, 'The *Jena* Symphony', *Music Review*, xviii (1957), 109–13.

impetus it received from Haydn and Mozart, has become the ultimate form of instrumental music – the *opera* of instruments as it were – all this is well – known to every lover of music.[5] The onerous task those musical heroes were happily able to perform in the symphony was to unite all the common instruments of the orchestra, voicing their individual characteristics in the performance of one great drama. Thus, disdaining the stiff, boring form of the old concerto grosso, they were able to put individual parts at the service of the whole, and these products of their genius rightly became the norm by which later composers conceived their symphonies. Herr Witt too has taken Haydn as his model and his Fifth Symphony once again demonstrates his worthiness to follow in the footsteps of the master.

The symphony begins with a short Adagio in D major[6] but continuing after the fifth bar in D minor. It is solemn in character but free from all grandiloquence, and does no more than announce what follows. The usual error of composers today, who so often squander all their force at the first charge, is thus completely avoided. After this Adagio comes an Allegro, likewise in D major, with a very pleasant theme:

Immediately after the first, rousing tutti the oboe enters with a simple, melodious phrase, while the first violins imitate the opening theme. This inspired idea produces an effect like a glimpse of bright sunshine through dark storm-clouds:

---

5 Hoffmann here evokes the whole critical tendency of the *AMZ* since its foundation in 1798, and also a text that he can be assumed to have known: Wackenroder's 'The Characteristic Inner Nature of the Musical Art and the Psychology of Today's Instrumental Music', which described modern symphonies in 1799 as containing 'not one individual emotion . . . but an entire world, an entire drama of human emotions'. See Schubert (ed., tr.), *Wackenroder's 'Confessions'*, 193.

6 Title page: SINFONIE / pour / 2 Violons [etc.] . . . / PAR / WITT. / No. 5. / N°. 2622. Prix fl.5– / A OFFENBACH sur le Mein, / chez Jean André. The plate number was 2622. The opening Adagio is 16 bars long, 4/4 time.

After another extremely attractive intermediary section in the dominant,[7] the leading voice and the bass imitate a phrase that has already occurred in a simple form in the fifteenth bar; it lacks novelty, therefore, but moves forward forcefully and so is ideally suited, as here, to lead to the close:[8]

The second half now brings further development of the opening theme, again in imitation between leading voice and bass, which alternately play the second half of the theme as a countermelody to the first, while the wind instruments provide the underlying harmony in held notes or occasionally take up the melody. The further progress of the Allegro follows the conventional pattern, with the first half coming back and moving to the close by way of the intermediary section, which now remains in the tonic.

The theme of the following Andante grazioso, in G major, is again most charmingly contrived and perfectly suits the inherently gentle nature of the key that the composer has chosen:

[7] That is, the second subject area.

[8] The last beat of the second bar of this example correctly reproduces both the *A M Z* text and Witt's original printed violin part, though a final c sharp''' seems needed.

Only at the appearance of the minor does the music lose its prevailing legato mood. The minor enters much too violently and harshly compared with the preceding major. One might liken it to a beautiful girl who in her sorrow howls and screams, instead of softly weeping. This minor section lasts for only twenty bars,[9] but long enough to do great damage to the overall effect, and a lighter, perhaps naive shading to it would certainly have benefited the subsequent return of the theme very much.

The Minuetto which follows has an expansive theme. In the second bar it is taken up by the bass in a sort of *al rovescio*,[10] and as a result the opening of this minuet acquires a proud, stately quality that contrasts very well with the gentle Andante.

The Trio is a solo for flute and bassoon and sounds very much like a waltz. This is a criticism that can also be levelled against many of Haydn's minuets, although in other respects these are always the tastiest dishes on a richly laid-out table. They suddenly strike the listener with some inspired twist of an initially quite ordinary-seeming idea, and particularly in the trios the deepest harmonic subtleties beneath the cheerful stream of artless melody are often detected only by the knowledgeable listener. That the minuet before us cannot quite satisfy the standard set by Haydn, the creator of this form,[11] the composer himself will certainly agree.

The final movement, in D major, has a melismatic theme[12] and is light and airy throughout. Here too one is reminded of Haydn's finales, but misses his far-reaching developments and ever new variations of the theme which keep the listener in suspense right to the last bar, however tenuous the thread of the music may appear. Here, for example, the connoisseur would expect a weightier intermediary section in longer notes,[13] followed by the return of the opening melismatic phrase, which would certainly have given rise to the most striking transformations and imitations. This expectation is not fulfilled, however, and the whole movement rushes by without arousing any great interest in the listener, although the conclusion is very brilliant and effective. In the symphony as a whole – the juxtaposition of movements, orchestration, etc. – Herr W. has shown himself to be an intelligent and thorough composer. His obvious endeavour to give the

---

[9] Actually nineteen bars. Witt's formal plan is unusual. The first and second subject areas (total fifty-one bars) proceed as for a sonata, but are followed by the section disliked by Hoffmann, carrying a G minor key-signature. The first subject is then restated.

[10] *al rovescio*: by inversion. Although Hoffmann describes the music as 'stately', the tempo indication is *Allegro più molto*: the key is D major.

[11] Literally, 'the creator of these pieces' [transl.].

[12] The movement is headed *Finale. Allegro* and is in 2/4 time. By 'melismatic' Hoffmann means what we would call *moto perpetuo*: running semiquavers dominate the texture.

[13] In fact there is a second subject, but it is soft and light in character.

whole work not only as much depth but also as great an appeal as possible shows that it is written for a *wide* public; and it will certainly not go unnoticed since, even moderately well performed, it is highly effective and therefore justly to be recommended to every orchestra.

The tempo of the first Allegro must not be taken too rapidly, and that of the Andante not too slowly, but the minuet and finale, so long as their essential character is preserved, can be as fast as the ability of the orchestra permits.

Sinfonie turque, No. 6[14]

Formerly the bass drum and the jangle of tambourine, triangle and cymbal were heard only rarely in the theatre, but gradually they became more and more frequent and finally even entered the concert-hall. It would have done well to lock its doors against them, for seldom is a concert-hall large or an orchestra loud enough to make the deafening sound of the bass drum and the jangle of the other so-called Turkish instruments even bearable. The functions of concert music and theatre music are different. In the overture to an opera the naive and boldly modulating music we now refer to as 'Turkish' music (although no original for this imitation exists) clearly proclaims the character of the work to every listener;[15] the bass drum, usually banished to the remotest corner of the orchestra, soon dies away in the spacious auditorium and never drowns the other instruments. In a concert and in the symphony, which usually serves as an overture to a wide variety of subsequent pieces, the strongly individual character of Turkish music, even discounting the cacophony of Turkish instruments, is not likely to be of great appeal to the listener. He does not wish to be transported to Turkey, as in the theatre, in order to listen to his concertos, arias, and the like, but merely expects to have his appetite whetted for musical pleasures of whatever kind. The specific character that should dominate in a symphony, as in a musical drama, and should captivate the listener by revealing its various nuances from every aspect, very easily becomes dull and one-sided if a single mannerism is dwelt upon.

Herr W., however, has now also written a *Sinfonie turque* with the bass drum and other accessories, thereby pandering to the taste of those who derive their musical, or rather unmusical, titillation in this way. That Herr

---

[14] Title page: SINFONIE TURQUE / pour / 2 Violons [etc.] . . . / composée / par / WITT. / No. 6. / N°. 2639. Prix f.5.– / A OFFENBACH sur le Mein, / chez Jean André. The plate number was 2639.

[15] e.g. Mozart, *Die Entführung aus dem Serail* (1782) and Boieldieu, *Le Calife de Bagdad* (1800).

W. would produce nothing inferior, nothing vulgar, even in this style, may be taken for granted in such an able composer, and this expectation is not at all disappointed in the present work.

After a short introductory section, Adagio in A minor,[16] of no great significance (as is quite right here) comes an Allegro, also in A minor, whose main subjects are not novel or particularly striking but do accurately capture the style adopted in this symphony:[17]

The latter subject recurs in the second part in A major, and the spirit of almost unrestrained gaiety continues in the major until the end of the Allegro, giving it added appeal and firmly holding the listener's interest.

The Adagio, in A major, is notable for its original opening. Basses, cellos, and violins play the basic chords pizzicato, while the violas move up and down mainly in thirds, also pizzicato. This appears as follows:

With the exception of a few bars the violas retain this figure throughout the movement, while flute, oboe, clarinet, and bassoon provide some extremely melodious phrases. Without being in the least shallow or hackneyed, this Adagio is intelligible and pleasing to anyone with a musical ear at

---

[16] Adagio: this is 15 bars long.
[17] The first example shows the beginning of the Allegro molto; the second shows bars 74–7 of the same movement.

all, and even the most fanatical friend of the bass drum will gladly accede to its remaining silent on this occasion.

The theme of the Minuetto, of no great moment although it falls pain-lessly upon the ear, is played by the second flute since the first flautist again has to take up the piccolo on which he doubles. The Trio consists of a very pleasant cello solo during which the bass drum and its appendages are not heard from at all.

The last movement again faithfully adheres to the adopted style:

Sixty bars before the end the music moves into a lively A major. In general the last movement is lightly handled, with no profound development of the theme, though it has considerable effect, to which the skilful orchestration contributes in no small measure. One peculiarity of this orchestration is that the four horns are crooked not in pairs at the tonic and dominant as usual but in the following way: *corno primo* in G, *corno secondo* in A, *corno terzo* in E, *corno quarto* in C.

The composer has very skilfully employed these different crooks for his purpose and combined the horns in chords in which they have to play only their easiest and best notes, so that their richness and power greatly heighten the effect of the whole. The use of these four horns, however, makes the symphony unsuitable for smaller orchestras, for if they cannot be obtained let no conductor imagine that a single one may be left out or replaced by another instrument. Otherwise the symphony is not especially difficult to perform, and since it is fully the equal of the Fifth Symphony in its flowing melody, though inferior to it in nobility of character, it can be highly recommended to any orchestra.

The two Adagios excepted, the tempos must be taken very fast.

Review of Fioravanti's *I virtuosi ambulanti*

Published: *AMZ*, xii, 27 December 1809, cols. 204–8   *Unsigned*
First reprinted: Ellinger 1912

The Bamberg theatre company almost collapsed in spring 1809 and Hoffmann used his contract to sever his links with it, retaining 'nothing more of my theatrical career than the title "musical director" which I shall preserve for future use' (letter to Hitzig, 25 May 1809: *HBW*, i, 285). He continued an active teaching and composing life. The editors of the *AMZ* sent him a letter in mid-June offering him the chance to review some Beethoven symphonies, which he accepted, and on 21 July he received from the *AMZ* a packet that must have contained two Beethoven symphonies (see pp. 452–4), Romberg's *Pater Noster* and Fioravanti's *I virtuosi ambulanti* (*The Wandering Players*). Hoffmann despatched his reviews of the Romberg and Fioravanti pieces exactly four months later.

Valentino Fioravanti (1764–1837) was a prolific and successful opera composer, though later eclipsed by the genius of Rossini. *I virtuosi ambulanti* was to be one of his most popular works, not least in German-speaking countries; Hoffmann himself conducted it in Leipzig on 11, 13, and 25 February 1814 for Seconda's company. It derived from a French libretto (see note 3) set to music in 1798 by Devienne, and was rewritten for Fioravanti by G. L. Balocchi. This French connection was probably exploited since *I virtuosi ambulanti* was written for the Parisian theatre for Italian opera, the Théâtre de l'Impératrice, where its première took place on 26 September 1807.

Fioravanti entrusted the publication of the work to Nicolas-Raphaël Carli ('Carli e Compagnia') in Paris, and Carli produced both a full score and a piano arrangement. Their plate numbers (59 to 80) indicate publication in 1807.[1] The piano arrangement, lacking most of the recitatives, also contained numerous other alterations, including transposition of the leading baritone part (Bellarosa) into the treble clef: as its use of separate pagination and titles for each number suggests, it was intended for piecemeal domestic performance. These musical arrangements and the piano reduction were credited to 'Pacini de Naples'; Antonio Pacini (1778–1866) was himself a composer, later eminent as a publisher in Paris, where he had settled in 1804. The score Hoffmann was sent for review was an unacknowledged reproduction of Pacini's version, with the sole addition of a German translation of the text, engraved in oblong instead of upright format, with continuous pagination and without separate titles.[2] Hoffmann, who does not mention the upward transposition of solo

---

[1] A. Devriès and F. Lesure, *Dictionnaire des éditeurs de musique français* (Geneva, 1979), i, 46.

male roles, concentrates admiringly instead on the essential theatrical quality of the work, ingeniously attempting to combine a basic account of the plot with his musical critique. The absence of recitatives, however, kept him and his readers ignorant of the opera's main intrigue, which hinges on the mistaken identity of a suitcase.

The reviewer is not familiar with the full score of the *Virtuosi ambulanti*; but he sees from the piano score in front of him that the libretto of *Les Comédiens ambulans* by Picard (translated into German by Treitschke for the Hoftheater in Vienna), previously set by Devienne, has been used again for this opera.[3]

It is a happy idea to drag life behind the scenes on to the stage, and thus force the actors to satirise themselves; in all the variations it has undergone, such as those of Cimarosa and Mozart, it has never failed in its effect on the public.[4] This opera too, a composition that places Fioravanti worthily beside those masters, is certain to find favour everywhere, so long as it is performed with vitality and comic force by good actors and singers. The whole work is easily and gracefully sustained, and demonstrates the composer's special talent for expressing comic pathos in music. The reviewer finds music particularly appealing when the melody seems familiar without actually reminding him of an existing theme, and thus becoming mere reminiscence. From this point of view the melodies in this opera are very appealing; together with the fact that the frequent melismas lie perfectly in the throat, as we say, this greatly facilitates their performance for the singers, although *German* singers will prefer to avoid the frequent *parlando* passages, for which they usually have no aptitude. In the very first number this *parlando* is employed in a most original way. Bellarosa, the director of the company, has hurried ahead of the cart (the Thespian wagon, loaded with scenery, actors, equipment, etc.) and can think of nothing better on a beautiful morning, described in a picturesque recitative with murmuring

---

[2] Title page: OUVERTURE ET AIRS / DE L'OPERA / I Virtuosi Ambulanti / PAR FIORA-VANTI. / ARRANGÉES POUR LE PIANO-FORTE / Avec les paroles Italiennes, Françaises et Allemandes. / PAR MR. L. WOLFF / . . . A LEIPZIG chez A. MEYSEL. The plate number was 67. If the German translation was by Treitschke, as Hoffmann's opening remarks possibly suggest, that name is certainly absent from the score. The French words were also pirated from the Paris edition, where they were credited to 'Desriaux', presumably Philippe Desriaux, librettist of Vogel's *Démophon* (1789) and Catel's *Sémiramis* (1802). This Leipzig score was advertised in the *AMZ Intelligenz-Blatt* in April 1809.

[3] *Les Comédiens ambulans*, words by L. B. Picard, music by François Devienne, in two acts, was first performed at the Théâtre Feydeau, Paris, on 28 December 1798.

[4] Mozart, *Der Schauspieldirektor* (1786); Cimarosa, *L'impresario in angustie* (1786).

brooks and twittering birds, than to practise his 'grand *aria principale*' of the next opera. The instruments play the melody of this aria without interruption, but he sings it a bit at a time, constantly inserting remarks about his performance:[5]

This continual alternation between singing and *parlando* provides not only the capable singer but also the good actor with the opportunity for an attractive comic exposition.

The Thespian carriage overturns; there are 'insults, blows, cries, tears'; finally in No. 5[6] the offended Lauretta, Rosalinda's rival for the position of *prima donna*, appears and pours out her wrath in a recitative. This, like Rosalinda's recitative No. 12,[7] contains the conventional phrases of opera seria recitative, and thus excellently satirises the empty formality of such compositions. Both the arias that follow are concertante pieces with an accompanying chorus,[8] and it is clear that the composer also intends to make fun of the now common practice of combining the chorus with the solo part. One can imagine nothing harmonically more inane than the

---

[5] The remarks include 'breathe here', 'observe the syncopation', 'the voice should fall artlessly'. 'Tre quarti d'aspetto' in the example means 'three-quarter profile'.

[6] Recitative, 'A me civetta?' and aria, 'Sono amabil, son graziosa.'

[7] 'No. 10' in *AMZ* text. Rosalinda's recitative begins, 'Ah, barbari! fermate'.

[8] Hoffmann refers to Lauretta's aria No. 5 (see above) and Bocchindoro's aria No. 7, 'Adorata eccelsa Diva'.

accompaniment provided by these choruses. On hearing them one realises that it is a very simple matter to write a concertante piece, so long as one uses the singers merely to reproduce here and there the chords underlying the melody and its melismatic decoration, which completely negates the higher ideal of a participating chorus, namely to express its own character yet lie close to the solo voice without smothering it. The composer also happily parodies the bad habit of singers who add embellishments everywhere with no regard for the words or situation. In the duet No. 6,[9] which is full of character and comic force and yet extremely graceful, Rosalinda criticises the interpretation of the words 'indietro perfidi! la borsa io cedo', and decides that on the word 'borsa' (money) there should be a cadenza, which she immediately puts to the test:[10]

The present reviewer would have exaggerated this cadenza even more, to make the point really obvious. Similarly Rosalinda wants a staccato passage on the word 'morir' (to die):

Particularly worthy of note is the trio No. 8,[11] in which the two sopranos have to sing their exercises at the request of the director. He characteristically gives expression to his approval and admiration entirely in short notes, and finally becomes so heated that he joins in with the beautiful roulades of the sopranos. In these roulades Lauretta and Rosalinda vary their figuration while Bellarosa firmly persists in his, so that both the rivalry of the ladies, vying for superiority like two nightingales, and Bellarosa's relationship to them, are very well expressed. In the aria No. 9[12] Fiordaliso gives the recipe for an opera in a most humorous way, and equally comical is Bellarosa's description in No. 11 of a theatre-director's tribulations[13]. He barks out his irritation and rage in short, rapid *parlando* notes, and when he has given vent to his feelings we hear again in longer notes, as a refrain, the words:

[9] Rosalinda and Lauretta, 'Miei signori, permettete'.
[10] In this example both *A M Z* and the piano score omit the last two quavers of the coloratura; they have been inserted from the full score [F.S.].
[11] Rosalinda, Lauretta, Bellarosa, 'Stiamo attente, e solfeggiamo.'
[12] 'Prià di tutto ad ogni istante'.
[13] Beginning with the recitative, 'Ah sfoghiamo ci un poco'; this is where Bellarosa vents his anger; the music example is taken from the succeeding aria.

Special praise should also be accorded the very pleasing duet No. 10, in which the reviewer questions only the ugly, easily avoided fifths in the voice parts in the sixth and seventh bars from the end,[14] and the canon No. 13 as far as the twenty-fifth bar, where another theme, too monotonous and repetitive, makes the singing dull and empty.[15]

The spirit that the composer has injected into even the smallest rôle is seen in the short aria of the peasant Gervasio. He has a lot of money in his knapsack and in order to avoid falling asleep and being robbed, he considers what he might get with the money: 'a little ass, a little house, a little wife'. The melody, constantly reiterating the same notes, perfectly expresses his stupidity and drowsiness, while the recurring figure in the violins approximates the effect of someone pinching himself on the nose in order to stay awake.[16]

14 Lauretta and Rosalinda, 'Già la notte s'avvicina.' The parallel fifths are the fault of the arranger, who freely adapted the conclusion of the 'duet' (actually a sextet with male chorus) and transposed the piece from C major to B flat major [F.S.].

15 'Trio and canon' for Rosalinda, Lauretta, and Bocchindoro, 'Talor dal grembo d'opaco nembo'. In bar 26 a tempo change should occur, from *Andante un poco sostenuto* to *Allegro*. In bar 27 Bocchindoro is joined by Bellarosa, Gervasio, and Podestà and in bar 28 by the other four soloists, so that ten soloists are singing from this point on, the male chorus also entering in bar 34. All this naturally gives the whole piece a different complexion from that suggested by the piano score with its three soloists and missing *Allegro* marking [F.S.].

16 Original key, D major; Gervasio in the bass clef.

But the simpleton nods off to sleep despite his house, ass, and little wife, which one assumed he would do as soon as he began to sing.

If Fioravanti has composed any longer comic operas with the same spirit, splendid humour, and melodic richness, then it would be a real gain if they could be transplanted to the German stage, which so often tires and bores us with the hybrid productions of inferior German and French composers.[17]

Without being too simple, the piano accompaniment lies very well under the hands, and even without knowing the full score it is clear that the arrangement has been made with understanding and skill. The engraving is clear and attractive, though not without mistakes. On page 11, system 2, bar 7, for example, there is a flat before the A which does not belong.[18]

Review of Beethoven's Fifth Symphony

Published: AMZ, xii, 4 and 11 July 1810, cols. 630–42, 652–9   *Unsigned*
First reprinted: Vom Ende 1899 (incomplete)

Beethoven's Fifth Symphony, in C minor, Op. 67, evolved during 1806–07 and was completed in 1808, being thus synchronous with the Sixth Symphony, the sonata for cello, Op. 69, and the Piano Trios Op. 70, whose review will be found on p. 300. The Fifth Symphony was first publicly performed (as No. 6) on 22 December 1808, and issued in published orchestral parts in 1809 (two editions, the second containing small modifications).[1] Although Hoffmann was sent these parts, together with a full score in manuscript copy, in July 1809 (the piano duet arrangement may have come later), he was not ready to send in the review until 6 May 1810. We do not know whether he had the opportunity to hear it performed in Bamberg.

The following review is Hoffmann's most remarkable achievement of its kind; it

---

[17] These comments found an echo in Milan, whence an *AMZ* correspondent wrote in July 1812, having heard four other Fioravanti comic operas including *Le cantatrici villane*, 'I very much like all those I have heard, if not unreservedly, then certainly for the most part, particularly for their facility and grace of style, and their lively comic force, which our earlier reviewer also rightly praises in the opera he discusses' (*AMZ*, xiv, 2 September 1812, col. 588). *Le cantatrici villane* was produced at the Bamberg theatre on 15 January 1811 [F.S.].

[18] This flat crept in as the too-hasty German engraver copied as an accidental what had in the French score been merely the key-signature.

[1] Twenty-one parts in all, announced in *AMZ*, April 1809, together with the parts of the Sixth Symphony. Title page: SINFONIE / Pour / 2 Violons [etc.] . . . / par / LOUIS VAN BEETHOVEN. / Propriété des Editeurs. / . . . / à Leipsic / chez Breitkopf & Härtel. / œuv. 67.

has always been recognised as such; and it is still yielding to new, intensive study.[2] There is a valid sense in which it exists in a symbiotic historical relationship with the Fifth Symphony: Hoffmann's interpretation is the critical benchmark to which all others must relate. Considering the specific way in which it grows out of now generally ignored early Romantic theory, this says much for its universality, and for the perspicacity of its judgement. Even within Hoffmann's reviews of Beethoven's works in general, the present essay retains a primary place: the review of the Trios begins by recalling it; and those of *Egmont*, the *Coriolan* overture, and the Mass in C beat something of a retreat by perforce considering the music as partner together with word and drama.

The basic ground-plan of the review of Op. 67 follows the tripartite *AMZ* scheme, as explained in the Prefatory Remarks to the Witt symphony reviews earlier. However, the first section, the exordium, attained such weight that it would later be recast for *Kreisleriana* (see p. 96). As a totality, the original review was, in 1810, the longest essay ever to have been devoted to a Beethoven work. However, it had been preceded by twenty-nine variously shorter or longer reviews of Beethoven scores in the *AMZ*, which certainly set the scene for Hoffmann's work in many respects. The most important of these were: the acceptance of Beethoven as an independent genius whose works demanded exceptional critical response; the formulation of the music's 'character'; the concern to relate 'character' to concrete musical devices; and the use of a repertory of critical words, or terms of reference in judgement. Even the idea that music 'raises us involuntarily to the light-filled regions of a higher, unknown world', and the direct association of music with the infinite, had appeared previously in the *AMZ*, though not especially in the context of Beethoven.[3]

Yet on close inspection Hoffmann's review betrays more differences than similarities with its predecessors, because its postulates, which infuse every detail of the writing, had not been previously set forth as necessary axioms. These postulates were large: that purely instrumental music possessed a supreme status; that one single piece of new music could bear the weight of the claim that instrumental music might supplant painting, drama, even poetry, as the purely Romantic art; that such music was a perfect embodiment of the tendency of Romantic poetry to be a 'progressive, universal poetry', whose 'particular essence is that it is always becoming, and that it can never be completed . . . It alone is infinite, as it alone is free' (Friedrich Schlegel, *Athenaeum* Fragment No. 116, 1798).[4] A consequence of this 'raising' and 'revelation' of instrumental music was the attribution to the composer Beethoven of a special type of creative perception, one which was conscious of an

---

[2] In particular the subtle and wide-ranging study that has informed the present Prefatory Remarks: Schnaus, *Hoffmann als Beethoven-Rezensent*; also Wallace, *Beethoven's Critics*.

[3] See the table of earlier reviews in Schnaus, *Hoffmann als Beethoven-Rezensent*, 15–17, and also 50f., 84f. For a complete listing of reviews, in all journals, related to Beethoven, see Donald W. MacArdle, *Beethoven Abstracts* (Detroit, 1973). The quotation is from *AMZ*, vi (1804), col. 356. See pp. 6–18 above for further background material.

[4] Behler and Struc (ed., tr.), *Schlegel. Dialogue on Poetry*, 140–1.

immanent, Romantic, infinite yet unified state of being. These factors, together with the idea of the composer as a 'cognitive vessel', have been discussed in the Introduction to *Kreisleriana*. Suffice it to say here that Hoffmann's essay was both an epoch-making account of a musical landmark, and an epoch-making statement of Romantic theory as such.

This approach explains Hoffmann's at first sight curious account of the third and fourth movements; of the final coda; and of the way he discusses motivic working throughout. Just as in the story *Don Juan* he created a particular (if highly influential) interpretation of the opera *Don Giovanni*, so in the present review he created a particular image of the symphony that exemplified an early Romantic view of creativity, and indeed of consciousness itself. The implications of this review can be regarded as having been 'composed out' in the *Kreisleriana* cycle.

The extraordinary imagery Hoffmann uses near the beginning links his reactions to the Fifth Symphony with his reactions to the music of Gluck. In *Ritter Gluck* (1809) the composer describes musical inspiration at length, including the idea, 'Rays of light shot through the night, and these rays of light were musical sounds that encircled me with lovely clarity . . .' Imagery of this order is never found in Hoffmann's reviews of music by other composers.

Sometimes, in the following, the writer uses *Thema* ('theme'), occasionally *Figur* ('figure'), but not *Motiv*. *Gedanke* ('idea') is also used, but more frequent is the multi-purpose *Satz*, which has been rendered in a number of ways, as shown on p. 17. The translation of terms has been made in collaboration with Professor Ian D. Bent.

The reviewer has before him one of the most important works by the master whose pre-eminence as an instrumental composer it is doubtful that anybody would now dispute; he is utterly permeated by the subject of the present review, and may nobody take it amiss if he exceeds the limits of conventional appraisals and strives to put into words all the profound sensations that this composition has given rise to within him.

When music is spoken of as an independent art the term can properly apply only to instrumental music, which scorns all aid, all admixture of other arts, and gives pure expression to its own peculiar artistic nature. It is the most romantic of all arts – one might almost say the only one that is *purely* romantic. Orpheus's lyre opened the gates of Orcus. Music reveals to man an unknown realm, a world quite separate from the outer sensual world surrounding him, a world in which he leaves behind all feelings circumscribed by intellect in order to embrace the inexpressible. How dimly was this peculiar nature of music perceived by those instrumental composers who tried to represent such circumscribed sensations or even events, and thus to treat sculpturally the art most utterly opposed to sculpture! Dittersdorf's symphonies of this type,[5] as well as all the newer *Batailles des Trois Empereurs* etc.,[6] should be condemned to total oblivion as ridiculous aberrations. In singing, where the juxtaposed poetry suggests precise moods through words, the magical power of music acts like the philosopher's miracle-elixir, a few drops of which make any drink wonderfully delicious. Any passion – love, hate, anger, despair, etc. – presented to us in an opera is clothed by music in the purple shimmer of romanticism, so that even our mundane sensations take us out of the everyday into the realm of the infinite. Such is the power of music's spell that, growing ever stronger, it can only burst the fetters of any other art.

It is certainly not merely an improvement in the means of expression (perfection of instruments, greater virtuosity of players), but also a deeper awareness of the peculiar nature of music, that has enabled great composers to raise instrumental music to its present level. Haydn and Mozart, the creators of modern instrumental music, first showed us the art in its full glory; but the one who regarded it with total devotion and penetrated to its innermost nature is Beethoven. The instrumental compositions of all three masters breathe the same romantic spirit for the very reason that they all intimately grasp the essential nature of the art; yet the character of their compositions is markedly different.

Haydn's compositions are dominated by a feeling of childlike optimism. His symphonies lead us through endless, green forest-glades, through a motley throng of happy people. Youths and girls sweep past dancing the round; laughing children behind trees, lying in wait behind rose-bushes, teasingly throw flowers at each other. A world of love, of bliss, of eternal youth, as though before the Fall; no suffering, no pain; only sweet, melancholy longing for the beloved vision floating far off in the red glow of evening, neither approaching nor receding; and as long as it is there the night will not draw on, for the vision is the evening glow itself illuminating hill and glade.

Mozart leads us deep into the realm of spirits. Dread lies all about us, but

---

[5] For example, *Trois simphonies, exprimant trois métamorphoses d'Ovide*, published in 1785 from a total of twelve that included the stories of Phaeton's fall, Actaeon's transformation into a stag, and the peasants transformed into frogs.

[6] Probably Jacques-Marie Beauvarlet-Charpentier, *La Bataille d'Austerlitz surnommé la Journée des trois Empereurs, symphonie militaire et historique à grand orchestre* (Paris, 1806), or the symphony by Louis-Emmanuel Jadin of the same name and date, or the piano arrangement of the latter, issued in Leipzig. Ironically, Hoffmann wrote his own occasional piano contribution to the genre, when necessity demanded, but under a pseudonym: *Deutschlands Triumph im Siege bey Leipzig* (Leipzig, 1814), signed Arnulph Vollweiler. It is now lost.

withholds its torments and becomes more an intimation of infinity. We hear the gentle voices of love and melancholy, the nocturnal spirit-world dissolves into a purple shimmer, and with inexpressible yearning we follow the flying figures kindly beckoning to us from the clouds to join their eternal dance of the spheres (as, for example, in Mozart's Symphony in E flat major, known as the 'Swan Song').[7]

In a similar way Beethoven's instrumental music unveils before us the realm of the mighty and the immeasurable. Here shining rays of light shoot through the darkness of night, and we become aware of giant shadows swaying back and forth, moving ever closer around us and destroying within us all feeling but the pain of infinite yearning, in which every desire, leaping up in sounds of exultation, sinks back and disappears. Only in this pain, in which love, hope, and joy are consumed without being destroyed, which threatens to burst our hearts with a full-chorused cry of all the passions, do we live on as ecstatic visionaries.

Romantic sensibility is rare, and romantic talent even rarer, which is probably why so few are able to strike the lyre that unlocks the wonderful realm of the infinite. Haydn romantically apprehends the humanity in human life; he is more congenial to the majority. Mozart takes as his province the superhuman, magical quality residing in the inner self. Beethoven's music sets in motion the machinery of awe, of fear, of terror, of pain, and awakens that infinite yearning which is the essence of romanticism. Beethoven is a purely romantic, and therefore truly musical, composer. This may well explain why his vocal music is less successful, since it does not permit vague yearning but can only depict from the realm of the infinite those feelings capable of being described in words, and why his instrumental music rarely appeals to the multitude. But even the multitude oblivious of Beethoven's depths will not deny him a high degree of invention; on the contrary it is usual to regard his works merely as products of a genius who ignores form and discrimination of thought and surrenders to his creative fervour and the passing dictates of his imagination. He is nevertheless fully the equal of Haydn and Mozart in rational awareness, his controlling self detached from the inner realm of sounds and ruling it in absolute authority. Just as our aesthetic overseers have often complained of a total lack of real unity and inner coherence in Shakespeare, when only profounder contemplation shows the splendid tree, buds and leaves, blossom and fruit as springing from the same seed, so only the most penetrating study of the inner structure of Beethoven's music can reveal its high level of rational

[7] Symphony No. 39 (1788), KV 543. See p. 97 n. 159.

awareness, which is inseparable from true genius and nourished by continuing study of the art. Beethoven bears the romanticism of music, which he expresses with such originality and authority in his works, in the depths of his spirit. The reviewer has never felt this more acutely than in the present symphony. It unfolds Beethoven's romanticism, rising in a climax right to the end, more than any other of his works, and irresistibly sweeps the listener into the wonderful spirit-realm of the infinite.

The first Allegro [con brio], C minor in 2/4 time, begins with the main idea consisting of only two bars, which subsequently appears again and again in a variety of forms. In the second bar a fermata, then the idea repeated a tone lower, then another fermata; both times strings and clarinets only. Not even the key is yet certain; the listener assumes E flat major. The second violins begin again with the main idea, then the key-note C played by cellos and bassoons in the second bar establishes the tonality of C minor; violas and first violins enter in imitation until the latter finally add two bars to the main idea, play them three times (the last time joined by the whole orchestra) and end with a fermata on the dominant, giving the listener presentiments of unknown mysteries. The beginning of the Allegro up to this pause determines the character of the whole piece, and the reviewer therefore inserts it here for the reader's inspection:

After this fermata, violins and violas remain in the tonic and imitate the main idea, while the bass here and there adds a figure that also copies it, until an ever-rising episode brings back earlier presentiments, this time more strongly and urgently. It leads to a tutti, the theme of which again follows the rhythmic pattern of the main idea and is closely related to it:

The first inversion above a D in the bass prepares the relative major E flat, in which the horn again imitates the main idea.[8] The first violins now take up a second theme, which is melodious but preserves the mood of anxious, restless yearning expressed by the movement as a whole. This theme is played by the violins alternating with the clarinet, while every three bars the cellos and basses interject the imitating figure previously referred to, so that the new theme is artfully woven into the overall texture. As a continuation of this theme the first violins and cellos play a two-bar figure five times in the key of E flat minor while the double-basses ascend chromatically.[9] A new episode leads to the close [i.e. the double bar] in which the wind instruments repeat the first tutti in E flat major, and finally the whole of the orchestra ends in E flat major with the frequently mentioned imitation of the main theme in the bass.

The second half begins with the main theme again, in its original form, but transposed up a third and played by clarinets and horns. The various elements of the first half follow in F minor, C minor, and G minor, but are differently arranged and orchestrated. Finally, after an episode again built only on a two-bar phrase taken up alternately by the violins and wind instruments, while the cellos play a figure in contrary motion and the double-basses rise, the following chords are heard from the whole orchestra [bar 168]:

[8] i.e. in bar 59; both horns are called for.
[9] i.e. bars 83–94. Second violins additionally play the figure and violas ascend with the double-basses. It is interesting that Beethoven altered the phrasing of this passage in order to counteract the symmetry implied by Hoffmann: see the Norton Critical Score, ed. Forbes, 130.

They are sounds that depict the breast, constricted and affrighted by presentiments of enormity, struggling for air. But like a friendly figure moving through the clouds and shining through the darkness of night, a theme now enters that was touched on by the horns in E flat major in the fifty-eighth bar of the first half.[10] First in G major, then in C major the violins play this theme in octaves while the bass[11] has a descending figure that to some extent recalls the tutti phrase at the forty-fourth bar of the first half [bar 179]:

The wind instruments take up this theme *fortissimo* in F minor, but after three bars the strings seize upon the previous two bars and alternate with the winds in playing them five more times, followed by further alternation of single chords in a gradual diminuendo. After the first inversion

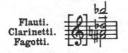

the reviewer would have expected G flat minor as the next chord in the sequence, which could then be changed enharmonically to F sharp minor if a modulation of the type used here was required to G major. The wind instruments which play the chord following this first inversion, however, are written thus [bar 215]:

Flauti.
Clarinetti.
Fagotti.

---

[10] Actually the fifty-ninth.
[11] The descending figure is played by violas, cellos, and double-basses.

The strings then play this F sharp minor chord

which is repeated four times by them and the winds alternating every bar. The chords for the wind instruments continue to be written as shown above, for which the reviewer can find no reason. Now the first inversion chord

is treated in the same way, gradually getting softer and softer. This again has an ominous, eerie effect. The full orchestra now bursts out with a theme in G major almost identical to that heard forty-one bars previously, in unison except for the flute and trumpet holding out the dominant D. After only four bars, however, this theme is interrupted by seven *pianissimo* diminished seventh chords [bar 233]

exchanged between strings with horns and the remaining winds. Then the bass[12] takes up the main idea followed in the next bar by the other instruments in unison; the bass and upper parts imitate each other in this way for five bars, combine for three bars, and then in the next bar the whole orchestra with timpani and trumpets comes in with the main theme in its original form.

The first half is now repeated with a few slight differences. The theme that earlier began in E flat major now enters in C major, and leads to a jubilant close in C major with timpani and trumpets. But with this close the music turns towards F minor. After five bars of the first inversion from the full orchestra [bar 382]

clarinets, bassoons, and horns softly play an imitation of the main idea. One bar's general pause is followed by six bars of

All the wind instruments repeat the imitation and now violas, cellos, and bassoons take up a theme that was heard earlier in the second half in G

[12] bar 240: the main idea is played by bassoons, horns, cellos, and double-basses.

major, while two bars later the violins enter in unison with a new counter-subject. The music now remains in C minor, and with slight changes the theme that began in bar 71 of the first half[13] is repeated by the violins, first alone then alternating with the wind instruments. The alternating phrases get shorter and shorter, first one bar, then half a bar. It becomes an irresistible surge – a swelling torrent whose waves break higher and higher – until the beginning of the Allegro is heard once more twenty-four bars from the end. There follows a pedal-point, above which the main theme is imitated, and finally the movement is brought to a strong and powerful close.

There is no simpler idea than that on which Beethoven has based his entire Allegro

and one perceives with admiration how he was able to relate all the secondary ideas and episodes by their rhythmic content to this simple theme, so that they serve to reveal more and more facets of the movement's overall character, which the theme by itself could only hint at. All the phrases are short, consisting merely of two or three bars, and are also constantly exchanged between strings and winds. One would think that such ingredients could result only in something disjointed and hard to follow, but on the contrary it is precisely this overall pattern, and the constant repetition of short phrases and single chords, which maintains the spirit in a state of ineffable yearning. Quite apart from the fact that the contrapuntal treatment betokens profound study of the art, the episodes and constant allusions to the main theme demonstrate how the whole movement with all its distinctive features was not merely conceived in the imagination but also clearly thought through.

Like the voice of a propitious spirit that fills our breast with comfort and hope, we now hear the lovely (and yet substantial) theme of the Andante [con moto], A flat major in 3/8 time, played by the violas and cellos. The further development of the Andante recalls several middle movements in Haydn symphonies, in that the main theme is varied in diverse ways between intervening episodes.[14] It cannot be compared with the opening

---

[13] Hoffmann refers to bar 423, a free extension of music originally heard at bars 63 and 71. His observation also implies that the rising quaver fourths in bars 418–22 are connected with the same interval in bars 63 and 71.

[14] e.g. Haydn symphonies Nos. 70, 90, 101, 103. Other similarities exist in the essentially ternary movement of No. 100.

Allegro in originality, although the idea of repeatedly interrupting the A flat major with a stately passage in C major for timpani and trumpets has a striking effect. The transition into C is twice achieved by enharmonic change [bar 28]

whereupon the stately theme enters and then the modulation back to the dominant chord of A flat major takes place in the following way [bar 41]:

The third time, flutes, oboes, and clarinets prepare the transition to the C major theme more simply, though with great effect [bar 144]:

All the material in this Andante is very melodious and the main subject is almost ingratiating. The very course of this theme, however, passing through A flat major, B flat minor, F minor, B flat minor and then back to A flat, the repeated juxtaposition of the major keys A flat and C, the chromatic modulations – all these again express the character of the whole work and make this Andante a part of it. It is as though the awful phantom that seized our hearts in the Allegro threatens at every moment to emerge from the storm-cloud into which it disappeared, so that the comforting figures around us rapidly flee from its sight.

The minuet[15] following the Andante is again as original and as captivating to the soul as one would expect from this composer in the movement that, according to the Haydn pattern which he followed, should be the most piquant and witty of all. The distinctive modulations; the closes on the dominant major, its root becoming the tonic of the following bass theme in the minor mode; this theme itself, repeatedly extended by a few bars at a time [see Ex. II]: it is particularly these features which express so strongly the character of Beethoven's music described above, and arouse once more those disquieting presentiments of a magical spirit-world with which the Allegro assailed the listener's heart. The theme in C minor, played by cellos and basses alone, turns in the third bar towards G minor; the horns then sustain the G while violins and violas, together with bassoons in the second bar and clarinets in the third, have a four-bar phrase cadencing on G. Cellos and basses repeat the theme but after the third bar in G minor it turns towards D minor, then C minor, and the violin phrase is repeated. Now, while the strings provide chords on the first crotchet of each bar, the horns play a subject that leads into E flat major [bar 19]. The orchestra takes it into E flat minor and closes on the dominant B flat major; in the same bar the cellos and basses take up the main theme again just as in the opening in C minor, but now in B flat minor. The violins etc. also repeat their phrase, and there follows a pause on F major. Cellos and basses repeat the theme [bar 52] but extend it by passing through F minor, C minor, G minor and then returning to C minor, whereupon the tutti that first occurred in E flat minor takes the music through F minor to a chord of C major [bar 97]. Just as they previously moved from B flat major to B flat minor, the cellos and basses now take up the C as the tonic of the C minor theme. Flutes and oboes, imitated in the second bar by clarinets, now have the phrase previously played by the strings, while the latter repeat a bar from the above-mentioned tutti. The horns have a sustained G, and the cellos begin a new theme [bar 105] to which is added first a further elaboration of the opening violin phrase and then a new subject in quavers (which have not yet been heard). Even the new cello theme contains allusions to the main subject and is thereby closely related to it, as well as by having the same rhythm. After a short repetition of the earlier tutti the minuet section closes in C minor *fortissimo* with timpani and trumpets.

[15] This description of the third movement, headed only Allegro by Beethoven, seems strange and is doubtless merely a term of expedience. A concert report in the seventieth issue of the *VZ* (12 June 1819), for example, mentions 'the very difficult minuet of Beethoven's *Sinfonia Eroica*'. It is quite clear from his analysis that Hoffmann was not thinking of a minuet in the proper sense [F.S.].

Cellos and basses begin the second section (the trio) with a theme in C major that is imitated by the violas fugally at the dominant, then by the second violins in an abbreviated form, and then by the first violins, similarly in stretto. The first half of this section closes in C major. In the second half cellos and basses start the theme twice but stop again, and only at the third attempt do they keep going. This may strike many people as amusing, but in the reviewer it produced an uneasy feeling. After several imitations of the main theme it is taken up by the flutes, supported by oboes, clarinets, and bassoons above a pedal G from the horns.[16] It dies away in single notes, first from clarinets and bassoons,[17] then from cellos and basses. The theme of the first section is repeated by the cellos and basses [bar 235] but instead of violins, wind instruments now have the phrase in short notes, ending with a pause.[18] After this, as in the first section, comes the extended main subject, but with crotchets and crotchet rests in place of the minims. The other elements of the first section, mostly abbreviated, also return in this form.

The restless yearning inherent in the theme now reaches a level of unease that so constricts the breast that only odd fragmented sounds escape it. A G major chord seems to be leading to a close, but cellos and basses sustain a *pianissimo* A flat for fifteen bars, the violins and violas likewise the C a third above, while the kettledrum plays the C first in the rhythm of the often-mentioned tutti, then once a bar for four bars, then twice for four bars, then on every beat. The first violins finally take up the opening theme and continue for twenty-eight bars with repeated allusions to it, ending on the dominant seventh of the home key. In the meantime the second violins and violas have been sustaining the C, the kettledrum its C in crotchets, and cellos and basses their pedal G likewise, after moving down the scale from A flat to F sharp and back to A flat. Now the bassoons come in, then one bar later the oboes, then three bars later flutes, horns, and trumpets, while the kettledrum plays its C in continuous quavers. This leads straight into the C major chord with which the final Allegro begins. Why Beethoven continued the kettledrum C to the end despite its dissonance with the chord is explained by the character he was striving to give the whole work. These heavy, dissonant blows, sounding like a strange and dreadful voice, arouse a horror of the extraordinary, of ghostly fear. The reviewer has previously

---

[16] bars 217ff.: Hoffmann's description omits the second statement of the trio material in bars 197ff.

[17] Actually one clarinet and one bassoon.

[18] It is noteworthy that Hoffmann omits mention of pizzicato in the strings at bars 231 and 244; he does not comment on the awkward extra two bars originally printed in error after bar 237, and pointed out by Beethoven to the publisher in 1810.

mentioned the intensifying effect of extending a theme by a few bars, and in order to make this clearer he illustrates these extensions together:

Ex. II

When the first half is repeated this phrase appears in the following form:

Just as simple and yet, when it is glimpsed behind later passages, just as potent as the theme of the opening Allegro is the idea of the minuet's first tutti:

With the splendid, exultant theme of the final movement in C major we hear the full orchestra, with piccolos,[19] trombones, and contrabassoon now added, like a brilliant shaft of blinding sunlight suddenly penetrating the darkness of night. The subjects of this Allegro are more broadly treated than the preceding ones, being not so much melodious as forceful and susceptible to contrapuntal imitation. The modulations are unaffected and clear. The first half particularly has almost the energy of an overture. It continues for thirty-four bars in C major as a tutti for the full orchestra. Then against a strong, rising figure in the bass a new theme in the leading voice modulates to G major and leads to the dominant chord of this key. Now another theme enters consisting of crotchets and triplets; in rhythm and character it is quite different from the previous ones, pressing urgently forward like the subjects of the first Allegro and the minuet [bar 44]:

[19] Actually only one piccolo is added to the two normal flutes.

With this theme and its further development through A minor to C major, the spirit returns to the mood of foreboding which temporarily receded amid the joy and jubilation. A short, furious tutti again takes the music towards G major and violas, bassoons, and clarinets begin a theme in sixths that is subsequently played by the whole orchestra. After a brief modulation into F minor with an energetic figure in the bass, taken up by the violins in C major and then by the bass again *al rovescio*,[20] the first half closes in C major.

This figure is retained at the beginning of the second half in A minor,[21] and the earlier characteristic theme consisting of crotchets and triplets is heard again. This theme is now developed for thirty-four bars in abbreviated and stretto configurations, in which the character already apparent in its original guise fully emerges, owing in no small measure to the interspersed secondary phrases, the sustained notes from the trombones, and the off-beat triplets from the timpani, trumpets, and horns. It finally comes to rest on a pedal G played first by cellos and basses[22] and then, when they join the violins in a closing unison figure, by the bass trombone, trumpets, horns, and timpani. The simple theme of the minuet

now returns for fifty-four bars, in the last two of which the transition from the minuet to the Allegro is repeated in a condensed form.

With a few minor differences and remaining in the principal key, the material of the first half is recapitulated, and a furious tutti seems to be leading to a close. After the dominant chord, however, bassoons, horns, flutes, oboes, and clarinets successively take up a theme that has previously only been touched upon [bar 317]:[23]

---

[20] bar 84: contrabassoon, cellos, and double-basses play the figure in inversion.
[21] i.e. on a chord of E major, its dominant.
[22] i.e. at bar 132; contrabassoon also plays the pedal G.
[23] Actual order of entries: bassoons, horns, flute I, clarinet I, bassoon I, oboe I, piccolo.

There follows another closing passage, but this time the phrase is taken up by the strings, then by oboes, clarinets, and horns,[24] then by the violins. Again the music moves towards a close, but with the final chord on the tonic the violins (after a *più stretto* a few bars earlier) launch *presto* into the phrase heard in the sixty-fourth bar of the Allegro, while the bass figure is the same as that in the twenty-eighth bar of the first movement Allegro, which vividly recalls the main theme, as has been noted above, by virtue of its close rhythmic relationship to it. With the opening theme of the final Allegro [bars 390 ff.] (the bass enters one bar later canonically imitating the upper parts)[25] the whole orchestra approaches the close, which is drawn out by a series of brilliant figures and comes forty-one bars later. The final chords themselves are oddly placed. The chord that the listener takes as the last is followed by one bar's rest, then the same chord, one bar's rest, the same chord again, one bar's rest, then the chord again for three bars with one crotchet in each, one bar's rest, the chord, one bar's rest, and a C played in unison by the whole orchestra. The perfect composure of spirit engendered by the succession of closing figures is destroyed again by these detached chords and rests, which recall the separate strokes in the symphony's Allegro and place the listener once more in a state of tension.[26] They act like a fire that is thought to have been put out but repeatedly bursts forth again in bright tongues of flame.

Beethoven has preserved the conventional order of movements in this symphony. They seem to follow a continuous fantastic sequence, and the whole work will sweep past many like an inspired rhapsody. The heart of every sensitive listener, however, is certain to be deeply stirred and held until the very last chord by *one* lasting emotion, that of nameless, haunted yearning. Indeed for many moments after it he will be unable to emerge from the magical spirit-realm where he has been surrounded by pain and pleasure in the form of sounds. As well as the internal disposition of orchestration, etc., it is particularly the close relationship of the individual themes to each other which provides the unity that is able to sustain *one* feeling in the listener's heart. In the music of Haydn and Mozart this unity prevails everywhere. It becomes clearer to the musician when he discovers

[24] bar 336: in fact the phrase is played by piccolo, oboe I, and horns together, without clarinets.

[25] Contrabassoon doubles cellos and double-basses; bassoons double violins.

[26] Here Hoffmann appears to recall the first movement progression at bar 196ff., which had an 'ominous, eerie effect'; also his summing-up of the first movement refers to the 'constant repetition of short phrases and single chords' that characterised the whole Allegro.

the bass pattern which is common to two different passages,[27] or when the similarity between two passages makes it apparent. But often a deeper relationship that is not demonstrable in this way speaks only from the heart to the heart,[28] and it is this relationship which exists between the subjects of the two Allegros and the minuet, and which brilliantly proclaims the composer's rational genius. The reviewer believes he can summarise his judgement of this composer's splendid work in a few words, by saying that it is conceived of genius and executed with profound awareness, and that it expresses the romanticism of music to a very high degree.

No instrument has difficult music to perform, but only an extremely reliable, well-trained orchestra animated by a *single* spirit can attempt this symphony; the least lapse in any detail would irredeemably spoil the whole work. The constant alternation, the interlocking of string and wind instruments, the single chords separated by rests, and suchlike, demand the utmost precision. It is therefore also advisable for the conductor not so much to play with the first violins more strongly than is desirable, which often happens, as to keep the orchestra constantly under his eye and hand. The way the first violin part is printed, showing the entries of the obbligato instruments, is useful for this purpose.

The engraving is correct and clear. From the same publisher this symphony has appeared for piano duet under the title: *Cinquième Sinfonie de Louis van Beethoven, arrangée pour le Pianoforte à quatre mains.* Chez Breitkopf et Härtel à Leipsic. (Price 2 thalers 12 groschen.)[29] Normally the reviewer is not especially in favour of arrangements, but it cannot be denied that the solitary enjoyment in one's own room of a masterpiece one has heard played by the full orchestra often excites the imagination in the same way as before and conjures forth the same impressions in the mind. The piano reproduces the great work as a sketch reproduces a great painting, and the imagination brings it to life with the colours of the original. At any rate the symphony has been adapted for the piano with skill and insight, and proper regard has been paid to the requirements of the instrument without obscuring the distinctive qualities of the original.

---

[27] '*Sätze*': Hoffmann could mean a unit as small as a phrase or as large as a complete movement.

[28] A common phrase of the period (see the superscription to Beethoven's *Missa Solemnis*), evoked by Hoffmann in 'Casual Reflections on the Appearance of this Journal' (p. 428).

[29] The duet arrangement was by Friedrich Schneider, and appeared in July 1809, according to G. Kinsky and H. Halm, *Das Werk Beethovens* (Munich, 1955), 160.

Review of Weigl's *Das Waisenhaus* (extract)

Published: A M Z, xii, 19 September 1810, cols. 809–19   *Unsigned*
First reprinted: Ellinger 1912

Hoffmann's critical activities were affected not only by what he heard, but also by what he was composing. This is especially apparent in the case of music for the theatre. Count Soden delivered his melodrama *Dirna* (on an Indian subject) to Hoffmann on 21 June 1809. The latter began work on the score straight away, and the piece was very successfully first performed in Bamberg on 11 October, even being favourably reviewed in the *AMZ* on 13 December 1809.[1] In a letter to the *AMZ* of 1 July 1809, Hoffmann expressed the desire to publish an article discussing 'the demands that the composer justifiably makes on the librettist of an opera', and 'today's degenerate form of opera, as well as the prerequisites for true operatic subjects and their treatment from the viewpoint of the librettist and the composer'. These ideas culminated in *The Poet and the Composer* (1813). But earlier groundwork came in a trilogy of reviews devoted to a German, a French, and an Italian opera, of which *Das Waisenhaus* (*The Orphanage*) was the first. The others were Gluck's *Iphigénie en Aulide* and Paer's *Sofonisba*.

Hoffmann probably received the score of Weigl's Singspiel in December 1809,[2] and sent off the finished review on the following 30 May. The opera itself was new, being first seen in Vienna on 4 October 1808; it received many performances, and *AMZ* reports came in from various of them;[3] it was staged at the Bamberg theatre, presumably in Hoffmann's presence, in December 1809.

As indicated in his letters of 28 March and 6 May 1810 *(HBW*, i, 309–11), Hoffmann's old friend Franz von Holbein (1779–1855) visited Bamberg,[4] and wrote the libretto *Die beiden Blinden* for the composer Peter von Winter. As this was a work Hoffmann subsequently likened to *Das Waisenhaus*, the friends must have had much to debate. Holbein was subsequently appointed to reorganise the Bamberg theatre (1810–12), became thereby the cause of Hoffmann's practical career in the

---

[1] Schnapp (ed.), *Hoffmann. Ein Dokumentenband*, 121–2, 129, 136. The text of *Dirna* has been published in the *Mitteilungen der E. T. A. Hoffmann-Gesellschaft*, xv (1969), 7–30.

[2] See *HBW*, i, 307. The piano score had been announced in *AMZ*, April 1809. Title page: Das Waisenhaus. / Ein Singspiel in zwey Akten / VON / Joseph Weigl / VOLLSTAENDIGER KLAVIERAUSZUG. / Nọ 1041–1053 Original-Ausgabe. Pᵉ f[ ] / WIEN / Im Verlage des Kapellmeisters Thadé Weigl [i.e. Taddäus Weigl, the composer's brother], am Graben Nọ 1212. A completely new edition in piano score was issued by Breitkopf & Härtel not long afterwards.

[3] *AMZ*, 2 and 23 November 1808 (Vienna); 19 April 1809 (Leipzig); 6, 13, 27 December 1809 (Berlin and Breslau); 14 March 1810 (Prague) [F.S.]. See also the review by Weber (1817) in *Weber: Writings*, 231–3.

[4] Holbein was on tour with Marie Renner, the actress, later his second wife. Hoffmann had written for him the part of Treuenfels in his first Berlin period opera, *Die Maske* (1799).

theatre (see p. 64), and wrote the libretto for his new opera *Aurora*, composed in 1811–12 but not performed until 1933.[5]

Das Waisenhaus, libretto by G. F. Treitschke, is extremely sentimental. Gustav, aged fourteen, has been brought up in the orphanage because his mother, Therese, married secretly and against her father's will. Therese has however taken employment at the orphanage in order to bring her son up surreptitiously. The father returns from exile in America, thinking his wife and son are dead, goes to the orphanage, and unwittingly selects Gustav for adoption. At the same time, Therese's father also comes to retrieve Gustav out of contrition at having had him brought up at the institution in the first place.

Frequent mention of this opera has already been made in these pages in reports of its performance. Up to now it has given pleasure everywhere and was bound to do so in view of its attractive music, which falls easily on every ear and commands a wide public.

The plan, the concept of an opera, as provided by the poet, must inspire the composer; and if it has the power to excite his imagination, then weak or ineffective details in its elaboration cannot destroy his inspiration. Animated by this concept and reacting to it alone, he creates a work that musically expresses the poet's idea; anything feeble or dull in the poet's realisation of the text is extinguished by the music, which powerfully and perfectly depicts the character, situation, etc. of the participants according to the idea underlying the whole. It has always greatly struck the reviewer how Mozart and other great composers were able to write masterpieces to bad texts; until now he has found every time that the whole work was based on a romantic concept, an absolutely indispensable requirement of opera, and that only the elaboration of this idea was deficient, usually because it was dashed off with too little care, as is conspicuously the case with *Die Zauberflöte* for example. Conversely, the most well-turned verses, the most carefully constructed scenes, even when the composer's needs in matters of form were adequately provided for, have often failed to inspire outstanding music, even from the best masters; and the fault lay always in the prosaic overall concept, for which no amount of ingenious working out could compensate. When a composer sets about writing an opera, his first thought is certainly not of individual verses and scenes. Rather is his spirit kindled by the overall imaginative idea from which the figures of the drama glowingly emerge, vividly expressing their character in musical sounds.[6] Following the poet's text, the composer then adjusts and rhythmically sets

---

[5] See the synopsis on p. 183. It was first published in 1984, edited by Hermann Dechant.

[6] This notion proceeded directly into *The Poet and the Composer*, as did later ones in the next paragraph.

out the music that the concept has given birth to; and happy is he should he then also find vigour and conciseness in the detail, so that instead of placing difficulties in his way it facilitates the composition and suggests to him many effective musical phrases. Of the text of the present opera, the reviewer now has to report that although the verses are somewhat better than average, it lacks precisely that from which the composer must draw his inspiration.

For a person of humane sensibility it is comforting and elevating to go into a hospital and see how every effort is made to reduce human misery; it is equally good to see a place where poor, orphaned children, instead of being abandoned to the rigours of the fate that has robbed them of their best support, can find shelter, protection, and care. Who can fail to admire the head of such an institution as he instructs his little ones with fatherly care, and who can remain unmoved by the innocence that draws them to him! But such scenes from ordinary life, showing people in the severest privations of their earthly journey, can hardly form an artistic subject for portrayal on the stage. As a subject for opera, which raises human nature to a higher power, where the language is song and (as when the fairy speaks in that tale)[7] chords echo every expression of feeling, and which only exists at all in the wonderful realm of romanticism, it is quite wrong to choose scenes from ordinary life which positively counteract any sense of the romantic. The plot of this opera is conceivable without the orphanage setting and the librettist seems to have introduced the throng of children merely to arouse emotion and to make the idea seem less hackneyed to the spectator. If the good headmaster can find nothing better to do on a fine spring morning than to increase his knowledge by reading for the benefit of his children; if the children, by marching up as though on parade and congratulating him on his birthday, then show the audience how well brought up and nicely dressed they are; then in real life that is all very laudable and good, but on the stage, in an opera? All the characters are of noble and virtuous disposition, or rather wear the uniform of virtue and nobility, as the orphans wear theirs, and the whole opera thereby acquires a tiring monotony not diminished by the comic but rather boring Thomas. Gustav, the chief character, is a delicate, tearful boy who is hardly likely to be turned into a soldier by his military father. His lachrymose nature seems in fact to be inherited from his father and mother, in both of whom it is a notable characteristic. The headmaster, briefly though he participates in the action, is clearly the best delineated. He exhibits a manly determination to promote the well-being of his pupils at all

[7] This tale has not been traced.

costs by disregarding Therese's lamentations when she opposes Gustav's adoption. The remaining characters (Sturm, Luise) are employed only for development at the end, or more just to complete the family group.

The reviewer has dwelt so long on the libretto of this opera in order to let full justice be done to the gallant composer, who has abundantly shown what he would have given had the dull, or rather completely non-operatic, overall idea not crippled the wings of his imagination. The music certainly contains pleasant, singable melodies even if here and there, as will be shown below, they are admittedly somewhat stale; the orchestration is brilliant, conceived from a deep knowledge of the instruments; the harmonic richness of the ensembles emerges clearly to the ear; and if the bright flame of that genius which irradiates the beholder of the infinite spirit-world of music in the operas of Gluck, Mozart, Cherubini, etc. is not seen in this opera, then the fault is that of the poet, whose concept failed to enkindle it in the composer. And for this reason, even if its pleasant outer polish commands universal applause in the short term, the composition will soon be extinguished by the cold water of the text.[8]

Review of Gluck's *Iphigénie en Aulide*

Published: *AMZ*, xii, 29 August and 5 September 1810, cols. 770–3,
     784–9   *Unsigned*
First reprinted: Süddeutsche Monatshefte, v (March 1908)

This review sets forth some of Hoffmann's most important beliefs concerning the nature of opera and operatic dramaturgy. It is also an essential companion to the tale *Ritter Gluck* (*AMZ*, February 1809). No detailed opera review by Hoffmann exists of any other work of which he thought so highly. Together with the preceding and the following reviews, the present essay forms a trilogy leading up to, but not wholly overlapping with, *The Poet and the Composer*. It was probably sent in for publication on 12 July 1810.

Iphigénie en Aulide, the first-performed of Gluck's seven late operas for Paris, received its première on 19 April 1774. The libretto was by M. F. L. G. Leblanc du Roullet. Its high quality and dramatic values (partly inspired by Diderot: see note 11) gave it lasting success in Paris. The problem of the reception of late Gluck in Germany has been mentioned on p. 177. *Iphigénie en Aulide* in particular was the

---

[8] There follows an account of the music, which has not been translated.

subject of a detailed essay in belittlement by J. N. Forkel which Hoffmann never tired of deprecating: see *Kreisleriana* p. 109 and 'Further Observations on Spontini's Opera *Olimpia*' p. 437. After sporadic performances at Kassel (1782) and Hamburg (1795), the opera had a series of initial runs at Brunswick and Schwerin (1806), Munich (1807), Vienna (1808), and Berlin (1809), mostly using a translation by J. D. Sander.[1] Hoffmann, however, had never had the chance to see it up to the time of writing.

Although *Iphigénie en Aulide* was published in a contemporary French full score, the piano score that Hoffmann was sent for review was the first complete issue anywhere in this convenient format.[2] Gluck's *Iphigénie en Tauride* (1779) had been published in piano score in Berlin already,[3] and Hoffmann's acquaintance with this opera in the theatre in Berlin in 1808 must lie behind *Ritter Gluck*, which criticises the Berlin performances. It is a work of literature in its own right, but can be read as a celebration of a great reforming visionary composer, whose spirit could be mortified but not destroyed by mediocre realisations of his work. In the present review Hoffmann again went on the offensive. He analysed the composer's achievement of dramatic truth and dismissed, by implication, the tendency of most of his contemporaries' operatic efforts. A vital concept first developed below in this connection was that of 'style', meaning something like 'authentic musico-dramatic language'. The same concept was further developed in 'Letters on Music in Berlin'.

A summary of the plot will be helpful. Act 1: The Greek fleet under Agamemnon is becalmed off Aulis: only he and the high priest Calchas know that in order to propitiate Diana the sacrifice of his daughter Iphigénie has been demanded. She arrives with her mother, Clytemnestre. Act 2: As Iphigénie is about to be married to Achille, a priest reveals that she is destined to be a sacrificial victim. Achille vows to defend her life; Agamemnon wrestles with conflicting loyalties. Act 3: Iphigénie is, however, willing to die. Her sacrifice is stopped only through divine intervention; the Greeks prepare to sail for Troy.

The rather objectionable form of opera introduced in recent times, in which dialogue interrupts the singing, has even further increased singers' inability to perform recitative; and this may well be the most weighty of many reasons why the masterpieces of Gluck, which cannot be compressed into

---

[1] See Alfred Loewenberg, *Annals of Opera 1597–1940* (3rd edn, London, 1978).
[2] He received it possibly on 22 December 1809: *HBW*, i, 307. Title page: IPHIGENIE / en Aulide / OPERA EN 3 ACTES / de M^r. le Chevalier Gluck. / arrangé pour le pianoforte / PAR M^r. GROSHEIM. / Prix 20 Francs. / A BONN CHEZ N. SIMROCK. This had been announced in the *AMZ* of October 1808, second *Intelligenz-Blatt*. See also Cecil Hopkinson, *A Bibliography of the Printed Works of C. W. von Gluck* (2nd edn, rev., New York, 1967), 41–2. The Grosheim piano score has its sung text in both French and German.
[3] Berlin, 1788 or 1789: *ibid.*, 61. A second piano score of this opera (1812) was reviewed by Weber: see *Weber: Writings*, 117. It is interesting to note that the insertion of the *Aulide* overture before *Iphigénie en Tauride* (see *Ritter Gluck*) was also made in this 1788–89 score.

such a form, are so rarely seen on the stage, except in a few of our major theatres in Germany (Vienna, Berlin, etc.). It is all the more praiseworthy to put these works, in good, complete piano scores, into the hands of those devotees of music who have not become alienated from the noble genius which lives and moves in Gluck's dramas. When a colossal painting is not exhibited in the lofty gallery which alone provides sufficient space for it, then a sketch, so long as it is accurate and suggests all the beauties of the original, will lift and gladden the heart of a sensitive observer in his own room.

When the reviewer had gone through the present score at the piano he was overcome by a feeling of profound melancholy, since it struck him yet again that whether through misguided artistic attitudes or through stupidity, composers of today are completely neglecting true opera seria, and that as a result the sublime heights that literature allied to music can attain on the stage will soon be totally lost to us.[4] In spite of the considerable progress of instrumental music, in spite of the great achievements of certain vocal pieces, we now search in vain for works conceived even remotely in that spirit, that genuinely tragic depth, expressed in the operas of earlier composers, even those who appear as dwarfs beside the giant Gluck. There are new, popular composers who, instead of thinking out the drama in all its parts and then expressing it in musical sounds, string together scene after scene with no regard for subject-matter, character, or situation; this only serves to encourage the singer to perform in a manner that glitters and impresses and sets the hands of the gallery in motion. It is very easy to attract the applause of the masses in this way, but even when such applause is his primary aim, the composer does not realise that the laurel branch that is thus accorded him can consist only of miserable sprigs from the full wreath received by the artful singer. It is above all the style that unifies and rounds the whole into a work of art, vividly expressing the character of the subject-matter, which is lacking in the majority of new operas, and no more splendid example of it is likely to be found than that of Gluck's dramas. Moreover, it is particularly the new recitatives and choruses which appear so dull and flat beside those of Gluck. It is here especially that the sparkling tinsel may momentarily blind, but can never long deceive. The colour and lustre of pure gold are everlasting only in pure gold.

Iphigénie en Tauride is clearly written with loftier simplicity, with loftier

---

[4] The plea for serious, even tragic opera, building on the dramaturgical foundations of late Gluck, remained the key demand by Hoffmann over the next eleven years. See the Introduction to *The Poet and the Composer*, and also 'Further Observations on Spontini's Opera *Olimpia*'.

tragic pathos; but *Iphigénie en Aulide* (the subject-matter alone determines this) is richer and more varied, and the reviewer cannot resist just a reference to some scenes bearing the unmistakable stamp of the sublimely lyrical inspiration that fired the composer when he created them.

The high priest, urged by the people to make known to them the will of their wrathful goddess, and seized with fear and trembling at the pronouncement revealed to him, offers up his prayer: 'Holy fear seizes my whole being.' The short G minor *a tempo* fills the listener's soul with awful premonition; he shudders with dread that Calchas will name the unhappy victim. Agamemnon adds his entreaty to the prayer of Calchas; Calchas asks 'Greeks, can you offer up to her this frightful sacrifice?' and then the people wildly cry 'Name to us the victim!' With these words the basses, then sopranos and altos, then tenors, enter in imitation at the fifth, and this fugue-like entry of the voices one after the other, as well as the theme itself, perfectly expresses the impatience of the people:

Calchas remains silent and the people entreat Diana: 'O Diana, grant us your favour.' For twelve bars, up to the words 'que notre fureur', this chorale-like passage is based on a melody of three bars, repeated twice in the tonic and then twice at the dominant. What sublime simplicity of idea and structure, and what effective part-writing for voices!

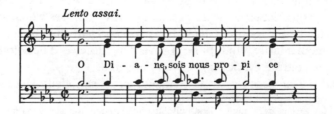

The chorus 'Que d'attraits!' refutes those who accuse Gluck's melody of lacking grace. It is equalled in its extremely simple structure and impressively solemn effect by the march No. 20. The reviewer also notes as particularly outstanding the splendid quartet No. 26,[5] with the chorus joining in later to thrilling effect, the scenes Nos. 27, 28, 29,[6] Agamemnon's great character scene No. 32,[7] Clytemnestre's scene No. 38,[8] the solemn chorus of the people on p. 124,[9] and the final scene beginning from Calchas's recitative.[10] Rather than go further into the inner detail of these compositions, which would exceed the scope of these pages, he would prefer to say something else about the character of Gluck's music in general, in comparison with our most recent operatic music.

Whereas the majority of our most recent operas are only concerts performed in costume on the stage, Gluck's opera is true musical drama, in which the action moves forward without stopping from one moment to the next. Whatever hinders this forward motion, whatever might reduce the listener's suspense and distract his attention to secondary matters – from the figure to its adornment, one could say – is most carefully avoided, and the extreme precision resulting from this vigorously sustains the whole. Thus there are no long ritornellos; most of the arias are in effect just *a tempos* interrupting the recitative at a point where the intensification of expression renders it appropriate; and superfluous repeats never carry the choruses and ensembles to a length that diverts the listener from the situation and from the momentum of the action. Only the highest artistic awareness, only an absolute mastery over the means of musical expression, can give rise to that noble simplicity with which the composer treats the most passionate moments of the drama. As a striking example of this the reviewer cites Agamemnon's scene No. 32, which he has already mentioned. In the recitative appear the words:

I shudder! Iphigénie, O heavens, crowned with garlands will offer her breast to the murderous blade, I would see her blood flow! – Inhuman father! do you not hear the cries of the Furies? The air resounds with the frightful hissing of their murderous

---

[5] 'Jamais à tes autels' (Act 2).

[6] Recitative and chorus, 'Princesse, pardonnez à mon impatience'; Clytemnestre, 'Par son père cruel'; recitative, 'Reine, rassurez-vous' and trio, 'C'est mon père.'

[7] 'Tu décides son sort.'

[8] 'Quels tristes chants' with chorus, 'Puissante Déité' (Act 3). It is strange that Hoffmann does not pick out 'the great passionate recitative of Clytemnestra' (Act 3 No. 37) which in *Kater Murr*, Part II, Julia sings in such a profoundly stirring manner to Kreisler's accompaniment [F.S.].

[9] 'Pour prix du sang.'

[10] No. 39, from 'Votre zèle des Dieux a fléchi la colère.'

serpents: avengers of parricides, they begin their torments. Inhuman ones, cease! the gods caused my crime, they guided my hand, they struck the blows, they alone destroy their victim! – What! nothing can deflect your anger, cruel ones! yet in vain your fury rises, the consuming remorse that weighs me down and excites my heart-rending anguish is more powerful than you! – With my guard, Arcas, etc.[11]

How gaudy and overladen the treatment of these words would be in the style of many composers popular today! After *shudder* a tremolo, then the *cries of the Furies*, the *murderous serpents* and so on. It would all be painted, and the painting itself would disappear under all the colours. Not so Gluck, who captures and depicts in music not the words but Agamemnon's state of mind, his struggle against the will of the gods. Thus the phrases that interrupt the declamation, from the words 'see her blood flow' to the word 'nothing', preserve the same figure, which well suffices to express the situation.

Only after the words 'yet in vain' does another figure enter, descending chromatically in sixths; this again (the last time shortened) continues as far as the words 'with my guard'; here, since Agamemnon is no longer expressing his inner feelings in a monologue but merely giving orders to Arcas, the usual *recitativo parlante* begins, with punctuating chords and no linking phrases. Merely by using declamation and modulating through a number of minor keys the composer achieves the utmost effect, since the force of the action is presented in its most essential terms, and thus the listener's heart, captivated by the unity and intensity of the whole passage, is deeply moved. The case is exactly the same in the previously-mentioned scenes with Clytemnestre and with Calchas, the words of which would have lured many composers into employing a hundred expressive devices that negate each

---

[11] This was set by Gluck as an 'obbligato recitative', accompanied but also interrupted illustratively by the orchestra. Diderot in 1757 had not only suggested Racine's *Iphigénie* (1674) as the basis for a regenerated French opera, but had also proposed obbligato recitative for the monologue by Clytemnestre whose words are similar to those above for Agamemnon: 'O mère infortunée! / De festons odieux ma fille couronnée / . . .': Denis Diderot, *Troisième entretien* to *Le Fils naturel*, in *Ecrits sur la musique*, ed. B. Durand-Sendrail ([Paris], 1987), 126.

other and thus destroy the momentum. As well as the force of the action, the characterisation also receives the greatest care, with no constraining deference to the individuality of the singers. It is not the *prima donna*, the *primo uomo* or the *primo basso* who should be heard, but Clytemnestre musically expressing her regal disposition, Iphigénie her childlike submission to the will of the gods, Agamemnon his forceful but deeply grieving spirit, Achille his love and his youthfully impetuous anger. It should be added that Gluck everywhere weaves a richly harmonic fabric and scorns all empty phrases, so that the setting overall, particularly in the splendid choruses, remains solid and strong while preserving the utmost precision and clarity. In saying this, the reviewer feels he has touched upon the most important reason why Gluck's operas are and will remain classical masterpieces which every young composer anxious to venture upon serious tragic dramas cannot study enough. Even if his wings are not strong enough to match the eagle's flight of that great genius, he will certainly rise above the mire in which the common herd so contentedly graze. He will at least acquire a certain style, which will give pleasure to the listener. This is why the reviewer considers it more valuable to study vigorous works of an earlier period than to pursue the high romanticism of Mozart without such a study. Only a romantic and profound spirit can fully appreciate the romantic and profound Mozart. Only a creative imagination equal to his, stirred by the genius present in his works, is permitted to express the highest things in art as he does. Even good composers in recent times, fired by the works of Mozart, have made the dangerous mistake of confusing them with the creative inspiration itself, of taking the means of expression for the expression, and have thereby fallen into meaningless rhetoric. The stage always has need of novelty and that is why so much music is composed. But rapid oblivion punishes the insipidity, the false style, or rather complete lack of style of many compositions that are not without felicitous moments and flowing melodies, but only pander to fashion and to the demands of vain singers. In the reviewer's opinion a deeper study and appreciation of the spirit of Gluck's dramas could disabuse many gifted young composers of prejudices and attitudes that cannot but lead them astray. Even if we failed to detect in their compositions the noble genius of that great master, then at least the unity and sustained character of their works would appeal to the listener more than clever bits and pieces, which will never produce the total impression on which a drama's success depends.

It is to be hoped that the apparent uniformity of Gluck's works, and especially the complaints of singers – that there is nothing brilliant for them to sing, that the recitative is too exhausting for them, etc. – as well as the fear of a reduced public attendance, do not deter theatre managements from staging them, and that the decline of true serious opera will thus be prevented.

But as the reviewer has already mentioned, even the publication of up-to-date piano scores performs a great service for the art. If a number of singers (competent amateurs) gather at the piano to perform the choruses and ensembles, the profound impression made by this deeply tragic work will create just as many enemies of the latest instrumental-singing (nowadays vocal music imitates instrumental music, and the singer the instrumentalist: it used to be the reverse) as it seems to win friends on the stage. For the piano score under discussion the reviewer can have nothing but praise: it is complete and very suitable for performance. In the overture the theme on page 5, bar 9,[12] could be differently arranged, since the octaves alternating with single notes in the bass do not adequately convey the imitation between the bass and the upper voice in the original. In the choruses the reviewer's eye cannot get used to reading all four voices in the treble clef, and he feels that at least the bass clef, surely familiar to every musically competent amateur, should be retained, since the treble clef certainly makes it harder for the bass to pitch his notes.[13]

The engraving is extremely attractive, and the words of the text fall clearly upon the eye.

Review of Paer's *Sofonisba*

Published: AMZ, xiii, 13 March 1811, cols. 185–93   *Unsigned*
First reprinted: Ellinger 1912

The plans to complete a trilogy of contrasting opera reviews (see the preceding two items) were held up, owing partly to the fact that the *AMZ* could not satisfy Hoffmann's request for a full score of *Sofonisba*. (The piano score that he requested on 2 December 1809 seems to have arrived within the month.) He also ordered Paer's *Sargino*, whose duet 'Dolce dell'anima' was to find mention near the opening of *Kreisleriana*, in 'Kapellmeister Kreisler's Musical Sufferings'; this appeared in the *AMZ* in September 1810. Although no personal diary for 1810 by Hoffmann has survived, we know that he was thrown predominantly back on to private teaching at this time.

---

[12] i.e. bar 88 of the overture.

[13] Not only were the chorus tenors and basses transposed into the treble clef (sounding down an octave) but also the rôles of Agamemnon, Calchas, and Achille.

Ferdinando Paer (1771–1839) enjoyed a successful career as opera composer in Vienna, Dresden, and finally Paris, where his relations in the 1820s with Rossini became almost litigious. Hoffmann encountered him in Warsaw following the French occupation in 1806, whence Paer had been brought personally by Napoleon. According to Hitzig, Hoffmann 'absolutely could not stand him, since he was just as saccharine a man as he was a composer'.[1] The present review is equally forcefully expressed. Paer's celebrated *Camilla* (1799) was in the Bamberg theatre repertory, and his *Achille* (1801) and *Sargino* (1803) were staged there in January and March of 1810. Hoffmann's tale about a mishap on stage during *Camilla* is worked into 'The Complete Machinist', p. 118.

La Sofonisba, a *dramma serio* with libretto by Domenico de' Rossetti, was composed for Bologna in 1805. In common with other Paer works, it had a considerable vogue, holding the stage in Italy until 1820, and being produced at (among other places) Dresden, Frankfurt, and Munich.

Sophonisba (253–203 BC) married Syphax (Siface in the opera), king of Numidia, and drew him away from his alliance with Rome. Syphax was captured by Masinissa, a prince allied to Rome, who subsequently tried to marry Sophonisba. Fearing that her influence on Masinissa would be as injurious to Rome as had been that on Syphax, Scipio Africanus claimed her as a captive of Rome. To elude capture, she drank poison.

The piano score reviewed by Hoffmann was announced in the *AMZ* in July 1809 and incorporated a German translation 'as used at the Frankfurt opera'.[2] We do not know exactly when Hoffmann completed the review.

It is well known that modern Italian music flatters the ear with pleasant melodies and gives singers the opportunity to show their skill with the utmost brilliance. But it neglects the genuinely dramatic element, the meaning of the action and situation, to the same degree that German composers make it their main concern and indeed in so doing often forget the singer's individuality and what his throat is capable of. By this criterion of Italian music Paer is certainly one of the best composers living today. He writes gratefully for the singer, his melodies are extremely graceful and his word-setting elegant; he also possesses a good knowledge of the instruments, revealed everywhere in his accompaniments which are richer than is usual for Italians. The thorough German listener, spoilt by Gluck, Mozart, and Haydn, will very soon notice his weakness in counterpoint, his lack of depth and originality, but will not complain about these shortcomings so

---

[1] Hitzig, i, 305, cited in *Schriften zur Musik*, 443.

[2] Title page: SOFONISBE / OPERA EN II ACTES / arrangé pour le PIANO-FORTE par / C. F. Ebers. / COMPOSÉ PAR / F. PAER. / Maitre de la chapelle de S.M.I. & R. &c. &c. &c. / Prix 20 Francs. / A BONN CHEZ N. SIMROCK. The plate number was 656.

long as Paer remains within the limits that nature has imposed upon him. Even if he does not command Paisiello's or Cimarosa's masterly lightness or their original, inimitable humour, his comic operas will nevertheless always remain exemplary.[3] His serious, heroic operas, however, will probably never satisfy German critics at least, since he is in no way capable of fulfilling the requirements of this genre.

It is an odd phenomenon that in his earlier compositions, especially in *Camilla*, Paer seemed to lean towards serious, German music, and in that particular opera was able to make the characters well defined and to write with a precision that is totally missing in his later compositions. In these one is faced with a diffuseness that nullifies the appeal of the most beautiful melodies, and instead of any individual style[4] only a mould into which the characters of the drama are poured and then turned out in identical shapes. If this is the case in *Achille*, an opera highly esteemed by every singer who can manage the main rôle, then it is even more true of *Sofonisba*. The tragic content of this opera is historical and sufficiently well known from Metastasio's dramatic version.[5] Graceful melodies, elegant workmanship, richly singable melismas, fiery brilliance of vocal writing and accompaniment everywhere, distinguish this opera from many of the insipid products of its time; but the dramatic element is so little heeded that the reviewer feels confident that if some other, even tragicomic text were put to the music, nobody on hearing it would remotely imagine the Romans, Numidians, and Carthaginians of the original. The composer's contrapuntal weakness referred to previously is apparent in the ensemble movements, particularly the choruses and *pezzi concertanti*[6] which the opera is full of; the mould is evident in the arias of the chief characters which, with their predictable and repetitive rallentandos after the main section, are all treated alike. That Paer is familiar with German music goes without saying; that he has also studied Mozart's works is borne out by his manner of orchestration and many passages in his comic operas. It is all the more incomprehensible why this knowledge and study have failed to deter him at least from his terrible prolixity and long ritornellos, which have rightly been so often ridiculed for

---

[3] For example *Le astuzie amorose*, also called *La locanda* (1792), *Una in bene e una in male* (1794), *Il principe di Taranto* (1797), *Il morto vivo* (1799), and *Poche ma buone, ossia Le donne cambiate* (1800), which last Hoffmann could have seen in Berlin (1807/08). The same opera was mounted in Bamberg in December 1808 as *Die bezauberten Weiber* [F.S., rev.].

[4] style: see Prefatory Remarks to the preceding review, of Gluck's *Iphigénie en Aulide*. 'Style' represents for Hoffmann everything that a serious opera by Paer lacked.

[5] Presumably his *Siface*, set by Francesco Feo (1723). The text of Paer's *Sofonisba* was based on an older libretto by A. and G. F. Zanetti, for Jommelli (1746). Gluck's *La Sofonisba* (1744) contains a mixture of Metastasio texts [F.S.].

[6] *pezzi concertanti*: concerted pieces, mixing soloists with chorus.

holding up the action and not infrequently forcing the unfortunate singer to stand waiting like a helpless puppet.[7]

The reviewer hastens to justify his opinion, which must seem harsh to many admirers of Paer's pleasant compositions, by a more detailed examination of the opera before him. On opening the piano arrangement he finds a number of examples even in the overture. Who would remotely anticipate a tragic opera recounting the struggle of love, jealousy, and heroic courage, on hearing the following music, the main themes of the Allegro in the overture?[8]

Ex. III

Transposition of the first subject to the bass, and its further treatment as for example:

---

[7] This point has already been made in 1808 in Hoffmann's 'Observations on Quaisin's *Le Jugement de Salomon*', p. 218 and note 2. Gluck's Preface to *Alceste* (published 1769) describes the first of the 'abuses' of Italianate opera as follows: 'I have been unwilling either to interrupt a singer in the greatest heat of dialogue in order to make him wait for a tedious ritornello, or to stop him in the middle of a word or on a favourable vowel, to display the agility of his fine voice in a long passage . . .'

[8] The overture begins with a Larghetto of twenty-six bars. The second part of Ex. III shows bars 73–7 of the Allegro, and Ex. IV shows bars 103–8.

Ex. IV

lend the overture a superficial scholarliness, an appearance of working-out. It is not in fact intended so seriously, and soon gives way again to jaunty, heterogeneous music.

The opera begins with a chorus of Romans, joined first by Scipione, then by Siface. Even in this chorus, with its recurring closes on the tonic and dominant, the harmonic substance is very scanty and the individual voices are not effectively arranged. Moreover, if one completely ignores the principle that the chorus should constantly express its character in sharp outlines, and if one is content merely to give the chorus chords that accompany the solo voice, then it is certainly easy to write a *pezzo concertante*. This treatment totally removes any possibility of the great effect such a choral piece can have if its requirements are strictly fulfilled. The criticism directed at this chorus also applies to the other choruses, but it is most conspicuously justified in the chorus and *pezzo concertante* containing the catastrophe of the work.[9] Here the people are seized with admiration and astonishment at Sofonisba's heroism: 'Oh true constancy and virtue! How it will always astound me!' But could there be music more ordinary and insignificant than the following?

[9] Act 2, No. 18.

mia   ti se - gui - rà,   l'al - ma mia   ti se - gui - rà.

pir o -gnor mi fa,   che   stu - pir   o -gnor mi fa.

The reviewer has added Siface's part in order to show how the 'O crudel' etc. ['O cruel one, my spirit will shortly follow you'] also has to blend into this passage. He prefers not to criticise the many melismas in the solo part to the words 'la mia tomba bagnerà' ('. . . will bathe my tomb'), which may indeed ill suit Sofonisba's melancholy state of mind; it is after all the composer's manner[10] that obliges him to write in this way rather than another.

The Numidian chorus, No. 5, has an exotic lilt. It recalls to some extent the triumphal chorus of Peruvians in Winter's *Opferfest*.[11] With reference to Scipione's aria, No. 3, the reviewer must point out that the composer likes to preserve the older pattern of bravura arias (with the exception of the da capo) and takes no notice of the justified objections to it raised in more recent times. He furnishes several such arias in this opera which, further-more, are extended to extreme lengths, as for example Masinissa's very long aria, No. 7, with its numerous, quite pointless repetitions.[12] Scene No. 4 is very melodious and tastefully set, but otherwise utterly devoid of all characterisation, a requirement surely deserving the highest priority here, where the central figure appears for the first time and reveals her heroic spirit in bold strokes. 'Gods – what voices I hear – ah! – how my heart leaps!' is merely a sequence of flourishes that certainly do not depict Sofonisba's

---

[10] manner: the appearance of *Manier* here marks the establishment of an important duality in Hoffmann's critical vocabulary: 'style' (*Stil*) versus 'manner' (*Manier*), later defined with great acuity in 'Letters on Music in Berlin' (p. 393), where 'manner' would be character-ised in musical composition as 'nothing but an expression of the artist's stereotyped subjectivity'.

[11] Paer's chorus No. 5 is a Tempo di Marcia in 2/4, 'Viva l'eroe.' Peter von Winter's *Das unterbrochene Opferfest* (*The Interrupted Sacrifice*) (1796) was in the Bamberg repertory and could have been seen by Hoffmann on 23 March or 7 May 1809, 18 January or 2 February 1810, and was noted as seen by him on 3 March and 2 April 1811 (*HTB*). The same Peruvian chorus appears near the end of his tale *Nussknacker und Mausekönig* (*Nutcracker and the King of Mice*) in a fantastic sequence: 'the procession of the Interrupted Sacrifice came along at the same time, surging towards the pyramid cake with drums beating and chorus singing . . .' [F.S.].

[12] Aria No. 3: 'Veggo dolente e misero'; aria No. 7, 'Amo un volto lusinghiero.'

anxious state in the proximity of battle.[13] Masinissa is to be sure a tender and sweet soprano hero; he proves this with his first notes on entering: 'Ah, why fly from me O queen?'[14] Sofonisba's ninth scene has incomparably more character than the one mentioned above. The wide intervals in the voice part at the beginning of the Andante maestoso really have something majestic about them. (Who can fail to think of Mozart's splendid aria in *Così fan tutte*, 'Come scoglio'?)[15] The melismas are also more in keeping here and very brilliant, but the recurring *più lento* is still present, however, and the chorus is simply too insignificant. In the tenth scene Masinissa swears eternal hatred of the Romans and eternal love of the Carthaginians, and for this Sofonisba is willing to marry him. But her husband [Siface], who was thought to be dead, appears at a very inopportune moment, which naturally gives rise to no little consternation among the people. Poor Siface is truly a model of self-restraint, however, for he waits for forty-three bars of Larghetto with many fermatas[16] and is content, while the lovers speak of 'sweet peace' and 'true happiness', to interject his 'Ah, who offers a sword?', before finally bursting out 'Wicked, worthless ones!' In the following trio, 'O qual barbaro cimento, qual tormento . . .' ('Oh what a cruel test, what torment'), in which the singers are inflamed by love, jealousy, hatred, and vengeance, we encounter this music:

---

[13] Sofonisba's recitative and cavatina, 'Lasciatemi, non temo': the words quoted come from an Allegro section (p. 32) heard against an offstage chorus.

[14] No. 5, 'Ah, perchè da me t'involi, o regina.'

[15] Aria of Fiordiligi, Act 1 No. 14. *Così fan tutte* was performed at Bamberg. See *The Poet and the Composer*, p. 203 and note 60.

[16] In the trio, 'Una soave calma'.

The latter extract is followed by the words 'O che affanno, che tormento' ('Oh what pain, what torment'), but then the next phrase comes straight from opera buffa:

Would not the words 'Oh what joy, what pleasure makes my heart rejoice' be much more suitable for this music, in which agonising pain is expressed so cheerfully and glibly?[17] The conclusion also contains a thoroughly hackneyed flourish.

Clearly on a much higher level is the duet No. 12, which is one of the best pieces in the opera, having at least a semblance of tragic music.[18] The quartet No. 15 is also one of the more significant items and will be found quite satisfactory if one applies the criteria given above.[19] Siface's scene No. 17 contains nothing distinctive and follows a predictable pattern, although the libretto provided ample opportunity for loftier expression of his anguished thoughts.[20] Among the linking passages in the recitative (page

---

[17] The words of the preceding music example read: 'Ah! At least finish my grief and put an end to my suffering!'

[18] For Sofonisba and Siface: 'Or verrai ferirmi ingrato.'

[19] For Sofonisba, Masinissa, Siface, Scipione: 'Che fatal e orrendo giorno!'

[20] Recitative, 'Ma qual mi stringe' and aria 'Da tanto duolo e spasimo'.

127, system 2) there occurs a chord sequence that the reviewer finds incomprehensible:[21]

By means of the examples quoted the reviewer believes he has adequately demonstrated the fairness of his judgement. He would add that those who in an opera expect only to be lulled by pleasant sounds, who desire only to admire the skill of the singers, in short who see the stage only as heightening the appeal of a nice concert by the visual pleasure of nice settings, costumes, etc., and to whom an opera is only a glorified concert, will find complete satisfaction in Paer's music. On the other hand those who have higher expectations, who demand from opera all the prerequisites of musical drama, and who therefore deeply revere the classical works of Gluck and Mozart, will hardly be able to sit through operas like this *Sofonisba*. An experienced, highly regarded, and well-known composer once said to the reviewer after hearing one of Paer's heroic operas (*Sargino*): 'It was all very nice and melodious, but heaven knows how it turned out, it sent me to sleep!'[22] The absence of that dramatic quality which springs from the utmost attention to every detail of character and every moment of the action, and which keeps the listener in a state of constant tension, could not be more tellingly exposed. The reviewer fully acknowledges Paer's merits listed above, but he feels that his opera seria, at least on the German and certainly on the French stage, with its strict demand for the style of lyric tragedy, will never create any special or lasting interest, and any temporary popularity will only be the result of chance circumstances such as the lustre of this or that singer.

The piano score is very well arranged, and can be highly recommended to all lovers of singing anxious to exercise their throats and to acquire the latest singing-style.

---

[21] Hoffmann's G in the second bar actually follows a $\frac{5}{3}$ on A, and the third bar should be shown to resolve onto F major, root position. The same sequence is repeated a fourth higher, circling round the tonic B flat, instead of F.

[22] The identity of the 'well-known composer' has not been discovered. Hoffmann could be referring to an incident in Berlin between February and June 1808. Ironically, he was to conduct *Sargino* in Dresden and Leipzig in 1813–14; see *HTB* 215, 2 July 1813: 'Thus I also conducted from the same spot where Paer directed the opera for the first time' [F.S.].

Review of Spohr's First Symphony

Published: AMZ, xiii, 27 November and 4 December 1811, cols. 797–
806, 813–19   *Unsigned*
First reprinted: Kroll 1909

As mentioned in the Prefatory Remarks to Weigl's *Das Waisenhaus* (above), Franz von Holbein took over the Bamberg theatre with effect from October 1810; not only did Hoffmann continue with stage composition (his music to J. Seyfried's melo-drama *Saul, König in Israel* was first heard on 29 June 1811) but he was pitched into all aspects of backstage and front-of-house activity. This has been briefly reviewed in the Prefatory Remarks to 'The Complete Machinist', p. 64. Holbein's memoirs also state that Hoffmann conducted certain performances. At the same time, Hoffmann commenced work on his *grosse romantische Oper, Aurora*, to which Holbein had contributed the libretto. Composition extended from 14 January 1811 for some fifteen months.

As the letter to *AMZ* of 2 August 1811 admits, Hoffmann not surprisingly fell behind in writing reviews (that of the Beethoven Trios was behindhand), but by 23 October he was ready to despatch that of the Spohr symphony:[1]

> It is a fine, important work, and I was all the more conscious of my duty to take great care; for this reason I did not want to write the review until I had heard the symphony performed several times by our excellent theatre orchestra. It was particularly the lack of simplicity and the tendency of the composer to modulate so quickly from key to key that I felt obliged to deprecate. Our most recent composers suffer from both these defects already, and for the sake of the wretched imitators one should not remain silent, even when an otherwise excellent composer commits them.

Louis Spohr (1784–1859), violin virtuoso, composer and conductor, was already a prominent German figure in 1811. He eventually completed nine symphonies (the second one not until 1820), ten operas, including *Faust* (1813) and *Jessonda* (1823), and a host of instrumental works. The genesis of the First Symphony in E flat, Op. 20, was a request for a work for the second music festival at Frankenhausen (Thuringia), of which Spohr was the musical director. The symphony was com-posed at Gotha, where Spohr was Konzertmeister, in March–April 1811, and first heard there on 25 April. The Frankenhausen performance, on 11 July, used an orchestra comprising forty-six violins, fifteen violas, seventeen cellos, ten double-basses, quadruple wind, a contra-bass-horn, and four timpani.[2]

---

[1] Hoffmann was sent a manuscript score and printed parts, title page as follows: PREMIÈRE / Symphonie / pour / 2 Violons [etc.] . . . / par / Louis Spohr. / Oe. 20. – Pr. 4 Rth. / . . . / Chez A. Kühnel, / Bureau de Musique à Leipzig. The plate number was 897.

[2] *ZEW*, 5 August 1811, col. 1236, cited in *Schriften zur Musik*, 447.

Spohr eventually read Hoffmann's review and wrote to the publisher, Peters, about it:

> Although the reviewer of my symphony dealt rather harshly with me and was deliberately blind to many good things in my composition (especially the Larghetto), he is nevertheless quite right in saying that the Scherzo is too long, and even in the Frankenhausen performance, therefore, as well as recently in Hamburg, I went straight through the first two sections [i.e. without repeats], whereby this defect was to a great extent remedied. Would it not be possible to erase the repeat signs in the copies not yet sent out?[3]

Hoffmann was indeed censorious, though he wrote as one who had himself composed a symphony in E flat five years earlier. The review seems almost teasingly ironic about it, as when in his introduction the writer implies that Spohr, as an expert, has avoided the over-use of a chromatically descending bass. In discussing the finale, he picks out this very cliché for mention.

This work, which is the first important work in this genre from a composer already highly acclaimed and popular, and which has been a brilliant success even before its appearance in print, is bound to attract the attention of the music-loving public. And the composer can count it a success indeed when his work, like the present one, does not leave the interest it arouses unsatisfied. The symphony is written in a substantial manner, orchestrated with an awareness of effect, and well proportioned in its parts. Despite its frequent striving for powerful expression, it generally keeps within the bounds of the calm dignity engendered by the chosen themes, which seems to suit the composer's genius more than the turbulent flames that stream forth in Mozart's and Beethoven's symphonies. For this reason the themes tend to be pleasant melodies rather than momentous utterances penetrating deep into the listener's soul, as is so much the case with those composers, and also with Haydn. The composer who writes a *first* symphony like this one certainly arouses the greatest expectations; one can entertain the hope of once again being able to hear well written symphonies, of which there are not many these days. The too frequent recurrence of certain favourite devices, such as a chromatically descending bass, and the repetition of hackneyed chord progressions, are easily avoided by a knowledgeable artist; and precisely because he is knowledgeable his themes are also devised with greater harmonic skill. The attention with which the reviewer has read and listened to this excellent composer's work and the esteem he has conceived for him as a result are borne out by the fact that he cannot resist discussing this substantial composition in more detail; and by allowing

---

[3] Letter of 1 January 1812; text kindly furnished by Dr Clive Brown.

himself small criticisms here and there he also hopes to illuminate individual moments of excellence in the work.

Like most larger-scale symphonies, it begins with a short Adagio introduction, in E flat major.[4] Beneath the tonic chord sustained by wind instruments the following figure is played in the bass:

This figure descends chromatically to the dominant and is imitated by the other string instruments, and then by clarinets and flutes. It continues until bar 13, combined with the secondary figure

introduced by the bass instruments in the third bar, and occurs in every bar except the seventh and eighth. The modulation leading away from the dominant back to the dominant chord closing the Adagio makes a very striking effect:

Ex. V

The reviewer, though, would have avoided the first appearance of the dominant in the ninth bar[5] since it is disconcerting, after an excursion promising great things, to find oneself back at the point one had reached quite smoothly a few bars before. The uncomfortable feeling of the closing cadences following in rapid succession on the same note is lessened by regarding the second B flat as the dominant of E flat minor:

One could not wish to hear a phrase more melodious and flowing, without degenerating into triviality and vapidity, than the theme of the following

---

[4] Twenty-two bars, 4/4 time.

[5] i.e. the first bar of Ex. V, after which Hoffmann provides the essential melody and harmony of bars 10 to 16.

Allegro, played by the strings above a *pianissimo* tonic sustained by the horns:

Ex. VI

In the first three bars the reviewer would have had the double-basses not playing quavers but sustaining the tonic very softly with the horns, or resting until the fourth bar and then coming in on G. The quavers spoil the serene nobility of the theme. In the eighth bar the flute enters *all'ottava* with the first violins; then follow one-bar phrases from clarinet and oboe; then the clarinet takes up part of the theme in canonic imitation with the flute; horns and bassoons join in, then a *pianissimo* timpani roll, until the full tutti finally bursts forth in the twenty-fourth bar. Violins and bass instruments alternately play a figure in semiquavers, while the wind instruments imitate the first two bars of the main theme. This gradual entry of the wind instruments leading to a full tutti has often been used to great effect by the best masters, and by his use of it here the composer has demonstrated his skill in the device. Quiet and restrained at first, the theme resembles a peaceful stream that gathers more and more strength as it flows on through the mountains and finally becomes a seething forest torrent. As far as the second theme in the dominant, again gentle and sustained, the music consists merely of developments of the abbreviated main theme, interwoven with a variety of secondary ideas. The first two bars of the theme, for example, which struck the reviewer at a glance as capable of all sorts of contrapuntal inversions, are taken up by the bass instruments in the following manner:

One can see that it perfectly supplies a characteristic bass-line without which the subsequent development would not get very far. This short passage, without being exactly original, is most effective, and the new contrasting material in the wind instruments particularly striking. The reviewer has quoted the full score to demonstrate also how intelligently the composer orchestrates. Such short, incidental figures for the violins as the following, however,

if not positively undesirable, seem to the reviewer of no particular value since they tend to make the music disjointed and fragmentary.

After the second theme a new section begins with a tutti (*fortissimo*, E flat minor) but remains in that key for only five bars. In the sixth there is an enharmonic change

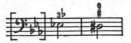

and then the section is brought back to the dominant by eight successive seventh-chords:

Ex. VII

The reviewer will have occasion below to say why he dislikes this entire modulation proceeding from the enharmonic change; but the feeble and hackneyed return from foreign regions to home territory also completely obliterates the intended impression. It is a brilliant meteor that disintegrates in a watery fog. The composer then surprisingly modulates again from the dominant to D flat major,[6] and the reappearance of the main theme in this remote key, and played by wind instruments, is most effective. After the music has returned to B flat major there follows a short, brilliant tutti and then the first half ends on a B flat pedal-point, over which the strings play the fruitful two opening bars and clarinets and horns a phrase that has previously occurred:

Ex. VIII

The second half begins with this same phrase in F minor but soon changes to C minor. In this key the main theme is developed in four-part fugue-like imitation, initially with a previously heard phrase combined with it as a countersubject in the wind instruments. The composer soon abandons this idea, however, and the bass moves to the root of A flat; then comes

---

[6] The progression in Ex. VII does not lead to B flat, but goes straight from the final dominant seventh on F to the new key of D flat, via a $\frac{4}{2}$ chord on G flat.

the same phrase that in the first half led to the first tutti[7] but here, more heavily orchestrated and enriched with a new figure in the violins and violas, it leads back to the opening.

Using the abbreviated main theme the composer modulates to G, as the dominant of C; the second theme returns in C major, begins again only slightly changed in C minor, ends in B flat as the dominant of E flat, and is finally repeated once more in E flat major. Then comes the tutti again, originally in E flat minor but now in A flat minor, then the same enharmonic change (A flat minor to G sharp first inversion) and again the eight seventh-chords leading the listener comfortably back to familiar territory [cf. Ex. VII]. The reviewer has already pointed out that the intended effect of the preceding enharmonic change is completely nullified by this sequential return over descending fifths in the bass. Even if that were not the case, the reviewer feels that one should be careful with strong spices. He would employ the most striking digressions, among which enharmonic ones are certainly to be included, only in the development section, before the recapitulation of the main subject; he would not want to be placed in the position of having to use them twice, as inevitably happens if they occur in the first half and therefore, according to the pattern dictated by convention and certainly by clarity, return in the second half in the tonic. It is difficult to use the same surprise twice. Following this pattern, then, the second half now remains in the tonic and comes to a brilliant and powerful close.

From this dissection of the first Allegro it is evident how much this worthy composer has striven for unity and clarity. The entire movement, however, would be much more of an entity, and yet also more incisive, if he had exploited the fruitful main theme in a few contrapuntal twists and turns, perhaps with fewer disconnected secondary themes interspersed. His development chiefly consists of abbreviations of the main subject divided between strings and wind, and no genuinely contrapuntal inversion occurs at all. Without parading a lot of useless erudition, it is certainly well to shape the main subject of a work so that it is susceptible of a multiplicity of contrapuntal treatments; every composer knows how often a phrase that in its initial form sounds not particularly original takes on in some inverted guise a whole new and striking character. Who has carried this art to a higher level, combined with the most songlike, flowing melodies, than the immortal Haydn!

The Larghetto, in A flat major, is arranged just like a number of symphonic andantes by this immortal composer; it is a charming canzonetta

---

[7] Similar to Ex. VIII and developed from the fourth and fifth bars of Ex. VI.

varied to the end in a multiplicity of ways.[8] First the obbligato cellos state the simple melody, accompanied only by the pizzicato double-basses:

Then the first violins take up the theme but modulate to the dominant, and from there the music moves to a chord of C, on which the following effective thematic imitation begins:

[8] As Spohr noted (see Prefatory Remarks), Hoffmann's account of the Larghetto (120 bars) does not suggest all its qualities. The form is sonata rondo (A:B:A:development:A),

Ex. IX

The transition leading back to the tonic is original and striking. After several further modulations, for example A flat minor, D flat major, E flat minor, etc., the pleasant main theme returns again, though now embellished with subsidiary figures from accompanying instruments, and the whole Larghetto closes *diminuendo* and *pianissimo*.[9] This second movement is very pleasant, well proportioned, and cleverly executed, matching the character of the symphony as a whole summed up by the reviewer above. It is lacking, however, in that significant quality which powerfully seizes and carries away the listener's spirit. Haydn's andantes often begin in a simple and childlike, almost frivolous way, but their meaning and character shine forth unawares and envelop the listener in their radiance. After the melodious theme in this Larghetto almost everything is said.

unusual for a slow movement of its date, and the fourth section develops over the space of thirty-five bars. The opening cello melody, alone accompanied by pizzicato double-basses, fortuitously duplicates the scoring of the slow movement of Méhul's Fourth Symphony in E (unpublished at the time; first heard in March 1810, Paris).

[9] Spohr writes *morendo*.

The theme of the following Scherzo allegro in E flat major is really playful and capricious:

At the fermata in the thirteenth bar the music seems to be veering towards A flat major, but passing through C minor, D minor, and G minor it goes into B flat major, in which key the first half ends.[10] The chief characteristic of the theme is the upbeat,

which made a powerful impression on the composer and therefore persists conspicuously in the development of the movement. It is not the theme itself that is developed but only a derivative of it. Because of the recurring upbeat, however, there is a close resemblance. As an illustration the passage following the fermata referred to above may serve all the better since it is also to be counted among the most successful in the whole movement:

<hr />

[10] The Scherzo is on the sonata pattern, both halves repeated (total 314 bars). The Trio, with both halves of its binary form repeated, totals 126 bars. The recapitulation of the Scherzo (157 bars) is written out without repeats.

Ex. X

The composer adheres strictly to the ideas he has chosen for his development. Only nineteen bars before the first half ends does there appear an odd eight-bar passage in 2/4 time, quite unrelated to the main theme. He has employed a number of devices, perhaps in an effort to add more spice, but in the reviewer's opinion unnecessarily. What the composer wanted has very often been achieved by Haydn without any change of time signature, and without the admixture of any heterogeneous music, merely by displacing the rhythm. This short passage rudely destroys the continuity. Before the end of the second half the same passage recurs in E flat major. The reviewer is less impressed by the Trio, since the added triplets in many ways give the music a confused, unrhythmical feeling, as for example

Passages for the wind instruments too, like the following one, are not effective at a very rapid tempo:

Furthermore, with its repeats the scherzo is 597 bars long,[11] and the reviewer feels that Haydn and Mozart quite rightly never tried to scherzo at such length. The tendency of the composer to modulate very quickly from one key to another is also mentioned here because it is most noticeable in the Scherzo. These quick transitions oblige the composer not only to touch on a large number of keys within a short passage, but also frequently to reiterate the same modulations later in the piece.[12] The true art of composition certainly does not lie in rapid transitions, in passing from one key to another. It is by quite simple means, merely by the music's originality and warmth, and the harmonic changes arising directly from it, that a composer of genius moves the enraptured listener.

The Finale[13] has a pleasant but, in the reviewer's opinion, rather too trivial theme. In particular there is a hopping quality in the similarity of note-values (crotchets) between upper and lower parts that is out of keeping with the character of the symphony as established in the first movement:

---

[11] Original text: '605' bars. If he miscounted slightly, Hoffmann incidentally provided evidence for us that musicians obeyed repeat marks as printed, evidence corroborated by Spohr in the letter (see Prefatory Remarks) attempting to get the marks erased after publication.

[12] The fourth movement modulates more extensively than the third.

[13] Sonata form, first half repeated, total 377 bars.

The music is again treated and orchestrated with much discernment, although it is less weighty than the first Allegro; the reviewer will therefore only touch upon the main features, without entering into a detailed explanation of the inner structure. Especially good is the imitation between winds and basses using the first bar of the theme, which carries the music along while the violins move in contrary motion:

The finale theme is also much more compatible than the previous movements with chromatically descending basses, which occur very frequently, perhaps too frequently. The following operative passages of the finale, if one may so put it, consist of triplet figures but conform very closely to the main theme, comprising for the most part merely embellished versions of the main theme itself, such as

It is clear that phrases like the following:

Ex. XI

can be used to traverse the remotest keys, and this does not fail to happen
here. B major, C sharp minor, etc. are touched upon until we reach the
dominant B flat with the main theme in the first violins and the violas
imitating skilfully in a canonic stretto.[14] The reviewer cannot complain
about the negligent orthography in the fourth bar of the above example,
since with our equal temperament it offends only the eye, but shortly after
that in the transition to the chord of B flat as the dominant of E flat minor the
bass should be written:[15]

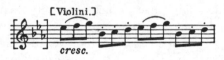

The theme sounds very charming played by clarinets, horns, and bassoons.[16] Violins and double-basses have single pizzicato notes and the cellos
supply a short counter-theme in quavers. The conclusion is based on the
perhaps too ordinary phrase

Ex. XII

and is altogether rather abrupt, owing to its brevity. Recent composers often
err in the most contrary ways, and in particular there are now overtures that
are almost incapable of coming to an end; one closing phrase follows
another, so that the listener grows weary and the effect of the whole piece is
spoilt, just as in the theatre long speeches that drag out the dénouement
destroy the audience's interest in the play. It is nevertheless true that after
many excursions the return to the tonic is very welcome, and the listener
may well savour this pleasure for a while especially when some closing
figure informs him that the movement will now remain in the tonic until the
end. Something brilliant and resounding is then needed, and if the music is
too abruptly cut off it seems to rush past the ear all the more rapidly.[17]

The reviewer reaffirms his sincere conviction that the symphony of this

[14] In the retransition to the recapitulation, bar 166.
[15] i.e. bar 147, where Spohr has a semibreve B natural leading to a B flat. In Ex. XI the
'negligent orthography' consists in juxtaposing enharmonic notations: the F sharp–G
sharp in the top part should have read G flat–A flat. Spohr, like Beethoven in analogous
cases, notates for ease of performance.
[16] i.e. as it appears beginning the recapitulation, bar 179.
[17] Spohr is exploring secondary modulations (G flat minor) only nineteen bars before the end.
The music of Ex. XII is merely part of the final cadential flourish; triplet rhythms have
predominated since the second subject group.

excellent composer, if well performed, is bound to provide the listener with much pleasure. It stands on a far higher level than so many loudly acclaimed works written in recent times. That is the reason why the reviewer has taken it upon himself to make such a rigorous study of this substantial work, and honestly to express everything he thought, everything he felt so deeply when he read, heard, and then re-read this symphony. How easy it is, on such a foundation as stands at the composer's disposal, to erect the most beautiful, masterly edifices!

So far as the reviewer can reliably discover, the symphony was originally intended for the large orchestra said to have been assembled in Frankenhausen, and this very circumstance could have tempted the composer to strive too hard for large-scale or extraordinary effects. The reviewer feels, however, that a work written for a very large or, as the orchestra gathered in Frankenhausen was somewhere referred to, for a *giant* orchestra[18] should be kept very simple and absolutely free of short, capricious figures. An altarpiece or a painting for a large room intended to be looked at by large numbers of people close up and far away requires large masses of light and shade, broad folds of cloth, sharp outlines of the figures; a small painting for a private room requires the most delicate execution. It is the same with music. Church and chamber, even opera-house and chamber, have hitherto been totally separate. The reviewer remembers a composer once looking through the opera *Virtù e costanza* of old Fux, which was about to be performed in the open air; he was not a little critical of the many long notes and sparse texture.[19] How surprised he was, though, that in performance the extreme simplicity of that great masterpiece delighted and enraptured thousands of listeners quite magically. It is particularly when several instruments move in different directions, however beautiful, however artistic their interplay may be considered, that a work for large orchestra easily

---

[18] See Prefatory Remarks.

[19] *Costanza e fortezza* [*recte*], *festa teatrale* composed by Johann Joseph Fux (1660–1741) for the coronation of Charles VI as King of Bohemia. The open-air performance was on 28 August 1723 in Prague. To Hoffmann's remark that he 'remembers' should clearly be added 'having read about'. He was obviously thinking of a passage from 'Herrn Johann Joachim Quantzens Lebenslauf', in F. W. Marpurg's journal, *Historisch-Kritische Beyträge*, i/5, 197–250, where we read on p. 216:

> I travelled . . . to Prague, to hear the great and splendid opera, which was being performed at the coronation of Emperor Charles VI in the open air by a hundred singers and two hundred instrumentalists . . . The concertante and contrapuntal writing for strings that occurred in the ritornellos, although it consisted for the most part of passages which on paper may often have looked quite stiff and dry, on such a large scale and with so many players as here produced a very good, indeed much better effect than a more *galant* melodic style decorated with many small figures and rapid notes would have had in this case. [F.S.]

becomes confused. For the combination of several lines moving in counter-point the reviewer prefers to listen to a string quartet, since only in that medium is the utmost purity and clarity to be attained.

The engraving is clear and falls well upon the eye. Formerly the bass-line was provided by the cellos in a single body with the double-basses; now they often supply middle voices and have solos to perform, so that they really deserve a separate part-book. Here the cello is still combined with the double-bass, which causes considerable trouble for the players.

Review of Beethoven's Overture to *Coriolan*

Published: AMZ, xiv, 5 August 1812, cols. 519–26   *Unsigned*
First reprinted: Vom Ende 1899

Hoffmann completed the opera *Aurora* by April 1812, and subsequently withdrew from practical theatre activity in favour of writing; in fact the present review was sent in to *AMZ* together with 'Thoughts about the Great Value of Music' (see the Introduction to *Kreisleriana*, p. 53). He was obliged to write out the score of *Coriolan*, since only the orchestral parts were published: the score was first printed in 1846. It is not known when Hoffmann heard the work, but he alludes to having done so. His review was written on 30 June 1812 and despatched next day (*HTB*, 163).

Beethoven's overture to *Coriolan* was his first not to have accompanied a musical stage work: only *Prometheus* and the three *Leonora* overtures antedate it. The score is dated 1807 and first performance was in March of that year; publication followed in January 1808.[1]

Heinrich Josef von Collin (1771–1811) was an influential friend of Beethoven's, as can be seen from his title as part of the dedication shown in note 1. Author of a series of verse plays on historical subjects, often extolling patriotism, his *Regulus* (1801) was his most popular production. The tragedy *Coriolan* (originally seen in 1802)[2] differs from Plutarch and Shakespeare in showing its hero choosing to die; thus – notes Maynard Solomon – the overture's 'closing, disintegrating passage . . . symbolises the death of the hero'.[3] Hoffmann's sensing of supernatural images in the music would have been rejected by Beethoven, who later wrote to Collin concerning magic in stage works: 'I am prejudiced against this sort of thing, because it has a soporific effect on feeling and reason.'[4]

---

[1] As a set of seventeen parts, entitled: Ouverture / de / CORIOLAN / Tragédie de Mr. de Collin / . . . / Composée et Dédieê / a Monsieur de COLLIN / Secrétaire aulique au Service de / Sa Majesté Imp. Roy. Ap. / par / LOUIS van BEETHOVEN / Op. 62. / A Vienne / Au Bureau des arts et d'industrie / A Pesth chez Schreyvogel & Comp. The plate number was 589.

[2] *Thayer's Life of Beethoven*, 416.

[3] Maynard Solomon, *Beethoven* (London, 1978), 203.

[4] Supposed date of origin, autumn 1808: *Letters of Beethoven*, i, 197.

The form of the overture is an unorthodox sonata, the development beginning after what Hoffmann calls 'the second period of the overture'; the opening material first reappears in the subdominant, bar 152.

Since it is the customary and by no means reprehensible practice to introduce every performance in the theatre with music, every really important play should have an overture conducive to the frame of mind that the character of the work requires. A number of tragedies have already been provided with overtures[5] and now the great Beethoven has furnished Collin's *Coriolan* with a splendid production of this type. The reviewer must admit, however, that Beethoven's purely romantic genius does not seem to him to be entirely appropriate to Collin's predominantly reflective poetry, and that this composer would seize the soul with his full force and properly arouse it for the scenes that follow if he were to write overtures to the tragedies of Shakespeare and Calderón, which express romanticism in the highest sense. The sombre gravity of the present composition, with its awe-inspiring resonances from an unknown spirit-world, foreshadows more than is subsequently fulfilled. One fully believes that the world of spirits ominously announced by subterranean thunder will draw closer in the play, that Hamlet's troubled shadow perhaps will steal across the stage, or that the terrible sisters will drag Macbeth down into Orcus. More emotion and brilliance would perhaps have better suited Collin's poetry. Nevertheless, apart from those expectations aroused only in a few critics who fully understand Beethoven's music, the composition serves very well to suggest the intended idea, namely that a great and tragic event is to form the content of the ensuing play. Even without having read the playbill nobody can expect anything else. This overture cannot be followed by domestic tragedy but only by high tragedy, in which heroes appear and perish.

The overture consists of only one movement, Allegro con brio, common time, in C minor, but the first fourteen bars are written in such a way that they sound like an andante leading into the Allegro. By its overall conception, but particularly by its original orchestration, this opening irresistibly seizes and captivates the spirit. Despite the *fortissimo* the first two bars, with the strings playing a low C, sound hollow and pungent, so that the F minor chord from the full orchestra on the first crotchet of the third bar breaks stridently in. The following deathly silence, the reiteration by the strings of the same hollow, eerie C, again a strident $\frac{6}{4}\natural$ on F, again the deathly silence,

---

[5] Perhaps Hoffmann was thinking of incidental music at the Berlin Nationaltheater. Reichardt, for example, had composed music to *Macbeth*, Goethe's *Götz von Berlichingen*, etc., Schiller's main plays too. An overture and entr'actes to *King Lear* (before 1806), once attributed to J. Haydn, may have been by W. G. or C. D. Stegmann. Any resident theatre conductor would if necessary compile or compose overtures, as part of his employment.

the C from the strings for the third time, the chord now intensified to a seventh, and finally two chords from the full orchestra leading to the Allegro theme: all adds to the expectation and tightens the listener's breast. It is the threatening rumble of an approaching storm. In order to make this clear, the reviewer quotes the whole opening:

Ex. XIII

The main theme of the Allegro bears a character of implacable unrest, of insatiable yearning, and though it is unmistakably the product of Beethoven's unique spirit, it vividly reminds the reviewer of Cherubini and clearly reveals to him the spiritual kinship of the two composers.[6] The further development of the overture is also closely related to Cherubini's overtures, particularly in its orchestration.

The transposition of this theme down by a tone (to B flat minor) immediately after the bar's rest is unexpected and heightens the tension created by the first few bars. The music moves towards F minor and then in a full tutti towards C minor. After the main theme has been briefly touched upon by the second violins and cellos

the first period of the overture closes on the first inversion of the dominant of the relative major key of E flat. Now the second main theme enters, accompanied by a figure that recurs frequently throughout the work, almost always in the cellos:

F minor, G minor, and C minor are touched upon, mostly in developments of this second theme, until the second period of the overture closes in G minor, with syncopated notes in the first violins accompanied by a new quaver figure in the cellos and violas [bar 102]:

---

[6] The Paris operas of Luigi Cherubini took Vienna by storm in 1803, when *Lodoiska*, *Eliza*, *Médée*, and *Les deux journées* were all seen; he was invited to Vienna shortly after and composed *Faniska* there (1806). Beethoven clearly regarded Cherubini as a rival at this time, and there are contradictory reports about his behaviour towards the visitor. See *Thayer's Life of Beethoven*, 381.

After the close on the dominant the figure just quoted, with the same accompaniment from cellos and violas, carries the music for thirty-four bars[7] through G minor, F minor, A flat major, D flat major etc. into F minor, in which key the beginning of the overture is repeated. The music moves towards C minor and the second theme, with the same accompaniment as in the first half, enters in C major but goes straight into D minor, E minor, and then immediately back to C minor [bar 200]:

Then comes the figure in syncopated notes with cello accompaniment which previously introduced the close in G minor but is now cut short in the following way [bar 237]:

Ex. XIV

---

[7] There are two main cadences in G minor, at bar 102 and bar 118. Hoffmann's 'thirty-four bars' indicates the space between bar 118 and the F minor recapitulation at bar 152.

The reviewer has included the oboes, trumpets, and timpani in order to let the reader appreciate the frightening effect of the dissonant C that he felt on hearing the overture performed. The distant horn octaves on G, followed quite unexpectedly by the second main theme in C major (as shown above), also heighten the sense of expectation again before the close. But this luminous C major was only a short-lived glimpse of the sun through dark clouds, for only four bars later the sombre main key returns and a theme [at bar 270] in syncopated notes similar to the figure frequently referred to[8] leads back to the beginning of the overture, now differently orchestrated. Oboes, clarinets, bassoons, and trumpets also intone the hollow C previously played by the strings alone. This is followed by short, disjointed phrases, whole bar rests, and finally the music dies away with these notes:

[8] i.e. as in Ex. XIV.

The reviewer should point out that he has quoted the complete score of the conclusion and that the entire remainder of the orchestra remains silent. These hollow sounds, the lugubrious tone of the bassoon sustaining the fifth above the key-note, the lament of the cellos, the short punctuations from the double-basses – all combine in a profound way to produce the most tragic effect, and the most tense expectation of what will be revealed to us when the mysterious curtain flies upwards.

The reviewer has endeavoured to give a clear idea of the inner structure of this masterpiece, and one will observe the extremely simple elements from which its artful edifice is built. Without contrapuntal devices and inversions, it is mainly the ingenious and rapid modulation which makes identical phrases appear novel on their return and draws the listener powerfully along. If several different elements were strung together then the perpetual modulations, hurrying without a pause from one key to the next, would turn the composition into a rhapsody devoid of stability and inner coherence, like many pieces by recent, derivative composers. But there are only two main themes here. Even the linking sections and the powerful tuttis remain the same, and even the type of modulation remains constant. As a result the theme becomes involuntarily impressed upon the listener and everything emerges clearly and intelligibly.

The reviewer must refer the reader to a study of the work itself in order to appreciate its deeply thoughtful orchestration, which he finds genuinely thrilling, since it would take too much space to illustrate the many inspired passages. Every entry of the wind instruments is calculated to produce the utmost possible effect. The E flat horns and C trumpets frequently play triads that make a profoundly awe-inspiring impression. The cello has been earning its place in the orchestra for some years now; previously nobody would have thought of treating it as a fully obbligato instrument, independent of the bass-line. In this overture it seldom plays *col basso* but has its own figures which are sometimes not at all easy to perform. The reviewer concedes that this way of treating the cello is an obvious gain for the orchestra: tenor figures played by the violas, usually too few in number and in any case muted in tone, often do not emerge clearly enough, whereas the penetrating, original sound of the cello has a radical effect. In a full tutti, however, he could never steel himself to deprive the double-basses of the cellos' support, since the higher octaves of the latter sharply define the notes of the former.[9] The reviewer is speaking here only of figures given to the cellos as an inner voice in the tutti, for it goes without saying that they can play bass-figures in the tutti that are unwieldy for the double-basses, while

---

[9] Beethoven himself does not separate cellos from double-basses in tuttis.

the latter play only the main notes, so that the clarity of the bass-line is unaffected.[10]

Having said that, the overture makes very heavy demands on the orchestra, like almost all the orchestral works of this extraordinarily thoughtful composer, although no individual part is especially taxing. Only the crispest precision and a total surrender by every player to the spirit of the composition, achieved by frequent, intensive rehearsal, can produce the irresistible effect that the master intends and has summoned all his abundant resources to create.

Review of Gyrowetz's *Der Augenarzt* (extract)

Published: AMZ, xiv, 30 December 1812, cols. 855–64						*Unsigned*
First reprinted: Ellinger 1912

This review and the following one seem to have been written in about August 1812; both were despatched to the *AMZ* on 5 September. The great, but unrealised, plan for a review at this time was for one of Beethoven's Fourth Symphony. This is mentioned in Hoffmann's letter to Härtel of 12 July (*HBW*, i, 341).

Adalbert Gyrowetz [Jírovec] (1763–1850) was Bohemian and studied in Prague; he worked as a musician in Vienna, Naples, Paris, London, etc., and was a friend of Mozart, Haydn, and Beethoven. He composed twenty-eight operas, of which *Der Augenarzt* was the twelfth, about forty symphonies, and much chamber music.

Although the present review is comparable with that of Weigl's *Das Waisenhaus*, Hoffmann's imagination now cannot resist burlesqueing the lachrymose genre; his stand elicited approval from a Leipzig correspondent to the *AMZ* in 1813.[1] But publicly *Der Augenarzt (The Oculist)* was extremely successful, to be seen in numerous theatres, and was staged in Vienna from its première on 1 October 1811 up to

---

[10] Here Hoffmann rewrites the bass part at bar 110, a *forte* tutti where Beethoven writes the quavers as shown for cello and double-bass together. It is interesting that Hoffmann does not regard Beethoven's taxing writing as a necessary artistic feature (elsewhere he attacks any tampering with masterpieces) but suggests the normal current double-bass player's technique of simplification. In the next sentence he compounds his illogicality.

[1] 'Concerning libretto and music, the reviewer is completely of the opinion of the critic of the piano score in these pages': *AMZ*, xv, 21 April 1813, cited in *Schriften zur Musik*, 451.

1817.[2] As one of the works Hoffmann conducted in 1813, it has been mentioned in the Introduction to *The Poet and the Composer*.

Publication of the piano score reviewed here was announced in April 1812; the outsize drawing of an eye decorating its title page is hardly likely to have put Hoffmann in a better temper than its plot.[3] Blindness on the musical stage seems to have been catching. Hoffmann mentions the immediate dispute over the source for *Der Augenarzt* (see below, and note 7). Alfred Loewenberg traced the idea to a French opéra-comique of 1802. But Méhul also composed a successful *Les deux aveugles de Tolède* (1806) and Armand-Emmanuel Trial an unsuccessful *Les deux petits aveugles* in 1792.

For a time sentimental family portraits took possession of our stage, until they foundered in the flood of their own tears. Now it seems they are hoping to be rescued by music, in order to grace the boards in the form of operas. The reviewer hopes, however, that this lachrymose phenomenon will soon be put to flight not only by good taste, which always triumphs in the end, but also by the more noble spirit of true music, which resides in every composer of merit. When we were obliged in Kotzebue's *Epigramm*[4] to see a blind man led about on the stage and then operated upon, none of us can have imagined that such a thing would be expected of us in an opera; and yet it has now come to pass. *Two* blind, orphaned children, a boy and a girl, have been taken in and brought up by a kindly clergyman; now they wander about with his daughter and have to beg for their food, but have fallen in love with each other and so lead a life of worry and anguish; then a clever surgeon carries out a successful operation upon them and as a reward receives the clergyman's daughter for his wife.

In Paris recently an aneurysm[5] was made the subject of a play, even though every conspicuous lapse of taste in that city is scourged by ridicule until it dies the most ignominious death. So if, before disappearing from it for ever, human misery now has to be portrayed on our stage in a surfeit of infirmities and their agonising cures, the reviewer has in mind a not unworthy subject for an opera that might almost surpass *Der Augenarzt* in its intensity of wretchedness. An old man, poverty-stricken but utterly vir-

---

[2] Loewenberg, *Annals of Opera*.

[3] Oblong folio score: Der / Augenarzt / ein Singspiel / in zwey Aufzügen / im vollstaendigen Clavier=Auszug / von / HERRN ADALBERT GYROWETZ / Kapellmeister des k.k. Hoftheater. / Wien bey Pietro Mechetti q^{m} Carlo, / am Bürgerspital Platz No. 1166. The plate numbers ran from 60 to 76.

[4] August von Kotzebue, *Das Epigramm* (1798), a comedy; translated at the time into English as *The Blind Boy*.

[5] aneurysm: 'morbid dilatation of an artery, due to disease, or to a tumour caused by rupture, of the arterial coats' (*Shorter OED*).

tuous, can barely support his family, which includes a very pretty sixteen-year-old daughter. There is a fire in which he saves a small child from the flames but in doing so seriously injures his leg; since he cannot pay skilled surgeons the wound deteriorates until he is close to death, despite the most solicitous care of his daughter. The misery of the family, which has now been joined by the rescued child since its parents lost their lives, mounts to breaking-point. They have eaten nothing for three or four days, when a young surgeon of extremely noble birth happens to catch sight of the beautiful young girl. He immediately falls in love, discovers the reason for her deep sorrow, hastens to bring wine, hot broth, and his surgical instruments, and saves the father's life by skilfully amputating the gangrenous leg, in return for which he receives the daughter for his wife. In addition some prince or count could easily be worked into the story who confers a generous gift upon the family. The description of the conflagration would provide a not contemptible Romance, and also the operation, with its chorus of surgical assistants, a fruitful *pezzo concertante*.

A certain Herr Emanuel Veith[6] claims authorship of *Der Augenarzt* but Herr von Holbein, who has adapted for the Vienna stage a Singspiel, *Die beiden Blinden*, now printed in his theatrical works, declares this to be a plagiarism since *Der Augenarzt* is that very Singspiel with a few alterations.[7] Now the reviewer believes that when the basic conception is misguided then its further exploitation is of no great consequence either, so that the plagiarism can be objectionable not to the public but only to Herr von Holbein. He must nevertheless give preference to the original in that, being much less operatically handled, it is more of an affecting drama in which the actors are occasionally seized by the particular desire to sing a ditty; the standards of genuine opera cannot then apply. But what is to become of music in our theatres when even *opera* lowers itself to the vulgar dealings of domestic ordinariness, which clips the spirit's wings and curbs its invention instead of letting it soar up into the romantic realm whose language is song? What incentive to delve into the mysterious depths of music and to awaken

---

[6] Johann Emanuel Veith (1787–1876), director of the royal veterinary institute in Vienna, later cleric, and author of works about medicine, veterinary science, and theology. His book on the cure of congenital blindness was published in 1846.

[7] Veith's libretto proclaimed: *Der Augenarzt. Ein Singspiel in zwey Aufzügen. Aus dem Französischen* (i.e. from the French). Hoffmann's colleague Franz von Holbein wrote *Die beiden Blinden* (The Two Blind Children) as a Singspiel early in 1810, if not before, and it was set by Peter von Winter. See *HBW*, i, 310; Sahlin, 162. Loewenberg (*Annals of Opera*) traced the source of *Der Augenarzt* to *Les Aveugles de Franconville* (1802) by Armand Croizette and A. F. Chateauvieux. The music, by Louis-Sébastien Lebrun, has disappeared. But it may be relevant that this French libretto was reissued in 1810.

the spirits residing at its heart can such a domestic concoction provide? Just as in one of Schiller's *Xenien* Shakespeare's ghost asks 'What can there be of greatness in this misery?'[8] so the ghost of Gluck or Mozart could also justly ask 'Is *singing* now to be the whining and wailing of misery?' The reviewer has the true purpose of opera, this highest pinnacle of chamber music, too much at heart not to be acutely sensitive to every deviation from it; he had to speak his mind about this tasteless libretto in order to direct any applause the opera has received in the theatre towards the gallant composer. The style of the composition vividly recalls *Die Schweizerfamilie*,[9] that delightful idyll in which homesickness, Emmeline's longing intensified to the point of somnambulism, and the way in which her dream is carried over into reality, invest the story with a truly romantic quality. As in *Die Schweizerfamilie* there is no shortage here of very delicately conceived melodies; and a proper economy (in the sense of not too much and not too little) governs the whole work, so that for the most part the reviewer can find fault only with details. If one could wish for greater characterisation of the individual rôles, the blame for this deficiency lies with the librettist, who gave his characters a rather generalised physiognomy; where the libretto provided only a flat surface, the composer would have had to give it depth entirely from his own resources.

Review of Méhul's Overture *La Chasse du jeune Henri*

Published: AMZ, xiv, 11 November 1812, cols. 743–7   *Unsigned*
First reprinted: Ellinger 1912

This is a valuable review, being virtually the only occasion on which Hoffmann dealt with instrumental tone-painting. (His sentences on Beethoven's 'Battle Symphony' are on p. 420.) Logically, one would expect him to have rejected this as vehemently as the Dittersdorf descriptive symphonies mentioned in the review of Beethoven's Fifth Symphony. He cannot call the Méhul piece 'romantic' because it is obviously circumscribed by its description of a hunt. Instead, he makes a distinction between naive imitation of details on one hand, and the attainment of a total impression on

---

[8]   From Epigram 405 in *Xenien*: 'Shakespeares Schatten'; *Musen-Almanach für das Jahr 1797* [F.S.].

[9]   Joseph Weigl, *Die Schweizerfamilie* (1809), 'the prototype of a German lyrical folk opera', 'was performed throughout the world during the nineteenth century': Rudolf Anger-müller, 'Joseph Weigl', *The New Grove*, xx, 297.

the other. He concludes by deciding that there is some validity in the latter approach. However, his reluctance to analyse poetic associations of orchestral tone-colour (see the opening paragraph) is a matter for regret.

Etienne-Nicolas Méhul (1763–1817) was the leading French composer during the age of Beethoven, responsible for many operas and four symphonies. His opera *Joseph* (1807), which Hoffmann conducted in 1813, was particularly successful in Germany. The opéra-comique *La Jeunesse de Henri IV*, text by Jean-Nicolas Bouilly, was written in 1791 as a pro-monarchist allegory, but not performed. It was revised in 1797 as *Le Jeune Henri* but proved a total failure as an opera. However, the overture became universally loved. In 1852 Berlioz wrote that 'Were it not for the concerts where the overture to *La Chasse du jeune Henri* and the first air from *Joseph* are occasionally heard . . . this generation would hardly know this great master.'[1] By 1880, however, only *Joseph* and Méhul's *Chant du Départ* were known.[2]

The overture is 525 bars long, scored for double woodwind, four horns, and timpani with strings.[3] Like the hunting-chorus in Haydn's 'Autumn' in *The Seasons* (published 1802) it uses the repertory of traditional horn signals to chart the progress of the hunt.

To the true composer music willingly reveals its secrets. He grasps its talisman and with it commands the listener's imagination, so that at his summons any scene from life may pass before the mind's eye, and one is irresistibly drawn into the colourful swirl of fantastic images. It may well be that it is in the knowledge of these mysterious charms and their proper application that the true art of musical painting lies. Melody, choice of instruments, harmonic structure – all must work together, and it would be a foolish delusion to try to evoke a particular image by imitating individual natural sounds without regard for the whole; the fusillades of violins and cannonades of kettledrums in many battle-symphonies are just as ridiculous as the blatant crowing of the oboe imitating St Peter's cock in that ancient oratorio.[4] On the other hand there are certain melodies which suggest solitude, or pastoral life, for example; a certain combination of flutes,

---

[1] Hector Berlioz, *Evenings with the Orchestra*, tr., ed. Jacques Barzun (Chicago and London, 1956), 345.

[2] Léon Pillaut, *Instruments et musiciens* (Paris, 1880), 359. But the overture was given at the 1867 Paris International Exhibition, by a monster orchestra of 3000.

[3] Hoffmann reviewed the set of parts published by Breitkopf & Härtel announced in 1812, rather than a score. Title page: OUVERTURE / à / grand Orchestre / du Jeune Henry Chasse / par / F. [sic] MÉHUL. The plate number was 1680.

[4] Some 'battle-symphonies' are noted on p. 237. As to the 'ancient oratorio', modern scholarship has still not uncovered the identity of Hoffmann's example. There is, however, a prominent oboe representation of a cock-crow in the opening accompanied recitative (evoking the dawn) of 'Summer' in Haydn's oratorio *The Seasons*. Hoffmann discusses this work briefly in 'Old and New Church Music', below.

clarinets, oboes, bassoons will intensify this feeling with extreme vividness. Similarly, certain horn melodies momentarily transport the listener into forests and fields, which may well be more than just a consequence of the horn's association with the forest-dwelling huntsman. Further elucidation of these ideas would lead the reviewer too far; he feels he has sufficiently indicated his opinions about musical painting, which must determine his appraisal of the overture under review.

Without the slightest prior knowledge of the composer's intention, every listener who responds to music at all is carried away by this overture into the merry tumult of the hunt. The reviewer ventures to assert this with confidence. The regal stag leaping forth from dense undergrowth is pursued and harried by frenzied hounds; the huntsmen gallop after them on snorting horses; suddenly the animal disappears, the dogs have lost the scent; they slink about searching and sniffing, while the huntsmen quietly wait; then the baying of hounds bursts out again, the animal bounds over walls and hedges, the horns ring out, the huntsmen overtake their prey, and jubilant fanfares proclaim the conquest. All this appears in the most brilliant colour, which shows how perfectly the composer chose the means to achieve his objective, and how he was able to sustain the whole in all its parts.

The overture consists of an Andante in 2/4 time (D major), followed by an Allegro in 6/8 time (also in D major). The Andante is a sort of pastorale and depicts the agreeable serenity of the countryside on a calm night.[5] Clarinet and bassoon begin alone with the following phrase, moving in octaves:

whereupon the violins enter, followed by cellos, oboe, and flute. After fifty-three bars the music is interrupted by a spirited horn fanfare (A major):

Four bars of andante seem to depict the huntsmen, still befuddled with sleep, mounting their horses, only to sink back again into their previous torpor during the following sixteen bars, before a second fanfare resounds from their livelier companions. Now they all shake off their sleep; the dogs, eager for the chase, set up their baying, the horns resound, and away they go

[5] Méhul left no written 'programme' of any kind.

into the green forest. The reviewer provides the first few bars of the Allegro
to show the original structure of this opening which so vividly portrays what
the composer had in mind [bar 109]:

Ex. XV

This section continues for fifty-two bars, with the D repeated in the bass throughout. Then, however, a crescendo from the whole orchestra leads into A major, and in this key the horns again take up a lively fanfare which is repeated by the entire orchestra.

The structure of the whole overture follows the pattern of this opening: ever more forcefully surging crescendos from the whole orchestra follow the horn fanfares without any admixture of contrasted figures affecting either the forward motion or rhythmical pattern; these then die away again in *pianissimo* single notes, and repeatedly alternate with spirited horn passages until the piece reaches its exuberant conclusion. Because of this structure the modulations in the overture are also kept simple (D major, A major, D minor, B flat major, D major), and for the same reason it is hardly surprising to find that contrapuntal devices have no place here.

The reviewer has often heard this overture, well known to be a favourite work of Parisian concert-audiences, in performances by very good orchestras, and has found that despite its uncomplicated style there are certain difficulties in obtaining really effective ensemble playing. In particular it calls for four good horn players, capable of performing their fanfares, on which the effect of the whole piece so largely depends, with facility, vigour, and the utmost purity. It is the firm conviction of the reviewer that this excellent composer, who has proven his worth in much profound and serious music (one thinks, for example, of his *Joseph*), has furnished in his brisk and brilliant hunting-piece a reliable model for those who wish, in striving to conjure forth particular pictures from the imagination, to paint in music. This gives the work a deeper significance for every student who aspires to further initiation in the temple of art, as well as providing pleasurable entertainment in the theatre and concert-hall.

Review of Beethoven's Piano Trios, Op. 70 Nos. 1 and 2

Published: AMZ, xv, 3 March 1813, cols. 141–54   *Unsigned*
First reprinted: Vom Ende 1899

Hoffmann soon became aware of the publication of these trios, in summer 1809,[1] since he ordered the second one on 30 May 1810 from the publisher. On 2 August 1811 he confirmed to the *AMZ* his continuing intention to review both trios, but

---

[1] Three separate parts were issued, for piano, violin, and cello; the trios were sold separately, with the following title page: Deux / TRIOS / Pour Pianoforte, Violon / et Violoncelle / composés et dédiés / à Madame la Comtesse Marie d'Erdödy / née Comtesse Niszky / par / Louis van Beethoven. / Propriété des Editeurs / Oeuv. 70 N° 1. [or 2] Pr. 1 Rth. 12 gr. [or 2

through various delays he began work only in September 1812, completing half the essay;[2] it was finished on 2 February 1813. In length, the review rivals those of symphonies by Beethoven, whether Hoffmann's own of the Fifth, or those by others of the Third and the Sixth.[3]

On one level, the whole review springs from a contradiction observed near the beginning: namely that the fortepiano (i.e. early piano) is very limited as a melody instrument but, at the same time, every Beethoven movement is based on 'a simple but fruitful and lyrical theme'. This leads Hoffmann throughout to consider (a) Beethoven's style both generally and in Op. 70, and (b) the piano as a medium, both generally and in Op. 70. Also acting as a unifying force is his simple concern to proselytise. The groundswell of this review builds on that of the Fifth Symphony by taking Beethoven's supreme Romanticism as a given fact, and then seeking to persuade the unconverted by stressing the traditional values in Op. 70, rather than any frightening aspects of its Romanticism. (The outstanding example of this is the treatment of the slow movement of Op. 70 No. 1, later to inspire the sobriquet 'Ghost Trio'.) Thus the factors of thematic unity and of counterpoint find much mention, as does the music's accessibility: 'the really musical listener will easily follow . . .'; 'no great difficulty in the piano part . . .'; the listener 'follows its amazing twists and turns' or 'understands all the most mysterious presentiments'; Op. 70 No. 1 'is less gloomy than many' Beethoven instrumental works. Allied to this is Hoffmann's determination to cite as much music in score as possible, since he knows that the publisher has issued only the parts; indeed he complains at the end of the near-universal absence of printed scores of Beethoven's music, which holds up the progress of knowledge and enlightenment.

Because it was so radically shortened for its incorporation into the fourth essay in *Kreisleriana*, this review gains commensurately more by being read in its totality. A few detailed changes, often only of a single word, are to be found between the two versions, so far as they may be compared.

The Op. 70 Trios were composed and first performed in 1808, the year of the completion of the Fifth and Sixth Symphonies. Op. 70 No. 1 has three movements, and Op. 70 No. 2 has four. Their outer movements are all in sonata form (subdivided as usual by Hoffmann into a first and second 'half'), but with sometimes marked idiosyncrasies.[4]

Some time ago the present writer reviewed one of Beethoven's most important works, the profoundly great Fifth Symphony in C minor. In doing so he tried to express as fully as possible his feelings about the spirit and style of

Rthlr.] / Chez Breitkopf & Härtel / à Leipsic. The plate numbers were 1339 (first trio) and 1340 (second trio).

[2] Hoffmann reviewed No. 1 first (*HTB*, 174–5), even though he was sent it only that August: *HBW*, i, 345.

[3] The Third Symphony review (18 February 1807) spread over fifteen columns; the Sixth Symphony review (17 January 1810) spread over twelve columns. See the table in Schnaus, *Hoffmann als Beethoven-Rezensent*, 16–17.

[4] See the discussion in Kerman, '*Tändelnde Lazzi*'.

this highly gifted master. After a keen study of his works the reviewer made the statement in that article that Beethoven, more than any other, is a purely *romantic* composer, and that this is why his vocal music, which does not permit a mood of vague yearning but can only depict from the realm of the infinite those feelings capable of being formulated in words, is less success-ful, and why his instrumental music is not understood by the multitude. The reviewer went on to say that even this multitude will not deny him a high degree of invention; that on the contrary it is usual to regard his works merely as the product of a genius who ignores discrimination and shaping of thought and blindly surrenders to his overpowering creative fervour and the passing impulses of his imagination. He is nevertheless fully the equal of Haydn and Mozart in rational awareness, his controlling self detached from the inner realm of sounds and ruling it in absolute authority.

The reviewer finds all these judgements increasingly substantiated with every new work by this composer that reaches his eyes and ears. These two splendid trios demonstrate once more how deeply in his heart Beethoven carries the romantic spirit of music, and with what sublime originality, what authority he infuses it into his works. Every true pianist must be overjoyed when a new work for his instrument appears from this composer, who is himself a virtuoso on the fortepiano and thus writes not only with a deep knowledge of what is performable and effective but also with a visible partiality for it.

The fortepiano is and will remain an instrument more appropriate for harmony than for melody.[5] The most refined expression of which the instrument is capable cannot bring a melody to life with the myriad nuances that the violinist's bow or the wind player's breath is able to call forth. The player struggles in vain with the insuperable difficulty presented to him by the mechanism, which by striking the strings causes them to vibrate and produce the notes. On the other hand there is probably no instrument (with the exception, that is, of the far more limited harp) that is able, like the piano, to embrace the realm of harmony with full-voiced chords and unfold its treasures to the connoisseur in the most wonderful forms and shapes. When the composer's imagination has struck upon a complete sound-painting with rich groupings, brilliant highlights, and deep shadows, he is able to bring it into being at the piano so that it emerges from his inner world in shining colours. A full score, that true musical book of charms preserving in its symbols all the miracles and mysteries of the most heterogeneous choir of instruments, comes to life at the piano under the hands of a master; and a

---

[5] Hoffmann here refers to the contemporary grand piano as 'Fortepiano', but subsequently just as 'Flügel', translated 'piano'. No difference of emphasis was intended between the two terms.

piece skilfully performed from a score, including all its voices, may be compared to a good copper engraving taken from a great painting. For improvising, then, for playing from a score, for individual sonatas, toccatas, etc., the piano is excellently suited. Trios, quartets, quintets, and so on, with the usual stringed instruments added, also belong fully in the realm of piano compositions, because if they are composed in the proper manner, that is to say genuinely in four parts, five parts, and so forth, then they depend entirely on harmonic elaboration and automatically exclude brilliant passages for individual instruments. The reviewer feels this to be an extremely important principle, and for this reason has an aversion to all piano concertos;[6] they are supposed to exploit the virtuosity of the individual player in solo passages and in melodic expressiveness, but the very best player on the very finest instrument strives in vain to equal what the violinist, for example, can achieve with little effort. Every solo, after a full tutti of strings and winds, sounds stiff and flat, and although one admires the facility of the fingers and suchlike, the heart is not really touched at all.

From what has been said about the spirit and character of Beethoven's music in general, and from the clearly indisputable assertion that he, a consummate master of composition and a virtuoso on the piano, will seize upon the most essential character of the instrument and cast it in the most appropriate form, one can abstract the underlying idea and the structure of all his piano trios, quartets, etc.[7] It is hardly possible to mistake it in fact, even if one has not yet seen or heard any works of this type by the composer. A simple but fruitful and lyrical theme, susceptible of the most varied contrapuntal treatments, abbreviations, etc., forms the basis of every movement. All the secondary themes and figures are closely related to the main idea, and everything is interwoven and arranged so as to produce the utmost unity between all the instruments. This describes the overall structure, but within this artful edifice there is a restless alternation of the most marvellous images, in which joy and pain, melancholy and ecstasy, appear beside and within each other. Strange shapes begin a merry dance, now converging into a single point of light, now flying apart like glittering sparks, now chasing each other in infinitely varied clusters. And in the

---

[6] In *Kreisleriana*, I–4, Hoffmann added a parenthesis at this point in which he excepted from this generality the concertos of Mozart and Beethoven, which he characterised as 'symphonies with piano obbligato'.

[7] The three piano and string Trios Op. 1 (1795) were the only true precedents for Op. 70. Beethoven had published a trio for piano, clarinet/violin, and cello Op. 11 (1798); and arranged his famous Septet for a piano trio with either violin or clarinet, as Op. 38. The only piano quartet issued so far was the (authentic) arrangement of the Op. 16 piano and wind quintet (1801). The youthful piano quartets WoO 36 were published posthumously in 1828.

midst of this spirit-realm that has been revealed, the enraptured soul perceives an unknown language and understands all the most mysterious presentiments that hold it in thrall. A composer has truly penetrated the secrets of harmony only if he can use its power to affect the human heart. For him the numerical relationships[8] that remain lifeless formulas for the pedant without genius become magical prescriptions from which he conjures forth an enchanted world.

The reviewer has found it necessary to preface all these remarks to his appraisal of the individual trios in order to make it absolutely plain how incomparably great Beethoven is in his piano works. He turns first to the Trio No. 1 in D major and quotes the opening of it here so that what he intends to say about it may be more closely seen.

Ex. XVI

The first four bars contain the main theme, and the seventh and eighth bars in the cello part contain the secondary theme. With the exception of a few subordinate figures inserted between appearances of the main material, the entire Allegro is woven from these two phrases. It is particularly useful, therefore, to have the idea that dominates the whole movement played in

---

[8] numerical relationships: harmony can be expressed and taught in numbers as 'figured bass'.

four octaves in unison; it impresses itself firmly and distinctly upon the
listener, who does not then lose sight of it but follows its amazing twists and
turns as though it were a silvery stream. This theme also completely
epitomises the character of the trio, which is less gloomy than many of
Beethoven's other instrumental works and expresses a genial serenity, a
cheerful, confident awareness of its own strength and substance. Apart
from the canonic imitation of the second theme there are no other contrapuntal passages in the first half of the Allegro, which is only seventy-three
bars long. The concluding idea, played first by the piano [bar 44] against the
cello and violin in octaves, and then by the latter instruments against
quavers from the piano in octaves, returns at the end of the second half in an
undeveloped though altered form. The first half in fact contains merely the
exposition of the piece. In the second half an ingenious, contrapuntal
texture now begins and continues until the entry of the main theme in D
major in its original form. The bass part in the piano takes up a figure that
seems almost like the second bar of the secondary theme (played in the first
half by the cello)[9] in contrary motion, while the cello and the upper part of
the piano alternately play an abbreviated version of the main theme, and the
violin adds an even shorter extract from the main theme in canonic
imitation.

[9] See bar 8 of Ex. XVI.

In the ninth bar [bar 82] the main theme played in unison in the bass of the piano and of the cello leads from D major to B flat major, and in this key it is immediately joined by the secondary theme. This is extended by the right hand of the piano against a held pedal point while cello and violin repeat the first bar of the secondary theme in thirds. Now a new theme enters, moving up and down the scale as far as the seventh and alternating between the upper and lower parts of the piano, while violin and cello further develop an idea from the secondary theme in alternation. The piano and the other instruments imitate this idea, which is only one bar long, until the musical argument seems to be dying away in a canonic stretto.[10] But it soon becomes livelier again; the violin takes up the first bar of the main theme, the upper part of the piano does likewise, and the cello plays the second bar of the secondary theme. A battle royal now develops between all the parts. Two bars, one bar, three notes of the main theme,

both forwards and backwards, are interwoven with each other in canonic imitation. This is the most original and ingenious part of the whole Allegro and the reviewer quotes it here for convenient inspection by the reader [bar 124].

---

[10] This 'canonic stretto' is at bars 120–4; the music is *fortissimo*, so Hoffmann's phrase 'dying away' refers to the reduced two-part texture.

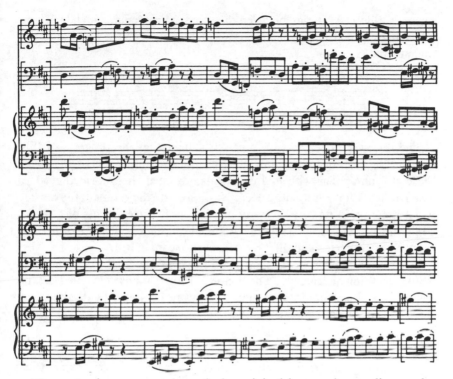

The main theme now returns in its original key, and according to the usual pattern followed by instrumental pieces of this type one would expect the first half to return and to remain in the tonic for the entry of the secondary theme. This is not the case, however. The ingenious composer surprises us with a sudden turn into D minor, in which key the [main] theme is repeated, whereupon the music moves into B flat major for the entry of the lyrical secondary theme. By means of a chromatically rising bass the music moves into A major and then back into D major [bars 181–98].

The closing theme of the first half follows in an altered form, in that the quaver figure is played first[11] by violin and cello in octaves, then by the upper part of the piano, and lastly in the bass of the piano. Following the repeat of the second half the secondary theme is heard once more[12] in G

[11] The violin and cello octave quavers at bar 203 actually follow a cello statement at 199. But in any case, Hoffmann's reference to 'closing theme' (*Schlussthema*) at this point is characterised solely in terms of the quavers, whereas in the exposition, his 'concluding idea' (*Schlussgedanke*) was characterised in terms of what occurred against those quavers. We shall find a similar inconsistency concerning the last movement of Op. 70 No. 2.

[12] The coda, here referred to, is twenty-one bars long.

major in canonic imitation between the three instruments, which leads the music back into D major, and the movement ends with the first bar of the main theme in unison.

The reviewer hopes that by precisely elucidating the progress of this outstanding piece he has not only given a sufficient impression of the trio to those still unfamiliar with it, but has also enabled the informed reader, when he hears or plays it, more deeply to appreciate the genius of the music, which emerges in its very diversity of contrapuntal treatments of a short, straightforward theme. To achieve this aim he has not hesitated to illustrate the most complicated and difficult part of the score in full.

The second movement, a *Largo assai ed espressivo*, bears a character of gentle, soothing melancholy. The theme is again composed in true Beethovenian style of two quite simple figures, only one bar long, divided between the piano and the other instruments.

These few harmonically fertile bars again contain the material from which the whole movement is fashioned. Primarily it is the cello figure in the ninth bar, with its counter-theme in the piano which blends in so beautifully, that repeatedly appears in imitation. The main theme in the second bar of the piano is also of potent effect when it is taken up and further developed by the cello [bar 26].

The modulation is not at all complicated, and the reviewer makes mention of only one other feature that distinguishes this movement from so many piano compositions. When the main theme is played by the violin and cello the piano usually accompanies it with a part in hemidemisemiquaver sextuplets to be played *pianissimo* and *leggiermente*.

This is almost the only way in which the *tone* of a good piano can be brought out in an arresting manner. If these sextuplets are played with a dexterous, light touch with the soft pedal down and the dampers raised, a susurration is produced that recalls the aeolian harp and glass harmonica[13] and has a quite wonderful effect when combined with the bowed notes of the other instruments. To the soft pedal and the sustaining pedal the reviewer added the so-called harmonica pedal.[14] As is well known this device shifts the keyboard sideways so that the hammers strike only one string, and from the beautiful

---

[13] Beethoven left no pedal indications at all. Although many piano pedals were available at the time (see p. 141 n. 244), the three that Hoffmann used here were considered the essential ones by Czerny and others. (1) The 'soft pedal' (*Pianozug, jeu céleste, jeu de buffle*) operated 'a strip of wood to which are glued tongues of leather about 2.50 cm in length which are interposed between the hammers and the strings to the extent of half their length for *piano* and produced to their full extent to muffle a further length of string for *pianissimo*.' (2) The 'sustaining pedal' (*Forte, grande pédale*) raised the dampers to prolong the tone. Rosamund Harding, *The Piano-forte: its History Traced to the Great Exhibition of 1851* (Cambridge, 1933), 44, 413–14. Jean-Louis Adam (*Méthode de Piano*, 1804/5) noted exactly the same effect of a glass harmonica produced by exactly Hoffmann's means. Harding, *The Piano-forte*, 125.

[14] The 'harmonica pedal' (*Verschiebung, Una Corda, shift*) slid the keyboard sideways 'so that one only out of a pair of unison strings is struck'. *Ibid.*, 44.

Streicher piano[15] floated sounds that surrounded the soul like hazy figures in a dream, enticing it into a magical world of curious presentiments.

The closing movement, Presto, in D major, again has a short, original theme that appears in a constant alternation of various transformations and ingenious allusions throughout the piece.

Just as the storm-wind drives the clouds before it producing abrupt alternations of light and dark, and just as figures take shape amid the ceaseless buffetting, then melt away and form again, so the music hurries impetuously forward after the second fermata. The music veers towards A major, F major, etc. with an octave passage in the piano, while violin and cello canonically imitate a new figure that ascends through the scale to the fifth. There follow imitations of the main subject, as for example [bar 76]

<hr>

[15] The Austrian firm Streicher was founded in 1802 and became the leading Viennese piano manufacturer. Their surviving grand pianos usually have four pedals: Una Corda, Bassoon, Soft, and Sustaining. See *The New Grove*, xviii, 267.

until in B flat major the whole first theme seems to be coming in but is extended in an original way that more than ever displays Beethoven's style, seen in his final movements particularly as a constant increase in intensity and momentum. The close of the first half leads into the main theme in such a way that there is absolutely no perceptible break separating the first half from the second,[16] as befits the restlessly driving character of the whole movement.

The second half begins with a development and imitation of the octave passage in the first half, and it would really lead the reviewer too far astray to analyse all the new devices and the original structure of the entire second half in sufficient detail to be understood; this could be done only through examples. He therefore contents himself with quoting from the second half just a single canonic imitation of a figure in crotchet triplets, which have not previously appeared, since it again epitomises the unmistakable characteristics of this composer [bar 194].

---

[16] Slight inaccuracy here again exists in the formal description: the 'main theme' is led into only when the exposition ('first half') is repeated. But the essential continuity obtains after both playings of the exposition.

Despite the geniality that prevails throughout the trio, not even excluding its melancholy Largo, Beethoven's spirit remains serious and solemn. The master seems to be implying that the deeper mysteries can never be spoken of in ordinary words, even when the spirit feels itself joyfully uplifted in moments of intimate familiarity with them, but only in expressions of sublime splendour. The dance of the High Priests of Isis can only be a hymn of exultation. The reviewer is convinced too that purely instrumental music, when its dramatic effect is to be achieved solely by itself as music rather than by some particular application, should avoid facetiousness and clowning.[17] The profounder mind seeks intimations of that joy, sublimer than the confines of this world allow, which comes to us from an unknown domain and kindles in the breast an inner bliss, a higher significance than feeble words, confined to the expression of banal earthly pleasures, can communicate. The reviewer intends to come back to this point again after

[17] clowning: Hoffmann uses '*Lazzi*', properly signifying 'stage business', particularly in the improvising parts of the Italian *commedia dell'arte* performance. So his meaning might include the mimetic aspects of playing showy piano music, as well as applying metaphorically to its substance. Kerman ('*Tändelnde Lazzi*') wonders whether Hoffmann half-alludes to the finale of Op. 70 No. 1.

reviewing the second trio, to which he now turns, in connection with the justified complaint that he must raise about the fact that so many good pianists can hardly be persuaded to perform Beethoven's compositions.

In the second trio, the flowing theme of the introductory section in E flat major, Poco sostenuto, common time, establishes a tranquil mood: it is played by the three instruments in canonic imitation.

In the eleventh bar, however, while the violin and cello only have single notes, livelier figures in semiquavers and semiquaver triplets appear in the upper part of the piano, until another pleasantly expressive theme leads to a pause on the dominant; thereupon an Allegro ma non troppo begins, in E flat major, 6/8 time.

Despite the 6/8 time, which normally produces a skipping, light-hearted effect, this movement maintains both in its initial form and in its various transformations a serious and – if one may use the expression – aristocratic character. The reviewer was inevitably reminded of several works by

Mozart in a similar rhythm, particularly the Allegro of the splendid symphony in E flat major, known as the 'Swan Song'.[18] He will speak, however, exclusively of the theme and not of the further development or structure of the movement, which again displays Beethoven's genius in the most original way. After a number of ideas in the upper part of the piano and violin taken from the main theme, such as the following:

a splendid second theme follows in the twenty-first bar [bars 39–40], still in the main key of E flat major, played first by the cello with piano accompaniment and then by the right hand of the piano and the violin *all'ottava*. The music now moves towards the dominant, and the theme of the introductory section, merely transposed into 6/8 time although allotted to different instruments, is heard again in canonic imitation [bar 53].

The way in which the music is arranged here makes it sound like an unexpected chorale that suddenly breaks through the artfully woven

---

[18] 'Swan Song': once-popular name for Symphony 39 (1788), KV 543. See p. 97 n. 159.

texture and stirs the spirit like a strange and wonderful vision. Only the more practised ear will immediately recognise the introductory section, so utterly different and new does it seem. It evinces the master's boundless wealth of invention and his penetration of the harmonic depths, that from a single idea a few bars long so many motives are generated, springing from it like the luxuriant blossom and fruit of a fertile tree. The first half ends in B flat major with a triplet figure from the piano while cello and violin allude briefly to the main theme, and the close leads straight back to the beginning of the first half. After the repeat the triplet figure is continued, with the cello and violin in imitation playing first a four-note then a two-note extract from the main theme.

The reviewer would also mention the enharmonic transition from D flat minor into B major in the eighteenth, nineteenth, and twentieth bars [of the development] which, though not remotely as crude as many modulations of this type in recent compositions, nevertheless has the most striking effect. In the twentieth bar the composer notates the piano and cello in C flat major, but has already allowed the violin to adopt B major [bars 113–15].

Clearly this was done because the violinist's intonation is greatly facilitated after the preceding rests, and because the piano can in any case be tuned only in equal temperament, which permits no distinction between B major and C flat major. The return to E flat minor is quickly achieved by three chords [bars 124–6].

After the main theme has re-entered in the tonic, the further working-out is with minor differences similar to that in the first half, except that the music remains in the tonic after the entry of the second main theme. Before the close the introductory section in common time comes back again, but after only nine bars the 6/8 time signature resumes, and the main theme in abbreviated form brings the Allegro to an end. The elements of which this movement consists are more heterogeneous than one is otherwise accustomed to in Beethoven's music, in that the second subject of the Allegro bears little relation to the first, and the third theme, taken from the introduction, appears to be totally unfamiliar.[19] Nevertheless it all constitutes a perfect and compelling whole, and the really musical listener will easily follow the admittedly complicated course of the Allegro, even if many things may not perhaps be clear at first to the less practised ear.

The following movement, Allegretto, in C major, 2/4 time, has an agreeably songlike theme and is fashioned in the manner employed by Haydn for many of his andantes, particularly in symphonies, consisting of varied intermediate sections in the minor, after each of which the main theme enters luminously in the major.

[19] The 'third theme' occurs at bar 53, so the 'second subject' meant here is the cello theme at bars 39–40.

In this Allegretto too the composer remains faithful to the true style of this genre, in that the three instruments are interwoven in such a way that only together can they render the overall conception of the music. Every figure is carefully weighed and effectively inserted in the appropriate place. Even the opening figure

frequently recurs in the subsequent working-out, more sharply defining the character of the piece, as for example at the end of the first minor section and in the conclusion. In order to avoid becoming too expansive the reviewer must advise the reader, both here and in the following Allegretto ma non troppo, in A flat major, 3/4 time, to make a thorough study of the work, which will delight and elevate every true musician. Only musical examples exceeding the reasonable limits of a review could make clear the further observations he would like to make. May he merely say that the splendid theme of this Allegretto, which is actually the piquant middle movement introduced by Haydn under the name 'Menuetto', again reminded him of the noble eagle's flight of Mozart's music.

The Trio[20] has a totally original structure, consisting of fragmented phrases alternating between the cello and violin and the piano.

---

[20] Trio: Beethoven indicates neither 'Menuetto' nor 'Trio'. The likeness which Hoffmann notices was more apparent from the way the music was printed out in the first edition than it is in some later editions, namely A B A B A where 'B' is the 'Trio'.

In this same Trio the composer executes the following modulation, audaciously confident of his power to rule the world of sounds [bar 97]:

Ex. XVII

One can see what a wealth of piquant effects the enharmonic system offers, but the reviewer may well share the view of every musician of taste when he entrusts the use of these devices only to the profoundly experienced master, and strongly warns against it all those not yet initiated into the innermost magic circle of the art. Only the artist who has bridled the eccentric flight of his genius by the most painstaking study of his art, who has thereby acquired the highest degree of rational awareness, and now rules the inner world of sounds, only he possesses the full and confident

ability to apply to their maximum effect the boldest devices that art affords
him. The pupil or the blind imitator without genius or talent is most likely
to blunder precisely where he intends to be most forceful.

In the final movement, Allegro, in E flat major, 2/4 time, everything the
reviewer has said in his remarks about the last movement of the first trio
again applies. There is a constant increase in intensity and momentum;
ideas and images rush past in ceaseless flight, coruscating and vanishing like
flashes of lightning; the most fevered imaginings are given free rein. And yet
this movement is again fashioned from a few short ideas and closely related
figures.

The first six bars seem merely to form an introduction to the simple theme itself which does not enter until the seventh bar; but it is this introductory idea, with its loudly punctuating chords from the violin, cello, and piano left hand, which is subsequently treated with the most varied transformations and allusions. After the violin takes up the theme, followed by the piano again, the cello merely plays the first bar while the violin imitates it in notes twice the speed (semiquavers); then in the thirty-first bar the introductory passage comes in again. A sort of cadenza from the piano in triplets leads into C minor, then the introductory passage again; a cadenza from the violin in G minor, and once again the introductory passage; then a cadenza from the cello. Now follows a new theme [bar 49] in crotchets, the comparative tranquillity of which lasts for only a few bars, however, since a new storm drives the music through G minor, G major, and C major, until the passage with which the Allegro began leads back again through G minor and C minor into the main key and the repeat of the first half. The second half begins with the same figure, and now it is the punctuating chords from the opening as well as the semiquaver figure, played by all three instruments in imitation, which give rise to the most artful and striking development through the most audacious of modulations. No proper conception of this original treatment is possible without seeing the score; the reviewer therefore quotes here the entire passage, since by so doing he hopes, even for those who know the trio, to facilitate the study and stimulate a deeper awareness of this great work [bars 128–66; see Ex. XVIII]. After an interruption of only eight bars, which themselves hint at the figure from the opening passage, the latter appears once more and with the gentle main theme leads back into the tonic.[21] The subsequent structure corresponds to

Ex. XVIII

---

[21] The retransition at bar 174 uses opening material, culminating in the recapitulation at bar 186 and the 'gentle main theme' at bar 192.

the first half, but with different modulations, and the lyrical middle section which occurred in G major in the first half [bar 89][22]

[22] This theme, heard first at bar 83 without the semiquavers shown here, has not actually found mention before; thus Hoffmann gives the original pitch-level of the exposition rather than that of the recapitulation, where it occurs at bars 281ff. and 341ff., in C and then E flat majors. Conversely, Hoffmann does not mention the recapitulation of the tranquil theme 'in crotchets', originally used at bar 49.

is not only repeated in C major but also, when the section returns to the tonic, further developed by all the instruments in imitation. Eventually it appears abbreviated in a sort of stretto, and then the introductory passage bursts forth again, alternating with the main theme and finally leading to the brilliant, breathless closing phrases with semiquavers in all the instruments.

In terms of mere dexterity, of the sort employing breakneck passages up and down the keyboard with both hands executing all sorts of odd leaps and whimsical flourishes, there is in these trios no great difficulty in the piano part, since the few runs, triplet figures and the like must be within the powers of any practised player; and yet they are in many ways extremely difficult to perform. Many so-called virtuosos dismiss Beethoven's piano works, not only complaining 'Very difficult!' but adding 'And most ungrateful!' As far as difficulty is concerned, the proper performance of Beethoven's works demands nothing less than that one understands him, that one penetrates to his inner nature, and that in the knowledge of the performer's own state of grace one ventures boldly into the circle of magical beings that his irresistible spell summons forth. Whoever does not feel this grace within him, whoever regards music solely as amusement, as a pastime for idle hours, as a passing gratification for jaded ears, or as a vehicle for his own ostentation, let him keep away from it. Only such a one could utter the reproach 'And most ungrateful!' The true artist lives only in the work that he conceives and then performs as the composer intended it. He disdains to let his own personality intervene in any way; all his endeavours are spent in quickening to vivid life, in a thousand shining colours, all the sublime effects and images the composer's magical authority enclosed within his work, so that they encircle us in bright rings of light, inflaming our imaginings, our innermost soul, and bear us speeding on the wing into the far-off spirit-realm of music.

That there are few such artists, such genuine virtuosos (for regrettably even in the world of art egoism and empty ostentation are rife), is no less certain than that one comes across few music lovers who feel appreciably moved or elevated by the profound genius of this composer. Since it became the fashion to use music as an incidental beguilement of boredom in society, everything is expected to be simple and pleasant, that is to say devoid of all significance and depth; and because, sadly, there are composers in plenty upon the earth who pander to the spirit of the age, a great deal of this flimsy stuff exists. Many not entirely bad musicians complain about the incomprehensibility of Beethoven's compositions, and of Mozart's too; this is the result, however, of subjective imbecility which prevents the whole from being seen and grasped as the sum of its parts. Thus weak compositions are always praised for their great *clarity*. The reviewer has been fortunate enough to hear a gifted lady, who plays the piano with virtuosity, perform several of Beethoven's compositions so excellently that it became very clear to him that only what the *spirit* provides is to be paid regard, and that all the rest cometh of evil.[23]

It is to be hoped that happier circumstances in the world of art will make it possible for publishers to issue Beethoven's instrumental works in score. What an inexhaustible storehouse for the proper study of music that would offer the artist and the knowledgeable listener! With this wish the reviewer concludes his essay, in which he has sought to express many of the feelings lying so deeply in his heart.

Review of Beethoven's Mass in C

Published: AMZ, xv, 16 and 23 June 1813, cols. 389–97, 409–14
First reprinted: Vom Ende 1899   *Unsigned*

As the Napoleonic era came to a close, the conditions developed for a period of religious feeling and renewal. Catholic and Protestant Europe alike were affected. Although not a worshipper, Hoffmann was bound to be concerned, as a Romantic thinker, with impulses that affected man's perception of the divine purpose. His concern with religious music and art eventually led to memorable results in the survey 'Old and New Church Music' (p. 351) and the story *Die Jesuiterkirche in G.* (*The Jesuit Chapel in G.*) in 1816. In the latter, his character of the Maltese painter speaks of the relation between these things in a passage that also recalls the final pages of *Kreisleriana*: 'To see Nature in her profoundest significance, the higher purpose which inspires all creatures to yearn for the higher life – such is the divine purpose of art . . . the power descends [on the initiated artist] like the Holy Spirit itself, to portray this divine glimpse in his works.'[1] As an amateur painter himself and a visitor of art-galleries, Hoffmann would have been only too aware of the success of an artist like Caspar David Friedrich in creating a visual language that was devotional, based on powerful feeling for nature, and suggestive of the infinite. To attempt to define the character of an authentic 'religious music' was of importance to him.

However, the tide of feeling in general had been flowing strongly against any vital form of religious music. When Beethoven tried to sell the present Mass to Breitkopf & Härtel in 1808 they responded bluntly, 'No demand for church works', and the composer gave them the score without fee, acknowledging 'the utterly frigid attitude

---

[23] Matthew 5, 37 (Sermon on the Mount): a favourite adage of Hoffmann's.
[1] *The Jesuit Chapel in G.*, tr. Ronald Taylor (London, 1985), 136.

of our age to works of this kind'.[2] Evidently by the time that Hoffmann wrote the review it had become 'fashionable to compose masses'; but their musical language was clearly inadequate to him.

In Protestant Germany the Enlightened call (starting in the 1760s) for a simple, devout form of church music had led to general acceptance of a plain, chordal style, with minimal adornment by instruments, and inspired by both Handel's and Palestrina's choral music. Word-painting was seen as inferior to 'subjective expression'.[3] About the place of fugue there was some dispute; about texts it was considered preferable to set the Scriptures rather than have recourse to poetic or dramatic treatment. This debate surfaces at the end of the review. Writing about a Beethoven Mass using full orchestra, highly affective melody and harmony, and resembling neither Handel nor Palestrina, Hoffmann began to work out a position. The contradictions involved, and the added fact that Beethoven had not written the kind of music that Hoffmann expected, meant that he felt obliged to return to such questions the following year.

The Mass in C was composed in 1807 but not published until October 1812;[4] the score was forwarded directly to Hoffmann by the *AMZ*. Occupied first with a commissioned translation of the *Méthode de violon* by Baillot, Rode, and Kreutzer, then with the review of the trios Op. 70, and then his move to Dresden in April 1813, he could not attend to the review until May. As it was, the bombardments hindered work (see p. 171). Prior to these military attacks, he had attended church performances of a requiem by Hasse and a mass by J. G. Naumann, both of which he enjoyed (*HTB*, 201–2).

Owing to the length of time that Beethoven's manuscript lay with its publisher, many references to it by the composer survive in letters. On 16 January 1811 he wrote: 'Gentleness is the fundamental characteristic of the whole work . . . cheerfulness pervades this Mass. The Catholic goes to church on Sunday in his best clothes and in a joyful and festive mood.'[5] Ample evidence of the publisher's need to make the work more attractive is seen from its title page, transcribed in note 4. The German half calls it, simply, 'Three Hymns', and the entire work is underlaid with additional German text. The second Hymn began at the *Credo* and the third at the *Sanctus*, which Hoffmann (see below) found appropriate enough.

No earlier mass by Beethoven is known to the reviewer, and his anticipation was all the keener, therefore, as to how this highly gifted composer had treated the simple, glorious words of the High Mass.

---

[2] *Letters of Beethoven*, i, 190–1. Originally, the work had been a private commission.

[3] See Georg Feder, 'Decline and Restoration', in Friedrich Blume *et al.*, *Protestant Church Music* (London, 1975), 320–40.

[4] Title page: MESSA / a quattro Voci coll'accompagnamento dell'Orchestra / composta da / Luigi van Beethoven. / DREY HYMNEN / für vier Singstimmen mit Begleitung des Orchesters, / in Musik gesetzt und / S⸿ Durchlaucht dem Herrn Fürsten von Kinsky / zugeeignet / von / Ludw. v. Beethoven. / 86⸿ Werk. PARTITUR Pr. 4 Rthlr. / Bey Breitkopf & Härtel. / in Leipzig. The plate number was 1667.

[5] *Letters of Beethoven*, i, 309.

Prayer and devotion stir the spirit to be sure, according to its habitual or momentary disposition, whether this is a result of mental and physical well-being or of mental and physical anguish. Sometimes, therefore, devotion takes the form of an inner contrition carried to the point of self-contempt and shame, an abasement of the sinner in the dust before the annihilating thunderbolt of the wrathful Lord of Worlds; at other times it appears as an uplifting urge towards the infinite, a childlike trust in godly grace, an intimation of the bliss to come. The words of the High Mass provide in one cycle only an inducement to devotion, a guide at most, and whatever one's mood they will arouse an appropriate resonance in the soul. In the *Kyrie* God's mercy is invoked; the *Gloria* praises his omnipotence and splendour; the *Credo* expresses the faith that gives the pious soul its firm foundation; in the *Sanctus* and 'Benedictus' God's holiness is praised and blessing promised to those who place their full trust in him; and then in the *Agnus Dei* and in the 'Dona nobis pacem' the Saviour is implored to grant comfort and peace to the pious, believing, hoping soul. Because of this universality, which does not encroach upon the deeper response, the inner significance that each of us brings to it according to his individual state of mind, the text is adaptable to the most varied musical treatment. This is why there are such wide divergencies in character and attitude of settings of the *Kyrie*, *Gloria*, etc., often by the same composer. One need only compare, for example, the two *Kyrie* settings in the C major and D minor Masses by Joseph Haydn,[6] or those of the 'Benedictus'.

It follows from this that the composer who undertakes the composition of a High Mass imbued by a true sense of devotion, as should always be the case, will primarily express his individual religious disposition, which every word readily bends to; and he will not be lured by the 'Miserere', 'Gloria', 'Qui tollis', etc. into wild alternations between the heart-rending misery of the contrite soul and clangorous jubilation. Confections of this latter sort such as those frivolously perpetrated in recent times, since it became fashionable to compose masses, the reviewer condemns as miscarriages begotten by an impure spirit.[7] But before paying his tribute of praise and admiration to the splendid works of Michael and Joseph Haydn,

---

[6] The D minor Mass ('Nelsonmesse', 1798) had been published in 1803. The *Missa in Tempore belli* (1796) in C was issued in 1802; but the *Missa Cellensis* ('Cäcilienmesse', 1766), also in C, had been issued in 1807.

[7] This tendency requires investigation. During 1810, for example, publication was announced in the *AMZ* of a German Requiem and a Te Deum by Benedict Hacker of Salzburg (*b*. 1769) and a Mass for male voices by the tenor and composer Benedikt Schack of Vienna (1758–1826). Hoffmann probably had in mind Luigi Cherubini's Mass in F, published in 1809, which he attacked in 'Old and New Church Music'.

Naumann,[8] and others, he cannot fail to recall the earlier works of the pious Italians (Feo, Durante, Benevoli, Perti,[9] etc.); their lofty and dignified simplicity, their wonderful artistry in penetrating right to the musical core without irrelevant frills, seems in more recent times to be completely disappearing. Even without wishing to preserve the original, pure church style merely because holy things disdain the motley adornments of earthly sophistication, it cannot be doubted that simple music in church is also more effective musically, since the faster the notes follow upon each other the more they die away in the high vaulting and destroy the clarity of the whole. Hence in part the great effectiveness of good chorales in church.

A gifted author (Tieck, in the second part of his *Phantasus*)[10] utterly condemns all recent church music and recognises only the old Italians. The reviewer willingly grants the sublime church pieces of former times pre-eminence for their rigorous, genuinely sacred style; nevertheless he thinks that although one should not make a display of the richness more recently acquired by music, chiefly in its use of instruments, it can be employed in church in an appropriate, dignified manner. The daring simile may be fairly apt that the church music of the earlier Italians is to that of the more recent Germans as St Peter's Church in Rome is to Strasbourg Cathedral.[11] The magnificent proportions of St Peter's elevate the spirit while preserving a balanced relationship, but it is with a strange inner disquiet that the observer stares at the cathedral rising high into the air with its audacious convolutions and extraordinary interplay of fantastic figures and flourishes. This very unease, however, arouses presentiments of unknown wonders, and the spirit willingly surrenders to the dream in which it seems to recognise celestial infinities. Now this is precisely the impression given by the pure romanticism living and moving in Mozart's and Haydn's fantastical compositions! It is easy to see why composers now will not so lightly undertake a mass or other liturgical setting in the lofty yet simple style of the

---

[8] Johann Gottlieb Naumann (1741–1801): distinguished and prolific composer active in Dresden but also celebrated for the opera *Gustaf Wasa* (1786), composed during his appointment to the King of Sweden.

[9] Francesco Feo (1691–1761), Neapolitan composer lauded by J. Fr. Reichardt in 1791 as 'one of the greatest of all composers of church music in Italy'; Francesco Durante (1684–1755), central figure in eighteenth-century church music, lauded by Rousseau, Burney, etc.; Orazio Benevoli (1605–72), Rome-based church composer, a Mass for four choirs by whom was brought back from Italy by Reichardt; Giacomo Perti (1661–1756), Bolognese composer distinguished for concerted as well as unaccompanied church music.

[10] Ludwig Tieck (1773–1853), influential Romantic author (see p. 204) whose *Phantasus* book 1, appeared in 1812. Its discussion on the subject of various genres of music, pp. 466ff., is referred to below in the Prefatory Remarks to 'Old and New Church Music'.

[11] The 'daring simile' was adumbrated in *Kreisleriana*, I–5, and the passage here later used in *Die Serapions-Brüder*.

old Italians. They usually lack the ability, for it is in such extreme simplicity that profound genius most powerfully takes wing; but they also frequently lack the necessary self-denial. Who does not enjoy dazzling all eyes with the riches at his disposal, and is content with the applause of a single know-ledgeable listener, by whom *intrinsic worth* without display is prized most highly, or rather prized at all? Since composers everywhere started making use of the same means of expression, we have almost come to the point where such a thing as style no longer exists. In comic opera we often hear solemn, plodding pieces, in serious opera frivolous ditties, and in church we hear oratorios and masses dressed as opera. When using the most highly figured melodies and the full resources of instrumental music, a rare depth of spirit and a high measure of genius are needed in order to remain serious and dignified, or, in other words, suitable for the church!

Mozart, however *galant* his style in the two better known masses in C major,[12] has splendidly overcome this problem in his Requiem; this is truly romantic–sacred music, proceeding from his innermost soul.

The reviewer need hardly point out how admirably Haydn too in many of his masses tells of the holiest and sublimest things in glorious sounds, although some people are inclined to find him too light-hearted here and there.

That Beethoven would rank beside Haydn in terms of style and compo-sure the reviewer had no doubt, even before he had read or heard a note of the present work; but he did find himself disappointed in his expectation with regard to its conception and expression of the Mass text. Elsewhere Beethoven's genius willingly sets in motion the machinery of awe, of terror. So, the reviewer thought, his spirit would also be filled with profound awe when contemplating celestial things, and he would express this feeling in sounds. On the contrary, however, the entire Mass expresses a childlike optimism that by its very purity devoutly trusts in God's grace, and appeals to him as to a father who desires the best for his children and hears their prayers.

Apart from this general character of the composition, its inner structure as well as intelligent orchestration (so long as one proceeds from the reviewer's premise above concerning the employment of rich musical resources in church) will be found entirely worthy of this great master.

In the entire work there is no movement that does not contain imitations and contrapuntal devices, although not one strictly worked fugue is to be found and older composers accustomed to the purest church style will

---

[12] Presumably the 'Credo' Mass, K V 257 (1776), published 1803, and the 'Coronation' Mass, K V 317 (1779), published *c.* 1802.

object to a number of offences against it: false progressions of fifths (that is from a diminished to a perfect fifth), for example, octave cadences,[13] false relations, and the like. The reviewer does not intend to mention these further, however, since he confesses to being a musical nonconformist himself in this respect, unless dealing with chorales where every chord falls weightily upon the ear;[14] he relies on what the genial old Haydn said when Albrechtsberger wanted to banish all fourths from the purest style.[15]

Now that he has expressed his thoughts about the character and structure of the work in general, the reviewer need only go into such detail as is necessary to support his judgement and to draw attention to a number of truly outstanding passages in which the composer's genius brilliantly shines forth.

Without any introduction the basses alone intone the *Kyrie*, and its attractive theme exactly represents the prayer of a child convinced that grace and favour will be granted him. The reviewer reproduces the first eleven bars in full score:

Ex. XIX

[13] octave cadences: possibly meaning those where the voices have parallel octaves, as in the *Credo*, bars 180–1, tenor and bass.

[14] Chorales at that time were sung very slowly by our standards, some two seconds per main beat, so that irregularities of counterpoint were obvious to the ear. See Feder, 'Decline and Restoration', 340. Earlier, Hoffmann has alluded to their 'great effectiveness' in church.

[15] Johann Georg Albrechtsberger (1736–1809), arguably the greatest theorist, organist, and

The violin motion characteristic of Haydn continues throughout the movement, in fact for the most part throughout the work. In the fifteenth bar the soprano solo takes up a figure with which the music modulates into E minor and which the bass, tenor, and alto imitate in canon one bar apart. Then in the style of a chorale, without additional accompaniment, the solo soprano, alto, and tenor sing 'Christe eleison' in E major, followed similarly by the chorus; this is of uncommon effect. The imitation passage recurs only as a soprano solo shortly before the end; the latter is treated in an original manner in that all the voices reiterate the dominant G while the instruments recall the first bar of the theme. This movement also contains a quite unusual modulation, since it moves straight from C major to E minor,

teacher of his time. The present tale was reported by Georg August Griesinger in his biography of Haydn, appearing as 'Biographische Notizen über Joseph Haydn' in *AMZ*, xi (1809), issues 41–7. 'Haydn was told that Albrechtsberger wanted to see all fourths banished from the strictest compositions. "What's the point of that?" replied Haydn, "Art is free . . . and I consider myself as competent as anyone to make up rules. Such artificial standards have no value; I would rather that someone tried to compose a genuinely *new* minuet."' *AMZ*, xi, 23 August 1809, col. 740 [F.S.].

then to E major – in which key four perfect cadences occur in rapid succession[16] – and then, after the main theme has been taken up once again in E major, very quickly back to C major [bar 77]:

The reviewer cannot recommend this modulation as an example to be copied.

The *Gloria* likewise begins without introduction, with a C major chord sustained by the singers and wind instruments, against which the violins shoot upwards in quavers. Fiery and brilliant, it rushes on as far as the seventeenth bar, whereupon singers and instruments suddenly fall silent and leave only the first violins together with the cellos descending in crotchets. This prepares the way for 'Et in terra pax', and the passage is too radical in its effect, too happily conceived in its simplicity, for the reviewer not to reproduce it here for convenient inspection by the reader:

---

[16] bars 40, 44, 56, 68.

The canonic imitation at the octave that now begins is broken off after being carried through the four voices, and the music continues through a series of modulations with alternating tuttis and solos until the 'Qui tollis' in F minor, which is an affecting melody given to the solo alto. With the 'Miserere' the tutti returns and the solo bass takes the music into A flat major. The 'Suscipe'

as well as the following imitation between the four voices in the 'Miserere' is composed with deep feeling in true church style. The 'Quoniam' is a highly jubilant unison and with the 'Cum sancto spiritu' a powerful fugue subject enters in C major.

After this subject has been carried through the four voices in the usual manner, however, the music is again quickly broken off and the basses alone repeat the theme of the 'Quoniam'. The other voices take up the first bar of the subject in inversion and the music moves through [bars 259–64]

to G major, whereupon a completely unfamiliar transition passage of fifteen bars begins, the motive of which occurs nowhere in the fugue. Then the tenors take up the fugue subject once again [bar 280] with a new countersubject in the basses, and after it has been carried through the four voices into A minor, the tenors begin a stretto which does not strictly follow the original subject but is nevertheless very ingeniously worked out:

With this canonic imitation of the second and third bars of the subject the music returns to C major and comes to a perfect cadence, from which the voices move straight on to a new phrase in minims for the 'Amen'. Now the

'Quoniam' comes in once again with the earlier theme; then the fugal subject follows in thirds, sung by sopranos and altos; then basses and tenors likewise in thirds; and again a perfect cadence in C major [bar 341]. The first violins continue with the fugal subject and the solo soprano enters in imitation. All the voices sing 'Amen' in semibreves, using the first bar of the fugue subject.

Now comes a sort of pedal point on the dominant, which lasts for only three bars, however, since the bass then continues in imitation of the theme. 'Amen' returns as a tutti in semibreves, and with this the whole movement ends. This 'Cum sancto' is the only movement that closely resembles a proper fugue. The reviewer has therefore dwelt longer on it in order to support his previously expressed judgement. He should add that he withholds censure of the many minor offences against strict style, since the freedom willingly allowed a genius who compensates in so many other ways can never, once it has been usurped, tolerate any constraint; in the awareness of its own strength it seems to be incapable of regarding unfettered licence as a sin against this or that convention. This remark is also intended to placate those too severe critics who otherwise would not be able to cease shaking their heads in wonder that this or that had been overlooked, etc.

The *Credo*, in C major, 3/4 time, is a vigorous and fiery movement with numerous neatly worked imitations that emerge splendidly. After the 'Et incarnatus' in E flat major has concluded with a heavy 'sepultus est', the solo bass begins the 'Et resurrexit' in common time accompanied by unison strings; this movement, too, is energetically and cleverly executed with alternating tuttis and solos as well as numerous imitations which reveal the composer's lively invention. With 'Et vitam' there enters another exultant fugue subject:

The listener eagerly awaits its further development and would gladly surrender himself to the flood-waves storming past; but here too the subject unfortunately breaks off after it has been carried through the four voices, and apart from a stretto and an imitation of the second bar by three voices the splendid theme is not used again.

Most composers make the *Sanctus* grand, sonorous, and fervent, but here, true to the work's overall character, it is gentle and moving, in A major, common time. The four-bar introduction is played by violas, oboes, clarinets in A, bassoons, and cellos,[17] and then the voices enter without any instrumental accompaniment. The reviewer mentions the original enharmonic change in the seventh bar, as well as the subsequent ingenious modulation[18] and the wonderful effect of the timpani strokes accompanying the voices alone in bars 13 to 15, only to draw the listener's attention to the great diversity of resources at the disposal of this highly gifted composer, enabling him to stir our hearts with unusual potency. The 'Pleni sunt coeli' is an exultant allegro and the 'Osanna in excelsis' a brief fugued section, again with a splendidly conceived theme:

One is sorry to hear this section rush past so rapidly. After being passed through the four voices, and after the sopranos alone have repeated one and a half bars of the opening, it suddenly breaks off and the end follows in five bars.

The 'Benedictus', gentle, flowing, and melodious, begins with a quartet of voices unsupported by any instruments, Allegretto, in F major. Subse-

---

[17] The horns also play.

[18] enharmonic change: from F sharp to G flat major, with flat seventh added. This is then reinterpreted as an augmented sixth on G flat in F major; the latter is itself reinterpreted as a flat sixth in the tonic of A. On 17 July 1812 Beethoven requested that this passage be clarified with an *ossia* in its notation for ease of performance, and the publisher complied with a three-bar appendix in sharp notation on p. [108] of the score.

quently a four-part chorus joins in, partly interrupting the four solo voices with short phrases and partly accompanying them. The first entry of this chorus in low, muted tones, after a completely unaccompanied passage from the alto, is of quite extraordinary effect:

The music moves forward in artful and highly melodious interplay between the four obbligato voices and the chorus. The whole movement expresses something indescribably moving, and the soul is surrounded by intimations of the infinite blessing that is poured upon those who come in the name of the Lord. After the 'Benedictus' the 'Osanna in excelsis' is repeated in its original form, in accordance with the usual pattern.

The *Agnus Dei*, in C minor, 12/8 time, expresses a feeling of profound melancholy which does not rend the heart, however, but comforts it and dissolves into unearthly ecstasy like sorrow from another world. Highly original and effective are the orchestration and structure of the first eight bars, which the reviewer is all the more justified in reproducing since they determine the character of the whole movement:

Ex. XX

Following on naturally from the *Agnus*, where the sopranos rise from G to the leading note, is the 'Dona nobis pacem', in C major, common time. This last movement too is worthy of the composer in its power and energy. The reviewer remains undecided, however, whether passages such as the following, which also occurs at the end of the *Agnus*, do not sound too operatic; at any rate he was strongly reminded of a similar figure in the well-known duet by the two basses in *Il matrimonio segreto*.[19]

Despite its brilliance and richness this work, clearly created by the composer with great love, is relatively speaking not so difficult to execute as are his instrumental compositions. Singers and instrumentalists accustomed to performing Haydn's church pieces especially will adapt to the composer's intentions without difficulty. If moreover the tempos are not too hurried, as so often tends to happen now unfortunately, and if the singers and instrumentalists, by precisely observing *piano* and *forte* and all the other expression marks, endeavour to do full justice to this work of genius, then it will move and uplift in a distinctive way not only enlightened listeners but also those who cannot penetrate to the inner essence of the composition.

Finally perhaps the reviewer may be allowed to say a few words about the German text that has been provided along with the Latin words of the High

[19] Domenico Cimarosa, *Il matrimonio segreto* (1792): duet in Act 2, 'Se fiato', including an Allegretto mosso section, 12/8, in C major. But Beethoven's use of a solo clarinet in this example parallels rather the Act 2 aria, 'Pria che spunti', using triplets in 4/4, albeit in E flat major.

Mass. As is well known, the three main parts of the Mass are the *Kyrie*, the *Credo*, and the *Sanctus*; between the first and second appears the Gradual (generally a church sinfonia) and between the second and third the Offertory (usually treated as a sacred aria). In the same way, probably in order to secure acceptance of this splendid music in Protestant churches and concert-halls as well, the German version also divides the whole work into three hymns, which in fact suits the composition very well. Now as for the words, in order not to injure the sense and significance of the whole they should be as simple as possible, and for the best and strongest effect purely biblical. Handel is known to have said of the bishop who offered to compose a text for his *Messiah*: 'Does he think he can invent better words than those I find in the Bible?'[20] Never has the real point of church texts been more truly expressed. Instead of displaying the utmost simplicity, however, the words of these German hymns are rather modern, affected, precious, and long-winded.[21] Thus the simple biblical 'Kyrie eleison, Christe eleison' is expanded to the following length:

Deep in dust we pray to thee,	Tief im Staub anbeten wir
Eternal Ruler of the world,	Dich, den ew'gen Weltenherrscher,
All-powerful Divinity.	Dich, den Allgewaltigen.
Who can name thee, comprehend thee,	Wer kann dich nennen, wer dich fassen?
Infinite Lord? O how mysterious,	Unendlicher! – Ach, unermessen,
Boundless is thy Majesty!	Unnennbar ist deine Macht!
Our childish prattle can but stammer	Wir stammeln nur mit Kindeslallen
The name of God.	Den Namen Gott.

The jarring effect of 'ănbēten' right at the start hardly needs to be pointed out.[22] In view of the original words the poet could perhaps have merely said: 'Tief im Staube beten wir: Herr, erbarme unser dich.' (Deep in dust we

[20] This is seemingly a garbled version of an anecdote related in Charles Burney, *An Account of the Musical Performances in Westminster Abbey* (London, 1785), 34; this book was published in German the same year by J. J. Eschenburg. 'At the coronation of his late majesty, George the Second, in 1727, HANDEL had words sent to him, by the bishops, for the anthems; at which he murmured, and took offence, as he thought it implied his ignorance of the Holy Scriptures: "I have read my Bible very well, and shall chuse for myself."'

[21] The addition of German words was mooted by Beethoven in 1808 and 1810; the publisher commissioned them from Dr Christian Schreiber, a theologian. The composer's own views on the German text – not unmixed – are in his letter of 16 January 1811. He found the *Kyrie* opening 'very appropriate'. *Letters of Beethoven*, i, 309.

[22] This line was fitted to the music in Ex. XIX as follows: Tief im | Staub an- | be-ten | wir.

pray: Lord, have mercy on us.) The reviewer, who certainly does not fail to
recognise the German poet's skill, finds on all sides corroboration of his
judgement above. He breaks off here, however, for he is convinced that
every musician and every informed listener who holds dear the real purpose
of church music and of texts appropriate to it will agree with him, and,
unless governed by unavoidable circumstances, will prefer to use the
original Latin text.

Review of Beethoven's Overture and Incidental Music to Goethe's *Egmont*

Published: AMZ, xv, 21 July 1813, cols. 473–81   *Unsigned*
First reprinted: Die Musik, 2 June 1902

Egmont is a five-act tragedy in prose, written by Goethe between 1775 and 1787.
First published in 1788, it was not staged until 1791; its early performance history
was problematic.

The action takes place in Brussels, set against the occupation and religious
oppression of the Netherlands by Philip II of Spain, and specific events that took
place between 1564 and 1568. The historical character Egmont, prince of Gavre
(1522–68), born in Hainaut, now in Belgium, was the governor of Flanders and
Artois. Goethe portrays him as freely impetuous, but much loved by his countrymen. He is romantically involved with a girl of the people, Klärchen. Philip II sends
in the Duke of Alba with an army to crush new uprisings, particularly in Flanders.
Egmont, who believes in toleration, is arrested and finally sent to execution as a
traitor. Klärchen, who has always seen Egmont as a force for liberty, unsuccessfully
tries to rouse the people to save him, and afterwards takes poison. Her spirit is seen
crowning the sleeping Egmont with laurel and prophesying the freedom of their
people.

Music for *Egmont* had been sought by Goethe from Philipp Kayser, who may have
composed a score in *c*. 1786–88; it is now lost.[1] J. F. Reichardt then produced music
for it, performed from 1796 to 1807 at the Weimar Hoftheater, and from 1801 at the
Berlin Nationaltheater.[2] In 1809, Austria went to war with Napoleon and lost at the
battle of Wagram, being thereafter obliged to form an alliance with France. The
Vienna Burgtheater defiantly responded with two productions, both with commissioned scores: *Egmont*, and *Wilhelm Tell*.[3] Beethoven seems to have worked hard on

---

[1] F. W. Sternfeld, 'Kayser, Philipp', *The New Grove*, ix, 837.

[2] Pröpper, *Die Bühnenwerke Reichardts*, ii, 299.

[3] *Thayer's Life of Beethoven*, 471, states that Gyrowetz won a commission for music to
    Schiller's *Wilhelm Tell*. But *The New Grove*, vii, 871, lists only a *Wilhelm Tell* ballet (1810)
    by Gyrowetz.

the music, writing the overture plus nine other items. The play (for the first time with its original text unaltered) with Beethoven's score was seen on 15 June 1810.[4] Goethe, for his part, is twice on record as having much praised this music, and specifically the melodrama sequence in No. 8.[5]

Goethe's tragedy contains two lyrics (Beethoven's Nos. 1 and 4), but also demands music for Klärchen's death in Act 5 (No. 7) and – yet more integrally – for the dream-sequence near the end as Egmont sleeps (No. 8). A 'victory symphony' is to sound as the hero goes to execution, whereupon the curtain falls (No. 9). Beethoven also composed the music for all four entr'actes. In these he was at pains to integrate music and drama in various ways, including written instructions to make his intentions clear.

Breitkopf & Härtel published the overture in orchestral parts (December 1810) and in piano arrangement (February 1811), then the incidental music in parts (January 1812) and piano arrangement (May 1812). No score was published until 1831. Hoffmann was sent a manuscript copy to work from, and this may be the reason why some of his comments appear to contradict later musical sources, as is explained in the notes. Yet there are signs, too, that he prepared hurriedly for the review, which he put to paper on 21 June 1813. For he was by then directing opera performances or rehearsals daily, including repertory new to him. One such sign is that he interpreted the overture's coda in terms of the play's opening, instead of pointing out that it is actually the 'victory symphony' from its close. Nonetheless, his brief interpretation of play and overture is interesting since it concentrates on the personal within the political, and stresses Klärchen as the 'nobler being' who more actively recognises her higher purpose.

An understanding of Hoffmann's sharp criticism of the two songs will be enhanced by reference to his review of Riem's *Zwölf Lieder*, p. 376.

It is without doubt a happy circumstance to see two great masters united in one splendid work, with the expectation that every demand of the discriminating music lover will be ideally fulfilled. Probably (the reviewer has no knowledge of the details at all) Beethoven was invited to compose incidental music for a production of *Egmont*, and he has demonstrated that out of many composers he was certainly the only one with a deep, inner grasp of its delicate yet powerful poetry; every note sounded by the poet echoed within his spirit as if on an equally tuned, sympathetically vibrating string, and thus took shape the music that now pervades and binds together the entire work like a ribbon of light woven from shining sounds. All the greater is the gain this composition brings for art, since it is a true but curious fact that not

---

[4] Not ready for the première, Beethoven's music was heard at the fourth performance of the run (i.e. 15 June), three weeks after the première had taken place.

[5] Letter to Marianne von Willemer, 12 July 1821; conversation with F. Förster, May/July 1821. See E. Beutler (ed.), *Johann Wolfgang Goethe, Gedenkausgabe der Werke, Briefe und Gespräche* (Zurich, 1948–), xxi, 451 and xxiii, 141.

one of Goethe's longer works specifically intended for music, or even just for musical embellishment, has yet enjoyed a proper classical setting. Although a master of the musical art[6] has intelligently set a number of Goethe's attractive lyrics, for example, and the songs from *Wilhelm Meister*[7] have proven to be real classics of their type, the music to *Claudine von Villa Bella*,[8] a gentle and appealing play aimed directly at the composer, is nevertheless a failure. The reviewer may say this freely, for the public has long since condemned the composition by totally disregarding and forgetting it. So far as the reviewer is aware, neither *Lila*[9] nor *Der Triumph der Empfindsamkeit*,[10] both of which perhaps with slight modification could provide splendid opera texts, has actually been set to music. The music to *Erwin und Elmire* is old-fashioned,[11] and only the amusing, truly Italian buffonade *Scherz, List und Rache* remains in the reviewer's memory, since he heard it more than once in Poznań several years ago; it was performed by the company of the theatre-director Carl Döbbelin which was resident there at the time, in the successful setting by an unknown master.[12] The score and written-out orchestral parts are said to have been accidentally burnt afterwards and to be no longer in existence.

Many good composers these days are at a loss for opera texts. Let them turn to the classical dramas of this great poet and try to win their still elusive fame by composing a work in which true inspiration shines. After this digression, which he hopes was permissible, the reviewer now turns to the work before him.

The aspect of Goethe's *Egmont* that must particularly stir every heart is

---

[6] J. F. Reichardt, whose four volumes called *Göthe's Lieder, Oden, Balladen und Romanzen* were issued in 1809–11. His *Göthe's lyrische Gedichte* had appeared in 1794.

[7] First issued as a musical supplement to the first edition of *Wilhelm Meisters Lehrjahre* (Berlin, 1795–96) [F.S.].

[8] Goethe's three-act Singspiel had been set by Johann André (Berlin, 1778), Ignaz von Beecke (Vienna, 1780), Gottfried Weber (Stuttgart, 1783), F. L. Seidel (date not ascertained), and Reichardt (Berlin, Nationaltheater, given from 1789 to 1799: Hoffmann could have heard this version). See *HBW*, i, 68 for a 1795 plan.

[9] Goethe's *Lila*, a *Singspiel mit Tänzen*, had been composed by Karl Seckendorff (Weimar, 1776) and by Reichardt (1791; not staged).

[10] *Proserpina*, within *Der Triumph der Empfindsamkeit*, had been set by Karl Seckendorff (Weimar, 1778).

[11] Goethe's two-act Singspiel was originally set by Johann André, and issued in piano score (1776); Reichardt's setting had first been published in 1791, but was not staged in Berlin. The Königsberg setting by C. D. Stegmann was also published (1776). There were other settings, e.g. by Anna Amalie von Weimar, Anton Schweitzer, C. C. Agthe, and August Bergt.

[12] i.e. Hoffmann himself, who arranged the text in one act, and had it performed either late in 1801 or early in 1802. See *HBW*, i, 157 for its later connections with Goethe. Other settings were by Philipp Kayser (1785–86) and Peter von Winter (1790).

the love of Egmont and Klärchen. Sublimely superior to her immediate
surroundings, this excellent girl can only attach herself firmly to the
patriotic hero with an ardour that is truly otherworldly; despising the petty
circumstances of this life and treading beyond all earthly things, she lives
only in him. And for him too, although he does not clearly realise it, she is
the nobler being that nourishes the heavenly fire smouldering in his breast
for freedom and fatherland. Fate requires his death if the highest of his
wishes is to be fulfilled; but she precedes him, and as a heavenly transfiguration of freedom itself she promises him the glorious reward of his martyr-
dom. He realises that the two sweetest desires of his heart are united, that he
is dying for the freedom for which he lived and fought, and thus goes to his
death with courage, since only a short time previously he was so unwilling to
part from the 'sweetly familiar habit of existence and activity'.[13] Many
composers would have given *Egmont* a warlike, proudly marching overture,
but our master has intelligently concentrated in his overture on that deeper,
truly romantic purpose of the tragedy, in short, on the love of Egmont and
Klärchen. Klärchen's passionate love is expressed just as strongly in the
dark key of F minor as her celestial transfiguration luminously shines forth
in the related keys of A flat major and D flat major.

The overture opens with a Sostenuto in 3/2 time and an F played by all the
instruments except the timpani and piccolo. A chorale-like idea begins,
magnificently effective in its utter simplicity in that, as we now expect from
this highly gifted composer, it accurately foreshadows the overall character
of the work:

Ex. XXI

After only fifteen bars the theme of the following Allegro enters in D flat
major, and is then taken up in bar 25 by the first violins and cellos in 3/4
time:

---

[13] Line spoken in the Act 5 prison scene, to Ferdinand.

Throughout the overture the composer maintains the simplicity with which
he began, frequently reintroducing the two themes from the Sostenuto and
weaving them into the Allegro. The reviewer will dispense with further
explication of individual details; he need only point out that they interfuse
and complement the whole in the classical manner typical of this composer,
and he can recommend the reader to give this sterling composition a careful
hearing. He feels he has so accurately defined the purpose to which the
composer was working that the listener, once imbued by the overture, will
automatically respond to echoes of it in many of Klärchen's speeches. Those
in the very first scene with Brackenburg and the mother[14] and those in the
first scenes of the fifth act[15] particularly recall its heart-rending sounds of
lamentation, as well as its chords proclaiming a higher existence which
occur in the transitions to major keys related to the main key in the minor.
In this regard the reviewer would mention only the idea starting from the
eighteenth bar of the Allegro, the transition into A flat major in the fiftieth
bar,[16] and the enharmonic contortions after the Sostenuto theme has been
repeated [bars 91 and 234]:

At the end of the Allegro this theme recurs in the main key of F minor,[17] and
the music dies away with long *ppp* chords from oboe, clarinets, and
bassoons.

---

[14] i.e. the third scene of Act 1, where Klärchen makes clear to her mother her rejection of her
   suitor Brackenburg, who still loves her.
[15] Where Klärchen's harangues to her countrymen to save Egmont fall on deaf ears.
[16] i.e. bar 74 of the whole work.
[17] At the climax at bar 275, with the theme from Ex. XXI.

Now, however, an Allegro con brio in F major begins, first *pianissimo* then growing louder and louder. Warlike and noisy, and bearing a direct relation to the high-spirited scenes at the beginning of the play, it brings the overture to a close.[18] Avoiding all contrapuntal devices, this last Allegro too is kept simple and is calculated, as it should be, purely to achieve the right effect.

In the first act occurs the song 'Die Trommel gerühret!'[19] The melody is very simple, in F minor, 2/4 time, but it is given a highly picturesque accompaniment of timpani rolls, piccolo skirls, and short chords from clarinets, bassoons, and horns. For a Singspiel the song would be a masterpiece; for a play, in the reviewer's opinion, it is much too elaborate. It is intolerable in an opera when some other motive for singing is sought than that which forms the basis of all opera, namely the heightened poetic state that in moments of passion spontaneously causes human language to become song. All the 'Shall we sing a little song?', 'Do sing my favourite song, dear daughter' and suchlike are utterly ridiculous, therefore, since in opera they nullify opera itself.[20] In a play, on the other hand, songs should actually be songs, just as they are sung in everyday life, and so any orchestral accompaniment, being a totally extraneous accretion, nullifies the general effect intended. Thus when Klärchen sitting quietly at home sings a soldiers' song about the beating of drums and the shrilling of fifes, and we actually hear them both, it is as though we are suddenly wrenched from the little room into which we have been permitted to peep, and deposited on an open plain with Brackenburg and Klärchen disappearing in the far distance. For songs of this sort occurring in plays the reviewer would provide at most only such accompaniment as could plausibly be performed by the characters on the stage.

'Die, poor wretch! Why do you hesitate? (He takes a flask from his pocket.) Not for nothing did I steal you from my brother's medicine chest, you healing poison! You shall once and for all consume and rid from me this fearfulness, this giddiness, this deathly sweat.'

With these words from the unhappy Brackenburg the first act comes to its

---

[18] This F major coda is actually identical to the 'victory symphony', No. 9.

[19] Sung by Klärchen as she winds thread; Goethe envisaged Brackenburg joining in at first, before being overcome with emotion. Its words express her dream of being a (male) soldier and fighting the enemy under her lover's command. Goethe refers to it as a *Lied*; there are two stanzas, ten and eight lines, set by Beethoven in two contrasting sections (minor–major) which are repeated *in toto*, plus a fifteen-bar coda.

[20] Hoffmann here parodies typical cue-lines in light opera, and alludes to his general theory of opera: see *The Poet and the Composer* and Introduction.

well-known close, and in the entr'acte the composer has very ingeniously contrived to depict in music his pain too, quite different from that of Klärchen. Brackenburg, an admirable young man of deep feeling but much too weak for the circumstances fate throws him into, seeks comfort rather in the thought of putting an end to himself than in possessing the strength and courage actually to carry it out. He has already tried to drown himself, but survived by swimming. He obtains poison which Klärchen laughingly takes away from him;[21] but when she has departed this life and left the remaining fatal potion for him he chooses to live. An Andante in A major accurately delineates Brackenburg's state of mind with a delicate theme consisting of broken phrases:

The lament dies away in disjointed sounds, and the cellos begin an Allegro con brio with semiquavers in A major portraying the inner ferment among the people, the unrest and confusion of spirit, as revealed in the first scenes of the second act.[22]

Orange's remarkable conversation with Egmont, who will not listen to his friend's warning voice, closes the second act; a Larghetto in E flat major, with interjections from horns and timpani, not only depicts Egmont's magnanimity, with its contempt of all petty suspicion, but at the same time leads to the third act which again begins with affairs of state. With regard to

---

[21] This is not seen, but related in Act 5 by Klärchen.

[22] Beethoven's No. 2, that is, prepares for the scene in the square in Brussels where news of spreading unrest is mingled with debate about the old constitution of the Netherlands.

the song 'Freudvoll und leidvoll'[23] the reviewer refers to his previous remarks about the first song, and would only add that he finds this song too protracted and operatically treated even in its melody. Reichardt has set it much better, with the utmost simplicity yet deepest feeling. At the end Beethoven's composition almost completely degenerates into an aria.

'Now let me die! The world has no joys after this!' cries Klärchen, and a jubilant Allegro in C major begins.[24] But after only two bars there is a fermata; a cadenza from the oboe, one more exhilarating bar, and the oboe plays another cadenza. Would it not have been a happier idea at this point to introduce the melody of the song 'Freudvoll und leidvoll'? The beginning of the Allegretto does in fact resemble that theme, but soon completely diverges from it. The following march is certainly a masterpiece. It has such a sombre, frightening, and in the louder passages even sinisterly jolly quality, that one imagines Alba's hirelings strutting in, relishing the prospect of pillage and murder. The march carries on in C minor even after the curtain has been raised, and as it dies away in short, disjointed phrases it corresponds perfectly to the dramatic action that follows, namely a depiction of the citizens' alarmed state.[25]

'This was the purpose? You summoned me for this? Am I defenceless then?' These words of Egmont are heard during the first three bars of the fourth entr'acte:[26]

---

[23] Sung in the second scene of Act 3 by Klärchen, at home. Her mother has again urged her to marry Brackenburg, to which she replies with this lyric, ten lines in irregular metre: 'Joyful and sorrowful, Thoughtful and glad, Hoping and doubting, now blithesome now sad; Now rapture enhances, now agony moves, Happy alone is the spirit that loves.' Beethoven's setting (No. 4) is through-composed, 46 bars long, accompanied by strings, woodwind, and horns.

[24] Hoffmann cites the last speech of Act 3, at Klärchen's moment of happiness in Egmont's arms. Beethoven's written instruction is: 'The orchestra comes in immediately after the last words from Klärchen, before the curtain has fallen; this is then lowered slowly so that it comes down fully only at the end of the second bar.' Maybe because he lacked this evidence, Hoffmann ignores the composer's way of catching the heroine's mood and developing it through musical means in this entr'acte (No. 5).

[25] The 'Marcia. Vivace' commences halfway through No. 5, and corresponds to the skilful march of Alba and his army up from Italy, referred to in Act 4. Beethoven's instruction, once again cementing music to drama, is: 'Here the actors enter from two different sides while the music is still playing; they slowly edge closer to the front of the stage until the music stops, when they begin to speak, although very slowly and nervously at first', i.e. because Alba has forbidden conversation on the streets.

[26] Again possibly owing to a discrepant source, Hoffmann totally mistakes the composer's intentions at the beginning of No. 6. The words cited by Hoffmann constitute Egmont's penultimate speech in Act 4, whereas Beethoven cites his final speech, adding, 'After these words the orchestra comes in immediately, even before the curtain has fallen.' At this point, Egmont realises he is under arrest and has been tricked.

Ex. XXII

The following Larghetto in 3/4 time, with muffled strokes from the timpani, announces the hero's demise. The following Andante agitato, however, relates entirely to Klärchen's state of mind and to the first scenes of the following fifth act. The reviewer reproduces its conclusion, which seizes the heart and mind with the simplest sounds, while the curtain rises and Klärchen enters with Brackenburg:

The music signifying Klärchen's death gives utterance to the most moving lament.[27] It is a Larghetto in D minor, 9/8 time, begun *pianissimo* by the horns alone. Then oboes, clarinets, and later the bassoons join in, but the strings not until the seventh bar. As the lamp goes out the horns alone are heard again, and finally the strings play a few pizzicato notes against a D minor chord held by horns and clarinets. The whole effect is conceived and presented in profoundest sympathy with the poet, who expressly placed store by the contribution of music here.

In the final scene, from the point where the author asks for music – namely when Egmont sits down on his bunk in order to sleep – the composer has treated Egmont's speech in the form of a melodrama and, in the reviewer's opinion, very rightly so. The musical phrases punctuating the speech are handled judiciously, not in the least obtruding but entirely conforming to the words; there is absolutely no suggestion of any lurid word-painting. The heavenly shining apparition of freedom is announced by a luminous chord of A[♮7] major, played by the wind instruments in semiquavers and quaver triplets. The remaining music is in keeping with the prescribed mime, but becomes particularly graphic at the point where the apparition indicates to the sleeping hero that his death will secure freedom for the Provinces and holds out to him the laurel-wreath of victory. The trumpet sounds and a sort of warlike march, albeit in simple, sustained chords, signifies with great emotion the apotheosis of the hero as he goes victoriously to his death for freedom. A drum is heard; at the Più Allegro, when the wind instruments have quaver triplets, the apparition disappears and the music dissolves in single notes.[28] Following exactly the spirit of the poet the composer ends with a rousing symphony, only fifty-five bars long and fashioned almost entirely from cadential figures.[29]

Elsewhere in Beethoven's instrumental music one is accustomed to a rich abundance of ingenious contrapuntal devices, audacious modulations, etc. The work under discussion here, however, shows how skilfully the com-

---

[27] In the third scene of Act 5 Klärchen takes poison, knowing Egmont has been condemned. She then goes out, leaving Brackenburg the final speech. Goethe here requests music 'indicative of Klärchen's death'; a lamp, left burning on the empty stage, flares up and then goes out. Beethoven's music (No. 7) specifically represents this, as his note in the score shows.

[28] Beethoven, that is, follows in No. 8 Goethe's instructions almost exactly, for after the visionary moment of triumph 'a warlike music of drums and pipes is heard in the far distance; at the faintest sound of the latter the vision disappears . . .' and Egmont awakes. The composer here specified '*pochi Violini*', a few violins only.

[29] i.e. the 'victory symphony', No. 9, played after the hero's last words: 'Courage, my friends! Your parents, wives, children, are behind you . . . Protect your hearths and homes! And to save your loved ones, fall joyfully, as I show by my example.'

poser is able to husband his resources and employ them at the most appropriate time; without in the least attempting to shine by itself, it follows exactly the spirit of the poet and conforms closely to his objectives. This is why the reviewer has also been at pains to pay due regard and tribute to the composer's effective aesthetic treatment of the material placed before him.

The piano scores of the overture and entr'actes are practical, and are arranged with taste and discernment. They deserve to be in the hands of every intelligent music-lover, just as every theatre-director desirous of presenting *Egmont* should put himself in possession of Beethoven's music; it is so intimately blended with the whole play that it must be regarded as an essential component of the work, on no account to be omitted.

'Old and New Church Music'

Published: A M Z, xvi, 31 August, 7, 14 September 1814, cols. 577–84,
    593–603, 611–19   *Unsigned*
First reprinted: Ellinger 1894

The second half of the year 1813 was occupied with Hoffmann's conducting duties, with the completion of Act 1 of *Undine*, and with *The Poet and the Composer*. Moreover, his writing continued to flourish with new items for the later *Fantasiestücke in Callot's Manier* such as *Der Magnetiseur* and 'Report of an Educated Young Man' (p. 136), the latter from January 1814. But after deteriorating relations with Joseph Seconda, director of the theatre company employing him, Hoffmann was sacked on 25 February 1814, with twelve weeks' notice.[1] Money earned from A M Z reviews thereafter became more important, and even after moving to Berlin in September, his surest source of income was to be from his pen. He was not permanently appointed to the Prussian Supreme Court until May 1816.

Having expressed some initial views on modern church music in the review of Beethoven's C major Mass (p. 325) Hoffmann explored the general subject further in a review of August Bergt's oratorio *Christus, durch Leiden verherrlicht* in December 1813.[2] He had also been attending rehearsals of choral music at the Dresden choral society (*Singakademie*) founded by Anton Dreyssig in 1807. These were a personal refuge from the war for him, but *Singakademien* were to form part of Hoffmann's plan for the future of church music in the present essay. Nobody was in much doubt

---

[1] See letter of 7 March 1814 to Rochlitz. The final break was provoked by an incident caused simply by the extreme cold in the theatre.
[2] Published in A M Z, xvi, 5 January 1814. The introduction to this review deals with Handel and *Messiah* in particular.

that practical suggestions were needed, for by 1800 'the practice of church music had reached a low ebb'.[3]

The way forward stylistically (see p. 372) was much clarified by a publication used throughout 'Old and New Church Music': J. F. Reichardt's *Musikalisches Kunstmagazin* (Berlin, 1782 and 1791). This anticipated early nineteenth-century journals by mixing music reviews with historical essays and substantial examples in music notation. In 1782, under the rubric 'Kirchenmusik', Reichardt published extracts from sacred works by L. Leo, Kirnberger, J. A. P. Schulz, and Handel, and concluded by giving reasons why they represented valid models: they rejected 'excessive liveliness', 'melodic opulence', 'harmonic emptiness', and 'mechanical artifice'. In 1791 Reichardt carried the subject forward with the conviction that 'genuine church music is the highest purpose of musical art'. He printed extracts gathered from his researches in Europe by Palestrina, B. Marcello, C. P. E. Bach, Porpora, Feo, and Fasch. But an artist like Hoffmann could use these only as a point of departure: the problem to him was how to move forward with new works worthy of the age and of the latest advances in musical art. (His own *Miserere* for chorus and orchestra had been completed in 1809; before that he had composed several masses, in 1802–05.)

Two Romantic writers before him, at least, addressed the subject of church music: W. H. Wackenroder in part of *Fantasies on Art for Friends of Art* (1799), and Ludwig Tieck in *Phantasus* (1812). (Tieck was also Wackenroder's collaborator and editor for the first of these.) In Wackenroder's 'Concerning the Various Genres in Every Art and Especially Concerning Various Types of Church Music',[4] three types of church music were isolated, without any composer being named: all were deemed equally valid, but variously popular. The most popular was the lightest, most elaborate type; the next was the slow, majestic type, using 'large masses of sound'; the least popular was the humble, penitential style, with 'old chorale-like' music with 'slow, deep chords [that] creep along in deep valleys like pilgrims laden with sin'. The first of these seemingly corresponds to the modern idiom of the later eighteenth century (e.g. Haydn's masses); the last surely to Renaissance and neo-Renaissance music, typically exemplified by Palestrina (whom Hoffmann also construed as a more chordal than a contrapuntal master). Hoffmann the individual could not however have identified with Wackenroder's belief that 'man finds everywhere in life excellent occasions to honour his God and to thank Him'.[5]

Tieck's analysis in *Phantasus* is more likely to have stimulated 'Old and New Church Music', having been explicitly criticised by Hoffmann in the review of Beethoven's Mass. Tieck's figure Ernst has experienced the revelation, through hearing the Papal choir in Rome, that earlier church music is the only true music. Not even Mozart's Requiem (the highest pinnacle to Hoffmann) can persuade Ernst – who is a musical 'Nazarene' – of the existence of a new and really spiritual music.[6]

---

[3] Feder, 'Decline and Restoration', 322.

[4] Schubert (ed., tr.), *Wackenroder's 'Confessions'*, 182–5.

[5] *Ibid.*, 183.

[6] Ludwig Tieck, *Phantasus. Eine Sammlung von Märchen, Erzählungen, Schauspielen und*

Later, Ernst divides church music into three periods, naming composers. The first was best represented by Palestrina. 'This vocal music, enduring, without rapid movement, sufficient in itself, evokes in our soul the image of eternity.' The next period was that of Leo and Marcello; it represented a retreat from the purest path; its music 'wants to rush back to that old innocence and conquer Paradise again'. Lastly came the 'gentle mixing of pain and joy in the loveliest melodies'. 'Pergolesi, often undervalued by the scholars, seems to me to have reached the highest in this.'[7]

Hoffmann's approach is much more detailed, and concentrates on those qualities he felt were genuinely religious about music of all periods; he ranges back to the ancient world and forward to Mozart and Haydn. (In ignoring Beethoven, he makes a tacit gesture of disapproval.) The research materials used by Hoffmann were lent to him in May 1814 by Breitkopf & Härtel, and consisted of manuscript and printed music. Quite a lot of what he discusses had never been published in any form. But another recurring theme of the essay is the relation between sacred art and church music, and these sections must have been informed not simply by Hoffmann's visits to the Dresden art-gallery, but by his discussions with painters in evolving what he reported was 'a very special hypothesis' (letter of 8 September 1813). The essay was finally written in July 1814. Parts of it and of the review of Beethoven's Mass in C were used for the second volume of *Die Serapions-Brüder* (1819).

The complaint of genuinely enlightened music lovers that works for the church have been in short supply in recent times is all too justified. Many have indicated as a reason for this shortage that present-day composers have completely neglected the profound study of counterpoint which is absolutely essential in order to write in the church style; and that their only concern is to dazzle and impress the multitude, or indeed for ignoble monetary gain to pander to passing taste and become merely popular composers instead of mature and serious ones. Such inferior and frivolous purposes can be served only by the theatre, however, not by the church; so that we see a hundred operatic efforts come and go, most of them failures, but not a single piece of church music. It cannot in fact be denied that for more than twenty years an unparalleled frivolity has been undermining every artistic aspiration. The sturdy industry of earlier men which guaranteed the quality of their works disappeared, and in place of strong, vivid forms previously summoned forth by the magic of artists we were greeted by nothing but gaudy finery whose glitter was supposed to invest lifeless puppets with a semblance of vitality. The deeper cause of this frivolity in art lay in the general tendency of the times. As though governed by demonic

Novellen (Berlin, 1812, 1816), i, 467–8. The 'Nazarenes' were German artists who practised Catholicism in Rome and channelled their work into Christian subjects inspired by the art of the Middle Ages.

[7] *Ibid.*, 471.

forces, everything conspired to hold men spellbound within their miserable, blinkered world, whose constant activity seemed to them the highest purpose of existence. And so they turned against all that was noble, true, and sacred; the divine spark which can be kept alive only by faith and love was extinguished, and the cold tongues of fool's fire that flared up in the hopeless desolation could never kindle that inner glow from which in everlasting incandescence true works of art arise. Even during such unhappy times, of course, that unseen church which rules eternally granted its loyal servants a full pardon, in order that they could express the feelings deepest in their hearts. But how few withstood the rigours of their circumstances! Their earthly demise meant spiritual transfiguration, in which they remain in perpetual communion with the faithful. One need only think of Mozart, still not generally accorded the recognition he deserves; of Vogel (Johann Christoph Vogel, composer of the sublime tragedy *Démophon*),[8] who is quite unknown in Germany although he was a German; of the excellent but now almost forgotten Fasch.[9]

It is clear that this frivolity, this criminal denial of the Power ruling over us which alone confers health and strength upon our works and deeds, this mocking contempt for wholesome piety originated in that nation which, incredibly, stood for so long before a bedazzled world as a model of art and science.[10] As a consequence of blindly aping her products, which with brazen insolence she set up as eternal models, science became contaminated by her loathsome affectation, and art by her frippery and foppery which took opium-induced vapourings for artistic inspiration. The unspeakable sacrilege of that nation finally brought about a violent revolution that swept across the earth like a devastating storm; but it was a storm that sent the dark clouds scudding, and now the dawn, sending its precursory glimmer through the black of night and promising comfort for the wounded hearts of the faithful, is about to break in all its splendour over our unhappy world. In this world the sovereignty of the eternal Power ruling over us will be proclaimed as with the thunderous sound of a thousand trumpets, so that men awaken from their apathetic stupor, hear the sound, comprehend the Word, and believe in themselves again; in this world the futility of our misguided cravings and of our obsession with earthly strivings for earthly goals will be starkly revealed; in this world the spirit, as if enlightened by a

---

[8] Johann Christoph Vogel (1756–88) was from Nuremburg, but active in Paris where his opera *Démophon* was given in 1789, and published in full score. His oratorio *Jephté* dated from 1781.

[9] Carl Friedrich Fasch (1736–1800) is discussed in note 29 below.

[10] Hoffmann indulges in one of his attacks on French culture and society in the aftermath of Napoleon's defeat and capitulation in February–March 1814.

bolt from heaven, will recognise its native land, and through this recognition gain the strength and courage to bear, indeed to resist, its earthly afflictions. And in this newly risen world of ours we will put a stop to the wanton debasement of art, so that the human breast will joyfully burst open to its deepest, most mysterious influence through music.

So let us now speak of music, music in the most profound and essential meaning of the word, that is to say when it takes the form of religious worship, of church music; for no longer will its words die away unheeded as they have before, when bitter frustration numbed into a state of torpid indifference even those more favourably disposed.

No art arises so directly from man's spiritual nature, and no art calls for such primary, ethereal resources, as music. Sound audibly expresses an awareness of the highest and holiest, of the spiritual power which enkindles the spark of life in the whole of nature, and so music and singing become an expression of the total plenitude of existence – a paean to the Creator! By virtue of its essential character, therefore, music is a form of religious worship, as already stated, and its origin is to be sought and found only in religion, in the church. As it acquired greater richness and power it showered its inexhaustible treasure upon mankind, and even the profane were then able with childish delight to bathe in its glow, which spread over life itself and all its petty, temporal affairs; but profanity, clothed in this finery, seemed to yearn for the higher realm of the spirit and to strive for admittance among its prodigies.

Because of its essential character music could not be the property of the ancient world, in which sensual embodiment was all, but found its place in the modern era. The two opposing poles of ancient and modern, or heathendom and Christendom, are represented in art by sculpture and music.[11] Christianity abolished the former and created the latter, together with its close neighbour painting. In painting the ancients knew neither perspective nor skill in colouring; in music neither melody (understood in the higher sense, as an expression of inner emotion without regard to words or their rhythmical value) nor harmony. But it is not this deficiency which characterises the lowly station that music and painting occupied at that time, but rather the fact that the first seedlings of those arts, lying in barren soil, as it were, could not flourish, whereas in Christendom they sprouted splendidly and bore blossom and fruit in luxuriant abundance. Both arts, music and painting, maintained their place in the ancient world only by appearance;

---

[11] This theory and its development may have been discussed with the artists Hoffmann knew in Dresden. For an overall perspective concerning art and sculpture, see Hugh Honour, *Romanticism* (Harmondsworth, 1979), esp. 295ff.

they were crushed by the power of sculpture, or rather, beside the weighty masses of sculpture they were unable to establish an identity. Neither art resembled in the least what we now know as painting and music, while sculpture retreated from the physical world, distilled into a spiritual form, as it were, by the tendency of the modern, Christian period to oppose all physicality. But those first raw seedlings of music, although their sacred mysteries were to be elucidated only by the Christian world, were already able to serve antiquity in their most distinctive capacity, that is to say in religious worship; for that is what its dramas really were. Even in earliest times they contained ceremonial representations of the sufferings and pleasures of a god. The declamation was supported by instrumentalists, and this fact alone proves that their music was purely rhythmical, even if it could not be demonstrated from other evidence that, as already mentioned, melody and harmony, the two axes about which our music moves, remained unknown to the ancient world. It may well be, therefore, that Ambrose,[12] and later Gregory (591),[13] used ancient hymns as the basis of their Christian hymns, and that we can still hear traces of that purely rhythmical singing in so-called plainsong, in antiphons.[14] But that means simply that they took over the seedlings they had inherited, and it is clear that further investigation of ancient music can be of interest only to the antiquarian. For the practising composer, however, the most sacred depths of his noble and truly Christian art are first revealed in Italy when Christianity shone forth in its greatest splendour, and the great composers, with the solemnity of divine rapture, proclaimed the holiest mysteries of religion in magnificent sounds not heard before.

It is remarkable that soon afterwards, when Guido of Arezzo[15] had penetrated more deeply into its mysteries, music became an object of mathematical speculation by the unlearned, so that its essential character, which had hardly begun to develop, was misunderstood. The magical accents of this spiritual language became audible and echoed forth across the earth; it had become possible to fix them in writing; hieroglyphics of sound (notation) had been devised to indicate their melodic and harmonic connections; but now the sign was mistaken for what it designated. Com-

---

[12] Saint Ambrose, Bishop of Milan (c. 340–97), traditionally thought to be responsible for 'Ambrosian' chant and also the authorship of the *Te Deum*.

[13] Gregory the Great, Pope and theologian (c. 540–604), traditionally credited with composing or editing the 'Gregorian' chant constituting the official music of the Catholic liturgy.

[14] antiphon: liturgical chant with prose text often sung in association with a psalm. Hoffmann's original text uses the slightly archaic term *canto fermo* throughout for 'plainsong'.

[15] Guido of Arezzo (c. 991 to after 1033), one of the most famous music theorists, author of *Micrologus*, and developer of the system of pitch notation using lines and spaces. Guido's coloured lines for C and F survive in the form of our C and F clefs.

posers became obsessed with harmonic affectations, and music thus reduced to a speculative science would have ceased to be music at all.[16] When these affectations had eventually reached an extreme, worship was profaned by what they foisted upon it in the name of music; and yet minds imbued with sacred art saw only music as true worship. So it could only be a short struggle, ending with the glorious victory of eternal truth over falsehood. Pope Marcellus the Second,[17] who was on the point of banning all music from the church and thus of robbing worship of its greatest glory, was reconciled with the art when the great Palestrina revealed to him the sacred wonders of music in its most essential form.[18] Now music would for ever be the most distinctive form of worship in the Catholic church; a profound awareness of the inner nature of music dawned in composers' minds, and from their hearts flowed a stream of immortal, inimitable vocal works born of genuinely holy inspiration. The six-part mass composed by Palestrina at that time (1555)[19] in order to allow the hostile pope to hear true music has become very well known by his name (*Missa Papae Marcelli*).

With Palestrina began what is indisputably the most glorious period in church music (and hence in music in general); in ever-increasing plenitude it maintained its pious dignity and strength for almost two hundred years, although it cannot be denied that even in the first century after Palestrina that lofty simplicity and dignity sank into a sort of elegance for which composers strove.

At this point it is appropriate, indeed necessary, to look more closely at the way in which this founding father of music composed. Without adornment and without the impetus of melody, chord follows upon chord; most of them are perfect consonances, whose boldness and strength stir and elevate our spirits with inexpressible power. That love, that consonance of all things spiritual in nature which is promised to the Christian, finds expression in chords which only came into existence with Christianity; thus chords and harmony become the image and expression of that communion

[16] affectations, etc: Hoffmann refers to the complex rhythmic, structural, and contrapuntal techniques of the early Renaissance in the music of figures such as Guillaume Dufay (c. 1399–1474), Johannes Ockeghem (c. 1420–97), and Jakob Obrecht (c. 1450–1505).

[17] Marcellus II, Pope briefly in 1555, had participated in the Council of Trent, which in fact restricted itself to general recommendations concerning music.

[18] Giovanni Perluigi da Palestrina (c. 1525–94), composer of 104 masses, active in Rome, and recognised in his own lifetime as a supreme figure in the sacred music of his century.

[19] The composition date of the *Missa Papae Marcelli* is unknown, but it could have been performed at a 'trial' on 28 April 1565 held to 'sing some masses and test whether the words could be understood', this being part of the effects of the Counter-Reformation and discussions of music at the Council of Trent in 1562 and 1563. As early as 1607 Agazzari claimed that this mass had prevented the Council abolishing polyphony in church. See the article by Lewis Lockwood in *The New Grove*, xiv, 122–3.

of spirits, of that bond with the eternal ideal which at once embraces and reigns over us. The music that is purest, holiest, and most suitable for the church must therefore be that which arises from the heart purely as an expression of that love, ignoring and despising all earthly things. Palestrina's simple, dignified works are conceived in the highest spirit of piety and love and proclaim godliness with power and splendour. His music can in fact be described by words with which the Italians have designated the work of many composers who are shallow and perfunctory beside him; it really is music from the other world (musica dell'altro mondo). The movement of the individual parts recalls plainsong; rarely do they exceed the compass of a sixth, and never does an interval occur that is difficult to pitch or, as they say, does not lie in the throat. It goes without saying that Palestrina, following the practice of the time, wrote only for voices, with no instrumental accompaniment. Praise of the highest and holiest should flow straight from the human breast, without any foreign admixture or intermediary.

Successions of consonant triads, particularly in minor keys, have become so alien to us in our present enfeeblement that many, their minds firmly closed to what is holy, see them only as a weakness of technique; but even disregarding any higher view, and considering only what it is customary in vulgar usage to call effect, it is obvious that in a church, in a large, resonant building, any blurring of the sounds by subtle nuances or short passing-notes would destroy the strength of the vocal line by making it unclear. In Palestrina's music every chord strikes the listener with full force, and even the most artful modulations could never affect the spirit in the same way as those bold, powerful chords, blazing forth like blinding shafts of light.

Palestrina is simple, true, childlike, good, strong, and sturdy. Truly Christian in his works, like Pietro von Cortona and our old Dürer in painting,[20] composing was to him a religious exercise. Reichardt in the fifth part of his Kunstmagazin has printed a splendid four-part Gloria from one of Palestrina's masses[21] which corroborates all that has been said. The reviewer has before him Palestrina's responsories sung by the choir on the last three days of Holy Week. The choir's responsories interrupt the priest's plainsong and, alternating with it, relate the biblical story of Christ's passion. The same arrangement, but with different words, is found in the Miserere (a point made only in passing for those unfamiliar with the Catholic

[20] Pietro da Cortona (1596–1669), painter and architect active in Rome; Albrecht Dürer (1471–1528), recognised by the Romantics as the father of German art; see 'A Memorial to Our Venerable Ancestor, Albrecht Dürer', and 'A Portrayal of How the Early German Artists Lived', in Schubert (ed., tr.), Wackenroder's 'Confessions', 112ff. and 164ff.

[21] J. F. Reichardt, Musikalisches Kunstmagazin (Berlin, 1791), 19; this four-part 'Gloria Patri et Filio' is not from a mass but a Magnificat [F.S.].

rite). In order to provide the reader with an example of the plainsong referred to above, part of an ancient Gregorian chant may be inserted at this point; an opportunity to illustrate one of Palestrina's responsories will present itself later.[22]

Di - xit Do-mi-nus   Do-mi-no me - o: Se-de a dex-te-ris me - is

Given that Palestrina's austere, noble style is the sincere and dignified expression of a spirit fired by the most ardent devotion, and given that the church is its only true home, then it comes as no surprise that it endured so long as the church continued to shine with the full flame of its original authority and dignity. The famous *Miserere* for two choirs by Allegri[23] is written exactly in the style of Palestrina, although it is inferior to his works in boldness and power; and despite its fame, which may have arisen from its wonderful performance by the singers of the Sistine Chapel, it must also yield to Leo's later *Miserere*.[24]

The composers of that time avoided all decoration and strove only to preserve a devout simplicity, until gradually the greater melodic impetus that compositions acquired brought about the first departures from that deep seriousness. But how dignified, how simple yet powerful the church style still remained is demonstrated by the works of Caldara, Bernabei, A. Scarlatti, Marcello, Lotti, Porpora, Leonardo Leo, Vallotti, and others.[25] It was still the practice to write solely for voices, without the accompaniment of other instruments, or with the organ at most, and this circumstance alone preserved the simplicity of the chorale-like singing, which was not overwhelmed by a hotchpotch of accompanying figures. These remarks are intended merely to clarify what follows concerning the relationship between old and new church music; they would expand into a pragmatic history of the subject, and it would lead too far for the scope of these pages, if the gradual transitions into later styles were to be demonstrated by listing the works of every composer. Let it suffice to make a few further observations

---

[22] The responsory referred to is actually by Ingegneri (see note 30, below). This example is the opening of Psalm 110 in the first psalm-tone [F.S.].

[23] Gregorio Allegri (1582–1652), composer and *maestro di capella* under Urban VIII; he was taught by G. M. Nanino, an eminent composer in the Palestrina tradition. Allegri's famous *Miserere* was also a famous secret, not being published until 1770, but performed each Holy Week in the Sistine Chapel.

[24] Part of Leo's *Miserere* is reproduced below.

[25] Antonio Caldara (*c.* 1670–1736); Ercole Bernabei (1622–87); Alessandro Scarlatti (1660–1725); Benedetto Marcello (1686–1739); Antonio Lotti (*c.* 1667–1740); Nicola Porpora (1686–1768); Leonardo Leo (1694–1744); Francesco Vallotti (1697–1780).

about those composers who will eternally remain our models and whose glorious age lasted until the middle of the eighteenth century.

Among the earlier composers of that age the great Alessandro Scarlatti shines conspicuously forth.[26] He is known to have written a number of operas at the end of the seventeenth century. But how small an influence the theatre exerted on the church at that time, or rather how little it could occur to a composer to carry worldly display into sacred matters, is shown by this composer's works for the church which, despite their melodic energy, stand beside Palestrina's works in their bold chord sequences and inner strength. The reviewer has before him an *alla cappella* mass for five and seven voices without any instrumental accompaniment which was composed at the beginning of the eighteenth century (1703) and is a model of genuine devotional style.[27]

Equally magnificent are the works of Leo; and who would not also admit, beside the great Handel, our deeply intellectual Sebastian Bach to the saintly throng of that age? His mass for two orchestras, eight solo and four ripieno voices[28] belongs among the few classical compositions for the church to have been offered to a wider public in engraved form.

Once again to sum up in a few words the spirit pervading the works of all the great composers referred to, it need only be said that the power of faith and love fortified their hearts and fired their urge to walk in communion with the highest, and to create works that should serve not worldly ends but to praise the ultimate reality of religion. These works therefore bear the stamp of authenticity, with no anxious striving for so-called effect; no contrived frivolity or orchestral mimicry defiles the purity of this heaven-sent music; nothing is heard of the so-called striking modulations, the gaudy figures, the feeble melodies, the impotent, confusing clamour of instruments that would stupefy the listener lest he notice the inner emptiness; and therefore only the works of these composers, and of the few who in the present age still remain faithful servants of the church now vanished from the earth, can truly elevate and edify the pious mind. Let the name of the excellent Fasch once more be mentioned here;[29] a master of the old tradition in the full sense of the word, his profound works were so little

---

[26] Scarlatti wrote many operas, cantatas, oratorios, motets, and ten masses; he was active chiefly at Naples.

[27] None of Scarlatti's masses is at present thought to come from 1703; the first *Missa Clementina* (1705) is for five voices.

[28] This short mass (*Kyrie, Gloria*) is by Johann Ludwig Bach, in all probability, though parts of the manuscript are in J. S. Bach's hand. It is Anhang 167 in the Schmieder *Verzeichnis*; it had been published in 1805.

[29] Carl Friedrich Fasch (1736–1800), a colleague of C. P. E. Bach at Frederick the Great's court, later active in Berlin as a central figure in the revival of choral music, including that of J. S. Bach. His Mass for four choirs with instruments was inspired by one by Benevoli

regarded by the feckless multitude after his death that owing to lack of
support the publication of his sixteen-part mass did not even take place.
The lowest point in this respect has been reached in most recent times
although, as was noted above, the enfeeblement of melody began by degrees
at an earlier date.

Before discussing in more detail the causes of this gradual decline in
church music, the reviewer feels it would be interesting for the reader to see
at a glance how the old authenticity and strength gradually degenerated into
the present affectation and sickliness. He therefore gives two examples from
different periods, although they do not in fact extend as far as the present
and thus leave out of account the worst excesses that have been perpetrated.

Palestrina lived and wrote in the sixteenth century, Vallotti in the eighteenth; here are two responsories by these composers to the same text.[30]

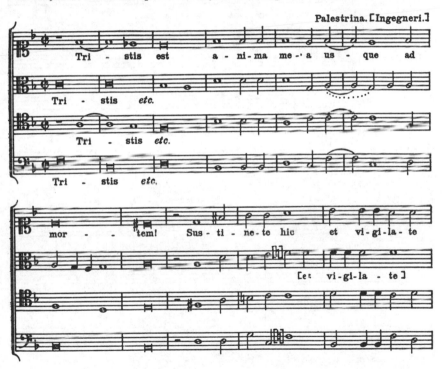

brought back from Italy by Reichardt. From 1789 he organised a choir which became the
basis in 1791 of the first *Singakademie* in Germany; by 1800 it had almost 150 members. Its
statutes (1816) stated, 'The *Singakademie* is an artistic society for the cultivation of serious
and sacred music, especially for music in contrapuntal style [*im gebundenen Stil*].' Feder,
'Decline and Restoration', 322.
30 The 'Palestrina' has been identified as by Marc'Antonio Ingegneri (*c.* 1547–92); active at
Cremona Cathedral, he published two books of masses; this piece dates from 1588
(*Schriften zur Musik*, 474).

Who can be unaware of the difference, and yet who does not still discern in Vallotti's composition the dignity and simplicity befitting the church?

Leonardo Leo was born in 1694, Sarti in 1730;[31] both composed a *Miserere*, and Sarti's has become well known. Here is the setting of the text 'Miserere mei, deus, secundum magnam misericordiam tuam.'

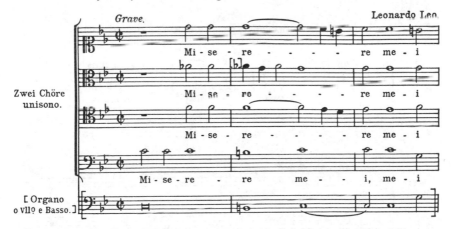

[31] Giuseppe Sarti (1729–1802), active in St Petersburg, wrote five settings of the *Miserere*.

(The following example is preceded by a twelve-bar ritornello.)

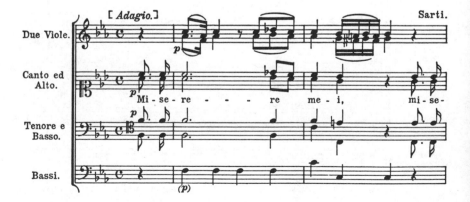

How forceful and sublime Leonardo's chorus sounds, and how weak Sarti's setting appears beside it.

Hitherto church music has been discussed only in its most essential form, namely as an act of worship in itself. At an early date, however, sacred drama developed; thus, though more like opera than worship, a form of church music came into being that could fill the mind with the subjects of holy scripture and so bring edification and spiritual elevation. It may well also have led eventually to the decline of the true church style. Music migrated from the church to the theatre and then, with all the empty ostentation it had acquired there, moved back into the church.

Among the earliest works of this type that attain a high level with regard to melodic evolution belong indisputably the oratorios of Caldara,[32] who lived and composed at the end of the seventeenth and beginning of the eighteenth centuries. An example of Caldara's noble and admirable oratorios is the sacred drama *Morte e sepoltura di Cristo*. The arrangement of this oratorio, in which recitatives alternate with arias, duets, and choruses, is very similar to that found in contemporary operas; the sacred dramas perhaps differed merely in their greater wealth of choruses. Much in this oratorio receives quite dramatic treatment. There is a *turba di popolo*, for example, which interrupts the recitative twice in succession and is written in the following way:[33]

---

[32] Antonio Caldara (*c.* 1670–1736) wrote forty-two oratorios, of which only one is lost.

[33] See the extensive notes on the manuscripts of this work in *Schriften zur Musik*, 475–8. A modern authority writes: '*Sepolcro* librettos . . . based on the theme of the Passion and Crucifixion of Christ . . . combine lamentation with interpretation of the Passion and Crucifixion. Numerous allusions to events of the Old and New Testaments are usually made in the course of the *sepolcro*', in the period 1660–1720. Howard E. Smither, *A History of the Oratorio*, i (Chapel Hill, 1977), 380–2.

As well as the wonderful harmonic elaboration of the choruses, the melodies in the arias, which breathe true piety emanating from the heart, cannot be praised highly enough. Even the orchestration, which seems sparse to us now, is full of imagination and feeling; one can already recognise the first signs of the extravagant richness that has characterised instrumental music in more recent times. The very first aria, for example, to the words

Deh sciogliete o mesti lumi	Oh sad eyes, set my afflicted
l'alma afflitta in onde amare	soul free on the bitter waters,
or ch'estinto è il mio Signor	now that my Lord is dead

is accompanied only by two violas providing the chords, while the bassoons and basses imitate a figure that is not taken up by the violins until the last eight bars.

The middle ground between music intended for actual worship and sacred drama is occupied in some ways by the famous psalms of Marcello,[34] which are set mainly in two or three parts, more rarely in four or five, and accompanied only by a continuo. This profound work stands at the head of those sacred hymns which were later composed in such numbers, such as

---

[34] Benedetto Marcello, *Estro poetico-armonico. Parafrasi sopri li primi venticinque* SALMI (8 vols., Venice, 1724, 1726). 'He attained a truly European fame with the composition of settings in cantata style of the first fifty psalms in Italian paraphrases . . . Enthusiastic letters from eminent musicians including Telemann, Mattheson, Bononcini, and Sarro were published with the psalms as successive volumes appeared.' Article by Michael Talbot in *The New Grove*, xi, 649.

Durante's Litanies, Pergolesi's *Stabat Mater*, Jommelli's so-called *Miserere* (*Pietà, Pietà, Signore*), and others.[35] It would lead too far afield to discuss this great work by the renowned Marcello in more detail; let it be remarked merely that it conceals a rich store of melodic distinction and strength which shines forth with increasing brilliance the closer one looks at the whole or the part.

Following these composers (Palestrina, Caldara, Marcello, etc.) the richness of melody brought with it increasing instrumental display, and it is all too clear that theatre music, to which oratorio had granted entry into the church, particularly encouraged this. At a very early date the strings were joined by a wind instrument whose origin is lost in the deepest darkness of antiquity, namely the trumpet. Although it still exists in its early form, this has been supplanted, or rather banished to a quite different region, by more convenient and mellifluous forms.[36] The way in which the trumpet was employed at that time (the end of the seventeenth century) may be demonstrated by a passage from a *Te Deum* by Ziani:[37]

It cannot be denied that the trumpet used by composers now has infinitely gained in power and nobility of effect. The trumpet apart, the bassoon usually just reinforced the bass; oboes reinforced the violins at the unison;

[35] Francesco Durante (1684–1755) wrote five Litanies. Giovanni Battista Pergolesi (1710–36), pupil of Durante, wrote the *Stabat Mater* shortly before his death; the *Miserere o Salmo L di Davidde* by Nicolò Jommelli (1714–74), dating from 1774, had been issued in score by Breitkopf & Härtel in 1804.

[36] It is difficult to know precisely what Hoffmann refers to by these 'forms', since the trumpet was in a period of rapid change. Many designs were made in order to facilitate hand-stopping, by curving the instrument and re-siting the crooks. The keyed trumpet was also familiar (this is the instrument for which Haydn's concerto was written). Even before 1800 such alterations won comments using epithets such as 'grace', 'sweetness', etc.

[37] Marc'Antonio Ziani (*c*. 1653–1715), active in Mantua and Vienna, known for his partiality for wind instruments (including the chalumeau).

and in three-part writing violas replaced second violins, which played in unison with the firsts.

Much richer in his orchestration than his predecessors was Handel, yet the works of this glorious composer preserve the spirit of piety and truth. Who can fail to think here of his *Messiah*, the oratorio of all oratorios,[38] for its genuinely biblical text, its melodic expression, its harmonic craftsmanship, and its stirring dignity and power? Who could find in it the briefest theme that in the slightest degree recalls the theatre, despite its wealth of melody and other musical artifice (in the higher sense of the word)? Alongside this great composer stands the immortal Hasse, even though he reached his goal along a different path.

Mention may be made here of a little-known work by Handel that admittedly cannot at all compare with *Messiah* in power and dignity, since its overall dramatic structure prevents it, but still contains many splendid and unrivalled things. This is the oratorio *Der für die Sünde der Welt gemarterte und sterbende Jesus*;[39] it is the only one Handel originally composed in German and now only needs changes in its occasionally inferior text for it to be performed again with the greatest effect.*

A composer of similar grandeur and power, particularly in his choruses, was the now almost completely forgotten Fux, and one can understand that an opera seria like *Virtù e costanza*,[41] composed in his style and performed in the open air by a huge orchestra, must have had a great effect.

---

* In Gerber's *Tonkünstler-Lexikon* this work is not listed among Handel's works and it has not become known in Germany at all. During his visit to London Haydn was presented with the original score by the Queen of England, and this score is probably to be found with the rest of Haydn's autograph remains in the possession of Prince Esterhazy.[40] Haydn gave the Härtel firm in Leipzig a copy of this original score, and thus Herr Härtel possesses a rarity whose publication – even if only of the choruses – would be of extreme interest to every admirer of true church music, particularly the musician able to plumb its sacred depths. As suggested above, it would only require changes in its text, which occasionally lapses into vulgarity and bad taste.

[38] This phrase, already used in Hoffmann's review of Bergt's *Christus*, parallels his 'opera of all operas', *Don Giovanni*.

[39] Text by Barthold Heinrich Brockes, composed probably 1716–17 in London; also performed five times in Hamburg in the next eight years. The text was set also by Keiser, Mattheson, and Telemann.

[40] This historical note was added by Hoffmann from information supplied by Härtel at the reviewer's request in a letter dated 19 July 1814. The gift from Queen Charlotte to Haydn is mentioned in Griesinger's biography of him. This score is now in Budapest, Országos Széchényi Könyvtára, and the copy taken from it (presumably Härtel's, used by Hoffmann) in the Nationalbibliothek, Vienna. See Bernd Baselt, *Händel-Handbuch. Band 2* (Kassel, Basel, London, Leipzig, 1984), 48–62.

[41] Johann Joseph Fux (1660–1741) wrote some eighty masses, requiems, motets etc. His *Costanza e fortezza* (Prague, 1723) was a *festa teatrale*: see p. 285 n. 19.

In the last half of the eighteenth century increasing enfeeblement and sickly sweetness finally overcame art; keeping step with so-called enlightened attitudes, which killed every deeper religious impulse, it eventually drove all gravity and dignity from church music. Even music for worship in Catholic churches, the masses, vespers, passiontide hymns etc., acquired a character that previously would have been too insipid and undignified even for opera seria. Let it be frankly admitted that even a composer as great as the immortal Joseph Haydn, even the mighty Mozart, could not remain untouched by the contagion of mundane, ostentatious levity. Mozart's masses, which he is known to have composed to a prescribed pattern on paid commission, are almost his weakest works. In one church work, however, he has revealed his innermost feelings; and who can remain unmoved by the fervent devotion and spiritual ecstasy radiating from it? His Requiem[42] is the sublimest achievement that the modern period has contributed to the church. Compelling and profound though Haydn's settings of the High Mass frequently are, and excellent though his harmonic development is, there is still hardly one of them that is completely without playfulness, without melodies quite inappropriate to the dignity of church style; and the tendency of Haydn sometimes to treat the human voice too much like an instrument, a criticism directed at him with justice, is evident from the hopping and leaping progress of his melody. The Creation[43] is not at all an oratorio in the pure church style, a fact long ago recognised by those with a true feeling for that style; but one does the composer great injustice to apply the standards of pure church music to The Creation and, particularly, The Seasons.[44] Pedantic scrutiny and classification in art seldom do any good. The music relates in no way to church worship and these so-called oratorios are nothing but the glorious expression of Haydn's view of life – and the world – emerging in music. The Seasons has appeared to some in a bad light, but only when a narrow view is taken.[45] There is no more splendid or more colourful picture of the whole of human life than that which the composer has musically delineated in The Seasons; and the playful wit only colours more vividly the motley figures from life who dance about us in brilliant circles. This wonderful music is charged with the same constant alternation of gravity, awe, horror, jollity, and exuberance as that which mundane

[42] Composed late 1791; completed by F. X. Süssmayr, published 1800.
[43] Die Schöpfung, composed 1796–98, published 1800.
[44] Die Jahreszeiten, composed 1799–1801, published 1802.
[45] Criticism centred on the various musical representations of the natural world. The most notorious one was of the croaking of a frog, the idea for which caused the composer himself to protest to his librettist, Gottfried van Swieten. Hoffmann ordinarily, of course, would be the first to condemn such 'imitations', taken by themselves.

activity gives rise to, and it relates to the church only to the extent that pious reflections play a part in the affairs of everyday life. It cannot be denied that the composer's individuality emerges even here, just as in his instrumental music, in a certain humorous, teasing jollity; but even in his most serious works for the church some things sound like dogs snapping beneath their master's table.

It is clear, to come back to pure church music, that Haydn's masses and church hymns cannot stand as models of church style, particularly when compared with that truly sacred music of former times which has now vanished from the earth; yet it goes without saying that they far outshine the most recent productions of this type, despite the fact that to the ignorant they opened the door to all sorts of theatrical gaudiness. How often the great Haydn has been imitated, or rather aped; but these so-called church composers merely nibbled at the shell without ever penetrating to the kernel, and the deeper spirit of harmony contained in his works never dawned on them. As a result tasteless, shallow, and feeble church compositions appeared of the sort that the present writer has heard in recent times in the Catholic churches of southern Germany, as well as in Bohemia and Silesia. Many an otherwise excellent composer has disgraced himself as soon as he set about composing a church work, and it is remarkable in this respect that even a serious-minded modern composer thoroughly versed in harmony can no longer write in the church style. Cherubini's three-part Mass,[46] much thought and art though it employs, utterly fails to satisfy the demands of true church music, and several of its movements are unconstrainedly theatrical.

A church composer not regarded according to his merits is the excellent Michael Haydn, who ranks fully with his famous brother in this field, and often far surpasses him in gravity of mood.

These suggestions – for the writer wishes all that he has said hitherto to be regarded only as such – will suffice to indicate the consequences that face church music at the present time. It is simply impossible for a composer today to write in the same way as Palestrina, Leo, and, later, Handel and others. Those times, particularly when Christianity still shone forth in all its glory, seem to have vanished from the earth for ever, along with that sacred dedication of artists. A musician today can no more compose a *Miserere* like that of Allegri or Leo than a painter can paint a Madonna like Raphael, Dürer, or Holbein. These two arts, painting and music, present differing patterns regarding their evolution through time. Who can doubt that the

---

[46] This Mass in F (soloists, chorus, and orchestra), originally published by the Imprimerie du Conservatoire, Paris, in 1809, was the first of Cherubini's mature sacred vocal works.

great painters of the early period in Italy scaled the highest summits of their art? Their works contain the utmost power and grace, and even in technical skill they surpass the modern artists who vainly strive to equal them in every detail. In drawing, skill in colouring, in short in every one of the elements which must harmoniously combine to form a perfect whole, the old masters are superior to the modern ones, and the unbiased observer will find this amply confirmed in any gallery displaying old and new paintings together.

With music, however, it is different. Man's frivolity was unable to withstand the spirit of the times marching onward in darkness; the more perceptive soul turned his glance away from the bewildering spectacle presented by men sundered from all holiness and truth, and only he discerned the shafts of light that pierced the darkness and proclaimed the existence of the spirit, restoring his belief in it. Our mysterious urge to identify the workings of this animating natural spirit, and to discover our essence, our other-worldly abode in it, which gives rise to the pursuit of knowledge, lay also behind the haunting sounds of music, which described with increasing richness and perfection the wonders of that distant realm. It is quite clear that in recent times instrumental music has risen to heights earlier composers did not dream of, just as in technical facility modern players clearly far surpass those of earlier times.

Haydn, Mozart, and Beethoven have evolved a new art, whose earliest beginnings can be traced only to the middle of the eighteenth century. It was not the fault of these composers, in whom the spirit was so gloriously manifest, that frivolity and ignorance squandered the wealth that had been so hard won, and that finally counterfeiters tried to give their tinsel productions the semblance of authenticity. It is true that singing was neglected almost exactly in proportion as instrumental music thrived, and that this neglect, which began with composers, was accompanied by the complete disappearance of good choirs brought about by circumstances within the church (dissolution of the monasteries etc.). The impossibility of returning to Palestrina's simplicity and grandeur has already been acknowledged, and it remains to be seen how far our newly acquired wealth can be carried into the church without unholy ostentation.

To the young composer anxious to know how he might begin to write church music of integrity and worth, one can only reply that he should search his soul and confirm that he possesses the spirit of truth and piety, that this spirit urges him to praise God and to speak of the wonders of the heavenly realm in the magical sounds of music, and that his composing consists only in writing down the sacred melodies that pour from his soul as though in devout ecstasy. Only if this is so will his church music be truly pious. Any external motive, any petty striving for worldly effect, any vain desire for admiration and applause, any facile show of acquired knowledge, will lead to error and irreverence. Sacred music that irresistibly inflames the congregation to devotion resides only in a truly pious mind kindled by religion.

If the young composer has not been corrupted by worldly superficiality, he will be miraculously uplifted by the works of the early composers; he will feel that what was merely a confused fancy in his own mind is brought sharply into focus. The study of counterpoint is nothing but the precise knowledge of inner structure needed by anyone who wishes to erect a building; but only a deeper, continuing study of the works of great composers provides the knowledge from which the artist must derive, or rather bring to life, his own creative strength. Thus the artist gifted with a childlike and pious mind cannot absorb the works of early composers too thoroughly: he must have them constantly in his thoughts. Then he will soon regard all superfluous, unholy display as empty and tasteless, and will never be tempted to beautify his work by such means.

Inventing genuinely religious melodies reveals the weakness of any composer who is less than sincere; it is the touchstone of the inner soul.[47] No amount of harmonic elaboration in the church style will disguise a profane theme; a fugue worked out strictly according to the rules cannot be religious; and artful imitations can often merely highlight even more starkly the original character of a jaunty theme borrowed from the concert-hall or theatre. The melody must flow directly from the pious mind. Nothing here can be artificially contrived; it will come only from true inspiration.

It is clear, however, that composers of today can hardly conceive of music other than in the finery heaped upon it by our present opulence. The brilliance of numerous instruments, many of which ring so splendidly through lofty vaulted spaces, shines forth everywhere; and why should we close our eyes to it when the onward march of progress itself has conferred this brilliance upon our mysterious art, in a modern age striving for inner spirituality? It is only the wrong use of this opulence that makes it harmful. By itself it is a splendid and valuable asset which the truly pious composer only employs to the greater glory of the celestial verities to which his hymns sing praise. But chromatic, intricate figures, particularly in the strings, are alien to all church music and are resorted to only by those who lack understanding; like glued-on pieces of rustling tinsel they mar the calm composure of the whole, smother the singing and, particularly in the high vault of a cathedral, only produce a confusing noise. In the same way

---

[47] This part of Hoffmann's theory relates to his view of compositional authenticity set out in 'Letters on Music in Berlin', pp. 392–3.

languid concert-melodies from the wind instruments sound weak and undignified in a church. It is certainly true that in loud passages for the violins rapid notes are of great effect; but for the church it is clearly better in such cases merely to break longer notes of a chord into shorter ones, crotchets into semiquavers, for example, than into other, more chromatic figurations. This passage, for example,[48]

rearranged in the following manner with dissonant running-notes,

verges on the theatrical and sounds confused in a church. As a general rule, in fact, those figurations are most suitable for church use which merely exploit the underlying chord without dissonant notes, since they do least injury to the power and clarity of the singing and often considerably strengthen the effect.

No one can deny that wind instruments often blend with voices admirably, and that modern composers have discovered much about their use that earlier ones did not imagine. Here mention may again be made of a masterpiece that combines the power and solemn dignity of the old music with the rich ornament of the new, and that can serve as a model in this respect, as also in its wisely handled orchestration, to church composers today: the profound and incomparably magnificent Requiem by Mozart. The *Tuba Mirum* may perhaps be the one movement that lapses into oratorio style, but otherwise the music remains genuinely devotional

---

[48] The example is from the *Dies irae* of Mozart's Requiem. Hoffmann's strictures against chromatic decoration relate back to Reichardt's rejection of 'opulence' and 'artifice' (see Prefatory Remarks).

throughout; pure devotion resonates through these awe-inspiring chords which speak of another world, and which in their singular dignity and power are themselves another world. The Requiem performed in a concert-hall is not the same music; it is like a saint appearing at a ball!

It is of course the great decline of church music in Catholic Germany, and even in Italy, that is the reason why the works of the early masters are heard either not at all, or only in an unworthy form; only in concerts can one now hope to hear older classical works[49] in even moderately worthy perform-ances! Music intended for worship is meaningless when played separately, because such music is *worship itself*, and thus seems like a mass celebrated in a concert, or a sermon preached in a theatre. Quite apart from this, however, it is impossible in concert performances, even good ones, for the spirit distracted in a thousand ways to be inflamed to devotion to the same degree that it is in church as a result of solemn worship. So the revival of early works in the concert-hall in no way compensates for their disappear-ance from the church.

The complete decline of singing is apparently being prevented by the admirable institution of choral societies;[50] but if these societies are to have any real influence on church music, they should not remain private under-takings, but should be established and maintained in some religious form by the state. These societies would then provide the musical service in Catholic churches and frequently perform music during the service in Protestant churches. *Concerts* in church, which one attends for the price of an entry-ticket, and where, just as in a theatre, there are often different categories of seats, inferior and superior, parterre and gallery, might then be seen as utterly unworthy and contrary to all Christian piety; they would be heard of no more and our holy places would no longer be desecrated by becoming pleasure-grounds of arrogance and ostentation. Even the rehearsals of these societies could be held in sanctified places and thus make conservatories of them, like those which used to exist in Italy and which produced the great composers of earlier times. It is true that Protestant worship actually opposes purely musical considerations, but with the recrudescence of true church music the spirit of the age would create splendour and joy here too,

---

[49] classical: i.e. permanent monuments of the art from any historical period.
[50] choral societies: that is, *Singakademien*, as discussed in note 29 above. Fasch's Berlin prototype was emulated in Würzburg (*Akademischer Chor*, 1801); Leipzig (*Singakademie*, 1802); Münster (*Singverein*, 1804); and Dresden (*Singakademie*, 1807). The last-named was described by C. M. von Weber in 1812; there were fifty-one members, who paid a subscription. Rehearsals were for two hours weekly, but with detailed optional coaching on a separate day: *Weber: Writings*, 115–17. Hoffmann wrote a *Hymnus* for the Dresden society in October 1813 (*HTB*, 229), now lost.

and sacred music would once again become part of the worship of the Protestant communion.

As the spirit of true music was further stimulated in this way among the people, so the error and irreverence that frivolity has brought into art would disappear: that is obvious. For musicians and composers, indeed for every genuine admirer of true church music, nothing would be more pleasing than if the works of the early masters, which we only come across now and then like hidden treasure, could be offered to the public in printed or engraved form, even if initially it only happened piecemeal, perhaps in the style of Reichardt's *Kunstmagazin*. For even that stimulus would not fail to have the most salutary consequences. Many a young composer knows Palestrina, Leonardo Leo, Scarlatti, etc. only by name, and is prevented from obtaining manuscript copies of their works, which have now become rarities, by his isolated situation; yet only those works will teach him what true church music is. Easier availability of such works, moreover, would bring about more performances, which otherwise would not have taken place.

The prevailing spirit of the age forever drives us on and on; the vanished figures will never return with the joy that infused their earthly lives; but truth is eternal, imperishable, and a wondrous community of spirits spins its mysterious thread around past, present, and future. The great masters live on in spirit. Their voices have not died away; it is merely that they cannot be heard through the seething clamour of frenzied activity that has broken over us. May the time of fulfilment of our hopes no longer be far away; may a devout life of peace and joy be dawning; and may music, free and strong, stir its seraph's wings and begin again its flight towards the world beyond, which is its home and from which consolation and grace shine down upon man's uneaseful breast.

Review of Riem's *Zwölf Lieder*, Op. 27 (extract)

Published: AMZ, xvi, 12 October 1814, cols. 680–92   *Unsigned*
First reprinted: Kroll 1909

This review was one of several Hoffmann wrote shortly before moving to Berlin on 24 September 1814; it was completed at the beginning of the same month. It is also his only review of original song settings with piano. His own song compositions had been Italian rather than German. Nevertheless, his customary exordium to the review is a valuable interpretation of the established nature of the Lied as it was practised by Herder, Wieland, Goethe, and Schiller, and by leading composers of Lieder such as J. A. P. Schulz, Reichardt, Mozart, Zelter, and the younger Beethoven. The above poets 'strove for the simplicity and the poignancy of the *volkstümliche Lied* [popular song] and not for the ambitious *Kunstlied* [art-song] with its demand for professional singers and accompanists'.[1] The following account is valuable in re-creating the prevailing mode of performance, i.e. before Franz Schubert and others accustomed audiences to the composer distorting the structure of a strophic poem.

> Wilhelm Ehlers . . . was often obliged to work with Goethe until far into the night, tirelessly rehearsing the same song until all nuances were most scrupulously rendered, and the most varied meanings of diffcrent stanzas brought into relief *to the same melody*. Goethe convinced him 'how objectionable was all so-called *Durchkomponieren* [through-composing] of songs which annihilates the general character of the poem, and postulates as well as excites a wrong interest in detail'.[2]

It is also apparent that Goethe (in a rehearsal of a Reichardt setting) demanded 'tempo changes from stanza to stanza'.[3]

Wilhelm Friedrich Riem (1779–1837) was educated under J. A. Hiller at St Thomas's School, Leipzig, and became organist at St Thomas's Church there until 1822, when he was made organist at Bremen Cathedral. He wrote principally for piano and chamber ensembles. The *Zwölf Lieder* Op. 27, settings of various poets, were published at about the same time that the present review appeared. Copies of the music are now exceedingly rare.[4] Therefore we have included the complete Lied quoted by Hoffmann.

Of the previous works of Herr R. the reviewer must confess that he recalls only a few early piano sonatas which did not exactly move him profoundly.[5] All the more agreeable is it now to make his closer acquaintance through this new work, which will be a source of great interest to every friend of music.

Herr R. has no lack of imagination, originality, or deep feeling, added to which a sound command of musical structure raises him far above so many who presume to compose Lieder and songs without possessing those qualities. Amid the welter of compositions of this sort Herr R.'s songs shine forth conspicuously. For this reason the reviewer may be permitted to appraise the work not by its outer dimensions but by its inner content, and to delve

---

[1] Frederick W. Sternfeld, *Goethe and Music. A List of Parodies and Goethe's Relationship to Music* (New York, 1954), 19.

[2] *Ibid.*, 20.

[3] *Ibid.*

[4] Title page: ZWOELF LIEDER / Alter und neuerer Dichter, / mit Begleitung des Pianoforte / in Musik gesetzt / von / W. F. RIEM. / 27tes Werk. Pr.1 Rthlr 8 gr. / Leipzig, / Bey Breitkopf & Härtel. The plate number was 1879.

[5] Breitkopf & Härtel had issued five sonatas, Opp. 1, 2, 3, 4, 7 (1803, 1804, 1805) [F.S.].

deeper into these ingeniously conceived songs than the scope of these pages normally allows for such works. May Herr R. thereby recognise the care and love with which we have played and sung his settings of these intimate Lieder, and may he accept in good part such remarks as our profoundest convictions give rise to, just as though two friends were cordially exchanging their opinions, and any differences were merely the result of differing points of view. Remarks, not censure, we would term the things we have in mind to say about so much in Herr R.'s compositions.

The reviewer has already referred to Herr R.'s compositions as *songs*, although the title expressly describes them as *Lieder*. With the possible exception of numbers 2, 4, and 5, there is no composition in the collection that could lay claim to the title of a true Lied; they more or less resemble musically developed arias, or seem like a free fantasy spontaneously arising in the musician's fingers and throat as he reads the poem. It would be appropriate here, so far as is possible without digressing unduly, to say a few things about the differences between an aria and a Lied; in doing so the true musical character and requirement of each will become self-evident.

The aria requires only a few words. Through them the poet gives clear expression to the inner state of mind determining and dominating his overall mood; but the gamut through which his emotions rise and fall, and often make themselves felt at individual moments in the most varied ways, is merely hinted at. The prevailing character established by the words dictates to the composer the underlying colour and tone (in the painter's sense) that he must work with and remain faithful to, if the whole is to be maintained in proper balance and not dissolve into confusion. Then, however, the composer fastens upon individual emotional impulses merely suggested by the words and uses the means of expression afforded to him by the inexhaustible riches of his art to bring that emotion to life in all its aspects, as they arise from the action, situation, etc. He plays upon the entire gamut of passions, so that all the inner resonances emerge in clear and striking colours; thus in an aria the words may be regarded merely as a symbolic indication of feelings that in the restless alternation of their subtlest nuances only music can convey. This is what gives rise to the musical devices – repetition of individual stanzas, even individual words – that characterise arias.

It is different with the Lied. Here the poet's proper object is to enunciate his inner experience purely in words, so that frequently many stanzas are needed to give full expression to every emotional impulse. The poet has done what in an aria the composer was required to do, and so the latter is now placed in the opposite position to that in an aria. The many words which must clearly convey every emotional impulse would bear down like lead weights upon the musical development appropriate to an aria and would hinder the composer's flight of fancy. In the Lied, therefore, all forms of broader development obscure the poet's intention, and the alien spirit appearing unannounced upon the scene destroys the magic of the words. The composer, stirred by the deeper meaning of the Lied, must bring all the emotional impulses into a single focus, as it were, from which the melody then radiates forth. Just as in an aria the words became a symbolic indication of the inner feeling, so now the notes become a symbol of all the various impulses of inner emotion contained within the poet's Lied. In order, therefore, to compose a Lied that fully matches the poet's intention, it is necessary for the composer not only to grasp its deeper meaning but rather to become the poet himself. The spark that kindled the Lied within the poet must glow again with renewed vigour within the composer and simultaneously with the words give rise to sounds that repose in the musician's soul like a wonderful, all-embracing, all-governing mystery. It is supremely in composing Lieder that nothing can be ruminated upon or artificially contrived; the best command of counterpoint is useless here; at the moment of inspiration the idea, which is all, springs forth in shining splendour like winged Minerva from the head of Jupiter.

The inner poet (as Schubert calls our miraculous ability to dream in his *Symbolik des Traumes*[6] – but is not every artistic conception like an exquisite dream unconsciously generated by the inner spirit?) expresses in his own magical way what normally appears inexpressible; thus a few simple notes often contain the profoundest meaning of the poem. Lieder of earlier composers were extremely simple, without ostentation or ornament and without contrived modulation, often remaining in the tonic throughout; compact in scale, usually with no ritornello and only accommodating one stanza; singable, that is to say without wide leaps and only covering a limited compass. But it should be obvious from what has already been said that all these characteristics proceed from the very nature of the Lied. To stir the innermost soul by means of the simplest melody and the simplest modulation, without affectation or straining for effect and originality: therein lies the mysterious power of true genius, such as that commanded by those excellent composers of the past, and by Reichardt and Zelter among the present generation. One need only think, for example, of Reichardt's 'Im Felde schleich' ich still und wild' and 'Freudvoll und

---

[6] G. H. Schubert, *Die Symbolik des Traumes*. See the similar quotation in 'Johannes Kreisler's Certificate of Apprenticeship' and a further one in 'Extremely Random Thoughts' (*Kreisleriana*, II–7 and I–5).

leidvoll',[7] so utterly simple and yet so deeply affecting. The fact that only true genius can achieve such things may well explain our paucity of real Lieder; and the custom of through-composing, which the reviewer finds abhorrent, unless the text lapses into drama and thereby ceases to be a Lied, is merely the resort of imbeciles incapable of encompassing the whole and heedful only of the part.[8]

[. . .]

No. 2, *Liedchen der Sehnsucht* [see below],[9] is a splendid, heartfelt, genuine Lied, and even if Herr R. had composed nothing but this his talent for composing Lieder would be proven.

[. . .]

Although the reviewer has found so many faults, at least as he sees them, in Herr R.'s compositions, he nevertheless repeats that Herr R. has shown himself in these same songs to be a composer worthy of note, who will certainly delight the music-lover with many works of interest, as he has indeed already done. That he has also done so here, the shortest of these twelve Lieder may demonstrate to all those who are willing to trust their own judgement.

---

[7] From J. F. Reichardt's settings of Goethe in *Göthe's Lieder, Oden, Balladen und Romanzen* (1809, 1811). The first, originally issued in 1781, is Goethe's *Jägers Abendlied*. The second is Klärchen's second song from *Egmont* [F.S.].

[8] Hoffmann here proceeded to a critique of each Lied in turn. We have included the totality of his remarks about No. 2, then reproduced his concluding paragraph.

[9] Words from J. G. von Herder, *Stimmen der Völker in Liedern*, rev. ed., Johann Müller (Tübingen, 1807) (see *Schriften zur Muzik*, 483).

1. lein, die mich er-freu-en soll, er - freu - en soll!
2. lein, die mir am Her-zen leit, am Her - zen leit!
3. lein, die ich im Her-zen trag', im Her - zen trag'!

4. In Zu - ver - sicht al - lein gen ihr ich hang', und

hoff' sie soll mich nicht ver - las - sen lang; sonst fiel ich

g'wiß in's bit-tern To-des Zwang, in's To - des Zwang.

Review of Boieldieu's *Le Nouveau Seigneur de village*

Published: *A M Z*, xvi, 5 October 1814, cols. 669–73   Unsigned
First reprinted: Ellinger 1912

This review and the thoughts provoked by the performance of Méhul's *Ariodant* (p. 401) are Hoffmann's only writings on French opéra-comique. As a genre using dialogue and composed music (particularly developed after 1755) this was the main model for the German Singspiel. The continuing popularity of French works in Germany has been documented in the Introduction to *The Poet and the Composer*. Although he seems not to have conducted Boieldieu's music, Hoffmann shows that he was familiar with the stylistic tendency of opéra-comique in the Empire period.

Adrien Boieldieu (1775–1834) became the leading composer of opéra-comique of his day. He was unusual in being trained outside Paris (in Rouen), and in his later employment at the St Petersburg court (1803–11). His best-known works include *Béniowski*, *Le Calife de Bagdad*, *Jean de Paris*, and above all *La Dame blanche* (1825). *Le Nouveau Seigneur de village* (*The New Village Squire*) was first mounted at the Opéra-Comique, Paris, on 29 June 1813. It held the stage until 1898 and was widely popular abroad, being translated into seven foreign languages. Reviewing it from a piano score lacking dialogue,[1] Hoffmann could not guess all the plot quite correctly.

The village locals are rehearsing for the arrival of their new squire, the marquis de Formann, in four days' time (quartet no. 1, 'Ainsi qu'Alexandre le Grand'). His valet Frontin is mistakenly taken for the marquis by Blaise (duet no. 2, 'C'est, dites-vous, du Chambertin?'). Frontin likes his new rôle (air no. 3, 'Paix, taisez-vous'), and goes to dress in his master's clothes. Babet tells her preferred suitor Colin about the traditional rights of the *seigneur* (couplets no. 4, 'Oh! vous avez des droits superbes'). Frontin is welcomed by the villagers (chorus no. 5, 'Célébrons'). But the true marquis enters unseen; he pretends to be a businessman, and decides to help Babet and Colin (trio no. 6, 'Mes bons amis'). After some comic scenes in dialogue the Bailli practises his welcome speech on the 'businessman' (duet no. 7, 'Ainsi qu'Alexandre le Grand'). Frontin's character is suspected by the Bailli, and the former makes advances to Babet (duet no. 8, 'Je vais rester'). All enter for supper, except the marquis. Babet is persuaded to sing about a local character, a figure of fun who gives himself airs (couplets no. 9, 'Monsieur Champagne') and all join in the refrain. Eventually the marquis makes his proper entrance and Frontin escapes (ensemble no. 10, 'Je perds les honneurs').

---

[1] Title page: Der Neue Gutsherr / (le nouveau Seigneur de Village) / Singspiel / im Clavierauszug / mit französich- [*sic*] und deutschem Texte / Musik von / ADRIEN BOILDIEU. [*sic*] / Preis 9 Francs. / Bonn bey N. Simrock. The plate number was 79 throughout. The text was by A. F. Creuzé de Lesser and E. G. F. de Favières, and the action (according to the printed libretto) is set in Germany. The Bonn score above agrees in order of musical items with the full score issued in Paris *c.* 1813, published by Boieldieu

The whole thing is a skilful tongue-in-cheek reworking of *ancien régime* motifs and characters, and it is unfortunate that Hoffmann was not given the wherewithal to form a more complete judgement.

French comedy has developed straight from the essential character of the French people, and from the life and movement of their conversation. In achieving the greatest possible smoothness, they bring about a situation where everything in conventional society flows neatly together; but in doing so of course the characteristic stamp of the individual is lost. It is the same in comedy, where the author strives only for a smoothly interlocking construction and not at all for depth and significance of the idea from which the work develops, or for detailed characterisation.

Genuine humour is alien to the French; its place is taken by jokes, just as sly tricks played by this or that character (pranks) have to take the place of intrigue in the higher sense. Just as alien to them as true humour, which proceeds from the deepest inner regions, is the romantic–fantastic element predominant in Italian opera buffa, arising partly from the quixotic dash of individual characters and partly from the mischievous play of chance.[2] It is evident from this that the French have no genuine opera buffa but only comedies with an incidental admixture of vocal music, which are then mistakenly called comic operas.

The music, which therefore appears not as an essential prerequisite but only as an incidental embellishment of the text, is subject to the same tendency. One could call it conversational; for here too the only object is that everything should flow together easily and smoothly, that nowhere should anything obtrude in an unseemly manner, and that the whole should be suitably amusing, that is, may be understood and enjoyed without any effort being needed, or indeed any particular attention being paid.

This fundamental tendency of the French opéra-comique springs too strongly from the character of the people for it ever to disappear. It cannot be denied, however, that within its continuing limits French music has for a number of years now possessed a new momentum, and that the great influence upon it of German music is unmistakable.[3] The psalmody of Lully and Rameau,[4] and lachrymose French romances, which despite the Gluck

jeune. The original was in one act, but the above piano score is divided into two acts between items 5 and 6.

[2] See *The Poet and the Composer* for Hoffmann's theory of opera buffa, and of ordinary dialogue operas.

[3] This observation is just; some of Mozart's works were already popular in Paris, as were certain other pieces by Peter von Winter, Joseph Wölfl, and Ludwig Lachnith (who arranged *Die Zauberflöte* for the Opéra as *Les Mystères d'Isis* in 1801). Haydn, naturally, had long been a favourite. Boieldieu has been called 'the French Mozart'.

[4] 'psalmody' was a regular jibe, even inside France, for the Baroque style of French recitative, especially as it was performed during the period of its decadence.

revolution were frequently still heard in later works,[5] have disappeared and been replaced by more lyrical melodies; just as the harmonic elaboration too has become richer and more varied after the German manner.

The imitation of German music has certainly produced a number of bizarre results; many French composers did not penetrate below the surface but merely adopted the foreign form and then tried to surpass the foreignism with even greater foreignisms. But the more enlightened among them have undoubtedly created things of real value from this and, as far as they were able, carried them over into French music.

Among these more enlightened ones the reviewer includes the composer of the present Singspiel, which is what has led him to make these remarks about French comic opera in general.

Boieldieu is to be sure a truly French composer; outstanding profundity and significance are not among his gifts, but besides showing a firm command of technique, his compositions are distinguished by a certain grace and deftness which will guarantee them ready acceptance everywhere.

He has already displayed these qualities in many larger Singspiels and *Le Nouveau Seigneur de village*, a Singspiel of modest proportions (only ten numbers), also contains much pleasure and amusement. It is particularly praiseworthy that the insignificant subject is not, like many others, hung about with cheap musical finery which only makes its poverty look more wretched.

So far as the reviewer can tell from the text of the piano score[6] the underlying basis of the work, in the typical French manner, is the joke that Monsieur Frontin, servant to the new squire whose arrival in the village is expected at any moment, passes himself off as his master, whereby all sorts of misunderstandings are created. Comedy of this sort is not likely to inspire the composer unduly.

In keeping with the insignificant subject the overture (A major, Allegro con moto) is cheerful but not without strength. It is to good effect, for example, that at the transition to the dominant the composer carries the music forward with the main theme extended and transferred to the bass.[7] If the reviewer were to find fault with anything it would be that the continuity is too often interrupted by a fermata. The music breaks off in this way after only nineteen bars, and then again eighteen bars later.

In Number 1, the introduction (D major), the *Bailli* (magistrate) studies

---

[5] romances . . . in later works: as heard in opéra-comique, especially by Dalayrac and Dezède.

[6] This also contains certain stage-directions that assisted Hoffmann.

[7] At bar 20, the 'false dominant': technically still in A major.

the speech with which he intends to welcome the new squire, while Colin (Lukas) and Blaise (Michel) pay court to Babet (Bärbchen), the former being the favoured suitor. The two of them turn to the Bailli as the father[8] and ask him to decide who should win the daughter; but he can think of nothing but Alexander the Great, with whose entry into Babylon he proposes to compare the squire's entry into the village. The composer has caught this situation with much skill and knowledge of effect. The music moves along, briefly digressing but immediately reverting, using only tonic and dominant, and makes very good motivic use of the Bailli's persistent phrase

The fact that there is no actual bass to be heard among the voices in this quartet, and that the key-note D is almost always sung at the upper octave, which sounds far too lightweight to German ears, can be attributed to the French manner.[9]

In Number 2, the little duet between Frontin and Blaise, Frontin as the squire drinks a quantity of wine on the pretext of precisely determining its variety and vintage. The composer has overlooked no facetious detail, and in things of this sort that may well be sufficient.

Number 3, an aria by Frontin, sounded to the reviewer almost like a companion piece to the well-known servant's aria in Méhul's *Une folie*.[10]

Number 4, an ariette by Babet, which in the third verse takes the form of a duet, will certainly appeal to those who like songs in such a sugary, typically French style. A thing like this must be sung by a woman, thoroughly in the French manner, and at the same time, if the reviewer may so put it, must convey a musical mincing; it is then capable of producing in many a delightfully ironic effect. It is again typical of the French manner

---

[8] Actually the Bailli is Babet's uncle.

[9] Even in the French full score the three male parts are all in the tenor clef. The 'French manner' was the tendency not to cultivate great distinctions between low and high male voices, at least in opéra-comique. (This was epitomised in the famous voice of Jean-Blaise Martin (1768–1837), combining a baritone with a tenor.) Hoffmann's 'upper octave' signifies middle d'.

[10] *Une folie* (1802), opéra-comique popular in German-speaking countries as *Je toller, je besser* or *Die beiden Füchse*. Hoffmann himself conducted it in 1813–14. By 'companion-piece' he means to draw a dramatic rather than a musical parallel between Boieldieu's No. 3 and Carlin's aria in *Une folie*, Act 1, 'De l'intrigue ô vastes mystères': servants imagining future contentment.

that there is a delicious *équivoque* (the reviewer prefers not to use the coarse German expression) underlying the whole piece.[11]

Number 5 is a short and jolly peasants' chorus, and Number 6 a very pretty, harmonically rich canon in three parts (soprano and two tenors: Babet, Colin, and the marquis). This canon could well be accounted the best piece in the whole Singspiel.[12]

Number 7, an amusing duet between the marquis and the magistrate, who does not recognise the real squire before his eyes and reads out to him the speech he proposes to make, is fittingly written with spirit, skill, and regard for the inevitable merriment that results.

Number 8 is a duet in which Frontin, thoroughly in character as the worthless young fellow who drinks and chases the girls, pays court to Babet. What could be more typically French than the theme of this piece?

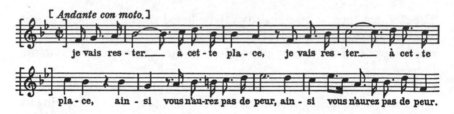

Number 9, a sort of vaudeville, brings the dénouement[13] in which the idle Frontin gets his comeuppance. Finally in the short closing number he assures the gentle public:

Je perds les honneurs, l'opulence	My honour gone, nought but a knave,
Et le rang, où j'étais monté:	Though wealth and status I now lack,
Mais si je trouve l'indulgence,	If your indulgence I can crave
Je n'ai pas perdu ma gaîté!	My jollity will soon come back!

This sort of thing always sets the hands in motion, and the melody of this closing number is again typically French.

The reviewer would add that the piano score is very well done, being neither too empty nor too full but perfectly satisfying the requirements of

---

[11] Joke about the ancient *droit du seigneur* enjoyed by the lord of the manor over women about to be married in his demesne.

[12] The piano score labels it 'Canon' (Andante grazioso, 6/8). After an introductory section in dialogue, the main eight-bar theme is expounded by the marquis alone. It is then sung in turn by Colin, Babet, and again the marquis, with decoration in the alternative voices. The coda contains chromatic harmony. Cf. Beethoven, *Fidelio*, No. 3, 'Mir ist so wunderbar.'

[13] Deprived of the full text, Hoffmann anticipates the dénouement slightly: see the Prefatory Remarks.

such versions. He concludes with the heartfelt wish that this trivial genre of operetta, just as it came from the French stage to ours, might disappear again as soon as possible, together with our blind reverence (admittedly extorted sword in hand) for everything else that comes from there; with its mawkishness and its inane joke-spinning, it is opposed to our conception of music and to our spirit in general.

'Letters on Music in Berlin. First Letter.'

Published: AMZ, xvii, 11 January 1815, cols. 17–27   *Unsigned*
First reprinted: Die Musik, 2 December 1907

The plural 'letters' surely signifies not just that Hoffmann intended the initial letter to be one of several, but also that he had something potentially ambitious and cumulative in mind. The *Kreisleriana* was almost finished, and *Undine* completely so. Taking musical performances rather than printed music as the point of departure, the author evidently planned to allow his deepest impressions of the art witnessed in a great city to engage him. The result, despatched on 10 December 1814, is unique in his work. After reflecting on aspects of instrumental music he turns to the problem of Gaspare Spontini's *Fernand Cortez*. This, his latest opera, received its Berlin première on 15 October 1814; it represented one avant-garde of its day. (Spontini was, indeed, to become an idol of the younger Berlioz.) So great was the dilemma its modernism caused him that Hoffmann was provoked into an analysis of the psychology of musical creativity itself. These paragraphs seem to be a most important contribution to a sub-literature that is still small. The fact that Hoffmann later came to recognise Spontini as Gluck's potential successor in the Romantic period (see p. 431) merely heightens the sense of authenticity of the earlier response. It may even be that Hoffmann was planning to use these or similar thoughts for the conclusion of *Kreisleriana*, since it was not until the following February that he decided to close that cycle with 'Johannes Kreisler's Certificate of Apprenticeship'.

We have described Hoffmann's welcome party to Berlin on p. 66. He was now working as *Kammergerichtsrat* (Supreme Court councillor), a post that his oldest friend Theodor von Hippel had procured for him.[1] His restlessness there was mitigated by the contacts he could now enjoy with many leading figures in the arts.

The present article proved to be the last review by Hoffmann for the *AMZ*. He promised to write for this journal about Beethoven's *Fidelio*, following its Berlin première in the autumn of 1815, but never did so.[2]

---

[1] See letter of 1 November 1814 (*HBW*, ii, 26–8) for reactions to this post, sent to Hippel. On the Berlin period in general, see Hewett-Thayer, *Hoffmann*, 77ff.

[2] See letter of 5 October 1815 (*HBW*, ii, 73). Only the story *Der Baron von B*. was afterwards sent to the *AMZ*, printed in vol. xxi, 10 March 1819.

You can imagine, now that I am burdened with numerous responsibilities of the sort customarily regarded as 'more serious', that I am revelling in the rich musical feast on offer here just as little as previously, when my state of mind restrained me from doing so. I permit myself only that music which I can rely upon either genuinely to stir my innermost emotions or at least significantly to enrich my artistic experience, and I am not often to be found either in the theatre or in the concert-hall.

After my long absence from Berlin,[3] it was with the gloomiest of expectations that I first entered the opera-house. How many glorious masters of the art are no more! Righini, Reichardt, Schick[4] have passed on, and I sorely miss several less generally well-known singers, such as the bass Franz,[5] who had so splendidly maintained his position in serious opera. Not even Franz has been replaced, and here too, as sadly almost everywhere now, manner has taken the place of style in singing. Nowhere is this more apparent than in recitative, in which Madame Schick was so unrivalled in her simple yet powerful and heart-stirring delivery. With the exception of a single survivor from the old, well-tried school,[6] whose appearance otherwise can no longer be counted a source of unalloyed pleasure, we have *no* female singer who can sustain and give full-breasted voice to the weighty masses of Gluck's music; only for the charming, light music of so-called operetta may there occasionally be some hope among the younger figures. With the men the situation is better, since several from the old days retain a rare vigour and depth, and still provide the connoisseur with real pleasure.

Always the old days this and the old days that, you will say, and perhaps you will think that like many others, victims of an unkind fate and grown grey before their time, I too, visited by many of the iniquities of this wicked age, have already become a poor *laudator temporis acti.*[7] So let me mention at once what I must acknowledge as a genuine innovation of recent times: I mean our orchestra. You know that for some time there has only been one

---

[3] Two previous residences are referred to. As a newly qualified lawyer he was employed in the Berlin Supreme Court from September 1798 to early summer 1800. The next one occurred after the Prussian defeat by France at Jena (1806), when he lost his post in Warsaw, as Prussia ceded influence there to France. He arrived in occupied Berlin in June 1807 and left a year later.

[4] Vincenzo Righini (1756–1812), composer, teacher, and conductor who came to Berlin in 1793 as director of the Italian opera. In 1811–12 he was joint Kapellmeister of the reorganised royal theatre. J. F. Reichardt (1752–1814), once a teacher of Hoffmann's, was famous for his operas and many publications; Margarethe Schick (1768–1809) sang in Berlin from 1793.

[5] Johann Christian Franz (1762–1814), bass singer in Berlin from 1786 [F.S.].

[6] Marianne Müller, retired in 1815 after a Berlin career starting in 1788 [F.S.].

[7] *laudator temporis acti*: a praiser of the good old days.

orchestra here, formed from the Royal Orchestra and that of the National Theatre.[8] This has had extremely beneficial results; in volume, intonation, precision of attack, expression, and fire, the orchestra here may not easily be bettered, despite the fact that strangely little notice is taken of it, and the so-called connoisseurs assume dubious expressions and speak only of the orchestras in Munich, Frankfurt, etc. A type of fault-finding seems to flourish in these parts which is almost never directed at the right target, and which allows really questionable things to pass unchallenged. This fault-finding does not proceed, of course, from a profound inner feeling for artistic truth, but only from a desire to be *saillant* and *pétillant*[9] (I know no German expression for these Gallic predicates). That is simply our way.

Many performances by this orchestra have swept me up into whole heavens of sound, full of luminous, glittering stars. But does this not also confirm a peculiar sign of the times, namely that instrumental music, taking ever bolder, ever braver flight, dashes singing to the ground with its powerful wings? Musical sound, with its immense primeval strength, is bursting the fetters of the word; but should the *vox humana* be quite silenced by this powerful force which, like a mighty sorcerer, summons forth all the resonances that nature holds concealed like a profound secret? This *vox humana* which, like a faithful echo of the first natural sounds, still floating on their mother's breath,[10] reawakens the sublimest inner presentiments?

Who else could come to mind, as I speak of the high degree of perfection with which instrumental music is now practised, but a splendid composer whom to my greatest joy I encountered again here after his long absence? You already know that Bernhard Romberg has been here for some time.[11] I knew that too, and yet I only became fully aware that he was in fact among us when I read the announcement of his concert. He has played in many other concerts, with a liberality befitting the true artist, but I wanted to see and hear him only in his own, where he himself was the focus of attention. I

[8] The orchestras were reorganised in June 1811. The Nationaltheater was founded in 1786 by Frederick William II; moved into the new Schauspielhaus in 1802. The Royal Opera was reopened in 1788, under Reichardt's direction, giving serious operas and some Italian opera. In 1807 the two companies merged as the Königliche Schauspiele, while retaining separation of repertories. Presumably the unification of orchestras was a further rationalisation.

[9] *saillant*: prominent; intrusive; *pétillant*: sparkling; bubbling.

[10] mother: Nature. The image of a primal, natural music recurs in Hoffmann.

[11] Bernhard Heinrich Romberg (1767–1841), celebrated cellist, composer of five symphonies, ten cello concertos, theatre works, and the *Méthode de violoncelle* (Berlin, 1840). After becoming chief Kapellmeister of the Berlin Königliche Schauspiele in 1816 he conducted the première of *Undine* on 3 August 1816.

say *see* and *hear* advisedly. The general desire not only to hear in a concert, but also to see, the pushing for seats in the hall, where this is possible, certainly does not arise merely from idle curiosity. One hears better when one sees. The secret relationship between light and sound is clearly demonstrated; both light and sound assume an individual form, and thus the soloist or singer himself becomes the sounding melody! That sounds strange, I admit; but see and hear our splendid Bernhard, then you will fully understand what I mean, and surely not accuse me of eccentric obscurantism. The total freedom of his playing and absolute mastery of his instrument obviate any struggle with the mechanical means of expression and make the instrument an immediate, unfettered organ of the spirit; this is after all the highest goal to which a practising artist aspires, and who has reached this goal more nearly than Romberg! He is in complete control of his instrument; or rather, with all its strength and grace and its rare abundance of sounds, it has become so much an extension of the artist that it seems by itself to vibrate with all the sensations of the spirit, seemingly with no expenditure of mechanical effort whatsoever.

It is not insignificant in this regard that Romberg never has music in front of him, but plays everything from memory, sitting clearly visible before the audience. You cannot imagine what a singular impression this made upon me. The sole passages of his concerto seemed like free fantasies, conceived at the moment of highest inspiration. All the wonderful figures, often flashing upward from the darkest depths to the most brilliant heights, seemed to burst forth from his elated spirit, and the notes seemed to be produced purely by the strength of his imagination, matching and following it in every nuance, before resounding from the orchestra.

This is why I say that one must not only hear this splendid musician playing, but also *see* him playing. Then one will be able even better to appreciate how high this artist stands, and how his playing bears witness to the greatest facility and absolute mastery of the means of expression. I wanted to single out this particular aspect of Romberg's playing since you already know, of course, that as required by that type of playing, Romberg possesses all the qualities one customarily extols in cellists to such a high degree that for the present at least he is unsurpassed.

Also in the concert, as was right and proper, a symphony composed by this artist was performed; it proved to me once again how the spirit of his playing also permeates his compositions. Both, his playing and his compositions, possess a quite distinctive clarity, grace, and elegance, and the symphony too, with its many melodious phrases and smooth modulations, had the most pleasurable effect. It is true that there were none of those deeper, heart-seizing impulses which Mozart's and Beethoven's symphonies give rise to, and the final movement particularly left me cold and unmoved; but there are certainly many who do not like descending into the awful abyss but prefer to remain on the sunlit surface, and they will hear in such music as this symphony far better things than those they normally consider good. The ordinary diet is enriched by some rare spices, and so the delicate stomach may gradually be strengthened.

Romberg had called the concerto he performed a *military* concerto.[12] Now you know what I think about things like that; I immediately looked for the bass drum, and sure enough, this phenomenon which for me at least is so alien to the concert-hall was duly located in a corner of the orchestra. Yet the noise was not excessive; the composer had intended only a moderate tumult, and the whole work, with its grace and cheerfulness, painted a picture of carefree, soldierly life, perhaps at summer camp, rather than of battle and slaughter. If music is to concern itself with such specific impressions, then it is quite true that more sharply defined rhythms can suggest a military quality, for quite apart from marching, they recall the more precise rhythm with which soldiers go about their lives in general.

The opening Allegro of this concerto was especially pleasing. I could not help thinking of Fouqué's tale *Die beiden Hauptleute*, and in the burning brilliance of the southern sun I saw Spanish regiments moving past with flying colours and jubilant hurrahs. You know that such images cannot appear to me unless I am genuinely aroused. So the military concerto, which I had in fact viewed with some misgiving, made such an agreeable impression on me that I was unable to enjoy to the same extent the *Rondoletto* which the artist went on to play. Although bright and attractive, it deviated into all sorts of intriguing byways. But my head was still full of the Spaniards, and their banners still fluttered before my eyes. The artist finally paid his tribute to lovers of musical curiosities by bringing forth even a pretty little bagpipe.[13]

There was also singing in the concert, and very good it was, although the pieces did not seem to me particularly well chosen. During the singing my thoughts wandered, to be honest, to something else, albeit related, to opera in fact, and I firmly resolved to pay closer attention to the posters from now on.

I then learned that Sacchini's *Oedipe à Colone* was to be given at the Schauspielhaus, and you can imagine that even urgent work could not

---

[12] This bears the opus number 31.
[13] Discovered by F.S. to be the Allegro of the *Capriccio sur des airs suédois*, later reviewed in the *AMZ* as both humorous and earthy (*Schriften zur Musik*. 493–4).

prevent me from hearing this opera. Do you still remember how we used to regard this old composer, and how we placed even Piccinni above him, not to mention Gluck?[14] We described his music then as insipid, affected, and goodness knows what else! But how I felt *now*, when after so many years I heard the opera again; so profound in its lofty, genuinely tragic expression and noble simplicity that Sacchini must in fact be ranked beside those composers! The choruses in the first act, as well as the scenes of Oedipus and Antigone, are quite splendid and achieve a striking effect. Although I missed Mme. Schick, and although the performance of Oedipus was mannered, pretentious, and contrary to the overall dramatic sense, this otherwise excellent production, to which the orchestra contributed most, aroused my innermost feelings, and its forceful sounds echoed in my mind long afterwards.

A few days later I heard Spontini's *Fernand Cortez* at the Opera House.[15] How can I convey to you the true character of this astonishing music? They say here, and well-nigh generally too, that Spontini composes in the grand, tragic style; and that he follows in Gluck's footsteps, except that his orchestration is much richer, often too rich, and his harmonic structure too contrived, particularly in its modulations.

This judgement seems to me to miss the point entirely. If one could accept that Spontini composed in a genuinely sustained *style* at all, then I would not call it grand and tragic so much as overpowering; but I must confess to feeling that one could justly censure him for lacking any sustained style, and could even claim that he possesses a manner rather than a style.

Do you not agree that true style in music proceeds from the liveliest awareness of a precisely delineated territory and its individual features? Such awareness is distinctive of the true master; with penetrating, clear-sighted vision he sees all these features and hears the sounds of love and hate, ecstasy and despair, in terms of a single native language. From deep within the artist's mind, objective, rounded forms emerge; but a vague fancy aroused merely by external stimuli flits back and forth across

---

[14] Hoffmann must have heard this opera by Antonio Sacchini (1730–86) in Berlin during his first residence there, during which time it was certainly staged. His earlier impressions are implicit in the penultimate essay in *Kreisleriana*.

[15] *Fernand Cortez*, first version, was first given at the Paris Opéra on 28 November 1809; the libretto was by Etienne de Jouy and J. A. d'Esmenard. It was reworked, again in three acts, in 1817, thereafter becoming one of Spontini's most influential works. Hoffmann may have conducted *Cortez* in 1813 (*HBW*, i, 409), and had already heard a rehearsal of it in Dresden that 'much edified' him (*HTB*, entry for 7 May 1813).

unbounded space, where multi-coloured figures, exiles from the farthest-flung spheres, mill together in a wild confusion of tongues.

It is surely when the inner spirit is enfeebled or impotent that it strives in vain to create from within itself, and to enable the *Gestalt*, as the painters say, to break free and assume independent life. Any truly objective character lies out of reach; its place is inevitably taken by a limited, subjective one, which remains always dependent; that which lacks colour is painted in a monotone, and remains colourless. This is how what we call *manner* arises; it is, I believe, nothing but an expression of the artist's stereotyped subjectivity.

Of style and manner understood in a higher sense, as the artist's inherent imaginative resources, one could assert that style engenders thoughts, whereas manner engenders whims. The former are given life by magical cross-fertilisation between the objective entities produced within the artist; the latter are motley capriccios that spring from the momentary, subjective stimulus of an individual mood, and say and signify nothing except that stimulus itself, which is incomprehensible once the moment has passed.

If true style in music consists, as I think it does, in reproducing the objective language of a particular territory in pure, unadulterated terms, then sustaining it depends primarily on inventing melody that in expressing the most varied passions and situations will in fact be and remain that language in its most distinctive character. Only the true genius solves this immense problem successfully, and again it has little to do with external, positive influences and forms, just as these can give little support and unity to the flimsy tissue if the problem has not been solved. To consider in more detail the particular territory of musical performance under discussion, namely grand, tragic opera, I need think only of Gluck, whose simplest, most artless melodies are full of a heart-piercing tragic pathos. And it is precisely in this respect that Spontini falls so far behind him; or I should say it is in this composer's inadequate or not wholly successful melodies that I find the lack of genuine style for which I have criticised him.

You will agree that I would have to point out each melody to you by reference to the score in order to prove my point fully. Since this is not possible, however, you may in the future, when you are familiar with this composer, assess the justice of my findings, which I have derived from the closest study of his music. With regard to melody, I find that Spontini replaces gravity and high tragedy by baroque incoherence, grace by Frenchified jauntiness, and simplicity by vacuity; but the melodies themselves are often woven from the most diverse elements, and so seem not to have emerged from the inner spirit already formed and fashioned, but to have been artificially fabricated according to external requirements.

Now as far as the harmonic substance of Spontini's music is concerned, it strikes me as so feeble, so stiff and rigid, that I feel the composer has no mastery of the magical realm of harmony at all. Only too clearly one sees everywhere an almost desperate straining after the most striking effect, but this is immediately negated by the effort being so visible. Spontini's transitions are almost always brutal, or rather they are not transitions at all. First a painful oscillation between tonic and dominant, then a sudden lunge into the remotest key possible, which in music is always the immediately neighbouring one.[16] The listener is restlessly tossed back and forth, and is unable to savour fully any important moment of the drama.

Who would disagree that in our wealth of instruments and their combined effects there lies a powerful, irresistible magic, and that the adornment of that glittering wealth becomes no genre of music better than that of heroic and tragic opera? It moved the immortal Gluck to enlarge the orchestra with instruments that at that time had never been heard in the theatre.[17] But this composer's music also shows that richer orchestration can be effective only when it renders more prominent the genuinely vigorous, inner harmonic structure, and when the use of various instruments according to their individual qualities proceeds from the deepest dramatic motives.

It is not, therefore, merely an increase in volume that bowls a listener over, but a more forceful unfolding of the underlying harmonic process, uninterrupted by strange leaps. Spontini, however, seems to aim merely at loudness; almost continuously we hear not only the standard complement of wind instruments, but also trombones, piccolos, drum, triangle, and cymbals, until the ears are deafened. Whenever any heightened dramatic expression is possible, every external resource is brought to bear, with the result that any climax becomes impossible.

The lack of clarity, not to say confused and confusing quality, in many passages of Spontini's music stems from its all too frequently repeated rhythmic convolutions, and also to a great extent from the strange figures, consisting of a hundred dissonant notes, with which the violins are tormented. In a large building particularly, one often hears merely a tuneless stridulation, in which the underlying harmony is lost.

---

[16] For example, C major and C sharp (D flat) major, the first with no sharps or flats, the second with seven sharps (five flats).

[17] In 'Further Observations on Spontini's Opera *Olimpia*', Hoffmann mentions trombones in the same context. In fact these were used by François-Joseph Gossec in Paris shortly before the advent of Gluck there in 1774, in Gossec's opera *Sabinus*. The music for chalumeau and cor anglais in the Vienna scores of *Orfeo* and *Alceste* was not without precedent in its demands; yet these instruments had to be cut from the scores when they were arranged for

Finally, the composer also seeks to bring forth unusual effects by choosing unusual keys, in which he writes entire movements. I do not want to call it criminal, but it is certainly misguided to place dramatic expression at risk, when proven practical experience shows that in strange keys like C sharp major, F sharp major, D flat minor etc. the wind instruments through no fault of theirs sound out of tune, and out of twenty-four violins perhaps six or eight cannot play the notes accurately.

For all these reasons it seems to me that Spontini's music is utterly devoid of inner truth, and that this is the obvious explanation why it fails to make a profound impression on the listener.

Do not think, however, unfavourable though my judgement of *Cortez* may seem to you, that I deny the composer all genius and talent; I would prefer to say that I consider him to be much better than he has hitherto shown himself. Even in *Cortez* there are frequently echoes (especially in the second act) that seem to have drifted across from some unknown region, suggesting the composer's true homeland which he disowns merely through obstinacy. Here and there (as, for example, in a trio in the second act)[18] there is a glimmer of more supple, almost Italianate vocal writing, but it is soon torn violently asunder.

Could Spontini's genius not create something quite different, which, even if it were not grand tragedy, would still be far better because it had genuinely issued from his inner feelings? Would not the spark fanned into life then also enkindle the listener's breast, as opposed to which an opera like *Cortez*, despite expending every resource to inject life and warmth, remains rigid and dead? Could the environment, the stage for which he originally wrote, not have exerted its influence on the composer?[19] This drunken sobriety, this cold ardour, this unsonorous noise, which is sadly to be found in so much modern music, had its starting point there! The rasp of trombones, dull thuds from the bass drum, incessant squeaking of the

---

Paris. For an account of the advanced texture of Gluck's orchestration, see Adam Carse, *The History of Orchestration* (London, 1925, reprinted New York, 1964), 155–60.

[18] The only writing in Act 2 of the 1809 version corresponding to this description is the short three-part 'Chœur No. 8', 'Elle craint l'amitié', sung by Amazily and a group of female chorus voices. However, there is a notable 'Trio Hymne No. 4' in Act 3, in C minor, unaccompanied, for Alvar and Spanish prisoners, praying 'avec une religieuse expression'. It begins 'Créateur de ce nouveau monde'.

[19] Hoffmann obviously refers here to the Paris Opéra, which in 1809 employed forty-nine string players (twenty-five violins), two harpists, and wind players to match. Paris was renowned as a centre of orchestral innovation; the early *Cortez* performances used, for example, two extra clarinets in F in the offstage ensemble. To approximate the effect of an offstage band in cases where one was unavailable, the score of *Fernand Cortez* (p. 394) recommends oboes and clarinets be muted with the aid of a leather bag.

piccolo, and above all, dances, dances, and more dances! What more is needed to coax them into believing? And they really do believe!

All that outer splendour and ingenious scenery can do to conceal inner poverty was done here, defying that stage of which I spoke above. You know that I am greatly fascinated by beautiful settings and tasteful costumes, and so I gladly abandoned myself to visual gratification and, wishing only for a measure of deafness, watched the colourful Mexicans and their even more colourful women gaily skipping and leaping about in their fantastic colonnades.

You will admit that such mutilated music as that of *Cortez* represents a very difficult challenge for singers and orchestra; but the precision, the very exuberance of the performance bore witness to the rare diligence with which the music had been rehearsed, and the fact that despite this a number of minor mistakes occurred was attributable not to the orchestra but entirely to difficulties unnecessarily introduced.

The singer who took on the main rôle[20] would certainly not have satisfied Spontini, in whose veins after all Italian blood flows. It cannot be denied that this woman has many natural gifts and a voice quite rich in tone; but I feel she has no clear conception at all of what singing is, or with those gifts she would strive with all her heart, with all the strength she possesses, to sing truly from the chest, and not to wail and moan with her throat constricted in what is presumably intended as expression. It is quite intolerable, especially in ensemble pieces, when the notes are constantly pulled up and down; this practice, known by the Italians as *cercar la nota*,[21] all too often degenerates into a wearisome hooting.

In contrast, the other parts were very well sung, particularly that of Cortez, and I have told you all this in so much detail, my dear friend, so that if you really come to B. as you intend, you will not neglect to make your way to the opera-house immediately *Cortez* is announced.

In many ways the production remains extremely remarkable, and it may well be extremely enjoyable too if one is still as childlike and ingenuous as a pretty young woman who sat in the stalls behind me, and who almost shouted with delight when the Mexican idol in the temple was thrown down. No doubt she saw it, following the well-known exegesis, as a clever allusion to the toppling of Napoleon's statue in Paris.

---

[20] Josephine Schulze, then only eighteen years of age [F.S.].
[21] 'A slight anticipation of the following syllable, performed as if searching for the precise note. The technique has something in common with portamento, but is not executed in as exact a manner.' William C. Holmes, in *The New Grove*, iv, 76.

Review of Mozart's *Don Giovanni*, 20 September 1815

Published: DW, 7 October 1815   *Signed:* R r
First reprinted: Zeitschrift für Musik, cvi, May 1939

During 1815 Hoffmann and his librettist la Motte Fouqué worked towards the acceptance of their *Undine* by Count Karl von Brühl, chief theatre manager (*Intendant*) of the royal Berlin opera. Since 1807 this consisted of the Nationaltheater and the Schauspielhaus companies together. As Hoffmann's letters show, things moved slowly. So when Brühl, shortly after receiving Act 1 of *Undine* in fair copy, requested Hoffmann to take over the opera reviews in the *Dramaturgisches Wochenblatt*, the latter had little choice. He submitted five during September 1815, of which this one was the fourth and longest, and four the next summer, including *Ariodant*, reproduced next. (The others are listed in the Appendix.) True to form, Hoffmann opened with a general question: the distortion of *Don Giovanni* in Germany, where it was produced in the vernacular in a variety of translations, but all with spoken dialogue. Not until 1845 was German text fitted to Mozart's sung recitatives; but in any case the opera easily fell prey to local and vulgar traditions, added episodes, obscene extemporisation by actors, and (see below) modifications of the ending.[1]

The Berlin performance employed the following, named by Hoffmann. Joseph Fischer (1780–1862), later the victim of 'Some Observations' (p. 408); Auguste Schmalz (1771–1848); Josephine Schulze (1796–1880), later an unrealised choice for Bertalda's rôle in *Undine*; Johanna Eunike (1798–1856), who created the rôle of Undine for Hoffmann; Carl Wilhelm Unzelmann (1753–1832); Friedrich Eunike (1764–1844), father of Johanna; Carl Wauer (1783–1857), the first Kühleborn in *Undine*; and Heinrich Blume (1788–1856).

When a new work reaches the stage, and one sees that all the effects intended by the author or, in the case of an opera, by the composer are carefully observed, and that the whole setting is devised with intelligence and thought, then it deserves the keenest public gratitude. But when an earlier masterpiece, long treated like a stepchild and made to wear the favourite's cast-offs, appears newly apparelled with love and care, then it shows that the management is aiming at a level much higher than usual, and that it is fully justified to expect from them all that befits true art.

This is the case with our present management, which has brought *Don Giovanni* to the stage in a new production that accords with the opera's profoundest meaning.

---

[1] All these are discussed in Julian Rushton, *W. A. Mozart. 'Don Giovanni'* (Cambridge, 1981), chapter 5.

Because of the very difficulty of this opera of all operas, whose poetic depths many spectators will appreciate only at odd moments, it has not hitherto been given the fully rounded interpretation one would wish for. It is an eternal truth that a poetic work proceeding from the innermost soul cannot be tampered with. Each of the wonderful sounds in *Don Giovanni* is mysteriously subsumed into the whole, like rays of light refracted into a single focus. So it is that *Don Giovanni* will always appear mangled and mutilated if it is not given according to the original score, i.e. with recitatives. The reviewer is well aware that this presents seemingly insuperable obstacles, but may he be permitted to suggest as a compromise that at least the main scenes, so far as they form a consecutive group, should proceed in recitatives.

He selects as examples just two such scenes, the first scene from the first act and the scene with Don Giovanni and Leporello beside the statue.[2] The first must not be interrupted by spoken dialogue until the stage changes after the duet. In the second, the two speeches from the statue produce an effect of profound horror only when Don Giovanni in his recitative first sings the note on which the dreadful warnings from the spirit-world are heard.[3]

This also provides the obvious practical advantage that the Commendatore can take up Don Giovanni's note, thus making his otherwise difficult entry quite easy.

It would be a simple matter to substitute German words for the Italian, and to rearrange the recitatives accompanied only by continuo bass for strings, if one feared that they would otherwise sound too empty. If they

[2] scene . . . beside the statue: Act 2 sc. 12, 'An enclosed churchyard with several equestrian statues, including that of the Commendatore. Moonlight.'

[3] These examples occur in Mozart in the reverse order, though in close proximity. Don Giovanni, in sung recitative, has just told of his latest attempted seduction, and laughs loudly after a joke. The Statue's voice is heard (second example), accompanied solemnly by wind instruments and string bass: 'Your laughter will be silenced before morning.' When Giovanni looks for the source of the voice, striking monuments with his sword, it utters again (first example): 'Impudent scoundrel!' (etc.)

were also sung in the manner in which Herr Fischer performs recitative, this scene would considerably gain in vitality.

Herr Fischer sings Don Giovanni throughout not only with all his characteristic virtuosity, but also in the precise character that Mozart has created. His delivery of the aria 'Treibt der Champagner',[4] apparently so light-hearted and yet portraying Don Giovanni's innermost nature so vividly, is quite unsurpassable. The verity of expression seizes one irresistibly, and thus could not fail to produce the loudest applause. Following calls of 'Da capo', Herr F. repeated the aria not only with Italian words but also with Italian spirit and fire.

Mlle. Schmalz performed excellently in the principal pieces, particularly the great scene in the first act, with its wildly headlong aria in D major,[5] which she embellished richly though within the spirit of the composition.

Indeed the music of *Don Giovanni* not only bears embellishment but here and there expressly requires it. It is self-evident, however, that such embellishment absolutely must proceed from the inner character of the composition, and that no arbitrary flourish or any figure occasioned merely by momentary fashion may be inserted. In order to embellish properly any vocal piece possessing character, one must thoroughly assimilate the composer's intention and then harness the artistic resources necessary to achieve it. Mlle. Schmalz embellished the aria, as has been stated, most appropriately.

What would the musically absorbed listener say, for example, if in the first duet[6] on the word

a singer saw fit to insert an endless cadenza running up and down from one blind alley to another, resolving on the tonic (B flat major), and then leaving Don Ottavio, who takes up Donna Anna's challenge merely with the words 'Io giuro', likewise resolving on the tonic, to stumble lamely after her? The

---

[4] Act 1 no. 11, 'Fin ch'han dal vino', in which he orders a feast and anticipates the wild enjoyment to come.

[5] Act 1 no. 10, 'Or sai chi l'onore', in which Donna Anna asks Ottavio to avenge her father's death. This is one of the arias 'Miss Amalie' sang in *Kreisleriana*, I–1, p. 86.

[6] Act 1 no. 2, duet for Donna Anna and Don Ottavio, 'Fuggi, crudele, fuggi', in which she first rejects Ottavio and, at a climactic later moment (see music example) makes him swear he will avenge the Commendatore.

reviewer has illustrated this bar in order to demonstrate how wisely the composer placed the dominant seventh chord as an earnest of that challenge, and he need hardly point out further that this very transition from the dominant seventh to the tonic heightens the dramatic force to the utmost effect.

Madame Schulze's full, steely voice was heard to great advantage in the rôle of Elvira, and she deserves particular gratitude for singing the aria in D major, 3/4 time,[7] which is of such splendid dramatic effect in its allotted place but is left out by the common generality of singers because it is said to be ungrateful, to use the favourite theatrical expression, but more likely because they cannot accommodate themselves to its style and syncopated rhythms.

Madame Eunicke is the Zerlina of all Zerlinas. It is simply not possible in either singing or acting to perform this rôle with greater vivacity, freshness, and charm, with more mischievous humour and irony (particularly in the scenes with Masetto), and in short with a profounder grasp of the composer's intention.

In the absence of Herr Gern, Herr Unzelmann took over the part of Leporello, and for that reason it cannot be regarded as his fault that he completely lacks the physical resources to carry off a rôle in which singing is so important. Herr Unzelmann's singing in the ensemble items was not only a nullity that would have been painful enough already, but with reckless naivety he also threw in some strange and highly audible notes that one would seek in vain in the score. His acting on the other hand was very amusing, although acting alone is not sufficient in this opera, since Mozart's music is of the kind where any part not performed with the security and strength demanded by the composer is most sorely missed. Herr U. has so much less reason to appear in operas when in plays he is able so often to put us into the warmest good humour and the most agreeable temper – truly the highest achievement of the comedian.

The Ottavio is one of Herr Eunicke's finest rôles and Herr Wauer likewise performed the part of Masetto extremely well in both singing and acting.

The very difficult scene in the finale of the second act was carried off superbly by Herr Blume. Apart from a single movement of the arm, when it grasps Don Giovanni's hand, the statue must not move at all; any declamatory raising and lowering of the arm after Don Giovanni has torn himself free would spoil the effect. Not even the head may move. The statue's coat

---

[7] Act 1 no. 8, 'Ah, fuggi il traditor'.

should look more as though hewn from stone, just as real feathers must not be seen to flutter on its helmet.

Of the stage settings, the arrangement of the dance in the finale of the first act is particularly praiseworthy; it could not be more intelligently fitted to the spirit of the whole, except that the chorus should not stand there so lifelessly in the closing Allegro.

The Gothic hall in the finale of the second act and Don Giovanni's table make a splendid effect. It is very unfortunate, however, that two intrepid servants remain standing not far from the statue and, their exceptional imperturbability truly putting to shame even Don Giovanni, who is impudent to the point of sacrilegious insolence, calmly get on with clearing the table as though a friendly neighbour had just walked in.

This time Don Giovanni had invited a good friend who had also brought a lady; thus the table was fully occupied, and with guests who were gracious in person and dress. Nothing appears more utterly opposed to Don Giovanni's character than to see him, as usually portrayed, sitting at table alone and bored and playing jokes on his servant. For this reason too the present production here cannot be praised too highly.

With regard to the concluding ballet the reviewer refers to his remarks above about the *faithful* interpretation of a masterpiece, although he willingly concedes that other more pressing theatrical considerations fully justify the addition of this ballet with music by another composer (Vogler). Let Minos[8] then finally pronounce judgement upon Don Giovanni, and let him accordingly be handed over by the demons for consumption by the hellish bow-wow.

Review of Méhul's *Ariodant*, 1 June 1816

Published: DW, 22 June 1816   *Signed:* Bl
First reprinted: Königsberger Hartungsche Zeitung, 28 October 1928

In spite of sets by Carl Friedrich Schinkel, this important Berlin première was unsuccessful and appears to have been the only performance. The cast included Josephine Schulze (Ina), Heinrich Stümer (Ariodant), Joseph Fischer (Othon), and Jonas Beschort (Edgard).

---

[8] We do not know the subject of the final ballet, but (see next review) can assume it was a classical subject involving Minos, king of Crete; Hoffmann cannot resist a facetious conclusion.

Ariodant, in three acts, was an outstanding product of opéra-comique, and a crucial work in Méhul's career. It was first seen at the Opéra-Comique, Paris, on 11 October 1799. The printed full score, to which Hoffmann obviously had access, contains a dedication to Cherubini, and a short essay entitled 'Quelques réflexions'. The librettist was François Benoît Hoffman (1760–1828), a seasoned dramatist, librettist, and critic.

Hoffmann's review contains a double purpose, because instead of reviewing the Berlin version as it stood he gallantly sought to convey an idea of the opera's unadulterated form. The German translation was by Joseph von Seyfried, but the musical reworking has remained anonymous; perhaps it was by Carl Herklots, who translated Méhul's *Stratonice* for its Berlin performance the previous year. The following summary will help to elucidate Hoffmann's comments.

Act 1: The action takes place at the castle of the Scottish king Edgard. The knight Othon, in love with Edgard's daughter Ina, has come to claim her in marriage. However, Ina's deeper affections lie with the courtier Ariodant. Othon is seized with passionate jealousy and anger, and he forces Ina's lady-in-waiting Dalinde to assist him in his vengeance. Act 2: Following nocturnal festivities, Othon arranges for Dalinde to dress in her mistress's clothes and receive him, in front of witnesses, into Ina's bedroom. Under the law this is enough to condemn Ina to execution. Act 3: Ariodant rescues Dalinde from her would-be murderers (paid by Othon) and the plot against Ina is revealed. Othon will be caught before he can flee the castle, and all ends happily.

The almost insurmountable difficulty of transplanting French opera successfully to the German stage, i.e. opera composed expressly for French singers, has probably never been more clearly demonstrated than in *Ariodant*. How limited is the composer who has at his disposal only tenors and earthbound sopranos who now and again screech up into the heights, as is the case with French opera. If composers as profound as Cherubini, or as learned and versatile as Méhul, could write for German singers, their distribution of voices would be made quite differently.

In *Ariodant* there is not a single true bass to be found among the solo parts, and for this reason Herr Fischer had to take the rôle of the Irish prince Othon, which is actually written for a high tenor (for the most part in the alto clef, after the French manner).[1] This Sieur Othon is the villain, the tyrant in the opera, but by perpetrating his evil deeds in a lyrical tenor voice he clearly sins against the old rule of our good friend Bottom, who says: 'This is Ercles' vein, a tyrant's vein; a lover is more condoling.'[2] Since Herr

---

[1] Actually Othon's part hardly exceeds g′, and requires vocal power well below middle c′: it is not a high part in the modern sense. The French tendency to cultivate mixed-range voices was mentioned also in the review of Boieldieu's *Le Nouveau Seigneur de village*, p. 385.

[2] *A Midsummer Night's Dream*, Act 1 sc. 2. Hoffmann quotes the same play satirically in *Kreisleriana*, at the end of I–6.

Fischer found it impossible to sing things that lay so far beyond his range, the unfortunate result was that major omissions had to be made, especially in the first act, of which only a miserable fragment could be given.

A splendid and deeply affecting G major Adagio[3] in 3/4 time begins with three obbligato cellos, and ends on the dominant seventh,

the curtain having risen seven bars previously. Then without any main Allegro (who composed the music performed here?) there follows a short [spoken] monologue by Othon, after which the orchestra enters *fortissimo* and Othon starts his recitative.

The reviewer believes that this opening must have the utmost effect, and quotes it here for the benefit of the musical reader.

After Othon's G minor aria,[4] frequently marked by accented F sharps and Gs, Dalinde appears and, after a very short dialogue, sings an aria. This is followed, after another brief dialogue, by a highly passionate, beautifully worked-out duet in E minor between Dalinde and Othon.[5]

Were it not too much for a journal not exclusively devoted to music, the reviewer would reproduce the theme as well as the section immediately following, with its basses and violins accompanying in close imitation. Let it suffice for him to assert that this movement is one of the most expressive and

---

[3] *D W* has 'Andante'.

[4] Aria 'Infortuné'.

[5] Duet 'O démon de la jalousie'.

dramatic of the whole opera. One should particularly notice the inspired stroke of the composer in being able to associate these three movements by using the first two bars of the example shown above. These bars serve as a short ritornello both to Dalinde's aria and to the duet, merely by changing the key. In a highly effective opening sequence Othon furiously cries 'Ariodant!', the movement commences [after the recurrent motif above] with the violins and violas alone, which are then imitated by a cello, and only when a few more words have been spoken does Othon begin the duet proper.

After this duet Dalinde leaves the stage. Othon delivers a short monologue, then Edgard appears and after a short dialogue sings a gently sustained aria accurately characterising the worthy king and father.[6] Edgard goes off and Othon remains alone, but soon Dalinde returns. Then, after they have both left, Ariodant appears, who brought us the first music after the overture.[7]

Instead of a succession of separate and mostly very substantial movements, we were greeted by the icy water of boring, inferior prose passages, so that any spark that the overture might have generated in us was soon extinguished. Even the splendidly fiery finale with the powerful and original closing chorus 'O kommt als Königin der Feste'[8] could not rekindle our spirits. The structure of the opening bars of this chorus bears witness to the composer's genius.

The second act begins with an eight-part, or rather a double chorus, which here was preceded by a dance and the Bard's Romance, also sung by a

---

[6] Aria 'D'un hymen'.

[7] Thus in Berlin, apparently, Ariodant's 'Plus de doute' followed the overture; in other words sixty pages of full score had been deleted.

[8] Chorus 'Venez, embellissez nos fêtes.'

tenor.[9] The dancing and singing make a lively effect, especially straight after the rise of the curtain. The members of the chorus stand stiffly and self-consciously behind the dancers and begin to stir only when they are permitted to sing. The Romance is accompanied by an obbligato harp, which the quite different sound and effect of the piano cannot in the least replace.[10]

Having referred to the most important changes individually, the reviewer must further point out that in several places a passage of music was inserted in place of a spoken episode or a melodrama; this divided the opera into proportions bearing no relation to each other.[11] At the beginning and end, long passages of prose hemmed in almost uninterrupted music, instead of the reverse, which would have been no detriment at all. An opera dismembered by speech is an absurdity to be sure, tolerated only out of habit. We expect to find ourselves in the higher realm of poetry, in which the language is music, and yet are flung back to earth at every moment.

The development of so-called operetta[12] introduced the ingenious idea of completely separating the music from the action, by conducting the latter entirely in prose and bringing it to a halt whenever the music starts. The arias not only depicted an inner state of mind, like the monologue, but contained the further elucidation of an aphorism or, following the elegant but cold Metastasio's example, an allegory ('Come una tortorella etc.')[13] or, as in a hundred German operettas:

Young lady: Oh how beautiful it is to live in the country. The croaking of the frogs, the cackling of the hens and geese, seem to me like music sweeter than any I can hear in the stuffy city opera-house.
Aria: Delightful are the joys, etc.

In order to remedy this ill to some extent finales were invented, and Dittersdorf, who does not deserve to be entirely forgotten, showed how

---

[9] In the full score the first double chorus is situated between the dancing and the once-famous Bardic Romance, 'Femme sensible'.
[10] Songs of the time, including 'Femme sensible', were sometimes published with accompaniment 'for harp or pianoforte'.
[11] melodrama: spoken declamation either alternating with instrumental music or superimposed on it. This technique was used in opera, including *Fidelio*, for particular effects.
[12] i.e. Singspiel, or opéra-comique.
[13] This example of a simile is not by Metastasio; Hoffmann re-uses his example from *The Poet and the Composer*. See p. 205 and note 68.

music can very often assist the action.[14] Méhul, and before him Cherubini, made use of melodrama at moments of emotion, to produce a climax by progressing from speaking to singing. How successful this idea was is strikingly shown, for example, by the scene in *Les deux journées* when Constanze stands before the tree in which Armand is hiding.[15] One thinks of the single note played softly by the violins with which the melodrama begins.

In *Ariodant* the prose is quite clearly intended to be connected as much as possible to the singing. The numerous interpolations of melodrama are designed to bring this about. In addition, however, the composer (as Cherubini often does) has employed the unusual device of not giving the movements a satisfying conclusion, or of immediately modulating into another key related to the next music, which follows after a short intervening dialogue.[16]

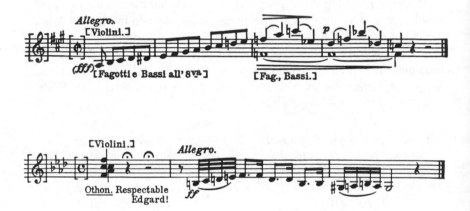

[14] Hoffmann had clearly somewhat revised his view of Dittersdorf, expressed in 1813 in *The Poet and the Composer*. At that time Dittersdorf's comic operas *Doctor und Apotheker* (Berlin 1787), *Betrug durch Aberglauben* (Berlin 1789), and *Hieronymus Knicker* (Berlin 1792) still received occasional performances in the Berlin repertory, while *Liebe im Narrenhaus* (Berlin 1791) and *Das rothe Käppchen* (Berlin 1791) had last been given in 1801 and 1807 respectively [F.S.].

[15] Cherubini, *Les deux journées ou Le Porteur d'eau* (*The Water-carrier*) (1800) was first staged in Berlin on 15 March 1802 in H. G. Schmieder's translation as *Der Wasserträger* and remained permanently in the repertory there. In May 1804 Hoffmann saw the opera in Warsaw. During his period in Bamberg performances took place at least six times, 1809–12. He conducted the opera seven or eight times in Dresden and Leipzig, 1813–14 [F.S.].

[16] First example: Act 2 sc. 2, end of Ina–Ariodant duet. Second example: Act 3 sc. 1, end of Edgard's aria. The technique had been tried out earlier by Grétry in *L'Amant jaloux* (1778), Act 3.

The reviewer feels he has adequately shown that Méhul, like every great composer, conceived and brought forth his work as a totality, so that any change inevitably destroys the inner structure, even though it may appear to be an improvement. In fact alteration or revision of any work is extremely dangerous and harmful. All composers, even those of lesser rank, see their works as complete and embody in them ideals which they endeavour to realise through the means at their disposal. It is remarkable that the composer himself is so often unable to make successful changes and revisions in his work, especially when he tries to tailor it to a particular requirement. His free-soaring genius has its wings clipped and is restrained by the shackles of convention. If this happens in the case of his own works, then how much more must it apply to those of others, which defeat the efforts even of great composers. Such failures have frequently occurred in recent times, since it is considered more convenient to lop off the giant's head than to enlarge the building in which he vainly tries to walk upright.

It is this total recasting of the opera *Ariodant* which, in the reviewer's opinion, explains why the public remained quite cool and even complained of boredom. In all other respects everything possible was done for the production, and none of the actors and singers can be accused of even the slightest negligence. Herr Fischer, as has already been mentioned, had a part in which he was quite unable to acquit himself as a singer. The fact that he nevertheless acted and sang with passion and dedication, particularly in the last duet,[17] showed that like every true artist he seeks honour not in constant applause but in portraying his allotted rôle as the overall effect dictates.[18] Madame Schulze and Herr Stümer also deserve all the more praise, since the public's coolness had not the least effect on them.

The costumes were excellent, and the settings, executed after drawings by Herr Schinkel, once again demonstrated the genius of that splendid artist. The final Gothic hall, particularly, with its opulent and fantastic decorations, created the most impressive effect. The reviewer could not feast his eyes on it enough; Dalinde's trial for her life could have lasted even longer.

The subject-matter of the opera, however, is simply too slight, and the question may well be posed, therefore, whether the opera would have been more effective even if it had remained faithful to the original. It is clear that the spirit of music cannot animate a totally inert substance; on the other

[17] Duet 'Eh bien, allez.'
[18] Hoffmann still hoped to retain Fischer for the 'ungrateful' rôle of Kühleborn in his *Undine* (3 August 1816). The phrase 'not in constant applause', in view of the following essay, 'Some Observations', must be taken with a large pinch of salt.

hand the *caput mortuum* precipitated from the words vanishes in the radiance of the musical sounds.[19]

Ariodant is one of the most consistent in style of Méhul's operas, serious, dignified, harmonically rich, and thoughtfully fashioned. Such an opera, which could provide real pleasure to every true connoisseur and which has had so much effort and money spent on its production, should not disappear from the stage. The reviewer feels that it would be worth the attempt to repeat *Ariodant* in a form that was faithful to the original, perhaps differently cast here and there. He has therefore given a detailed account of what has been omitted and changed, so that the musical specialist who is unacquainted with the musical score might be made aware of the intrinsic musical qualities of the opera.

After the opera came the ballet *Die Olympischen Spiele*, but the reviewer would have to forgo any judgement of it, even if, as was not the case, he had seen it, since he has not even the smallest understanding of dancing and pantomime. Let competent critics express their opinion of this ballet.[20]

'Some Observations on the Comments made by the Royal Chamber Singer Herr Fischer in No. 32 of the *Gesellschafter*, Concerning the Artist's Relationship to the Public'

Published: Der Freimüthige, xv, 2 March 1818   *Signed:* B.
First reprinted: von Maassen (ed.), *Hoffmanns Sämtliche Werke*, iv

In January 1816 Hoffmann sent the revised second and third acts of *Undine* to Count von Brühl, who thereafter set the wheels in motion for its production; the successful

---

[19] *Caput mortuum*: 'Residuum remaining after the distillation or sublimation of any substance' (*OED*). Hoffmann seems to mean that after the 'reaction' between music and words has taken place, which ought to be a perfect process, there can remain, as here hypothesised, a dead residuum. But even this is transformed by the irradiation of the music. The chemical metaphor extends back to the word 'spirit', which is also understood as 'spirituosity' or even 'alcoholic quality' [ed. and transl.].

[20] The playbill states: 'After that, for the first time: *Die Olympischen Spiele* (*The Olympic Games*). Pantomimic Divertissement by Herr Anatole. In which Herr Anatole and Madame Anatole-Gosselin, first dancer at the Royal [Academy] of Music in Paris will dance a *pas de deux* which they had the honour of performing on the occasion of the first appearance at the Grand Opera in Paris of His Majesty the King', i.e. the restored Louis XVIII [F.S.].

première was on 3 August of that year. Joseph Fischer was Hoffmann's first choice for Kühleborn's rôle, and at first agreed to take it on; but by 29 May Brühl reported to Hoffmann: 'Herr Fischer . . . still urgently wants to be informed about some vocal pieces in which he could bring to bear not simply his talent for musical declamation, but also for artistic singing. This is the usual weakness of this singer, whose vanity is revealed everywhere . . .' Having agreed to write another scene, 'in which Kühleborn stops his frightening ghostly music and becomes a friendly singer', Hoffmann automatically compromised the opera, for 'the unity of character I was specifically aiming at will be interrupted' (letter of 1 June). But Fischer withdrew even so.

A number of revenge attacks followed (of which the present article is one) that led to Fischer's Berlin career coming to an end.[1]

Fischer's original article contains the following sentences relevant to the response it was to provoke:

> Posterity weaves no wreath for the actor; he addresses himself only to the moment at which he performs; how deeply hurtful, I would even say humiliating, is the feeling that must possess him in the face of the coolness, so numbing and arresting every upward impulse, with which artistic achievements are greeted here . . . Loud applause is essential to the artist; it lifts him up, fires him, inspires him. Indeed he may *demand* it as acknowledgement of the respect he pays the public by his performance, as a receipt for what they have heard, as it were, after an important scene or aria, for example . . . The sensitive artist expects this applause, and if he does not get it – for whatever reasons it may be – he goes elsewhere if he can . . . What esteem, on the other hand, the artist enjoys in France, England, Italy, even in Vienna, Munich, etc. . . .; here [in Berlin] when a foreign visitor . . ., overcome by his emotions, permits himself a spontaneous murmur of approval, a sibilant hissing is usually heard which has an ice-cold effect on the actor and transports him from Rome, Athens, or wherever his inspiration had carried him, rapidly back to reality. There even seems to be a sort of etiquette applied here; for example, *never* applaud a recitative or individual solo scene, and *rarely* an ensemble scene . . . The effect that a singer who is also an actor might hope for from a recitative is also negated by the fidgety use of libretto-booklets, which so distract attention from the performer that characterisation and acting become almost superfluous, not to mention the irritating noise of pages

---

[1] See Hewett-Thayer, *Hoffmann*, 89–90. In February, March, and May 1817 Hoffmann published coded attacks on Fischer in the *DW* in part of 'Die Kunstverwandten', the preliminary version of *Seltsame Leiden eines Theater-Direktors* (1819). Circumstantial proof of Hoffmann's authorship of the present article exists in the anonymous contribution to *Bemerker* no. 3, supplement to issue 44 of the *Gesellschafter* dated 18 March 1818: 'The author of the second outburst in the *Freimüthige* has clearly not forgotten that Herr Fischer turned down the rôle of Kühleborn in *Undine*.' The complete text is in Schnapp (ed.), *Hoffmann. Ein Dokumentenband*, 499.

being turned in unison which fills the air like the crashing of waves . . . One could almost assert that seldom or never is loud applause elicited here purely by the artist's power over his listener's spirits; personal attitudes from middle-class life have a great influence in it. How often have I myself heard deliberations and debates about it in the stalls: 'Shall we applaud *him*?' – 'Heaven forbid, I can't stand him!' Or, 'Listen, we must get *him* to take a bow today, he's a terrific fellow!' – 'What! He's arrogant enough already!' and suchlike. Many more instances could be adduced to bring it home to the assembled multitude that the artist who devotes his whole life to providing them with pleasure and enjoyment, . . . that this artist feels himself entitled to demand similar respect and attention . . . But I will conclude this essay which, flowing as it does from my innermost feelings, may seem to some perhaps too long, with the master's famous words: 'The public is the artist's mistress!' Will the most ardent love not eventually cool, however, when bestowed upon a coy or even coquettish beauty who greets profound emotion with indifference or mocking jibes?[2]

It is interesting to compare some of Fischer's comments with the 'type of fault-finding' mentality criticised by Hoffmann in his 'Letters on Music in Berlin' three years before, p. 389.

How splendid and how gratifying it is, when a great artist is not above instructing his public himself as to how they have to behave towards him and receive his performances. Herr F. has bravely set about this somewhat distasteful task and for doing so deserves the warmest gratitude from all true friends of art. Yet how often the weightiest of words, hardly have they been uttered, are seized by stormy gusts and scattered like chaff! How often the rising wave envelops the boldly venturing mariner! May it therefore not seem a vain exercise briefly to repeat Herr F.'s admonitions, whereby various erroneous opinions that were previously held might be utterly discredited, and most earnestly to remind the public of the duties it has wickedly neglected with respect to Herr F.

Many people, and even the present writer, as he must confess with deep shame, were previously under the impression that a true actor should be thoroughly immersed in the work being performed, that his inspiration should radiate from within him, and that only this produces dramatic fire and truth, by conjuring forth the ideal world in which he lives and moves in brilliantly shining colours. How unsophisticated! The only thing that lifts up, fires and inspires the poor actor for whom posterity weaves no wreath (the names of Garrick, Ekhof, Schröder,[3] etc. were forgotten long ago), and

---

[2] Original text reproduced by F.S. in *Schriften zur Musik*, 511–13.

[3] David Garrick (1717–79); Konrad Ekhof (1720–78), 'father of German acting'; Friedrich Ludwig Schröder (1744–1816), famous actor and director in Vienna and Hamburg.

who addresses himself only to the moment, is *loud* applause from the public, and this he may *demand*. The actor displays respect for the public merely by appearing at all, and they must thank him for it. (Contractual obligation – a salary approaching that of the highest civil servants – such petty details are clearly irrelevant here.)[4] So *loud* applause must be accorded:

1) when the actor appears, in gratitude for his appearance, for the memory of his last performance, and to show that the same high standard is hoped for today;
2) after every aria, principal scene etc., as a receipt for what has been heard;
3) after every high point within a recitative, aria, ensemble, etc.

No member of the audience who stupidly forgets his higher responsibilities towards the actor and wishes to hear the music without disturbing interruptions may show this by hissing when applause breaks out; and even less may he turn the pages of his libretto-booklet, since it produces a noise like the crashing of waves. Both of these sounds have an ice-cold effect on the actor and transport him from Rome, Athens or wherever his inspiration had carried him (thanks to loud applause) rapidly back to reality. Admittedly it is in the latter dimension that clapping also takes place, but that is different.

Who would be so malicious as to liken the actor whose art is sustained by loud applause to a tightrope-walker, who the more he is clapped the higher he jumps?

Herr F. complains that the public here is so barbarous and cold as completely to neglect the deserving actor, and this with obvious reference to himself; it is odd then that at the same time he implies that when he was greeted with loud applause on his first appearance after completing a tour, he did not wish to express his *thanks*, but had something quite different in mind.

One can hardly believe that such an actor as Herr F., with his incomparable talent and scintillating genius, would not reap the loudest applause every time he appeared. A man who, with these qualities, which he possesses in exceptional measure, combines the most charming modesty and the most benign geniality! Who has even the slightest knowledge of theatrical affairs and does not know that Herr F., concerned solely with the art of giving pleasure to the public, will cheerfully undertake any rôle, however unsuited it may be to displaying the full range of his enormous talent? Was this not the case just recently with *Tancredi*,[5] a rôle which was so

---

4 Fischer's 1817 contract specified 250 thaler a month, plus 1000 thaler annual private allowance, plus two months a year allowed for guest appearances elsewhere. 4000 thaler was worth perhaps £600 at the time in England [F.S., rev.].

5 Rossini, *Tancredi*; his first important opera seria (1813), written for a female contralto in the title rôle; first Berlin performance 5 January 1818.

utterly incompatible with the voice and the whole temperament of this superb actor that he must have foreseen its unfavourable outcome, particularly in view of the universally condemned shallowness and insignificance of the entire opera? Does not Herr F. often remain purposely in the background in order to allow lesser talents to shine? Does he not sacrifice himself? Weighed down by countless rôles and perpetually treading the boards, does he not devote his whole existence to providing the assembled multitude with enjoyment and pleasure?

It would indeed be the most outrageous injustice to neglect such a great actor as Herr F. That would make the public here a sad exception from all the others, who always maintain a keen regard for truly great talent.

Only one circumstance comes to mind in which a genius might not be recognised, and might even be ostracised to some extent: that is when an actor of great talent, consumed by the demon of artistic vanity, caring nothing for the work, rôle, situation, fellow actors, or anything around him, and considering himself and his own personality as the focal point at which every strand converges or diverges, tries to thrust himself forward at every opportunity with petulant arrogance and to lecture the public with resentful expostulations! Nay, his great talent would then serve only to increase the profound dismay in the breast of every listener who sees, not the work of art that he was expecting to enjoy, but a conceited histrion performing his somersaults. Such a talent would be like a superb old-master painting which a mischievous boy has daubed over with hideously bright colours. But where is such a caricature of an actor to be found who, even if his great talent never ceased to be respected, would still not rely upon the sincere applause that flows from the heart, and at some point would not feel a surge of long-suppressed revulsion at his own overweening insolence!

Yes! As already stated, it would be the most outrageous injustice if the incomparably huge talent of Herr F., the greatest actor of our time, were not appreciated in full measure. But this deficiency occurs only to the extent to which the applause he receives falls short of the level expected; until now it has clearly been inadequate, and it is very right and proper that Herr F. has now indicated what the correct amount should be. May it be permitted, however, also to say something on behalf of our poor, uneducated public.

Herr F. is an exceptional man, and is the first truly *great* actor and singer who has trodden our stage (the likes of Marchetti, Schick, Bethmann, Fleck, Iffland,[6] etc. cannot be regarded as great talents); so it is because of

---

[6] Maria Marchetti-Fantozzi (1767 to after 1812), formerly leading soprano at the Berlin Italian opera; Margarethe Schick (1768–1809), already eulogised in Hoffmann's 'Letters on Music in Berlin'; Friederike Bethmann (1766–1815), celebrated actress and singer in Berlin; Ferdinand Fleck (1757–1801); August Wilhelm Iffland (1759–1814), perhaps the

our childish awkwardness, arising from lack of experience, that we do not know how to treat Herr F. in the manner to which he is accustomed. If Frederick the Second, also an exceptional man, were suddenly to appear at a gathering of honest burghers, would one expect them to behave in a manner comparable with court ceremony – however much trepidation, awe, or reverence they felt? May it be hoped, therefore, that Herr F. will attribute it only to this circumstance and not to ill will if we seem to offend him, and that he will take a kindly interest in our improvement. The vulgar remarks which Herr F. says he heard from the public ('Shall we applaud *him*', etc.) must have been the cause of the slight mistake which seems to be worrying him.

It is a very similar one to that made by the former Turkish ambassador here, Achmet Effendi. One evening many years ago there spread through the theatre a fragrant haze of Turkish tobacco. It was soon noticed that the good Achmet was sitting in his box contentedly puffing at his long pipe. Now the man was a distinguished Turkish guest, and since he was also quite a comical sight with his short, fat figure, his huge turban, and his protruding eyes, police and public were happy to tolerate this brazen exception to the rule. Soon after that, however, some people in the parterre felt the unmistakable effect of a shower-bath and, on looking up, realised that the good Achmet was spitting on their heads. There were shouts, there were curses! This time the police went up to the Turk and put it to him that although they were willing to overlook his smoking, spitting was right out of the question. Whereupon Achmet Effendi stretched out his arm, pointed down to the parterre and, surveying the police with an expression of earnest solemnity, said 'Peasants!' The good man thought that those below were merely common people, their heads to be regarded merely as cabbage heads, and the whole place a spittoon for his convenience. We all make mistakes!

What are we to do then? Grovel abjectly in the dust and plead: 'Good F., most excellent of actors, forgive us our sins; but do not think we are all tanners with palms like leather, O noble soul! Many of us merely wield the pen rather than the scraping-iron or sledge-hammer and could easily clap our hands raw. Permit us, O magnanimous one, to divide into gangs, so that in the manner of a well-drilled firing-party we can provide you with continuous clapping, O beloved actor! If this you cannot do, then we must bid you a fond farewell! Fly! Fly from our barbarian land!' May Herr F. kindly accept a well-intentioned word of advice from the innermost heart of

most famous actor and director of his time in Germany, and latterly chief director of the Berlin Nationaltheater.

one of his warmest supporters, not to go about it in the wrong way if he wishes to educate us or others, or else the rod will very easily turn against the schoolmaster himself. Because of the calls of *da capo* which he found so irritating, Herr F. wanted to put into practice in the evening what he had advocated in the morning, and in doing so ran into all sorts of odious misfortunes.

Finally it must be noted that Herr F. has demonstrated in his essay not only that he has a fine command of language but also that he is a skilled and cultivated stylist. All the more to be denounced, therefore, is the impudence of the person to whom Herr F., perhaps under the pressure of leaving for a tour, assigned the task of inserting an address of thanks to the public in the *Hamburger Correspondent*, and who composed the following rigmarole, which was printed in No. 185, 19 November 1817, of that journal:

> While not wishing to neglect to offer an esteemed public my most heart-felt gratitude for the flattering reception they have given me here as sincerely and unambiguously as I have ever been able in a case where my own sense of performance is so difficult to objectify, the recollection I carry of my recent sojourn here will nourish the dearest of my desires, should I perhaps return, to be gratified once more by a continuation of the good fortune I have enjoyed.
>
> 18 November 1817
>
> > J. Fischer
> > Royal Prussian Chamber Singer[7]

Anyone who may have concluded from this article that the worthy actor F. does not know how to handle a pen properly will now recognise with real pleasure that this newspaper announcement was not written by him, and must perceive how the great F. is as accomplished in his literary refinement as he is in his art.

'A Letter from Kapellmeister Johannes Kreisler (Contributed by E. T. A. Hoffmann)'

Published: Der Freimüthige, xvi, 29 and 30 April 1819
First reprinted: Ausgewählte Schriften, ed. Z. Funck [C. F. Kunz, *pseud.*] (Stuttgart, 1839)

Hoffmann's creative work resulted in, among other things, the first volume of *Die

---

[7] *Staats- und Gelehrte Zeitung des Hamburgischen unpartheyischen Correspondenten*, 185, 19 November 1817 [F.S.].

Serapions-Brüder at Easter 1819; and, as the opening of the article below reminds the reader, the definitive second edition of *Fantasiestücke in Callot's Manier* came out early in the same year. This occurrence perhaps prompted not just this 'letter' but the start of work on *Kater Murr* in May. Illnesses (which, paradoxically, tended to promote Hoffmann's writing) affected him seriously in spring 1818 and again a year later. This was the reason he did not personally attend the concert on 10 March referred to. It was of vocal music performed by artists from the royal Berlin opera, but also contained music played on the armonica (glass harmonica) by the actress Friederike Krickeberg. In her private reply to Hoffmann, dated 8 May, she explained her early musical training at home, then later on the armonica with Carl Leopold Röllig, and the effects of playing on 10 March in the opera house.[1]

Alec Hyatt King's brief history of the musical glasses may be read in *The New Grove*, xii, 823–5. The semi-mechanical version invented by Benjamin Franklin and named 'armonica' by him, dates from 1761. In this, the glasses were mounted horizontally on a spindle and made to revolve with the aid of a foot-pedal. Mozart composed three works involving armonica: the Adagio, KV 356/617a; the Adagio and Rondo with four instruments, KV 617; and the Fantasie K. Anhang 92. Dating from 1791, they were probably all written for the famous exponent Marianne Kirchgessner (1769–1808), mentioned in Hoffmann's article.

The said Kapellmeister Kreisler has become well known to all those who have read a certain fantastical book, a new edition of which has only recently appeared. It is printed on such smooth paper that one hardly understands how the letters can lie on it so nice and straight without sliding off. Well, this fellow Kreisler has written to a friend, with whom he is of one heart and mind, and among other things the letter contains the following:

'Tell me, my dearest Sir and Friend, tell me in the name of heaven the story behind the concert you had at the Opera House on the tenth of March. As you know, I was not there myself; it was bad weather, my umbrella was out on loan, and then it struck me, overcome as I was by a certain laziness – the most natural tendency of all human kind – that the distance from my lodgings to the Opera House really was a bit too far, although it can hardly amount to fifty paltry miles. Now I read conflicting reports about this concert, which leave me quite bothered and confused.

'Haude and Spener, in No. 31 of their journal,[2] make it clear that Frau K.'s armonica playing was rather lacking in effect, and ask how it is that the armonica in general is no longer so effective as formerly; perhaps our nerves have become hardened or softened, or perhaps the fault lies in our ear-

---

[1] *HBW*, ii, 207–10. Hoffmann's reply to this is in *Mitteilungen der E. T. A. Hoffmann-Gesellschaft*, xxviii (1982), 10.

[2] i.e. *Berlinische Nachrichten von Staats- und gelehrten Sachen*, 13 March 1819 [F.S.].

drums, now that they have been spoiled by all the drum-beating, trumpeting, tromboning, and keyed-bugling. On the other hand the *Freimüthige für Deutschland*, in No. 62 of that journal,[3] calls the armonica the most beautiful and sonorous of all instruments, and praises the inspired fingers of this gifted artist which summoned forth the instrument's ethereal echoes.

'I for my part, not having heard these ethereal echoes, must agree with Messrs. Haude and Spener that the astonishingly magical effect produced by the armonica years ago is now completely a thing of the past. But I am sure that our nerves have remained exactly the same, and that our eardrums, however battered they may be by drums and trumpets, are certainly still able to detect ethereal echoes too.

'Please permit me, my worthiest Friend and Sir, a few words to explain what my musical convictions are in this matter. Sound is to music exactly what colour is to painting. Both, colour and sound, are capable in themselves of an incalculable variety of sublime beauties, but they represent only the raw material which must first assume an ordered pattern before it can exert a deep and lasting effect on human minds. The intensity of this effect is determined by the degree of beauty and perfection the pattern achieves.

'It is not the colour green, it is the forest with the graceful splendour of its foliage which awakens delight and sweet melancholy in our breast. A deep blue sky will soon become desolate and sad unless the clouds tower upward in their myriad changing forms. Just imagine, my friend, if this were applied to art! How soon would it weary you, or what sort of sensory irritation would it instantly cause, to see the most beautiful colours without any pattern? Think of Père Castel's absurd ocular harpsichord![4] Well, it is just the same in music. Musical sound will stir our hearts profoundly only when it takes the form of melody or harmony – in short, of music.

'Now if the *Freimüthige für Deutschland* calls the armonica the most beautiful and sonorous of all instruments, then as a hardened musician I would reply that from the musical point of view the armonica is one of the most feeble and imperfect instruments there are! Of the welter of trivial ariettas and variations and polonaises and other insipid trifles that are normally played on it I will say nothing except to remark that, to a finer ear at least, any melody on the armonica sounds stiff and awkward. The fault lies in the instrument's mechanism, which makes it impossible even for the

---

[3] Dated 27 March 1819 [F.S.].

[4] The 'ocular harpsichord' was invented by Louis-Bertrand Castel (1688–1757) – a writer, mathematician, and theorist – and developed over a period of almost thirty years. Each of the twelve semitones of the musical scale was matched to a different colour, these covering the spectrum from red to violet. Some harpsichords used paper strips, others coloured glass.

most practised player to connect the notes together in an artistic sense. This mechanism also precludes any rapid execution. On the other hand, the armonica affords the advantage of the organ, that the note continues as long as one's finger touches the glass. This property means that the characteristic quality of the instrument can be fully exploited only in slow music written in strict style.

'So that you may immediately understand what I mean, my dear fellow, without a lot of further explanation, I would refer you to the long, canonically worked Benedictus by the founding father Palestrina,[5] which lies before me on my desk; it must be the despair of every pianist, yet is perfectly suited to the armonica and may be performed on it with great effect. But I know you have no armonica yourself, and if you take my worthy example to this or that gentleman, or to this or that lady, adept in fingering the glasses, they will complain inordinately about wide-spread chords etc., in short about the impossibility of playing it. And yet it depends only on dividing the four parts correctly between the two hands. But that is another matter! *Hinc illae lacrimae*,[6] my dear fellow!

'Perhaps you feel, my friend, that the armonica is capable in such music of developing a wealth of harmonic richness, and that no instrument in the world, the organ excepted, can make a chorale sound more beautiful; but even here one deficiency destroys any longer-term effect.

'This deficiency lies in the instrument's limited compass; it possesses no powerful bass register at all, with the result that music played on it in a contrapuntal style, such as chorales,[7] sounds thin and, to use a term from art criticism, "young".

'Now if it is true that the armonica has such limited capabilities in music, then it is clear that the admiration and wonderment created by its novelty was aroused merely by its tone. This admiration and delight in formless matter could not possibly endure, however, and diminished all the more rapidly the longer every desire for a musical pattern remained unsatisfied. In addition, the armonica's popularity rose during the period of delicate

---

[5] Giovanni Perluigi da Palestrina (*c.* 1525–94). As we saw in 'Old and New Church Music', Palestrina's music was conceived of primarily as slow and chordal in the early nineteenth century. 'Canonically worked' means using exact imitation between voices, like a complex round. Such Benedictus movements occur in the *Missa ad fugam* (1567) and the Mass on *Già fù chi m'ebbe cara* (1600).

[6] *Hinc illae lacrimae*: Hence all those tears shed.

[7] contrapuntal style . . . chorales: Hoffmann here and twice more uses the loose phrase *im gebundenen Stil*. This meant a continuous, unbroken style, implying thereby strictly composed polyphonic (contrapuntal) part-writing, whether in vocal, keyboard, or instrumental music. The *AMZ* in 1801, for example, said this style was typical of J. S. Bach (vol. iii, 14 Jan. 1801, col. 259).

nerves, and when it was claimed that the armonica exerted a magical influence on the nerves, the instrument could not fail to captivate every sensitive soul. For any young lady of breeding it would have been most ill advised, as soon as the glasses were even touched, not to fall into a tolerably convincing swoon; she would have risked becoming an immediate object of indifference to any young man of refinement, however long he had courted her with amorous glances. Even ladies of more mature age fancied themselves transported back ten or fifteen years by all the pangs of blessed rapture, and received a heart and a novelette into the bargain! Of the use made of the instruments by Mesmer I prefer not to think![8]

'Now, it seems, the age of delicate nerves and swoons is just about over.

'I must also make mention of the great evil that pieces are constantly coaxed from the armonica that are quite unsuitable for the instrument, and that one almost never hears compositions in a strict, contrapuntal style. This is for the simple reason that players are not capable of performing such things.

'However easy it may seem to you, worthiest Friend and Sir, to play such music as Palestrina's Benedictus, I can assure you that it is a quite singular business and that few understand it properly. Mlle. Kirchgessner played very poorly in the contrapuntal style, and Pohl[9] not much better; Frau K., as already stated, I did not hear for lack of an umbrella, and I must therefore withhold all judgement of her.

'The best armonica player of recent times I have heard was a fine man of gentle and pleasing character who, returning home from the French war, resided for a few days in the same house as me. I am referring to none other than my inestimable friend, the Bashkirian Colonel Tetulow Pripop who, unjustly, has become little known in the musical world. This man was totally obsessed by the armonica which he found in my house; he played the whole day long, and was able to elicit from the instrument the strangest sounds one could ever hear; the melodies and chords he produced also rejoiced in the most amazing originality. The distinctive, inimitable sound which other good armonica players achieve only now and then, and which insensitive people claim to resemble the scraping of a knife across a window-pane, was so completely within the colonel's power that he was able to produce it uninterruptedly.

'The manservant to my dear Tetulow Pripop, a jolly young fellow with a most endearingly tigerish physiognomy, was so beside himself at his

[8] Franz Anton Mesmer (1734–1815), 'the originator of "magnetism" . . . developed an enduring devotion to the instrument and used it to induce a receptive state in his hypnotic subjects.' The New Grove, xii, 824.

[9] C. F. Pohl the elder, who often performed in Berlin [F.S.].

master's virtuosity that with loud howls he threw himself down and kissed his feet. Yet it was not surprising that this person was so deeply moved, since he too was musically gifted and was able, when playing his long, narrow, Bashkirian pipe, to awaken truly idyllic sensations in the breast. One was momentarily transported to the most beautiful toad-pond a sensitive soul had ever sat beside.

'I will eternally remember the occasion when Tetulow Pripop played the armonica for the last time. Overcome by profound emotion, he had removed his large, pointed fox-fur cap as well as three smaller caps he was wearing beneath it; he sat there in his red cape, conjuring forth the most exquisitely ethereal harmonies, at which his tiger was also moved to wail and moan dreadfully.

'Finally, as though in heart-breaking grief at the departure of their beloved friend, the majority of the glasses burst into pieces.

'Thereupon the Bashkirian Colonel Tetulow Pripop pulled on a pair of white kid-gloves and hurried away to his regiment.

'I have never seen the good man since.

'Do write, my dearest Sir and Friend, to Herr Gerber in Sondershausen,[10] and tell him to grant due recognition to my worthy Colonel Tetulow Pripop in any new edition of his *Tonkünstler-Lexikon*. Farewell etc. etc.'

'Further Observations on Herr Konzertmeister Möser's Concert on 26 March this Year [1820]'

Published: VZ, 30 March 1820   *Signed:* Hnn
First reprinted: Dresdner Neueste Nachrichten, 4 March 1933

Karl Möser (1774–1851) was an important violinist, who had been a child prodigy. Hoffmann met him in Warsaw in 1806[1] when Möser's quartet played at the musical society of which Hoffmann was an organiser. After touring and then working in St

---

[10] Ernst Ludwig Gerber (1746–1819), famous scholar and owner of a substantial music library. His *Neues historisch-biographisches Lexikon der Tonkünstler* (Leipzig, [1812–14]) updated the work cited in *Kreisleriana*, p. 152.

[1] Möser, who became a friend of Hoffmann's, was written by the latter into the story *Der Baron von B.*, which is about the historical Baron Charles Ernest de Bagge (1722–91). See Hoffmann's letter to Härtel of 12 January 1819. According to F. J. Fétis's *Biographie universelle des musiciens* (Brussels, 1840), vi, 430, Möser's life was reputedly 'filled with amazing adventures'.

Petersburg (1807–11) Möser became Konzertmeister to the Berlin court orchestra. His quartet began chamber concerts, which by 1816 had become symphonic concerts.

The author omitted mention of Möser's violin concerto and sundry other solo items in the concert, presumably because he genuinely was appreciative of Beethoven's 'Battle Symphony', Op. 91, properly called *Wellingtons Sieg oder die Schlacht bey Vittoria*. His reasoning may be compared with that employed in the review of Méhul's *La Chasse du jeune Henri*. In its time *Wellingtons Sieg* was as popular as its two originators intended it to be: the idea for the work and indeed its formal details were provided by the man who commissioned it for his mechanical orchestra ('Panharmonicon'), Johann Nepomuk Maelzel (1772–1838). Various difficulties made a normal orchestral version desirable, and the first performance was in Vienna on 8 December 1813 with an ensemble including Hummel, Meyerbeer, Spohr, and Salieri. The work mixes absolutely literal musical imitation (e.g. the trumpet signals of each army) with other sections of more abstract and developed music.

The battle at Vitoria, N E Spain, took place on 21 June 1813, and was the decisive battle of the Peninsular War that broke Napoleon's power in Spain.

Herr Konzertmeister Möser is adept, in each of his concerts, his musical banquets, at following the finest, most exquisite foods with a particularly spicy dish which cannot but stimulate the most jaded palate. So in his recent concert, after productions displaying all the brilliance and splendour of consummate virtuosity, he had chosen a piece of music that could in fact be given nowhere, in view of the drastic effect it had, but in a hall that leads directly into the open air. The work in question was Beethoven's *Schlacht bei Vittoria*.

However much one may object with justice to this sort of musical painting, genius unfurls its powerful wings in all kinds of ways, and even the strangest flight arouses wonder and admiration, precisely because it is so bold and powerful.

True musical painting must not mimic individual sounds of nature but strive to evoke in the listener's mind the sensation that would occupy it in reality. In the aforementioned composition that great composer Beethoven has fulfilled this condition with brilliant success; and through the intelligent manner in which Herr M. directed the performance, entering fully into the composer's thoughts and intentions, everything came so vividly to life that anyone who had ever been present at a battle, or at least nearby one, could not but forget concert-hall and music and, with no great effort of imagination, experience those dreadful moments once more in his mind.

The present writer observed with real amusement a military man of high rank who stood completely lost in his thoughts; when with attack after attack the storm of dissonances rose to its highest point, indicating the crisis of the battle, he reached involuntarily for his sabre, as if to lead his battalion into the decisive charge. A gentle smile passed over his face when at that moment he realised how his senses had been deceived.

It is to be hoped that Herr M. will be willing very soon to give another performance of this highly original piece of music in the same manner; many people missed it because of doubt as to whether the concert would take place.[2] He would thereby satisfy the heartfelt wish of many true friends of art.

The infantry columns seemed too far away, their gunfire (reproduced by so-called *rattles*) was too weak.

Concert under the Direction of Spontini, 3 August 1820

Published: VZ, 5 August 1820   *Signed:* Hff.
First reprinted: Euphorion. Zeitschrift für Literaturgeschichte, xlv, 1950

The years 1820 and 1821 saw Hoffmann's close and creative involvement with the composer whose work he had publicly denigrated in 'Letters on Music in Berlin'. Gaspare Luigi Pacifico Spontini (1774–1851) rose from the humblest background in Maiolati, near Jesi, to become a musical power in three lands: his native Italy, France, and Prussia. In Italy he composed operas for Rome, Palermo, Venice, and Naples. On moving to Paris in 1803 he established his position in opéra-comique before his great triumph, *La vestale*, was first given at the Opéra in 1807. It was quickly followed by *Fernand Cortez* (the opera to which Hoffmann's earlier article refers). King Frederick William III of Prussia heard this work in Paris in 1814 and immediately had it mounted in Berlin. The king's continuing enthusiasm eventually succeeded in attracting Spontini to Berlin as General-Musikdirektor, and he arrived on 28 May 1820. Within a few days he had arranged a meeting with Hoffmann, since the latter's name had reached him even in Paris as one who might act as translator for his new opera, *Olimpia*. The reasons for Hoffmann's agreement to this proposal are discussed below, p. 431. But even before he had met the composer he wrote a public 'Greeting to Spontini' couched in effusive terms: it appeared in the *VZ* on 6 June.[1]

The present review draws attention to a central feature of Spontini's musical personality: his tightly disciplined manner of rehearsing and conducting. 'The same

---

[2] That is, people assumed it might be cancelled owing to poor weather.

[1] Opening 'Welcome to our midst, you great, glorious master!', this short piece brought against Hoffmann various charges of opportunism that persisted after his death. It is translated in full in Dennis Albert Libby, 'Gaspare Spontini and his French and German Operas', unpublished Ph.D. dissertation, Princeton University, 1969, i, 264–5.

laborious accuracy which he showed in composing was carried over into every detail of the performance', resulting in the 'complete fusion of the vocal and instrumental, the dramatic and the musical elements'.[2]

The 'song' sung for the king's birthday had been composed for him two years before: *Borussia. Preussischer Volksgesang*.[3] Spontini's note at the end of the printed score set out his desired distribution of forces for the first performance: one hundred strings; fifty trumpets; twenty other wind instruments; a choir of 130. (The wind instruments include high clarinets in F, basset-horns, double bassoon, bass-horn and ophicleide.) There are four verses and a choral refrain. The 'festive march' was Spontini's *Grosser Sieges- und Festmarsch*,[4] scored for strings, wind instruments and percussion, including similar forces to the preceding. After 106 bars of an Allegro brillante, 6/8 time, in C major, there enters an unexpected Andante religioso, 3/4, F major, with the melody known in England as *God Save the King* and in Germany as *Heil dir im Siegerkranz*.

On Thursday 3 August, in celebration of the honoured birthday of His Majesty the King, a song was sung, a speech was given, and a festive march newly composed by Spontini was played.

Was that all that happened in celebration of the great day of joy? Many may have asked that question, and with much shaking of heads wondered, when they heard that choir and orchestra consisted of three hundred and fifty persons, whether such large forces were necessary.

This reporter would add, however, that the strength, fire, and sublime exuberance which have won universal admiration for Spontini's works are also evident in this song, which in the simplicity and dignity of its thought bears the stamp of true inspiration and genius. And the splendid composer is able to transmit this inspiration, this fire glowing within his works to those chosen to perform them. In his hand the baton becomes a veritable magic wand, with which he wakens into life dormant forces which then rise up in majestic awareness of their power.

The normal orchestra was reinforced, but in addition a second orchestra was installed in the theatre on a raised platform, consisting of the music sections of the local guard and grenadier regiment. And these two orchestras, together with the singers who filled the entire stage in the most glorious

[2] Philipp Spitta, 'Spontini', in *Grove's Dictionary of Music and Musicians* (5th edn, London, 1954), viii, 22.

[3] Full score, issued after Spontini's appointment in Berlin: Borussia. / Preussischer Volksgesang / für / Solo-Gesang und Chor mit vollständigem Orchester / . . ., issued by Schlesinger with plate number S 1066.

[4] Full score: Grosser / Sieges= und Festmarsch / componirt und ehrfurchtsvoll zugeeignet / S.<u>r</u> Majestät Friedrich Wilhelm III / König von Preussen / . . ., issued by Schlesinger with plate number 1062. The string and timpani parts were issued separately, and do not appear in the full score.

harmony, performed this truly popular song with fiery energy and deep feeling. The two orchestras also played the festive march in the same manner, the unexpected entry of *God Save the King* giving it a truly splendid brilliance.

One could not deny, therefore, that the effect calculated by our excellent Spontini was in fact overwhelming. Only that which is conceived and brought to life with inspiration can awaken inspiration, and so it was that this inspiration was expressed in the liveliest manner by the tumultuous applause of an enraptured public.

Anyone who felt that too little was done will now concede that the most splendid tribute was paid, and with us will thank this great composer, of whom we can be fully justified in expecting that he will provide us, in his intense enthusiasm for art, with many further pleasures.

It is the fault of no one that the little opera *Aline*,[5] after this colossal performance, had a rather feeble effect; our opera company at the moment has the semblance of a sickly child, of an abandoned orphan, deprived of its best protectors.

'Casual Reflections on the Appearance of this Journal'

Published: Allgemeine Zeitung für Musik und Musikliteratur, 9 and 16 October 1820

Signed: Hffmnn.

First reprinted: Cäcilia, 1825, issue 9

The present essay appeared in the second and third issues of the Berlin *Allgemeine Zeitung*, but these proved to be also the last. Since the Second World War the remaining known copies have disappeared.

Carried off with a light touch, 'Casual Reflections' nonetheless addresses at least two questions of permanent interest. The first is Hoffmann's philosophy as a writer about music. Now at some considerable remove from the days of his *AMZ* essays, and having since received his share of critical comment about *Undine*,[1] he considers

---

[5] *Aline, Reine de Golconde*, three-act opera by Henri-Montan Berton (1767–1844), a popular 'magic' opera with oriental setting, seen in Berlin since 1804, a year after its première in Paris at the Opéra-Comique.

[1] See the reviews of *Undine* in Schnapp (ed.), *Hoffmann. Ein Dokumentenband*, from the Berlin *VZ* (pp. 443 and 445–6); the *DW* (pp. 447 and 452–7); the *AMZ* (pp. 450 and 476–80, Weber's review).

the practice of writing about music from both sides. Instead of adopting the yardstick of Romantic theory, however, he now sees the critic more empirically, as an almost-enchanted facilitator, who reveals hidden structures. This method, he perspicaciously adds, can 'lead people to *listen* well'; there is no narrow restriction to those of Romantic sensibility.

The second question is concerned with Spontini and 'effect'. This article was presumably written after the laborious work on *Olimpia*, Acts 1 and 2, had ended; its manuscript score must still have been with him. (There is an implied reference to it, in fact, near the end, explained in note 21.) We saw in the Prefatory Remarks to *Kreisleriana*, II–6, that 'effect' was a special critical term (*Effekt* rather than *Wirkung*), denoting superficial attractiveness. Hoffmann related it to the practice of followers of Goethe and Mozart, particularly in the slavish emulation of the latter's harmony and use of wind instruments. The implied criticism of Spontini here was made overt in 'Letters on Music in Berlin', where remote and difficult keys were named as 'effective' devices, in *Fernand Cortez*. In 'Casual Reflections', the author seems to accept – albeit with a certain chagrin – that orchestration and instrumentation must move with the times; he recalls that even old Reichardt was once accused of sounding like a fire-alarm; and perhaps admits to himself that he was indeed guilty of inflexibility in the earlier verdicts.[2] It is by no means certain that, in private, Hoffmann railed against Spontini's 'effects', of whatever hue, as was reported by Rellstab in 1827.[3]

The sense of Hoffmann summing up aspects of his critical career is enhanced by the repeated allusions to his past writings, detailed in the notes.

What is that incantatory formula with which authors customarily conclude their prefaces? 'And now go forth, my dear child, which I have cherished and protected with such care', etc. And since nothing is more natural, it has become the convention to compare the intellectual with the physical act of giving birth.

Upon both lies the curse of original sin, that is to say the pain and torment of labour, counterbalanced by paternal pride and an abundance of blind love for the new-born creature. In truth, however, it is not a child which the author of a finished book sends out into the world, but a fully grown man whose whole physique lies open to view, within and without. With a work

---

[2] I am indebted here to the stimulus of Michael Walter, 'Hoffmann und Spontini', in Alain Montandon (ed.), *E. T. A. Hoffmann et la musique. Actes du colloque international de Clermont-Ferrand* (Berne, 1987). Walter goes further, however, and sees a more detailed sub-text connecting other parts of 'Casual Reflections' with Spontini, with 'Letters on Music in Berlin', and with the charges of opportunism levelled against Hoffmann in the wake of Spontini's appointment in Berlin.

[3] e.g. 'If only I could take from the man the single word "effect", but with that he ruins everything.' Ludwig Rellstab, *Über mein Verhältniss als Kritiker zu Herrn Spontini . . .* (Leipzig, 1827), translated in Libby, 'Gaspare Spontini', i, 272.

such as that just making its first appearance here, the situation is different again, totally different. The publisher builds as pretty a cradle as he can, the editor places the embryo in it, and as soon as the tiny creature begins to stir he asks suitable godparents, just like real godparents, to provide the infant with the necessities of life, care, and upbringing. The thing may now develop and thrive according to its nature right under the eyes of the invited guests. There is an extended christening feast, and it is the responsibility of the hosting godparents to ensure that the food remains elegant and tasty, and that the drink never lacks fire and spirit; then the guests will not stay away, and the little one sitting at the front also eating and drinking will enjoy nourishing and palatable food and will continue to grow into a healthy adult.

But why this sour expression, my dear composer?

'Yet another new anatomical slab on which our works will be clamped down with their limbs forcibly stretched out and dissected with ruthless cruelty. Ha! I can already see false relations and hidden consecutive fifths[4] severed from the flesh of their harmonic context and quivering under the glinting knife of the anatomist!'

So that is the source of your displeasure? Oh my dear old composer! I am convinced that you will write, or must already have written, a work which proceeded directly from your innermost heart. If it was perhaps an opera that you wrote, then first you absorbed the poetic idea underlying the whole with all its deepest implications; then the genius of music stirred its powerful wings; and even the fetters now and then imposed upon it by inferior passages of the libretto were unable to curb its bold flight, as it carried upward into higher regions every radiance of that poetic idea.[5] All love, all yearning, all desire, ecstasy, hate, delight, despair seemed transfigured in the splendour of music's higher realm, and the human heart, stirred in a curious way, perceived the divine even amid the worldly. I believe that in the sacred hours of inspiration it was given to you to conceive the music in such a way as your controlling, ordering intellect deemed most truthful. Yes, intellect! I am afraid that this sometimes rather grumpy taskmaster cannot be ignored. He examines the supports of our building with a sharp eye; if he finds them too thin or weak he kicks them down, and if the entire edifice collapses he says that it was of no value anyway! It is better for it to be done by our grumpy friend within us than by others from

---

[4] false relations: piquant clashes of harmony produced as the consequence of chromaticism in the part-writing of any piece (cf. Mozart's 'Dissonance' Quartet, KV 465). Consecutive fifths: infringement of the most basic rules of counterpoint.

[5] Compare the similar observation and metaphor of *caput mortuum* at the end of the 1816 review of Méhul's *Ariodant*.

outside! Enough, my dear composer. You have done a thorough job, I am sure, and it goes without saying that you are perfectly aware of having composed your music in accordance with its underlying idea, in that way and no other. So here you find your work not lying on an anatomical slab under the murderous hands of a barbaric anatomist, but standing before an allied spirit who casts a sharp eye over it and, instead of ruthlessly cutting it to pieces, puts into words all that he discovers in it, the entire edifice with all its wonderful intricacies. Do not say, dear composer, that it is hardly a pleasure to have everything one has thought and felt analysed like a mathematical problem. It is the pleasure of being fully understood by a kindred spirit which prevents any concern about such pedantic analysis from arising. Think of your work, my dear composer, as a beautiful and imposing tree which has sprung from a tiny seed and now extends its blossom-laden branches high into the blue sky. Curious people stand and stare and cannot understand the miracle by which the tree came to grow in such a way. But then this kindred spirit comes along who is able, by means of a mysterious magic, to let the people see into the depths of the earth, as through crystal, so that they discover the seed, and realise that from this very seed the entire tree sprang. Indeed they will see that tree, leaf, blossom, and fruit could take only that form and colour and no other.[6]

You will appreciate, my dear composer, that I was just reflecting on the form which criticisms of musical works should take, and that I prefer to consider as such only those essays which really penetrate to the heart of the work and reveal its deepest impulses; they not only cheer the composer, should the trumpet of his praise not always sound, as well as his fellow artists, but they also acquaint others with much that they would otherwise miss. What is certain is that criticisms of this sort can lead people to *listen* well. Listening well is a skill which may be acquired, if one is so disposed, but composing well oneself is certainly not. The latter activity presupposes a small matter which one shrewd old composer candidly referred to in a polite letter to a young gentleman of quality, who had asked in great desperation how in the name of heaven he could set about delighting the world with a musical masterpiece. The musician replied: 'If only Your Lordship would be so good as to possess genius, then everything would etc. etc.'[7]

Finally I must confess to you, my dear composer, that it strikes me as very curious how often a few songs or an album of polonaises or, had they not

---

[6] Compare the passage in the review of Beethoven's Fifth Symphony discussing Shakespeare's 'inner coherence' as a 'splendid tree, buds and leaves, blossom and fruit . . .'

[7] Hoffmann quotes himself from *Kreisleriana*, II–6: 'Just make sure, my dear fellow, that you are a musical genius, and then the rest will take care of itself!'

gone out of fashion, minuets, can bear criticism very well, far better than many works lasting three hours, by which time one has heard enough and more than enough. Even a whole bush of rootless sprigs stuck into the loose soil can never become a vigorous, living tree.

There is nothing more gratifying than to give voice to one's feelings about an art which is so dear to one's heart; but how is this to be achieved? Talking is far better than writing, but it seems that one must write, since it is nowadays well-nigh easier to find people who read than people who listen; and musicians will always much prefer to listen to notes than to words, and suffer as unwillingly in speech as in music those excessively audacious modulations which the winged word all too lightly permits itself. One must ensure, however, that the dead letter carries within it the power of coming to life in the reader's mind, and making his heart respond to it! So does this also mean articles on musical subjects not based on any particular work? Nothing is more boring than articles of that sort, you say? Quite right! Especially in the style in which they are couched in *Hildegard von Hohenthal*[8] by the hero of the novel; he lectures his aristocratic pupil, for whom incidentally he bears a not entirely respectable affection, on the mathematical aspects of musical science in such a way that one cannot understand how she could bear such a pedant! Everything has its proper time and place. When a house is built, scaffolding is necessary; it would indeed be strange, however, to seek and find the architect's merit not in the building but in the scaffolding! There is a way of discussing musical matters, whether in speech or in writing, which satisfies the initiated without being incomprehensible to the people in the temple forecourt. The latter in fact may well derive considerable pleasure and unwittingly receive a measure of enlightenment without putting on priestly vestments at all.

No art, and music least of all, suffers pedantry, and a certain latitude of mind is sometimes precisely what makes a great genius. An old gentleman was once caused to blush when he discovered hidden consecutive octaves between the upper and lower parts, as though an obscenity had been uttered in polite company. What Kirnberger[9] would have said about Mozart's harmony! Not to mention his orchestration. Tamino passes through fire and water to the sounds of flute and kettledrum, with a gentle accompaniment

---

[8] Novel by Wilhelm Heinse (published anonymously, Berlin, 1795–96), in which Heinse expresses his thoughts on musical aesthetics. He shows the young composer Lockmann repeatedly giving long theoretical lectures to the highly gifted singer of the title, with whom he is in love. See i, 42–52, 101–45; ii, 386–413; iii, 35–76 [F.S.].

[9] Johann Philipp Kirnberger (1721–83), musical theorist and author of *Die Kunst des reinen Satzes in der Musik* (1771–79). 'He was criticised for being inflexible, conservative, tactless, and even pedantic': Howard Serwer in *The New Grove*, x, 81.

from *pianissimo* trombones![10] We know that the ordeal by fire and water of good taste now requires an entire arsenal of wood and brass weaponry, which is being daily augmented by strange inventions such as keyed bugles, flugelhorns, etc.,[11] cleverly made conspicuous by their dissonance. We know that every wind player, since he is no longer allowed to rest, wishes he had the lungs of Rameau's nephew,[12] or of the bewitched fellow who with his breath set in motion six windmills eight miles away.[13] We know that the pages of many scores now appear so black that a cheeky flea can relieve itself on them with impunity, since nobody notices it. And why? For effect – effect! Now creating an effect is certainly one of the most wonderful mysteries of composition, for the reason that the human heart is also a most wonderful mystery. From the heart to the heart, we say, and yet we cannot say which has the greater effect, an entire thunderstorm of kettledrums, bass drums, cymbals, trombones, trumpets, horns, etc., or the sunbeam of a single note from the oboe or some other instrument of refinement. Frederick the Great called a *crescendo* that Reichardt included in one of his arias a fire-alarm,[14] and he left the room in anger after he had been prevailed upon to listen to an act from one of Gluck's operas, saying that it all sounded to him not like music but like a confused cacophony; only Hasse and Graun were true composers, that is to say noble, simple, and melodious![15] 'Go back to the simplicity of the early masters', I hear you cry, my dear old composer, to your young followers. 'No more of this jangle and clatter, forget all your modern music, forget Mozart and Beethoven, and the sooner

---

[10] i.e. in Mozart's *Die Zauberflöte*, Act 2, the 'trials' scene. Pamina accompanies Tamino.

[11] keyed bugle: early nineteenth-century short bugle (originally military) fitted with between five and twelve keys to provide a chromatic scale; it was just entering its first wave of popularity. A German *Flügelhorn* would have been similar to this in 1820. But Hoffmann must have been aware of the historic invention of the valve (*c*. 1814) by Heinrich Stölzel, first applied to the French horn. Stölzel entered the royal orchestra in Berlin in 1818, and a Prussian patent for the valve was issued the same year to him and Friedrich Blühmel jointly.

[12] See *Kreisleriana*, I–1, p. 85 and note 136.

[13] 'When they had walked two miles they saw a man sitting on a tree who was shutting one nostril, and blowing out of the other. "Good gracious! What are you doing up there?" He answered: "Two miles from here are seven windmills; look, I am blowing them till they turn round."' From 'How Six Men Got On in the World', in *Grimm's Fairy Tales*, tr. Margaret Hunt, rev. James Stern (New York, 1944), 345. Identified by Georg Ellinger, this story was originally published in 1819.

[14] This is literally taken from 'Bruchstücke aus Reichardt's Autobiographie', *AMZ*, xv, 29 September 1813, identified by F.S.

[15] *Ibid.*, 15 September 1813, relating to the year 1776, when the king 'did not let [Reichardt] finish speaking, but with vehement expressions of abuse launched into a violent attack on Gluck'; he admired J. A. Hasse (1699–1783) chiefly, then C. H. Graun (1703/4–59), his own Kapellmeister.

the better.' But you must tell us, my old friend, which early masters you mean. If you define the age in which the true art of music came to an end, and say whatsoever is more than this cometh of evil,[16] then you incorporate within you an entire *académie française*, setting boundaries around art which nobody may cross without having to pay a penalty! What do you think of Fux, Keiser, or later of Hasse, Handel, Gluck and the rest? Undecided? Incidentally, nobody had any belief in the Chevalier initially,[17] despite his chivalrous nature. In Forkel's *Beiträge* his overture to *Iphigénie en Tauride* was very wittily compared to the noise of peasants in a village inn.[18] And yet if Gluck were living today, is it not possible that even he, as far as orchestration is concerned, would unfortunately be found wanting? We know that before he died he had planned an opera, *Die Hermannsschlacht*, for which he wanted a special instrument making, copied from the Roman *tuba*.[19] In view of this intention, his death was probably well timed.

Do not take me, my stern old friend, for a delinquent who does not honour the fathers, or who does not feel deeply in his heart that the lives of all of us are sustained by their creative achievements, and that we cannot cut the cord by which they lead us without danger of stumbling. And yet – now that I come to look at you more closely, Sir, you appear all at once quite youthful! Well, I have long been accustomed to such phantasmagoria. My younger brother was a droll young fellow. As a boy of five or six he would put on grandfather's wig and lecture us older ones with a vexed countenance, whereupon we could not help bursting out with laughter![20]

'Secure your windows and doors, you composers, there's a bogeyman abroad!'

---

[16] See *Kreisleriana*, I–1, p. 92 and note 151.

[17] In 1756 Gluck received the papal title of Cavalicre dello Sperone d'Oro (Knight of the Golden Spur).

[18] Hoffmann again recalls *Kreisleriana*, I–5, p. 109 and note 175. Gluck's *Iphigénie en Aulide* (*recte*) was attacked in Forkel's *Musikalisch-Kritische Bibliothek*, i, 53–173. The music Forkel likened to carousing peasants, on p. 167, was not from the overture but the solo for Achille with chorus, 'Chantez, célébrez votre Reine', Act 2 sc. 3. In fact it is martial in style, not folk-like.

[19] Gluck died in 1787. See Friedrich Rochlitz, 'Glucks letzte Pläne und Arbeiten', *AMZ*, xi, 22 March 1809. An anonymous Viennese correspondent reported on the projected *Die Hermannsschlacht* with its 'large horns, after the style of Russian hunting-horns' which would be specially made. Similar things were reported in 'Bruchstücke aus Reichardt's Autobiographie', *AMZ*, xv, 13 October 1813 (identified by F.S.). For an illustration of a French copy of a Roman trumpet made in the 1790s for ensemble use, see 'Buccin' in *The New Grove*, iii, 403.

[20] Hoffmann's fantasy here centres on the perpetual freshness or 'youth' of the (Gluckian) masterpiece, just as in *Ritter Gluck* the spirit of the composer lived on. Walter, 'Hoffmann und Spontini', considers that Hoffmann thinks here of Spontini as a successor to Gluck, whose image thereby is rejuvenated through later art.

Is it possible for any magazine to exist, any artistic journal, without some trivial tittle-tattle? In the midst of composing, the musician is accosted by this or that reporter and must answer his questions whether he wishes to or not. The said reporter then announces to the world that the great X, as he can testify from his own observation, composes in a not very clean morning-gown of coloured calico, uses very finely ruled Venetian music-paper, has excellent black ink, for some curious reason writes the viola part below the bassoon part, thus breaking up the string section,[21] but is otherwise a splendid and good-hearted fellow. He does not think very highly of A, he did not really want to express an opinion about B, he seems to like C, but what he said about D should be passed over in silence for now, and so forth.

That is why I say 'Secure your . . .' But no – no! There is a sort of acceptable tittle-tattle which, rather than being malicious, serves to make even stronger the spiritual bond between the multitude and the beloved, revered composer, and this may well appear in these pages. It is after all the legacy of our weaker nature that we cannot separate the composer's work from his person, and that when we think of the one we always think of the other, for otherwise portraits of popular composers would not be so eagerly sought and purchased. 'What does he look like', we all tend to wonder, 'this man who is capable of giving me such profound pleasure?' And if somebody well acquainted with the composer sets forth in kindly terms a detailed account of his particular character, if he paints a complete picture of the man in vivid phrases, then whoever has already taken him to his heart will feel an even greater intimacy with him.

In the days when the science of physiognomy flourished, people also tried to reveal the inner man by the study of handwriting,[22] and it is quite true that many characteristic features are revealed in this. It is likely that they are even more glaringly expressed in musical handwriting, and it would be welcome if these pages were to contain occasional facsimiles of great composers. One should not tell tales out of school, and so it is not really possible to discover how, that is by what procedure, this or that composer writes his works down. Each one has his particular method, and it would

---

[21] Michael Walter, 'Hoffmann und Spontini', has noted that this disposition of a full score was characteristic of Spontini, who placed the violins at the top, followed by woodwind, upper brass, bassoons, violas, voices, and bass. Trombones and timpani, if present, went below the bassoons. See the illustration in *The New Grove*, xviii, 20; timpani here are near the basses, however.

[22] Hoffmann knew Lavater's *Physiognomische Fragmente* (Leipzig and Winterthur, 1775–78) in his youth, as is seen from the letter to Hippel of 18 July 1796. 'On the Character of Handwriting' is in the *Dritter Versuch* (1777), part IV, fragment IV [F.S.].

indeed be most intriguing to trace precisely how that procedure has influenced and continues to influence the works themselves. But personal confessions are not very likely to be forthcoming, and such things should therefore be said or written only about dead composers!

Yet thought follows upon thought, and so etc.

'Further Observations on Spontini's Opera *Olimpia*' (extract)

Published: Zeitung für Theater und Musik zur Unterhaltung gebildeter, unbefangener Leser, 9, 16, 23, 30 June, 14, 21, 28 July, 4, 18, 25 August, 1, 8, 22 September 1821   *Unsigned*
First reprinted: E. T. A. Hoffmanns musikalische Schriften, ed. Edgar Istel (Stuttgart, [1907])

That Hoffmann had by 1816 come to appreciate *La vestale* (1807) by Spontini is shown in his brief notice of a performance of it on 28 June that year. This opens with the confession that it is an 'overwhelming masterpiece', which the reviewer has repeatedly enjoyed. In his letter to Count von Brühl of 8 June 1820, Hoffmann set out the nature of his new commitment to the recently arrived composer and his *Olimpia* (see p. 421 above). First he confirmed that he had met the composer personally, and had been at pains to deny the 'misunderstanding' that he was hostile to his music. He continues:

> the revision of such a large work is a very arduous task, that is, if one intends to take it seriously and provide not a pedantic translation, but a work in which from a poetic and musical point of view it is not apparent that it has been translated from a foreign language . . . I should have been reluctant to undertake it if Spontini's great mastery did not merit such a sacrifice.[1]

Examining the reasons for Hoffmann's espousal of this cause, Dennis Libby particularly isolates the startling ascendancy of the operas of Rossini.[2] London and Paris may have welcomed them earlier, but *Tancredi*, his first universal success (1813), reached Berlin in 1818. *L'inganno felice* (1812) was then seen in Berlin in September 1820, closely followed by *Otello* in January 1821. (Hoffmann refers to the

---

[1] Translated in Libby, 'Gaspare Spontini', i, 266.
[2] *Ibid.*, i, 271ff.

latter in his essay.) *Il barbiere di Siviglia* (1816) had its Berlin première on 18 June 1822, precisely a week before the writer's death.[3]

Rossini represented for the composer of *Undine* a profound betrayal of true opera. His denunciation of Paer's art in *Sofonisba* had been blistering enough (see p. 262), but that of Rossini is applied like a flail. Thus an analysis of the present essay shows that Hoffmann 'saw in Spontini one who, under the proper German influence, could re-establish the superiority of the tragic opera'. He 'is not trying to write a dispassionate appraisal of Spontini, but to promote him as the leader of a cause. His critical method is directed to this end. The praise is lavish, the censure muted . . .'[4]

Yet there are several historical questions that remain unresolved. One is the fact that Hoffmann must have known that to assist Spontini was to court disfavour with the latter's sworn enemy, von Brühl. Another is the impact of Weber's *Der Freischütz* on Hoffmann's position. With supreme irony, this great landmark in German Romantic opera received its première in Berlin only thirty-five days after Spontini's and Hoffmann's *Olimpia* was seen for the first time on 14 May 1821.[5] Unfortunately, Hoffmann's last illness and his creative work did not permit him the time to write the review of *Der Freischütz* which he had assured his friend Weber he would write.[6]

Hoffmann's translation (or, as he termed it, 'adaptation') of Acts 1 and 2 proceeded until about 20 September 1820 (*HBW*, ii, 272). Act 3, which Spontini was reworking, still had not been made available. The task was completed only in the following January. Because Hoffmann's musical description of Act 3 within 'Further Observations on Spontini's Opera *Olimpia*' breaks off at the point where he and Spontini were to rewrite their version to create a happy ending, it is very possible that Hoffmann actually wrote his blow-by-blow account of the score (*not reproduced here*) in 1820 rather than 1821.[7] The first part of the essay (*below*) thus conjecturally came into being after the second part, being stimulated by the new Rossini opera, *Otello*, in January 1821.

Opinions have differed as to Hoffmann's achievement in *Olimpia*. He declared in a letter to Hippel of 24 June 1820 that he was determined not to change a single

---

[3] Loewenberg, *Annals of Opera. Otello, L'inganno felice* and later importations were given in German.

[4] Libby, 'Gaspare Spontini', i, 274–5.

[5] The French original was entitled *Olimpie*. The Berlin version, whose title we have used, appears as follows in its piano score: OLIMPIA/ grosse Oper in 3. Acten. Hoffmann's name does not appear on the title page. The publisher was Schlesinger, and the plate number 1158.

[6] See Weber's letters and diaries documenting his relationship with Hoffmann, including visits to his house, in Schnapp (ed.), *Hoffmann. Ein Dokumentenband*, 542, 650–2. The whole question is explored in Wolfgang Kron, *Die angeblichen Freischütz-Kritiken E. T. A. Hoffmanns* (Munich, 1957), which shows that Hoffmann did not write the antipathetic reviews of Weber's opera.

[7] Walter, 'Hoffmann und Spontini'. Walter also adduces evidence concerning Hoffmann's attitude to the way Spontini composed the end of Act 3, to original verses by Hoffmann. The latter appear in Friedrich Schnapp, 'E. T. A. Hoffmanns Textbearbeitung der Oper *Olimpia* von Spontini', *Jahrbuch des Wiener Goethe-Vereins*, lxvi (1962), 126–43.

musical note in the process, and also to replace 'French clichés' with 'powerful words'. Georg Ellinger accused the results of having 'un-German constructions' and other unpleasant stylistic faults.[8] Michael Walter has analysed the nature of the adaptation in the light of its effect in inclining the work towards Romantic opera, away from its roots in Voltaire's tragedy.[9]

Hoffmann's synoptic opening history of opera was evidently written with his copy of Gerber's dictionaries in one hand. There is little point in calling attention to all its dubiosities. But its resolute tracing of the elements most significant for Romanticism as Hoffmann saw it creates a striking parallel with 'Old and New Church Music', and anticipates Wagner's *Oper und Drama*.

Spontini's latest opera has already been reviewed in these pages, but may the person entrusted with translating the French text into German be permitted to add a few further comments about a work he has had the opportunity to acquaint himself with in great detail. The translator worked on the principle that a translation of the words into another language could satisfy the composer only if it were founded on precise knowledge of the musical requirements as a whole; he began this very difficult and thankless task, therefore, by assiduously studying the score and making himself thoroughly familiar with this truly colossal work. The task can be called difficult because the choice of words depends not only on requirements dictated by melody, rhythm, and correct accentuation according to note-values and intervals, but also on instrumental motives emerging from the overall musical edifice. Frequently a preferred poetic equivalent has to be rejected because its sound is lost in the interplay between singers and orchestra. Furthermore, it would be a simple matter to take the confused metres found in French opera texts, especially in recitatives, which strictly speaking are not metres at all, and recast them as neatly regular German verses. But this would totally change the rhythms within the work; quavers, for example, would have to be contracted into crotchets, etc., minims or semibreves split into crotchets, quavers, etc. This has happened frequently in many translations of foreign operas, and with great injustice to the composer, since the original character of the composition is thereby considerably obscured. On the other hand the translator could regard the composition as a sacrosanct entity, in which nothing whatsoever may be reshaped or altered; he could conscientiously adhere to the composer's intentions, never forgetting that everything must be subservient to the effect of the music. But then it seems almost impossible that anyone reading

---

[8] See Libby, 'Gaspare Spontini', i, 268. In 1834 Hoffmann's version was extensively revised for stage use.
[9] Walter, 'Hoffmann und Spontini'.

the translation without regard for those musical considerations would not be able to criticise the translator, and rightly so, for cobbling clumsy verses and choosing strange words. This is why such a task must be called ungrateful.

Let the gentle reader not take these comments amiss, but regard them as something more than a mere *captatio benevolentiae*,[10] although the translator keenly perceives he has great need of that as well.

Yet if the translator's work was difficult and thankless, he can give his heartfelt assurance that love and joy in the task increased in direct proportion as he became increasingly familiar with a work that can claim and maintain a worthy place among the first music-dramas[11] ever created; indeed, when he had studied the wonderful structure of the work in all its aspects, and its vigour and exuberant energy were revealed to him for the first time, he felt more than adequately rewarded for all his efforts.

The operas that preceded *Olimpie*, *La vestale* and *Fernand Cortez*, have already given the most convincing proof that Spontini's compositions have in view nothing but dramatic expression of the greatest intensity and perfection. Such music must not deliquesce into meaningless flourishes and short-lived titillations;[12] no, it must stir the listener's deepest feelings. Every passion, every situation the drama gives rise to emerges more clearly and forcefully from the edifice of sounds, and the highest potency of art is achieved when the listener, utterly captivated and completely caught up in the action, is no longer aware of the individual threads comprising the overall fabric.

Since true art reasonably demands that drama, whatever form it may take, is expressed in a genuinely dramatic language, the composer is to be highly praised who upholds the truth at a time when luxurious fashion stands opposed to everything that is significant, serious, and communicated by the innermost heart. Only those who do not wish to see stage drama conceived in terms of music would not gladly endorse this praise; they can find pleasure only in meaningless sequences of trifling vocal concertos, whose outer trimmings consist of scenery and costumes.

The curious split that has occurred in music recently is quite remarkable. May the writer be permitted to say a few words on this subject.

Think of that unforgettable period when Gluck, the mighty reformer of

---

[10] *captatio benevolentiae*: reaching after goodwill (rhetoric).

[11] *Tondichtungen*: Hoffmann's word here seems to recall his term *Tongedicht*, also translated 'music-drama', in *Kreisleriana*, II–6, where it referred to Gluck's operas.

[12] Here and below he surely thinks of the latest works of Rossini, which are the reverse of his ideal of 'music-drama', an all-involving totality.

dramatic music, with his giant's strength demolished the musical edifice erected by Lully and Rameau[13] and cast it aside. Lully had fashioned operatic music into a precise form; melody was replaced by a certain psalmodic motion of the upper voice which one still finds in the ancient antiphons of Catholic worship; harmony, to the extent that it embraces orchestration, was reduced to an ordinary figured bass accompaniment divided between the instruments without any other motives being introduced. A musician today cannot help smiling when he looks at the scores of Lully's highly acclaimed operas, such as *Atys*, *Phaëton*, *Roland*, etc., and simply cannot understand how it was that this empty, monotonous singsong, always from the same formal mould, could be regarded as music for almost a hundred years, at least by the French. It is characteristic of that nation to look upon form as an indispensable requirement of art and then, thereby led astray, to ignore content in favour of form and to mistake the latter for the former. Rameau, although he also followed Lully's principle, was richer, especially in his harmony, and in particular made use of motives arising from the dramatic action. For this his enemies accused him of lacking good melodies (one can imagine what they considered to be good melodies), and consigned his chords to the Iroquois, where they belonged; for this too, Kapellmeister Campra was unable to judge Rameau's first opera otherwise than he did.[14]

Rameau was fifty years old, without having written anything but keyboard pieces, when he came to Paris and set about composing the opera *Hippolyte et Aricie*, to a text by the Abbé Pellegrin. After the first performance of this opera the Prince de Conti asked the ageing Campra what he thought of the music. Campra replied that there was so much music in it that one could make ten operas from it! Thus Rameau was considered rich, excessively rich, because they took Lully's music as the yardstick.

However empty, however monotonous, and however lifeless in dramatic terms the compositions of these old coryphaei of French music may seem to us, one cannot deny them one great merit, one that gives their works value at least for demonstrating an important aspect of musical grammar which cannot be studied carefully enough. It is the merit of absolutely correct

---

[13] Jean-Baptiste Lully (1632–87), founder of French opera in its definitive form (though born in Italy). Created thirteen *tragédies en musique* and two *pastorales* between 1672 and 1686, which had been preceded by many ballets and also collaborations with Molière. Jean-Philippe Rameau (1683–1764), creator of over twenty-six stage works for the Paris Opéra between 1733 and 1764.

[14] The foregoing criticisms and the following anecdote are from 'Rameau' in Gerber, *Historisch-Biographisches Lexicon der Tonkünstler . . . Zweyter Teil* (Leipzig, [1792]), cols. 227 and 228.

declamation, not only according to the value of syllables but also according to the gradation of intervals. The psalmodic motion of Lully's melodies, bereft of other motives, can be seen merely as a series of notes serving as a vehicle for correct declamation (recalling the probable form of ancient music without melody and harmony); and even if Rameau went further in introducing motives, the principle, as already stated, remained the same.

Many poets are able to hear nothing but themselves, and consequently no music either; they regard opera merely as an insane farrago of confused rantings, or disparage it in other common and unpleasant terms. Indeed, such librettists would be quite happy with the aforementioned principle, that music should renounce all its essence and identity, and be employed not to illuminate the drama but to convey and accompany the *words* of the drama; they would like to see this principle continue too, from which may heaven preserve the rest of us.[15]

Then Gluck appeared! Like Rameau, he was already fifty years old when he began the cycle of operas that established his fame and immortality, with *Orfeo*, composed in 1764[16] in Vienna. Ten years later he went to Paris. In this sixty-year-old man the fire of youth burned like an unquenchable naphtha-flame, but mature experience, the resolute independence of a man at one with himself and with all his ambitions gave this flame strength and constancy. So firm was his grasp of the glories of music in all its quintessential needs that genuinely musical drama sprang forth from him like a brilliant meteor! The music was enkindled not by words but by ideas, and what it created was not a series of notes determined by the sequence of words, but true melody which translated those ideas into vivid reality, without doing the slightest injury to the underlying basis of correct declamation. He brought to bear all the possibilities of harmony and orchestration, all the resources available to composers at that time, in order to express the extremes of dramatic intensity inflaming his fervent and fertile imagination. So it was that his vocal style and orchestration seemed unprecedented, that he found what the normal orchestra offered him inadequate, and that as well as employing the wind instruments quite unconventionally he introduced into the orchestra instruments not otherwise usual in such contexts, such as trombones.[17] And yet his spirit was looking forward to even more radical departures with regard to orchestration. It is well known that when he died, Gluck had a whole opera worked out in his head without having written down a single note. This opera was to be called *Die Her-*

[15] This vital distinction should be compared with the opening of *Kreisleriana*, II–6.
[16] *Orfeo ed Euridice* (1762) is recognised as Gluck's first 'reform' opera: he was in his forty-eighth year, being born in 1714.
[17] See 'Letters on Music in Berlin', note 17.

mannsschlacht, and he was intending to include some totally new brass instruments, to be modelled on the pattern of the Roman tuba, in order to introduce their plangent tones during the wildest battle-choruses and thus intensify the effect to an unprecedented degree.[18]

It could not have been otherwise. The effect of Gluck's operas, completely overwhelming the listener's mind and senses, was such that those whose ear was dulled by Lully's and Rameau's largely trite and sentimental, psalmodic vocal style could never comprehend this great composer's works; proceeding from their own preconception, and applying this as a measure of what is acceptable in art, they condemned him. Others, clinging tenaciously to the earlier form they regarded as inalienable, and obstinately ignoring every other, denounced his works merely for opposing what had previously stood for truth and beauty. To those endowed with greater vision a new world of sound was inaugurated with splendour and glory, filling them with the sublimest rapture. By one party, therefore, Gluck was praised to the skies, while the other condemned him to the depths of Orcus.

Even though nothing during this same period in Germany was of lower esteem than French taste, even though the works of the fiery Hasse, the sensitive Graun,[19] and other splendid opera composers of the time were dissimilar in every respect to French compositions, and even though much in the works of German composers contained the utmost dramatic expression (particularly in the recitatives, which must still be regarded as models today), there was nevertheless a very precise pattern to which everything had to conform, and whatever offended against this pattern was rejected. Thus even in Germany no composer was more harshly treated than Gluck, until the shining light of his genius broke through and sent the dark, demonic horde fleeing to their nocturnal abode. Forkel, for example, in his *Musikalisch-Kritische Bibliothek* compared the magnificent opening of the second part of the overture to *Iphigénie en Aulide* with the wrangling of peasants in a tavern, and then adduced a hundred passages, with musical extracts provided, in order to show how crude, vulgar, shallow, lacking in expression, and striving for effect with overloaded orchestration and musical barbarisms the composer's music was, and how limited was the extent of his theoretical knowledge.[20] Similarly an earlier composer pronounced the dreadful anathema on poor Gluck, that this unjustifiably acclaimed musician had as much understanding of counterpoint as his (the older

---

[18] See 'Casual Reflections on the Appearance of this Journal', note 19.
[19] *Ibid.*, note 15.
[20] *Ibid.*, note 18.

composer's) cook.[21] These bitter attacks were very much provoked by a pamphlet originating from a certain abbé (whose name momentarily escapes the present writer)[22] which he launched upon the public on the subject of Gluck's *Iphigénie*; in it the composer was elevated above all the clouds and stars in such an exaggerated, effusive, amateurish, and unartistic manner that, in Germany at least, it could only do him harm, without at all helping him to the fame that his works by themselves would necessarily have earned him. The aphorism holds eternally and universally true: Against my enemies I can defend myself, but may God protect me from my friends!

Before the reviewer begins to speak of Piccinni and of the quarrel in Paris (dispute between the Gluckists and Piccinnists)[23] it occurs to him that the scope and arrangement of the journal for which this essay is intended oblige him to break off for today and save the remainder for next week. May the gentle reader not lose patience and regard this major digression, or rather this extended prolegomenon, as idle or superfluous. The reviewer has the confidence to assure him, with hand on heart, that when he finally turns to the work under discussion itself many a reference to what has already been said, many a *fiat applicatio*,[24] will not go unnoticed by the sympathetic reader.

In Italy at that time the glorious music of the early native composers still resounded. With regard to singing, Italy was then still the cradle, the nursery of music, and the greatest German masters (Gluck, Handel, Hasse, etc.) pilgrimaged there and set operas, in order at the fountainhead to fathom the mystery that gave Italian vocal music that inimitable vigour, that irresistible magic which delighted the world. A number of German composers left Italy as initiates in that mystery. And Gluck too may well have plumbed its depths (the reviewer has none of his earlier operas such as *Demetrio* to hand). He would not otherwise have been capable of writing an aria in Italy that was widely held to be by the highly popular Sammartini, and received rapturous applause during rehearsals; only when the opera was performed was it realised, as Gluck intended, that this aria, composed

---

[21] 'The relationship between Gluck and Handel [in London, 1745–46] has often been misunderstood owing to the false emphasis placed on Handel's remark to Susanna Cibber, related by Burney: "[Gluck] knows no more of contrapunto as mein cock [?cook]" . . . [which overlooks the] cordial relationship between the two.' Winton Dean, 'Gluck', *The New Grove*, vii, 456.

[22] Abbé François Arnaud (1721–84): *Lettre à Mme D'[Augny] et à la comtesse de B. . . . sur l'Iphigénie de Gluck* (1774); reprinted in his *Oeuvres complètes*, ii [F.S., rev.].

[23] See note 177 to *Kreisleriana*, I–5, 'Extremely Random Thoughts'.

[24] *fiat applicatio*: let it be applied.

exactly after the conventional Italian manner, distorted the entire dramatic structure of the opera.[25]

In the depths of his serious, German spirit, Gluck recognised the danger in which genuinely tragic opera was placed by the seductive attractions of such sensual, predominantly rich vocal writing. This made him resolve to avoid with care any tendency in that direction and, keeping dramatic considerations constantly in view, never to sacrifice any situation or effect to the voice. Gluck is melodious, as only a tragic composer can be; indeed, when they fulfil a dramatic need his melodies have a sweetly southern nuance, as for example in Renaud's entry into Armide's enchanted garden.[26] But the tragic gravity and profound significance investing Gluck's melodies will not permit a single flourish to creep in, if it is there merely as a passing titillation of the ear, without relation to the whole. Those who enjoyed only the latter in Italian music, therefore, could not but find Gluck's compositions graceless, dry, and unmelodious.

For this reason Gluck's enemies were convinced that in order to check his increasingly meteoric, increasingly irresistible progress an Italian master should be set in opposition to him, and so it was that Madame du Barry summoned Piccinni to Paris.

If the hope was to diminish Gluck's fame by reference to a principle established and perpetuated by his enemies, the choice could not in fact have been better. Piccinni was a consummate master of the ravishing charm of Italian melody, and yet he was far from allowing it to hinder or overwhelm the drama. Also, Piccinni had grasped the essence of opera, his characters are distinctive and convincing, and his dramatic movements are of striking expressiveness. Thus the first opera that Piccinni brought to the Paris theatre in 1778[27] could not fail to be greeted with the most rousing applause, and was given seventy-five performances in succession. It is well known that the public then divided into two different parties, that of the Gluckists and that of the Piccinnists, who fought each other with such zeal that bloody heads frequently resulted. Such battles can only be seen as foolish, if the intention is to tear the well-earned laurel-wreath from the head of one great and venerated composer, merely to bestow it upon another, equally venerated but following a different direction. Gluck,

---

[25] Anecdote taken from Gerber, 'Gluck', in *Neues Historisch-Biographisches Lexikon der Tonkünstler . . . Zweyter Teil* (Leipzig, [1812]), cols. 344–5. Gerber actually relates that Gluck wrote the aria (in his own opera) in the conventional manner since he had heard that people were taking exception to his own musical style.

[26] *Armide* (1777), Act 2 sc. 3, celebrated solo 'Plus j'observe ces lieux'.

[27] *Roland, tragédie-lyrique* (1778). Piccinni wrote it in Paris following his arrival there at the end of 1776.

bowed with age, quitted the arena and moved back to Vienna. And yet he stood firm, lived on, and still stands firm and lives on through the immortality of his works. It could not be otherwise. Though Piccinni might surpass him in the grace and charm of his vocal style, it was in profundity of thought and soul-stirring power of expression that the great Gluck emerged as the conquering hero of true art.

The ability to combine the most ravishing and enchanting vocal style of the Italians with the deep expressiveness of the Germans, together with the richness meanwhile gained by instrumental music, was vouchsafed a later composer; both singing and accompaniment were then brought forth as a single organic entity, derived from the same germ.

Fiery imagination, deeply felt humour, and extravagant abundance of ideas, pointed this Shakespeare of music in the direction he had to follow: Mozart broke new ground, and became the incomparable creator of romantic opera. Because Mozart emerged in Germany, where people have a profound appreciation of real works of art, but do not give each other bloody heads on that account, there could not be a dispute like that of the Gluckists and Piccinnists in Paris. There was also no particular opponent to Mozart whom his detractors had placed at their head; nevertheless his first works were tepidly received. *Don Giovanni* failed at its first performance in Vienna,[28] and there were many who called the great composer a lunatic who could only write confusing rubbish that was without rhyme or reason and that nobody could play. In Milan (if the reviewer is not mistaken it was in that city) Mozart's *Don Giovanni* was abandoned after nine fruitless rehearsals, as being completely unperformable music.[29] Even in Germany Mozart was not fully understood until much later, and even today there are musicians who refer to Gluck in order to demonstrate Mozart's irregularities. Surely, to draw a comparison between these two composers is like comparing Aeschylus with Shakespeare, or *Oedipus* with *Romeo and Juliet*.

Such a comparison furnishes proof of total want of sensibility capable of appreciating art in all its ramifications.

Fights and feuds have always existed in art, and they have a salutary effect,

---

[28] *Don Giovanni* was written for Prague (1787). In fact in Vienna (Burgtheater) it was performed fifteen times in 1788, but thereafter not until 1792. The music was found 'learned' by Zinzendorf and 'too difficult for the singers' by Joseph II. See Deutsch, *Mozart*, 314–15.

[29] The first Milan performance of *Don Giovanni* was in 1814. Hoffmann actually refers to a report about Florence, published in F. X. Niemetschek, *Mozart* (Prague, 1798), 68, reproduced in *Schriften zur Musik*, 542, and Loewenberg, *Annals of Opera*, col. 454.

since strength is increased by struggle, and the victory of truth and beauty greatly assists the progress of art.

At the present time there are no real fights and feuds in music, merely a bewildering but frictionless disunity, since we have no new works that stand so utterly opposed to each other as those of Gluck and Piccinni. At that time both factions had a common basis in the guiding principle of dramatic convention; they both set out from this, and the dispute merely concerned which composer achieved the greater things. Now it is different, since that basis has been lost. The genius of art has flown its southern home and, half in sadness, half in anger, looks back to the degenerate race that has rejected it! One can hardly understand how it could have happened, that in the country that gave birth to the greatest composers, whose immortal works should still dazzle the world, all authenticity in art could so completely disappear! Rossini, admittedly a frivolous composer and therefore not worthy of true art, has actually stood the principle on its head; accordingly, in an opera, which should be a drama, what matters is neither character, nor situation, nor any other requirement of the drama; accordingly, the words, regardless of rhythm and declamation, serve only as an incidental vehicle for strings of notes, forming successions of flourishes that titillate the ear, or justified merely by fashionable taste or by the particular idiosyncrasies of some adulated *prima donna*. It is also curious that Rossini, and with him the latest Italian composers too, with crass stupidity trample underfoot that flowing vocal style which was previously regarded in Italy as an indispensable prerequisite of any composition. One need only think of the grotesque leaps and roulades of Rossini and his ilk, of the clumsy violin figures, and of the odious trills that often take the place of melody and then incite female singers to a surfeit of gurgling. When Rossini actually does conceive a melody that is sweet in the better sense, it usually appears in a completely inappropriate place, or it abruptly breaks off without any of the further development that gave significance to the heavenly melodies of the earlier Italians, and gave them intimate appeal to heart and mind; instead, a rapid succession of unconnected flourishes merely beguiles the ear for a moment. It is said that Rossini does have a sense of the dramatic, and only panders to popular taste in order to make money; the third act of his *Otello*[30] genuinely seems to evince this sense. All the more blameworthy is it then, if Rossini has genius within him and deliberately trims its wings, so that it cannot take flight even despite the weight of metal dragging it down to earth.

---

[30] See the Prefatory Remarks. *Otello*, given in Berlin in 1821, was first performed in 1816, and remained the standard setting prior to Verdi's (1887).

But how could it happen that this degenerate taste has found so many supporters even in Germany, where previously only truth and gravity were valued in art? Quite naturally, so it seems. Because of the huge increase in musical activity, and precisely because music has become an *activity*, the taste of that mysterious entity known as the public has become so diluted that it has not been preserved in any recognisable pattern. How many there are who pursue musical *activities* without any inner calling, without any genuine artistic feeling, merely because of fashion, or out of vanity, or the like! And yet any gentleman or lady who with little talent can amuse the most elegant tea-circle, or who has perhaps performed a solo at the choral society, and also strums badly but charmingly on the piano, is able to speak and pass judgement about the works of great composers, as though he or she were accustomed to passing in and out of the hallowed temple of Isis, and ordering breakfast or tea there with complete ease and equanimity. Can such clever and well-bred art-fanciers have even the slightest inkling of the real grandeur and purpose of musical drama, let alone comprehend it? Is it not exactly what one would expect, that to such art-worshippers and the effete artists associated with them, who are not actually artists at all, Rossini's sugary lemonade, which they gulp down with no ill effects, tastes better than the fiery and powerful wine of great dramatic composers, which gives them headaches owing to their effeteness?

Directly opposed to them are the rigorists who ruthlessly condemn all music of recent times, who frequently consider Gluck too *galant*, who demand that composers should forgo all their hard-won musical resources, to whom a crowded full score is an abomination, etc. Their watchword is simplicity, for which, however, they often mistake emptiness and insipidity. Then again there are the malcontents who generally concede that dramatic music took proper form only at the time of Gluck, and that it received special impetus from Mozart, but to whom nothing in the world is right, and who attach a 'but' to the most deserved praise. Around this banner rally those musicians in particular whose works are stillborn children which no divine breath can quicken into life. On the other hand there are the musical visionaries[31] – But enough of this. It is clear that the babel of tongues that now obtains in artistic criticism arises from the most varied motives.

Finally, let us turn to the composer whose latest work is intended to be the central subject of this essay, in order to construe his inner character, as it emerges from his works.

---

[31] visionaries: does Hoffmann mean himself? Does he perhaps refer to C. M. von Weber's *Der Freischütz* (June 1821)?

Just as was the case with Gluck and Mozart, Spontini at an early date composed a series of operas which made his name well known, indeed famous. But these works have not made their way in the world; they do not belong to it since they are determined by the time and place and form dictated by their origin; they did not seek the universal, and did not contemplate it or achieve it.[32] But suddenly the composer surprises us with a work that springs upon the world in shining array, like Minerva from the head of Jupiter, a work of full maturity and truth, an offspring of the delight that aroused his genius at the first moment of fully awakened consciousness. And with this work begins a cycle of creations that by virtue of their character and their demeanour seem to belong to a different composer, and by virtue of their universal rather than individual appeal establish their creator in the world.

But the flame can and will never take hold unless the divine spark reposes in the breast; the genius is born, the sapling rises from the single seed and puts forth leaves and blossom and fruit, and the life-giving rain merely provides nourishment, so it can better germinate and develop. The sudden enhancement of a composer's powers, therefore, can never be attributed to continued study alone, however high his attainment.

To quote an example from Mozart's works, if one compares the score of *La finta semplice*[33] with the score of *Don Giovanni* it hardly seems possible that one and the same composer produced both works. And yet it is obvious why that divine spark residing in the breast cannot glow and catch fire in the very first works of a composer. In any art it is inadequacies of technique which send a student back to the form and example of existing works; only by degrees does the embryo take shape within, and eventually develop the strength to walk by itself, without the need of leading-strings. Instinct matures into awareness of truths, and from this awareness emerge distinctive ideas, the personal expression of these truths which no longer looks back to received notions or to defined forms that find their justification merely in what temporary artistic convention seems to demand.

It was this inner instinct, therefore, ripened to the fullest possible awareness of artistic truths, which set the great composers on the road that led to immortality, and Spontini in *La vestale* gave conspicuous notice that he had developed this awareness to the most acute degree.

It has previously been stated that Spontini's works have no other aim or

---

[32] Spontini wrote eleven Italian operas (1796–1802). In Paris he wrote three one-act opéras-comiques, including *Milton* (1804), which Hoffmann was commissioned to translate in 1821. See letter of 10 Sept. 1821, showing that he apparently started this. *La vestale* was Spontini's next work (1807).

[33] Mozart's second opera, KV 51 (1768), written in his thirteenth year.

intention than dramatic expression of the greatest intensity and perfection, and that to achieve such expression using the resources provided by one's inner vision is the characteristic strength of true genius.

It has likewise already been suggested that the earlier Italians also placed great store by dramatic expression, but could not entirely free themselves from external forms or from the momentary allurements of sweetness and sentimentality, which did considerable harm to that expression. Gluck rose up like a hero and with his pure and unadulterated drama demolished all pretence. But since Gluck's time instrumental music has become more prominent, and Mozart showed how the so-called accompaniment must contribute as much to the overall character as the vocal part. It is clear that Spontini has deeply absorbed the works of the great and glorious composers of his native country, but it is equally clear that the works of Gluck and Mozart have exerted the most decisive influence on him.

Spontini recognised the quintessential nature of dramatic composition, and the Minerva in shining array, offspring of inspiration and delight, was opera, in which everything – singing, orchestration, modulation, rhythm – radiated from a single focus of dramatic expression. His genius fashioned this expression in quite new and distinctive forms incorporating all the long-accumulated riches of art, and brought them brilliantly to life.

As long as man remains confined by mortality and incapable of full spirituality, of fully transporting himself into another world, he will be influenced, the external world surrounding him will act upon him, and without intending to he will from time to time, however extreme his originality, pay homage to the conventions prevailing at the time. Spontini cannot deny the Italian in him, which does him no dishonour at all as far as melodious vocal writing is concerned; where it is appropriate (and elsewhere it does not occur) it rather gives his works a special charm, an enchanting grace and felicity. But a certain expansiveness in the layout of arias, duets, etc., is also characteristic of that taste. Furthermore it cannot be denied that perhaps without him being aware of it or thinking about it, the taste of the French public for which he first composed also influenced him. This influence is particularly apparent in a certain highly characteristic light-heartedness, which appears alien and strange to us Germans. It is the *gaieté française*, which to us remains as inexplicable as it is inimitable. Even Gluck tended towards the French taste, albeit in a different way that corresponded to his time, namely in the shaping of his melodies. Equally, French audiences, just like German ones, are probably pleased more by violence than by power, more by thunder suddenly bursting upon a profound silence than by a crescendo pushed to the limit. His unusual way of treating the chorus, differing from that in German music but sanctioned by French and Italian taste, should also be borne in mind.

At this point the question naturally arises whether Spontini's first great serious opera would not have turned out differently had he spent the period during which he lived in Paris in Vienna, or here in Berlin, where the works of Gluck and Mozart are those most frequently given. The alien influences would not have been able to affect him, and he would have had no need of them. His spirit, having grasped the essential nature of musical drama, would have been refreshed and purified by the genuinely tragic gravity and deep significance that, as has been pointed out, pervade Gluck's works. However, Spontini is now in Germany, is now here in Berlin, and is just beginning his cycle of classical works; from the three masterpieces that have opened the series, we can draw not merely the hope but the confident expectation that he will compose operas *for us* that will also belong to that invisible church whose members are transfused by the celestial fire of art and desire nothing but the purest integrity and truth.

The distinctive character of his composition, therefore, follows from this premise:

that in Spontini, a true genius who bears the divine spark within him, the essence of opera has been revivified, fully in the spirit of the great composers of the past, yet in the form evolved by great composers in the progressive period of art.

His melodies and rhythms are determined solely by considerations of dramatic expression, and the orchestration should enhance this expression in such a way that every instrument contributes its individual character to the whole, or rather emerges as an integral component of the whole.

Again, it follows from this that melody can never be dictated by the requirements of fashionable taste, pampered ears, or vain singers; and that in the orchestration very dissimilar figures must often be given to widely separated instruments in order to achieve a *single* objective, so that anyone incapable of comprehending the whole will often call the score cluttered and confusing. The same criticism was levelled at the great Mozart, and his bold reply when the Emperor Joseph maintained that there were too many notes in the composer's score is well known.[34]

From what has been said, however, it can be seen that the critic who takes perhaps too strict a view of tragic opera will deprecate the treatment of some

---

[34] Joseph II, apropos *Die Entführung aus dem Serail*: '"Too beautiful for our ears, and far too many notes, my dear Mozart", Joseph II is supposed to have said after the first performance, on 16 July 1782; whereupon Mozart is said to have replied, "Exactly as many, Your Majesty, as are needed."' Alfred Einstein, *Mozart. His Character. His Work* (London, 1946), 458.

arias, duets, etc., as too expansive and Italianate, and some rhythms as too jaunty.

May these observations about the fundamental nature of Spontini's works suffice in a general way, although much more could be said on this subject.

SOURCES AND SUPPOSITIVE REVIEWS*

Friedrich Schnapp

Music is in fact the only art which is so rarely discussed on an elevated
level, and this probably stems from the fact that musicians, as a rule,
cannot write.

Hoffmann to Cotta, 11 June 1814

As a music critic, the writer and composer Hoffmann exerted an epoch-
making influence.

Generally speaking, creative artists are rarely expected to show any depth
of understanding, let alone objective evaluation, of other masters (particularly those close to them). Hoffmann as a practising musician, however,
does not belong with those who go their way in perfect assurance and with
splendid singleness of mind overlook or ignore whatever is confusing or
distracting to their purpose. Instead, he commands that sensibility and
receptivity essential to the observer of art. With the benefit of his practical
experience, his deep knowledge, and his own artistic gifts of the highest
order, he sharply distinguishes the trivial from the mediocre, the good from
the excellent, the valuable from the priceless, and allots to each its due.
When the leap of his imagination takes him to the highest summits of music,
he is able to recognise and express in words what remained hidden from
most and dimly suspected by a few. ('You have even written about my poor
efforts', Beethoven thanks him early in 1820. 'Allow me to say that this is
very pleasing to hear from a man graced with such excellent qualities as
yourself.')

A large part of the riches which we possess in Hoffmann's reviews lay
buried for a long time. It took the work of several generations to recover it.

The author himself never remotely considered collecting his criticism
together. Only four essays which had appeared in the *AMZ* were thought
by him worthy of revival in his writings: in the first volume of *Kreisleriana*
(1814) he included his reviews, greatly condensed and reworked, of Beethoven's Fifth Symphony (p. 234) and two piano trios Op. 70 (p. 300); five

---

* Taken from the *Schriften zur Musik*. Footnotes are by Friedrich Schnapp (1900–83), except
those indicated 'D.C.' (David Charlton).

447

years later the articles on Beethoven's Mass in C major (p. 325) and on 'Old and New Church Music' (p. 351) were recast in dialogue form and used for the second volume of the *Serapions-Brüder* (1819).

One year after Hoffmann's death J. E. Hitzig, in his book *Aus Hoffmann's Leben und Nachlass* (2 vols., Berlin 1823) based on his knowledge of Hoffmann's diaries, published seven more reviews which had appeared in the *AMZ*, reprinted the 'Letter from a Monk' (p. 213), and made reference to the *Gruss an Spontini*. After that, however, it was left to literary and musicological research to discover his remaining writings of this type, forty-five in number. This was a particularly difficult task since only very few of the pieces bear the name of their author. Some of the others are provided with easily recognisable ciphers such as Hff., Hffmnn., Hnn. or J. Kr. (Johannes Kreisler); a larger number of articles are signed with invented names, however, and the majority have no signature at all.[1]

The credit for identifying Hoffmann's anonymous articles on music and musicians, which appeared in seven different journals, belongs to a number of scholars: Carl von Ledebur (1806–72), Georg Ellinger (1859–1939), Eduard Grisebach (1845–1906), Edgar Istel (1880–1948), Hans von Müller (1875–1944), Erwin Kroll (1886–1976), Carl Georg von Maassen (1880–1940), Felix Hasselberg (1893–1945), Wolfgang Kron (b. 1927), Klaus Kanzog (b. 1926), and the present writer.

Documentary corroboration of the authenticity of these new discoveries was frequently found in letters, diary entries, and other sources. In many cases, however, there is only the indirect evidence of style and content to indicate Hoffmann's authorship, as in six reviews in the *AMZ* (Weigl (p. 252), Gluck (p. 255), Stiastny, Ogińsky, Ambrosch, André, and Riotte), all nine contributions to the *Dramaturgisches Wochenblatt* (1815–16), the essay 'Some Observations on the Comments made by . . . Herr Fischer' (p. 408), and the *Rüge*.[2] The evidence in these cases is nevertheless so convincing as to leave scarcely any doubt.

While recognising the achievements of research, it should not be forgotten that in the years between 1864 and 1933 numerous musical articles were wrongly attributed to Hoffmann. A list of spurious writings, with details of their first republication under Hoffmann's name, or their first attribution to Hoffmann, will be of value, since some of these articles still occasionally cause confusion.

1   Review of Beethoven's Sixth Symphony, *AMZ*, 17 January 1810
      Vom Ende 1899, pp. 75–84

---

[1]   See the Appendix for the complete list of Hoffmann's criticism [D.C.].
[2]   See the Appendix under Meyerbeer [D.C.].

2   Review of F. Schneider's Piano Sonata (*Grande sonate pathétique*) Op. 14, *AMZ*, 14 February 1810
    Kroll 1909, p. 124: 'Absolute authenticity . . . can however not be claimed'; Kroll nevertheless attributes the review to Hoffmann.

3   Review of A. Romberg's *Das Lied von der Glocke*, *AMZ*, 28 March 1810
    Vom Ende 1899, pp. 281–3

4   Review of F. H. Himmel's *Vater unser*, *AMZ*, 1 August 1810
    Kroll 1909

5   Review of A. Romberg's *Die Macht des Gesanges*, *AMZ*, 6 March 1811
    Vom Ende 1899, pp. 282–5 ·

6   Review of B. A. Weber's *Deodata*, *AMZ*, 7 August 1811
    Ellinger 1894, p. 210: the criticism 'can be attributed with the greatest probability' to Hoffmann.

7   Review of Beethoven's *Christus am Oelberge*, *AMZ*, 1 and 8 January 1812
    Vom Ende 1899, pp. 279–81

8   Review of M. Haydn's Requiem, *AMZ*, 18 March 1812
    Ellinger 1894, p. 201: 'Hoffmann's authorship cannot be entirely certain'.

9   Review of Beethoven's Fantasia for Piano, Chorus, and Orchestra Op. 80, *AMZ*, 6 May 1812
    Vom Ende 1899, pp. 140–4

10 Review of F. Dotzauer's three quartets Op. 19, *AMZ*, 11 November 1812
    Kroll 1909

11 Review of Bach's English Suite in D minor, *AMZ*, 27 January 1813
    Ellinger 1894

12 Review of T. Haslinger's *Ideal einer Schlacht*, *AMZ*, 16 June 1813
    Ellinger 1912, vol. xiii, pp. 153–4

13 Review of Weber's *Der Freischütz*, *VZ*, 21 June 1821
    Ellinger 1894, pp. 153, 222

14 Review of Weber's *Der Freischütz*, *VZ*, 26 and 28 June 1821
    Max Maria von Weber, *Carl Maria von Weber. Ein Lebensbild* (Leipzig, 1864), vol. ii, pp. 324f.

15 Review of Weber's *Der Freischütz*, *VZ*, 7 July 1821
    Max Dubinski, 'Hinter den Kulissen', *Berliner Börsen-Courier*, 15 August 1911

16 'Es giebt Leute, die sagen . . .' [Invitation to the violinist Boucher], *VZ*, 7 July 1821
    Hirschberg 1922, vol. xiv, p. 169. On p. x Hirschberg notes: 'Not entirely certain whether by Hoffmann'; personally, however, he is 'firmly convinced' that Hoffmann is the author.

17 Review of Weber's *Der Freischütz* and Cherubini's *Lodoiska*, *VZ*, 13 November 1821
    Felix Hasselberg, 'E. T. A. Hoffmann über Weber und Cherubini', *Blätter für Musik*, supplement to the *Königsberger Hartungsche Zeitung*, 9 April 1933

18   Review of Weber's *Der Freischütz*, *VZ*, 25 December 1821
     Hasselberg, as for item 17 above

In his important essay 'E. T. A. Hoffmann als Musikschriftsteller für Breitkopf & Härtel 1809–1819' (*Süddeutsche Monatshefte*, March 1908, pp. 283–95) Hans von Müller sharply warned against the irresponsible attribution of anonymous reviews to Hoffmann and in no uncertain terms went on to dismiss Vom Ende's edition of the musical writings as a 'Cologne Carnival production'. Nevertheless he expressed the opinion that between 1809 and 1814 there must have been 'at least one hundred reviews' in the *AMZ*, of which twenty-two or twenty-three were then identified. (In fact there are no more than twenty-eight, or thirty-four if the double reviews are counted twice. In all Hoffmann wrote forty-one contributions to the *AMZ*, including the musical tales.)

Dazzled by Müller's revelations, Kroll in his 1909 dissertation named a further twelve reviews (!) in the *AMZ*. These are not given in the above list, however, since the youthful author referred to them only with extreme caution: 'The following reviews *could* have been written by Hoffmann' etc. (p. 124).

Both Ellinger and Kroll were discerning enough not to take Vom Ende's 'discoveries' seriously, and to make a critical examination of their own conclusions at a later date. As a result, Ellinger's edition of Hoffmann's works contains only nos. 12–15 from our blacklist.

For proof that Hoffmann did *not* discuss the Berlin productions of Weber's *Der Freischütz* we are indebted to Wolfgang Kron's brilliant study, *Die angeblichen Freischütz-Kritiken E. T. A. Hoffmanns* (Munich, 1957).

The present writer accepts responsibility for rejecting the review of Haslinger's *Ideal einer Schlacht*.

The reviews collected in this book fall into two groups: the first, following the early-Romantic prelude, 'Letter from a Monk' (1803), extends from early in 1808 until autumn 1814 and consists predominantly of reviews of musical works; the second embraces the years 1814–15 to 1821 and chiefly contains reports of opera and concert performances in Berlin.

When Hoffmann sent his tale *Ritter Gluck* to the editor of the *AMZ*, Friedrich Rochlitz, on 12 January 1809 (incidentally, his first literary masterpiece had not been written at Rochlitz's suggestion, as the latter subsequently claimed), he simultaneously offered his services as a contributor to the journal: 'Perhaps I could also become more closely connected with the editors of the Musikalische Zeitung and occasionally provide essays and also reviews of lesser works.'[3] Hoffmann may have felt equipped for such tasks since, as secretary of the Musical Society in Warsaw from 1805 to 1806, he had already served as reviewer of the theoretical lectures given there, and had also been active himself in the field of musical criticism and composition theory (see the account of Quaisin's *Le Jugement de Salomon*, p. 217).

Rochlitz took up the offer at once, and Hoffmann replied on 29 January:

The conditions on which you are willing to accept me as a contributor to the Musik[alische] Zeitung are, as I see them, entirely adequate and very agreeable. Here [in Bamberg] I can hear frequent and good performances, and thus also form careful opinions, of symphonies, overtures, quartets, quintets, as well as piano sonatas, piano quartets and trios; but of church music only masses of a smaller scale . . .

Hoffmann's musical criticisms in the *AMZ* then began with a sample article, the review of two symphonies by Friedrich Witt, which appeared on 17 May 1809. On 15 April 1809 Hoffmann had suggested to the journal's editors that he might also discuss vocal works, 'indeed whole *operas* in piano arrangements or in score, as well as *church pieces* in the same form'. Rochlitz or the publisher Gottfried Härtel, however, had reserved a particularly important task for their new contributor. On 23 June Hoffmann notes in his diary: 'Received *an extremely agreeable letter* from the editors of the Musikal-[ische] Zeit[ung] – They ask whether I would be willing to review the Beethoven symphonies –'. Eight days later, on 1 July, he replied: 'The proposal from the highly respected editors of the Musik[alische] Zeitung regarding the suggested review of Beethoven's symphonies is most flattering to me, and I count myself honoured by the kind trust in my ability which their proposal carries with it.'

Hoffmann had thus moved into the front rank of reviewers for the most important musical journal in Germany.

It was nevertheless inevitable that he was not always given masterpieces to pronounce upon, and that inferior works were sometimes allotted to him. As early as 15 April 1809 he declined to review the *Harmonie ou Sonate en B* for wind instruments by H. A. G. Tuch, with the comment: 'Tuch's Harmonie is very insignificant and I have therefore been able to say nothing about it.' Later, in autumn 1814, he rejected three other compositions – flute pieces by R. Dressler, *Siegeslied der Deutschen* for four voices by B. A. Weber, and *Das Räthsel unsrer Zeit* for voice and pianoforte by F. H. Himmel – remarking that these three works were 'so utterly insignificant

---

[3]   The full text of this and subsequent letters will be found in *HBW* [D.C.].

that even the smallest space devoted to their advertisement in the [A]MZ would have been a waste' (letter to Härtel of 12 September 1814).

In the above-mentioned letter of 1 July 1809 Hoffmann referred to his ability 'to play the piano with some virtuosity', and undertook 'if need be to make careful appraisals even of large-scale keyboard works'; on 1 July 1812 he wrote to the editors: 'It would be very agreeable to me to receive for review vocal pieces such as operas, or best of all, church music.' On 16 April 1814 he offered to review for Härtel 'some of the latest *large-scale vocal works* in the sacred or secular style', and repeated this offer on 12 June: 'Should you wish to give me any reviews in the domain of *vocal music*, I would be delighted.'

Hoffmann could not complain of a shortage of commissions; in fact he soon fell into arrears in completing them and repeatedly had to make excuses. In 1819, when Rochlitz had already given up the editorship of the *AMZ*, there was still in Hoffmann's Berlin apartment a long-overdue accumulation of works awaiting review, which he would gladly have been rid of (letter to Härtel of 12 January 1819).

Of reviews and articles planned, the following remained unwritten:

On the Bamberg Theatre (particularly on the opera productions there)

Letter to Rochlitz of 29 January 1809: 'There is a great deal one can say about the theatre here which must also be of general interest; it will not be possible without speaking of myself, and I find it an uncommonly gratifying token of your trust that, notwithstanding this fact, you call upon me to compose such an account ... In so far as I mention myself in this account, I shall faithfully and conscientiously adhere to the judgement of the public, and thus be merely the organ of general opinion.'

Review of Beethoven's Sixth Symphony

Letter to Härtel of 30 May 1810, in which Hoffmann confuses the numbers and speaks of the 'Fifth Symphony', the review of which had already been written and published. (Oddly this same confusion in numbering is found in the programme for the performance of both symphonies at the Theater an der Wien on 22 December 1808.) We know fortuitously that the Erfurt organist and composer M. G. Fischer reviewed the 'Pastoral' symphony (*AMZ*, 17 January 1810).[4]

Review of Cherubini's Mass (probably the *Messe à 3 voix et chœurs avec accompagnemens* in F major, published in Paris in 1809)

---

[4]   See *HBW*, i, 292, note 4. Hoffmann wrote a letter to the *AMZ* on 1 July 1809 accepting the offer to review Beethoven's Fifth Symphony. Härtel subsequently wrote the following to Rochlitz on its second page: 'Herr Fischer in Erfurt informs me just now that he is busy with the review of the *Sinfonia pastorale* by Beethoven.' [D.C.].

Letter to Härtel of 12 July 1810; Hoffmann mentions the Mass with a few critical comments in the essay 'Old and New Church Music', p. 371.

Review of Beethoven's Fourth Symphony

Letters to the editors of the *AMZ* of 2 August 1811 and 12 July 1812.[5] The symphony was not reviewed in the *AMZ*.

Essays on musical performances in Berlin

Letter to the editors of the *AMZ* of 10 December 1814.

Review of Beethoven's *Fidelio*

Letter to the editors of the *AMZ* of 5 October 1815, in which Hoffmann promises 'to deliver an essay which will not be without interest, since I have obtained a full score of the opera *Fidelio* for close inspection, and consequently can provide a thorough appraisal of this masterpiece.[6] I will deliver this essay soon after the performance, and also attend to the reviews entrusted to me.' (Unfortunately neither of these promises was carried out.)

Opera music in recent times

Letter to Härtel of 12 January 1819: 'I have in mind to make use of some of the new productions here in Berlin (Das Fischermädchen – Lila etc.) in order to express my thoughts about the direction which opera music has taken in recent times. Would such an essay be agreeable to you? Should any important new piece of choral music be suitable for review in the form of a substantial article, I beg you to honour me with the commission.'

(A shorter discussion by Hoffmann of J. P. Schmidt's opera *Das Fischermädchen*[7] had already appeared in the *VZ* of 3 December 1818; he did not review F. L. Seidel's music for Goethe's *Lila*, performed in Berlin on 9 and 15 December 1818.)

Review of Weber's *Der Freischütz*

Letter from Weber to Friedrich Kind of 21 June 1821: 'I am still anxious to hear what Hoffmann has to say', to Friederike Koch of 9 August 1821: 'Hoffmann wanted to write about the Freischütz, but appears to have forgotten it. My friend Wollank could perhaps remind him of it, and also himself at the same time.'

A notice of the *Entr'actes pour des pièces de théâtre, à grand orchestre, livres 1–4*

---

5 Hoffmann wrote out his own score for study purposes: see below [D.C.].
6 See *HBW*, ii, 73. He had obtained the manuscript copy from the Berlin opera library. The soprano Anna Milder-Hauptmann, for whom Beethoven had written the title part, was temporarily residing in the same house as Hoffmann [D.C.].
7 i.e. of the opera's première, in Berlin [D.C.].

by J. C. Stumpf, which Hoffmann sent to the editors of the *AMZ* on 15 April 1809, and which for some reason was not published, is lost.

The following remarks indicate how conscientiously Hoffmann approached his task as a reviewer:

... since it goes without saying that it is my duty, if I do not have the score to hand, to write out doubtful passages in score myself [from the parts] ...

What I must most respectfully beg, however, is that the time allowed to me for completing reviews is not too short, for otherwise I cannot be as thorough as I would wish; moreover when large-scale works are submitted to me, perhaps some smaller vocal pieces or piano arrangements of operas could also be included for review, since through such reviews I may perhaps be able to engender an improvement in the quality of German song.   (To Rochlitz, 29 January 1809)

against expectation, however, I have not had an opportunity to hear good performances of the two quartets by Haensel and Dotzauer, and have therefore had to forgo their review.

The winter concerts have now come to an end and it would present difficulties to arrange good performances of symphonies and the like ... full scores of the works to be reviewed would be welcome, since they facilitate their study greatly.

(To the editors of the *AMZ*, 15 April 1809)

I still have the opportunity to arrange performances of orchestral works before the onset of autumn, and this, as well as the desire to make a careful study of these important compositions [Beethoven symphonies] in advance and if need be to write out some passages in score [from the parts], prompts me to request *early* despatch of the pieces to be reviewed.   (To the editors of the *AMZ*, 1 July 1809)

Could you, Sir, not send me the score of *Sofonisba* by Paer? It would be extremely useful in connection with my review of the piano arrangement.

In order to review Beethoven's Symphony No. 6 [Hoffmann erroneously writes: No. 5], I must write out the whole work in score from the parts.

(To Härtel, 30 May 1810)

[The Symphony No. 1 by Spohr] is a fine, important work and I was all the more conscious of my duty to take great care; for this reason I did not want to write the review until I had heard the symphony performed several times by our excellent theatre orchestra.   (To Rochlitz, 23 October 1811)

worked very hard on the score of the overture to Coriolan by Beethoven for the purpose of my review.

(Diary entry of 28 June 1812: full transcript in *HTB*, 162)

In the case of symphonies, however, I must ask you where possible to send a copy of the score, in order that I might look over the composition more quickly and appraise it more thoroughly.   (To the editors of the *AMZ*, 1 July 1812)

For the purpose of my review I have had to write out both works [the *Coriolan* overture and Beethoven's Fourth Symphony] in score myself.
(To Härtel, 12 July 1812)

I must again refer to my repeated request, in the case of items in several parts, to be so good as to send me the score, if it is available.   (To Härtel, 5 September 1812)

(At this point we may recall an observation by Spohr in his *Flüchtige Bemerkungen auf einer musikalischen Reise*, dated Würzburg, 10 November 1815:[8] 'As a reviewer he [Joseph Fröhlich] seems to work fairly conscientiously, yet I noticed that like many other reviewers even he puts into writing opinions about works of which he has not been able to examine the score. Anyone who knows how difficult it is to get to know a work merely by reading it, even with the help of the score, must be very surprised that these gentlemen proceed by laying the separate parts beside each other and then looking at them in turn. In the case of a work in many parts, even reading the score does not permit the formation of a reliable judgement; one must also have heard it, and in a good performance!')

. . . but for this [writing the article on 'Old and New Church Music'] I require the help of several musical items which I could perhaps obtain from your good self, as shown in the list which Herr Rochlitz has given you for this purpose.
    In this connection I am returning some of the pieces of music sent to me, of which some have already been reviewed in the [A]*MZ*, and others are impossible for me to review since I have no opportunity to hear them.   (To Härtel, 15 April 1814)

pressure of duties constantly increased, so that it became impossible for me to find the free time and energy needed to produce anything for the [A]*MZ*; I did not want to send something mediocre or superficial.
(To the editors of the *AMZ*, 5 October 1815)

I certainly never praise a work of art if I have no feeling for it.
(To J. P. Schmidt, 8 September 1816)

When Hoffmann left Leipzig on 24 September 1814, in order to become a civil servant again in Berlin, he promised Härtel or Rochlitz that he would write reports from the Prussian capital about the musical life there – a promise which in the event he fulfilled with only a single article, the 'first' of

---

[8]   Louis Spohr, *Selbstbiographie* (Kassel and Göttingen, 1860), i, 227.

the 'Letters on Music in Berlin' (p. 387). It naturally seemed to Hoffmann more sensible and convenient to publish such reports in Berlin papers from then on.

He spent barely a year – from September 1815 to July 1816 – as a regular contributor of reviews. They appeared in the *Dramaturgisches Wochenblatt in nächster Beziehung auf die königlichen Schauspiele zu Berlin*, a theatrical journal published from 8 July 1815 to 28 June 1817 and edited by Dr Konrad Levezov, a schoolmaster and former teacher of the theatre-manager Count von Brühl, and by Dr Franz Horn, a writer and former schoolmaster. From the beginning Hoffmann clearly concerned himself in Berlin only with musical events with which he was particularly in sympathy.

In both groups of Hoffmann's critical writings on music, the reviews and the articles, there is an unmistakable striving for fairness in his appraisal of works and artists. From his elevated standpoint Hoffmann sees the particular against the background of the general. He likes to introduce his reviews with expertly sketched historical summaries, or with basic discussions of the nature of the genre concerned. For this reason even his reviews of forgotten compositions by lesser masters are still worth reading, precisely because his judgements 'by postulating universal principles [are given] the more general interest of a musical treatise', as he himself puts it in a letter to the editors of the *AMZ* (of 2 February 1813). By nature devoid of envy, Hoffmann was always pleased to recognise the merits of others; but he also showed sympathy towards modest accomplishments, so long as he could discern honest endeavour. His taste and feeling for quality were developed to a high degree.

It has often and rightly been pointed out by his admirers that he was one of the first to appreciate Beethoven's true greatness. His acquaintance with Beethoven's compositions probably dates from the time when he lived in Warsaw (1804–07). 'Even at this early date', according to Hitzig's testimony,[9] he arranged a performance of a Beethoven symphony 'by which he was greatly impressed'. Overwhelmed as he was by the feeling of 'infinite yearning' which surrounded him, the Romantic visionary, when he entered this 'realm of the mighty and the immeasurable', Hoffmann the musician immediately realised that there could be no talk here of caprice or unbridled flight of fantasy. Although there is a 'restless alternation of the most marvellous images, in which joy and pain, melancholy and ecstasy appear beside and within each other', Beethoven is nevertheless 'fully the equal of Haydn and Mozart in rational awareness, his controlling self detached from

[9]   Hitzig, ii, 299.

the inner realm of sounds and ruling it in absolute authority' ('Beethoven's Instrumental Music', pp. 102 and 98).

Certainly Hoffmann's deepest affection was for Mozart, the 'Shakespeare of music', whose all-embracing mastery, sparkling imagination, pervasive humour (in Hoffmann's sense), and boundless fertility of imagination constantly inspire him with new enthusiasm. For Hoffmann, 'true humour in music, as in general, arises only from profound gravity, from the alert, active recognition of a higher order'.

Beside Mozart and Beethoven, however, he places another name. It is his 'splendid old friend Sebastian', by whom he feels himself 'borne high into the air on powerful wings' (manuscript of 'Kapellmeister Johannes Kreisler's Musical Sufferings'); and, a few years later, after a study of Beethoven's piano compositions, he concludes: 'How pale and insignificant everything seems that does not come from you, from the intelligence of Mozart, or from the mighty genius of Sebastian Bach' ('Beethoven's Instrumental Music', p. 100). Hoffmann *was* a visionary; he knew nothing by Bach other than some chorale settings, the motets, and, along with a few other keyboard works, the 'Goldberg' Variations.

APPENDIX: CATALOGUE OF HOFFMANN'S MUSIC CRITICISM

This appendix lists all Hoffmann's reviews of music and opera as contained in the *Schriften zur Musik*, in order of composer. Works reviewed within articles bearing a different title are included. Where Hoffmann is concerned with a performance rather than the printed score, this is indicated by (perf.).

The many works alluded to in 'Old and New Church Music' are not included. Page numbers refer to the present book.

Ambrosch, Joseph Karl
Songs by J. A. Hiller and V. Righini, with vocal variations (*AMZ*, 30 Nov. 1814)

André, Johann Anton
Piano variations on *Ah vous dirai-je Maman* and on *O du lieber Augustin* (*AMZ*, 22 Feb. 1815)

Beethoven, Ludwig van

Overture to *Coriolan*, Op. 62	page 286
Fifth Symphony, Op. 67	page 234
Piano trios, Op. 70	page 300
Overture and incidental music to Goethe's *Egmont*, Op. 84	page 341
Mass in C major, Op. 86	page 325
Wellingtons Sieg, Op. 91 (perf.)	page 420

Bergt, August
Christus, durch Leiden verherrlicht (*AMZ*, 5 Jan. 1814)

Boieldieu, Adrien
Le Nouveau Seigneur de village   page 382

Braun, Carl Anton Philipp
Fourth Symphony (*AMZ*, 9 June 1813)

Pustkuchen, Anton Heinrich
Choralbuch für die Gesangbücher der reformirten Gemeinden im Fürstenthum Lippe; *Kurze Anleitung, wie Singe-Chöre auf dem Lande zu bilden sind* (*AMZ*, 2 Dec. 1812)

Quaisin, Adrien
Le Jugement de Salomon   page 217

Reichardt, Johann Friedrich
Piano sonata in F minor (*AMZ*, 25 May 1814)

Riem, Wilhelm Friedrich
Zwölf Lieder, Op. 27   page 376

Riotte, Philipp Jakob
Nine variations for piano on a theme from Weigl's *Die Schweizerfamilie* (*AMZ*, 22 Feb. 1815)

Romberg, Andreas
Pater noster (*AMZ*, 3 Jan. 1810)

Romberg, Bernhard Heinrich
Symphony (perf.)   page 390
'Military' concerto for cello, Op. 31 (perf.)   page 391
Rondoletto (perf.)   page 391

Sacchini, Antonio
Oedipe à Colone (perfs.) (*DW*, 30 Sept. 1815; 8 June 1816)

Schiller, Friedrich von
Die Braut von Messina   page 213

Schmidt, Johann Philipp Samuel
Die Alpenhütte (perf.) (*Berlinische Nachrichten von Staats- und gelehrten Sachen*, 12 Sept. 1816)

Schneider, Friedrich
Piano duet sonata, Op. 29 (*AMZ*, 6 Apr. 1814)

Spohr, Louis
First Symphony   page 271

Spontini, Gaspare
Fernand Cortez (perf.): See 'Letters on Music in Berlin' page 392

La vestale (perf.) (*D W*, 20 July 1816)
Preussischer Volksgesang and *Grosser Sieges- und Festmarsch*
(perfs.): See 'Concert under the direction of Spontini,
3 August 1820'   page 421
Lalla Rûkh (perf.) (*Zeitung für Theater und Musik*, 24 Feb.
1821)
Olimpia   page 431

Stiastny, Bernard
Il maestro ed il scolare for two cellos (*A M Z*, 26 Oct.
1814)

Stiastny, Jan
XII pièces faciles et progressives for cello and
double-bass (*A M Z*, 26 Oct. 1814)

Weber, Bernhard Anselm
Sulmalle (perf.) (*D W*, 14 Oct. 1815)

Weigl, Joseph
Das Waisenhaus   page 252

Wilms, Jan Willem
Symphony, Op. 23 (*A M Z*, 9 June 1813)

Winter, Peter von
Das unterbrochene Opferfest (perf.) (*D W*, 23 Sept. 1815)

Witt, Friedrich
Fifth and Sixth Symphonies   page 221

SELECT BIBLIOGRAPHY

The most complete and recent critical bibliography of Hoffmann is Gerhard R. Kaiser, *E. T. A. Hoffmann* (Sammlung Metzler, vol. ccxliii, Stuttgart, 1988). Works in all languages on Hoffmann are regularly listed in the *Mitteilungen der E. T. A. Hoffmann-Gesellschaft*.

Abraham, Gerald (ed.), *The Age of Beethoven 1790–1830* (*New Oxford History of Music*, vol. viii, Oxford, 1982)

Allroggen, Gerhard, *E. T. A. Hoffmanns Kompositionen: ein chronologisch-thematisches Verzeichnis seiner musikalischen Werke mit einer Einführung* (Regensburg, 1970)

'Hoffmann', in *The New Grove*

[*AMZ*] *Allgemeine musikalische Zeitung* (Leipzig, 1798–1848)

Anderson, Emily *see* Beethoven, *The Letters*

Baudelaire: Selected Writings on Art and Artists, tr., ed. P. E. Charvet (Harmondsworth, 1972)

Bauman, Thomas, *North German Opera in the Age of Goethe* (Cambridge, 1985)

Beethoven, Ludwig van, *The Letters of Beethoven*, tr., ed. Emily Anderson (London, 1961)

Symphony No. 5, Norton Critical Score, ed. Elliot Forbes (London, 1971)

Behler, Ernst and Roman Struc (tr., ed.), *Friedrich Schlegel. Dialogue on Poetry and Literary Aphorisms* (University Park, Pennsylvania, and London, 1968)

Benz, Ernst, *The Mystical Sources of German Romantic Philosophy*, tr. B. R. Reynolds and Eunice M. Paul (Allison Park, Pennsylvania, 1983)

Blum, R., K. Herloßsohn, and H. Marggraff (eds.), *Allgemeines Theater-Lexikon oder Encyklopädie alles Wissenswerthen für Bühnenkünstler, Dilettanten und Theaterfreunde* (7 vols., Altenburg and Leipzig, 1839–46)

Callot, Jacques *see* Daniel (ed.)

Cardinal, Roger, *German Romantics in Context* (London, 1975)

Castein, Hanne *see* Hoffmann, *Kreisleriana*

Cooper, J. C., *An Illustrated Encyclopaedia of Traditional Symbols* (London, 1978)

Daniel, Howard (ed.), *Callot's Etchings* (New York, 1974)

Dechant, Hermann, *E. T. A. Hoffmanns Oper 'Aurora'* (Regensburger Beiträge zur Musikwissenschaft, vol. ii, Regensburg, 1975)

'Entstehung und Bedeutung von E. T. A. Hoffmanns Oper *Aurora*', *Mitteilungen der E. T. A. Hoffmann-Gesellschaft*, xxxi (1985), 6–14

Deutsch, Otto Erich, *Mozart. A Documentary Biography* (Stanford, 1965)

Diderot, Denis, *Rameau's Nephew*, tr. L. W. Tancock (Harmondsworth, 1966)

[*DW*] *Dramaturgisches Wochenblatt in nächster Beziehung auf die Königlichen Schauspiele zu Berlin* (Berlin, 1815–17)

Ellinger, Georg, *E. T. A. Hoffmann. Sein Leben and seine Werke* (Hamburg and Leipzig, 1894)

(ed.), *E. T. A. Hoffmanns Werke* (Berlin, Leipzig, Vienna and Stuttgart, 1912)

Feder, Georg, 'Decline and Restoration', in Friedrich Blume *et al.*, *Protestant Church Music* (London, 1975), pp. 320–40

Forbes, Elliot *see* Beethoven, *Symphony No. 5*; *Thayer's Life of Beethoven*

Forkel, Johann Nikolaus, *Musikalisch-Kritische Bibliothek* (Gotha, 1778–79, reprinted Hildesheim, 1964)

F.V.M.T. and U.C.B. (trs.), *The Disciples at Saïs and Other Fragments by Novalis* (London, 1903)

Garlington, Aubrey S., Jr, 'E. T. A. Hoffmann's "Der Dichter und der Komponist" and the Creation of the German Romantic Opera', *Musical Quarterly*, lxv (1979), 22–47

Gerber, Ernst Ludwig, *Historisch-Biographisches Lexicon der Tonkünstler* (Leipzig, [1790–92], reprinted as *Historisch-Biographisches Lexikon der Tonkünstler (1790–1792)*, ed. Othmar Wessely (Graz, 1977))

Neues historisch-biographisches Lexikon der Tonkünstler (Leipzig, [1812–14], reprinted Graz, 1969, ed. Othmar Wessely)

HBW see Schnapp (ed.), *Hoffmanns Briefwechsel*

Hewett-Thayer, Harvey, W., *Hoffmann: Author of the Tales* (Princeton, 1948)

Hirschberg, Leopold (ed.), *Ernst Theodor Amadeus Hoffmanns sämmtliche Werke* (Berlin and Leipzig, 1922)

[Hitzig, Julius Eduard], *Aus Hoffmann's Leben und Nachlass* (Berlin, 1823)

Hoffmann, E. T. A., 'Über die Aufführung der Schauspiele des Calderón de la Barca auf dem Theater in Bamberg', in *Die Musen*, i (1812) [reprinted in Schnapp (ed.), *Nachlese*]

The Serapion Brethren, tr. Alexander Ewing (London, 1886)

Fantasie- und Nachtstücke, ed. Walter Müller-Seidel (Munich, 1960)

Kreisleriana, ed. Hanne Castein (Stuttgart, 1983)

'Don Giovanni', in *Six German Romantic Tales*, tr. Ronald Taylor (London, 1985)

see also Kent and Knight (tr., ed.); von Maassen (ed.); Schnapp (ed.)

Hosler, Bellamy, *Changing Aesthetic Views of Instrumental Music in Eighteenth-Century Germany* (Ann Arbor, 1981)

HTB see Schnapp (ed.), *Hoffmann. Tagebücher*

Kent, Leonard J. and Elizabeth C. Knight (tr., ed.), *Selected Writings of E. T. A. Hoffmann* (Chicago and London, 1969)

Kerman, Joseph, '*Tändelnde Lazzi*: On Beethoven's Trio in D Major, Opus 70, No. 1', in Malcolm Hamrick Brown and Roland John Wiley (eds.), *Slavonic and Western Music. Essays for Gerald Abraham* (Ann Arbor and Oxford, 1985)

Kolb, Jocelyne, 'E. T. A. Hoffmann's *Kreisleriana*: à la recherche d'une forme perdue?', *Monatshefte*, lxix (1977), 34–44

Kroll, Erwin, *E. T. A. Hoffmanns musikalische Anschauungen* (Königsberg, 1909)

Kron, Wolfgang, *Die angeblichen Freischütz-Kritiken E. T. A. Hoffmanns* (Munich, 1957)

le Huray, Peter and James Day, *Music and Aesthetics in the Eighteenth and Early-Nineteenth Centuries* (Cambridge, 1981)

Libby, Dennis Albert, 'Gaspare Spontini and his French and German Operas' (unpublished Ph.D. dissertation, Princeton University, 1969)

Loewenberg, Alfred, *Annals of Opera 1597–1940* (3rd edn, London, 1978)

Maassen, Carl Georg von (ed.), *E. T. A. Hoffmanns sämtliche Werke* (Munich and Leipzig, 1912)

MacArdle, Donald W., *Beethoven Abstracts* (Detroit, 1973)

Mitteilungen der E. T. A. Hoffmann-Gesellschaft (Bamberg, 1938–   )

Mollenauer, Robert, 'The Three Periods of E. T. A. Hoffmann's Romanticism: An Attempt at a Definition', *Studies in Romanticism*, ii (1963), 212–43

Müller-Seidel, Walter (ed.) *see* Hoffmann, *Fantasie- und Nachtstücke*

Nachlese see Schnapp (ed.), *Hoffmann. Nachlese*

Negus, Kenneth, *E. T. A. Hoffmann's Other World* (Philadelphia, 1965)

Niemetschek, F. X., *Leben des k.k. Kapellmeisters Wolfgang Gottlieb Mozart . . .* (Prague, 1798; 2nd edn 1808)

Nock, Francis J., 'E. T. A. Hoffmann and Shakespeare', *Journal of English and Germanic Philology*, liii (1954), 369–82

Novalis (pseudonym of Friedrich von Hardenberg) *see* F.V.M.T. and U.C.B. (trs.)

Peters, Diana Stone, 'E. T. A. Hoffmann: The Conciliatory Satirist', *Monatshefte*, lxvi (1974), 55–73

Pröpper, Rolf, *Die Bühnenwerke Johann Friedrich Reichardts (1752–1814)* (2 vols., Bonn, 1965)

Raraty, Maurice Michael, 'E. T. A. Hoffmann and the Theatre. A Study of the Origins, Development and Nature of his Relationship with the Theatre, and its Impact on his Imaginative Literary Work' (unpublished Ph.D. dissertation, Sheffield University, 1963)

(ed.), *E. T. A. Hoffmann. Prinzessin Brambilla* (Oxford, 1972)

Reichardt, Johann Friedrich, *Musikalisches Kunstmagazin* (Berlin, 1791)

Ritter, Johann Wilhelm, *Fragmente aus dem Nachlasse eines jungen Physikers* (Heidelberg, 1810, reprinted Heidelberg, 1969)

Rohr, Judith, *E. T. A. Hoffmanns Theorie des musikalischen Dramas* (Baden-Baden, 1985)

Rusack, Hedwig, *Gozzi in Germany. A Survey of the Rise and Decline of the Gozzi Vogue in Germany and Austria* (New York, 1930)

Sahlin, Johanna C. (ed., tr.), *Selected Letters of E. T. A. Hoffmann* (Chicago and London, 1977)

Saul, Nicholas, *History and Poetry in Novalis and in the Tradition of the German Enlightenment* (Institute of Germanic Studies, University of London, Bithell Series of Dissertations, vol. viii, London, 1984)

Schafer, R. Murray, *E. T. A. Hoffmann and Music* (Toronto, 1975)

Scher, Steven Paul (ed.), *Zu E. T. A. Hoffmann* (Stuttgart, 1981)

Schlegel, Friedrich *see* Behler and Struc

Slusser, George Edgar, '*Le Neveu de Rameau* and Hoffmann's Johannes Kreisler: Affinities and Influences', *Comparative Literature*, xxvii (1975), 327–43

Schnapp, Friedrich (ed.), *E. T. A. Hoffmann. Nachlese. Dichtungen, Schriften, Aufzeichnungen und Fragmente* (Munich, 1963, reissued Darmstadt, 1966)

E. T. A. Hoffmanns Briefwechsel (vols. i, ii, Munich, 1967, 1968)

E. T. A. Hoffmann. Tagebücher (Munich, 1971)

E. T. A. Hoffmann. Schriften zur Musik. Aufsätze und Rezensionen (rev. edn, Munich [1977])

Der Musiker E. T. A. Hoffmann: Ein Dokumentenband (Hildesheim, 1981)

Schnaus, Peter, *E. T. A. Hoffmann als Beethoven-Rezensent der Allgemeinen Musikalischen Zeitung* (Freiburger Schriften zur Musikwissenschaft, vol. viii, Munich and Salzburg, 1977)

Schriften zur Musik see Schnapp (ed.), *Hoffmann. Schriften zur Musik*

Schubert, G. H., *Die Symbolik des Traumes* (Bamberg, 1814)

Schubert, Mary Hurst (tr., ed.), *Wilhelm Heinrich Wackenroder's 'Confessions' and 'Fantasies'* (University Park, Pennsylvania, and London, 1971)

Strunk, Oliver (tr., ed.), *Source Readings in Music History. The Romantic Era* (New York, 1965)

Sulzer, Johann Georg, *Allgemeine Theorie der schönen Künste* (2nd edn, Leipzig, 1792–99, reprinted Hildesheim, 1967–70)

Taylor, Ronald, *Hoffmann: a Study in Romanticism* (London, 1963)

'Music and Mystery: Thoughts on the Unity of the Work of E. T. A. Hoffmann', *Journal of English and Germanic Philology*, lxxv (1976), 477–91

Thayer's Life of Beethoven, rev., ed. Elliot Forbes (Princeton, 1970)

The New Grove Dictionary of Music and Musicians, ed. Stanley Sadie (London, 1980)

[Triest, Johann Karl Friedrich], 'Bemerkungen über die Ausbildung der Tonkunst in Deutschland im achtzehnten Jahrhundert', *AMZ*, iii (1801), issues 15 to 26, 7 January to 25 March inclusive

Vom Ende, Hans (ed.), *E. T. A. Hoffmann's musikalische Schriften* (Cologne and Leipzig, [1899])

[*VZ*; *Vossische Zeitung*] *Königlich privilegirte Berlinische Zeitung von Staats und gelehrten Sachen. Im Verlage Vossischer Erben* (Berlin, 1751–1934)

Wackenroder, Wilhelm Heinrich *see* Schubert, Mary Hurst (tr., ed.)

Wallace, Robin, *Beethoven's Critics* (Cambridge, 1986)

Walter, Michael, 'Hoffmann und Spontini. Zum Problem der Romantischen Oper', in Alain Montandon (ed.), *E. T. A. Hoffmann et la musique. Actes du colloque international de Clermont-Ferrand* (Berne, 1987), 85–119

Warrack, John (ed.) *see* [Weber]

Watts, Pauline, *Music: The Medium of the Metaphysical in E. T. A. Hoffmann* (Amsterdam, 1972)

[Weber] *Carl Maria von Weber: Writings on Music*, tr. Martin Cooper, ed. John Warrack (Cambridge, 1981)

Wessely, Othmar *see* Gerber

Zeydel, Edwin H., *Ludwig Tieck, the German Romanticist* (2nd edn, Hildesheim and New York, 1971)

[*Z E W*] *Zeitung für die elegante Welt* (Leipzig, 1801–59)

INDEX

With acknowledgements to Hedwig Charlton